GREEKS, ROMANS, AND CHRISTIANS

ESSAYS IN HONOR OF ABRAHAM J. MALHERBE

Greeks, Romans, and Christians

Edited by
David L. Balch
Everett Ferguson
Wayne A. Meeks

FORTRESS PRESS   **MINNEAPOLIS**

GREEKS, ROMANS, AND CHRISTIANS
Essays in Honor of Abraham J. Malherbe

Book design and cover design by Publishers' WorkGroup

Library of Congress Cataloging-in-Publication Data
Greeks, Romans, and Christians: essays in honor of Abraham J. Malherbe / edited by David L. Balch, Everett Ferguson, Wayne A. Meeks.
    p.   cm.
Includes bibliographical references and index.
ISBN 0-8006-2446-7 (alk. paper)
    1. Christianity and other religions — Greek.   2. Christianity and other religions — Roman.
3. Philosophy, Ancient.   4. Civilization, Greco-Roman.   5. Bible. N.T. — Criticism, interpretation, etc.   6. Greece — Religion.   7. Rome — Religion.   8. Theology — Early church, ca. 30–600.
I. Malherbe, Abraham J. II. Balch, David L. III. Ferguson, Everett, 1933-   . IV. Meeks, Wayne A.
BR128.G8G72   1990   90–42906
270.1 — dc20   CIP

The paper used in this publication meets the minimum requirements of American National Standard for Information Sciences—Permanence of Paper for Printed Library Materials, ANSI Z329.48–1984.

Manufactured in the U.S.A.   AF 1-2446

94   93   92   91   90   1   2   3   4   5   6   7   8   9   10

CONTENTS

PART FOUR
HELLENISTIC SOCIAL BEHAVIOR

PART FIVE
ARCHAEOLOGY

PREFACE

These chapters are presented to Abraham J. Malherbe on his sixtieth birthday to honor the scholar who is a mentor for some of us and a deeply respected colleague for all. During three decades, his own writings have taught us new ways of understanding early Christian texts and communities in relationship to Greco-Roman philosophy, literature, and culture. His willingness over those same decades to give constructive critiques of our essays, dissertations, and books has sometimes generated, and always deepened, our own abilities to interpret texts in that Hellenistic environment. We also recognize his devotion to the church, which has been as genuine as his commitment to quality education.

Malherbe grew up in a large family in Pretoria, South Africa. He attended an Afrikaans medium primary school and then received his high school education at the Afrikaanse Hoër Seunskook, from which he graduated in 1947. He worked for the Surveyor General and then became a draftsman in the Electricity Supply Commission until he left South Africa for the United States in 1951.

In America, Malherbe studied at Abilene Christian University (ACU), where Everett Ferguson was a fellow student and LeMoine G. Lewis, a respected teacher. There he met and married Phyllis Melton; they have three children—Selina, Cornelia, and Abraham Johannes (Jan). After graduating magna cum laude from ACU in 1954, Malherbe studied at Harvard Divinity School, where he earned an S.T.B. degree in 1957 and was the Harvard Divinity School Commencement Greek Orator. He also worked on the Corpus Hellenisticum Novi Testamenti project with W. C. van Unnik at the University of Utrecht from 1960 to 1961. In 1963, he received a Th.D. from Harvard Divinity School, where he studied with A. D. Nock, about whom we have all heard many stories. After Nock's death, Malherbe completed his dissertation under the direction of Helmut Koester. Its central theses, relating the Christian apologist Athenagoras to the Middle Platonist Albinus, were published in *Vigiliae Christianae* in 1969. From 1956 to 1962, he was also the minister for the Church of Christ in Lexington, Massachusetts.

Malherbe has taught at ACU and Dartmouth College and, since 1970, at Yale Divinity School (YDS). In 1981, he became the Buckingham Professor of New Testament Criticism and Interpretation at YDS and served for two years (1987 to 1989) as the associate dean for academic affairs.

Malherbe's earliest book, *The World of the New Testament*, included his central professional interest in the Cynics and Epicureans. His often-cited *Social Aspects of Early Christianity* contains both his revisions of Adolf Deissmann's view concerning the social level of early Christians and suggestions about early house churches' similarity to trade guilds. Interests both in ancient epistolography and in the Cynics came to fruition in a collaborative work with some of his students, an edition and translation of *The Cynic Epistles*. Continuing an early focus on church history, he collaborated with Everett Ferguson on a translation with commentary of *Gregory of Nyssa: The Life of Moses*.

Recently Malherbe has published four books. The first, *Moral Exhortation: A Greco-Roman Sourcebook*, grew out of a "Hellenistic Moralists" course that has stimulated many college, divinity school, and doctoral students through the years, one result of which has been a number of dissertations by graduate students at Yale. His lifelong fascination with Paul's early Thessalonian correspondence became *Paul and the Thessalonians: The Philosophic Tradition of Pastoral Care*, which is concerned not with Paul's theology but with his practice of pastoral care, with his nurture of new converts in the Christian community. Malherbe's insistence on studying primary Greek and Latin texts shows itself again in his edition, with translation and introduction, of *Ancient Epistolary Theorists*. Some of his important essays have been collected in *Paul and the Popular Philosophers*, which focuses on the Cynics and the diatribe, Paul's Thessalonian and Corinthian correspondence, the Pastoral Epistles, and the presentation of Paul as a philosopher in the book of Acts, all of which relate Greco-Roman philosophy and ethics to early Christian texts and communities. Finally, we eagerly anticipate his Anchor Bible commentary on the Thessalonian letters and his Hermeneia commentary on the Pastorals.

The editors are grateful to Fortress Press. We treasure the memory of Dr. John A. Hollar, who encouraged and supported the publication of this volume to honor our esteemed colleague, teacher, and mentor, Abraham J. Malherbe.

David L. Balch
Everett Ferguson
Wayne A. Meeks

CONTRIBUTORS

David E. Aune
Professor of Religious Studies
Saint Xavier College
Chicago, IL 60655

David L. Balch
Associate Professor of
    New Testament
Brite Divinity School
Texas Christian University
Fort Worth, TX 76129

Everett Ferguson
Professor of Church History
Abilene Christian University
Abilene, TX 79699

Benjamin Fiore, S.J.
Professor
Canisius College
Buffalo, NY 14208

John T. Fitzgerald
Associate Professor
Department of Religious Studies
University of Miami
Coral Gables, FL 33124

Susan R. Garrett
Assistant Professor of
    New Testament
Yale Divinity School
New Haven, CT 06511

Ronald F. Hock
Associate Professor of Religion
University of Southern
    California
Los Angeles, CA 90089

Carl R. Holladay
Associate Professor of
    New Testament and
    Associate Dean
Candler School of Theology
Emory University
Atlanta, GA 30322

Pieter W. van der Horst
Reader in New Testament
    and Early Judaism
Faculty of Theology
University of Utrecht
3508 TC Utrecht, The Netherlands

Luke Timothy Johnson
Professor of Religious Studies
Indiana University
Bloomington, IN 47405

Marinus de Jonge
Professor of New Testament and
    Ancient Christian Literature
Faculty of Theology
University of Leiden
2318 VE Leiden, The Netherlands

Hans-Josef Klauck
Professor
Biblisches Institut
Lehrstuhl für neutestamentliche
    Exegese
Katholische Theologische
    Fakultät der Universität Würzburg
D-8700 Würzburg, West Germany

Helmut Koester
John H. Morison Professor of New
    Testament Studies and Winn
    Professor of Ecclesiastical History
The Divinity School
Harvard University
Cambridge, MA 02138

William S. Kurz, S.J.
Associate Professor of
    New Testament
Marquette University
Milwaukee, WI 53233

Bernard C. Lategan
Professor
Department of Biblical Studies
University of Stellenbosch
7600 Stellenbosch, South Africa

Dieter Lührmann
Professor of New Testament
Philipps-Universität
3550 Marburg/Lahn, West Germany

Wayne A. Meeks
Woolsey Professor of
    Biblical Studies
Yale University
New Haven, CT 06520

Jerome H. Neyrey, S.J.
Professor
Weston School of Theology
Cambridge, MA 02138

Thomas H. Olbricht
Chair, Religion Division
Pepperdine University
Malibu, CA 90265

Stephen L. Peterson
Librarian
Yale Divinity School
New Haven, CT 06510

Stanley K. Stowers
Associate Professor of
    Religious Studies
Brown University
Providence, RI 02912

Willem S. Vorster
Professor
Institute for Theological
    Research
University of South Africa
0001 Pretoria, South Africa

L. Michael White
Associate Professor of
    Religion in New Testament
    and Christian Origins
Oberlin College
Oberlin, OH 44074

INTRODUCTION

To honor Abraham J. Malherbe, the contributors have chosen to write a book that focuses on the interaction between Greco-Roman culture and early Christianity, especially as this involves Hellenistic philosophy, literature, rhetoric, anthropology, ethics, and urban life. Ten of us have focused on the philosophers: David E. Aune evaluates the possibility that Cynic images of Heracles influenced the formation of Christology, especially in Hebrews. Ronald F. Hock studies the previously neglected, but best documented of all, imperial Cynics, Athenaeus's Cynulcus, to shed new light on the intellectual world, as well as the culinary customs, of a learned symposium. Willem S. Vorster argues that Stoics and Christians valued blessedness/happiness both as an inner state of mind and as it relates to conduct. David L. Balch examines the Stoic Posidonius's views of providence in nature and history, as well as his opposition to images of the gods, which are all reflected in the Areopagus speech of Acts 17, although images were philosophically supported by later Stoics like Dio Chrysostom and by Epicureans. Carl R. Holladay studies the form and function of 1 Corinthians 13; the section is epistolary parenesis in which Paul presents himself in the first person singular as a paradigm of parental love to his addressees, as Epictetus does in the catechetical relationship reflected in his *Discourses* and as Isocrates had done in the epistle to Demonicus. Susan R. Garrett evaluates the relationship between popular philosophical portraits of the afflicted sage and influences from Jewish apocalyptic as they overlap in 2 Corinthians 4. Jerome H. Neyrey, S.J., relates Epicurean denials of theodicy to Christian affirmation of the same in the Areopagus speech of Acts 17. Benjamin Fiore, S.J., shows that Plutarch's polemic against Epicureans can help us understand the discussions of incest, lawsuits, and frequenting prostitutes in 1 Corinthians 5–6. Hans-Josef Klauck, who has just published a commentary on 4 Maccabees, compares discussions of "brotherly love" in the Middle Platonist Plutarch and 4 Maccabees to analogous values in the Johannine epistles. Everett Ferguson uses Hellenistic number symbolism to clarify a passage in the *Epistle of Barnabas*, concluding that the author was not a chiliast.

Several of the contributors focus on Hellenistic literature and rhetoric to clarify portions of Acts and Paul's epistles. William S. Kurz, S.J., explicates ancient paradigmatic functions of narrative to clarify the purpose of Luke-Acts; further, he relates this Hellenistic rhetorical emphasis to contemporary concern for implicit moral exhortation to implied readers. John Fitzgerald, Jr., employs epistolary theorists to interpret the different subjects and styles of Paul's "mixed letter" in 2 Corinthians 10–13. L. Michael White refers to the Hellenistic moral paradigm of friendship in order to interpret the communal ideal of virtue in the Christ-hymn of Philippians 2. Thomas H. Olbricht interprets Malherbe's favorite epistle, 1 Thessalonians; starting with the perspective developed in Aristotle's *Rhetoric*, Olbricht delineates a new genre, "church rhetoric," to analyze the power of parenesis in 1 Thessalonians. Dieter Lührmann emphasizes the importance of ethical instruction to former pagans in the foundation of the church at Thessalonica.

Two authors give highly original, provocative interpretations of Hellenistic anthropology in Paul and Hebrews. Stanley K. Stowers argues that Paul opposes a Stoic and Epicurean view of human reason as a therapy of the passions, a view reflected in 1 Corinthians 8, 2 Corinthians 10, and Rom 14:1; this view of reason as a fortress of the wise is elitist and individualistic, whereas the goal of Paul's work was communal. Pieter W. van der Horst surveys Greco-Roman literature, including rabbinic texts, from 500 B.C.E. to A.D. 200 and beyond, concluding that many philosophers, physicians, and poets held that the contributions of men and women to the formation of a fetus were strictly equal, while others denied that females contribute to embryogenesis; the author of the Epistle to the Hebrews did write that Sarah "received strength for a seminal emission" (11:11).

Several contributors deepen our understanding of Hellenistic social behavior as it is reflected in early Christian texts and archaeological evidence. Wayne A. Meeks adopts the social psychologist Herbert H. Hyman's concept of "reference groups" and asks about the size of Paul's and his communities' moral world, concluding that the dominant reference groups and individuals in his admonitions are peculiar to the movement, although his stance is not simply countercultural. Bernard C. Lategan investigates the nature and style of Paul's ethic in Galatians, finding that Paul emphasizes freedom and creativity, empowerment and participation. Luke Timothy Johnson examines the rhetorical, moral, and religious logic of the ancient world's assumption that a wise person is also taciturn; the letter of James shares much of this logic but has its own startling, distinctive approach to speech. Marinus de Jonge shows that there is a remarkable continuity of ideas about sexual morality between Hellenistic moralists like Musonius, Hellenistic Jews like Philo and Josephus, and early Christians like the author of the *Sentences* of Sextus; therefore, the study does not allow a conclusion concerning the Jewish or Christian origin of the *Testaments of the Twelve Patriarchs*.

Helmut Koester discusses an important Corinthian sanctuary in the interest of learning more about the urban world of the apostle Paul.

Finally, Stephen Peterson has compiled a bibliography of Abraham J. Malherbe's works.

The chapters of this book employ the style of the *Journal of Biblical Literature* 107 (1988) 579–96 and, secondarily, that of the *Chicago Manual of Style*, which means, for example, that Arabic numbers, not Roman ones, are employed in citing Greco-Roman texts. Many authors refer to the translations of Latin and Greek texts in the Loeb Classical Library (Cambridge: Harvard University Press; London: William Heinemann). This book cites these with the following form: "trans. Oldfather in LCL." Abbreviations of Greco-Roman texts follow the *Oxford Classical Dictionary* and the *Theological Dictionary of the New Testament*.

GREEKS, ROMANS, AND CHRISTIANS

PART ONE

SCHOOLS OF HELLENISTIC PHILOSOPHY

DAVID E. AUNE

1

HERACLES AND CHRIST
Heracles Imagery in the
Christology of Early Christianity

By the middle of the second century A.D., Justin Martyr recognized the existence of formal parallels between the career of Jesus and a motley assortment of Greek gods and heroes, including Heracles: "In saying that the Word, who is the first offspring of God, was born for us without sexual union, as Jesus Christ our Teacher, and that he was crucified and died and after rising again ascended into heaven we introduce nothing new beyond [what you say of] those whom you call sons of Zeus" (*1 Apol.* 21.1; trans. Hardy). The parallels include virginal conception, death, resurrection, and ascension. Elsewhere Justin, apparently threatened by such parallels, defends the uniqueness of Christ by arguing that the similarities between Heracles and Christ were the result of imitation: "And when they tell that Herakles was strong and travelled over all the world, and was begotten by Zeus of Alcmene, and ascended to heaven when he died [ἀποθανόντα εἰς οὐρανὸν ἀνεληλυθέναι], do I not understand that the Scripture which speaks of Christ, 'strong like a giant to run his race,' has been in like manner imitated [μεμιμῆσθαι]?" (*Dial.* 69.3). Later, Celsus lists major figures in mythology whom the Greeks thought were originally mortals and eventually became immortals or gods (the Dioscuri, Heracles, Asclepius, and Dionysus), but whose divinity was rejected by Christians (Origen *C. Cels.* 3.22); Origen, using the traditional strategies of Christian apologists, attempts to refute the divinity of each (3.42).[1]

This evidence indicates that during the second and third centuries A.D., Christians and pagans alike saw Heracles and Christ as religious rivals. In this chapter I will explore some of the reasons for the similarities that early Christians perceived between Heracles and Christ. Did the Greeks transform Heracles in conformity with traditions about Christ? That is impossible, if only because the basic features of the Heracles legend were fixed long before

---

1. The argumentative strategy of the Greek apologists consists primarily of attempts to point out the immoral behavior of divinized heroes and gods, thereby discrediting them; cf. Clement of Alex. *Protrepticus* 2.22–23, 26–28, 30; Athenagoras *Legatio* 29. On Tertullian, see Gordon J. Laing, "Tertullian and the Pagan Cults," *TAPA* 44 (1913) xxxv–xxxvii.

the first century A.D.[2] Two other possibilities remain. Either the similarities between Heracles and Christ are phenomenological parallels that cannot be explained by theories of literary dependence and/or Christians have conceptualized the role of Jesus in light of aspects of the Heracles myth—that is, Christ is, at least to some extent, an imitation of Heracles.

ASPECTS OF THE HERACLES LEGEND

Heracles was the single most popular hero in Greek and Roman antiquity. This popularity is reflected in the favorite ancient expletive "O Heracles!",[3] in the many folktales and myths in which he functions as the protagonist, in the many local cults in which he was honored (usually as a hero, occasionally as a god), in literary adaptations (primarily in comedies and satyr plays),[4] and in artistic representations (which often reveal more than literary sources).[5] Such artistic illustrations of his exploits go back to the eighth century B.C., and Heracles himself goes back at least to the Mycenaean period, if not earlier.[6] There were, in fact, Heracles-like figures in the ancient Near East, known primarily from iconographic sources.[7] The Old Testament figure of Samson clearly belongs to this Levantine Heracles tradition.[8] By the fourth century A.D., early Christians connected Samson with Heracles (Augustine *Civ. Dei* 18.19).[9]

---

2. The emperor Julian (late fourth century A.D.) embellished the legend of Heracles in the light of Gospel traditions about Jesus; cf. Marcel Simon, *Le Christianisme antique et son contexte religieux: Scripta Varia* (WUNT 23; Tübingen: J. C. B. Mohr [Paul Siebeck], 1981) 1. 258. Julian mentions the journey of Heracles over the sea in the golden cup of the sun and says, "I believe by the gods, that it was not a cup but I am convinced that he traveled over the sea as upon dry land. For what was impossible to Herakles?" (Julian *Or.* 7.219D; cf. Mark 6:48 *par.*).
3. Aelius Aristides (*Or.* 40.1) refers to this exclamation as "the daily praise [of Heracles] by all men." Cf. Sophocles *Philoctetes* 174; Aelius Aristides *Or.* 40.14; Libanius 18.186.
4. G. Karl Galinsky, *The Herakles Theme: The Adaptations of the Hero in Literature from Homer to the Twentieth Century* (Oxford: Basil Blackwell, 1972).
5. Frank Brommer, *Vasenlisten zur griechischen Heldensage* (3. Aufl.; Marburg: Elmert, 1973); idem, *Denkmälerlisten zur griechischen Heldensage I* (Marburg: Elmert, 1972); Jane Henle, *Greek Myths: A Vase Painter's Notebook* (Bloomington: Indiana University Press, 1973) 57–74, with extensive bibliographies on 204–8; John Boardman, *Athenian Black Figure Vases* (New York: Oxford University Press, 1974) 221–25.
6. Martin P. Nilsson, *The Mycenean Origin of Greek Mythology* (Berkeley: University of California Press, 1932) 187–220.
7. Walter Burkert, *Structure and History in Greek Mythology and Ritual* (Berkeley: University of California Press, 1979) 80–83.
8. Othniel Margalith has written a series of articles in which he attempts to demonstrate the ultimate dependency of many stories connected with Samson to Heracles traditions from Minoan-Mycenaean civilization: "Samson's Riddle and Samson's Magic Locks," *VT* 36 (1986) 225–34; idem, "More Samson Legends," *VT* 36 (1986) 397–405; idem, "The Legends of Samson/Heracles," *VT* 37 (1987) 63–70.
9. Samson is depicted in the guise of Heracles in the frescoes of the Via Latina catacomb; cf. Simon, "Remarques sur la Catacombe de la Via Latina," *Le Christianisme antique et son contexte religieux* (Lief. 108/9; Stuttgart: Anton Hiersemann, 1988) 286–96; cf. Abraham J. Malherbe, "Herakles," *RAC* 581–83.

Further, Heracles was traditionally associated with the Tyrian god Melkart, the Baal of the Old Testament.[10]

Yet Heracles differed decisively from other Greek heroes. The worship of most Greek heroes centered at their tombs, where their physical remains were thought buried. Heracles, however, had no tomb. There are several reasons for this unique state of affairs. Martin Nilsson argues that since Heracles originated in folklore and was never an actual historical individual, it is not surprising that he was not localized in the same way that other heroes were.[11] According to a widespread ancient view, his mortal part was consumed on the pyre on Mount Oeta, whereas his immortal part was carried off to heaven (Seneca *Hercules Oetaeus* 1966–69), so no physical remains were left for burial (Diodorus 4.38.5). Friedrich Pfister correctly suggests that such *Entrückungslegende* (ascension legends) were a mythological way of rationalizing cultic offerings of both Olympian and chthonic types to a single deity.[12]

In fact, Heracles received sacrifices in many different places, sometimes as a hero, but sometimes also as a god.[13] Herodotus, who thought that there were originally *two* Heracleses, one an ancient Egyptian god and the other the son of Alcmene, justified his view by appealing to two ways in which Heracles was worshiped: "And further: those Greeks, I think, are most in the right, who have established and practise two worships of Heracles, sacrificing to one Heracles as to an immortal, and calling him the Olympian, but to the other bringing offerings as to a dead hero" (2.44; trans. Godley in LCL).

The implications of these two apparently contradictory types of sacrifice are reconciled in an interpolation in Homer's *Odyssey* (11.602–4), where the εἴδωλον (phantom) of Heracles is said to be in Hades, whereas the hero himself reportedly lives with the immortal gods on Olympus. Pindar, who regarded Heracles as the embodiment of heroic humanity, expressed this ambiguity by designating Heracles as a ἥρως θεός, a "hero-god" (*Nem.* 3.22)—that is, "a hero who has become a god in reward for his sufferings and prowess."[14] Like Herodotus, the Stoic philosopher Cleanthes proposed that there were in fact *two* different figures named Heracles—one the god and the other the hero.[15] Arrian proposed *three* different figures named Heracles: the son of Alcmene, the Tyrian Heracles, and the Egyptian Heracles (*Anabasis Alexandri* 2.16). This tendency was taken to extremes by the rationalist

---

10. Herodotus 2.44; 2 Macc 4:19; Josephus *Contra Ap.* 1.118–19; *Ant.* 8.146; Arrian *Anabasis Alexandri* 2.16.1–8; Aelius Aristides *Or.* 40.10.

11. Nilsson, *Mycenean Origin*, 187–220 (on Heracles). Nilsson argues that Heracles' connection with Thebes (the site of his birth) and Tirynsis was the result of the Greek propensity to localize heroes, and that all local cults were secondary institutions.

12. Friedrich Pfister, *Der Reliquienkult im Altertum* (Giessen: Töpelmann, 1909–12) 480–88.

13. The distinction between a hero and a god was maintained primarily through distinctive sacrificial protocol; cf. W. K. C. Guthrie, *The Greeks and Their Gods* (Boston: Beacon Press, 1950) 220–21; Paul Stengel, *Die griechischen Kultusaltertümer* (München: Beck, 1920) 138–44.

14. C. W. Bowra, *Pindar* (Oxford: Clarendon Press, 1964) 45f.

15. J. von Arnim, *Stoicorum Veterum Fragmenta* (Stuttgart: Teubner, 1964) 1. 115f. (frag. 514).

Roman mythographer Varro, who thought that forty-three different figures bearing the name Heracles should be distinguished.[16]

Heracles, whose name means "glory of Hera" (which is odd, since Hera was his chief antagonist), was the son of Zeus and Alcmene. Because Alcmene's husband, Amphitryon, had sexual relations with her shortly after Zeus visited her, she conceived and bore twins. Whereas Alcides (Heracles' original name) was the son of Zeus, his twin, Iphicles, was the son of Amphitryon. The adventures of Heracles may be grouped into three types of activities:[17] (1) the Twelve Labors (the so-called canonical tasks assigned to him by Eurystheus to purify him for killing his wife and children, the completion of which earned him immortality); (2) the πάρεργα, or "subsidiary activities" (the uncanonical deeds that punctuated, but were incidental to, the completion of the Twelve Labors); and (3) his military expeditions, as a prototype of Alexander and the embodiment of the Stoic ideal of kingship (Dionysius Hal. *Ant. Rom.* 1.41.1–44.2). These are framed by stories of his birth and youth on the one hand and of his self-immolation and apotheosis on the other.

The complexity of Heracles' mythological character is such that only a few relatively late accounts make any attempt to synthesize the many mythic episodes that came to be associated with his life and adventures.[18] With the exception of Euripides' *Alcestis*,[19] literary adaptations of the Heracles theme fail to provide complete and balanced portraits of the hero's major traits but tend to explore only a restricted selection of his traditional characteristics. There is a very real sense in which his personality was a pastiche of Greek social and cultural values, thereby accounting for his enormous popularity. One consistent trait of Heracles is his massive physique and physical strength,[20] though Cynics pointedly rejected the athletic image of Heracles with bulging muscles (Dio Chrys. *Or.* 8.30). He was also given to excess. In a fit of madness, he murdered his wife, Megara, and his sons, a deed for which he had to seek purification through performing the Twelve Labors. He is also portrayed as a world conqueror and a civilizer of humankind (Euripides *Hercules Furens* 851f., 875ff., 1252, 1309). In Seneca, Heracles claims,

16. Cf. Augustine *Civ. Dei* 18.12. Herodotus (2.43.1, 4) distinguishes between an Egyptian Heracles (probably Khonsu; cf. 2.42.3, 5), one of the Twelve Gods, and the Greek Heracles; cf. Charlotte R. Long, *The Twelve Gods of Greece and Rome* (Leiden: Brill, 1987) 147.

17. On the Twelve Labors, see Frank Brommer, *Herakles: Die zwölf Taten des Helden in antiker Kunst und Literatur* (2. Aufl.; Köln und Wien: Böhlau Verlag, 1972). On the uncanonical deeds, see Frank Brommer, *Herakles II: Die unkanonischen Taten des Helden* (Darmstadt: Wissenschaftliche Buchgesellschaft, 1984).

18. The three most extensive syntheses are found in Diodorus 4.8–39 (cf. 40–53) on Heracles' role in the adventures of Jason (an account perhaps dependent on an encomium on Heracles by Matris of Thebes; cf. Schwartz, PW 5. 673ff.), Apollodorus 2.4.5–2.8.5 (dependent on Pherecydes), and Aelius Aristides *Or.* 40, a eulogy in honor of Heracles.

19. Galinsky, *The Herakles Theme*, 66–72.

20. Cf. the Farnese Heracles, by Lysippus, which depicts a weary Heracles with exaggerated musculature leaning on his club draped with a lion skin (J. J. Pollitt, *Art in the Hellenistic Age* [Cambridge: Cambridge University Press, 1986] 50, plate 41).

Peace has been given to earth, to sky, to sea; all monsters have I subdued and in triumph come again. (*Hercules Oetaeus*, 794f.; trans. Miller in LCL)

Further, when Heracles conquered Hades, he conquered death itself:

He has crossed the streams of Tartarus,
subdued the gods of the underworld, and has returned. (Seneca *Hercules Furens* 889f.)

His love for his nephew, though he sired sixty-eight sons, is held up as exemplary, as is his grief over the death of his brother, Iphicles (Plutarch *De fraterno amore* 492C–D).

Whereas the adaptations of the Heracles theme in Homer and Hesiod focused on the hero's external actions and adventures, without particular moral purposes or concerns, Heracles' inner life, including his intellect, emotions, and conflicts (though of little interest to Cynics), was explored and developed by Greek tragedians. The mature Heracles was thought skilled in prophecy and proficient in logic (Plutarch *De E apud Delphos* 387D; cf. Hippolytus *Ref.* 5.26.26–28). He was associated by some with eloquence and dialectic (Lucian *Hercules* 4).[21]

Heracles' attainment of immortality was regarded in the tradition as a consequence of the successful completion of the Δωδεκάθλος, or Twelve Labors (Lucian *Deorum Concilium* 6). Consequently, the message conveyed was that through toil and suffering, a human being can become a god. This is perhaps the central reason for the great popularity of Heracles; according to W. K. C. Guthrie, "the career of Herakles offered new hope to the ordinary man."[22]

There was a widespread view in the Hellenistic world, justified by the allegorical interpretation of the Twelve Labors, that Heracles achieved the status of the Olympian gods through *virtue*.[23] This view was reflected in the Prodicus myth (see below) and was reinforced by the allegorical understanding of his divine sonship as παιδεία or ἄσκησις (Dio Chrys. *Or.* 2.78; Epictetus *Diss.* 2.16.44). Deification for merit was a Stoic topos,[24] and one that cohered with a Euhemeristic interpretation: "Human experience moreover and general custom have made it a practice to confer the deification of renown and gratitude upon distinguished benefactors. This is the origin of Hercules, of Castor and Pollux, of Aesculapius, and also of Liber" (Cicero *De nat. deor.* 2.24.62; trans. Rackham in LCL). Euhemerism is also reflected in

---

21. Ragnar Höistad, *Cynic Hero and Cynic King* (Lund: Carl Blom, 1948) 69–72.
22. Guthrie, *The Greeks and Their Gods*, 239.
23. Dionysius of Hal. *Ant. Rom.* 1.40; Plutarch *De Is. et Osir.* 361E; *Reg. et Imp.* 229F; Augustine *Civ. Dei* 18.8. According to Seneca (*De prov.* 1.5), only the wise and good man is truly the offspring of God and truly like God. It is for this reason that Seneca used Heracles as the paradigmatic Stoic wise man in his tragedies; cf. Emil Ackermann, "Der leidende Hercules des Seneca," *Rheinisches Museum für Philologie* 67 (1912) 425f.
24. Cicero *De nat. Deor.* 1.15.38–39 (Von Arnim, *Stoicorum Veterum Fragmenta* 1. 448); 2.62.

Scaevola, used by Varro, who in turn is quoted by Augustine. Augustine thinks that the public should *not* be told that "Hercules, Aesculapius, Castor, and Pollux are not gods, for it is related by the learned that they were men and passed on from the mortal state" (*Civ. Dei* 4.27; trans. Wiesen in LCL). According to Dio Chrysostom (*Or.* 1.59–60), Heracles was not only king of all Greece, but of the entire world as well. The myth of Heracles' choice, composed by Prodicus,[25] is also found in other versions (including one that some have attributed to Antisthenes (Dio Chrys. *Or.* 1.69–84),[26] changes an earlier conception that Heracles completed his Twelve Labors through necessity (ἀνάγκη), and emphasizes the fact that his deeds were accomplished *voluntarily*.

CYNIC AND STOIC CONCEPTIONS
OF HERACLES

Heracles was considered "the greatest example [παράδειγμα] of this [that is, the Cynic] lifestyle" (Julian *Or.* 6.187C), and in Lucian's *Vitarum Auctio* (8), Diogenes the Cynic is made to claim that he patterns his life after Heracles.[27] Elsewhere, Lucian suggests that the austere Cynic Peregrinus,[28] who reportedly carried a club, as Heracles did, committed suicide by self-immolation, following Heracles to the point of imitating his death (*De morte Per.* 21, 24, 36).[29] Lucian quotes Peregrinus as saying that "one who had lived as Heracles should die like Heracles" (33). Lucian mentions the philosopher Sostratus, who was nicknamed Heracles: "I have written about Sostratus elsewhere, and have described his size and excessive strength, his open-air life on Parnassus, his bed that was no bed of ease, his mountain fare and his deeds (not inconsistent with his name) achieved in the way of slaying robbers, making roads in untravelled country and bridging places hard to pass" (*Demonax* 1; trans. Harmon in LCL).

Like Heracles, the Cynic lived simply and endured pain and suffering in order to be liberated from the constraints of physical life. Cynics proclaimed this message of liberation to all who would listen. When Dio Chrysostom describes the exile of the Cynic sage Diogenes from Sinope, he has Diogenes describe his hunger, thirst, and poverty and then describes the labors of Hera-

25. Xenophon *Mem.* 2.1.34; Diels-Kranz, *Fragmente der Vorsokratiker* 2. 313–16 (frag. B.2); cf. Philostratus *Vit. soph.* 1. praef., 12. Justin uses the myth in a positive way in 2 *Apol.* 12.

26. The doxography on two types of training attributed to Antisthenes in Diogenes Laertius 6.70–71 is probably an early example of Cynic propaganda, which at the same time reflects the Cynic idealization of Heracles; cf. Höistad, *Cynic Hero*, 37–47. Julian adapted the Prodicus myth, placing himself in the role of Heracles (*Or.* 7.229C–234C).

27. The most detailed study of this subject is Höistad, *Cynic Hero*, 22–73.

28. Abraham J. Malherbe, "Self-Definition among Epicureans and Cynics," *Self-Definition in the Greco-Roman World* (vol. 3 of *Jewish and Christian Self-Definition*; ed. B. E. Meyer and E. P. Sanders; Philadelphia: Fortress, 1982) 51.

29. Although there is evidence for Cynic and Stoic suicides, there is little evidence to suggest that these were done in imitation of Heracles; Peregrinus is unique.

cles. The audience would naturally see the implicit comparison with Dio's own experience of exile by Domitian (*Or.* 8). The Cynic emphasis on παρρησία, "frank speech," is a characteristic also found in Heracles (Philo *Quod omn. prob.* 99, with a citation from Euripides). Heracles, though at one time a slave of Syleus, also acted as if he were free, and even acted as if he were the master of Syleus (100–104). Philo compares the Xanthians to Heracles: "Now these to escape the merciless cruelty of tyrannical enemies chose death with honour in preference to an inglorious life, but others whom the circumstances of their lot permitted to live, endured in patience, imitating the courage of Heracles, who proved himself superior to the tasks imposed by Eurystheus" (120; trans. Colson in LCL). Begging was approved by Cynics so that the proceeds could be used to do the sort of things Heracles did (Ps.-Diogenes *Ep.* 10.1 [Hercher, *Epistolog. Graec.* p. 238]). Cynics were encouraged to see parallels between themselves and Heracles: "But as for you, consider the ragged cloak to be a lion's skin, the staff a club, and the wallet land and sea, from which you are fed. For thus would the spirit of Heracles, mightier than every turn of fortune, stir in you" (*Ep.* 26 [Hercher, p. 241]; trans. Malherbe).

Heracles became the model of the courageous and victorious conqueror and so became the exemplar for generals, kings, and emperors. Dio Chrysostom (*Or.* 1.84; cf. Seneca *Hercules Oetaeus* 1330) referred to Heracles as "the savior of the world and of humanity" (τῆς γῆς καὶ τῶν ἀνθρώπων σωτῆρα), and Julian (*Or.* 7.220A) similarly described him as "the savior of the world" (τῷ κόσμῳ σωτῆρα). The term σωτήρ, however, refers to the actions of the ideal king and philosopher, a supreme benefactor for his people, and so has more political and moral than religious overtones. Isocrates, in giving advice to Philip of Macedon, used his mythical ancestor Heracles as a pan-Hellenic example of the wise ruler who embodied φιλανθρωπία (*Or.* 5.109–115). Alexander the Great claimed to be a descendant of Heracles[30] and depicted him on his coins, perhaps thereby presenting himself as the hero.[31] Alexander purportedly had a son named Heracles by Barsine of Pergamon (Diodorus 20.20, 28). Plutarch has Alexander claim to be a conscious imitator of Heracles, Perseus, and Dionysus (*De Alexandri magni fortuna* 1.10.332A). Like Heracles, Alexander toiled greatly, performed great deeds, and ultimately was thought to have been apotheosized. The Antigonids emphasized their descent from Heracles and used his club as an emblem on their coinage. The Roman emperor Caligula reportedly dressed himself up on different occasions as Heracles, the Dioscuri, and Dionysus (Philo *Leg ad Gaium* 78–85, 90). "Heracles" was a title of honor given to Nero by acclamation (Dio Cassius 62.20.5): "Hail to Nero, our Heracles!", and Suetonius reports that he planned

---

30. Arrian *Anabasis Alexandri* 3.3.2; 4.10.6; Julius Caesar saw a statue or picture of Alexander in the temple of Heracles at Gades (modern Cádiz), placed there in all likelihood because of the supposed genealogical relationship between Heracles and Alexander (Suetonius *Iul.* 7.1; Dio Cassius 37.52.2).

31. Pollitt, *Art in the Hellenistic Age*, 25, plates 13a and 13b.

to emulate Heracles by killing a lion in an amphitheater with a club or his bare
hands (Suetonius *Nero* 53). Domitian dedicated a temple to Heracles with a
cult statue bearing his own features (Martial *Ep.* 9.64, 65).[32]

Cynics and Stoics alike used Heracles as a symbol for the human desire to
achieve final peace and reward after great toil (πόνος).[33] Antisthenes, whom
Diogenes Laertius regarded as the teacher of Diogenes and, consequently, the
founder of Cynicism,[34] "demonstrated that pain is a good thing by instancing
the great Heracles and Cyrus, drawing the one example from the Greek world
and the other from the barbarians" (Diog. Laert. 6.2; trans. Hicks in LCL).
Antisthenes was a prolific writer who wrote three or four lost treatises on
Heracles that probably depicted the hero as an example of the Cynic emphasis
on mastering human frailties.[35] He perhaps continued the allegorical treatment of Heracles found in the writings of such Sophists as Herodorus and
Prodicus. Prodicus had earlier produced an epideictic speech entitled "The
Training of Heracles by Virtue" (Xenophon *Mem.* 2.1.34), in which the hero's
education in virtue was presented as an allegorical story of a choice between
two roads, the path of virtue or the path of vice (2.1.21–33). Diogenes, who
supposedly wrote a tragedy entitled *Herakles*, was the only fourth-century
Cynic to write on Heracles.[36] The intellectual Cynic philosopher Dio Chrysos-
tom adapted (or was perhaps dependent on an earlier adaptation by
Antisthenes for) the story of Prodicus, in which the choice between a life of
virtue or vice became a choice between kingship and tyranny, represented by
Trajan and Domitian, respectively (*Or.* 1.48–84).[37] Heracles, Odysseus,
Socrates, and Musonius Rufus were widely tauted as moral examples (Origen
C. Cels. 3.66). Those who died a noble death—Heracles, Asclepius, and
Orpheus—were also held in high esteem (7.53).

Cynic propaganda concerning Heracles had several objectives.[38] First, it
attacked the traditional view of Heracles as suffering against his will (Sophocles *Trachiniae*; Euripides *Hercules Furens*), though *voluntary* suffering was
acceptable (Dio Chrys. *Or.* 8.35; Epictetus 3.22.57; 3.26.31). Second, it
attacked the popular conception of Heracles as a muscle-bound moron,

---

32. Cf. Martial *Ep.* 101, in which the poet compares the deeds of Alcides *minor* (Heracles) with
Alcides *maior* (Domitian).

33. Donald R. Dudley, *A History of Cynicism* (Hildesheim: Georg Olms, 1967 [orig. pub. 1937])
13, 43.

34. Dudley rejects the relationship between Antisthenes and Diogenes as a fiction sponsored by
Stoics to establish continuity between themselves and Socrates, and considers Diogenes the real
founder of Cynicism; cf. Dudley, *A History of Cynicism*, 1–16 (also the view of F. Sayre, *Diogenes
of Sinope: A Study of Greek Cynicism* [Baltimore: Johns Hopkins University Press, 1938], who,
however, regards Crates as the founder of Cynicism). This view is problematic, however, since
the asceticism of Diogenes has links with a pre-Cynic "Socratic" asceticism.

35. Diogenes Laertius 2.61; 6.16, 17, 104f.; Socrates and the Socratics *Ep.* 9.4 (Hercher, 617).

36. Diogenes Laertius 6.80; Galinsky, *The Herakles Theme*, 107, suggests that this lost work was
more a didactic treatise than a tragedy.

37. Cf. C. P. Jones, *The Roman World of Dio Chrysostom* (Cambridge: Harvard University
Press, 1978) 116–19.

38. Höistad, *Cynic Hero*, 59f.

athlete, glutton, and boor (as he was depicted in comedy, satyr plays, and
Euripides' *Alcestis*). Third, Heracles is understood from an individual ethical
point of view, with divine sonship referring to proper moral training (Dio
Chrys. *Or.* 4.29, 31; Diogenes Laertius 6.70–71).

HERACLES AND THE GOSPELS

There have been a number of attempts during this century to demonstrate
that the legend of Heracles has had a significant impact on the formulation of
the life of Jesus as portrayed in the canonical Gospels.[39] In two articles published in 1907 and 1912, Emil Ackermann called attention to, but did not
attempt to explain, various similarities between aspects of the life of Jesus and
the life of Heracles, though he restricted his data relating to Heracles to the
tragedies of Seneca.[40] Theodor Birt pushed the parallels further by implying,
though not explicitly claiming, that the Gospel tradition (which he referred to
as "proto-Matthew" and "proto-Mark") was dependent on the Heracles
legend.[41]

Perhaps the most bizarre attempt to link the figure of Heracles to that of
Jesus was that of Friedrich Pfister in 1937;[42] Pfister suggested that the author
of the "Urevangelium" (from which each of the Synoptic Gospels was derived)
modeled the story of Jesus after a Cynic-Stoic Heracles biography. Under
four main headings ("Birth Story," "Youth," "Mature Activities," and "Death
and Ascent to Heaven"), Pfister lists twenty-one parallels between the lives of
Jesus and Heracles. These parallels are of mixed quality. A few are excellent,[43] whereas many are very weak or not really parallels at all;[44] others reveal

39. A brief review and critique of this liteature is found in Marcel Simon, *Hercule et le Christianisme* (Paris: Editions Orphrys, 1955) 49–74; a briefer survey is found in Malherbe, "Herakles,"
568–73.

40. Emil Ackermann, "De Senecae Hercule Oetaeo," *Philologus Supplementband* 10 (1907)
323–428; idem, "Der leidende Hercules des Seneca," 425–71. Although the authenticity of
Hercules Oetaeus continues to be disputed, the issue of authorship is irrelevant to the study of
parallels with the Gospels.

41. Theodor Birt, *Aus dem Leben der Antike* (3. Aufl.; Leipzig: Teubner, 1922).

42. Friedrich Pfister, "Herakles und Christus," *Archiv für Religionswissenschaft* 34 (1937)
42–60; Pfister concluded on p. 58: "The comparison made by us indicates without doubt, in my
opinion, that there is much more here than fortuitous coincidences and typological similarities,
but that there must have existed a documentary dependence that stems from a Cynic-Stoic Heracles biography antedating the Synoptic Gospels."

43. Pfister, "Herakles und Christus," 46–47: Both Jesus and Heracles, it is claimed, were born to
maidens who had no previous sexual intercourse with their husbands (Luke 1:26; Matt 1:24–25;
Apollodorus 2.4.7–8); both were called "son of God" (Luke 3:23; 4:22; Ovid *Met.* 15.49). the
phrase "it is finished" (*peractum est*) is uttered by Heracles just before his death three times in
Seneca *Hercules Oetaeus* (lines 1340, 1457, 1472), whereas the corresponding term in Greek,
τετέλεσται, is used twice by Jesus in John 19:28, 30, just before he expires.

44. According to Pfister, just as Herod killed the children of Bethlehem but Jesus was saved by
the flight to Egypt, so Hera sent two serpents into the room of the infants Heracles and Iphicles,
but Heracles strangled them. Another foolish parallel he adduces is that the followers of Christ
were called Christians, just as the descendants of Heracles were called Heraclidae.

only that the more general figure of the hero or divine man has influenced some of the more legendary features of the Gospel narratives.[45] The basic weakness of Pfister's proposal, however, is that his so-called Urevangelium is essentially a synthesis of material from all the Gospels, whereas his Cynic-Stoic "life of Heracles" is a pastiche of themes and motifs culled from a wide selection of Greco-Roman texts. Yet as H. J. Rose suggested, and Wilfred Knox has argued in more detail,[46] the legendary elements in the Gospels are often the result of the influence of themes and motifs widely associated with the lives of heroes in the Greco-Roman world, of which Heracles was certainly the most prominent.

This leads us to consider a very different, more detailed, and nuanced approach to the problem, the proposal made by Arnold J. Toynbee.[47] Toynbee discussed various ways in which saviors sought salvation in a disintegrating Hellenistic society by means of the "time machine," that is, by archaism (escape from the present to an ideal past) or futurism (escape from the present to an ideal future). In comparing Jesus with a variety of Hellenistic saviors, all historical figures (for example, Aristonicus, Eunus, Catiline, Agis, Cleomenes, the Gracchi, and Cato Minor), Toynbee enumerates eighty-seven points of comparison.[48] Discounting literary dependence, Toynbee proposes that "the Gospels contain, embedded in them, a considerable number and variety of elements which have been conveyed to them by the stream of 'folk-memory,'" and "the Gospels contain elements which are not 'historical' in the conventional usage of that word."[49] Toynbee then asks whether "folk-memory" has channeled elements from pagan authors to the Gospels or whether the Gospels and pagan authors are mutually dependent on "folk-memory."[50] The possible common source he proposed is the legend of Heracles, particularly the portrait of *Hercules Philosophus*. Toynbee finds twenty-four points of correspondence between the Jesus of the Gospels and the Heracles of Greek legend.[51] Because many of these features also characterize pagan historical heroes, Toynbee concludes: "this finding suggests that the legend of Heracles may be an important common source from which the story of Jesus on the one side and the stories of the pagan historical heroes on the other side may have

---

45. See the critiques of Pfister's proposal by H. J. Rose, "Herakles and the Gospels," *HTR* 31 (1938) 113–42; Simon, *Hercule et le Christianisme*, 51–55; Malherbe, "Herakles," 569–72.

46. Wilfred L. Knox, "The 'Divine Hero' Christology in the New Testament," *HTR* 41 (1948) 229–49; on p. 233 Knox observes: "In any case Heracles will supply most of our parallels and this is only natural in view of his popularity in the Stoic and Cynic circles which stood nearest to Judaism and Christianity; in spite of all condemnations of pagan mythology we find an affinity between Jewish-Christian and pagan language which can hardly be due to chance."

47. Arnold J. Toynbee, *A Study of History* (Oxford: Oxford University Press; London: Humphrey Milford, 1939) 6. 376–539.

48. Toynbee, *A Study of History*, 6. 376–406.

49. Toynbee, *A Study of History*, 6. 457.

50. Toynbee, *A Study of History*, 6. 464.

51. Toynbee, *A Study of History*, 6. 469–475.

derived some of their common features, independently of one another, through separate channels of the stream of 'folk-memory.'"[52] Marcel Simon considers Toynbee's approach infinitely more satisfying than that of Pfister and expresses general agreement with "the hypothesis of spontaneous imitation through the channel of popular tradition which he [Toynbee] has developed with such penetration, method and persuasive force."[53] The really difficult task in analyzing the Gospels, according to Simon, is to determine with precision where historical reality ends and fiction begins.[54]

One major problem with Toynbee's approach, however, is that he nowhere recognizes that those features of the Heracles legend that have analogies in the Gospels also have many parallels in the lives of other mythical heroes. This suggests that the Heracles legend was not as influential in the accounts of pagan historical heroes and the Gospel accounts of Jesus as the pattern or morphology implicit in the "lives" of ancient heroes. Lord Raglan proposed a pattern of twenty-two elements that he applied to twenty-one traditional heroes and gods, including Theseus, Romulus, Heracles, Perseus, Zeus, and Jason.[55] Although there have been a number of other attempts to deal with the problem of the significance of the morphology of the hero,[56] no thoroughly satisfying explanation has yet been proposed for why communal re-creations of the lives of heroes exhibit so many stereotypical features in common.

HERACLES IMAGERY IN HEBREWS

Early Christians gave expression to their conception of the ultimate religious significance of Jesus by utilizing a variety of metaphors and symbols. Because the coherence of Christology based on such figurative language lies on a different level than that of the logic and consistency expected in theological or philosophical discourse, there are many apparent inconsistencies in the christological imagery of such major segments of the New Testament as the Pauline letters, Johannine literature, and the anonymous Letter to the Hebrews. Hebrews is distinctive in that it places a greater emphasis on the historical Jesus than any other document in the New Testament outside the Gospels and the Acts of the Apostles.[57] Although the author uses traditions

52. Toynbee, A Study of History, 6. 475.
53. Simon, Hercule et le Christianisme, 63.
54. Simon, Hercule et le Christianisme, 65.
55. Fitzroy William Sommerset (Lord Raglan), The Hero: A Study in Tradition, Myth and Drama (New York: Vintage, 1956).
56. Archer Taylor, "The Biographical Pattern in Traditional Narrative," Journal of the Folklore Institute 1 (1964) 114–29; Jan de Vries, Heroic Song and Heroic Legend (trans. B. J. Timmer; New York: Oxford University Press, 1963); Joseph Campbell, The Hero with a Thousand Faces (Princeton: Princeton University Press, 1968).
57. This topic has not yet been adequately investigated; for discussions of the problem, see Olof Linton, "Hebréerbrevet och den 'historiske Jesus.' En studie till Hebr. 5:7," STK 26 (1950) 338ff.; M. B. Hansen, "Den historiske Jesus og den himmelske upperstepraest i Hebraeerbrevet," DTT 26 (1963) 1–22; Ulrich Luck, "Himmlisches und irdisches Geschehen im Hebräerbrief. Ein Beitrag zum Problem des 'historischen Jesus' im Urchristentum," NovT 6 (1963) 192–215; Erich

14 ESSAYS IN HONOR OF ABRAHAM J. MALHERBE

similar to those found in the canonical Gospels,[58] it is also probable that he drew upon Jesus traditions from unknown sources. Several such christological traditions in Hebrews exhibit themes and motifs that are associated with ancient conceptions of Heracles.

Two of the central christological metaphors of Hebrews are son and high priest.[59] The author sometimes uses the title Son of God when speaking of Jesus as a preexistent divine being (1:2),[60] but at other times he suggests that Jesus became the Son of God at the end of his earthly career (1:4–5; 2:9; 5:5; 6:20; 7:28).[61] The Stoic philosopher Cornutus, in the first century A.D., describes Heracles as "the Logos permeating everything, giving nature its force and cohesion."[62] Seneca, a contemporary of Cornutus, claims that God, the *divina ratio* who is the author of the world, can be called by many names, including Heracles (*De beneficiis* 4.7.1–8.1). Seneca, who wrote two tragedies with the "historical" Heracles as the protagonist (*Hercules Furens* and *Hercules Oetaeus*), thus puts himself in the position of implying a kind of doctrine of incarnation for Heracles.[63] Although the author knows the redemptive pattern also found in Phil 2:5–11, 1 Tim 3:16, and Col 1:15–20, he has not fully integrated it with adoptionistic traditions.

A distinctive feature of Hebrews is that Jesus is presented as having undergone a process of "education" in suffering through which he learned obedience and ultimately attained perfection.[64] Heb 5:8–9 states that "although he was a Son, he learned [ἔμαθεν] obedience [ὑποκοή] through what he suffered [ἔπαθεν]; and being made perfect [τελειωθείς] he became the source of eternal salvation to all who obey him." Although the author clearly portrays Jesus as a human being, he also is careful to mention his sinlessness (4:15). According to Heb 2:10, it is clear that "perfection" was the result of the suffering that Christ experienced: "For it was fitting that he [that is, God] . . . should make the pioneer [ἀρχηγός] of their salvation perfect through suffering [διὰ παθη-

---

Grässer, "Der historische Jesus im Hebräerbrief," ZNW 56 (1965) 63–91; B. L. Melbourne, "An Examination of the Historical-Jesus Motif in the Epistle to the Hebrews," AUSS 26 (1988) 281–96.

58. Grässer, "Der historische Jesus," 73–87, discusses three traditions found in Hebrews: (1) Jesus' descent from Judah (Heb 7:14). (2) The allusion to Gethsemane (Heb 5:7); Harold Attridge, however, argues correctly that "this picture of Jesus at prayer cannot be simply derived from any known tradition on the subject" (*The Epistle to the Hebrews* [Philadelphia: Fortress, 1989], 148). (3) Jesus' death "outside the gates" (Heb 13:12).

59. Most recently, see M. C. Parsons, "Son and High Priest: A Study in the Christology of Hebrews," EQ 60 (1988) 195–215.

60. Martin Hengel, *The Son of God* (trans. J. Bowden; Philadelphia: Fortress, 1976) 86–88.

61. Cf. John Knox, *The Humanity and Divinity of Christ* (Cambridge: Cambridge University Press, 1967) 34–49; J. D. G. Dunn, *Christology in the Making* (Philadelphia: Westminster, 1980) 51–56.

62. Cornutus *Theologiae Graecae compendium* 31; cf. Simon, "Christianisme antique et pensée païenne: Recontres et Conflits," *Le Christianisme antique et son contexte religieux*, 1. 256f.

63. Simon, "Christianisme antique," 257.

64. Oscar Cullmann, *The Christology of the New Testament* (Philadelphia: Westminster, 1963) 97f.; Attridge, *The Epistle to the Hebrews*, 153.

μάτων]." Jesus is presented in this way for parenetic reasons; he is an appropriate model for his followers.[65]

It is also important to observe that the suffering involved does not appear limited to Passion week, but includes unspecified experiences throughout Jesus' life.[66] This becomes clear in Heb 6:1, where, through a play on words, the author contrasts "the elementary doctrine [ἀρχῆς] of Christ" with "maturity" (τὴν τελειότητα) expected of Christians. According to Heb 12:5–11, God trains or disciplines sons because God loves them. This point is clearly expressed in Heb 12:7: "It is for discipline [παιδείαν] that you have to endure. God is treating you as sons; for what son is there whom the father does not discipline [παιδεύει]?" Here παιδεία, an important term in the Greek educational tradition, refers to the positive results of suffering. Dio Chrysostom (relying on earlier Cynic tradition) used the tradition of the divine-human sonship of Heracles as an allegory for two types of παιδεία or ἄσκησις, "training, education" (Or. 4.29–32; cf. Diogenes Laertius 6.70–71), that is, the Cynic theory Διὸς παῖς = πεπαιδευμένος.[67] This equation is found in Dio Chrysostom (Or. 4.31; trans. Cohoon in LCL): "Men of old called those persons 'sons of Zeus' [Διὸς παῖδας] who received the good education [ἀγαθῆς παιδείας] and were manly of soul, having been educated [πεπαιδευμένους] after the pattern of the great Herakles." A similar correlation between suffering and training is discussed by Epictetus (3.22.56f.; trans. Oldfather in LCL): "Does he [the Cynic] call upon anyone but Zeus? And is he not persuaded that whatever of these hardships he suffers [πάσχῃ], it is Zeus that is exercising [γυμνάζει] him? Nay, but Heracles, when he was being exercised by Eurystheus, did not count himself wretched, but used to fulfil without hesitation everything that was enjoined upon him: and yet is this fellow, when he is being trained [ἀθλούμενος] and exercised [γυμναζόμενος] by Zeus, prepared to cry out and complain?"

The term ἀρχηγός is used of Jesus twice in Hebrews (2:10; 12:2) and several other times in early Christian literature (Acts 3:15; 5:31; 2 Clem. 20:5).[68] It can mean "pioneer leader, founding leader," or "initiator, founder, originator."[69] Aelius Aristides (Or. 3.27) refers to Heracles as "the common leader of all men," and in Or. 40.14 claims that "he was the best champion of

65. Grässer, "Der historische Jesus," 70–72.

66. Cf. T. Moses 3.11 (trans. Charlesworth), where it is said of Moses that he "suffered many things in Egypt and at the Red Sea and in the wilderness for forty years." On this, see David L. Tiede, "The Figure of Moses in The Testament of Moses," Studies on the Testament of Moses (ed. G. W. E. Nickelsburg; Cambridge: Society of Biblical Literature, 1973) 89.

67. Höistad, Cynic Hero, 56–59.

68. Cf. the survey of opinions collected by G. Johnston, "Christ as Archegos," NTS 27 (1981) 381–85. Johnston's proposal that ἀρχηγός is dependent on the Hebrew term נשׂיא or שׂר is briefly but effectively rebutted by Herbert Braun, An die Hebräer (HNT 14; Tübingen: J. C. B. Mohr [Paul Siebeck], 1984) 404.

69. Johannes Louw and Eugene Nida (eds.), Greek-English Lexicon (New York: United Bible Societies, 1988) 1. 36.6, 68.2.

human nature and guided all men toward the best."[70] In the Greek world, ἀρχηγός is used of the god or hero who founded a city or nation, sometimes giving it his or her name (for example, Athena, Zeus, Apollo, Dionysus, and Moses).[71] The term ἀρχηγός in this sense is also applied to Heracles. In his speech to the citizens of Tarsus, Dio Chrysostom refers to "founders" (ἀρχηγοί) of their city (*Or.* 33.1) and then speaks of the possibility of an invisible visitation by ὁ ἀρχηγὸς ὑμῶν Ἡρακλῆς, "your founder Heracles" (*Or.* 33.47).[72]

In Heb 12:3–4, Jesus is set forth as one who endured in spite of abuse, hostility, and suffering and received a heavenly reward: "consider him who endured from sinners such hostility [ἀντιλογία] against himself, so that you may not grow weary or fainthearted. In your struggle against sin you have not yet resisted [ἀνταγωνιζόμενοι] to the point of shedding your blood."[73] This emphasis has a parallel in Aelius Aristides (*Or.* 40.22), who gives the gist of a divine voice he heard from the Metroon (a temple dedicated to the Great Mother): "It exhorted me to endure the present circumstances, since Heracles also endured his, although he was the son of Zeus." (Compare with the phrase καίπερ ὢν υἱός in Heb 5:8.) The motif of undeserved hostility and abuse dished out by outsiders occurs frequently in Cynic *chreiai* (Dio Chrys. *Or.* 8.36; 9.8).[74] The motif of the innocent suffering of Heracles was introduced by fifth-century Athenian dramatists, and the notion of φιλανθρωπία through suffering became part of the Heracles image;[75] in Euripides' *Hercules Furens*, Heracles is portrayed as a suffering human benefactor (lines 851ff., 875ff., 1252, 1309), and in Sophocles' *Trachiniae*, as a suffering god. According to Höistad, "In the final scene of Euripides' play [*Hercules Furens*] the problem of innocent suffering finds a purely immanent solution exemplary for all humanity. Heracles has descended to the world of man, exposed himself to the same sufferings and the same capricious fate as man must face."[76] Dio Chrysostom depicted the various experiences of Heracles as including loneliness, poverty, nakedness, homelessness, and suffering (*Or.* 1.59–65).

Although the suffering, death, and exaltation of Jesus are primarily in view in Heb 12:3–4, elsewhere the unknown author provides scattered indications

70. Charles A. Behr, *P. Aelius Aristides, the Complete Works* (Leiden: Brill, 1981, 1986), 1:203; 2:241.
71. G. Delling, *TDNT*, 1. 487f.; Attridge, *The Epistle to the Hebrews*, 87. Ernst Käsemann, *The Wandering People of God* (trans. R. A. Harrisville and I. L. Sandberg; Minneapolis: Augsburg, 1984) 128–33, emphasizes the importance of construing ἀρχηγός against the background of Gnostic tradition, a view shared by Braun, *An die Hebräer*, 58f., but opposed by Otto Michel, *Der Brief an die Hebräer* (12 Aufl.; Göttingen: Vandenhoeck & Ruprecht, 1966) 144.
72. For other references to Heracles as ἀρχηγός, see Attridge, *The Epistle to the Hebrews*, 88, n. 104.
73. The author makes elaborate use of other *exempla* in Heb 11:1–40; cf. Michael R. Cosby, "The Rhetorical Composition of Hebrews 11," *JBL* 107 (1988) 257–73.
74. Höistad, *Cynic Hero*, 198f.; Julian *Or.* 7.214D–215A.
75. Höistad, *Cynic Hero*, 24–28.
76. Höistad, *Cynic Hero*, 27.

DAVID E. AUNE   17

that he knew a connected form of the story of Jesus. In a chreia in Dio
Chrysostom, *Or.* 8.11, a person reportedly asked Diogenes if he had come to
watch the Isthmian games (ἀγῶνα). He replied that he was there as a partici-
pant (ἀγωνιούμενος). The man laughed and asked who Diogenes' competi-
tors [ἀνταγωνιστάς] were, to which he replied "hardships" (πόνους) (12; cf.
15), such as hunger, cold, thirst, exile, and loss of reputation (16).[77] In Heb
12:4, the verb ἀνταγωνίζεσθαι reflects either an athletic or military image,
and the reference to "shedding your blood" in the same verse can refer to box-
ing imagery, but also (but less probably) to military conflict.[78]

According to Heb 4:14–16, Jesus is a great high priest who has "passed
through the heavens" and who can understand our weaknesses since he has
himself experienced temptation just as we have. Through prayer expressed
boldly (μετὰ παρρησίας),[79] Christians can therefore find "grace to help in time
of need" (4:16). One important function of Heracles was as a helper and giver
of strength in the difficulties of life, a conception that first appears in Pindar.
Heracles is given the epithet πᾶσιν ἀρωγέ, "helper in everything," in Orphica
Hymni 12.6. There are several examples of prayers and references to prayer
to Heracles for help in the trials of life.[80] It was a widespread practice to
promise a tithe to Heracles if he would send good luck.[81] In what appears to
be a Cynic polemic against popular conceptions of Heracles, Dio Chrysostom
(*Or.* 8.28; LCL trans. with modifications) says, somewhat disparagingly, "All
pray to him that they may not themselves suffer [ἄθλιοι]—to him who in his
labours suffered [ἀθλήσαντι] exceedingly great." According to Aristides, *Or.*
40.16 (trans. Behr), Heracles' help was not limited to the duration of his life
on earth: "Not only could one say all this about the god, some of whose deeds
took place while he lived among mankind, and others of which he still now
clearly performs by himself."

The kinds of help that Heracles was expected to provide are expressed in
the following apotropaic inscription used as a motto inscribed on many door-
ways:[82]

ὁ τοῦ Διὸς παῖς καλλίνικος Ἡρακλῆς
ἐνθάδε κατοικεῖ, μηδὲν εἰσίτω κακόν.

77. G. Mussies, *Dio Chrysostom and the New Testament* (Leiden: Brill, 1972) 226f.
78. Attridge, *The Epistle to the Hebrews*, 360.
79. Although the Cynic emphasis on παρρησία, "boldness, freedom," involves primarily speech,
here παρρησία is a characteristic of how one approaches God (cf. Heb 3:6; 10:19–22).
80. Note the beginning of the prayer in Pindar *Nem.* 7.94–97 (trans. Sandys in LCL: "And thee,
O blessed Heracles, it beseemeth to persuade the consort of Hera and the grey-eyed maiden; for
full often canst thou grant to mortals relief from distress inexplicable." Cf. the prayer in the
Homeric *Hymn to Herakles* 9 (LCL trans.): "Hail, lord, son of Zeus. Give me success and prosperity [ἀρετήν τε καὶ ὄλβον]"; and Julian *Or.* 7.220A (trans. Wright in LCL): "Now when we
meditate on this, may Heracles be gracious to you and to me!"
81. Dionysius Hal. *Ant. Rom.* 1.40.5–6; Cicero *De nat. deorum* 3.36.88; Macrobius *Sat.* 3.12.2;
Plautus *Truc.* 2.7.11; Tertullian *Apol.* 14.1; 39.15.
82. Diogenes Laertius 6.50; G. Kaibel, *Epigrammata Graeca* (Berlin, 1878), 1138 (inscription on
a house wall at Pompei); Diogenes *Ep.* 36.1 (ed. Hercher, 249).

"The son of Zeus, gloriously triumphant Heracles,
dwells herein. Let nothing evil enter."

Two of Heracles' most popular epithets (mentioned together in Aristides *Or.* 40.15), which were often used synonymously, are reflected here: καλλίνικος, "exquisite victory," is explicitly mentioned; and ἀλεξίκακος, "averter of evil," is clearly implied. In this latter role, it is somewhat surprising that the name Heracles is missing from the Greek magical papyruses, though his apotropaic function, and therefore his ability to provide assistance to worshipers in time of need, is capitalized on in Orphica, *Hymni* 12.13–16:

> Immortal, world-wise, boundless and irrepressible,
> come, O blessed one, bringing all charms against disease;
> with club in hand, drive evil bane away
> and with your poisonous darts ward off cruel death.[83]

The obedience of Christ to the will of the Father is emphasized in Heb 5:8–9 and 10:5–10. In the first passage, Jesus is said to have learned obedience (ὑπακοή) through his sufferings (cf. Phil 2:8). Antisthenes, against the popular view of πόνος as a κακόν and using Heracles as an example, argued that pain had a positive value and could be considered a *good* thing [ὁ πόνος ἀγαθόν] with positive benefits (Diogenes Laertius 6.2). In Judaism, suffering was widely regarded as punishment for sin, yet suffering could have a positive effect in cleansing a person of sin.[84] This obedience must in part be understood as an expression of endurance, a quality emphasized by Cynics. Obedience to the will of Zeus is a frequently mentioned characteristic of Heracles, who always obeyed the commands of Zeus (Diodorus 4.11.1; Epictetus 2.16.44; 3.22.57; Menander Rhetor 2.380).

In Hebrews, the author describes the exaltation of Jesus in terms of the metaphor of heavenly enthronement *ad dextram dei* (Heb 1:3; 8:1; 10:12; 12:2), a conception that the author links with the metaphor of Jesus' presence in the most holy place (heaven) as high priest (cf. 6:20; 9:24). The resurrection of Jesus receives scant formal attention just once (Heb 13:20, as part of a benediction that concludes with a doxology). The exaltation is described in different language in Heb 4:14–16: Jesus, the Son of God, is a great high priest who has "passed through the heavens [διεληλυθότα τοὺς οὐρανούς]," essentially a description of the exaltation as an ascension.[85] Jesus' exaltation is also described in Heb 2:9 as a reward for suffering: Jesus was "crowned [ἐστεφανωμένον] with glory and honor because of the suffering of death [διὰ τὸ πάθημα τοῦ θανάτου]." The same sentiment is reflected in Heb 12:2, where

83. Apostolos N. Athanassakis, *The Orphic Hymns: Text, Translation, and Notes* (SBLTT 12; Missoula: Scholars Press, 1977).

84. E. P. Sanders, "R. Akiba's View of Suffering," *JQR* 63 (1972–73) 333; George Foot Moore, *Judaism* (Cambridge: Harvard University Press, 1927) 2. 248–56; E. E. Urbach, *The Sages* (Cambridge: Harvard University Press, 1987) 444–48.

85. Michel, *Der Brief an die Hebräer*, 204f.; Braun, *An die Hebräer*, 124.

Jesus' present status is the result of his endurance of suffering and death; he is described as "the pioneer and perfecter of our faith, who for the joy that was set before him endured the cross, despising the shame and is seated at the right hand of the throne of God."

Although the notion of resurrection is largely absent from Heracles legends,[86] the notion that he was raised to Olympus with divine status was an integral part of the Heracles myth.[87] The early tradition that Heracles had died (Homer *Iliad* 8.117–19), a view that some thought contradicted the belief that Heracles was a god, was recognized as a problem by the scholiast: "Some affirm that Homer was unaware that Heracles was apotheosized since he says that he died. Yet saying that he did not escape death does not indicate ignorance of his deification."[88] Death and ascension to heaven resulting in deification are connected in the late account of Apollodorus (2.7.7; trans. Simpson): "Heracles commanded Hyllus, his elder son by Deianira, to marry Iole when he reached manhood, then went to Mount Oeta (in Trachis) and there constructed a pyre, climbed upon it and ordered it to be ignited. When no one would light it, Poeas, who was passing by in search of his flocks, set fire to it. Heracles then bequeathed his bow to him. While the pyre was burning a cloud is said to have enveloped Heracles and to have raised him up to heaven [εἰς οὐρανὸν ἀναπέμψαι] with a crash of thunder. Thenceforth he was immortal." Diodorus transmits a less mythological version, observing that people generally thought that Heracles "had been transferred [μεθεστάσθαι] from among men into the company of the gods" (3.38.5; cf. Justin *Dial.* 69.3).

Despite the widespread popularity and symbolic value of the figure of Heracles in the Greco-Roman world, there is no convincing evidence that Heracles imagery played any significant role in the formation of legendary episodes about Jesus found in the canonical Gospels. The phenomenological similarity between aspects of the lives of Jesus and Heracles are rather to be attributed to the more general tendency of traditions about great personalities to conform to the morphology of Greco-Roman heroes through the folkloristic process of the communal re-creation of tradition. In contrast, the similarities between Heracles imagery and the Christology of Hebrews that have been explored above suggest that many of the important and vital functions attributed to Heracles as a Hellenistic savior figure were understood by some early Christians as applicable to Jesus to an even greater extent than they were to Heracles.

86. Josephus (*Ant.* 8.146) refers to a Tyrian festival called τοῦ Ἡρακλέους ἔγερσις, "the raising of Heracles" (cf. Pfister, "Herakles und Christus," 58f.). This is probably part of the cycle of death and rebirth associated with many Near Eastern fertility cults.

87. Homer *Odyssey* 11.602–4; Diodorus 4.39.2–4; Hesiod frag. 25.24–28 Merkelbach and West; Hesiod *Theogonia* 950–55; Seneca *Agamemnon* 812–16; *Octavia* 210–12.

88. W. Dindorf, *Scholia Graeca in Homeri Iliadem* (Oxford: Clarendon Press, 1875) 2. 153; cf. *Inscriptiones Graecae* 14, 1806; *Corpus Inscriptionum Graecarum* 6438: οὐδεὶς ἀθάνατος, καὶ ὁ Ἡρακλῆς ἀπέθανε, "no one is immortal; even Heracles died."

2

A DOG IN THE MANGER
The Cynic Cynulcus among
Athenaeus's Deipnosophists

Problems of evidence constantly dog the student of imperial Cynicism. To
begin with, the evidence remains scattered through countless sources, for
Cynics of this period had no Diogenes Laertius to collect their materials, as
had the early Cynics (Diogenes Laertius bk. 6), and modern collections likewise focus on the earlier period. In addition, the evidence itself is problematic
in several ways. For example, it is sometimes so brief that little more than a
name remains for some Cynics, such as a Plenetiades in Plutarch (*Def. Orac.*
413A) or a Rhodius in Lucian (*Toxaris* 27). The evidence may be largely
anecdotal, raising problems of overall coherence, as happens in the case of
Demonax (Lucian *Demon.* 12–67). At times the evidence becomes opaque, at
least insofar as the personalities of imperial Cynicism often write pseudepi-
graphically, as is the case for the Cynic epistles that use the names, say, of
Diogenes or Crates. The evidence may be tendentious, whether positively, as
in Epictetus's familiar but highly Stoicized portrait of the ideal Cynic (*Diss.*
3.22), or negatively, as in Lucian's scathing and personal attack on Peregrinus
in his *De morte Peregrini.*[1]

Consequently, given these problems with the evidence, it is surprising that
scholars have neglected one imperial Cynic, Athenaeus's Cynulcus, the best
documented of all imperial Cynics and one, moreover, who, because of his
important role in Athenaeus's *Deipnosophistae* (*The Learned Dinner Guests*),
is provided with a detailed and coherent context. Accordingly, after some
introductory and orienting remarks about Athenaeus and his *Deipnosophistae,*
this chapter will turn to Cynulcus and his context: the intellectual world of a
learned symposium.

I wish to thank my friend and colleague Professor Edward N. O'Neil of the University of
Southern California classics department for his reading of an earlier draft of this chapter and for
offering many helpful suggestions and improvements.
    1. My own interest in imperial Cynicism derives, of course, from Professor Abraham J.
Malherbe's work, and in particular from his article "Gentle as a Nurse: The Cynic Background of
1 Thess. 2," *NovT* 12 (1970) 203–17, an article that decisively influenced my intellectual development. It is appropriate, then, for me to turn to imperial Cynicism to honor Professor Malherbe.

ATHENAEUS AND HIS *DEIPNOSOPHISTAE*

Little information survives about Athenaeus outside the·*Deipnosophistae*, his only extant work. The *Suda* (1.69 Adler) says only that Athenaeus was a grammarian (γραμματικός) from Naucratis, in Egypt, and flourished during the reign of Marcus Aurelius (A.D. 161 to 180). But, as W. Dittenberger points out, even this basic information clearly derives from the *Deipnosophistae* itself.[2] Athenaeus is explicitly connected with Naucratis (*Deipnos.* 3.73a; 11.480d), the reign of Marcus Aurelius is probably an inference from statements about Galen and Oppian (1.1e; 13b),[3] and the *Deipnosophistae* as a whole betrays Athenaeus's standing as a grammarian. Consequently, with the *Suda* dependent on the *Deipnosophistae*, we are left with only the work itself for information about it and its author.

Fortunately, more information than that gleaned by the *Suda* is scattered throughout the *Deipnosophistae*. One obvious inference is that Athenaeus had left Naucratis at some time for Rome, where he found a friend and probably a patron in a Roman aristocrat named Larensis, who is undoubtedly the pontifex P. Livius Larensis known from an inscription.[4]

Larensis is important for Athenaeus for two reasons. On the one hand, his exceptionally large library (*Deipnos.* 1.3a)—and one with a large collection of ancient Greek writings (4.160c)—probably served Athenaeus's needs as he wrote the (now lost) treatise "On Those Who Ruled in Syria" (5.211a) and especially so as he composed the quotation-rich *Deipnosophistae*.[5] At any rate, Larensis's library seems a more likely location for Athenaeus to have worked than the more famous library at Alexandria, as some have suggested.[6]

On the other hand, Larensis, because of his interest in intellectual life (*Deipnos.* 1.2c), gathered about himself a large and diverse group of profes-

---

2. W. Dittenberger, "Athenäus und sein Werk," *Apophoreton, überreicht von der Graeca Hallensis* (XLVII, Versammlung deutscher Philologen und Schulmänner; Berlin: Weidmann, 1903) 1–28.

3. On this inference, as well as the interpretation of the *Suda* article presupposed here, see Dittenberger, "Athenäus," 2–4.

4. The identification goes back to H. Dessau, "Zu Athenaeus," *Hermes* 25 (1890) 156–58, and has been accepted ever since: Dittenberger, "Athenäus," 16–17; K. Mengis, *Die schriftstellerische Technik im sophistenmahl des Athenaios* (Studien zur Geschichte und Kultur des Altertums 10, 5; Paderborn: Ferdinand Schöningh, 1920) 30–31; G. Bowersock, *Greek Sophists in the Roman Empire* (Oxford: Clarendon, 1969) 20, n. 4; and B. Baldwin, "The Minor Characters in Athenaeus," *Acta Classica* 20 (1977) 37–48, esp. 37.

5. These are the two certain writings of Athenaeus. Scholars, however, often identify a third, an exegesis of a passage in the poet Archippus (cf. *Deipnos.* 7.329c and M. Wellmann, "Dorion," *Hermes* 23 [1888] 179–93, esp. 179; G. Wentzel, "Athenaios [nr. 22]," *RE* 4 [1896] 2026–33, esp. 2026; and W. V. Christ, W. Schmid, and O. Stählin, *Geschichte der griechischen Literatur* [6th ed.; Handbuch der Altertumswissenschaft; Munich: Beck, 1924] 2.1. 791). But Athenaeus is recounting a conversation, and although the speaker is not identified here, it is more likely that the treatise belongs to the speaker than to Athenaeus himself. This situation is clearly the case for an alleged fourth writing (cf. *Deipnos.* 4.155a and Christ, Schmid, and Stählin, *Geschichte*, 792, n. 1), where the speaker, the grammarian Plutarch, is presumably the author.

6. Christ, Schmid, and Stählin, *Geschichte,* 791. For Athenaeus's use of Larensis's library, see also Mengis, *Die schriftstellerische Technik,* 31.

sional intellectuals and, because of his wealth and hospitality (1.3c–d), hosted them at symposia (1.2b). The intellectuals—grammarians, philosophers, orators, physicians, jurists—dined on foods of unimaginable variety as they discussed a like variety of topics of conversation, or ζητήσεις (cf. 1.2b). Indeed, for most, these conversations proved more nourishing than the foods, for, as Larensis put it, "We live by ζητήσεις" (9.398b; cf. 6.270c; 7.275b).

Many of the conversations naturally deal with matters related to the symposia—wines; foods of all kinds, but especially fish; hand washing; cups; chefs; cooking utensils; entertainers; wreaths; and libations. But many other subjects transcend the symposium setting and include Homeric heroes, religious processions, large ships, parasites, fish dealers, slaves, and hetaerae.[7] Especially significant is the fact that all the conversations are spiced with copious quotations from ancient Greek literature.

These many conversations by the intellectuals gathered at Larensis's symposia were used by Athenaeus for his own literary symposium,[8] which he wrote shortly after the death of the Emperor Commodus, or about A.D. 193 to 197 (cf. Deipnos. 12.537f.), as Dittenberger has persuasively argued.[9] This work, which contains fifteen books[10] and fills seven Loeb volumes,[11] consists of Athenaeus's regaling his friend Timocrates (1.1a et passim) with the conversations of the Deipnosophists, though the conversations are now organized as if they came from a single, if lengthy, symposium.[12] Thus, as J. Martin argues, the conversations are so organized that they deal first with various preliminary

7. The fullest summary of the subjects discussed in the Deipnosophistae is that by Wentzel, "Athenaios," 2028–31.

8. For literary analyses of the Deipnosophistae, including its relation to other symposiac writings, see esp. Mengis, Die schriftstellerische Technik, 45–108, and J. Martin, Symposion: Die Geschichte einer literarischen Form (Studien zur Geschichte und Kultur des Altertums 17; Paderborn: Ferdinand Schöningh, 1931) 270–80.

9. See Dittenberger, "Athenäus," 4–14, 20–26. He argues vigorously against a later date of shortly after 228, as do, for example, Wentzel, "Athenaios," 2033, and Mengis, Die schriftstellerische Technik, 33–36. The later date arises when the principal speaker, Ulpian of Tyre, whose death is noted at Deipnos. 15.686c, is identified with the famous jurist of the same name. The latter was once thought to have been murdered in 228—hence the dating—but new evidence pushes his death back to late 223 or early 224 (see P.Oxy. 2565 and T. Honoré, Ulpian [Oxford: Clarendon, 1982] 40–41). In any case, the identification, as Dittenberger points out, is most unlikely due to sharp differences between the two Ulpians in terms of education, social rank, occupation, and manner of death; Athenaeus's note about Ulpian's death hardly suggests murder. In addition, as Dittenberger also points out, all the people mentioned in the Deipnosophistae who lived during imperial times fit the 190s better than a period after 228, or 223–224. Accordingly, those persuaded by Dittenberg include Christ, Schmid, and Stählin, Geschichte, 793; J. Werner, "Athenaios (nr. 3)," Der kleine Pauly (5 vols.; Stuttgart: Druckmüller, 1964) 1. 702–3, esp. 702; B. Baldwin, "Athenaeus and His Work," Acta Classica 19 (1976) 21–42, esp. 29–34; and Honoré, Ulpian, 12–15. But if the two Ulpians are not to be identified, they may still, concedes Dittenberg, have been related, as father and son or as uncle and nephew—a possibility accepted by Baldwin, "Athenaeus," 34, and Honoré, Ulpian, 14.

10. For evidence that originally there may have been thirty books, see Wentzel, "Athenaios," 2027, and Christ, Schmid, and Stählin, Geschichte, 791, n. 5.

11. Athenaeus the Deipnosophist (trans. Gulick in LCL).

12. Martin, Symposion, 270. Cf. Mengis, Die schriftstellerische Technik, 3.

matters of a symposium (bk. 1–5); then with the dinner proper, or δεῖπνον (bk. 6–10); and finally with the drinking party, or πότος (bk. 10–15).[13]

As Timocrates eagerly listens to Athenaeus recount the many conversations along with their accompanying quotations from ancient Greek literature, the purpose of the work begins to emerge: to provide Timocrates (and the reader) with an exhaustive treatment of the symposium—a Περὶ συμποσίων, as Martin puts it[14]—that will contain all the literary lore necessary to attend a learned symposium, so that he will have an appropriate literary citation for any likely food served or for any likely topic discussed, and even for an unexpected noise during the symposium (cf. *Deipnos.* 8.361f–362a).

Such a purpose—or indeed any purpose—for the *Deipnosophistae* has not usually concerned scholars. They have instead regarded the work solely as a source of fragments of earlier writers—some 1,250, according to one estimate.[15] In this sense, the *Deipnosophistae*, scholars admit, is invaluable and in fact unrivaled.[16] Otherwise, however, scholars dismiss Athenaeus as a mere copier of others' collections of quotations,[17] as literarily inept, and as prone to blunders,[18] and the conversations in which the quotations occur as "unbelievably boring."[19]

Interest in the individual deipnosophists has been sporadic and usually pursued in terms of the question of Athenaeus's dates—as is especially the case with the principal deipnosophist, Ulpian of Tyre[20]—or simply in terms of establishing the deipnosophists' likely historical existence. The latter problem reflects a reaction to G. Kaibel, the Teubner editor of the *Deipnosophistae*, who proposed that the Deipnosophists were a combination of fact and fiction, a group of individuals who were made up of names and characteristics from persons of previous centuries. For example, the grammarian Plutarch of Alexandria (*Deipnos.* 1.1c et passim) has the name of the famous philosopher from Chaironeia, and the physician Daphnus of Ephesus (1.1d et passim) is modeled on the first-century physician Rufus, also of Ephesus.[21] But the work of Dittenberger and others has demonstrated that the deipnosophists are in fact individuals of Athenaeus's own time.[22]

13. Martin, *Symposion*, 274–75. Cf. Mengis, *Die schriftstellerische Technik*, 7–19.

14. Martin, *Symposion*, 271.

15. W. M. Edwards and R. Browning, "Athenaeus (1)," *OCD* 139.

16. So, e.g., Wentzel, "Athenaios," 2028; Dittenberger, "Athenäus, 8; and Werner, "Athenaios," 702.

17. Christ, Schmid, and Stählin, *Geschichte*, 793.

18. Martin, *Symposion*, 272; Werner, "Athenaios," 702; and esp. Mengis, *Die schriftstellerische Technik*, 1–2, 5, and passim.

19. Honoré, *Ulpian*, 12.

20. On the importance of Ulpian for dating Athenaeus, see note 9 above.

21. *Athenaei Naucratitae Deipnosophistarum Libri XV* (3 vols.; ed. G. Kaibel; Bibliotheca Teubneriana; Leipzig: Teubner, 1887–90) 1, praef. vi–vii.

22. Dittenberger, "Athenäus," 14–26, and Baldwin, "Minor Characters," 37–48. See also Mengis, *Die schriftstellerische Technik*, 23–45, who, except for Larensis, Galen, Ulpian, and Cynulcus, is less optimistic about their historicity.

As already noted, an inscription has established the reality of Athenaeus's host, Larensis. The probabilities also favor the historical existence of a Plutarch of Alexandria[23] and a Daphnus of Ephesus,[24] as well as that of the principal subject of this chapter, the Cynic Cynulcus—"eine zeitgenössische, geschichtliche Person," as K. Mengis describes him.[25]

B. Baldwin, however, goes somewhat further than merely establishing the deipnosophists as Athenaeus's likely contemporaries; he also recognizes Athenaeus's value as a witness for intellectual life in the imperial Rome of the Antonines and Severans.[26] To be sure, Baldwin limits himself to the largely prosopographical matters of "provenance, chronology, and attainments."[27] Nevertheless, the recognition is surely correct, and hence it is the purpose of this chapter to build on Baldwin's work by focusing on one of the deipnosophists, the Cynic Cynulcus, whose role in the symposia at Larensis's house helps us not only in discerning his personality and character but also in sharpening our understanding of a Cynic view of the dominant literary culture of Rome.

There are, of course, problems—both textual and literary—in carrying out this project, and a brief discussion of them is in order before proceeding. The text of the *Deipnosophistae*[28] survives in only one manuscript, Codex Marcianus Graecus 447. The manuscript is early (it was copied by John the Calligrapher in the late ninth or early tenth century)[29] and also damaged; it is missing the first two books and the beginning of the third (1.1a–3.73e), as well as parts at the end (15.700e–f). Fortunately, an epitome survives, made from a complete text, perhaps by Eustathius in the twelfth century,[30] so that at least the general contents of the whole remain intact. However, the epitomizer seemingly cut short the opening roster of the deipnosophists (1.1c–f) and eliminated the conversational form. Consequently, it is only by accident that any of the material in the epitome can be assigned to a particular speaker (1.11b, 26c–27d; 2.49a–c, 50f–51b, 58c).

More serious problems, however, arise at the literary level. Some are due to Athenaeus's literary habits, and especially frustrating is his habit of identify-

23. Baldwin, "Minor Characters," 47.

24. Dittenberger, "Athenäus," 17.

25. Mengis, *Die schriftstellerische Technik*, 37. So also Dittenberger, "Athenäus," 17, and Baldwin, "Minor Characters," 42.

26. Baldwin, "Athenaeus," 42. See also the brief comments by Dittenberger, "Athenäus," 26–28, and Mengis, *Die schriftstellerische Technik*, 45.

27. Baldwin, "Minor Characters," 47.

28. On the textual tradition, see the brief, but excellent, discussion in Wentzel, "Athenaios," 2026–27.

29. On the identification of the copyist, and hence a more precise date for the manuscript (between A.D. 895 and 928), see N. Wilson, "Did Arethas Read Athenaeus?" *JHS* 82 (1962) 147–48.

30. See N. Wilson, *Scholars of Byzantium* (Baltimore: Johns Hopkins University Press, 1983) 163, 201–2. He, however, remains skeptical.

ing speakers only by the indefinite pronoun τις (someone).[31] But he also, on occasion, drops the conversational format in favor of an alphabetical arrangement for especially numerous items, as happens, for example, in the long discussion of fish (*Deipnos.* 7.277a–330b).[32] Moreover, no speaker appears at all in book 12, as Athenaeus seemingly prefers to speak directly to Timocrates on those who were renowned for gluttony (12.510a–554f).

Even when the conversations are assigned, however, they sometimes are hardly conversational, having only an address,[33] and at other times they are impossibly long and too filled with lengthy quotations to be plausible conversations—even for deipnosophists and their prodigious memories.[34] Finally, there are the problems of adopting a literary form to preserve the conversations. Athenaeus followed many of the literary conventions of the symposium form, including, for example, the arrival of an uninvited guest—in this case, the musician Amoebus (*Deipnos.* 14.622c–623d)—and the presence of a requisite Cynic in the figure of Cynulcus.[35]

This rehearsal of problems, as well as the discussion of the document as a whole, should serve to emphasize how far apart the actual conversations of the deipnosophists at Larensis's house are from their literary treatment in the *Deipnosophistae*. Athenaeus was, to be sure, present during these conversations, but in writing the *Deipnosophistae* he has rearranged them, has often been vague or cavalier about preserving their attributions, has sometimes stripped them of their conversational form or otherwise extended them beyond plausible bounds, and has set them all within the form and conventions of the literary symposium. In addition, the single manuscript of the *Deipnosophistae* to survive is incomplete, so that a welcome, if sharply curtailed, epitome of the lost portions is alone available.

However, although this situation certainly invites caution about using the *Deipnosophistae* for a reconstruction and analysis of the intellectual world centered at Larensis's house, there is also no reason for despair. Although some conversations are lost or their attributions dropped or only vaguely identified, the sheer bulk of the *Deipnosophistae* makes this evidence less problematic than it seems at first, and even this evidence is valuable for a general sense of intellectual activity at Larensis's symposia. Likewise, Athenaeus's tendency to transform conversations into learned treatises is also not complete, for many conversations—and particularly those involving sharp disagreement among the deipnosophists—remain intact,[36] and even the

31. See *Deipnos.* 3.115b; 4.156c; 8.362a, 366a; 9.384a, 384f, 385a, 385b, 396a, 396b, 398b, 401b, 408b; 10.421a, 426a, 426b, 426c, 446b; 13.561b; 14.613c, 640b; 15.666a, 686c, 699d, 699e.

32. At times, however, the catalog does include snippets of the conversations (e.g., *Deipnos.* 7.298d–299c; 307f–308c).

33. See further Mengis, *Die schriftstellerische Technik*, 57–62.

34. See Mengis, *Die schriftstellerische Technik*, 24.

35. On the literary conventions used by Athenaeus, see Martin, *Symposion*, 277–80, and Mengis, *Die schriftstellerische Technik*, 93–108.

36. Even Mengis, *Die schriftstellerische Technik*, 68, acknowledges the transcriptional quality of such conversations and points in particular to those between Ulpian and Cynulcus.

treatiselike sections indicate the general tenor, if not the actual words, of the discussions at Larensis's house. Finally, although the presence of a Cynic like Cynulcus may be due to literary convention, Cynulcus himself, as we will see, is hardly conventional. In short, Athenaeus's *Deipnosophistae*, for all its problems and shortcomings, still provides us with a rare glimpse into the intellectual life of Rome in the late second century, and a still rarer—and coherent—glimpse of an imperial Cynic in this milieu. Accordingly, we can turn now to the learned world of the deipnosophists and to Cynulcus's active, if ambivalent, role within it.

CYNULCUS'S LIFE BEFORE AND OUTSIDE LARENSIS'S SYMPOSIA

The total number of deipnosophists at Larensis's symposia cannot be fixed precisely.[37] The roster at the beginning (*Deipnos.* 1.1c–f) lists fourteen individuals, but it is also vague and, as already indicated, incomplete. Thus, it speaks vaguely of numerous orators (1.1d), but Ulpian of Tyre is the only one listed, and no other orator appears. Eight other individuals, who are not listed here, do appear in the course of the work, and still four others, identified only by profession, appear as well. Thus, we have, besides Larensis and Athenaeus, at least twenty-six deipnosophists who can be grouped by profession as follows: nine grammarians,[38] six philosophers,[39] five physicians,[40] and two musicians,[41] as well as several single representatives: one orator (Ulpian), one jurist,[42] and one individual—a Roman named Magnus (3.74c)—whose profession is not given. And there is the chef, named Sophon (14.622e), whose literary learning and admiration of the ancient chefs (9.376c–380c et passim) justify his inclusion among the deipnosophists.

The roster also speaks vaguely of Cynics in the plural (*Deipnos.* 1.1d)—as do several other passages (4.160b; 7.275b; 13.612f)—and, indeed, one other Cynic does appear briefly (7.307f). However, he remains unnamed and otherwise unidentified, so Cynulcus, like Ulpian among the orators, becomes the sole representative of his group. Some information about him and his life before and outside of Larensis's symposia is noted in passing in the course of

37. See Mengis, *Die schriftstellerische Technik*, 24. For a fuller discussion of all the deipnosophists than is possible here, see Mengis, *Die schriftstellerische Technik*, 23–45, and esp. Baldwin, "Minor Characters," 39–48.
38. The roster lists four: Plutarch, Leonides, Aemilianus, and Zoilus (*Deipnos.* 1.1c). But also appearing are Arrian (3.113a), Myrtilus (3.83a), Palamedes (9.397a), Varus (3.118d), and an unnamed grammarian (7.276c).
39. The roster lists, besides Cynulcus, three: Pontianus, Democritus, and Philadelphus (*Deipnos.* 1.1d). But also appearing are two unnamed philosophers: an Epicurean (7.298d) and a Cynic (7.307f). In addition, the Platonic allegiance of the physician Daphnus is noted (1.1e).
40. The roster lists three: Daphnus, Galen, and Rufinus, though an unnamed physician also appears (*Deipnos.* 15.665f).
41. The roster lists only one: Alceides (*Deipnos.* 1.1f). But Amoebus also appears (14.622c).
42. The roster lists Masurius as a jurist but also as a poet (*Deipnos.* 1.1c).

the conversations, and it is to this information that we now turn before resuming the analysis of the deipnosophists and Cynulcus's place among them.

Cynulcus is the name by which our Cynic is usually identified, but it turns out to be only a nickname. Larensis says, however, that he preferred this name to the one given him at birth by his mother (*Deipnos.* 4.160d), but Larensis does not reveal the given name. That name appears later as Theodorus (15.669e, 692b). The preferred name Cynulcus, which means "leader of dogs," is clearly apt for a Cynic, or "doggish," philosopher with followers, as Athenaeus notes, who are more numerous than Actaeon's hounds (1.1d). Cynulcus's preference for it, however, may have had less to do with its aptness than with its literary flavor, as it probably derives from Parmeniscus's *Cynicorum Symposium*, where the name is also applied to a certain Carneius (4.156e). In addition, nicknames, as we will see, are quite popular among Larensis's deipnosophists.

Although we know the name given Cynulcus at birth, we do not know—in contrast with most of the other deipnosophists—where he was born. To be sure, at one point Cynulcus refers to the Cynic Cercidas as ὁ ἐμὸς Μεγαλοπολίτης (*Deipnos.* 8.347d), which might suggest that he was a "fellow citizen" of Cercidas at Megalopolis and hence a native of this Greek city. But he may be simply identifying himself with this expession because Cercidas was a "fellow Cynic."[43] Wherever he was born, however, Cynulcus's early years included a good education, as is clear from his referring to having read the poetry of Callimachus as a boy, thereby indicating study with a grammarian (15.669c). His literary education is worthy of note, for imperial Cynics—with notable exceptions, such as Demonax—were typically depicted as uneducated.[44]

At any rate, Cynulcus eventually—like Athenaeus himself and many of his fellow deipnosophists—took up residence in Rome (see *Deipnos.* 3.121f: τὰ νῦν). Earlier, perhaps, or during this sojourn, he seems also to have visited Athens (3.98b) and Corinth (13.567b–c). Just when and where he took up Cynic philosophy is never said, but at least at Rome, Cynulcus has not only become the leader, as already indicated, of a large band of Cynics (1.1d) but also involved himself quite fully in the life of the city. He learned some Latin (3.121e; 15.701b); spent time in the marketplace, where he mingled with the crowds and heard a Sophist nicknamed Plethagoras (6.270d); and befriended a physician, who helped with a prank on Ulpian. The latter had bruised his ankle but had described it using a word (ὑπώπιον) more appropriate for a black eye, prompting Cynulcus to ask the physician for some eye salve and to use, when asked about it, a word (πρόσκομμα) more appropriate for a foot injury (3.97f). Cynulcus likewise criticized Ulpian's language at the baths and during a festival (3.97d–e). He was no less critical of the language of the

---

43. So also Kaibel, *Athenaeus,* 3.561, and Mengis, *Die schriftstellerische Technik,* 36.
44. See, e.g., Dio *Or.* 32.9; Lucian *Fug.* 12; *Vit. Auct.* 11; and Alciphron *Ep.* 2.38. On Demonax, see Lucian *Demon.* 3.

Sophist Pompeianus of Philadelphia when the latter, on arriving at Rome, began his encomium of the city with an ill-chosen word (3.98c).

These chance references to Cynulcus's literary education and to his activities in Rome are few, but they do suggest a person who was born into the privileged classes and who later played a role in the intellectual life of the Roman aristocracy. This role is especially evident in the prank played on Ulpian, for it not only shows Cynulcus to be a friend of a physician but also shows him to have been known to Ulpian's circle of friends, since otherwise the prank would not have worked. Therefore, it is not surprising that a prominent aristocrat like Larensis would have included Cynulcus among the regular guests at his symposia. It is only here, of course, in the learned setting of Larensis's house—at what must have been regular, perhaps daily, symposia[45]—that the evidence about Cynulcus is sufficient to permit a clear and coherent description of him. Since that description is so tied to the setting, a few brief comments on the setting itself—its host, as well as the dominant ethos that he and the other deipnosophists created there—are in order.

LARENSIS AND THE LITERARY WORLD
OF HIS SYMPOSIA

Larensis's prominence is apparent from the priestly office the emperor Marcus Aurelius gave him (*Deipnos.* 1.2c) and from the governorship that he had at one time in the province of Moesia (9.398e). In addition to these public roles, Larensis also seems to have been an amateur intellectual as well, and with this intellectual interst he is reminiscent of Lucian's host in the *Convivium*, Aristaenetus, who likewise gathered about himself a group of intellectuals. However, whereas Aristaenetus was especially interested in philosophy—he even named his son Zeno and his daughter, Cleanthis (*Conv.* 5)—Larensis is particularly partial to the literary studies of the grammarian. In fact, he is said to have mastered both Greek and Latin literatures, thereby earning the nickname "Asteropaeus," in that his command of both languages recalled Asteropaeus's ability to throw spears with either arm (*Deipnos.* 1.2c; cf. Homer *Il.* 21.164: περιδέξιος). At any rate, Larensis can mine Latin literature for a description of life among the ancient Romans (6.273a–274e), and he surpasses most professional Roman grammarians in his knowledge of Greek poets and historians (4.160c). His love of Homer, Athenaeus notes, was especially keen (14.620b).

Reinforcing Larensis's grammatical or literary interests—and thereby establishing a grammatical rather than, say, a philosophical or medical ethos to the intellectual discussions at the symposia[46]—are not only the nine gram-

---

45. Various passages suggest the regularity of Larensis's symposia: *Deipnos.* 1.2b; 8.331b; 9.396b, 397a, 399a; 15.665a.
46. On grammarians and their literary ethos, see S. F. Bonner, *Education in Ancient Rome: From the Elder Cato to the Younger Pliny* (Berkeley: University of California Press, 1977) 212–49;

marians but also Ulpian, who, though an orator by profession, acts more like a
grammarian, as is immediately evident from his nickname "Keitoukeitos"
(*Deipnos.* 1.1e). This name is formed from the phrase κεῖται ἢ οὐ κεῖται,
which itself is part of a standard question: "Is a word *found or not found* in an
ancient author?"

Ulpian, it is said, asks this grammatical question (ζήτησις) everywhere—in
the streets, public walks, bookshops, baths (*Deipnos.* 1.1d)—and, not surprisingly, at symposia, too. Indeed, he had a rule not to eat anything before asking
whether the word for a food, drink, method of preparation, serving dish, or
cup "is found or not found" in Greek literature (1.1e). Moreover, since Ulpian
is Larensis's "master of ceremonies" (ὁ τῶν δείπνων ταμίας [2.58b]), this
question dominates the symposia and so sets the grammatical tone of the
intellectual discourse. Thus, when the appetizers are served, he asks if the
word for "appetizer" (πρόπομα) is found in some author (κεῖται παρά τινι
[2.58b]), and likewise for swine's "matrix" (μήτρα [3.96f]), "puddings" (χόν-
δροι [3.126f]), "tender" ham (τακερόν) and "fatted" geese (σιτευτοί [9.366a,
384a]), "pheasants" (φασιανικοί [9.386e]), and meats from animals that had
been "choked" (πνικτά [9.396a]), to name just a few. The other deipnosophists are expected to answer these ζητήσεις with quotations from the ancient
authors (οἱ ἀρχαῖοι or οἱ παλαιοί)—usually poets and historians (ποιηταὶ καὶ
συγγραφεῖς). These authors not only bear witness to the words' early usage;
they also justify the deipnosophists' using them as well. In any case, the grammarian Aemilianus recites several lines containing the word "pudding" from
the comic poets Antiphanes, Alexis, and Aristophanes (3.127b–c), and Ulpian
himself recalls a passage from the historian Phylarchus that has the word
"appetizer" (2.58c). Only then, however, can the symposium proceed. Otherwise, as Ulpian puts it rather dramatically at one point, "I will choke myself to
death unless you say where you can find such strangled meats in literature"
(9.396a; cf. 9.401d). Fortunately, a deipnosophist could—in Strattis, Eubulus,
Aristophanes, and Antiphanes (9.396a–b).

Neither Ulpian nor the other deipnosophists limit their ζητήσεις to the
foods served, however, but also seek literary precedent for any number of
words that had been used in their conversations or were otherwise prompted
by the activities of the symposium. Thus, when Magnus refers to Aristomenes
of Athens as a freedman of Hadrian, Ulpian asks if the word "freedman" (ἀπε-
λεύθερος) is found in any ancient author (*Deipnos.* 3.115b). When the grammarian Myrtilus uses ὀλβιογάστωρ (finding happiness in the belly) as an
epithet for Ulpian, the latter is not angered by the epithet but merely asks for
attestation of it in ancient literature (9.386c, e). When water for the hands is
brought in, Ulpian asks if "wash-basin" (χέρνιβον) is mentioned by any
ancient author (9.408b).

and R. A. Kaster, *Guardians of Language: The Grammarian and Society in Late Antiquity* (Berkeley: University of California Press, 1988) esp. 201–30.

Answers to these ζητήσεις—and they number in the hundreds in the course of the *Deipnosophistae*—always contain one quotation from literature, although there are usually many quotations. They also include, in passing, much else that further underscores the grammarians' hold on the intellectual ethos of Larensis's symposia. Thus, the deipnosophists frequently comment on the attribution or authenticity of a literary work (4.137e, 144e, 166d; 6.264a; 7.277d, 283a; etc.) or even of a line in a work (5.177c–178a). Or they discuss the spelling of a word (3.95f; 6.228d; 7.324d; 9.366a; etc.), or its accent (7.323c; 9.388f; 11.485a; etc.), gender (3.119b; 9.366a; 11.484c; etc.), case endings (3.127d; 7.299a; 9.392b; etc.), and etymology (7.308b; 8.362e; 9.367a; 11.783b; etc.). In addition to these technical concerns of the grammarian, the literary ethos is also apparent from slaves who have names taken from literature (for example, Strombichides [3.98a; cf. 6.230d]), as well as from slaves who themselves can recite literature (for example, Myrtilus's slave who answers Ulpian's questions with lines from the poets [3.108d–f] and Larensis's chef who, as already noted, is as able as any of the deipnosophists to quote ancient literature).

To function in such a thoroughly literary atmosphere clearly required considerable intellectual skills, and the most obvious one was to have been widely read in this very literature. The deipnosophists clearly were qualified. The grammarian Democritus, for example, says that he had read and excerpted eight hundred Middle Comedies (*Deipnos.* 8.336d). Plutarch claims to have read all the commentaries of Hegesander (3.83b) and Myrtilus, the whole history of Phylarchus (13.610d). Ulpian speaks of searching through books in Alexandria and Rome until he found a single word (15.640b) and on another occasion speaks generally of his wide reading (πολυαναγνωσία [14.654a]).

In addition to being widely read, however, the deipnosophists had to be exceptionally skilled at being able to recall what they had read at the appropriate time during the symposia. Throughout the symposia they display formidable memories, ready with quotations that are apt, often lengthy, and sometimes quite amazing, as when Larensis recites lines from his beloved Homer that begin and end with the same letter or whose first and last syllables spell a name (*Deipnos.* 10.458a–f). The rare occasions when their memories fail (3.83a, 127c; 8.332c, 359d–e; 9.401b) only confirm their outstanding facility with ancient Greek literature.

The word the deipnosophists used to describe exceptional performance in this sort of intellectual milieu is πολυμάθεια (great learning). Athenaeus defines this word most clearly when discussing a pretender to this learning, a certain Calliphanes, who copied out the beginnings of many poems and then recalled three or four lines from them on various occasions (*Deipnos.* 1.4c).[47] Several of the deipnosophists, however, fully deserved to be characterized as

---

47. See also G. Anderson, "Lucian's Classics: Some Short Cuts to Culture," *BICS* 25 (1978) 59–68. He notes that Lucian also tended to quote from the first or opening lines of literary works.

possessing πολυμάθεια: Democritus, certainly, for having read eight hundred Middle Comedies, and in fact he is so described (1.1d); his fellow Nicomedian, the philosopher Pontianus (1.1d); the jurist Masurius (1.1d); the grammarians as a group, including, as the context suggests, Larensis (14.648d–e); and, of course, Ulpian (14.649e).

The reason the deipnosophists valued πολυμάθεια so highly was their love of what was ancient. Indeed, Ulpian is described in just this way—as φιλάρ-χαιος. Hence he will say no word that cannot be found in ancient Greek literature (*Deipnos.* 3.126e); hence the motivation for the question that produced his nickname "Keitoukeitos" (1.1e); and hence the enthusiasm and competition among the deipnosophists to answer the question, or at least to supplement it (2.51b; 3.126b; 5.221f; 6.271b–272d; 9.397c; etc.). Citations from the ancient poets and historians for a word or subject brought applause from the others, as happens, say, to Plutarch after his meticulously illustrated catalog of cups (11.461e–503f).

The attachment to the ancient Greeks, however, was more than linguistic. The deipnosophists discuss the life of the Homeric heroes (*Deipnos.* 1.8e–19a, 24b–26c; cf. 5.186d–193c) and express interest in ancient symposia (4.134d–156a), ancient chefs (9.382b–383f), and even the wine mixtures used by the ancients (10.426c–427c). Especially enlightening, however, are certain ζητήσεις discussed by the deipnosophists: Did the ancients use silver plates (6.228c–231b)? Did they have slaves (6.264c–266f; 267e–270a)? And did they drink from large cups (11.460b–461e)? These questions, not to mention their negative answers, show that the ancient poets and historians also served as norms for the deipnosophists. As Democritus put it after citing the poets Cratinus, Crates, and Telecleides on the question of slaves, "The ancients (οἱ ἀρχαῖοι) teach us through their poetry" (6.268d)—in this case, to live moderately enough so as to need no slaves.

In other words, the symposia at Larensis's house were not simply occasions to display the deipnosophists' wide reading and sharp memories. They were also occasions, through that very πολυμάθεια, to reconstruct the world of the ancients—their people, their events, and above all their language and literature—and so to allow the deipnosophists to inhabit that world again. At the symposia they could once again hear and use the ancient Greek in all its purity and could at least reaffirm the values of that otherwise vanished world in the face of a contemporary social world dedicated to extravagance and excess—a world where, as Larensis notes, many Romans owned ten thousand or even twenty thousand slaves (*Deipnos.* 6.272e).

CYNULCUS, THE DOG IN
LARENSIS'S MANGER

Such, then, is the highly erudite, but also utopian, world of Larensis's symposia where we must place Cynulcus. Scholarly treatments of this Cynic are brief and tend to generalization. Accordingly, they characterize Cynulcus as a clownish figure much like the Cynic Alcidamas of Lucian's *Convivium*,[48] although they also note his role as Ulpian's chief opponent.[49] This latter role is usually regarded positively, since it is claimed to enliven the otherwise overly learned discussions of Ulpian and the others.[50] More perceptive, however, is Mengis's view that Athenaeus, in making Cynulcus an opponent of Ulpian, has been inconsistent, turning what was originally only a noisy mischief maker who hated πολυμάθεια (*Deipnos.* 13.567b; cf. 13.610b) into a Cynic polyhistor who can match Ulpian ancient quotation for ancient quotation.[51]

This characterization of Cynulcus—as clown and critic, but also as inconsistent—is open to criticism. For example, the characterization as clown is only partially true. He is, to be sure, once made the butt of a joke, when someone poured perfume over him as he dozed toward the end of one symposium (*Deipnos.* 15.686c–d), and on occasion he is an object of laughter (4.156c, 158d, 165b). These lighthearted moments notwithstanding, Cynulcus is no Alcidamas. On the contrary, he is, as we will see, a serious critic of Ulpian and the Atticizing world he and the others are recreating at Larensis's house. In addition, to characterize Cynulcus simply as a critic of Ulpian is to underestimate the extent to which, as we will see, Cynulcus is an opponent of all the deipnosophists; and to see him simply as a critic is to miss the extent to which, as we will see, he himself was criticized. Finally, the charge of inconsistency is more apparent than real, for a learned Cynulcus who hates learning is, as we will see, less a fault of Athenaeus than a sign of the complexity of Cynulcus's character.

Therefore, given these shortcomings in the scholarly assessment of Cynulcus, it is best to begin afresh with the evidence. One promising way to organize and analyze the evidence is to ask this question: How, precisely, does Cynulcus fit into the world of the deipnosophists? The answer, to put it briefly at the outset, is like the proverbial dog in the manger. In some ways, of course, he fits in quite well, but overall his role at the symposia is such that neither he nor the other deipnosophists are able to eat as they want. Cynulcus's ambivalent position in this world requires elaboration.

That Cynulcus can—and often does—fit quite well into the literary ethos of Larensis's symposia is easy to document. To begin with, we have already noted his literary training as a boy (*Deipnos.* 15.669c), and other evidence shows that he shares many of the characteristics of the other deipnosophists. He, like them, continues to read widely (4.160a; 7.275b; 15.671d, 678f) and even recommends a book he has because it contains a rich source of ζητήσεις (7.276a). At the symposia he, too, displays a fine memory for literature. Thus,

---

48. See, e.g., Christ, Schmid, and Stählin, *Geschichte*, 792; Mengis, *Die schriftstellerische Technik*, 27; and Martin, *Symposion*, 278.
49. See, e.g., Dittenberger, "Athenäus," 22, and Werner, "Athenaios," 702.
50. See esp. Werner, "Athenaios," 702.
51. Mengis, *Die schriftstellerische Technik*, 27.

he can remember the exact book—the twenty-third—in which Phylarchus wrote that hetaerae are not to be seen on the streets of the cities of Ceos (13.610d). He regularly begins his comments with an apt quotation from some poet (3.108f, 122f; 4.164d–e; 9.385b; 13.566e, 610b; 15.697b), engages in the asking and answering of ζητήσεις (3.123a–e; 4.165b–c; 15.669d), and generally reflects the intellectual perspective of the grammarian (3.98c–99e, 108f–109b, 122a–c; 4.158a–d; 13.567c–f; 15.698a–699c). Indeed, after he supplies Ulpian with an ancient reference to some religious festival, all the deipnosophists admire him for being well-educated (εὐπαίδευτος [7.275b–276a]).

Significantly, however, the deipnosophists use only εὐπαίδευτος, and herein lies the first indication that Cynulcus does not fit in as well as the evidence so far presented might suggest. The deipnosophists deny him the recognition he sought: the possession of πολυμάθεια. In fact, after a recital of nine authorities on behalf of lentils, which he supposes will display his πολυμάθεια (Deipnos. 4.158a–d), the grammarian Plutarch only laughs. Cynulcus immediately follows up with a similar display of literary learning on the subject of moderate eating (4.158d–159d), but none of the deipnosophists applaud (4.159e)—as they do after, say, Plutarch's discussion of cups (11.503f).

In order to explain this withholding of praise from the obviously learned Cynulcus, we need to turn to relations among the deipnosophists and especially to those with Cynulcus. Relations among the deipnosophists are surprisingly rancorous. Sometimes the reasons are personal (for example, Myrtilus's hatred for Ulpian [Deipnos. 13.571a]), but typically they are professional, as in the attacks on philosophers (3.104b–c; 4.160e–164d; 11.504c–509e; 13.610d–612f). The rancor is especially evident, however, in the epithets that the deipnosophists hurl at one another. Thus, Myrtilus calls Ulpian a "licker of fat" (κνισολοιχός), a "toady for fat" (κνισοκόλαξ [3.125b]), and a "glutton" (ὀλβιογάστωρ [9.386c]). Ulpian calls Aemilianus a "late-learning" Sophist (ὀψιμαθής [3.127b]), and Pontianus calls Ulpian a "drunk" (ἀρρυθμοπότης [9.445e]). Still, for all the animosity, the relations do not remain strained for long.

Not so, however, with Cynulcus. He has more confrontations than anyone else. He attacks the grammarian Arrian for having many students and charging high fees (Deipnos. 3.113d–e). He expresses the wish—albeit wittily—that Plutarch hang himself (4.156a). He criticizes Magnus sharply for his attack on philosophy (4.164e–165b). He withholds his praise of Democritus and instead complains about his speaking interminably (6.270a–c) and later accuses him of being gullible about what he reads in Aristotle (8.352d). He hurls an epithet at an unnamed Epicurean (7.298e), and he levels an especially sharp denunciation of Myrtilus's morals (13.566e–571a) and his πολυμάθεια (13.610b–d).

Not surprisingly, the deipnosophists reserve a great proportion of their attacks for Cynulcus. For example, Magnus assails him (and Cynics generally) for unwashed feet, parasitical ways, and hypocritical attachment to self-sufficiency (αὐτάρκεια [*Deipnos.* 3.113f; 4.160e–164d]). Myrtilus likewise lashes out in denunciation of Cynulcus (and Cynics generally). Even Larensis at one point puts Cynulcus in his place by citing still earlier authors than Cynulcus had for a certain word (4.160d). Then, of course, there is the most persistent clash of all—that between Cynulcus and Ulpian. Athenaeus terms their relationship—and only theirs—as a "rivalry" (φιλονεικία [15.669b]) and otherwise draws frequent attention to their relationship. He observes that they are always at war with one another (6.270c), that they are armed against one another (3.106f, 127a; 15.669b, 701b), and that they are often annoyed or angry with one another (3.97c, 121f; 15.671d). Their conversations are filled with epithets for one another (3.97c, 100b, 126a; 4.165c; 6.270c; 8.347d).

Why, then, are the relations especially acrimonious between Cynulcus and the other deipnosophists, and betwen Cynulcus and Ulpian in particular? Why do they all, as Athenaeus says, run down or inveigh against him (κατα-τρέχειν: *Deipnos.* 1.1e; 4.164d, 175e; 7.278f)? The answer lies in drawing attention to three especially frequent features in Athenaeus's portrait of Cynulcus: the puns on the "doggish" character of his philosophy; his sharp criticism of the πολυμάθεια of Ulpian and the others; and his habit of eating first, as it were, and asking ζητήσεις later.

The puns on Cynulcus's Cynicism, or doggishness, are frequent and betray a deep dislike on the part of the other deipnosophists toward Cynics and Cynicism. Cynulcus must have been an object of this dislike every time they mentioned his name, itself a pun on his philosophy with the meaning, as already noted, "leader of dogs" (*Deipnos.* 1.1d et passim). The dislike surely surfaces in the puns they use. Thus, Ulpian addresses Cynulcus as a dog (ὦ κύον [3.100b; 6.270c]), although on other occasions he is more literary in his referring to him as a "dog-fly" (κυνάμυια [3.126a; cf. Homer *Il.* 21.394, 421) and as a "fearless dog" (κύον ἀδδεές [15.697e; cf. Homer *Il.* 21.481). Magnus calls him a "pot-bellied" dog (γάστρις κύων [4.160e]). Other puns refer to Cynulcus's barking or being rabid (3.99e), but more often they speak of feeding the hungry Cynic as one would dogs—by throwing him bones, bread, or scraps (3.96f–97a, 114a; 6.270d). Myrtilus presents a particularly elaborate comparison of Cynics and dogs, but again the voraciousness of both is emphasized (13.611b–c). The effect, however, of Cynulcus's name and the other puns is to identify him very closely as a Cynic.

The identification of Cynulcus with Cynicism is apparent also in his typically Cynic praise of the simple life (*Deipnos.* 4.156c–159d) and of virtue (13.566e–571a). Far more central to his identity and role as a Cynic, however, is his persistent opposition to the excesses, as he perceived them, of the πολυμάθεια produced by literary study. We have already noted his criticism of Ulpian's and Pompeianus's language outside the setting of Larensis's symposia (3.97c–f), and that criticism continues inside. Indeed, it is this criticism that specifically accounts for the strained relations between Cynulcus and the other deipnosophists.

Several passages present Cynulcus's opposition to the dominant literary ethos established by Ulpian and the others. For example, Cynulcus says that Ulpian is wasting his time on ζητήσεις in which he constantly asks κεῖται, οὐ κεῖται (found or not found) of virtually every word that is used by the other deipnosophists. Ulpian is, in effect, gathering "thorns" (ἄκανθαι) rather than flowers. What is more, by investigating single words, he is unable to make lengthy speeches (λόγοι διεξοδικοί) or recall coherent stories (ἱστορίαι [*Deipnos.* 3.97c–d]). He is, to use a word applied to Pompeianus, who is himself an Ulpianic Sophist (3.98c), a "word-hunter" (ὀνοματοθήρας [3.98a]).

Elsewhere, Cynulcus repeats and develops this criticism. He uses the word ἄκανθαι again—in fact, the word is seemingly a technical term for this sort of literary investigation (see *Deipnos.* 6.228c; 9.385b—but now it is in the sense of the spines of fish. Ulpian, he argues, prefers the unnourishing or inedible parts of some fish and thus ignores the large fillets (8.347d–e). In other words, as a word-hunter (15.671f), Ulpian is more likely to produce thorns than flowers, and bones than meat. When Myrtilus turns to the poets to attest the name of his hetaera Ocimon in the presence of his students, Cynulcus regards this πολυμάθεια as not only useless, but dangerous as well (13.567b–c). In fact, it is for Myrtilus, whose πολυμάθεια is illustrated in a long catalog of hetaerae (13.571a–599e), that Cynulcus reserves his harshest words: nothing is more empty than (this sort of) πολυμάθεια that cannot teach wisdom. What is the benefit (ὄφελος), he asks, of such catalogs? A grammarian like Myrtilus, he adds, cannot instill virtue with these catalogs. Conversely, he cannot catalog what is really useful—the names of those in the Trojan horse or the companions of Odysseus—and he does not know that no hetaerae appear on the streets in the cities of Ceos (13.610b–d).

At one point Cynulcus's criticism of the deipnosophists' πολυμάθεια extends to them all. He had spoken on the simple life, but they all laughed. Consequently, they are, he says, uneducated (ἀπαίδευτοι), because they do not read those books that alone can educate (παιδεύειν) those who desire virtue (*Deipnos.* 4.159f–160a). In other words, throughout the *Deipnosophistae,* Cynulcus plays the role of critic of the dominant literary ethos of the symposia; he charges that ethos, exemplified in the deipnosophists' πολυμάθεια, with a preoccupation with words and a corresponding neglect of their responsibility for instilling morality.

But Cynulcus's role as critic does not end with this explicit attack on Ulpian and the other word-hunters. It surfaces also when he deliberately uses Latin words instead of their Greek equivalents (*Deipnos.* 3.121e; 15.701b; cf. 4.159f). The sound of Latin is a barbarism to Ulpian, who in anger strikes his pillow and threatens to leave because he cannot digest such language (3.121f). Far more important in this respect is another of Cynulcus's habits—his desire to eat rather than talk. The importance of this behavior is evident from the

number of times Cynulcus (or the Cynics) expresses this desire. Thus, while
Ulpian was talking about fried fish, Cynulcus shouts that he wants to eat bread
(3.108f). After salt fish is brought in and the grammarians Leonides, Varus,
Plutarch, and Myrtilus, as well as the physicians Dionysocles and Daphnus, all
discuss this food (3.116a–120a), Cynulcus asks for a drink to wash away the
salty discourse (3.121e). Similarly, after Plutarch's long discussion of ancient
symposia (4.134d–156a), it is Cynulcus who comments that his lengthy talk
had meant fasting for him (4.156a). Again, Democritus's discussion of slaves
(6.262b–270a) ends with praise from the other deipnosophists, but Cynulcus
describes the discussion as interminable and says it has left him hungry
(6.270b–e). When Ulpian asks one of his ζητήσεις—in this case, Where is
"oil-pickle" (ὀξάλμη) found in Greek literature?—Cynulcus shouts some lines
from the poet Metagenes: "Let's dine first, then ask me anything you want, for
now I'm hungry" (9.385b–c). Finally, when the δεῖπνον (dinner) itself gets
under way, Athenaeus notes that the Cynics were enjoying themselves more
than the others, since they supposed that they were celebrating the Eating-
Festival (φαγήσια [7.275b]).

This desire to eat on the part of Cynulcus (and the other Cynics) prompts
the comparisons with voracious dogs, as already noted, but it also serves to
distinguish Cynulcus (and the other Cynics) from the other deipnosophists.
Cynulcus realizes that they are not hungry (*Deipnos.* 4.159e), and he speaks of
Ulpian as one who feasts (ἑστιᾶν) on words (7.275b) and as one who thirsts
(διψᾶν) for them (3.122f). In fact, Ulpian himself recognizes the difference
between Cynulcus and the other deipnosophists precisely at this point, and his
words to Cynulcus are worth quoting: "The marketplace is full of vegetables
and bread. But you, you Cynic/dog, are always starving and do not permit us
to partake of—better, be fed by—fine and abundant words. Indeed, fine
words are food for the soul." Then, after turning to his slave, he adds:
"Leucus, if you have any scraps of bread from the manger, give them to these
Cynics/dogs" (6.270c–d).

Baldwin's recognition of the value of Athenaeus's *Deipnosophistae* as a
source for the intellectual life of Rome in the last years of the second century
has by now been amply demonstrated. Indeed, this source, for all its problems and shortcomings, provides an unusually detailed and coherent view of a
vital intellectual milieu centered around the symposia hosted by the prominent aristocrat P. Livius Larensis for upwards of thirty intellectuals of various
kinds. The variety, however, turned out to be of little importance. Ulpian and
the grammarians established a literary ethos at the symposia in which the
ζήτησις, or question seeking the attestation in ancient Greek literature of virtually every word and action at the symposia, dominated the conversations and
so required wide reading and a ready memory on the part of all the intellectuals if they wanted to participate, much more if they wanted to receive
applause for having such literary erudition, called πολυμάθεια.

Thus, although philosophers, physicians, musicians, and others attended the symposia, their role was at most to supplement the literary ethos by adding, say, some medical reflections on the food being served. Only one philosopher, the Cynic Cynulcus, the subject of this chapter, dared to challenge this ethos. Given his formal literary training under a grammarian and his continued reading in Greek literature and possession of a quick memory, he could, to be sure, fit into this milieu by answering and asking ζητήσεις. Nevertheless, more typical is Cynulcus's opposition to this form of intellectual culture, a role he played outside the symposia, too, as we saw in his ridicule of Ulpian and Pompeianus for the silliness of trying to use ancient Greek in a later setting. But it is within the symposia that his opposition is more fully expressed. He charged the word-hunting Ulpian with preferring thorns to flowers and bones to fillets, the catalog-forming Myrtilus with neglecting what is beneficial and conducive to morality, and all the deipnosophists with being uneducated with respect to books that produce morality.

This criticism, not surprisingly, led to strained relations with the other deipnosophists, but Cynulcus's critical role was not alone responsible for his isolation among the deipnosophists and their withholding of recognition of his πολυμάθεια. The deipnosophists returned the attack but focused, primarily through their puns, on Cynulcus's Cynicism, emphasizing in particular Cynic voraciousness and so portraying him as a glutton. Cynulcus, however, seemingly reveled in his Cynicism not only by preferring his nickname (meaning "leader of dogs") to his given name Theodorus but also by using Cynic voraciousness—that is, emphasizing his preference for eating over talking—to function as yet another way of criticizing the word-hungry Ulpian and his fellow deipnosophists. In short, whether it was through his verbal attacks on the Atticizing excesses of the deipnosophists or through his Cynic habit of desiring to eat rather than participate in the ζητήσεις for each of the foods served, Cynulcus truly functioned at Larensis's symposia as a dog in the manger.

WILLEM S. VORSTER   3

STOICS AND EARLY CHRISTIANS ON BLESSEDNESS

The interest of scholars in Cynicism and Stoicism in their study of early Christianity during the last century and the early twentieth century was to a great extent replaced in the mid-twentieth century by studies of Judaism as the context of the interpretation of Christianity, and Cynicism and Stoicism were therefore also often neglected. There is currently a renewed interest in the Greco-Roman context within which Christianity originated.

In spite of the conviction about the apocalyptic nature of the preaching of Jesus, for example, which had dominated scholarship since the late nineteenth century, it was recently asserted that "a Cynic Jesus does appear to fit the Hellenistic cast to Galilean culture much better than the apocalyptic Jesus."[1] This is only one of many recent attempts to place Jesus, Q, and aspects of early Christianity in a Greco-Roman context.[2]

In this respect the Cynics and Stoics are of special interest, both because of their ways of life and also because of their views. It is nevertheless widely agreed that both Jewish and Greco-Roman contexts are necessary for the interpretation of the spread and beliefs of early Christian thought patterns. This is substantiated by the wide-ranging interests of New Testament scholars in matters such as Judaism, Gnosticism, mystery religions, healing cults, and Hellenistic philosophical thought. One should, therefore, welcome the renewed interest in Cynicism and also take cognizance of the ongoing interest in Stoic philosophy and the New Testament. But, in contrast, there also seems to be reason not to jump to conclusions too quickly about the Cynic character of the teaching of Jesus, and so-called parallels between Christian and Greek philosophical thought.

The purpose of this chapter is to explore the way in which Stoics and early Christians conceived blessedness, that is, happiness.[3] I am interested in how

1. B. L. Mack, "The Kingdom That Didn't Come: A Social History of the Q Tradents," *1988 SBLSP* (Atlanta: Scholars, 1988) 1. 608.
2. See, for example, F. G. Downing, "Cynics and Christians," *NTS* 30 (1984) 584–89; idem, *Christ and the Cynics: Jesus and Other Radical Preachers in First-Century Tradition* (JSOT Manuals 4; Sheffield: JSOT, 1988); and the work being done in the *Corpus Hellenisticum* project.
3. *Blessedness* and *happiness* are translation equivalents for exactly the same terms and con-

38

Stoics and early Christians constructed their views on happiness and how these views fitted into their views on reality. This is not an attempt to investigate influences or parallel thought patterns in the first instance. Although there might be similarities between the two systems of thought, I am convinced that most of the statements about happiness in the New Testament have their background in Jewish wisdom and eschatological, including apocalyptic, thought.[4]

The chapter has three parts. The first deals with Stoic views on happiness. Although reference will be made to different members of the Stoic tradition, I will use Epictetus as my main representative. In the second section, early Christian views on happiness will be dealt with. Again, I will restrict my discussion to the treatment of a limited amount of material in the New Testament. In the last section, I will focus on a few parallel statements concerning happiness in Stoicism and the New Testament.

The Stoics believed that the ultimate end of life, τὸ τέλος, was happiness. According to Cicero (*Fin.* 3.26), the *sapiens* (wise person) is always happy, because the final aim in life is to live in accordance with nature. It naturally follows, he asserts, that all wise persons at all times enjoy a happy, perfect, and fortunate life, free from hindrance, if they live in agreement and harmony with nature. This, in short, is a summary of the Stoic view of blessedness. According to Luke 6:20–22, in contrast, Jesus taught that those who are poor and hungry, those who weep, and those who are hated, rejected, insulted, and accused of being evil because of the Son of Man are happy. They are regarded as happy because God will take care of their needs. How do these two views compare? Are they totally different, contradictory, or perhaps related?

STOICS ON BLESSEDNESS

Different terms are used in Greek literature for happiness. In Homer, the gods are called οἱ μάκαρες (Blessed Ones). They live a life of happiness beyond care (*Od.* 5.7). The term μάκαρ is later used to denote the godlike blessedness of humankind hereafter in the isles of the blessed (Hes. *Op.* 141). Its cognate μακάριος similarly first describes the blessed state of the gods and is then used of the dead who have obtained this blessed state. From the time of Aristotle onward it becomes a much weaker term and is used as an everyday

---

cepts in Greek and will be used as synonyms in this chapter. Even in the New Testament there is no reason to attach some special "religious" connotation to words such as μακάριος. The so-called difference between *happiness* and *blessedness*, or *happy* and *blessed*, as translation equivalents for Greek and Hebrew words in the Bible, derives from the erroneous idea that the אשרי formulas originated in the cult as blessing formulas. See n. 21 below.

4. See, for example, C. H. Maahs, *The Makarisms in the New Testament: A Comparative Religions and Form Critical Investigation* (diss. Eberhard-Karls-Universität, Tübingen, 1965), and C. Kähler, *Studien zur Form- und Traditionsgeschichte der biblischen Makarismen* (diss. Friedrich-Schiller-Universität, Jena, 1974).

word for happiness. Aristotle still ascribes full blessedness (μακάριος) to the gods only and uses the term εὐδαιμονία for the happiness of humans.[5] It is the latter term that became the leading word for inner happiness in Greek philosophy.

Happiness is defined in Stoic terms as εὐδαιμονία, being the goal of life. From Zeno, the founder of the Stoic school of philosophy, through the middle and later Stoa, the theme of εὐδαιμονία runs like a golden thread. In order to understand the term properly, one has to see it within the frame of reference and thought within which it was used. Happiness in the Stoic sense of the word is directly linked to the moral purpose of humankind (προαίρεσις), a deliberate choice that must be in harmony with nature (κατὰ φύσιν). It is furthermore related to what is good and to virtue (ἀρετή). In short, happiness is governed by reason (λόγος). All these different concepts are integrated into a view of reality that will now receive our attention, mainly in the writings of Epictetus, a contemporary of early Christian authors.

Epictetus (55 to 135 C.E.) was born at Hierapolis in Phrygia. The son of a slave woman, he was a slave himself, and from the Phrygians he inherited an intense interest in their deities and a passion for his personal god. He was taken to Rome and was brought up in the house of Epaphroditus, a powerful freedman of Nero. Because of his interest in philosophy, he was allowed to take lessons from Musonius Rufus, a very important Stoic philosopher of the time. He was granted his freedom and was later banished from Rome with other philosophers in 89. He went to Nicopolis in Greece and started his own school. Epictetus suffered from bad health and was lame.[6]

He wrote nothing himself, but fortunately his pupil Flavius Arrian recorded and published his notes as discourses (diatribes), of which four complete books are extant. Arrian also summarized the basic ideas of Epictetus in the ΕΓΧΕΙΡΙΔΙΟΝ, or *Manual*. A number of other fragments also exist.

Epictetus was a representative of Stoic philosophy and agreed with most of the main teachings of the school. He also regarded himself as a Cynic, a messenger from Zeus whose purpose it was to teach people how to live and to make decisions between good and evil (*Diss.* 3.22). As a philosopher, he reflected on physics, logic, and especially on ethics. His views of reality are dominated by his theology.

According to Epictetus, the universe is the work of God and the product of divine providence. This explains the order and unity in the universe. God has not only taken care of everything that happens; he has also given humankind the faculties to understand it (*Diss.* 1.6) and to live a life in harmony with

5. See F. Hauck, "μακάριος κτλ.," *TWNT* 4. 365–67 for a detailed discussion and references. In the second century C.E. Lucian maintains in his *Bis accusatus sive tribunalia* 1 (trans. Harmon in LCL): "Plague take all philosophers who say that bliss is to be found only among the gods!" See also his *De sacrificiis* 2 (trans. Harmon in LCL).

6. See K. von Fritz, "Epictetus," *OCD* 324; E. Ferguson, *Backgrounds of Early Christianity* (Grand Rapids: Eerdmans, 1987) 291–93.

nature (1.4.18), that is, orderly and self-sufficient (3.7–8):[7] "Assuredly from the very structure of all made objects we are accustomed to prove that the work is certainly the product of some artifice, and has not been constructed at random" (*Diss.* 6.8; trans. Oldfather in LCL).

People fit into this orderly universe as beings with all sorts of faculties, which allow them to make judgments and choices, right or wrong. That is why people should be educated in order to reach their goal in life, which is happiness (Epictetus *Diss.* 2.9.29). Certain things are good, whereas others are evil. And in addition, there are virtues and vices, as well as things that are indifferent. To be free is to be master of oneself (Epictetus frg. 35). Some things are under our control, whereas others not, and one has to know how to deal with the things that are under one's control while accepting those that are not (Epictetus *Diss.* 1.1; also Epictetus *Ench.* 1). Epictetus asserts, "Remember that you are an actor in a play, the character of which is determined by the Playwright: if He wishes the play to be short, it is short; if long, it is long; if He wishes you to play the part of a beggar, remember to act even this role adroitly; and so if your role be that of a cripple, an official, or a layman. For this is your business, to play admirably the role assigned to you; but the selection of that role is Another's" (*Ench.* 17).

Within this framework, Epictetus maintains that some things are under the control of humans, whereas others are not: "Under our control are conception, choice, desire, aversion, and, in a word, everything that is our own doing; not under our control are our body, our property, reputation, office, and in a word, everything that is not our own doing. Furthermore, the things under our control are by nature free, unhindered, and unimpeded; while the things not under our control are weak, servile, subject to hindrance, and not our own" (*Ench.* 1.1; see also *Diss.* 1).

In accordance with ancient Stoic views,[8] Epictetus maintains that false judgments give rise to unhappiness. The most important faculty that the gods have given humankind is the faculty to make correct judgments concerning external impressions. The first task of the philosopher is to test the impressions and discriminate between good and evil, as well as to apply nothing that has not been tested (*Diss.* 1.6.7).[9] Since wealth, health, fame, and so on are not under the control of humans, it is important to realize the significance of being able to use external impressions correctly. Happiness depends on

---

7. There is a very close relationship between nature and reason in Stoicism. Seneca puts it as follows: "Man is a reasoning animal. Therefore, man's highest good is attained, if he has fulfilled the good for which nature designed him at birth. And what is it which this reason demands of him? The easiest thing in the world—to live in accordance to his own nature" (*Ep.* 41.8–9; trans. Gummere in LCL).

8. See M. L. Colish, *The Stoic Tradition from Antiquity to the Early Middle Ages* (2 vols.; Leiden: Brill, 1985) 1. 42.

9. See also Seneca *Ep.* 95.57: "Peace of mind is enjoyed only by those who have attained a fixed and unchanging standard of judgment; the rest of mankind continually ebb and flow in their decisions."

correct judgments about external impressions (2.19.32). People are to con-
template making right judgments.

The Stoics also taught that all events in nature are good. Evil does not stem
from nature but from the acts of humans.[10] "The nature of the good as well as
of the evil lies in a use of the impressions of the senses" (Epictetus *Diss.*
2.1.4). Prudence, courage, temperance, and justice are the four virtues of
Stoicism. For our purpose it is important to note that prudence is a synthesis
of speculative and practical wisdom.[11] People have to strive for wisdom and to
avoid vice. That is done by moral choice (προαίρεσις).

Προαίρεσις has an intellectual basis in Epictetus; it is not merely a matter
of will (*Diss.* 1.29). It is preceded by διαίρεσις, the distinction between what
is under one's control and what is not (2.6.24). Moral purpose concerns the
making of good judgments (3.9) in harmony with nature (1.4.18).

By constructing reality as a self-sufficient, orderly universe under the providence of the Divine, in which people control certain things in accordance with
moral purpose, the Stoic becomes a person whose ultimate goal in life is happiness. Despite his bodily problems and the fact that he grew up as a slave,
Epictetus had an extraordinarily optimistic view of reality.[12] As a Stoic he
believed in the possibility of being happy irrespective of one's position in life:
"Show me a man who though sick is happy (εὐτυχοῦντα), though in danger is
happy, though dying is happy, though condemned to exile is happy, though in
disrepute is happy. Show him! By the Gods, I would fain see a Stoic!" (*Diss.*
2.19.24).

It is within this frame of reference that Epictetus understands happiness as
the goal of life. The terms he employs for happiness include γαλήνη, words
related to the stem εὐδαιμον-, εὐδία, εὔροια κτλ., εὐσταθ-, εὐτυχ-, and words
related to the stem μακαρ-. These words give an idea of the semantic field
within which happiness functions in Epictetus. The words related to the stem
εὐδαιμον- dominate the statements of Epictetus on happiness, whereas terms
such as μακάριος κτλ. are used as close synonyms. He maintains: ὁ γὰρ θεὸς
πάντας ἀνθρώπους ἐπὶ τὸ εὐδαιμονεῖν, ἐπὶ τὸ εὐσταθεῖν ἐποίησεν (For God
made all mankind to be happy, to be serene) (*Diss.* 3.24.4).

God has made humankind to be happy and not to be unhappy, and for that
reason God has put some things under the control of people and others not.
Because they are begotten by God, humans have reason (λόγος) and intelligence (γνώμη) in common with the gods, which is a divine (θεία) and blessed
(μακαρία) relationship. Only some are inclined to this relationship. Others
are inclined to the body, which humans have in common with all living
creatures. They cannot be happy. One should concentrate on the things that
are under human control and act accordingly (Epictetus *Diss.* 1.3.3). Moral

10. See Colish, *The Stoic Tradition*, 42–50.
11. See Colish, *The Stoic Tradition*, 43.
12. See A. Bonhöffer, *Epiktet und das Neue Testament* (Giessen: Töpelman, 1911) 347–53.

purpose is the highest of all things. When it is attended to—that is, when one makes right decisions—a person becomes good and is fortunate and happy. When moral purpose is ignored, evil arises.

Virtue can produce happiness, calm, and serenity. This explains the necessity to make progress toward virtue: "For it is always true that whatsoever the goal toward which perfection in anything definitely leads, progress is an approach thereto" (Epictetus *Diss.* 1.4.4). Progress occurs where people turn their attention to their moral purpose, cultivating and perfecting it in harmony with nature, free and unhindered. Therefore, people must strive to avoid things that are not under their control, because those are the things that make humans unfree (1.4.18–19). Possessions, children, marriage, slaves, and friendship are of no use if a person does not attend to the things that can produce happiness. Humans should know what God is, what humanity is, and also what is good and what is evil. Ignorance of these things produces unhappiness: "Some persons, like cattle, are interested in nothing but their fodder; for to all of you that concern yourselves with property and lands and slaves and one office or another, all this is nothing but fodder" (2.14.24–25).

Happiness does not reside in the body, in possessions, in an office, in external appearance, or in royalty.[13] Happiness is found in freedom from the things that enslave humans (Epictetus *Diss.* 3.22.26–40). Suffering, death, bad health, a crippled body, exile, and so on cannot be reasons for humans to be unhappy. These things are not under human control. Happiness can only be reached by attending to that which is under one's control. This does not mean that Epictetus accepted life passively. On the contrary, because of his views on reality, he believed in the active participation of humans in their perfection and happiness.

Because of his belief in divine providence, the intellectual ability of humans, and the importance of moral purpose, Epictetus could accept life as a gift from God that has to be lived in accordance with nature. Happiness is the ultimate goal of life. It is not a disposition in the first instance. According to Epictetus, as a state of mind, happiness is something that has to be achieved. It is an activity. This is in line with the Stoic concept of εὐδαιμονία as the ultimate goal of life: "*Eudaimonia* is in Stoic ethics, according to our analysis, primarily to act virtuously so that one's life flows smoothly (εὔροια) in accordance with the universal nature (ὁμολογία), and secondarily it is possibly a state of exhilaration (χαρά, εὐφροσύνη etc.) which comes into being as an ἐπιγέννημα ["subsequent manifestation"] of virtuous activity."[14]

Happiness, according to Epictetus, is practical wisdom.[15] In accordance

13. According to Dio Chrysostom *Or.* 3.1 (trans. Cohoon in LCL), "Man's happiness is not determined by any external possessions, such as gold plate, cities or lands, for example, or other human beings, but in each case by his own self and his own character."
14. D. Tsekourakis, *Studies in the Terminology of Early Stoic Ethics* (Wiesbaden: Steiner, 1974) 97.
15. This is a common theme in Stoicism. See Cicero *Fin.* 3.26.

44   ESSAYS IN HONOR OF ABRAHAM J. MALHERBE

with his view of reality, he taught people how to live and how to make
judgments that could help them in achieving the ultimate goal in life, that is,
happiness.

EARLY CHRISTIANS ON BLESSEDNESS

Unlike in Stoicism, in the New Testament εὐδαιμονία is not used to
express happiness.[16] Μακάριος and χαίρω dominate the semantic field of happiness in these writings. Other terms functioning in the same semantic field in
New Testament writings are ἀγαλλίασις, ἀγαλλιάω, ἀσμένως, ἀσπάζομαι,
εὐφραίνομαι, εὐφραίνω, εὐφροσύνη, ἡδέως, ἱλαρός, ἱλαρότης, μακαρίζω,
μακαρισμός, σκιρτάω, συγχαίρω, συνήδομαι, and χαρά.[17] Because of the
lack of space, I will have to limit my discussion of happiness in early Christian
perspective to a few important aspects.

As in Stoicism, New Testament beliefs about happiness are motivated by
conceptions of reality and symbolic universes. Because New Testament writings are in the first place religious texts, it is not amazing that happiness is
related to God as the giver of happiness.

According to the New Testament, early Christians regarded themselves as a
community of joy and happiness. The coming of Jesus inaugurated a new era,
that is, an era of happiness. He made the blind see again and the lame walk;
he cured those who suffered from illnesses, made the dead come alive, and
made the good news known to the poor (Matt 11:5). The days of fasting were
something of the past, because the bridegroom had arrived, it was said (see
Mark 2:18). The teaching and the deeds of Jesus created a new world view for
a group of people who most probably despaired because of their socio-
economic and political situation. In their interpretation of the life and the
works of Jesus, and of his message concerning the kingdom of God, followers
of Jesus saw the basis for a new conception of happiness. Although it had a
present aspect in that his coming gave reason for happiness, his teaching
about the kingdom of God most probably also included a future aspect—that
real happiness would come in the end (see Matt 8:11–12; Mark 14:25).

After the death of Jesus, happiness was motivated christologically. His
complete life was seen as the sole basis of happiness. Especially in the case of
Luke, we notice how the life of Jesus from his birth to his resurrection is
described from the perspective of joy and happiness.[18] The infancy narrative
was written from the perspective of joy (see Luke 1:14, 41, 44, 46–55, 68–79;

16. The observation of Bonhöffer, *Epiktet*, 245–46, that the absence of εὐδαίμων κτλ. in the
Greek Bible is deliberate because of reservations about the term δαίμων by Jews and Christians,
is out of place. Words have meaning in contexts, and demons were part of the symbolic universe
of early Christians.
17. See J. P. Louw and E. A. Nida (eds.), *Greek-English Lexicon of the New Testament Based on
Semantic Domains* (2 vols.; New York: United Bible Societies, 1988) 1. 302–304.
18. Luke is called the evangelist of joy, and scholars even speak of the Lukan theology of joy.
See A. B. du Toit, "Freude," *TRE* 11. 585–86; H. Conzelmann, "χαίρω κτλ.," *TWNT* 9. 350–62.

2:10), and so was the rest of Luke's story of Jesus. Jesus started his mission, according to Luke, with a sermon in the synagogue of Nazareth concerning the good news of the liberation of the oppressed that he brings about (Luke 4:18–19, 21). The Gospel ends on a happy note when the followers of Jesus are seized by the happiness of Easter (see χαρά in Luke 24:41, 52). Lukan Christians are happy because Jesus is born, because he brings a message of happiness and makes people happy, and because Jesus is raised from the dead. Happiness in Luke has both a present and a future character.

In Paul, happiness becomes happiness "in Christ" or "in the Lord" (see especially Phil 3:1; 4:4, 10). Because of the death and resurrection of Jesus, believers share in Christ, that is, in his suffering and in his triumph (see Romans 8), and that is why Christians become a community of happiness (see 1 Cor 12:26; 2 Cor 2:3) even when they suffer (see 2 Corinthians 10). Happiness is, however, also something to be hoped for (Rom 12:12). Happiness in spite of suffering and happiness in suffering is quite a common theme in early Christian thought (see Matt 5:11; Luke 6:22; Jas 1:2–4, 12; 1 Pet 1:6–8; 4:12–14).

In the Johannine writings, special emphasis is laid on happiness as something that is fulfilled in the present. It is not something for which Christians have to wait. It is given in Christ (see John 16:24; 17:13; 1 John 1:4). This is quite a different perspective from that which we find in Revelation, where real happiness will come on the "new earth" and in the "new heaven" when all unhappiness will be removed forever.

In short, happiness is to be found in Christ. He is the inaugurator of happiness. In sorrow or pain, poverty or sadness, he is the reason why Christians can be happy. In Christ, God gives happiness. Happiness is both present and eschatological. In this sense, happiness appears to be a state of mind.

There is a certain tension between a world view that emphasizes present happiness and one that projects happiness into the future, especially if the future is seen in apocalyptic terms. Both strands of tradition are present in early Christian documents, and in some cases the interpretation of statements about happiness becomes a moot point. It is not always clear whether present happiness is an intimation of future happiness or whether the present is seen in relation to the future when full happiness will be reached. Two symbolic universes may be involved. This needs to be discussed now with respect to some of the so-called macarisms, or beatitude formulas, in the New Testament. I shall concentrate mainly on the macarisms that Jesus expressed according to Matthew (5:3–12) and Luke (6:20–25) and discuss happiness in terms of wisdom theology and apocalyptic theology.

There are several problems involved in the interpretation of these macarisms, and opinions differ greatly.[19] This is not the place to discuss all the

19. See, for example, U. Luz, *Das Evangelium nach Matthäus (Mt 1–7)* (EKK 1/1; Zürich: Benzinger, 1985) 198–218.

issues, because I am only interested in showing how different views of reality influence our understanding of early Christian views concerning happiness. Should the macarisms of Jesus be seen from the perspective of wisdom theology or from the perspective of apocalyptic theology? Are the macarisms in Matthew 5 and Luke 6 "entrance requirements," or are they "eschatological blessings"?[20]

The macarism was known to both the Greek and Semitic worlds. In Classical Greek, the formula was introduced by ὄλβιος or by μάκαρ followed by a relative clause and a finite verb, mostly in the third person. In Hebrew, the formula was introduced by אַשְׁרֵי followed by a participle, a noun, or a pronoun. Unlike the בָּרוּךְ formula, the אַשְׁרֵי formula is not a blessing formula, in spite of the fact that it has often been viewed in this manner.[21] The "congratulation" of happiness never refers to God. It always refers to the "life-enhancing" behavior[22] of the believer; that is, coming to Zion (Ps 65:5), fearing God (Ps 94:12), studying and obeying the Torah (Prov 29:18), caring for the poor (Ps 41:2), finding wisdom (Prov 3:13), listening to wisdom (Prov 8:33), and so on. These formulas appear almost exclusively in the Psalms and Wisdom literature of the Old Testament. In these contexts, the formulas normally have a parenetic function of religious and moral exhortation. Persons who abide by the rules of moral conduct are happy. Happiness corresponds with Israel's understanding of "well-being." It concerns everything that makes people happy: life, security, deliverance, posterity, military success, prosperity, and so on. "Any hint of an eschatological hope is rare" (for example, Isa 30:18; 32:20; Dan 12:12).[23] This is in accordance with the use of macarism formulas in practical wisdom in Egypt.[24]

In the intertestamental literature, beatitude formulas are used in two different ways. In continuity with Old Testament usage, macarisms appear in Wisdom literature, where they have a parenetic function. They are also used in apocalyptic writings, where they are future oriented, and their function is to encourage. Guelich correctly observes that the context of these beatitudes is different from that of those used in Wisdom literature.[25] The persons who are called lucky in apocalyptic writings are those who are in distress and under pressure. The promise of happiness concerns otherworldly happiness. There is no hope in this world, but in the world to come, the roles will be changed, and the "underdogs" who are righteous will be happy.

---

20. See R. A. Guelich, "The Matthean Beatitudes: 'Entrance-Requirements' or Eschatological Blessings?" *JBL* 95 (1976) 415–34.

21. See H. Cazelles, "אַשְׁרֵי" *TWAT* 1. 481–85; R. A. Guelich, *The Sermon on the Mount: A Foundation for Understanding* (Waco: Word Books, 1982) 64. Because it was related to the cult, אַשְׁרֵי was translated as "blessed" in the sense of somebody who receives a blessing. This was also transferred to the Greek μακάριος, by which the Hebrew word is normally translated.

22. L. G. Perdue, "The Wisdom Sayings of Jesus," *Foundation and Facets Forum* 2 (1986) 17.

23. Guelich, *The Sermon*, 63.

24. Cazelles, "אַשְׁרֵי" 484.

25. Guelich, *The Sermon*, 65.

The difference between the two usages is important, since wisdom theology and apocalyptic theology are based on two different world views. Reality is constructed in two totally different ways, even though one often finds wisdom traits in apocalyptic theology (for example *1 Enoch*). Wisdom theology underscores the order and unity in God's creation. The sages believed that deeds have effects both for people and for their environment. That is why one should live as a *sapiens* (wise person) by pursuing wisdom. Deeds, good or bad, have their consequences. Apocalyptic theology, in contrast, puts its hope in the world to come, and actions are motivated by hope of a better future.

Let us now turn to the beatitudes in Matthew 5 and Luke 6. It is not clear how many of these statements originated with Jesus and what their original wording was. However, what is clear is that Matthew and Luke interpreted the macarisms differently and wanted their hearers/readers to understand them in particular ways. Whereas Luke places the emphasis on the socio-economic pressures of poverty, unhappiness, hate, insult, and rejection because of the Son of Man, Matthew seems either to have retained the original parenetic character of the macarisms or to have ethicized them. He refers to the "spiritually poor," the "humble," and those who seek "righteousness" and "show mercy," and in this manner seems to have the emphasis fall on "life-enhancing behavior."[26] This explains why the macarisms have often been understood as "entrance requirements" for the Kingdom in the mouth of Jesus.[27]

The apodoses of the macarisms are normally interpreted eschatologically because of the use of the future tense, the *passiva divina* (passive as circumlocution for naming God), and the reward in heaven. It is nevertheless remarkable that in both Matthew and Luke, it is said that the kingdom *belongs* (present tense) to the μακάριοι (Matt 5:3, 10; Luke 6:20). It is possible to argue that in Matthew the connection between moral conduct and heavenly recompense is emphasized, whereas Luke stresses the promise of eschatological blessings to the "underdogs." This does not imply that both Matthew and Luke interpreted the macarisms in line with the intertestamental apocalyptic use of the beatitudes. On the contrary, one can make out a strong case that these macarisms should be read as wisdom sayings in both Matthew and Luke, even though it is clearly possible to interpret them apocalyptically.

When the focus is placed on the parenetic function of the macarisms, blessedness or happiness is not simply a state; it implies conduct, a goal that is to be achieved. In terms of Matthew, the goal is to become τέλειοι (5:48). This is in line with other μακάριος statements in the teaching of Jesus, which also reflect the wisdom perspective: "Happy is the person who takes no offense at me" (Matt 11:6 || Luke 7:23); "Happy are the eyes that see what you

26. See G. Strecker, *Die Bergpredigt: Ein exegetischer Kommentar* (Göttingen: Vandenhoeck & Ruprecht, 1984) 29–30.

27. See Luz, *Das Evangelium*, 202–4, for a short review of different interpretations.

see and the ears that hear what you hear" (Matt 13:16 || Luke 10:23); "Happy is the person who comes in the name of the Lord" (Matt 23:39 || Luke 13:35); "Happy are those who hear the word of God and keep it" (Luke 11:28); "Happy are those servants whom the master finds awake when he comes" (Luke 12:37); and "Happy is the servant whom the master will find so doing when he comes" (Luke 12:43).

These sayings can be regarded as wisdom sayings declaring well-being to those who engage in proper conduct. "The state of blessing already exists, though the tangible rewards may still lay [lie] in the future."[28] Happiness is not something that the followers of Jesus will receive in the afterlife; it is a state that they already experience. Being poor, hungry, marginalized, and so on does not imply unhappiness. On the contrary, because they are members of the kingdom of God, they are happy. This is true of both Matthew's and Luke's versions of the macarisms in spite of their differences with regard to who the blessed are.

It is furthermore remarkable that Matthew presents the Sermon on the Mount as a speech of Jesus the teacher (Matt 5:2), underscoring the fact that he was a teacher of wisdom. Taking into account how much of the teaching of Jesus can be regarded as wisdom theology simply strengthens the possibility of interpreting the macarisms of Matthew 5 within this framework.[29] The macarisms that were included in Q would most probably have been understood as wisdom sayings of Jesus the teacher of wisdom, because Q was most probably a wisdom document.[30] In this framework, Christians are expected to live as sages irrespective of their socioeconomic or political situation. Under all circumstances they can be happy. Well-being is connected to conduct. Deeds have effects.

If, however, we interpret these sayings within an apocalyptic framework, happiness has a totally different connotation. Happiness is then related to the hope of an afterlife. Some day the followers of Jesus will be happy. They must bear with their poverty, hunger, and so on, because in the afterlife things will change, and they will receive full happiness.

This is not the place to determine whether early Christians understood their happiness only from the perspective of wisdom theology or whether they understood it apocalyptically. I am convinced that both trends were present in early Christianity. It is clear from the New Testament that there were wisdom, as well as apocalyptic, trajectories in early Christianity. The point I wish to underline is that happiness can be conceived differently within early Christian perspectives because of the different world views that were involved.

Although early Christians did not have a particular doctrine about happi-

---

28. Perdue, "Wisdom Sayings," 17.

29. Perdue, "Wisdom Sayings," 3–35, gives a very useful survey of the wisdom teaching of Jesus.

30. See J. Kloppenborg, *The Literary Genre of the Synoptic Sayings Source* (Ph.D diss., University of St Michael's College, 1984); idem, "Blessing and Marginality: the 'Persecution Beatitude' in Q, Thomas and Early Christianity," *Foundations and Facets Forum* 2 (1986) 35–56.

ness, they undoubtedly formed part of a tradition where happiness was related to God as the giver of happiness. In the New Testament, happiness is related to the coming of Jesus and to his teaching.

PARALLEL STATEMENTS ON BLESSEDNESS

A few examples of parallel statements about happiness in Stoic and early Christian writings will help give an idea of corresponding views. These will then be viewed against the background of the foregoing discussion of happiness in Stoic and early Christian perspective.

In a recent article on Cynics and Christians, F. Gerald Downing claims that Cynics and early Christians had similar ideas about true blessedness. Epictetus, for one, he argues, was sure that true happiness "lay in the right relation with deity."[31] Downing furthermore draws attention to the fact that Cynics, like Christians, were ready to invite trouble. Epictetus, for example, said, "Think the matter over more carefully, know yourself, ask the Deity, do not attempt the task without God. For if God so advises you, be assured that He wishes you either to become great, or to receive many stripes. For this too is a very pleasant strand woven into the Cynic's pattern of life; he must needs be flogged like an ass, and while he is being flogged he must love the men who flog him, as though he were the father or brother of them all" (*Diss.* 3.22.53–54). The acceptance of one's role in life and of brotherly love enabled Cynics (and Stoics) to live happily.

Especially with regard to Q and "special Matthean" material, there seems to be a close relationship between Cynic and Christian views about happiness, according to Downing. Neither of the two groups was interested in wealth and property as grounds for happiness, and both relied on their gods to take care of their needs and problems: "Consider the beasts yonder and the birds, how much freer from trouble they live than men, and how much more happily also, how much healthier and stronger they are, and how each of them lives the longest life possible, although they have neither hands nor human intelligence. And yet, to counterbalance these and their other limitations, they have one very great blessing—they own no property" (Dio Chrys. *Or.* 10.16). This reminds one of the teaching of Jesus about trust in God for daily needs in Luke 12:22–31. Cynics and early Christians may also be compared with regard to their practical life-styles as the pursuit of wisdom.[32]

Let us now turn to a few μακάριοι statements in the New Testament that can be compared with similar statements in Dio Chrysostom:[33]

31. Downing, "Cynics and Christians," 587. Cynics and Stoics are one and the same in Downing's article, as can be seen from the sources he uses.

32. See Downing, "Cynics and Christians," 588 and n. 20 on 592.

33. I found the works of scholars involved in the *Corpus Hellenisticum* project most helpful in my search for parallel statements on happiness. See, for example, G. Mussies, *Dio Chrysostom and the New Testament* (Leiden: Brill, 1972). See also P. W. van der Horst, "Musonius Rufus and the New Testament: A Contribution to the Corpus Hellenisticum," *NovT* 16 (1974) 306–15;

Happy are the poor in spirit. (Matt 5:3)

Happy are you [scil. the good king] in your gracious and excellent nature, and happy are we who share its blessings with you. (Dio Chrys. *Or.* 1.36)

Happy are you poor, for yours is the kingdom of God. (Luke 6:20)

I desired to show in some way or other that poverty is no hopeless impediment to a life and existence befitting free men who are willing to work with their hands, but leads them on to deeds and actions that are far better and more useful and more in accordance with nature than those to which riches are wont to attract most men. (Dio Chrys. *Or.* 7.103)[34]

It is more blessed to give than to receive. (Acts 20:35)

Therefore he finds greater pleasure in conferring benefits than those benefited do in receiving them. (Dio Chrys. *Or.* 1.23)

Happy is the person who does not feel guilty about what he approves. (Rom 14:22)

Whose life is safer than his whom all alike protect, whose is happier than his who esteems no man an enemy, and whose is freer from vexation than his who has no cause to blame himself? (Dio Chrys. *Or.* 1.35)

In spite of similarities, it is obvious that statements concerning happiness in Stoicism and early Christianity differ because of the broader framework in which they were conceptualized, as well as the way in which both groups constructed reality. Stoics and Christians had similar views on certain conditions for well-being, but they nevertheless did not share the same world view.

From the above treatment of happiness in Stoic and early Christian thought, it has become clear that both Stoics and Christians held happiness in high esteem. To be happy is the goal of life for Stoics, and for Christians, happiness is something that believers receive from God. Happiness is not something that God alone has.[35] It is part and parcel of a life in Christ. Inner

---

"Hierocles the Stoic and the New Testament: A Contribution to the Corpus Hellenisticum," *NovT* 17 (1975) 156–60; and "Cornutus and the New Testament: A Contribution to the Corpus Hellenisticum," *NovT* 23 (1981) 165–72. See furthermore J. N. Sevenster, *Paul and Seneca* (Leiden: Brill, 1961).

34. See also Epictetus *Diss.* 3.20.12, 15. Further possible parallels are given in Downing, *Christ and the Cynics,* 19–20. Of special interest is Musonius. Although his teaching about happiness is in agreement with almost everything the Stoics taught, he nevertheless says (Musonius 7) that the aim of life is to become a good person and to live richly. A. C. van Geytenbeek, *Musonius Rufus and Greek Diatribe* (Assen: Van Gorcum, 1963) 22–25, gives a useful survey of Musonius's views on happiness.

35. In Philo, for example, happiness (μακαριότης) belongs to God alone. It is only when the divine nature becomes part of earthly life that earthly beings like humans have part in divine blessedness. See Philo *Abr.* 202: ἄλυπος δὲ καὶ ἄφοβος καὶ παντὸς πάθους ἀμέτοχος ἡ τοῦ θεοῦ φύσις εὐδαιμονίας καὶ μακαριότητος παντελοῦς μόνη μετέχουσα ("But the nature of God is without grief or fear and wholly exempt from passion of any kind, and alone partakes of perfect happiness and bliss." Trans. Colson in LCL.) See also Philo *Vit. Mos.* 2.184.

happiness is not only a disposition in Stoicism; it is something that humans have to attain by living in accordance with nature, that is, by virtue and moral purpose. Because happiness is a gift from God and is found in the believers' relationship with God, it seems that happiness, according to early Christianity, is an inner state of mind, a condition. There is, however, also another side to the picture. Early Christians were also happy because of their conduct. Deeds have consequences, and proper conduct leads to happiness. Except for those who saw life in an apocalyptic perspective, both early Christians and Stoics had an optimistic view of life. They both accepted life as it was and tried to live happily. To be happy is to become wise in the eyes of both Stoics and early Christians.

Christianity originated in a society that was dominated by Judaism. This explains the many Jewish traits in the understanding of a happy life by early Christians. One should nonetheless not disregard the Greco-Roman influence in Galilee, where the ministry of Jesus took place. His preaching about the kingdom of God created a new understanding of life for the underdogs of lower Galilee, who were his first followers. These people were probably acquainted with ideas about happiness in the Greco-Roman perspective, and they probably shared some of these with their non-Jewish contemporaries.

Professor Abraham J. Malherbe has contributed greatly to the fact that the study of Greco-Roman documents of the period of the development of early Christianity has become a sine qua non for students of the New Testament and early Christian writings. With his motto *ad fontes*, he has opened the Greco-Roman world to many. I am grateful that I can share many of his views and, therefore, present this essay with admiration to him.

DAVID L. BALCH

4

THE AREOPAGUS SPEECH
An Appeal to the Stoic Historian
Posidonius against Later Stoics
and the Epicureans

"Luke describes the Athenians . . . as those delighting in novelties. . . . There is
therefore a subtle turning of the tables; the pagan philosophers who question
the apostle do not themselves hold to the legitimating tradition; it is Paul who
does." °

C. K. Barrett asks why Luke mentions Epicureans and Stoics in Acts 17:18
and suggests the following: "In view however of this relation between the
Areopagus address and Stoicism it is not unreasonable to think that Luke
mentioned the Stoics in v. 18 in order to prepare for the allusions, and to suggest that he mentioned the Epicureans for the same reason."[1] The Stoics are
right: "The human race *is* one, it *was* made for a special relation with God,
and it is man's business to discern this relation and to live in accordance with
it. . . . But they worship God in ignorance, and what lies ahead of the human
race is not (as they think) an *ekpurosis* [conflagration] and a new beginning of
the age-old cycle, but the judgment of the world through Jesus Christ."[2]
Epicureans opposed superstitious popular religion, as Paul does, but they, too,
will come under judgment.[3]
    In a seminar at Yale University some years ago, Abraham J. Malherbe
raised this very question and suggested that the Stoic Posidonius might shed
new light on the speech. Posidonius was not only a Greek empirical scientist
who traveled about 100 B.C.E. to Gades (the present Cadiz on the Spanish
coast northwest of Gibraltar) to investigate the ocean tides,[4] but also was the

---

° Abraham J. Malherbe, "'Not in a Corner': Early Christian Apologetic in Acts 26:26," *Paul
and the Popular Philosophers* (Minneapolis: Fortress, 1990) 152.
    With this essay I express gratitude to a mentor who has not only taught students distinctive
exegetical emphases but who has also continued to devote time, care, and attention to us beyond
graduate school.
    1. C. K. Barrett, "Paul's Speech on the Areopagus," *New Testament Christianity for Africa and
the World* (ed. M. E. Glasswell and E. W. Fashole-Luke; London: SPCK, 1974) 69–75, at 73.
    2. Barrett, "Paul's Speech," 73–74.
    3. Barrett, "Paul's Speech," 74–75.
    4. See Jürgen Malitz, *Die Historien des Poseidonios* (Zetemata 79; Munich: C. H. Beck, 1983)
13.

only important philosopher of antiquity known to us who also wrote a political history of his own time.[5] In this chapter I argue that Posidonian texts clarify four aspects of the Areopagus address because they are related to contemporary philosophical debates—debates concerning providence in nature, debates concerning providence in history, and debates concerning whether or not the divine is to be worshiped by images in temples. Fourth, although I agree with Wolfgang Nauck that Hellenistic-Jewish mission preaching influenced the form of the Areopagus speech, I will discuss the analogy of Dio Chrysostom *Olympic Oration* 12, a Stoic speech influenced by the Stoic Posidonius on the topic of our "sources for the knowledge of God." Other points of contact between this speech and Posidonian thought could be developed, but I focus on these.

We know Posidonius only from fragments of his works quoted by other authors. Two recent editions approach the sources quite differently. Willy Theiler[6] includes all those passages that modern scholars have *argued* reflect Posidonian ideas and texts, whereas L. Edelstein and I. G. Kidd[7] edit only those fragments that *name* Posidonius as the source. The differences are dramatic; for example, Theiler's edition of Posidonius, Ἱστορία ἡ μετὰ Πολύβιον (History after Polybius' Histories) has 104 pages of Greek and Latin texts; Edelstein-Kidd's has merely 14. I will cite both editions so that the nature of the sources on which the interpretation is based will be clear. Because these Posidonian texts are scattered as fragments among the many authors who cited Posidonius, I will quote them extensively in an attempt to provide a clear environment for these four themes in the Acts speech. Many of the comparisons I make between Posidonius and the Areopagus speech will be based on texts that name Posidonius as the source, but in several instances, I consider Theiler's arguments persuasive.

5. Malitz, *Die Historien*, 7, 409.
6. Willy Theiler, *Poseidonios: Die Fragmente*, vol. 1: *Texte;* vol. 2: *Erläuterungen* (Texte und Kommentare 10.1 and 10.2; Berlin: Walter de Gruyter, 1982).
7. L. Edelstein and I. G. Kidd, *Posidonius: I, The Fragments* (2d ed.; Cambridge Classical Texts and Commentaries 13; Cambridge: Cambridge University Press, 1989); I. G. Kidd, *Posidonius: II, The Commentary* (2 vols.; Cambridge Classical Texts and Commentaries 14A and 14B; Cambridge: Cambridge University Press, 1988). For different approaches to the issue of sources for Posidonius, see Olof Gigon, "Der Historiker Poseidonios," *Studien zur antiken Philosophie* (Berlin: Walter de Gruyter, 1972) 242–58, esp. 247–49; and I. G. Kidd, "Posidonian Methodology and the Self-Sufficiency of Virtue," *Aspects de la philosophie hellénistique* (Entretiens sur l'antiquité classique 32; Geneva: Fondation Hardt, 1986) 1–28. When quoting Posidonius, I will first cite the ancient author who excerpts him; second, the testimony (= T) or fragment (frag.) in the edition by Theiler (= Th.); and third, the fragment in the second edition by Edelstein-Kidd (= E.-K.), if the latter prints the text.

POSIDONIUS:
PROVIDENCE IN NATURE

Martin Dibelius[8] and Walther Eltester[9] have written illuminating articles on the Areopagus speech. Their outline of the speech is as follows. First is the introduction (Acts 17:22b–23). Next is the body, with three main themes: (1) God, Creator and Lord of the cosmos, needs no temples, for God does not need anything (vv. 24–25); (2) this Lord created humans to seek God (vv. 26–27); and (3) humans are the "offspring" of God, which excludes all worship of images (vv. 28–29). Last is the conclusion: God commands repentance and has appointed a person to judge the world (vv. 30–31). Hildebrecht Hommel gives the speech the title "On the True Knowledge of God Which Every Human Can Attain."[10]

Acts 17:26

These scholars distinguish a "historical" from a "philosophical" interpretation of the speech, a distinction that largely depends on the exegesis of Acts 17:26b. Do the προστεταγμένοι καιροί refer to "allotted [historical or apocalyptic] periods" of the nations, perhaps parallel to the καιροὶ ἐθνῶν ("times of the Gentiles") in Luke 21:24, or do they refer philosophically to "appointed seasons" of the agricultural year? Second, do ὁροθεσίαι τῆς κατοικίας αὐτῶν refer to the "boundaries of their [the nations'] habitation," or do they refer philosophically to the "boundaries" of the torrid/tropic, temperate, and frigid/arctic geographical zones on earth provided by the deity, the temperate zones of which are "for human habitation"?

Following Dibelius, Eltester points to persuasive parallels for the philosophical interpretation of Acts 17:26b. For example, God gave Solomon knowledge of "the alternations of the solstices and the changes of the seasons [μεταβολὰς καιρῶν], the cycles of the year" (Wis 7:18). Appealing for order in the Corinthian church, 1 Clement refers to the harmony of the universe: "The earth teems according to his will at its proper seasons [τοῖς ἰδίος καιροῖς], and puts forth food in full abundance for men and beasts. . . . The

8. Martin Dibelius, "Paul on the Areopagus," *Studies in the Acts of the Apostles* (trans. Mary Ling; New York: Scribner's, 1956) 26–77, originally published in *Aufsätze zur Apostelgeschichte* (hrsg. H. Greeven; Göttingen: Vandenhoeck & Ruprecht, 1953) 29–70. See the review by A. D. Nock in *Gnomon* 25 (1953) 497–506.

9. Walther Eltester, "Gott und die Natur in der Areopagrede," *Neutestamentliche Studien für Rudolf Bultmann* (2d ed.; ZNTW Beiheft 21; Berlin: Alfred Töppelmann, 1957) 202–27, whose outline of the speech is on 203–4.

10. Hildebrecht Hommel, "Neue Forschung zur Areopagrede Acta 17," ZNW 46 (1955) 145–76, reprinted with "Nachträge" in his *Sebasmata: Studien zur antiken Religionsgeschichte und zum frühen Christentum* (WUNT 32; Tübingen: J. C. B. Mohr [Paul Siebeck], 1984) 2. 83–117, at 159. Alfons Weiser, *Die Apostelgeschichte* (Ökumenischer Taschenbuchkommentar zum Neuen Testament 5/2; Gütersloh: Echter, 1985) 2. 472–73, 478–80, denies that the Lukan gospel assumes human knowledge of God without the revelation of the gospel; see p. 457 on alternative ways to outline the Areopagus speech.

seasons [καιροί] of spring, summer, autumn and winter give place to one another in peace" (*1 Clem.* 20:4, 9; trans. Lake in LCL). These parallels are even more convincing because of the identical thought in Paul's speech to pagans at Lystra (Acts 14:17): "[God] leaves a witness, doing good and giving you rains from heaven and harvest seasons [ὑετοὺς διδοὺς καὶ καιροὺς καρποφόρους], satisfying your hearts with food and gladness."

However, Eltester[11] rejects Dibelius's interpretation of the ὁροθεσία as "boundaries" of the geographical zones on earth. He rather appeals to material assembled by Hermann Gunkel that refers to the battle of God in the beginning and in the end time with chaos, the primeval sea (Gen 1:9–10; 7:11; 8:1), for which God has set "boundaries":

> You have bound the sea with your power, you have broken to pieces the heads of the dragons in the water.... You have made all the borders [ὅρια] of the earth; you have made summer and spring. (Ps 73:13, 17 LXX, a parallel to *both* ideas in Acts 17:26b)

> You have set a boundary [ὅριον] which they [that is, the waters, the abyss] shall not pass; neither shall they turn again to cover the earth. (Ps 103:9 LXX)

> Or who shut in the sea with doors, ... and prescribed bounds [ὅρια] for it, and set bars and doors, and said, "Thus far shall you come, and no farther?" (Job 38:8–11)

Eltester[12] observes that whereas the texts cited above and Acts 17:26b are optimistic, Luke can image the end time in precisely the opposite way: "And there will be signs in sun and moon and stars, and upon the earth distress of nations in perplexity at the roaring of the sea and the waves, men fainting with fear and with foreboding of what is coming on the world; for the powers of the heaven will be shaken" (Luke 21:25–26). This demonstrates that the ideas that Eltester suggests lie behind Acts 17:26b were known to the author, but they have been combined with other, Greek concerns. *1 Clement* 20, concerning God's gift of the "seasons," was quoted above; the same chapter contains the reference to "boundaries," now with Stoic accents: "The unsearchable places of the abysses ... are controlled by the same ordinances. The hollow of the boundless sea is gathered by his working into its allotted places, and it does not pass the barriers placed around it, but does even as he enjoined on it; for he said, 'Thus far shalt thou come, and thy waves shall be broken within thee'" (*1 Clem.* 20.5–8, quoting Job 38:11; cf. *1 Clem.* 33.3).[13]

Finally, Harald Fuchs[14] discusses Dio Chrysostom's *Or.* 40.35–41, a Stoic

11. Eltester, "Gott und die Natur," 209–19.
12. Eltester, "Gott und die Natur," 219–20.
13. Eltester, "Gott und die Natur," 221.
14. Eltester, "Gott und die Natur," 225, citing Harald Fuchs, *Augustin und der antike Friedensgedanke: Untersuchungen zum neunzehnten Buch der Civitas Dei* (Berlin: Weidmann, 1965) 101–5. See also J. J. Thierry, "Note sur τὰ ἐλάχιστα τῶν ζώων au chapitre xx de la Ia Clementis," *VC* 14 (1960) 235–44, who shows in what ways *1 Clement* 20 is Stoic.

speech written in the same decade as Luke-Acts and *1 Clement*.[15] Like the author of *1 Clement*, Dio is appealing for concord between two parties, in this case for harmony between two cities:

> Do you not see . . . the everlasting concord of the elements . . ., air and earth and water and fire . . . which are preserved themselves and also preserve the entire universe [σῴζοντα τὸν ἅπαντα κόσμον]? . . . you should observe that these things, being by nature indestructible and divine and regulated by the purpose and power of the first and greatest god [τοῦ πρώτου καὶ μεγίστου γνώμῃ καὶ δυνάμει κυβερνώμενα θεοῦ], are wont to be preserved as a result of their mutual friendship and concord for ever. . . . The stars make way for the sun and do not feel they are being mistreated or destroyed through that god's power [διὰ τὴν ἐκείνου τοῦ θεοῦ δύναμιν]. . . . Moreover, the earth is content with having drawn the lowest place, like a ship's prop, and the water with having been poured about it. (Dio Chrys. *Or.* 40.35, 36, 38, 39; trans. Crosby in LCL)[16]

The ancient Near Eastern myth of God's battle with chaos, which results in its being confined within fixed boundaries—a myth reflected in the texts quoted from Genesis, Psalms, and Job—is partially analogous to the harmony and order regulated by the deity that Dio Chrysostom appeals to, and Clement has combined the two world views. Eltester[17] judges, however, that Clement has not successfully transformed the Stoic tradition by the biblical understanding of the earth and seas as God's creation that reveals God's power and goodness.

Dio's thirty-sixth oration has similar ideas.[18] He quotes a "song of the Magi" (36.39–60) that "contains Stoic elements . . . probably due to a Magian (born or adopted) who seized on elements capable of being combined with his own beliefs, just as Philo seized on Logos speculation,"[19] and, I add, just as Luke and Clement combined OT language and images with partially analogous Stoic elements. Dio first explains the Stoic view that the cosmos is orderly and has been divided into many plants and animals, as well as into air, earth, water, and fire, "being nevertheless by nature in all these forms one thing [ἕν] and governed by one spirit and force" (36.30). This doctrine harmonizes the human race [γένος] with the divine; both are endowed with reason. The wisest and eldest ruler and lawgiver of all ordains friendship and concord for all; he is the leader of all the heaven and lord of all being, the father of gods and men (36.32). The cosmos is the home of Zeus, the father of all (36.36), who governs as king (36.37). The universe is constantly moving (κινήσεις); the courses of Helius and Selene are "clearly perceived by humans," although

---

15. Anthony R. R. Sheppard, "Dio Chrysostom: The Bithynian Years," *L'Antiquité classique* 53 (1984) 157–73, at 160–62, dates *Or.* 40 in 100–101 C.E., agreeing with von Arnim.

16. See Diog. Laert. 7.155 for Stoic doctrine of the place of water in relation to the five zones.

17. Eltester, "Gott und die Natur," 226: "es [ist] Clement nicht gelungen."

18. Sheppard, "Dio Chrysostom," 158, 173, observes that *Oration* 36 postdates Dio's return to Prusa from exile in 97 C.E.

19. A. D. Nock, *Conversion* (Oxford: Oxford University Press, 1963; originally published 1933) 43.

many are ignorant (ἀγνοεῖν) of the movement of the entire universe (36.42). These Magi tell of the generation of the cosmos by Zeus and Hera from "one seed for the entire world" (ἕν σπέρμα τοῦ παντός [36.56]). This particular myth may have originated with Dio's Greek sources or with the Persian Magi, but the emphasis on the oneness and unity of the cosmos, including the divine and humans, is orthodox Stoic doctrine.[20] Christian readers knowing the Septuagint would understand the ἐξ ἑνός of Acts 17:26a to refer to Adam; whether they would also perceive it to refer to Stoic oneness, or even to the Zeus of Dio in Or. 36.56, or to both Adam and the unity of the cosmos would depend on how close the actual readers are to the audience of Stoics (and Epicureans) Luke supplies in Acts 17:18.

Acts 17:27a

The Lord set (ὁρίσας) these seasons and boundaries "that they should seek [ζητεῖν, a telic infinitive dependent on ὁρίσας] God" (Acts 17:27a). Seeking God is, of course, known in the Hebrew Bible, but there it is typically a matter of the *will*, whereas in this speech it is a matter of *thinking*, a consequence of reflection on the annual seasons and geographical boundaries of 17:26b.[21] Hommel emphasizes the occurrence of the thought in the Stoic Posidonius, for example, as quoted by Dio Chrysostom in Or. 12.27–30 (frag. 368 Th.):

> Now concerning the nature of the gods in general, and especially that of the ruler of the universe, first and foremost an idea regarding him and a conception of him common [ἐπίνοια κοινή] to the whole human race, to the Greeks and to the barbarians alike, a conception that is inevitable and innate [ἔμφυτος] in every creature endowed with reason ... has rendered manifest God's kinship with man. ... How could they [ancient persons] have remained ignorant [ἀγνῶ-τες] and conceived no inkling of him who had sowed and planted and was now preserving and nourishing them ...? They dwelt upon the earth, they beheld the light of heaven, they had nourishment in abundance, for god, their ancestor, had lavishly provided and prepared it to their hand.

Theiler prints this as a Posidonian fragment, although Edelstein-Kidd do not. But it is a Posidonian thought, as is clear from the one fragment we have from Posidonius's work Περὶ τοῦ Ὠκεανοῦ ("On the Ocean"), where he is concerned with boundaries (ὅροι) in the sense of the arctic, temperate, and tropic zones of our earth (Strabo Geog. 2.3.2; frag. 13 Th./49 Edelstein and Kidd). Strabo systematically *criticizes* this work of Posidonius, including a conclusion concerning design or providence that the Stoic scientist draws in the fragment: "For such a distribution [of animals, plants, and climates] is not

20. See Diog. Laert. 7.140: Posidonius asserts that the sympathy and tension in the cosmos prove that it is one and forms one united whole (using the favorite verb ἑνόω). See Diog. Laert. 7.143, 151; and Sextus Empiricus 9.60, 75, 78–80, 111, 120, 132.

21. Dibelius, "Paul on the Areopagus," 32; and Hommel, "Acta 17," 164, citing Cicero *Tusc.* 1.68, and Seneca *Ep.* 95.47 (on which see Hommel's "Nachträge," 115). See also Sextus Empiricus 9.60, 75–110.

58   ESSAYS IN HONOR OF ABRAHAM J. MALHERBE

the result of design [τοιαῦται διατάξεις οὐκ ἐκ προνοίας γίνονται]—just as the differences of race [τὰ ἔθνη διαφοραί], or of language, are not either— but rather of accident and chance [ἀλλὰ κατὰ ἐπίπρωσιν καὶ συντυχίαν]" (*Geog.* 2.3.7; trans. Jones in LCL; frag. 13 Th./49 E.-K.). The Posidonian reasoning that Strabo here opposes has close analogies to the way the thought develops from Acts 17:26b to 27a. Similarly, when Strabo is describing the country near Toulouse, he observes that the necessities of life are interchanged by everyone with ease, and that the advantages are common to all; the people till the country diligently and devise civil modes of life. "Therefore in the cases of this sort, one might believe that there is confirmatory evidence for the workings of Providence [τὸ τῆς προνοίας ἔργον ἐπιμαρτυρεῖσθαι], since the regions are laid out, not in a fortuitous way [οὐχ ὅπως ἔτυχεν], but as though in accordance with some calculated plan [μετὰ λογισμοῦ]" (Strabo *Geog.* 4.1.14; frag. 28b Th./cf. 248 E.-K.).

A Stoic audience would not be aware of the dragon of chaos whose boundaries were set by God as celebrated in Genesis and Psalms but would be aware of the geographical/climatic "boundaries" clarified by Posidonian science. Luke's Stoic audience would be prepared to conclude from these natural phenomena that they rationally demonstrate God's providence to one seeking the divine. Eltester has clarified the origin of the language in Acts 17:26b, but since the author of this sermon is combining ancient Near Eastern and Greek theologies, it still needs to be observed that the portion of the audience mentioned in 17:18 accustomed to Stoic ideas would think of the Posidonian "boundaries," the tropic, temperate, and arctic zones on our planet that point to rational thought in the cosmos.[22]

POSIDONIUS: PROVIDENCE IN HISTORY

Posidonius's perception of providence in nature raises two questions: (1) whether Posidonius related his scientific investigations of the climate zones on earth and of the ocean tides to his writing of history, and (2) since Acts 17:26b–27a reflects this Stoic science, whether the Areopagus speech is related to the rest of Luke's "narrative" (διήγησις; Luke 1:1; cf. Acts 1:1).[23]

Posidonian science, philosophy, and history are related. If a debated passage in the prooemium of Diodorus Siculus (1.1.3; frag. 80 Th.) has its source in Posidonius,[24] he understood historians to be "ministers of Divine Provi-

22. Cf. Dibelius, "Paul on the Areopagus," 304.
23. Jacob Jervell, *The Unknown Paul: Essays on Luke-Acts and Early Christian History* (Minneapolis: Augsburg, 1984) 17, thinks that "this speech is more or less a foreign body within Acts, not a typical missionary speech, and from the point of view of composition and structure no lines lead from this speech to the other parts of Acts." Cf. Dibelius, "Paul on the Areopagus," 52, 58, 64.
24. Cited by Malitz, *Die Historien des Poseidonios,* 412–13; denied by David E. Hahm, "Posidonius's Theory of Historical Causation," *ANRW* 2.36.3 (1989) 1358, n. 51.

dence" (ὑπουργοὶ τῆς θείας προνοίας). The idea occurs again later: when some who were involved in the slave revolts ate a fish sacred to Artemis, they experienced great pain, the divine power holding them up as "an example [τὸ δαιμόνιον ... εἰς παραδειγματισμόν] to deter the others, leaving all those who had acted so madly to suffer unsuccoured. And since in keeping with the retribution visited on them by the gods, they have also received abuse in the pages of history [διὰ τῆς ἱστορίας βλασφημίας], they have indeed reaped a just reward" (Diodorus 34/35.9; trans. Walton and Geer in LCL; frag. 142 Th.). But neither of these texts names Posidonius as the source. The following key text does: "Nicolas the Peripatetic and Posidonius the Stoic both say in their *Histories* that the Chians were enslaved by Mithridates the Cappadocian and handed over in chains to their own slaves, to be transported to Colchis; so truly did the Deity vent his wrath [τὸ δαιμόνιον ἐμήνισε] upon them for being the first to use purchased slaves, although most people did their own work when it came to menial services" (Athenaeus *Deip.* 6.266ef; trans. Gulick in LCL; frag. 250 Th./51 E.-K.).[25] Theiler and Malitz[26] accept the final lines on the Deity as Posidonian, whereas Kidd (in his commentary) and Hahm reject them.

The question at issue between Theiler and Kidd has to be how or in what manner Posidonius presented providence in his *History*, not whether he did; that is, did Posidonius's stories present the consequences of virtuous and vicious actions subtly, as in the first part of the quote from Athenaeus, or were the results more crudely, directly emphasized, as in the second part? Malitz[27] emphasizes that Posidonius was understood as a philosopher in antiquity— that he wrote history as a Stoic. The consequences of irrational, immoral conduct are clear in the fragment on the philosopher Athenion, whom the Athenians allowed to become a "god-king" and tyrant opposed to the Romans: the Roman praetor Orbius slaughtered hundreds of them (Athenaeus *Deip.* 5.211d–215b; frag. 247 Th./253 E.-K.). And the first Sicilian slave war shows that history in a larger sense becomes judge of those who are the source of the slaves' misery.[28]

That Posidonius advocated Stoic views on providence is clear not only from

25. Kidd, *Commentary*, 2.1. 277, however, argues that "the remark about the animosity of τὸ δαιμόνιον in relation to the inauguration of bought slaves comes from Athenaeus and not from Posidonius." Edelstein placed these words in the text; after his coeditor's death, Kidd wrote the commentary alone and denies the words are genuine. Hahm, "Posidonius's Theory of Historical Causation," 1358, n. 52, also denies they are Posidonian; but Malitz, *Die Historien des Poseidonios*, 420, n. 81, considers them genuine.

Kidd, *Commentary*, 2.1. 277, notes that "this is the latest datable event which can with certainty be assigned to the *History* from the surviving fragments. Moreover, Malitz (70) has pointed out the curious fact that Athenaeus no longer cites Posidonius for any subsequent event in the eighties and seventies, but only Nicolaus alone. This raises the question whether the *History* continued much after 86 B.C."

26. Malitz, *Die Historien des Poseidonios*, 421–22.

27. Malitz, *Die Historien des Poseidonios*, 411.

28. Malitz, *Die Historien des Poseidonios*, 422.

the narrative but also from his metaphysical statements. Several sources, especially Cicero and Philo,[29] clarify the debate between Stoics and Epicureans about providence: "Next I [Lucilius Balbus, the Stoic] have to show that the world is governed by divine providence. . . . The doctrine is hotly contested by your [Epicurean] school, Cotta, and it is they no doubt that are my chief adversaries here" (Cicero *Nat. D.* 2.73; trans. Rackham in LCL).[30] Posidonius treated providence under three different aspects. Fate is "third from Zeus; for first there is Zeus, second nature, and third fate [εἱμαρμένην]" (frag. 382a Th./103 E.-K.).[31] "Heaven . . . is the ruling power of the world" (τὸν οὐρανὸν . . . τὸ ἡγεμονικὸν τοῦ κόσμου; Diog. Laert. 7.139; frag. 347 Th./23 E.-K.). "That all things happen by fate" (καθ᾽ εἱμαρμένην . . . τὰ πάντα) is maintained . . . by Posidonius in his *De fato,* book 2 (Diog. Laert. 7.149; frag. 381 Th./25 E.-K.). "Fate is defined as an endless chain of causation" (εἱμαρμένη αἰτία τῶν ὄντων; Diog. Laert. 7.149).[32] "What is more, they say that divination in all its forms is a real and substantial fact, if there really is Providence [πρόνοια]. And they prove it to be actually a science on the evidence of certain results: so . . . Posidonius in the second book of his *Physical Discourse* and the fifth book of his *De divinatione* [Περὶ μαντικῆς]" (7.149).

Two recent articles interpret Posidonius's historical explanations by stressing his analysis of psychological factors.[33] Klaus Bringmann analyzes Posidonius's narration of (1) the first slave war in Sicily (136 to 132 B.C.E., assuming that Diodorus's stories in books 33 through 37 have their source in Posidonius),[34] (2) the Athenian revolt against Roman rule led by Athenion in 88 B.C.E, (3) Demetrius II (in Diodorus 33.4, 9), and, finally, (4) the positive

29. Malitz, *Die Historien des Poseidonios,* 344–50, on the relation between providence and divination. Max Pohlenz, *Die Stoa: Geschichte einer geistigen Bewegung* (Göttingen: Vandenhoeck & Ruprecht, 1959) 1. 98–101, as well as the notes in 2. 55–58, which often cite Cicero *Nat. D.* 2 and Philo *Prov.* See K. Reinhardt, "Poseidonios von Apameia," *Paulys Realencyclopaedia* (1953) 22.1. 697–718, who adds Sextus Empiricus *Math.* 9.60–194.

30. Cited by W. C. van Unnik, "An Attack on the Epicureans by Flavius Josephus," *Romanitas et Christianitas: Studia Iano Henrico Waszink* (ed. W. den Boer et al.; Amsterdam: North-Holland, 1973) 341–55, at 344. Van Unnik interprets Josephus *Ant.* 275–81, the only place where Josephus takes sides against a philosophical school (the Epicureans) by naming it. Josephus quotes Daniel's prophecy as fulfilled to prove them wrong about providence.

31. In Aetius *Placita* 324b11, a text emphasized by Malitz, *Die Historien des Poseidonios,* 421.

32. Cf. Strabo *Geog.* 2.3.8; frag. T 30b Th./T 85 E.-K.

33. Hahm, "Posidonius's Theory of Historical Causation," and Klaus Bringmann, "Geschichte und Psychologie bei Poseidonios," *Aspects de la philosophie hellénistique* (Entretiens sur l'antiquité classique 32; Geneva: Fondation Hardt, 1985) 29–66.

34. Bringmann announces (32, n. 6) that he will quote only Edelstein-Kidd but then repeatedly cites the fragments of Posidonius in Diodorus edited by Theiler. He argues (47) that it is the psychological analysis that distinguishes the excerpts of Posidonius in Diodorus 33–37. Hahm, "Posidonius's Theory of Historical Causation," 1347, n. 38, admits that some of the Diodoran fragments are genuine and cites Kidd's similar conclusion, so he seems reluctantly to agree. Gigon, "Der Historiker Poseidonios," 247 (cf. also 261), writes that Diodorus, bk. 33–37, is the most important witness to Posidonius's *History*; and Kurt von Fritz, "Poseidonios als Historiker," *Historiographia Antiqua, Commentationes Lovanienses in honorem W. Peremans septuagenarii editae* (Symbolae, A. 6; Leuven: Leuven University Press, 1977) 179, argues that Diodorus 34 is essentially Posidonian.

example of Viriathus (in Diodorus 33.1, 7). Bringmann concludes that psychological factors in the personality of the protagonists in the narrative, not the social circumstances, are the key to Posidonius's analysis.[35] Unlike Thucydides, Posidonius expresses human character not only by narrating the history of national politics but also by private and social factors.[36]

David E. Hahm goes further. Like Bringmann he analyzes the Athenion episode, and in addition, he analyzes the Roman consul Marius's internal psychology. His conclusion about Posidonius's method of explaining success or failure is as follows: "The central importance of character in explaining both human actions and their consequences may be confirmed by the large number of allusions to it in the surviving fragments. Posidonius seems to have been obsessed with the duty to identify the character of both individuals and nations and to correlate character with behavior and with success or failure."[37] Hahm continues, "The character traits of nations and social groups . . . could be discovered in their constitutions, laws, and customs. This is presumably the reason that Posidonius pays so much attention to ethnology in both his 'History' and 'On the Ocean.'"[38] Critically, however, even if a historian like Diodorus were inspired by Posidonius to emphasize providence in his preface, "Diodorus's commitment to demonstrating the role of divine providence in the interrelations of world events is hardly an adequate statement of Posidonius's purpose in writing history. In fact, a survey of the explicitly attested fragments turns up no mention of god, fate, or providence as a force in history, and even chance (τύχη) is mentioned only in a popular characterization of Athenion. . . .[39] These same fragments suggest that Posidonius was able to account for events quite adequately without mentioning god, fate, or divine providence."[40] This does not deny the role of god in history, Hahm argues, since human minds are fragments of the universal world soul, the divine mind; when human minds think or act, the divine mind thinks and acts. "The process of human decision-making was, in fact, identical with the operation of fate and divine providence in the universe. Divine providence was not an alternative causal explanation of historical events, but another description of the psychological theory of explanation that we have been investigating. . . . [T]hrough their minds men not only can, but of necessity do, control their

35. Bringmann, "Geschichte und Psychologie," 29–30.
36. Bringmann, "Geschichte und Psychologie," 35.
37. Hahm, "Posidonius's Theory of Historical Causation," 1342.
38. Hahm, "Posidonius's Theory of Historical Causation," 1344.
39. But see C. D. Gilbert, "Marius and Fortuna," CQ 23 (1973) 104–7.
40. Hahm, "Posidonius's Theory of Historical Causation," 1358. He must deny that the last part of the fragment on the Chians' enslavement by Mithridates is genuine (see note 25 above). Again, the editor of the fragments judges what is Posidonian, for example, in Seneca Ep. 90 (frag. 447 Th./284 E.-K.). Edelstein-Kidd omit Ep. 90.28 (with its reference to "what the gods are and of what sort they are; what are the nether gods, the household deities, and the protecting spirits; what are the souls which have been endowed with lasting life and have been admitted to the second class of divinities"), while Theiler includes it. See H. Dörrie, "Der Begriff 'Pronoia' in Stoa und Platonismus," Freiburger Zeitschrift für Philosophie und Theologie 24 (1977) 60–87.

destinies and the destinies of others. Even if some Stoics could submit passively to the dictates of fate, those in a position of power could not."[41]

Bringmann and Hahm have shed light on Posidonius's contribution to
understanding human actions and their consequences, and these two interpreters have helped us see what is new in Posidonian historiography—for
example, that Posidonius even describes "changes in character due to external
circumstances,"[42] which was rare and which modern interpreters often deny
was even done by ancient historians and biographers.

Nevertheless, not only has Hahm overstated his case by focusing on
Anthenion and Marius and then drawing conclusions on the basis of these
individual tyrants, but he also virtually ignores Posidonius's Stoic metaphysical
statements, as well as his narration of consequences larger than individual,
psychological ones.[43] Further, the certainty that Posidonius argued for the
presence of design or providence in nature (Strabo *Geog.* 2.3.2; frag. 13
Th./49 E.-K., quoted above) suggests that he would have looked for the same
in history, although perhaps not in the direct way Athenaeus expresses it.

Hahm is simply incorrect that in "the explicitly attested fragments [one]
turns up no mention of god, fate, or providence as a force in history,"[44] as
Athenaeus's citation of Posidonius in his discussion of slaves demonstrates.
Kidd[45] observes that the topic begins in Athenaeus 6.262B but turns to Roman
customs in 272D: many own large numbers of slaves. At 273A, Athenaeus
contrasts this with Posidonius's report of the moderation and virtue of early
Romans with regard to numbers of slave attendants:

> The Romans of early times [οἱ ἀρχαῖοι 'Ρωμαῖοι], however, were moderate and
> highly virtuous in all things. Scipio surnamed Africanus, for example, when
> dispatched by the Senate to pacify the kingdoms of the world and entrust them
> to their rightful rulers, took as retinue only five slaves, as we are told by Polybius
> and Poseidonius. (Athenaeus *Deip.* 6.273B; frag. 125c Th./265 E.-K.)

> But today, though they select what is useful, they are also borrowing from their
> enemies' pernicious ideals. As Poseidonius says, their ancestral traits used to be
> rugged endurance, a frugal manner of life, a plain and simple use of material
> possessions in general, a religion, moreover, wonderful in its devotion to deity
> [εὐσέβεια μὲν θαυμαστὴ περὶ τὸ δαιμόνιον], upright dealing [δικαιοσύνη], and
> great care in avoiding wrongdoing in their relations with all men; associated with
> these qualities was the pursuit of agriculture. This may be seen in the ancestral
> festivals [πατρίων θυσιῶν] which we celebrate. . . . What we say in prayers or
> do in the sacred office is plain and frugal. . . . [T]he utensils which we bring are
> of earthenware or bronze, and in them are the simplest foods and drinks in the

41. Hahm, "Posidonius' Theory of Historical Causation," 1359, 1360.
42. Hahm, "Posidonius's Theory of Historical Causation," 1334, n. 20, repeating von Fritz,
"Poseidoniios als Historiker," 183, 186–87, 193.
43. See esp. Gigon, "Der Historiker Poseidonios," 254.
44. See note 40.
45. Kidd, *Commentary*, 2.2. 910–11.

world, because we think it absurd that while we bring to the gods offerings ordained by ancestral custom, we should indulge ourselves in exotic luxuries. (Athenaeus *Deip.* 6.274A; frag. 81 Th./266 E.-K. [who edit only the first half])

But in earlier times [πρότερον], the inhabitants of Italy, according to Poseidonius, even those who were very well off for a livelihood, trained their sons in drinking water, mostly, and in eating whatever they happened to have. (Athenaeus *Deip.* 6.275A; frag. 81 Th./267 E.-K.)

Theiler argues that another text from Plutarch is a Posidonian description of these ancient Romans:

Furthermore, his [king Numa's] ordinances concerning images are altogether in harmony with the doctrines of Pythagoras. For that philosopher maintained that the first principle of being was beyond sense or feeling, was invisible and uncreated, and discernible only by the mind. And in like manner Numa forbade the Romans to revere an image of God [εἰκόνα θεοῦ] which had the form of man or beast. Nor was there among them in this earlier time any painted or graven likeness of Deity [οὔτε γραπτὸν οὔτε πλαστὸν εἶδος θεοῦ πρότερον], but while for the first hundred and seventy years they were continually building temples and establishing sacred shrines, they made no statues in bodily form for them, convinced that it was impious to liken higher things to lower, and that it was impossible to apprehend Deity except by the intellect. (Plutarch *Numa* 8.7–8; trans. Perrin in LCL)[46]

Given the certainly genuine Posidonian texts, Theiler also includes several Diodoran texts that contrast the ancient, virtuous founders of Rome with the power- and money-hungry Roman magistrates of the present, who love luxury and subject allies to rapacity and lawlessness (πλεονεξίαν τε καὶ παρανομίαν; Diodorus 34/35.33.5; frag. 178 Th.; cf. 37.8; frag. 215 Th.). Malitz[47] quotes a Diodoran passage about the cause of this decline: "The primary cause [αἰτίαν] of the war [that is, the Marsic or Social War of 91 B.C.E.] was this, that the Romans abandoned the disciplined, frugal and stern manner of life that had brought them to such greatness, and fell [τὸ μεταπεσεῖν] into the pernicious pursuit of luxury and license [τρυφῆς καὶ ἀκολασίας]. The *plebs* and senate being at odds as a result of this deterioration [ἐκ γὰρ τῆς διαφθορᾶς] ..." (37.2.1; frag. 211a Th.). The differences between Diodorus's own reflections and the following excerpt, Malitz[48] suggests, make the latter's Posidonian origin manifest:

In days of old [τὸ παλαιόν] the Romans by adhering to the best laws and customs, little by little became so powerful that they acquired the greatest and most splendid empire known to history. But in more recent times [ἐν δὲ τοῖς νεωτέροις καιροῖς], when most nations had already been subjugated in war and

---

46. See Theiler, *Poseidonios*, 282, and Malitz, *Die Historien des Poseidonios*, 317, n. 97.
47. Malitz, *Die Historien des Poseidonios*, 385.
48. Malitz, *Die Historien des Poseidonios*, 386–97.

there was a long period of peace, the ancient practices gave way at Rome [μετέ-
πεσεν ἐν τῇ Ῥώμῃ τὸ τῆς ἀρχαίας ἀγωγῆς] to pernicious tendencies. After the
cessation of warfare the young men turned to a soft and undisciplined [εἰς τρυ-
φὴν καὶ ἀκολασίαν] manner of life, and their wealth [πλοῦτον] served as pur-
veyor to their desires. Throughout the city lavishness (πολυτέλεια) was preferred to frugality, a life of ease to the practice of warlike pursuits. (Athenaeus
Deip. 37.3.1–2; frag. 211b Th.)

Owning many slaves is one sign of this luxury; for example, Syrian kings
from Posidonius's homeland give away gold, silver, slaves, horses, and camels
(Athenaeus *Deip.* 5.210e; frag. 157b Th.). The present Roman way of life is
indicted:

In answer to this Larensis said: "But every Roman, as you are well aware, good
Masurius, owns an infinite number of slaves; in fact there are very many who
own 10,000, 20,000 or even more—not to bring in revenue, as in the case of the
opulent Greek Nicias; but the majority of Romans have the largest numbers to
accompany them when they go out. Moreover, most of these Athenian slaves,
counted in myriads, worked in the mines as prisoners. Poseidonius, the philosopher, at any rate (whom you have constantly quoted), says that they revolted.
(Athenaeus *Deip.* 6.272ef; frag. 193 Th./cf. 262 E.-K.)[49]

Edelstein-Kidd include only the latter part of this fragment, but Theiler is
correct that the whole reflects Posidonian ideas; it fits the Posidonian contrasts
between (1) early simplicity/present luxury and (2) few slaves in early
Rome/myriads now. As a Stoic, Posidonius valued simplicity and self-
sufficiency and had a negative attitude toward having too many slaves and mis-
treating them.

This negative judgment on luxury has consequences for Roman piety. The
Posidonian fragment quoted above concerning practices of the ancient
Romans (Athenaeus *Deip.* 6.274a; frag. 81 Th./266 E.-K.) includes praise of
their simple piety. Posidonius contrasts this, too, with present practices:

In the second book he [Posidonius] says: In the Roman capital, whenever they
hold a feast in the precinct of Hercules, it is given by the general who for the
time being is celebrating a triumph, and the preparation for the banquet is
worthy of Hercules himself. For honeyed wine flowed copiously throughout the
entire meal, and the food consisted of large loaves and boiled smoked meat, as
well as roast meat from the freshly sacrificed victims, in extravagant plenty. And
among the Etruscans sumptuous tables (τράπεζαι πολυτελεῖς) are prepared
twice a day, and richly coloured rugs are spread, and there are silver cups of
every kind, and a host of handsome slaves stands by, dressed in rich garments.
(Athenaeus *Deip.* 4.153cd; frag. 82 Th./53 E.-K.)

Probably because of this Posidonian criticism of luxurious piety and

49. Malitz, *Die Historien des Poseidonios,* 384–85, 402–3; cf. Diodorus 34/35.2.25–27; frag. 136c
Th.

because of its enlightened, "scientific" approach, Theiler includes another
Diodoran fragment critical of "superstition," the story of a hermaphrodite in
Syria. An Arabian woman married and had two children. Then an extra-
ordinary event happened: she changed sexes (Diodorus 32.10; frag. 85 Th.).
Similar events happened in Epidaurus and Naples:

> And this is the reason why we have considered these shifts of sex worthy of
> record, not for the entertainment, but for the improvement of our readers. For
> many men, thinking such things to be portents [τέρατα], fall into superstition
> [δεισιδαιμονοῦσιν], and not merely isolated individuals, but even nations and
> cities. At the outset of the Marsian War, at any rate, there was, so it is reported,
> an Italian living not far from Rome who had married an hermaphrodite similar
> to those described above; he laid information before the senate, which in an
> excess of superstitious terror and in obedience to the Etruscan diviners ordered
> the creature to be burned alive. Thus did one whose nature was like ours and
> who was not, in reality, a monster, meet an unsuitable end through misunder-
> standing [ἀγνοίᾳ] of his malady. Shortly afterwards there was another such case
> at Athens, and again through misunderstanding [ἄγνοιαν] of the affliction the
> person was burned alive. There are even fanciful stories [μυθολογοῦσιν]. . . .
> Let this much then be said by way of remedy to superstitious fears [πρὸς διόρ-
> θωσιν δεισιδαιμονίας]. (Diodorus 32.12; frag. 85 Th.)[50]

For the topic of this chapter, it is not irrelevant that the Rhodian Posidonius
refers to a superstitious, ignorant murder in Athens.

The following, then, are certainly Posidonian ideas. Posidonius is a Stoic
whose metaphysic places providence third after Zeus. Posidonius saw evidence of this rational design in the climatic "boundaries" on earth, where
humans inhabit temperate, not frigid or torrid, zones. He understood a
people's character to be revealed in their "constitution" and customs, which,
in the case of the ancient Romans, involved a simple diet, a nonluxurious life-
style without many slaves, and a marvelous piety. However, this early Roman
simplicity has, at least since the destruction of Carthage,[51] degenerated into
luxurious, lawless, greedy, power-hungry Roman governance of the empire
and a lavish piety in the present, which has consequences like slave revolts and
the hatred of the Romans by those whom they rule (for example, by Sicilian
slaves and the Athenians). The consequences of offending against rational,
moral providence include the psychology of individual slave owners and
tyrants but reach beyond to include the decline of the whole empire, so that
Bringmann's emphasis on psychological factors to the virtual exclusion of

50. Cf. Diodorus 34/35.2.37 and 24b (frag. 136e Th.) on Ennus's spiritual enthusiasm and 36.13
(frag. 200 Th.) on Battaces, a priest of the Mother of the Gods who played on the Romans' "fear in
matters of religion."
51. Malitz, *Die Historien des Poseidonios*, 365, 409: "The reconstruction of the *History* allows no
doubt that he understood the period he narrates as an epoch of decine. It cannot be due merely
to the literary taste of the excerpters that with few exceptions the power is in the hands of evil
figures, whose viciousness is only exceeded by their successors" (my trans.).

social ones is one-sided. Hahm's conclusion is naive: Individual "men not only can, but of necessity do, control their destinies and the destinies of others. Even if some Stoics could submit passively to the dictates of fate, those in a position of power could not."[52] Rather, Posidonius shows both that (1) the immoral conduct of tyrants like Athenaion and Marius have psychological *and social* consequences[53] and that (2) the present immoral conduct and luxurious piety of a nation like Rome, measured by its own earlier virtuous way of life, leads to decline and to revolts of slaves, of cities like Athens, and even of allies like the Italian Marsic peoples.[54]

These observations strongly suggest that Posidonius meant the passage about the Chians' being "handed over in chains to their own slaves"[55] to express the providential, rational consequences of immoral conduct, probably expressed by Posidonius's narrative itself and addressed to contemporary Roman magistrates,[56] to which Athenaeus felt compelled to add an explicit remark about the Deity venting its wrath for their having been the first to purchase slaves.[57] One purpose, then, of Posidonius's history is as follows: "I shall make mention of certain men to serve as models [παραδείγματος ἕνεκα], both because they merit my praise and for the good it does to society, in order that the denunciations of History may lead the wicked to turn from their evil course [διὰ τῆς κατὰ τὴν ἱστορίαν βλασφημίας ἀποτρέπωνται τῆς ἐπὶ τὴν κακίαν ὁρμῆς], and the praises that its enduring glory confers may persuade the good to aspire to high standards of conduct" (Diodorus 37.4; frag. 212 Th.). Posidonius's *History* demonstrates that "Fortune [τύχη] is wont to veer towards what is morally fitting, and to involve those who have contrived some injustice against others in the same difficulties themselves. . . . Perhaps for the present they exercise tyrannical power, but later they will have to render an accounting for their tyrannical crimes" (Diodorus 37.17; frag. 227 Th.).

To the Stoics whom Luke presents as the audience in Acts 17:18, the Areopagus speech appeals not only to a Posidonian understanding of divine providence in nature (17:26b–27a) but also, at its close (17:31),[58] to a Stoic

---

52. Hahm, "Posidonius's Theory of Historical Causation," 1358.

53. Von Fritz, "Poseidonios als Historiker," 179, 183, 186–87, 193.

54. Given some of the hideous historical events Posidonius narrates, Malitz, *Die Historien des Poseidonios*, 4 and 416 with n. 48, wonders about the unresolved inner contradiction involved in Posidonian theodicy in decline.

55. Athenaeus *Deip.* 266ef (cited n. 25 above).

56. Malitz, *Die Historien des Poseidonios*, 416, suggests that many of humbler origin could find themselves in the pages of Posidonius's *History*. Gigon, "Der Historiker Poseidonios," 251, notes Posidonius's preference for characters whose beginning is humble but whose gifts elevate them to historically active figures, for example, Viriathus and Ennus.

57. Cf. Diodorus 34/35.2.47; frag. 137 Th.

58. See esp. Paul Schubert, "The Place of the Areopagus Speech in the Composition of Acts," *Transitions in Biblical Scholarship* (ed. J. Coert Rylaarsdam; Chicago: University of Chicago Press, 1968) 235–61, at 251–53, 255; and H. Conzelmann, *Die Apostelgeschichte* (HNT 7; Tübingen: J. C. B. Mohr [Paul Siebeck], 1963) 101–4. Both scholars understand Acts 17:30–31 as the goal and climax of the speech, against Hommel, "Neuere Forschungen," 158–59 (and in addition his "Nachträge," 114), and Dibelius, "Paul on the Areopagus," 56–57.

understanding of providence in history.[59] As the Stoic Posidonius narrated, those who are impious or unjust will be judged. Examples of such judgment with negative consequences may be seen both in Posidonius's narration of Rome's decline and in Acts 12:20–23; Luke narrates a positive example in the "growth" of the church.[60] Thus, the Deuteronomic emphasis that obedience brings blessings and disobedience brings curses[61] is "translated" into the Stoic, Posidonian assertion that one's δικαιοσύνη (17:31)[62] is to be judged (κρίνειν). The theological accents are still quite different, of course. For Luke, this is not the early Christian, imminent, apocalyptic judgment but one at the end of the epoch of the Church.[63] For Posidonius, the providential consequences are immanent, within history. Luke has modified the apocalyptic expectation but not arrived at a Posidonian immanent view.

From a Posidonian point of view, descriptions of providence in nature and in history are compatible; Posidonius attempted to observe the one as a scientist and to narrate the other as a historian. Therefore, Jacob Jervell is incorrect that the Areopagus speech is "a foreign body within Acts."[64] Luke connected the Posidonian view of nature in Acts 17:26b–27a to a climax in 17:31 that, at the conclusion of the epoch of the Church, God will judge the world in righteousness by one appointed, a conclusion compatible with the rest of Luke's two-volume work. And against Dibelius and Hommel, Conzelmann[65] has shown that 17:30–31 is indeed the goal and climax of the speech: it reflects the mission preaching of the two-part credo seen in 1 Cor 8:6 and 1 Thess 1:9–10.[66]

POSIDONIUS: OPPOSITION TO IMAGES OF THE DEITY

The Deity is not "like gold, or silver, or stone, a representation by the art and imagination of humans" (Acts 17:29; cf. 17:23–25 and 7:48). One source of this opposition to images and even temples is Stoic. Zeno (335 to 263 B.C.E.), founder of Stoicism, is accused by Plutarch as follows:

59. Cf. John T. Squires, The Plan of God in Luke-Acts (diss., Yale University, 1988).
60. See David L. Balch, "Comments on the Genre and a Political Theme of Luke-Acts," SBL 1989 Seminar Papers (ed. David J. Lull; Atlanta: Scholars, 1989) 343–61.
61. On Luke's relation to the Deuteronomic pattern, see James A. Sanders, "The Ethic of Election in Luke's Great Banquet Parable," Essays in Old Testament Ethics: J. Philip Hyatt in Memoriam (ed. James L. Crenshaw and John T. Willis; New York: Ktav, 1974) 247–71, esp. 255, 258, 266.
62. Cf. Athenaeus Deip. 6.274A (frag. 81 Th./266 E.-K.), on the ancient Romans' justice (quoted above, 62).
63. E. Grässer, "Die Parusieerwartung in der Apostelgeschichte," Les Actes des Apotres: Traditions, rédaction, théologie (ed. J. Kremer; Gembloux: Duculot, 1979) 99–127.
64. See note 23.
65. See note 58.
66. Cf. U. Wilckens, Die Missionsreden der Apostelgeschichte: Form und Traditionsgeschichtliche Untersuchungen (WMANT 5; Neukirchen: Neukirchener Verlag, 1961) 72–90.

Moreover, it is a doctrine of Zeno's not to build temples of the gods [ἱερὰ θεῶν μὴ οἰκοδομεῖν], because a temple not worth much is also not sacred, and no work of builders or mechanics is worth much. The Stoics, while applauding this as correct, attend the mysteries in temples, go up to the Acropolis, do reverence to statues [τὰ ἕδη], and place wreaths upon the shrines, though these are works of builders and mechanics. Yet they think that the Epicureans are confuted by the fact that they sacrifice to the gods, whereas they are themselves worse confuted by sacrificing at altars and temples which they hold do not exist and should not be built. (Plutarch Stoic. Rep. 1034B; trans. Cherniss in LCL)[67]

Plutarch, a Middle Platonist, satirizes the dispute between Stoics and Epicureans about temples and statues of the gods. The Epicureans did believe that the gods exist and have human shape (Cicero Nat. D. 1.18.46–49), which is open to ridicule (1.15.71; 1.27.75–77):

> We have an idea of god implanted in our minds, you say. Yes, and an idea of Jupiter with a beard, and Minerva in a helmet; but do you therefore believe that those deities are really like that? The unlearned multitude are surely wiser here—they assign to god not only a man's limbs. For they give him bow, arrows, spear, shield, trident, thunderbolt; and if they cannot see what actions the gods perform, yet they cannot conceive of god as entirely inactive. Even the Egyptians, whom we laugh at, deified animals solely on the score of some utility which they derived from them; for instance the ibis. . . . [T]hese animals are at all events deified by the barbarians for the benefits which they confer, but your gods not only do no service that you can point to, but they don't do anything at all. "God," he says, "is free from trouble." Obviously Epicurus thinks, as spoilt children do, that idleness is the best thing there is. (Cicero Nat. D. 1.36.101–2)[68]

Stoics reverence statues of the gods and goddesses in temples, neither of which, they think, should ever have been made, whereas Epicureans offer sacrifice before the human shapes of divinities who do nothing. Some early Stoics, in theory but not in practice, held the view expressed in Acts 17:29. According to Plutarch in a text that may have had a Posidonian source,[69] the early Roman emperor Numa held such a view in both theory and practice. Other texts show that the question of images' validity was seriously discussed:

> What then? Does it not seem to you that the feeling of the atheists [ἀθέων] compared with the superstitious [δεισιδαίμονας] presents just such a difference? The former do not see the gods at all, the latter think that they do exist

---

67. Cited by J. Geffcken, Zwei Griechische Apologeten (Leipzig: Teubner, 1907) xx. See J. Geffcken, "Der Bilderstreit des heidnischen Altertums," ARW 19 (1919) 286–315, who discusses Posidonius on 295ff. See esp. Abraham J. Malherbe, "Pseudo-Heraclitus, Epistle 4: The Divinization of the Wise Man," JAC 21 (1978) 42–64. Cf. Varro; the texts are in Menachem Stern, Greek and Latin Authors on Jews and Judaism: Edited with Introductions, Translations and Commentary (Jerusalem: Israel Academy of Sciences and Humanities, 1974) 1. 207–11.
68. Cited by Geffcken, Apologeten, xxi.
69. Kidd, Commentary, 2.2.910–11.

and are evil. The former disregard them, the latter conceive their kindliness to be frightful, their fatherly solicitude to be despotic, their loving care to be injurious, their slowness to anger to be savage and brutal. Then again such persons give credence to workers in metal, stone or wax, who make their images of gods in the likeness of human beings [ἀνθρωπόμορφα τῶν θεῶν τὰ εἴδη ποιοῦσι], and they have such images fashioned, and dress them up, and worship them. But they hold in contempt philosophers and statesmen, who try to prove that the majesty of God is associated with goodness, magnanimity, kindliness, and solicitude. So the atheists have more than enough of indifference and distrust of the Beings who can help them, whereas the superstitious experience equal agitation and fear towards the things that can help them. Or, in fine, atheism is an indifferent feeling towards the Deity, which has no notion of the good, and superstition is a multitude of differing feelings with an underlying notion that the good is evil. (Plutarch *Superst.* 167DE; trans. Babbitt in LCL)[70]

Here Plutarch assumes the Stoic view that images of the gods are not like human beings, a contrast to the opinion and feelings of the "superstitious." This is so widely accepted that the satirist Lucian can poke fun at these images (*Iup. trag.* 7–12; *Gall.* 24) in a way reminiscent of Isa 44:9–20, referring to the "mice and rats" in them, a contrast to their "ivory and gold" exteriors (*Gall.* 24).[71]

One important source of this Stoic critique of images was Posidonius, who in the seventh book of his *History* described the campaign of Antiochus Sidetes in 134 B.C.E. that resulted in the capitulation of Jerusalem.[72] He may have taken the opportunity to describe the Judeans and their leader, Moses, who said

that the Aegyptians were mistaken in representing the Divine Being by the images [εἰκάζοντες] of beasts and cattle as were also the Libyans; and that the Greeks were also wrong in modelling gods in human form [ἀνθρωπομόρφους τυποῦντες]; for, according to him, God is this one thing alone that encompasses us all and encompasses land and sea—the thing which we call heaven, or universe, or the nature of all that exists [ἕν τοῦτο μόνον θεὸς τὸ περιέχον ἡμᾶς ἅπαντας καὶ γῆν καὶ θάλταν, ὃ καλοῦμεν οὐρανὸν καὶ κόσμον καὶ τὴν τῶν ὄντων φύσιν]. What man, then, if he has sense, could be bold enough to fabricate an image [εἰκόνα πλάττειν] of God resembling any creature amongst us? Nay, people should leave off all image-carving [ξοανοποιίαν], and, setting apart a sacred precinct and a worthy sanctuary, should worship God without an image [ἔδους χωρίς]. (Strabo *Geog.* 16.2.35–39; frag. 133 Th.)[73]

70. Cited by Geffcken, *Apologeten*, xxi.
71. Cited by Geffcken, *Apologeten*, xxi.
72. Theiler, *Poseidonios*, 2. 96.
73. A. D. Nock, "Posidonius," *JRS* 49 (1959) 1–15, at 5–9, agrees that this is a Posidonian fragment, or rather from a Jew who was aware of Posidonian ideas. See Eduard Norden, "Jahve und Moses in hellenistischer Theologie," *Festgabe von Fachgenossen und Freunden: A. von Harnack zum siebzigsten Geburtstag dargebracht* (Tübingen: J. C. B. Mohr [Paul Siebeck], 1921) 292–301. Opposed to Posidonian derivation are H. Conzelmann, *Heiden-Juden-Christen: Auseinandersetzungen in der Literatur der hellenistisch-römischen Zeit* (BHT 62; Tübingen: J. C. B. Mohr [Paul Siebeck], 1981) 63–69; John G. Gager, *The Origins of Anti-Semitism: Attitudes toward*

Later, tyrannical men (the Maccabees), who opposed their neighbors, and superstitious men, who instituted dietary laws and circumcision, came to the priesthood (16.2.37). But Moses and other prophets were "deemed worthy to be kings, on the ground that they promulgated to us ordinances and amendments from the gods" (16.2.39). In this text, Posidonius's opposition to images of the gods may be reflected in his description of Moses, itself quite remarkable in view of the usually garbled view of Judaism expressed by pagan writers.

John G. Gager's arguments that many of the ideas in this passage that have been specifically attributed to Posidonius are generally Stoic are strong. Divination was supported not only by Posidonius but by other Stoics as well. The same is true of the pattern of an ideal beginning followed by subsequent degeneration. It is the pattern of Roman history narrated in Posidonian texts cited above; in the text from Strabo just quoted that sketches Jewish history; and in Acts 7:20–45, a text with close parallels to the view of Moses and his "successors" found in Strabo. However, the assumption that "decline" has occurred is not specifically Posidonian.

One of Posidonius's definitions of god is striking: "Posidonius said that god is intelligent and fiery pneuma, without form [οὐκ ἔχον μὲν μορφήν], but changing into what he wishes and assimilating to everything" (Aetius *Placita*

Judaism in Pagan and Christian Antiquity (New York: Oxford University Press, 1983) 72–74; and Matthias Klinghardt, *Gesetz und Volk Gottes: Das lukanische Verständnis des Gesetzes nach Herkunft, Funktion und seinem Ort in der Geschichte des Urchristentums* WUNT, 2. Reihe, 32; Tübingen: J. C. B. Mohr [Paul Siebeck], 1988) 288–93. Cf. Stern, *Greek and Latin Authors on Jews and Judaism*, 1. 261–67, 294–311.

Norden concludes that Polybius first wrote about the Jews in relation to Antiochus the Great's victory over the Egyptian Skopas in 198 B.C.E. Then Posidonius, either in his work *History after Polybius* or in his *On Divination*, expanded Polybius's narrative, after which Strabo took it over with little editing.

Klinghardt, *Gesetz und Volk Gottes*, 292, n. 40, observes that Posidonius's *History* ends at 86 B.C.E. (see note 25 above) but that this fragment narrates Pompey's conquest of Jerusalem in 63 B.C.E., which is a strong argument against its Posidonian origin. However, Malitz, *Die Historien des Poseidonios*, 30–32, discusses the *History*'s date of publication; it must have been published after "On the Ocean," as well as after the work on psychology and the one on divination. He observes, too, that the fragments reach to 86, but the lack of reference to *History* by Posidonius's admirers (e.g., Cicero) argues against its publication by that date. Therefore, Malitz assumes that Posidonius worked on his *History* until the end of his life (between 51 and 45 B.C.E.); that he published sections of it periodically, not at one final date; and that he never finished it. Gigon, "Der Historiker Poseidonios," 245, writes that there are many indications that Posidonius often narrated events earlier than 145 B.C.E. and after 86 B.C.E. Von Fritz, "Poseidonios als Historiker," 172, observes that Posidonius worked on historical questions into the final year of his life; he also notes Posidonius's interest in ethnography and religion "vor allem bei den Juden" (176).

In its context, the fragment justifies Pompey's conquering of the Jerusalem "tyrants" (16.2.37, 40). Might this be Posidonius's narration of his friend's virtuous conquest? Gigon, "Der Historiker Poseidonios," 249, 256, 258, says it is obvious that Posidonius must have written of Pompey's two visits to him. See H. Strasburger, "Posidonius on the Problems of the Roman Empire," *JRS* 55 (1965) 40–53, at pp. 44, 46.

Malitz's arguments, in *Die Historien des Poseidonios*, 7–9, 303, 310–11, with his n. 62 and n. 64, that Posidonius was not anti-Semitic deserve a hearing. He emphasizes that the *charges* against the Jews in the Posidonian fragment in Diodorus 34/35.1 (frag. 131a Th.) are *rejected* by the Syrian king Antiochus VII.

1.7.19; frag. 349 Th./101 E.-K.).[74] This is supposedly also true of the Stoa in general (Diog. Laert. 7.134: ἀμόρφους), but "in fact there is little other evidence. . . . [W]e have no reason to doubt that this was a Stoic view, but it may have been Posidonius who pressed this aspect of god."[75] Posidonius's metaphysical foundation would support the general Stoic notion that those are wrong who are "modelling gods in human form" (ἀνθρωπομόρφους τυποῦντες, quoted above from Strabo). It could have led either Posidonius or a Jew who knew his thought to eulogize Moses for his rejection of anthropomorphic images of the deity.

However, instead of opposing popular religion, as one would expect, Stoics after Posidonius effected a rapprochement with it, including a defense and explanation of religious images and temples.[76] Dio Chrysostom's *Oration* 12 is such an apology, a "Verteidigungsrede für die Idole"[77] delivered in 97 C.E.[78] In the holy place Olympia and in view of the statue of Zeus by Pheidias, acknowledged as a wonder of the world, Dio sought to interpret images as one aspect of true religion. Dio's discourse is both dependent on Posidonius (Dio Chrys. *Or.* 12.27–37; frag. 368 Th.; and Dio Chrys. 12.60–61; frag. 369 Th.) and on Dio's own quite different development of such ideas.[79] This oration on sources for the knowledge of God has the following outline: (1) the first source of knowledge is an idea innate in all humankind [τὴν ἔμφυτον ἄπασιν ἀνθρώποις ἐπίνοιαν]; and (2) a second source is the idea that has been acquired, and indeed implanted, in men's souls [ἐπίκτητον . . . ἐγγιγνομένην ταῖς ψυχαῖς] through narrative accounts, myths, and customs (12.39).[80] The first idea (1) is treated in 12.27–37, the section Theiler edits as Posidonian. Theiler also includes one later paragraph, 12.60–61 (against images). The second part of the oration (2), which treats the second source of the idea of God, falls into three sections: (a) art (poetry and sculpture), (b) law, and (c) philosophy. Law is treated briefly (12.40, 48), as is philosophy (12.47); then both are dropped. The rest of the oration deals with poetry and sculpture.

Against the defense of images by contemporary Stoics like Dio in the second part of this oration, Acts pictures Paul presenting the ancient, authentic, philosophical opinion,

> stressing Christianity's continuity with . . . the pagan philosophical tradition. . . .
> By having Paul explicitly quote from popular Stoicism (Acts 17:28), Luke aligns

74. This translation is the paraphrase by Kidd, *Commentary*, 2.1. 409. This text is emphasized and related to Quintilian *Instit. or.* 10.1.16 by Hommel, "Neue Forschung," 166, n. 43.
75. Kidd, *Commentary*, 2.1. 410.
76. Malherbe, "Pseudo-Heraclitus, Epistle 4," 46.
77. Geffcken, "Bilderstreit," 300.
78. Sheppard, "Dio Chrysostom," 158–59, dates it to 97 C.E. Max Pohlenz, "Paulus und die Stoa," *ZNW* 42 (1949) 95, now in *Das Paulusbild in der neueren deutschen Forschung* (ed. K. H. Rengstorf; Darmstadt: Wissenschaftliche Buchgesellschaft, 1969) 553, dates it to 96.
79. See Hermann Binder, *Dio Chrysostomus und Posidonius: Quellenuntersuchungen zur Theologie des Dio von Prusa* (Borna-Leipzig: Robert Noske, 1905) 13–46, 90–94.
80. Binder, *Dio Chrysostomus*, 16; see also 44–45.

him with a venerable philosophical tradition in a manner reminiscent of the
apologists. It is noteworthy that Luke describes the Athenians and resident
aliens as those delighting in novelties . . . (17:21). There is therefore a subtle
turning of the tables: the pagan philosophers who question the apostle do not
themselves hold to the legitimating tradition; it is Paul who does.[81]

Dio concludes his speech claiming that he is "guarding the customs" (ἔθη
. . . διαφυλάττεις [Or. 12.85; cf. 12.46, 57]). Paul makes the same claim in
Acts 17 (compare Acts 6:14; 7:53; 21:21, 24), appealing to Posidonian tradition
(Posidonius himself may have appealed to the early Roman emperor Numa).
The Athenians are fascinated by novelties [καινότερον] (17:21). Jews and
Christians, too, polemicized against images and temples for the divine and
even intensified such arguments, but they were joining a debate already in
progress in Greco-Roman culture.[82] Understanding Luke's picture of Paul in
Athens depends on recognizing this appeal to the true, ancient philosophical
tradition, parallel to Luke's picture of Paul in continuity with true Judaism.

THE AREOPAGUS SPEECH
AGAINST THE DEFENSE OF IMAGES
BY DIO CHRYSOSTOM, *ORATION* 12

One of the best treatments of the Areopagus speech is that of Wolfgang
Nauck.[83] He has demonstrated that the speech belongs to a category with
precedents in Hellenistic-Jewish mission literature, which has influenced the
form not only of the Areopagus speech but also of other Christian missionary
documents. As examples of this form he gives the Jewish texts *Apostolic Constitutions* 7.34.1–7; 8.12.8–16; Keduscha of Jozer; the first two of the Eighteen
Benedictions; two fragments of a Sybilline writing preserved in Theophilus of
Antioch, *To Autolycus* 2.36; the Prayer of Manasseh; Aristobulus (preserved in
Clement *Strom.* 1.22.150); and Eusebius's *Preparation for the Gospel* 8.9–10;
13.12. Christian examples of the type are in *1 Clem.* 19.2–20.12; 33.2–8 and
the Epistula Apostolorum.[84] These texts have the following order of motifs:
(1) *creatio* (references to God's creation of humans in God's image), (2) *con-
servatio* (times and boundaries), and (3) *salvatio*. One conclusion that may be
drawn is that the short reference to salvation at the end of the speech (Acts
17:30–31) is not a foreign element; rather, it is required by the pattern.[85]

Nauck points out that the Jewish form has antecedents in the Hebrew
Bible, in Pss. 33; 74:12–17; 89; 148. Gerhard von Rad shows that the salvation
motif dominates in these texts,[86] but Nauck notes that creation becomes more

---

81. Malherbe, "'Not in a Corner,'" 152.
82. Geffcken, *Apologeten*, xxii.
83. Wolfgang Nauck, "Die Tradition und Komposition der Areopagrede," *ZTK* 53 (1956) 11–52.
84. Nauck, "Die Tradition," 17–18, 24–26, 29, 34–35. Except for Aristobulus and the Keduscha
of Jozer, he translates these texts into German (46–52).
85. Nauck, "Die Tradition," 30–31.
86. Nauck, "Die Tradition," 29.

prominent in the Prayer of Manasseh and that this motif dominates in the Areopagus speech; that is, the latter is more Hellenistic.[87] The Hellenistic element is further evident in that the standard reference to the "image" of God in human beings has been replaced by a quote of Aratus *Phanomena* 5 in Aristobulus[88] and in Acts 17:29, which asserts that we are God's "offspring" [γένος]. The form is, then, neither strictly Jewish[89] nor exclusively Stoic;[90] it is rather a Jewish form in the process of being Hellenized.

Nauck is basically correct, yet he is too negative about the possibility of Hellenistic-Stoic models having influenced the form.[91] The influence of a Stoic model on Acts 17 can be convincingly shown. Dio Chrysostom's *Oration* 12, which is dependent on Posidonius,[92] presents a Stoic model that was important in producing this speech, as were the protoypes in the Hebrew Bible. It will be the primary purpose of the rest of this chapter to develop this thesis. This section will not do a detailed exegesis of the Areopagus speech but rather will comment on it verse by verse to exhibit contacts and contrasts with Dio's *Oration* 12.

Acts 17:19–20

Luke places the Areopagus speech in a "trial" setting in Acts 17:19–20. Ἐπιλαβόμενοι means to "seize" in arresting (see also Acts 16:19; 17:6; 18:17; 21:30; Luke 23:26).[93] Ἄρειος πάγος refers to the "judgment seat" of the Areopagus council that supervised education. In 17:22, ἐν μέσῳ means "among some members of the court," not "in the middle of the hill." One of Luke's purposes is to show that several Roman courts had already declared Paul harmless (16:21, 35; 17:8; 19:23–41; cf. Luke 23:29, 47; 25:15, 25; 26:31).

There is a fascinating parallel in Dio *Oration* 12.49, 52, 63. Dio supposes that Pheidias, the famous sculptor of the statue of Zeus at Olympia, was to be questioned before "judges" in a law court (δικαστά) at a trial (ἀγῶνα; 12.49–50). A "fine" is the possible penalty (12.63); therefore, the oration consists of what Pheidias might have said in his "defense" (12.52, 84). The subject of the trial is an exact parallel to Acts 17:22–31: "Was the shape [εἶδος] you by your artistry produced appropriate to a god, and was its form [μορφή] worthy

---

87. Nauck, "Die Tradition," 32.
88. Nauck, "Die Tradition," 34–35, a fragment in Eusebius *Praep. Ev.* 13.12, translated by A. Y. Collins in *The Old Testament Pseudepigrapha* (ed. James H. Charlesworth; New York: Doubleday, 1985) 2. 841.
89. Bertil Gärtner, *The Areopagus Speech and Natural Revelation* (ASNU 21; Uppsala: C. W. K. Gleerup, 1955).
90. Dibelius, "Paul on the Areopagus."
91. See, for example, Nauck, "Areopagrede," 33: "Die Annahme einer Abhängigkeit der Rede von hellenistisch-Stoischen Vorbildern ist . . . unnötig."
92. Pohlenz, "Paulus und die Stoa," 91; Hommel, "Neuere Forschungen." Dio 12.27–37 = frag. 368 Th.; Dio 12.60–61 = frag. 369 Th., with commentary in Theiler's vol. 2.
93. Cf. Rudolf Pesch, *Die Apostelgeschichte* (EKKNT 5; Neukirchen-Vluyn: Neukirchener, 1986) 2. 134–35.

of the divine nature?" (Dio Chrys. *Or.* 12.52; cf. 25, 44, 46, 54, 55, 61–62).[94] Did the earliest, divine people fear "never to be able adequately to portray by human art [τέχνη] the Supreme and most Perfect Being?" (12.52). Do humans "attribute to God a human body . . . in their lack of a better illustration?" (12.59). Pheidias objects, "If you find fault with me for the human figure, you should make haste to be angry with Homer first" (12.62, and see 12.63, 77, 78). "But if, again, anyone thinks that the material used is too lacking in distinction to be in keeping with the god, his belief is true and correct. . . . Gold and silver [*sic:* "stone"] are trivial and worthless things, but the essential substance" (12.80–81). Dio's discourse is a defense of images; Acts 17:22–31 is a Hellenistic-Jewish-Christian attack on the practice. Luke does not mention Epicureans and Stoics (17:18) only to show that he was aware of which schools of thought had most influence at that time. Dio's discourse shows that images of the gods were discussed at the time Acts was written, and precisely in this context, he attacks Epicureans (Dio *Or.* 12.36–38).

Acts 17:21

As noted above, the Athenians, not Paul, want to hear something new in Acts 17:21.

Acts 17:22

In Diodorus 32.12 (frag. 85 Th.), discussed above, these "very religious" (κατὰ πάντα ὡς δεισιδαιμονεστέρους) Athenians are "superstitious" in a negative sense: through misunderstanding (ἀγνοίᾳ) at Athens, a hermaphrodite was burned alive, a story Posidonius told to remedy superstitious fears (πρὸς διόρθωσιν δεισιδαιμονίας). Strabo (*Geog.* 16.2.37), perhaps repeating Posidonius, praised Moses' worship of God without an image, but judged his successors to be "superstitious." This same Stoic philosopher may have idealized Numa; he says Numa, like Moses, built temples but rejected images of the Gods.[95] Paul, in the Areopagus speech, is making a similarly critical evaluation of contemporary Stoics over against their earlier, wiser teacher, Posidonius. However, the superstition being criticized included not only the images Posidonius rejected but even temples, an idea of the founder of Stoicism, Zeno.

Acts 17:23

Paul proclaims a God whom they worship as "unknown" (ἄγνοια in Acts 17:23 [twice], 30). In some texts, incorrect worship of God leads to immorality (for example, Romans 1–2; Strabo *Geog.* 16.2.35, followed by 16.2.37,

---

94. Dio does not expect the reader to assume that Pheidias was literally put on trial. How does this influence our understanding of Luke's intention when he is narrating Paul's trial?

95. See note 46.

39–40; and also Dio Chrys. *Or.* 12.29, 36–37). Dio asks, "How then could they [the first humans] have remained ignorant [ἀγνῶτες] and conceived no inkling of him who had sowed and planted and was now preserving and nourishing them?" (*Or.* 12.29). Dio polemicizes against the Epicurean worship of the "female divinity depraved and monstrous, representing a kind of wantonness or self-indulgent ease and unrestrained lewdness, to which they gave the name of Pleasure. . . . [The universe has] no master to take thought for it now [μηδενὸς μήτε νῦν προνοοῦντος]" (12.36–37).

Immorality is, however, not the consequence in Acts 17:22–31 or 14:15–17. The Lycaonian people mistakenly believe that "the gods have come down to us *in the likeness of humans*" (οἱ θεοὶ ὁμοιωθέντες ἀνθρώποις; Acts 14:11, my emphasis). And in Acts 17:18, some mistakenly believe that Paul is "a preacher of foreign divinities" (ξένων δαιμονίων; cf. Dio Chrys. *Or.* 12.26, 45). Thus, in these two speeches in Acts, one emphasis is on "turning to God from idols" (1 Thess 1:9).

Acts 17:24

As in the Hellenistic-Jewish missionary form, in Acts 17:24 there is a reference to God's creating the cosmos. Dio repeatedly refers to an analogous, although quite different, idea (*Or.* 12.27, 34, 75, 84). God is the source of human intelligence and capacity to reason (12.28). The earliest humans learn through their senses that the cosmos is a "cunning creation" (12.37). Homer refers to God as a consummate artist, to which poetic line Dio adds a reference to "the most perfect artificer" who fashioned the whole cosmos (12.81–82). Bertil Gärtner[96] notes that the Hebrew Bible's emphasis on creation often occurs in the context of the ridiculing of idols (Isa 40:12–26; Deuteronomy 32; Jeremiah 10), which is not the case in the latter part of Dio's speech. But that a Stoic could draw this conclusion is shown by Strabo (*Geog.* 16.2.35, 37), dependent on Posidonius. First, Moses is praised, as are his early successors, "but afterwards, in the first place, superstitious men were appointed to the priesthood, and then tyrannical people; and from superstition arose abstinence from flesh, from which it is their custom to abstain even today, and circumcision and excisions and other observances of the kind. And from the tyrannies arose the bands of robbers." Martin Dibelius[97] also observes that the term *cosmos* is Hellenistic (it occurs in the LXX only in Ps 49:2, in Wisdom, and in the Maccabean books), whereas the Hebrew Bible would speak of heaven and earth.

Acts 17:24b. He is "lord of heaven and earth." He is "ruler of the universe" (a technical term in Dio *Or.* 12.27). "More than wise intention and preparation" occurs in the world (12.33), for there is one "directing the entire heaven

96. Gärtner, *Areopagus Speech*, 41.
97. Dibelius, "Areopagus," 41.

and universe, even as a skillful pilot commands a ship [σοφοῦ κυβερνήτου νεὼς ἄρχοντος]" (12.34). As already noted, the Epicureans deny this (12.37, where several technical terms are used). "God governs all" is an introductory statement in Pheidias's defense (12.55), which is striking, since the attack on images is often associated with an affirmation of providence.[98]

Acts 17:24c. There is no Jewish demand for abolition of temple services that corresponds to Acts 17:24c.[99] Compare the Posidonian parallels cited in the discussion of Acts 17:22 with Seneca's *Ep.* 90.28–29, "not a village shrine, but the vast temple of all the gods, the universe itself," and *Ep.* 95.48, "let us forbid men ... to throng the doors of temples.... God is worshipped by those who truly know him."

The Septuagint does use χειροποίητος, which occurs both in Acts 17:24 and 7:41 (cf. 19:26), in a polemic against images, as in Isa 16:12 and Bel 5, "I may not do honor to idols made with hands, but to the living God, who has created heaven and the earth and has sovereignty over all flesh." Christ becomes the temple not made with hands (Mark 14:58; 1 Cor 5:1). Dio (*Or.* 12.69) concedes that the sculptor's art is "dependent on the workman's hand," the result of which admits of no movement. However, the best substance that could have come into human hands is the matter of the entire universe (12.80, 82).

God's not "needing" anything is a late idea, which is admitted even by Gärtner; it appears in the Septuagint only in 2 and 3 Maccabees, and only in Acts 17:24c in the NT, although it becomes common in early Christian literature. Dio, given the argument for images in the latter part of his treatise, does not refer to it.

Acts 17:25

Acts 17:25 says, "He gives to all life and breath and everything."[100] Dio notes that the earliest humans were "nourished by the unceasing inflow of their pneuma, sucking in moist air as infants suck in their food" (*Or.* 12.30). "When a babe is born, air breathes into it and quickens it" (12.31). God is the "Giver of our material and physical life ..., Father and Savior and Guardian of humankind" (12.74), who gives and bestows blessings (12.77). The more immediate background of πνοή is, of course, Gen 2:7, but in this apologetic situation, that does not exclude a reference in the direction of the Stoic

---

98. H. W. Attridge, *First Century Cynicism in the Epistles of Heraclitus* (HTS 29; Missoula: Scholars, 1976) 16–23.

99. Gärtner, *Areopagus Speech*, 42. Cf. note 67 above.

100. See M. Dibelius, "Die Christianisierung einer hellenistischen Formel," *Botschaft und Geschichte* (Tübingen: J. C. B. Mohr [Paul Siebeck], 1956; originally published 1915) 14–29, on Marcus Aurelius 4.23: ἐκ σοῦ πάντα, ἐν σοὶ πάντα, εἰς σὲ πάντα; and Rom 11:36; 1 Cor 8:6; and Col 1:16–17.

"breathing in" of the Logos, especially in light of the Aratus quotation in Acts 17:18.

Acts 17:26

"And he created out of one the whole race of humans," says Acts 17:26. Both Dibelius[101] and Max Pohlenz[102] take ἐξ ἑνός as neuter and philosophical, which aligns it with orthodox Stoic doctrine.[103] Dio refers to "God their ancestor" (*Or.* 12.30) and to Zeus "their first and immortal parent" (12.42).

In arguing that all humans have an innate idea of God, Dio suggests, "Men could not help admiring and loving the divinity [θαυμάζειν καὶ ἀγαπᾶν τὸ δαιμόνιον], also because they observed the seasons [ὥροι] and saw that it is for our preservation that they come with perfect regularity and avoidance of excess in either direction" (12.32).

Acts 17:27, 28, 29

The phrase, "to seek God," is included in Acts 17:27. Philo (*Spec. Leg.* 1.32) says that "seeking" involves two questions, God's existence and essence, but his *Abr.* 79–80 limits human knowledge of God unless revelation occurs.[104] 1 Cor 1:22 observes that "Greeks seek wisdom," whereas Wis 13:16 asserts that Greeks are led astray to idols while "seeking" God. Dio (*Or.* 12.28) imagines that the earliest humans were so close to God that they did not need to seek.

In Acts 17:27 the purpose of seeking God is "that they might feel after him [ψηλαφήσειαν] and find him." The sensuous verb led Gärtner to wonder whether this might not be a Stoic interpolation.[105] Norden[106] long ago pointed to Dio's *Or.* 12.60–61: "All men have a strong yearning to honour and worship the deity from close at hand, approaching and laying hold of him [ἀπτομένους] with persuasion. . . . For as infant children, when torn away from father or mother . . . stretch out their hands, . . . so also do men to the gods, rightly loving them for their beneficence and kinship."

Acts 17:27c. "Yet God is not far [οὐ μακράν] from each one of us," says Acts 17:27c. All interpreters see here a parallel in Dio's *Or.* 12.28: "For these earlier men were not far from [οὐ μακράν] the Divine being or beyond his borders apart by themselves, but had grown up in the very center of things, or rather had grown up in his company, and had remained close to him in every

---

101. See Dibelius, "Paul on the Areopagus," 35–37.
102. Pohlenz, "Paulus und die Stoa," 88.
103. See note 20 and the discussion above of Posidonius's view of providence in nature as the context for Acts 17:26.
104. Gärtner, *Areopagus Speech*, 111, 118, 155, 157.
105. Gärtner, *Areopagus Speech*, 178.
106. Eduard Norden, *Agnostos Theos: Untersuchungen zur Formengeschichte Religiöser Rede* (Stuttgart: Teubner, 1956; originally published 1912) 16–17.

78 ESSAYS IN HONOR OF ABRAHAM J. MALHERBE

way." Gärtner[107] quotes Adolf Bonhoeffer as insisting that the polemic against idolatry becomes incomprehensible if this is read in a Stoic way, but both have overlooked Strabo's *Geog.* 16.2.35, where exactly these two points of view are combined by the Stoic Posidonius.

Acts 17:28a. "For in him we live and move and are [ἐν αὐτῷ γὰρ ζῶμεν καὶ κινούμεθα καὶ ἐσμέν],"[108] says Acts 17:28a. Astoundingly, Hommel[109] traces one root of this idea to Plato's *Timaeus:* "And when the Father that engendered it [Soul] perceived it in motion and alive [κινηθὲν αὐτὸ καὶ ζῶν], . . . He too rejoiced" (37C; trans. Bury in LCL). Dio (*Or.* 12.43) says the poets encourage us not to withhold gratitude from Zeus, who is "of the same blood besides being the author of life and being [αἴτιον ζωῆς καὶ τοῦ εἶναι]." Pohlenz[110] suggests that the triad in Acts reflects Posidonius's *Allgefühl* of the cosmos as a living organism with all its parts in sympathy; Pohlenz refers to several texts, including Epictetus 1.14.6, which reads: "But if our souls are so bound up with God and joined together with him as being parts and portions of his being, does not God perceive their every motion as being a motion of that which is his own and of one body with himself?" (trans. Oldfather in LCL). In contrast, Dio must concede that the sculptor's hand produces something that has "no movement" (*Or.* 12.70) and that his art cannot portray the movement of the god of war (12.79). Correspondingly, Gärtner makes the intriguing observation that all three verbs of Acts 17:28a are prominent in the Jewish polemic against idolatry: images do not move, are dead, and are nothing (Wis 13:6ff.; 15:16–17; Jub. 20:7–8; Epistle of Jeremiah 8, 24, 26; Bell and the Dragon 5).[111] The Areopagus speech would then be advancing to the conclusion in Acts 17:29, which refers back to an introductory theme in vv. 24–25. But the Aratus quotation in v. 28 and the development of the thought from v. 28 to v. 29 is difficult unless the similarity between humans and God provided by the common γένος is that both are "living."[112]

Acts 17:28c. "For we are indeed his offspring [γένος]," says Acts 17:28c. Dio has parallel language (*Or.* 12.27, 29, 39, 43, 47, 61, 75, 77). The gods love humans because of this kinship (Dio *Or.* 30.26). The quotation of Aratus in Acts 17:28c is only copying the same lines that Aristobulus had employed earlier.[113] Aristobulus used the quotation to "show that the power of God pervades all," so not in the OT sense suggested by Gärtner.

---

107. Gärtner, *Areopagus Speech,* 164, n. 1, quoting G. von Rad, "Das theologische Problem des alttestamentlichen Schöpfungsglaubens," *ZAW* Beiheft 66 (1936) 138–47.
108. Cf. H. Hommel, "Platonisches bei Lukas. Zu Acta 17.28a (Leben-Bewegung-Sein)," *ZNW* 48 (1957) 193–200.
109. Hommel, "Neue Forschungen," 104.
110. Pohlenz, "Paulus und die Stoa," 90.
111. Gärtner, *Areopagus Speech,* 197, 219–20; see 183 on the difficulties of ἐν αὐτῷ.
112. Gärtner, *Areopagus Speech,* 193.
113. See note 88.

Acts 17:29. The polemic against idols in Acts 17:29 was discussed in "Posidonius: Opposition to Images of the Deity." It can be added that "deity" is neuter here.

Acts 17:30–31

Nauck[114] notes that references to judgment and appeals for repentance are standard in the conclusion to this form, so Acts 17:30–31 is not merely an epilogue.[115] On the contrary, Luke has a speaker interrupted in order to emphasize the idea being discussed.[116] Further, the section of this chapter entitled "Posidonius: Providence in History" suggests that the reference to God's judgment would not surprise a Stoic audience.[117] Both Posidonius and Josephus[118] write of God's providence in history, God's retribution toward those who do evil. Against the Epicureans, who teach that nature and history occur fortuitously, God has a plan, and according to Posidonius, Josephus, and Luke, God judges human beings. The Stoics are surprised not by the proclamation that God judges the world but by the proclamation of the resurrection (Acts 17:18, 31–32).

Professor Malherbe's suggestion that one ought to compare Posidonius with the Areopagus speech provides exegetical insights, just as many of his other suggestions to graduate students at Yale have proven fruitful. Posidonius and his Stoic readers concluded that, for a rational person "seeking God," the climate "boundaries" (cf. Acts 17:26) on earth suggest providence in nature. Further, both Posidonius and Acts narrate human history under divine judgment. As the unjust Chians were handed over in chains to their own slaves (within history), so also the God proclaimed by Paul to the Areopagus court has fixed a day on which one appointed will judge the world in righteousness (at the end of the period of the church; Acts 17:31). Third, Posidonius was one of the few philosophers in antiquity to stress that God is "without form," on the basis of which opinion he criticized representing the divine with images of animals or humans, a true philosophical opinion according to Acts 17:25 and 29, despite the later Stoic rejection of this opinion argued in the second part of Dio Chrysostom's *Oration* 12. Luke-Acts guards the legitimate philosophical tradition against the Athenians who delight in novelties.

114. Nauck, "Areopagrede," 33.
115. Pace Hommel, "Neue Forschungen," 159. See note 58 above.
116. M. Dibelius, "Speeches and Ancient Historiography," *Studies in the Acts of the Apostles* (London: SCM, 1956) 138–85, at 160.
117. Pace Barrett, "Paul's Speech."
118. Josephus is discussed by van Unnik, "An Attack on the Epicureans" (see note 30 above).

1 CORINTHIANS 13
Paul as Apostolic Paradigm

If the general reader finds 1 Corinthians 13 inspiring, the scholar finds it baffling.[1] The exegetical anomalies it presents relate not only to its content but also to its form and function. Its highly rhetorical (some would say lyrical) form sets it apart from its immediate context (chap. 12 and 14), if not from the rest of the epistle, which is seen by some to be tiresomely prosaic by comparison. To account for its alien literary quality, scholars have variously classified it formally as hymnic,[2] rhetorical,[3] and diatribal.[4]

Given the interconnection between form and function, the chapter's formal distinctiveness has rendered its function ambiguous. Even the most casual reader notices that the text reads quite smoothly from 1 Cor 12:31 to 14:1, and the editorial transitions bracketing the chapter have struck critical exegetes as artificial.[5] At best, its literary function is explained as a typical Pauline digression;[6] at worst, as an interpolation.[7]

1. For a history of interpretation, cf. H. Riesenfeld, "Etude bibliographique sur la notion biblique d' ἀγάπη, surtout dans 1 Cor 13," ConNT 5 (1941) 1–27; J. T. Sanders, "First Corinthians 13: Its Interpretation since the First World War," Int 20 (1966) 159–87; and O. Wischmeyer, Der höchste Weg: Das 13 Kapitel des 1 Korintherbriefes (SNT 13; Gütersloh: Gütesloher Verlagshaus Mohn, 1981) esp. 11–16 and literature cited on 11, n. 1.

2. A. Robertson and A. Plummer, First Epistle of St. Paul to the Corinthians (ICC, 2d ed.; Edinburgh: T. & T. Clark, 1914) 285: "a psalm in praise of love" (cf. Psalm 45); F. R. M. Hitchcock, "The Structure of Paul's Hymn to Love," ExpTim 34 (1923) 488–89; N. W. Lund, "The Literary Structure of Paul's Hymn to Love," JBL 50 (1931) 266–76; H. Lietzmann and W. G. Kümmel, An die Korinther I–II (HNT 9, 5. Aufl.; Tübingen: J. C. B. Mohr [Paul Siebeck], 1969) 65: "Das hohe Lied der Liebe."

3. A. Harnack, "Das hohe Lied des Apostels Paulus von der Liebe (I Kor. 13) und seine religionsgeschichtliche Bedeutung," SPAW 1 (Berlin, 1911) 132–63, esp. 153, n. 4: "Poesie im strengen Sinn ist der Hymnus freilich nicht, sondern 'Rede' (daher ist auch die Bezeichnung Hymnus nicht ganz korrekt)."

4. E. Lehmann and A. Fridrichsen, "1 Kor. 13: Eine christlich-stoische Diatribe," TSK 94 (1922) 55–95.

5. J. Weiss, Der erste Korintherbrief (MeyerK 5, 9. Aufl.; Göttingen: Vandenhoeck & Ruprecht, 1910; repr. 1970) 310.

6. J. Héring, The First Epistle of St. Paul to the Corinthians (London: Epworth, 1964) 134. W. Wuellner, "Greek Rhetoric and Pauline Argumentation," Early Christian Literature and the Classical Intellectual Tradition (ed. W. R. Schoedel and R. L. Wilken; Théologie historique 54; Paris: Editions Beauchesne, 1979) 177–88, esp. 184, sees 1 Corinthians 13 (along with 1:19–3:21

Given this formal distinctiveness and functional ambiguity, the chapter's authenticity has quite naturally been questioned,[8] though not seriously in recent scholarship. In spite of the exegetical confusion, a scholarly consensus has emerged in certain respects. Few any longer regard it as hymnic.[9] Most would agree that it is rhetorical, though in what sense is disputed.[10] Virtually all agree that it is a self-contained unit.[11] Few, if any, would now deny its Pauline authorship. There is little agreement, however, regarding its literary function. As yet, no fully satisfactory explanation has been offered to account for its placement between chap. 12 and 14.

Any plausible explanation must take seriously the rhetorical complexion of the passage without denying its alien literary quality. Adequate account must also be given of the immediate literary context in which it is now placed. The rhetorical complexion of the chapter has long been recognized by those who have investigated it against its Greco-Roman background.[12] Rhetorical

and 9:21–10:13) as a digression, "one of the means traditionally used in epideictic discourse," and it functions to amplify "by intensifying the point Paul leads up to with a series of seven rhetorical questions (12:29–30), the premise of *agape*" (187). Earlier, A. Fridrichsen, *Le problème du miracle dans le christianisme primitif* (Strasbourg: Faculty of Protestant Theology, 1925; *The Problem of Miracle in Primitive Christianity* [Minneapolis: Augsburg, 1972] 138–41) had also analyzed chap. 13 as a digression (παρέκβασις) whose purpose was to provide variation and lyrical effect. Unlike Wuellner, Fridrichsen recognized the parenetic (and polemical) element in chap. 13, noting especially the internal connection between the content (especially vv. 4–7) and the rest of the epistle.

7. Weiss, *Der erste Korintherbrief*, xliii; also 311: "Kap. 13 macht durchaus den Eindruck einer 'Einlage'—nicht anders wie Kap. 9, einer Digression, die sich von dem Hauptthema unbillig weit entfernt." Noting the similarities between 1 Corinthians 13 and 9, Weiss conjectures that both belonged originally to the same letter. Also treating chap. 13 as an insertion is H. Mosbech, "1 Kor. 13," *TT* 3, ser. 5 (1914) 193–263 (as noted by Riesenfeld, "Etude bibliographique," 10). Lehmann and Fridrichsen, "1 Kor. 13," 67, argue that chap. 13 was a diatribe composed and inserted into the epistle by an unknown Stoic Christian who found Christian "enthusiasm" unappealing. Also C. K. Barrett, *The First Letter to the Corinthians* (2d ed.; New York: Harper & Row, 1973) 297. M. Dibelius, "Zur Formgeschichte des Neuen Testaments," *TRu* N.F. 3 (1931) 231, sees the chapter as a sermon previously prepared by the apostle but placed here as a self-contained unit.

8. E. L. Titus, "Did Paul Write 1 Corinthians 13?" *JBR* 27 (1959) 299–302. Lehmann and Fridrichsen, "1 Kor 13," 60, doubted chap. 13's Pauline authorship, but Fridrichsen later retracted this view. Cf. prescript to E. Hoffmann, "Zu 1 Cor. 13 and Col. 3, 14," ConNT 3 (1939) 28; also Fridrichsen, *The Problem of Miracle*, 139.

9. Sanders, "First Corinthians 13," 159: "First Corinthians 13 is not a hymn, as it is often thought to be."

10. J. Weiss, "Beiträge zur paulinischen Rhetorik," *Theologische Studien* (ed. C. R. Gregory et al.; Göttingen: Vandenhoeck & Ruprecht, 1897) 165–247, esp. 196–200; C. Clemen, *Primitive Christianity and Its Non-Jewish Sources* (Edinburgh: T. & T. Clark, 1912) 67–68.

11. H. Conzelmann, *A Commentary on the First Epistle to the Corinthians* (Hermeneia; Philadelphia: Fortress, 1975) 217.

12. J. J. Wettstein, *Novum Testamentum Graecum* (Amsterdam, 1751–52; repr. 2 vols.; Graz: Akademische Druck, 1962) 2. 154–58; Weiss, "Beiträge," 196–200, provides a stylistic analysis that was later incorporated into his commentary, esp. pp. 309–12. Harnack, "Das hohe Lied," esp. 161–63, notes the chapter's rhetorical quality but argues for Paul's dependence on Jewish traditions instead of Greek philosophical or Hellenistic religious traditions. As already noted, Lehmann and Fridrichsen, "1 Kor 13," adduce numerous Stoic parallels. Riesenfeld, "Etude bibliographique," 12–14, identifies several scholars who investigated links with various Greco-

analysis of the passage can now be extended even further because of recent research on the literary forms and epistolary function of parenesis.[13] This chapter seeks to move the discussion further in this direction by analyzing certain features of 1 Corinthians 13 from the perspective of epistolary parenesis.

This analysis begins with two unassailable premises: (1) the placement of the chapter within an epistolary setting and (2) the parenetic function of the epistle, in part if not in whole.[14] It proceeds with the methodological assumption that close attention to the formal structure of Pauline parenesis can illuminate the form, function, and content of 1 Corinthians 13.

THE INTRODUCTORY FORMULA
(1 Cor 12:31)

The shift from the second person plural to the first person singular, which continues into 1 Cor 13:1–3, has always struck commentators as inexplicably abrupt. Not surprisingly, ingenious efforts have been made to account for this, either by altering the punctuation,[15] taking ζηλοῦτε as an indicative,[16] or

---

Roman traditions: Fridrichsen, *Le problème du miracle*, 97–105 (*Problem of Miracle*, 137–47); Clemen, *Primitive Christianity*, 51; G. Rudberg, *Hellas och Nya Testamentet* (Stockholm, 1929) esp. 118–19, 149–50; W. Jaeger, "Tyrtaios über die wahre ἀρετή," SPAW (Philosophisch-historische Klasse; Berlin, 1932) 537–68; E. Hoffmann, "Zu 1 Cor. 13 und Col. 3,14," 28–31, with p. 32 containing an excerpt from Rudberg's work on 1 Corinthians 13; also Hoffmann, "Pauli Hymnus auf die Liebe," *Deutsche Vierteljahrschrift für Literarische-wissenschaftliche und Geistesgeschichte* 4 (1926) 58–73; Hoffmann, *Die Sprache und das archaische Logik* (Heidelberg Abh. z. Philosophie und ihrer Geschichte; Tübingen, 1925), cf. p. 33, n. 3. In addition, cf. R. M. Grant, "Hellenistic Elements in 1 Corinthians," *Early Christian Origins* (Chicago: Quadrangle, 1961) 60–66.

13. Abraham J. Malherbe, *Ancient Epistolary Theorists* (SBLSBS 19; Atlanta: Scholars, 1988); Malherbe, "Hellenistic Moralists and the New Testament," ANRW (pt. 2, vol. 2; ed. W. Haase and H. Temporini; Berlin: Walter de Gruyter, forthcoming); L. T. Johnson, "II Timothy and the Polemic against False Teachers: A Re-examination," *JRelS* 6–7 (1978–79) 1–26.

14. On the epistolary form and function of 1 Corinthians, cf. N. Dahl, "Letter," *IDBSup* (Nashville: Abingdon, 1976) 539–40; B. Fiore, *The Function of Personal Example in the Socratic and Pastoral Epistles* (AnBib 105; Rome: Biblical Institute Press, 1986) 168–76. Characteristic features of parenesis are noted by Malherbe, "Hellenistic Moralists"; cf. literature cited therein, esp. Schubert and Bjerkelund.

15. Lehmann and Fridrichsen, "1 Kor 13," 65–70, offer this alternative punctuation: ζηλοῦτε δὲ τὰ χαρίσματα τὰ μείζονα καὶ ἔτι ⟨τι⟩ καθ᾽ ὑπερβολήν· ὁδὸν ὑμῖν δείκνυμι ("Strive for the higher gifts and everything utterly superlative; I will show you the way"). Cf. Conzelmann, *First Corinthians*, 215, n. 50. Another possibility is represented by p⁴⁶ D°, which read εἴ τι, thus καὶ εἴ τι καθ᾽ ὑπερβολὴν ὁδὸν ὑμῖν δείκνυμι ("and if there is anything that surpasses this, then I will show you the way"). But Héring, *The First Epistle*, 134, n. 1, objects that the phrase introduced by εἴ τι would then have no verb, in which case ζηλοῦτε (1 Cor 12:31a) would be implied, a comma would have to be inserted after ὑπερβολήν. Accordingly, the translation would read: "And if you seek something extraordinary, I will show you a way." Barrett, *The First Letter to the Corinthians*, 297, notes the difficulty: what appears to be a Western reading is supported by p⁴⁶. This reading is also preferred by BDF, paragraph 272 and apparently followed by J. F. Moulton, W. F. Howard, and N. Turner, *A Grammar of New Testament Greek: Syntax* (Edinburgh: T. & T. Clark, 1963) 3. 221: "If there is anything beyond, I show you the way." But the papyrus itself is not clear. These are the very lines that are damaged in the papyrus.

16. G. Iber, "Zum Verständnis von I Kor. 12,31," ZNW 54 (1963) 43–52. In this case, 1 Cor

dismissing the sentence as an awkward editorial transition designed to incorporate the otherwise literarily extrinsic chap. 13 into the discussion of spiritual gifts.[17]

When, however, the structure of this introductory verse is viewed in the light of Paul's parenetic method, it reveals a typical Pauline move. Adducing himself or certain aspects of his behavior either to illustrate his teaching or to buttress his parenetic appeals is a typical feature in the Pauline letters.[18] Characteristically, this is accomplished by Paul's shifting from the language of moral imperative to self-referential language. This can be done in brief, relatively undeveloped form[19] or in much more elaborately constructed literary periods.

The most notable instance of the latter occurs in 1 Corinthians 8–10, a section whose overall structure is strikingly similar to chap. 12–14. The following similarities may be noted: (1) Both sections are introduced with the same stereotypical formula (περὶ δέ), indicating that Paul is now addressing himself to another in the list of questions submitted to him by the Corinthians. (2) In both sections, there follows the citation of a slogan that was apparently in current use within the church. In each case, the slogan is introduced only to be corrected. (3) Then comes a discussion of the topic at hand, τὰ εἰδωλόθυτα (meat offered to idols) in one case and τὰ πνευματικά (spiritual gifts) in the other. Obviously, each discussion has its distinctive shape, but generally, both discussions are characterized by the use of imperatives— specifically, the use of the second person plural. In each case, Paul is addressing the church directly. (4) In both of these major sections, there is a conspicuous shift midway in the discussion from the use of imperatives to the use of examples that illustrate the appeal. Grammatically, this is signified by a shift from the second person plural to the first person singular. The shift, in each case, has been marked in our editions by a chapter beginning, that is, chap. 9 and 13. What is significant for our purposes is that the shift to the first person singular in chap. 9 has usually been taken at face value by commentators, whereas this has not been the case with the shift at 13:1. (5) At this point, the structure of the two sections diverges somewhat. In the first section (chap. 8–10), after introducing the first paradigm, Paul introduces an example from history. In 10:1–22 the behavior of disobedient Israel is rehearsed in the Exodus midrash, after which the moral implications are drawn out. After this,

---

12:31a would describe an existing attitude rather than function as an ethical imperative. The μείζονα χαρίσματα, in this case, would be the gifts already being pursued, and 12:31b would be seen as Paul's typical counterargument correcting the Corinthians' misguided direction. Cf. Conzelmann, *First Corinthians*, 215, n. 52.

17. Héring, *The First Epistle*, 134; Weiss, *Der erste Korintherbrief*, 309; Wuellner, "Greek Rhetoric," 184. See note 6 above.

18. Cf. Fiore, *Function of Personal Example*, 164–90.

19. Cf. 1 Cor 7:1–7. The imperative is stated in v. 5: μὴ ἀποστερεῖτε ἀλλήλους κ.τ.λ.; then v. 7a refers to Paul's own practice: θέλω δὲ πάντας ἀνθρώπους εἶναι ὡς καὶ ἐμαυτόν. Also, cf. 1 Cor 10:31–11:1; Phil 3:12–17.

there is a return to the original topic as imperatival language is resumed. In the second section (chap. 12–14), however, there is a conspicuous reversion back to the second person plural at 14:1, where the discussion of spiritual gifts is resumed. (6) The two sections conclude in slightly different fashion. In the first section, the moral imperative is fused with the moral paradigm Paul, and the section concludes with an explicit appeal to imitation. In the second section, Paul refers to his own status in the community but issues a warning.

To be sure, these two sections exhibit important structural differences, and their structural similarity should not be exaggerated. Nevertheless, the pattern of argument in 1 Cor 8:7–13 should be noted. The language of ethical imperative becomes explicit in 8:9: "Only take care lest this liberty of yours somehow become a stumbling block to the weak" (βλέπετε δὲ μή πως ἡ ἐξουσία ὑμῶν αὕτη πρόσκομμα γένηται τοῖς ἀσθενέσιν). The curious oscillation between the second person singular in vv. 10–11 and the second person plural in vv. 9 and 12, however striking, does not diminish the force of the imperative, nor does it alter the fact that Paul's remarks are obviously directed to his readers. Suddenly, however, the language shifts to the first person singular in the concluding verse (8:13), where Paul's remarks become self-referential.[20] This shift marks the transition to chap. 9, where Paul gives a highly detailed, personal account of his own apostolic behavior. The function of this chapter is clear: Paul adduces himself as the concrete paradigm of voluntary, responsible self-restraint for the self-indulgent Corinthians. Paul introduces the concluding athletic metaphor and then personalizes it to illustrate and highlight his own conduct; it thus serves as a fitting and graphic climax to the chapter.[21]

What is worth noting in this connection is that this pattern of argument is not uniquely Pauline but thoroughly typical of Greco-Roman parenesis.[22] The use of ethical paradigms in parenesis to exemplify the moral teaching being commended has long been recognized.[23] Plutarch's fondness for adducing named individuals as ethical paradigms typifies the conviction shared by Greco-Roman moralists that example was far superior to precept and logical analysis as a means of illustrating and reinforcing appeals to pursue a particular mode of life, normally the life of ἀρετή (virtue).[24]

---

20. Weiss, *Der erste Korintherbrief,* 311, however, characterizes the *I* in 1 Cor 8:13 and 13:1–13 as "nicht individuell sonder typisch."

21. On the use of athletic metaphors, cf. Fiore, *Function of Personal Example,* 206, n. 46.

22. Cf. Fiore, *Function of Personal Example,* esp. 26–44.

23. Cf. Malherbe, "Hellenistic Moralists," and literature cited therein. Also, A. Lumpe, "Exemplum," *RAC* (1966) 1229–57; H. Schlier, "δείκνυμι," *TDNT* 2 (1964) 25–33, esp. 32–33; and K. O. Wicker, "Mulierum Virtutes (Moralia 242E–263C)," *Plutarch's Ethical Writings and Early Christian Literature* (CHNT 4; Leiden: Brill, 1978) 112. Also H. D. Betz, P. Dirkse, and E. W. Smith, Jr., "De Sera Numinis Vindicta (Moralia 548A–568A)," *Plutarch's Theological Writings and Early Christian Literature* (CHNT 3; Leiden: Brill, 1975) 198 (cf. esp. *Moral.* 551A); and Betz, *Nachfolge und Nachahmung Jesu Christi im Neuen Testament* (BHT 37; Tübingen: J. C. B. Mohr [Paul Siebeck], 1967) esp. 107–36. M. Hadas and M. Smith, *Heroes and Gods* (New York: Harper & Row, 1965) 3–9, discuss charismatic figures as ethical paradigms.

24. According to Aristotle *Pr.* 18.3 (916b 26–36), in speeches and tales, examples have greater appeal than syllogistic arguments. Cf. Plutarch *Moral.* 550D, 551A–B. In 576E; 576F–577A;

One well-established form of example was for moralists to present themselves as paradigms for their readers. Even though some moralists were reti-
cent to do this, others were not.[25] In rhetorical education, rhetoricians
instructed the pupils in good rhetorical theory and method, but even more
important, they were expected to embody these principles and exemplify them
both in speech and character.[26] What is stated as a theoretical principle in
Isocrates[27] is reinforced later by Quintilian.[28] The theory becomes rendered as
practice in Isocrates' portrait of Nicocles as the ideal ruler whose life serves as
the moral paradigm of the precepts he teaches.[29] In *Praecepta Gerendae
Reipublicae,* Plutarch not only offers advice about proper conduct in public
life but also adduces himself as an example to the addressee, Menemachus.[30]
Also in the context of letter writing, the moralist could use self-description in
providing examples for the readers. Especially notable in this regard was
Seneca, whose letters attest to and illustrate the central importance of his own
example in giving moral instruction.[31]

Numerous examples of this use of personal example in parenetic contexts
could be offered, but none more instructive than Epictetus. Apart from the
fact that he is roughly contemporary with Paul, the catechetical relationship
reflected in his *Discourses* bears strong similarities to that of Paul and his
readers.

We may cite two instances, one in which Epictetus adduces himself as an

---

583F–585D Epameinondas exemplifies the Socratic paradigm; in 84C–E and 85A–B ἀνὴρ ἀγαθὸς
καὶ τέλειος exemplifies the pursuit of ἀρετή. Cf. generally Wicker, "Mulierum Virtutes,"
112, who refers in n. 21 to *Alex.* 1; *Pomp.* 8; *Cim.* 2; *Per.* 1–2; *Moral.* 505A–511E; 768B–D;
770D–771C.

25. Cf. H. D. Betz, *"De Laude Ipsius* (Moralia 539A–547F)," *Plutarch's Ethical Writings,*
373–82. Cf. esp. Plutarch *Moral.* 539D–E. Fiore, *Function of Personal Example,* 51, 66–67, notes
Isocrates' general reluctance to present himself as an example; Isocrates prefers instead to be
oblique in this respect. Even so, in *Ep.* 8.10 he becomes explicit in encouraging his readers to
imitate his character. But as Fiore (67, n. 46) concludes, "In general, however, from the evidence
of the Isocratean corpus, he seldom offered his own example and action as a model for others to
follow."

26. Fiore, *Function of Personal Example,* 33–34.

27. Isocrates *Adv. soph.* 16–18 (trans. Norlin in LCL; cited in Fiore, *Function of Personal Example,* 33–34): "and it is necessary for the disciple . . . on the one hand to learn the forms of speech
. . . and for the teacher on the other hand . . . to himself provide the example so that the ones who
are able to be impressed might also imitate."

28. Quintilian *Inst.* 2.2.8 (trans. Butler in LCL; cited in Fiore, *Function of Personal Example,*
34): "For however many models for imitation he may give them from the authors they are reading,
it will still be found that fuller nourishment is provided by the living voice, as we call it, more
especially when it proceeds from the teacher himself, who, if his pupils are rightly instructed,
should be the object of their affection and respect. And it is scarcely possible to say how much
more readily we imitate those whom we like."

29. Isocrates *Nicocles* 27–47, esp. 35, 37–38. Cf. Fiore, *Function of Personal Example,* 45–56.

30. Plutarch *Moral.* 811B–C, 816D–E; cited in Fiore, *Function of Personal Example,* 70, 72.

31. Cf. Fiore, *Function of Personal Example,* 87–100, esp. 89–90, who notes esp. *Ep.* 71.7; 6.3–5.

example in a parenetic context.[32] Using many of the typical hortatory devices, such as the imperative mood and rhetorical questions, he exhorts the reader to refrain from inordinate desires that would lead to theft or adultery. Once he frames the exhortation, he then cites an incident from his own life to illustrate it. He had an iron lamp that was stolen, but deciding that the blame lay not with the thief but with his own misguided values in owning an expensive lamp, he replaced it with an earthenware lamp. Typically, he states the principle gnomically—"A man loses only what he already possesses"—and concludes that "our losses and our pains have to do only with the things we possess" (Epictetus Diss. 1.18.15–16). Here we have a clear case of a teacher drawing from his own life experience to provide an ethical paradigm for his moral exhortation.

The other instance is less direct, but nonetheless illuminating. In the well-known passage entitled Περὶ Κυνισμοῦ (Epictetus Diss. 3.22.1–109), where the Cynic philosophical life-style is delineated, Epictetus provides the reader with a specimen Cynic discourse in which the Cynic preacher, earlier designated as ἄγγελος τοῦ θεοῦ (messenger of the deity) and κατάσκοπος (scout [3.22.23–25]), boldly proclaims the Cynic message of salvation. In the opening section, the hearers are accosted for forsaking the true path leading to virtue and following another way (ὅδος [3.22.26]). They are also censured for refusing to believe when another, presumably the Cynic preacher, points out (δείκνυμι) the way to serenity and happiness (3.22.26). There follows a list of named individuals who serve as examples of the misdirected seeker: Myron and Ophellius, otherwise unknown but presumably dissipated athletes; Croesus, typifying unhappy wealth; Nero and Sardanapalus, the pitiable rulers; and Agamemnon, the unhappy warrior-king. The true nature of the good has eluded them all (3.22.32). The diatribal form of the discourse becomes explicit when Agamemnon becomes the interlocutor and asks the preacher, "In what, then, is the good [τὸ ἀγαθόν], since it is not in these things? Tell us, Sir messenger and scout!" (3.22.38; trans. Oldfather in LCL). The Cynic preacher gladly obliges with a sermon on the nature of the good and happy life. The hearers are enjoined with a loosely connected set of ethical imperatives concluding with the following exhortation: "Poor wretches, develop this, pay attention to this, seek here your good" (3.22.44). The question is then put: "And how is it possible for a man who has nothing, who is naked, without home or hearth, in squalor, without a slave, without a city, to live serenely? Behold, God has sent you the man who will show in practice [τὸν δείξοντα ἔργῳ] that it is possible" (3.22.45–46). Then follows this rather remarkable statement in which the moral imperative is illustrated by the example of the Cynic preacher himself. With typical Cynic boldness, the preacher proclaims:

32. Epictetus Diss. 1.18.15–16. Also, cf. 1.10.7–13; 12.12–16; 16.15–21; 17.13–19; 19.4–6; 21.1–4; 22.13–16; 25.23–24; 27.7–21; 28.28–33; 29.7–8, 20–29, 60–64; also Seneca Ep. 6.3–5; 92.11–13, 21–22.

"Look at me," he says, "I am without a home, without a city, without property, without a slave; I sleep on the ground; I have neither wife nor children, no miserable governor's mansion, but only earth, and sky, and one rough cloak. Yet what do I lack? Am I not free from pain and fear, am I not free? When has anyone among you seen me failing to get what I desire, or falling into what I would avoid? When have I ever found fault with either God or man? When have I ever blamed anyone? Has anyone among you seen me with a gloomy face? And how do I face those persons before whom you stand in fear and awe? Do I not face them as slaves? Who, when he lays eyes upon me, does not feel that he is seeing his king and master?" (3.22.47–49; cf. 4.8.30–31)

Here, the dramatic shift to the first person singular highlights the paradigm and renders in concrete form the specific life-style that is being enjoined. This text vividly illustrates the formal structure of the parenesis employed by Paul in 1 Corinthians 8–10 and 12–14.

Having examined the structure and literary function of the introductory formula, we can now turn to its content. The phrase ὁδὸν δείκνυμι (I show a way) is capable of being used in a literal and a metaphorical sense. The myth of Heracles at the crossroads illustrates how easily these two senses of ὅδος can merge.[33] Frequently, the phrase functions as a technical term for "teach."[34] But what is remarkable, and all too seldom noticed, is that δείκνυμι in the NT is ordinarily used to refer to that which is graphically concrete or, if not, should be.[35] Only once does it function as a synonym for διδάσκειν (Matt 16:21). If it is used here in the normal NT sense, its demonstrative rather than pedagogical force is focal and should be rendered *show* in the sense of "display," "point out," or "demonstrate." That the phrase can be used in parenetic contexts where a particular ethical life-style is being promulgated, and indeed in a context where the preacher himself provides the paradigm, is clear from the passage from Epictetus cited above. On this showing, what fol-

33. Xenophon Mem. 2.1.21, 23; 2.1.11; 1.7.1. Also, cf. Diogenes Laertius 7.121. References cited in Weiss, Der erste Korintherbrief, 310.

34. Epictetus Diss. 1.4.10: οὐ θέλεις δεῖξαι αὐτῷ τὸ ἔργον τῆς ἀρετῆς, ἵνα μάθῃ ποῦ τὴν προκοπὴν ζητῇ (Are you not willing to show him the work of virtue, that he may learn where to look for his progress?); 1.4.29: ὦ μεγάλου εὐεργέτου τοῦ δεικνύοντος τὴν ὁδόν (O great benefactor who points the way! [of Chrysippus, whose teachings have been unfolded in the previous sections]); 1.4.32: τὴν ἀλήθειαν; Lucian Men. 4: καί τινα ὁδὸν ἁπλῆν καὶ βέβαιον ὑποδεῖξαι τοῦ βίου (to show me a plain, solid path in life). Also, cf. Weiss, Der erste Korintherbrief, 310. Also, Lehmann and Fridrichsen, "1 Kor 13," 66, refer to Marcus Aurelius 3.11.2: ἐλέγχειν ὁδῷ καὶ ἀληθείᾳ (to test methodically and truthfully); also 5.3; 6.22; and conclude, "Dem stoischen Verfasser ist das ὁδὸν δείκνυμι die gegebene Formel, um eine vorzutragende Lehre einzuführen" (66).

35. Matt 4:8 par. Luke 4:5: all the kingdoms of the earth; Matt 8:4 par. Mark 1:44 par. Luke 5:14: a cleansed leper; Mark 14:15 par. Luke 22:12: a large upper room; Luke 20:24: a denarius; Luke 24:40 par. John 20:20: the hands and feet of the risen Lord; John 5:20 (twice); 10:32: the Father's works; John 14:8–9: the Father alone; Acts 7:3: the land of promise; Heb 8:5: the architectural pattern of the tabernacle; James 2:18; 3:13: works born of faith. Especially instructive is the use of the word in connection with visions or visionary experiences (Acts 10:28; Rev 1:1; 4:1; 17:1; 21:9–10; 22:1, 6, 8).

lows in 1 Corinthians 13 is less a didactic explanation than it is a paradigmatic exhibition.

The Pauline expression καθ' ὑπερβολήν ordinarily functions adverbially (Rom 7:13; 2 Cor 1:8; Gal 1:13), but because of its distance from δείκνυμι, it appears to function attributively here. But if used as an attributive, it would most naturally be understood as a superlative.[36] Following ἔτι, this would be awkward, unless ἔτι were taken temporally. A much smoother meaning may be provided if ὑπερβολήν is understood as a technical rhetorical term.[37] Paul's use of rhetorical figures of speech is pervasive in 1 Corinthians, and the choice of a rhetorical figure of speech here would be typical of his style throughout the epistle.[38] This suggestion that ὑπερβολή be taken in its technical rhetorical sense should not be pushed too far, however. In any case, whether καθ' ὑπερβολὴν ὁδόν is translated as "more excellent way" or "a way expressed in hyperbole," Paul himself intends to "point out the way" to the Corinthians and chooses to do so first by referring to himself.

THE APOSTOLIC PARADIGM
(1 Cor 13:1-3)

The apostolic paradigm is introduced in 1 Cor 13:1-3, where the first person singular, introduced in 12:31, continues. It is not in itself remarkable that Paul employs the first person singular, but why he does so is. Commentators have long noticed Paul's use of the first person singular here, but it is ordinarily taken in a general rather than a strictly autobiographical sense.[39] In

36. W. Michaelis, "ὁδός," *TDNT* 5 (1967) 85, n. 151, quoting Schlatter, "A ὑπερβολή is a throw which goes beyond that of others. . . . What takes place καθ' ὑπερβολήν is done with surpassing force and elan. . . . The phrase is hard to link with the idea of a 'way.' Thus it should be taken with ὁδὸν δείκνυμι rather than with ὁδόν. Probably something like: "Now in superlative fashion do I show you the way." Or, as Barrett, *The First Letter to the Corinthians*, 297, renders it, "Beyond all this, beyond all that I have so far said, I show you a way." C. Spicq, *Agape dans le nouveau testament* (EB; 3 vols.; Paris: J. Gabalda, 1958–59) 2.65, argues that καθ' ὑπερβολήν is not comparative but superlative. Conzelmann, *First Corinthians*, 216, n. 53, argues for a comparative sense because of ἔτι: "From the standpoint of content it is pointless to argue about this; naturally, this 'higher way' is the highest. It acquires a certain significance only when to the comparative contained in καθ' ὑπερβολήν we supply τῶν χαρισμάτων, 'than the gifts' (R. Reitzenstein, "Die Formel 'Glaube, Liebe, Hoffnung,' bei Paulus," *Nachrichten von der Königlichen Gesellschaft der Wissenschaften zu Göttingen* [1916] 367–416, here esp. 398, n. 2). Then faith, hope, and love are not themselves χαρίσματα." Thus Conzelmann (216) concludes that "καθ' ὑπερβολήν goes attributively with ὁδόν: a still more excellent way."
37. Cf. Isocrates *Ep.* 4.88; Aristotle *Rhet.* 1413a29; Demetrius *Eloc.* 52; Strabo 1.2.33; 3.2.9 (apud LSJ).
38. Cf. 1 Cor 4:6, esp. the use of αἱ ὁδοί; also Fiore, *Function of Personal Example*, 178–80, esp. 179.
39. Weiss, *Der erste Korintherbrief*, 311. Wischmeyer, *Der höchste Weg*, 90–91, moves beyond traditional interpretations that see the *I* here as the "typical I," an equivalent of "one." She sees the first section move toward a climax in v. 3b, which is seen to reflect Paul's own apostolic experience. The first person singular in vv. 1–3 she regards neither as an autobiographical *I* in a pure sense nor as a mere figure of speech, but rather as a "generalizing 'I'": "Vielmehr handelt es sich um ein generalisierendes 'Ich' in einer theologischen Grundsatzrede, die zwar nicht autobiographisch abgezielt ist, wohl aber die eigene Person und die eigene Erfahrung direkt in den

spite of the repeated use of the first person singular in vv. 1–3, these verses are not ordinarily thought to refer to Paul's own apostolic experience. This may be a classic example of the *sensus literalis* being ignored in favor of a far more problematic interpretation.

Whether the activities mentioned in 1 Cor 13:1–3 are taken as seven different items or whether they form subgroups (as is more likely the case), for our purposes what distinguishes them is that each appears to be self-referential in the sense that they function as part of Paul's own self-presentation. As such, they are directly anchored in his own apostolic behavior.

First, the "tongues of men and of angels" (ταῖς γλώσσαις τῶν ἀνθρώπων ... καὶ τῶν ἀγγέλων [1 Cor 13:1a]) apparently refers to "the gift of tongues,"[40] even though the phrase is crafted in the form of hyperbole. On his own testimony, Paul possessed the gift of tongues (14:18) and even exercised it (14:6), even though he attached little importance to it, at least before the Corinthians.

Second, Paul's prophetic status (προφητείαν [1 Cor 13:2]) some may have questioned (14:37), but the very questioning suggests that Paul claimed it. This is a claim no one can seriously question (cf. 1 Cor 2:2–16; 7:40; 14:6; also Gal 1:15–16).

Third, "to know all mysteries" (ἐὰν ... εἰδῶ τὰ μυστήρια πάντα [1 Cor 13:2]) is also self-referential, recalling no doubt Paul's earlier description of the content of his preaching as "the mystery of God" (τὸ μυστήριον τοῦ θεοῦ [2:1]). This provides the ultimate certification of his claim. The language of 2:9–10 is hardly surprising: the apocalyptic mysteries formerly hidden from the view of all are now revealed "to us through the Spirit" (ἡμῖν ... διὰ τοῦ πνεύματος [2:10]). Whomever else ἡμῖν includes, it at least includes Paul, who placed himself among the circle of inspired prophets to whom God's mysteries have been revealed. His oracular utterance in 15:51, "Behold, I tell you a mystery" (ἰδοὺ μυστήριον ὑμῖν λέγω), operates from the same assumption. He reckons himself among those appointed "as stewards of the mysteries of God" (ὡς ... οἰκονόμους μυστηρίων θεοῦ [4:1]). Paul was in the position, at least theoretically, to know "all mysteries" (τὰ μυστήρια πάντα).

Fourth, in spite of Paul's consistent reluctance actually to claim "knowledge of God" for himself (cf. Gal 4:9), we can still interpret "all knowledge" (πᾶσαν τὴν γνῶσιν; 1 Cor 13:2) with reference to Paul himself. "Knowledge" is num-

---

Zusammenhang der theologischen Rede einbezieht." Also, cf. Fiore, *Function of Personal Example*, 183–84.

40. The expression χαλκὸς ἠχῶν ἢ κύμβαλον ἀλαλάζον (a noisy gong or a clanging cymbal) may recall the liturgical practices of pagan cults or the philosophical tradition in which gifted speakers were described in such terms. Dio Chrysostom *Or.* 8.2 records Diogenes' judgment of Antisthenes: "For when he [Diogenes] contrasted the man Antisthenes with his words, he sometimes made this criticism, that the man himself was much weaker; and so in reproach he would call him a trumpet because he could not hear his own self, no matter how much noise he made" (ἔφη αὐτὸν εἶναι σάλπιγγα λοιδορῶν· αὐτοῦ γὰρ οὐκ ἀκούειν φθεγγομένου μέγιστον). Cited in Lehmann and Fridrichsen, "1 Kor 13," 73.

bered among the gifts accessible to all Christians (1 Cor 12:8), but 13:2 may also refer to the earlier discussion in 2:6–16, especially to vv. 8–10, where Paul asserts that what the principalities and powers did not know (ἔγνωκεν)—that is, the content of the divine mystery—inspired prophets do know. It is they, after all, who are said to "know the things given to us by God" (ἵνα εἰδῶμεν τὰ ὑπὸ τοῦ θεοῦ χαρισθέντα ἡμῖν [2:12]). The final claim in 2:16 is equally explicit: "For who has known the mind of the Lord so as to instruct him? For we have the mind of Christ" (τίς γὰρ ἔγνω νοῦν κυρίου ὃς συμβιβάσει αὐτόν; ἡμεῖς δὲ νοῦν Χριστοῦ ἔχομεν).

Fifth, faith capable of removing mountains (ἐὰν ἔχω πᾶσαν τὴν πίστιν ὥστε ὄρη μεθιστάναι [1 Cor 13:2b]), an expression firmly anchored in the synoptic tradition (Matt 17:19–20; 21:21; and parallels), appears to signify the ability to perform miracles of healing, and exorcisms in particular. That Paul possessed such powers is clear from his own writings (2 Cor 12:12; Rom 15:19), and this picture is reinforced by Acts (14:3; 16:16–24; 19:11; 28:3–6). To be sure, Luke-Acts is not only more explicit in portraying Paul as an exorcist (Acts 16:16–24) but also places a far higher premium on the value of such powers as a means of authenticating Paul's apostolic status than Paul apparently did. Even so, Paul does not completely ignore such powers when he describes his own apostolic conduct.

Sixth, relinquishing all possessions (κἂν φωμίσω πάντα τὰ ὑπάρχοντά μου [1 Cor 13:3a]) is reminiscent of other passages in Paul's writings where his voluntary pauperization for the sake of the gospel figures prominently. This is especially the case in the περίστασις catalogs, where he defines the shape of his apostolic existence. His decision not to accept pay for his apostolic work he regarded as absolutely fundamental to his apostolic commission (1 Cor 9:12; cf. 2 Cor 11:7–11), and the point is reinforced, not diminished, by his custom of working with his own hands to support himself. 1 Cor 4:11 suggests that the image he projected of himself was that of vagabond and pauper. The list of apostolic tribulations in 2 Cor 6:3–10 concludes with the image of Paul as poverty-stricken. Also relevant here are the items mentioned in 2 Cor 3:9b–10. Even if they are hypothetical in some sense, even if the section is rhetorically constructed, and even if the reality described is the perceived reality of Paul's opponents, the image is still fundamental. How impoverished Paul actually was is less important than the fact that he was perceived to be. In 13:3 the statement is hyperbole, after all.

Seventh, whether the last item in the list also refers to Paul's own apostolic experience depends on how we resolve the well-known textual difficulty (1 Cor 13:3): "that I may glory" (ἵνα καυχήσωμαι) or "that I may be burned" (ἵνα καυθήσομαι). But the reverse may actually be true: the clue to resolving the textual problem may lie in recognizing the thoroughly self-referential character of the phrase. Actually, the decision is not difficult on strictly text-critical grounds: "that I may glory" (ἵνα καυχήσωμαι) enjoys better textual support,[41] but it appears to be theologically incompatible with Paul's severe critique of καύχησις, especially in 1 Corinthians 1–4. The other reading, "that I may be burned" (ἵνα καυθήσομαι), by contrast, has weaker textual support and appears to reflect a later situation, when death by fire became a living reality for Christians.[42] This latter reading also represents the kind of correction we would expect from a pious scribe who found martyrdom virtuous and boasting vicious, especially if he had come under the influence of the story of the three Hebrew children, which is known to have influenced later Christian martyrology (Dan 3:1–3). Bruce Metzger is right when he concludes the following: "The argument that the presence of the statement, 'that I may glory,' destroys the sense of the passage loses some of its force when one observes that for Paul 'glorying' is not invariably reprehensible; sometimes he regards it as justified (2 Cor 8:24; Phil 2:16; 1 Thess 2:19; 2 Thess 1:4)."[43]

Metzger might have noted further, however, that Paul does not simply boast on occasion but does so precisely in contexts where he discusses his own apostolic ministry. If 1 Cor 13:1–3 are self-referential, and if these verses refer primarily to certain aspects of Paul's own apostolic behavior, "that I may boast" (ἵνα καυχήσωμαι) is not unexpected but wholly compatible with other passages where his apostolic behavior is under consideration.

The other part of the phrase, "if I hand over my body" (ἐὰν παραδῶ τὸ σῶμά μου), strikingly resembles the language in 2 Cor 4:7–15, another description of Paul's apostolic life-style, where the concern is what disposition is made of his life as the ministerial vessel (εἰς θάνατον παραδιδόμεθα διὰ Ἰησοῦν [4:11]). The ultimate referent is undoubtedly Christ (cf. Rom 4:25; 8:32; Gal 2:20), and thus the choice of language itself shows how thoroughly Paul's apostolic self-understanding has been transformed by his theology of the cross. His use of similar language in other contexts suggests that his apostolic behavior may also be the referent here. The use of "glory" (καυχάομαι) is not surprising—indeed, is fully expected—in light of 1 Cor 15:31, where apostolic dying (καθ' ἡμέραν ἀποθνήσκω) and boasting of the fruits of his apostolic labor (νὴ τὴν ὑμετέραν καύχησιν ... ἣν ἔχω ἐν Χριστῷ Ἰησοῦ τῷ κυρίῳ ἡμῶν) are explicitly linked. The choice of the aorist in 1 Cor 13:3 (παραδῶ) instead of the usual present with which he profiles his daily apostolic dying would be consistent with the hyperbolic style employed in the first three verses. It would refer to the ultimate handing over, death itself.

Not only does each of the protases appear to be constructed with Paul him-

---

41. The textual support for καυχήσωμαι is stronger (p[46] ℵA B 6 33 69 1739° cop[sa,bo] goth[mg] Clement Origen Jerome and Greek mss[acc. to Jerome]), although the evidence for καυθήσομαι is not unimpressive (C D F G K L Ψ most minuscules it vg syr[p,h] goth[txt] arm eth[pp] and numerous patristic writers including Tertullian Aphraates Cyprian Origen Basil Chrysostom Cyril Theodoret Euthalius Maximus-Confessor John-Damascus). So, B. M. Metzger, A *Textual Commentary on the Greek New Testament* (New York: United Bible Societies, 1971) 563–64.

42. Although Conzelmann, *First Corinthians*, 222–23, esp. nn. 44–48, defends this reading on other solid grounds.

43. Metzger, *Textual Commentary*, 564.

self as the primary referent, but the apodoses do as well. The double metaphor "noisy gong or clanging cymbal" (χαλκὸς ἠχῶν ἢ κύμβαλον ἀλαλάζον
[1 Cor 13:1]) in this case would not be intended to recall images from pagan
worship, as is often suggested, but would recall the philosophical tradition in
which identical language was used to caricature the empty-headed Sophist.[44]
2 Corinthians, of course, provides the most explicit evidence that Paul's
rhetorical prowess left much to be desired, at least in the opinion of his
detractors,[45] but his fear that the cross could be emptied of its power through
rhetorical eloquence is already full-fledged in 1 Cor 1:17. His insistence that
his preaching was not characterized "by persuasive words of wisdom" (ἐν πει-
θοῖς σοφίας λόγοις [2:4]) would only give point to the apodosis in 13:1. Apostolic behavior unmotivated by love would indeed be deserving of the charge
that his words were hollow and his preaching empty. The charges need not
have been brought already by opponents. Paul's own charges made in 1:17–25
would be brought against himself and sustained. If this cluster of ideas under-
lies 13:1, it may force a re-reading of the protasis: "speaking with tongues of
men and angels" may not refer to glossolalia at all but may be a way of
expressing his mode of preaching or teaching in the form of hyperbole; that is,
"if I speak with rhetorical flourishes, but have not love."

Similarly, the apodoses in 1 Cor 13:2–3 may equally be construed as self-
referential, since the former phrase "I am nothing" (οὐθέν εἰμι) occurs in
almost identical form in reference to Paul in 2 Cor 12:11 (εἰ καὶ οὐδέν εἰμι),
where he is charged by his opponents with being "nothing," and the latter
phrase "it profits me nothing" (οὐδὲν ὠφελοῦμαι) appears to anticipate 1 Cor
15:32, "what does it profit me" (τί μοι τὸ ὄφελος).[46] It is also conceivable,
though perhaps not demonstrable, that each of these two apodoses encapsu-
lates charges brought against Paul, which he concedes would have substance
were his prophetic and healing ministry found to be motivated by anything
other than love (cf. 2 Cor 6:6).

On this reading of the passage, in the threefold refrain, "if I have not love"
(ἀγάπην δὲ μὴ ἔχω), Paul is seen to be articulating the primal impulse
motivating his apostolic behavior. This is so self-evident that it hardly needs
restating, except for the fact that "love" here is so seldom understood as refer-

---

44. Plato Prt. 329A. Spicq, Agape, 2.146, notes, "After Plato . . . the description of an 'empty'
sophist or rhetor as a gong, lyre, cymbal, or trumpet became a commonplace of literature and
philosophy." Pliny Hist. nat. pref. 25 reports that Tiberius used to call the grammarian Apion cym-
balum mundi. Tertullian De Pallio 4 (PL 2.1098a) speaks of the philosopher Empedocles in his
doubtful capacity: "Digne quidem, ut bacchantibus indumentis aliquid subtinniret cymbalo inces-
sit" (Worthily, indeed, in order that at the bottom of his Bacchantian raiment he might make some
tinkling sound, did he walk in cymbals!).

45. 2 Cor 2:17; 4:2; 10:1; esp. 10:10; 11:6; also 12:16.

46. On οὐθέν εἰμι and οὐδὲν ὠφελοῦμαι, cf. Epictetus Diss. 1.24.18; 2.19.10, 24.25; 3.1.10; esp.
4.8.25, of Socrates, who said, "If a man can trust me, what I am engaged in amounts to nothing; if
I wait for somebody else to help me, I am myself nothing. If I want something and it does not
happen, it follows that I am miserable." Also, cf. Ench. 24.4. Cf. Lehmann and Fridrichsen,
"1 Kor 13," 72. Also, cf. 1 Cor 7:9; Acts 25:11; Gal 6:3.

ring specifically to Paul's own apostolic self-understanding. As is often the case, what is implicit in 1 Corinthians becomes explicit in 2 Corinthians. In 2 Cor 2:4, Paul openly expresses his love for the church, but nowhere does he become more explicit than in the outburst in 2 Cor 11:11: "And why? Because I do not love you?" (διὰ τί ὅτι οὐκ ἀγαπῶ ὑμᾶς). Equally explicit is 2 Cor 12:15: "if I love you the more, am I to be loved the less?" (εἰ περισσοτέρως ὑμᾶς ἀγαπῶ[ν], ἧσσον ἀγαπῶμαι). The reminder in the preceding verse that parents should provide for their children (12:14) renders ἀγάπη more specifically as parental love. Given Paul's reminder in 1 Cor 4:15 that he had fathered the Corinthians, and given the pervasiveness of the father-children metaphor in both epistles, this may serve to establish the metaphorical assumption underlying 1 Cor 13:1–3. The final warning in 1 Cor 4:21 appears to recall the image of the father who must discipline the proverbial misbehaving child (cf. Prov 19:13; 23:13–14; 29:15), yet the alternative to stern paternal discipline is to come to the Corinthians "in love" (ἐν ἀγάπη), presumably fatherly love.

If the father-children relationship defines the nature of ἀγάπη as paternal love, the benediction in 1 Cor 16:24 would then be seen as a father's final reminder to his children. What is more, it would place 13:1–3 even more firmly within the parenetic tradition in which the father's giving advice to his children may have provided the original *Sitz im Leben* of such advice. Isocrates' epistle *Ad Demonicum* best illustrates this genre of epistolary parenesis, where the life of ἀρετή is praised and promulgated; then illustrated with concrete paradigms, first Heracles and Theseus; then illustrated by the example (παράδειγμα) of the pattern of the life of Isocrates' own father, Hipponicus, whom Demonicus is encouraged to imitate (9–11).[47] When, therefore, Paul characterizes his own apostolic ministry as having been carried out "in genuine love" (ἐν ἀγάπη ἀνυποκρίτῳ [2 Cor 6:6]), he is stating positively what is stated negatively and hyperbolically in 1 Cor 13:1–3: ἀγάπη is the primal impulse of his apostolic behavior, particularly toward churches he has fathered. The ethical paradigm could hardly be depicted more graphically.

The carefully crafted structure of 1 Cor 13:1–3, then, consists of three present general conditional sentences, complete with protases and apodoses, with varying complexity. The verses are hypothetical, but they are rendered so because of their hyperbolic form, not because they have an imaginary subject. The first person singular is conspicuous, and the primary referent is Paul. Each of the activities is framed with specific reference to a concrete subject: Paul himself.

It is Paul who speaks, who as a prophet is privy to the mysteries of God, who therefore knows the mind of God, who exercises healing faith, who dispossesses himself of what is rightfully his, who hands over his body to an

47. Cf. Fiore, *Function of Personal Example*, 35, 64.

apostolic ministry that is his only boast. But the structure suggests that the claim is not simply "If I perform my apostolic work, unmotivated by ἀγάπη, my apostleship evaporates into vacuous speech and a hollow life-style." Rather the hyperbole recasts the self-portrait so that each item is stretched to the limit of incredibility because it is recast with the assumptions of the Corinthian enthusiasts. That is, even if he were to allow his apostolic work to be shaped by the assumptions of those Corinthians who are not content with speaking, but insist that an apostle must speak with eloquence surpassing human capabilities; who are not content with prophecy that enables them to understand the divine mysteries and have knowledge of God's will, but must experience the fullness of the eschaton now and know *all* prophecy, know *all* mysteries, have *all* knowledge; who are not content with simple miracles, but insist on the most dramatically convincing signs; who are not content with being poor but insist on possessing now *all* the eschatological riches; who are not content to yield their "bodies" to Christian service, but insist on unqualified suppression of the body and all somatic desires, it would be for nought. In other words, even if his own apostolic existence were redefined according to the assumptions of the Corinthian enthusiasts, yet were unmotivated by ἀγάπη, it would be for nought.

CHARACTERIZATION OF ΑΓΑΠΗ
(1 Cor 13:4–7)

Having introduced the personal paradigm, Paul now turns to a detailed characterization of the primal impulse of his apostolic ministry. What gives definitive shape to his own apostolic behavior, especially his behavior toward the Corinthians, he now enjoins upon them (1 Cor 14:1), expecting it also to give definitive shape to their own behavior toward one another. The personal paradigm is carried over into the characterization but does not dominate it, because the shift now moves toward its implementation. How this is achieved structurally is especially noteworthy.

It should be noticed first, however, that the discussion in 1 Cor 13:4–7 is not totally alien to the rest of the epistle. Although the immediate frame of reference of the appeal here is 1 Corinthians 12–14, the scope is much broader. Early in the epistle, the discussion in chap. 13 is adumbrated when Paul introduces the LXX quotation in 2:9, insisting already that ἀγάπη, not γνῶσις, is the sole prerequisite for participating in the divine mystery. When the epistle begins to address questions raised by the Corinthians, the antithesis of ἀγάπη and γνῶσις is advanced: "knowledge inflates, love edifies" (ἡ γνῶσις φυσιοῖ, ἡ δὲ ἀγάπη οἰκοδομεῖ [8:1]). The second half of this antithesis may be said to form the topic sentence of chap. 14. It is stressed in 8:3 that only if one loves can one experience the knowledge of God, albeit only passively. What is more, the epistle concludes on the same note (16:14, 24). Thus, what actually turns out to be a recurrent theme of the epistle as a whole reaches its fullest and richest expression here.

The fundamental reference point of the characterization in 1 Cor 13:4–7 is ἀγάπη. Certain, though not all, parts of the characterization appear to be taken directly from previous sections of the epistle itself: "is not jealous" (οὐ ζηλοῖ [13:4]) recalls 3:3 directly (ὅπου γὰρ ἐν ὑμῖν ζῆλος καὶ ἔρις, οὐχὶ σαρκικοί ἐστε) and 1:10–17 indirectly; "is not boastful" (οὐ περπερεύεται [13:4]) may be taken as being synonymous with "is not inflated" (οὐ φυσιοῦται [13:4]), which specifically relates to 4:6, 18, 19; 5:2; 8:1; "is not rude" (οὐ ἀσχημονεῖ [13:5]) recalls the language of 7:3b, though the sense is different; "does not seek its own" (οὐ ζητεῖ τὰ ἑαυτῆς [13:5]) directly recalls 10:33, which we will note in more detail later; "is not irritable" (οὐ παροξύνεται [13:5]) appears to have no exact counterpart; similarly, "is not resentful" (οὐ λογίζεται τὸ κακόν [13:5]) has no direct counterpart, but may anticipate 14:20 and should perhaps be taken with the following phrase; and "does not rejoice at wrong" (οὐ χαίρει ἐπὶ τῇ ἀδικίᾳ [13:6]) appears to recall the discussion in 6:7–8.

Other parts of the characterization, notably those stated positively, employ terms used elsewhere by Paul to characterize his own apostolic ministry: "patient" (μακροθυμεῖ [1 Cor 13:4]) and "kind" (χρηστεύεται [13:4]) figure centrally in the apostolic profile sketched in 2 Cor 6:3–10, especially v. 6: "in forbearance" (ἐν μακροθυμίᾳ) and "in kindness" (ἐν χρηστότητι). The fact that these two expressions appear beside "in genuine love" (ἐν ἀγάπῃ ἀνυποκρίτῳ [2 Cor 6:6]) should not go unnoticed. The second part of the antithetical parallelism in 13:6, "rejoicing in the truth" (συγχαίρει δὲ τῇ ἀληθείᾳ), anticipates the language of 2 Cor 13:8. The chiastic arrangement of 1 Cor 13:7 causes "bears all things" (πάντα στέγει) to be parallel to "endures all things" (πάντα ὑπομένει). There is an explicit connection between "bears all things" (πάντα στέγει) and "we endure anything" (πάντα στέγομεν) in 9:12, where Paul employs the term in reference to his own apostolic conduct. In his description of his apostolic demeanor elsewhere, "endurance" (ὑπομονή [13:7]) figures prominently (2 Cor 6:4; 12:12). The two middle parts of the chiasmus, "believes all things" (πάντα πιστεύει) and "hopes all things" (πάντα ἐλπίζει), are more elusive, though elsewhere Paul employs both terms self-referentially in contexts where he discusses his apostolic ministry. "Hope" (ἐλπίς) may recall 9:12 or even 15:19, though both are indirect parallels, at best. In 2 Cor 1:7, Paul reaffirms his steadfast hope for the Corinthians; in 2 Cor 10:15, he expresses hope specifically for their growth in the faith. In 1 Thess 2:19, his church, the fruits of his apostolic work, becomes his "hope, joy, and crown" (ἐλπίς, χαρά, στέφανος). "Believes all things" (πάντα πιστεύει) may anticipate 1 Corinthians 15, where the constancy of Paul's own faith (v. 11) informed by his belief in the risen Lord contrasts with the potential vanity of the Corinthians' faith if it becomes shorn of belief in the resurrection (vv. 14, 17).

These one-for-one correspondences, however, should not be pushed too far. Every item in the characterization need not be specifically anchored within the Corinthian situation. This would be placing undue constraints on Paul. There may be an underlying Stoic characterization of the moral ideal that accounts for certain features, as well as the form, of the characterization.[48] Still, if so, its present form appears to be redacted specifically by Paul to the Corinthian situation. What cannot be denied is that those parts of the characterization that surface as distinctively reflecting the Corinthian situation are prominent enough to suggest that in the characterization, Paul has fused both negative and positive paradigms. Those items reflecting his own apostolic behavior serve to illustrate the positive profile that ἀγάπη produces; those negative items depicting unedifying behavior of the Corinthians seem to illustrate the negative profile that results from the absence of ἀγάπη—and the presence of γνῶσις.

Thus, although it is true that certain of the motifs employed in these verses are typical items found in vice/virtue lists, and therefore are of more general character, they are nevertheless quite distinct in both form and function. We see, then, that the present form of Paul's characterization of ἀγάπη in 1 Cor 13:4–7, even if it exhibits an underlying Stoic complexion, is achieved by blending two strands: (1) that which typifies Paul's own behavior is stated positively and is therefore exemplary, and (2) that which typifies the present behavior of the Corinthians is stated negatively and is therefore blameworthy.

This antithetical structure in which behavior to be avoided is set in contrast to behavior to be pursued is perhaps one of the most distinctive features of parenesis. Although Paul has creatively modified the form, it is nevertheless striking because we see in it the fusion of apostolic paradigm, illustrating the positive ideal, with the addressees' present behavior, illustrating the negative paradigm.

This fusion achieves its sharpest focus in the phrase "seeks not its own" (οὐ ζητεῖ τὰ ἑαυτῆς [1 Cor 13:5]), a phrase that underscores one of the most conspicuous shortcomings of the Corinthians (some of them, at least) by recalling a phrase used earlier in 1 Corinthians 10. In 10:24, the following prohibition is given: "Let no one seek his own good but the good of his neighbor" (μηδεὶς τὸ ἑαυτοῦ ζητείτω ἀλλὰ τὸ τοῦ ἑτέρου). To buttress this prohibition—that is, this negative ethical imperative—Paul makes his instinctive move by concluding the section with a final appeal couched in identical terms, but this time he phrases it so as to adduce his own apostolic behavior as the paradigm: "just as I try to please all men in everything I do, not seeking my own advantage, but that of the many, that they may be saved" (καθὼς κἀγὼ πάντα πᾶσιν ἀρέσκω μὴ ζητῶν τὸ ἐμαυτοῦ σύμφορον ἀλλὰ τὸ τῶν πολλῶν ἵνα σωθῶσιν [10:33]). He thus exemplifies the ideal that he urges upon the Corinthians, as the explicit imitatio Pauli motif in 11:1 makes clear. In 13:5 the phrase is stated in the

48. Lehmann and Fridrichsen, "1 Kor 13," 70–79.

indicative, but its earlier occurrence has already shown how the ethical imperative becomes illustrated and concretized by the apostolic paradigm. Thus, what is here stated in a gnomic way and therefore expresses a general truth has already been actualized in Paul's own apostolic conduct (10:33). That this conduct has been adduced as being exemplary for the Corinthians provides the compelling basis enabling them to reproduce this outlook within their own behavior.

THE FINALITY OF LOVE AND THE
APOSTOLIC PARADIGM
(1 Cor 13:8–13)

In 1 Cor 13:8–13, the language of vv. 1–3 is recalled, confirming Johannes Weiss's suggestion that the three sections of the chapter are arranged in an a-b-a pattern.[49] In vv. 1–3 the hyperbole served to highlight the "gnostic" propensity for making absolute claims. Verses 8–13 counter this propensity by underscoring the partial quality of human existence, especially existence "in Christ" (ἐν Χριστῷ).

The section begins with a declaration of the absolute finality of ἀγάπη: "love never fails" (ἡ ἀγάπη οὐδέποτε πίπτει). Spiritual gifts such as prophecy, tongues, and knowledge have no ultimate finality. They are temporary scaffolding belonging to "this age." Even as they are practiced and experienced "now," they are intrinsically partial. The eschaton will only dramatically reinforce their penultimate quality. The Corinthians have erred because they have reversed this fundamental eschatological truth. For them, essentially partial gifts possess finality, and these gifts are worth making ultimate claims about, when in fact ἀγάπη alone can be seen to possess such finality. It alone reveals the interior of the Christ-event that turned the ages. The quintessential eschatological reality, then, is ἀγάπη, and it is the only such reality to have invaded the now in any absolute sense. For this reason, it alone can be called the earmark of existence "in Christ" (ἐν Χριστῷ). It alone should become the ultimate reality of Christian existence. It alone should be primal.

At this point, Paul makes the instinctive shift to self-referential language by contrasting the "then" and the "now" of his own life. The key term is "child" (νήπιος), for it captures the fundamental misconception of the Corinthians. Their failure to apprehend the finality of ἀγάπη accounts for their puerile behavior in being preoccupied with the partial, as well as for the glaring imperfections in their corporate behavior. It is this that renders them immature children who apparently still "think as children" (cf. 1 Cor 14:20). Paul's "maturity," by contrast, consists in his recognition of the ultimate finality of ἀγάπη, as well as in his recognition that Christian knowledge, in particular, is partial. "Now" this knowledge can only be experienced passively, not grasped

---

49. Weiss, *Der erste Korintherbrief*, 311; also Lund, "Literary Structure," 266–76.

actively. Ultimate knowledge is beyond the reach of this age. Ἀγάπη alone has penetrated this age. Paul's assertion "Now I know in part" (ἄρτι γινώσκω ἐκ μέρους) expresses his present apostolic outlook. His maturity recognizes knowledge for what it is: excessively inflating and incurably partial. The Corinthians' immaturity causes them to misconstrue knowledge as the gift possessing absolute finality. The surpassing superiority of ἀγάπη lies not in the fact that it alone extends to the eschaton but that it alone represents the extension of the eschaton into the present.

Whether or not this interpretation of 1 Corinthians 13 captures the subtlety of Paul's line of argument, it at least takes seriously the self-referential language and its parenetic function. There is no longer any mystery about ἀγάπη. It has been introduced as the primal impulse of Paul's own apostolic behavior, without which the stereotypical charges leveled against him by unknown opponents would be true. Were his apostolic work not motivated by love, he would be nothing more than an empty-headed Sophist fond of peddling the gospel, and his words would be "empty," as some charge in 2 Corinthians. Equally clear is the fact that the Corinthians' own glaring imperfections, despite their claims to the contrary, only serve to underscore the conspicuous absence of love within their corporate life. For this reason, no substantial "upbuilding" is occurring.

In 1 Corinthians 14, Paul does not "descend back to the plane of reality," as K. Barth suggests,[50] because chap. 13 is grounded in the concrete reality of his own apostolic experience. From this Paul plunges ahead into a discussion of what the corporate life of the Corinthians would be were they to "pursue love," as he has done. Without launching into a detailed analysis of chap. 14, we may simply note that the discussion is notable for the way in which Paul refers to himself and his behavior. Repeatedly, as in 14:6–12, he proposes what he would do to bring about more edifying conditions were he in their situation (similarly, in 14:14–15, 18–19). As noted earlier, chap. 14 may be seen as the working out of the second half of the antithesis introduced in 8:1–2: "love builds up." In chap. 14, Paul proceeds to instruct the Corinthians how love can and should become a concrete reality in their corporate life as a congregation. Although love is not mentioned in chap. 14 after v. 1a, it functions as the crucial middle term.

---

50. K. Barth, *The Resurrection of the Dead* (New York: Revell, 1933) 88: "After chapter xiii 1 Cor xiv signifies once more a descent to the plane of the rest of the Epistle, which was left at xii.31."

SUSAN R. GARRETT   6

THE GOD OF THIS WORLD AND
THE AFFLICTION OF PAUL
2 Cor 4:1–12

Paul saw suffering and struggle as the hallmarks of his apostolic existence
(for example, 1 Cor 4:9–13; 2 Cor 4:7–12; 6:4–10; cf. Phil 1:29–30). He wrote
to the Corinthians that the apostles were exhibited by God as "last of all,
like persons sentenced to death" (1 Cor 4:9a). The relevance of popular
philosophical portraits of the afflicted sage for understanding this aspect of
Paul's discourse has long been recognized.[1] In his teaching and publications,
Abraham J. Malherbe has helped us to understand how remarkably nuanced
and varied is Paul's adaptation of such philosophical portraits.[2] The recent
work of one of Malherbe's former students, John T. Fitzgerald, on Paul's use
of the *peristasis*-catalogs, or "hardship lists," prevalent in Hellenistic moral
philosophy has deepened our understanding still further.[3]

To be sure, some scholars have rejected the theory of Hellenistic philosophical influence, arguing that the proper interpretive background for Paul's
ideas about the endurance of suffering is rather to be found in Judaism. Wolfgang Schrage, for example, argues that Paul's hardship lists derive not from
Stoicism but from Jewish apocalypticism, which Paul has interpreted in light
of his Christology.[4] But, though some of his arguments are persuasive,
Schrage's approach reflects an unwarranted tendency "to see an unbridgeable

1. This relevance became known especially through the work of Rudolf Bultmann, in his dissertation *Der Stil der Paulinischen Predigt und die kynisch-stoische Diatribe* (FRLANT 13;
Göttingen: Vandenhoeck & Ruprecht, 1910) 19, 71–72. For a history of research prior and subsequent to Bultmann (focusing on scholarly attention to Paul's use of *peristasis*-catalogs, or "hardship lists"), see John T. Fitzgerald, *Cracks in an Earthen Vessel: An Examination of the Catalogues
of Hardships in the Corinthian Correspondence* (SBLDS 99; Atlanta: Scholars, 1988) 7–31.
2. Works by Malherbe pertinent to the topic include "The Beasts at Ephesus," *JBL* 87 (1968)
71–80; "'Gentle as a Nurse': The Cynic Background to I Thess ii," *NovT* 12 (1970) 203–17;
"Antisthenes and Odysseus, and Paul at War," *HTR* 76 (1983) 143–73, esp. 170–71; *Moral Exhortation: A Greco-Roman Sourcebook* (Philadelphia: Westminster, 1986) 141–43; and *Paul and the
Thessalonians: The Philosophic Tradition of Pastoral Care* (Philadelphia: Fortress, 1987) 47–48,
52–60, and passim.
3. Fitzgerald, *Cracks in an Earthen Vessel.*
4. Wolfgang Schrage, "Leid, Kreuz und Eschaton: Die Peristasenkataloge als Merkmale paulinischer theologia crucis und Eschatologie," *EvT* 34 (1974) 141–75.

99

gap between Stoicism and Jewish apocalypticism."[5] As divergent in many respects as these two realms of discourse were, Paul was at home in both. Consequently, he was, as Fitzgerald remarks, "capable of blending highly heterogeneous material in remarkable ways."[6] To identify either the Jewish or the Hellenistic philosophical background as the single or dominant set of traditions controlling Paul's discussion of his suffering is to sell short the richness of his thought. The endurance of affliction (θλῖψις, παθήματα, πληγαί, and so on) was a frequent topic of discussion in the works of Jewish and Hellenistic philosophical writers alike. Many from both traditions agreed that the proper response to hardships was "patient endurance" (ὑπομονή, μακρο-θυμία, καρτερία, and so on). Moreover, both Jews and Greeks could speak of hardships as a *test* of virtue or faith.[7] Such terminological and conceptual overlaps made it easy for Jewish writers familiar with Hellenistic philosophical discussions of hardships to move back and forth between semantic fields (4 Maccabees is a case in point).

One passage in Paul's writings that seems to exhibit elements of both streams of tradition is 2 Cor 4:1–12. Here Paul employs a *peristasis*-catalog to shed the best possible light on his own "weak" condition, which has come under fire. But Paul prefaces this typical Hellenistic literary device with the apocalyptic-sounding comment that the "perishing" fail to comprehend his message because "the god of this age has blinded their minds" (4:4). Moreover, within the hardship list itself, Paul claims that the living are always being "given over to death" (εἰς θάνατον παραδιδόναι [4:11]). Here παραδιδόναι echoes not only texts describing the "giving over" of Jesus to death (for example, 1 Cor 11:23) but also passages referring to the "giving over" of persons to Satan for the affliction or destruction of the body.[8] How do these seemingly disparate elements cohere? In the following analysis of 2 Cor 4:1–12, I shall

5. Fitzgerald, *Cracks in an Earthen Vessel*, 29. An analogous charge can be made against Karl Theodor Kleinknecht's *Der leidende Gerechtfertigte: Die alttestamentlich-jüdische Tradition vom "leidenden Gerechten" und ihre Rezeption bei Paulus* (WUNT, 2d ser.; Tübingen: Mohr [Siebeck], 1984). Kleinknecht argues that Paul's self-understanding and the intended meaning of his words (*Aussageintention*) differ sharply from anything found in the Cynic-Stoic tradition, though he concedes that some (minimal) Hellenistic philosophical influence may have been mediated to Paul through a Jewish stream of tradition in which the "suffering righteous one" played the dominant role. See pp. 226–33, 257–68, 294, 346, 365, 384–85.

6. Fitzgerald, *Cracks in an Earthen Vessel*, 29.

7. For hardships as a "test" in the writings of the moralists, see, for example, Epictetus *Diss.* 1.18.21–23; 3.10.11; 3.12.11; 4.8.31; Seneca *Ep.* 13.1–3; *Prov.* 1.6; 4.5–8, 12; Dio Chrys. *Or.* 3.3. See also R. Liechtenhan, "Die Ueberwindung des Leides bei Paulus und in der zeitgenössischen Stoa," *ZTK* 30 (1922) 381–82. For Jewish and Christian notions of hardship as "testing," see, for example, *Pss. Sol.* 16:14–15; *T. Jos.* 2:7; 4 Macc 17:11–16; Wis 3:5–6; Sir 2:1–5; Judith 8:25–27; 1 Pet 1:6–9; see also note 28 below.

8. For example, 1 Cor 5:5; Job 2:6 LXX; *T. Job* 20:3. Some such "giving over" to satanic authority is also implied by Luke 22:31–32: here Satan "demanded to have" (ἐξαιτήσαι) the apostles — that is, demanded that God give them over into Satan's authority. Cf. *T. Job* 20:2–3: καὶ ἀπελθὼν [ὁ Σατανᾶς] ᾐτήσατο τὸ σῶμά μου παρὰ τοῦ κυρίου ἵνα ἐπενέγκῃ μοι πληγήν· καὶ τότε παρέδωκέν με ὁ κύριος εἰς χεῖρας αὐτοῦ χρή(σα)σθαι τῷ σώματί μου ὡς ἠβούλετο, τῆς δὲ ψυχῆς μου οὐκ ἔδωκεν αὐτῷ ἐξουσίαν.

argue that Paul's interpretation of his own situation vis-à-vis his opponents in Corinth synthesizes Jewish and Stoic views of the endurance of affliction. Whether deliberately or by "second nature," Paul uses each set of traditions to interpret the other. He casts himself into the role of the afflicted righteous one, who is mocked by the devil's allies. Paul's faithful endurance in the face of suffering and ridicule demonstrates his superiority to the diabolical forces that oppose him, much as the sage's endurance demonstrates superiority over the passions. As allies of Satan, Paul's opponents focus on the transient and perishing, and so are caught in ignorance. They are unable to see past Paul's weakness. By contrast, as an ally of God, Paul has knowledge of eternal realities.

2 COR 4:1–12: AN OVERVIEW

2 Cor 4:1–12 ties together several important themes of 2 Corinthians 1–3. The first two verses (4:1–2) reiterate the point that Paul's ministry is backed by the authority of God, who has established it to supersede the ministry of the old covenant (a "ministry of death" [3:6–8]). Paul's emphasis on the integrity of his methods (4:2) may be refutation of explicit charges leveled against him (3:1; 5:12; 12:16);[9] or it may be an accusation against his detractors: *they* are the ones who engage in shameful, secret actions, and *they* are the ones who practice cunning and tamper with God's word (cf. 2:17; 11:3, 13–15). In any case, vv. 1–2 contribute to the nuanced self-commendation that is a major thrust of 2 Corinthians 1–7.[10]

The next verses (2 Cor 4:3–4) repeat the motif found in 3:14–15 of "hardened" or "veiled" minds (νοήματα). Paul's wording in 4:3 suggests that he is making a concession (εἰ δὲ καί, "but even if"). Perhaps he has himself been charged with preaching a veiled gospel.[11] He counters that those who reject his gospel as "veiled" are to be numbered among the perishing.[12] They are

---

9. See, for example, Peter Marshall, *Enmity in Corinth: Social Conventions in Paul's Relations with the Corinthians* (WUNT, 2d ser., 23; Tübingen: Mohr [Siebeck], 1987) 272.

10. Fitzgerald, *Cracks in an Earthen Vessel,* 148–53, passim; also Marshall, *Enmity in Corinth,* 265–77, passim; Linda L. Belleville, "A Letter of Apologetic Self-Commendation," *NovT* 31 (1989) 142–63.

11. Cf. Victor Paul Furnish, *II Corinthians* (Anchor Bible 32A; Garden City, NY: Doubleday, 1984) 247; C. K. Barrett, *The Second Epistle to the Corinthians* (New York: Harper & Row, 1973) 130.

12. The syntax of 2 Cor 4:3–4 is awkward. In the phrase ἐν τοῖς ἀπολλυμένοις of v. 3, the ἐν stands for the dative (cf. 1 Cor 1:18) and may be translated simply "for" or "to" (so Furnish, *II Corinthians,* 219; see also BDF § 220[1]). The subsequent ἐν οἷς (v. 4) could introduce a subgroup (the "unbelievers," οἱ ἄπιστοι) among the "perishing"; or ἐν οἷς could be resumptive (cf. the RSV: "in their case"), so that ἄπιστοι of v. 4 is synonymous with οἱ ἀπολλύμενοι. However one construes the grammar, contextual considerations suggest that Paul is referring specifically (if obliquely) to his opponents. The suggestion of John A. Bain ("2 Cor iv.3–4," *ExpTim* 18 [1906–1907] 380) that οἱ ἀπολλύμενοι be taken as a neuter ("by the things that are perishing") is to be rejected, inasmuch as it does not take into account Paul's usage of this term elsewhere (see esp. 2 Cor 2:15).

unable to see the truth of Paul's claims because their minds (νοήματα) have been blinded by the god of this world. Who are these persons? Paul's use of the terms "the perishing" (οἱ ἀπολλύμενοι) and "unbelievers" (οἱ ἄπιστοι) might seem to indicate that he is referring to the unconverted generally. However, the polemical tone of Paul's statement (cf. 6:14–15; 11:3, 12–15) suggests that he has a very specific group in mind: namely, those in Corinth who are undermining his work by accusing him of being weak, vacillating, and obscure.[13] As David Rensberger observes, "Those who reject the Gospel of Christ and the Apostle of Christ belong in the category of 'unbelievers,' whether nominally Christians or not."[14] The repetition of the motif of veiled minds from the discussion of the Mosaic covenant in 3:14–18 suggests that these detractors associate themselves with Moses in some way.[15] They are likely the same opponents whom Paul rails against in 2 Cor 10–13 (probably the fragment of a letter written after the composition of chapters 1 through 9, when the opposition of these persons to Paul had deepened considerably).[16] Paul does not regard ones controlled by the devil (4:4) as merely passive victims: they threaten the salvation of the Corinthians, whose minds also can be led astray (2 Cor 11:3: φοβοῦμαι δὲ μή πως . . . φθαρῇ τὰ νοήματα ὑμῶν).

The contrast between ignorance and knowledge and between hiddenness and revelation that figured so prominently in Paul's discussion of the old and new covenants (2 Cor 3:7–18)[17] is carried through in the opening verses of chapter 4. Paul's reference to the rejection of his gospel by the perishing (4:3–4) echoes both 1 Cor 1:18 (the perishing regard the message of the cross as foolishness) and 2 Cor 2:15–16 (the perishing perceive Paul as one who exudes the stench of death). The parallels suggest that in 2 Cor 4:4 also, Paul

13. For Paul's use elsewhere of ἀπολλύμενοι or ἀπώλεια in reference to opponents, see Phil 1:28; 3:19. In 1 Corinthians, ἄπιστος always refers to the unconverted (1 Cor 6:6; 7:12, 13, 14, 15; 10:27; 14:22, 23, 24), but in 2 Corinthians the other two occurrences of the term (2 Cor 6:14, 15) probably refer to Paul's opponents.

14. David Rensberger, "2 Corinthians 6:14–7:1—A Fresh Examination," *Studia Biblica et Theologica* 8 (1978) 30.

15. Dieter Georgi assumes that Paul's opponents in 2 Corinthians make much of their Jewish heritage (*The Opponents of Paul in Second Corinthians* [Philadelphia: Fortress, 1986] esp. 250–71). Georgi entertains the possibility of an allusion to the opponents in 2 Cor 4:3–4 but then rejects it (353, n. 3).

16. For a defense of this "two-letter hypothesis," see Furnish, *II Corinthians*, 35–41. Despite the vastly different tone of chap. 1–9 and chap. 10–13 in 2 Corinthians, in both sections Paul repudiates opponents who commend themselves (3:1; 10:18; cf. 5:12) while maligning Paul as weak, vacillating, and deceitful (1:17; 4:2; 7:2; 10:2, 10; 12:11, 16–17). Thus, the two groups of opponents are probably identical. See Georgi, *Opponents*, 229–30; Furnish, *II Corinthians*, 45, 48–54; and Rensberger, "2 Corinthians 6:14–7:1," 30, 42–43. For a bibliography and a breakdown of the types of proposals regarding the opponents Paul is addressing, see Furnish, *II Corinthians*, 49.

17. This contrast between ignorance and knowledge is highlighted in the discussions of 2 Cor 3:1–4:6 in Richard B. Hays, *Echoes of Scripture in the Letters of Paul* (New Haven: Yale University Press, 1989) chap. 4; and of 2 Cor 2:14–6:10 in J. Louis Martyn, "Epistemology at the Turn of the Ages: 2 Corinthians 5:16," *Christian History and Interpretation: Studies Presented to John Knox* (ed. W. R. Farmer, C. F. D. Moule, and R. R. Niebuhr; Cambridge: Cambridge University Press, 1967) 269–87.

is reacting against the charge that the messenger and his message are *weak* and *shameful.* The perishing look to the cross and see humiliation rather than Christ's glory, which must be divinely revealed. They look to Paul and see only a devastated and decomposing "outer nature" (4:16). In their state of blindness, they see only the visible and transient; hence they regard Paul's afflicted condition as a disgrace. Paul, by contrast, is the recipient of divine knowledge: knowledge of things unseen and eternal (4:6, 18). Paul explains the contrast between his knowledge and his opponents' ignorance as the consequence of differences in alliance: Paul is allied with God and Christ, whereas those who reject Paul are allied with the god of this age.

Paul is eager to counterbalance allegations that he is weak and dying, inasmuch as he wants the Corinthians to be proud of him, as he is of them (2 Cor 1:14). In 4:7–12 he furthers this aim by launching into a *peristasis-*catalog, which functions to turn his liability (weakness) into an asset. Paul had already made an analogous rhetorical move in 2:14–16, where he described himself as a conquered captive led by God in a triumphal procession, "the very showpiece of God's triumph."[18] For first-century readers, the imagery would have evoked strong emotional reactions: the captured prisoner being led to death was the most abject of beings. The powerful connotations of the metaphor are exploited by Seneca in a description of the sage's indifference to hardships and vicissitudes: "Let me be placed upon a foreign barrow to grace the procession of a proud and brutal victor; no whit more humble shall I be when I am driven in front of the chariot of another than when I stood erect upon my own" (*On the Happy Life* 25.4).[19] So also in 2 Cor 2:14–16, Paul's paradoxical assertion of his own joyful attitude as he is led to death serves to display "his serendipity, capacity, and worth."[20] In 4:7–12, Paul's use of the *peristasis-*catalog works in a similar way, to demonstrate his composure and to exhibit him as one whom adversity cannot conquer. Like the moralists, Paul stresses that hardships are an opportunity for the demonstration of power.[21]

---

18. Fitzgerald, *Cracks in an Earthen Vessel,* 162; see the full discussion of the term θριαμβεύω on 161–64 and in Scott Hafemann, *Suffering and the Spirit: An Exegetical Study of II Cor 2:14–3:3 within the Context of the Corinthian Correspondence* (WUNT, 2d ser., 19; Tübingen: Mohr [Siebeck], 1986) 18–39. Hafemann points out that the one being led in a triumphal procession would typically be executed at its conclusion.

19. Translated by Basore in LCL.

20. Fitzgerald, *Cracks in an Earthen Vessel,* 163.

21. Fitzgerald, *Cracks in an Earthen Vessel,* 166 (citing Epictetus *Diss.* 2.1.39; Seneca *Ep.* 71.26) 205, passim. Fitzgerald (156–57, 166–72) highlights Paul's insistence that his capacity to perform his tasks derives from God (see, for example, 2 Cor 1:3–4; 3:5–6; 4:7) and remarks that such attribution of one's sustaining power to the divinity is also common in the moralists (see, for example, Seneca *Ep.* 41.4–5; Aelius Aristides *Or.* 24). By ascribing his power to God, Paul not only expressed a genuine theological conviction that God uses human weakness to show forth strength but also rendered his self-commendation less offensive. Marshall, *Enmity in Corinth,* 359, comments that there is no "reversal of values" in Paul's citation of his hardships: "Paul boasts in his shame and appears to agree with his enemies that these things are truly disgraceful. There is little of the Cynic spirit in his parade of shame." Schrage, "Leid, Kreuz, und Eschaton," 146–50, makes a similar point but unjustifiably infers from it that one must exclude the possibility of Stoic influence on Paul.

Thus, he appropriates the charge of his detractors and makes it work in his favor. By evoking images of the afflicted but invincible sage, the *peristasis-catalog* in vv. 7–12 serves to portray Paul as unconquerable, his weakness and exposure to death notwithstanding. But Paul's allegation that his detractors have been blinded by the god of this age gives an eschatological (and very un-Stoic) cast to his rhetoric. An examination of Paul's references to the character of Satan elsewhere in his letters will contribute to a deeper understanding of this harsh allegation.

PAUL'S VIEW OF SATAN

The phrase "god of this age" (ὁ θεὸς τοῦ αἰῶνος τούτου) is a hapax legomenon in Paul's writings. It refers to Satan.[22] Like the title "ruler of this world," which occurs in the Fourth Gospel and in the *Martyrdom and Ascension of Isaiah,*[23] the designation "god of this age" presupposes a dualistic frame of reference: *this* age (or *this* world) is implicitly contrasted with another.[24] Paul's other uses of "this age" indicate that it refers to the present reign of sin and death.[25] Although future victory over the powers of death is assured (1 Cor 15:21–28, 53–57; cf. Rom 8:38–39), the present is a time of inescapable suffering for the people of God.[26] Had the (spiritual) "rulers of this age" understood that Christ's death would ensure their own destruction, they would never have allowed him to be crucified (1 Cor 2:6, 8).[27] As "god of this age," Satan blinds the minds of some of Paul's hearers, lest they perceive that Christ died to rescue them from the age's dominion (cf. Gal 1:4). Now that

22. Cf. Martin Dibelius, *Die Geisterwelt im Glauben des Paulus* (Göttingen: Vandenhoeck & Ruprecht, 1909) 64. Furnish, *II Corinthians,* 220, comments that "the dualism apparent here is characteristic of Jewish apocalypticism" and that "the dualism of Christian Gnosticism as known from the Nag Hammadi texts involves a view of the created order as inherently inferior and by nature evil—a view which is foreign to the thought-world of early Jewish and Christian apocalypticism."

23. John 12:31; 14:30; 16:11 (discussed in B. Noack, *Satanás und Sotería: Untersuchungen zur neutestamentlichen Dämonologie* [Copenhagen: G. E. C. Gads, 1948] 60–61, 77–78); *Mart. Isa.* 1:3; *Asc. Isa.* 10:29 (cf. 9:14); cf. Luke 4:6; Eph 2:2; Ign. *Magn* 1.2. On the use of this title in Johannine Christianity, in Gnosticism, and in early rabbinic Judaism, see Alan F. Segal, "The Ruler of this World," *The Other Judaisms of Late Antiquity* (Brown Judaic Studies 127; Atlanta: Scholars, 1987) 41–77.

24. Dibelius, *Geisterwelt,* 65–67, points out that the notions of a temporal dualism (this age/the coming age) and of a physical one (this world/the heavenly world) easily blend into one another; Paul sometimes interchanges the words *world* and *age* (compare 1 Cor 1:20b; 2:12; and 3:19 with 1:20a; 2:6; and 3:18). Regarding the combined influence on 2 Cor 4:16–18 of Hellenistic anthropological dualism and apocalyptic thought, see Kleinknecht, *Der leidende Gerechtfertigte,* 261–63, 277; also Furnish, *II Corinthians,* 261, 289–90. In general, on the similarities between certain patterns of Greek thought and apocalyptic eschatology, see John J. Collins, "Apocalyptic Eschatology as the Transcendence of Death," *CBQ* 36 (1974) 21–43.

25. The expression ὁ αἰὼν οὗτος is found in Rom 12:2; 1 Cor 1:20; 2:6, 8; 3:18; 2 Cor 4:4.

26. Cf. Liechtenhan, "Ueberwindung des Leides," 382–84; Kleinknecht, *Der leidende Gerechtfertigte,* 203.

27. Dibelius, *Geisterwelt,* 88–99. As Dibelius points out, the references to the abolition (καταργεῖν) of these "rulers" makes little sense if they are conceived as earthly (i.e., mortal).

the crucifixion and resurrection have occurred, Satan engages in "damage containment." He strives to keep as many as possible from escaping his dominion and seizes every opportunity to capture one of the saved (2 Cor 2:11; cf. *T. Dan* 6:3–4).

Like many of his Jewish and Christian contemporaries (or near contemporaries), Paul believed that Satan "tempts" or "tests" (πειράζειν) the righteous.[28] Satan ruthlessly uses physical and emotional violence to lead the faithful astray into immorality, idolatry, or apostasy—knowing, it seems, that those weakened by long affliction are most likely to forsake the way of righteousness.[29] As a number of writers make clear, the proper response to satanic testing is "patient endurance" (ὑπομονή, μακροθυμία, or καρτερία).[30] By showing endurance, the righteous will gain the ability to "stand,"[31] and on the day of judgment the accuser will have no ammunition with which to convict those who have endured.[32] Hence Paul rejoices when he learns that "the tempter" has not succeeded in using affliction to lead the Thessalonians astray into apostasy: "for now we live, if you stand fast in the Lord" (1 Thess 3:8). The Thessalonians' hopeful endurance (cf. 1:3: ἡ ὑπομονὴ τῆς ἐλπίδος) ensures that they will be unblameable on the day of judgment (3:13).

28. See 1 Cor 7:5; 1 Thess 3:5; and note that Paul's wording in 1 Cor 10:13 ("God will not let you be tested" [οὐκ ἐάσει ὑμᾶς πειρασθῆναι]) may indicate that Paul was reluctant to name God as the author of temptation or testing (cf. Jas 1:13). Non-Pauline texts featuring Satan as tester include *Mart. Isa.* 5:1–16; *Jub.* 17:16 (modeled after the Job account); Mark 1:13; Matt 4:1–11; Luke 4:1–13; 22:31–32; 1 Pet 5:8–9; Rev 3:9–10. Secondary discussion of Satan as one who "tests" include H. Seesemann, πεῖρα κ.τ.λ., *TDNT* 6 (1968) 23–36; Noack, *Satanás und Soteria*, 20–22, 62–65; and K. G. Kuhn, "New Light on Temptation, Sin, and Flesh in the New Testament," *The Scrolls and the New Testament* (ed. Krister Stendahl; New York: Harper & Bros., 1957) 94–113.
29. On Satan's use of affliction, see *T. Job* 16:2–4; 20:1–2; 38:2; 1 Thess 3:4–5; 1 Pet 5:8–9. A belief in Satan's desire to make the faithful "blaspheme" or "deny Christ's name" is probably reflected in the Christian notion of the "unforgivable sin." See Mark 3:28–29 and parallels; 2 Tim 2:12; Rev 2:10, 13; 3:8–10 (all of which presuppose a situation of θλῖψις or πειρασμός); *Herm. Vis* 2.2.7–8. In Heb 10:26–29, neither "blasphemy" nor "denying the name" is mentioned explicitly, but these may nonetheless be in view: note the ensuing exhortation to endure suffering and avoid apostasy (vv. 32–39). In Acts 26:11, Paul reports that he formerly tried to make Christians blaspheme (cf. 1 Tim 1:13). Is Luke implying that Satan had been the agent behind Paul's actions?
30. See Rom 5:3; 12:12; *T. Job* 1:3; 4:6, 8; 5:1; 7:13 (ὑποστῆναι); 26:6; 27:7 (ἡ καρτερία), 10 (ἡ μακροθυμία is "superior to everything"); Jas 1:12–15 (cf. *Life of Adam and Eve [Apocalypse]* 19:3, where the temptation in the Garden is in view); Jas 5:10–11 (recalling the ὑπομονή of Job); 1 Pet 5:9; Rev 1:9; 2:2–3, 19; 3:8–10; 13:10; 14:12; Ign. *Magn.* 1.2. Passages that stress the need for "patient endurance" in times of suffering, but that do not explicitly mention Satan or "testing," include Ps 9:18; Sir 2:14; 16:13; 2 Macc 6:20; 4 Macc 1:11; 5:23; 7:22; *Pss. Sol.* 14.1; Matt 10:22; 24:13; 2 Cor 1:6; 6:4; Acts 14:22.
31. See 1 Cor 10:12–13; 1 Thess 3:8; Eph 6:11. For use of ἵστημι to indicate blamelessness in judgment contexts, see Rom 14:4; Jude 24.
32. For Satan's role as accuser, see Zech 3:1; *Jub.* 1:20; 48:15; *Mart. Isa.* 3:6 (through the person of a false prophet); Rev 12:10. Dibelius, *Geisterwelt*, 119, points out how closely related are Satan's roles as tempter and accuser. He argues (p. 53) that in 2 Cor 2:10–11, Paul envisions Christ (the world judge) and Satan (the accuser) both observing the Corinthian church. Paul seeks to effect reconciliation "in the presence of Christ" (v. 10)—supposing that if there is no reconciliation, Satan the accuser will prevail. Note that Rom 8:33–34 sounds like a counterclaim to the common notion that *Satan* is at God's hand, condemning God's elect (cf. esp. Rev 12:10).

Satan uses not only affliction but also *deceit* to achieve his goals. Frequently the devil tells lies or changes into other forms.[33] The *Testament of Job*, for example, refers to the devil's power as that "by which human nature is deceived" (ἐν ᾗ πατηθήσεται ἡ ἀνθρωπίνη φύσις [3:4]).[34] In this retelling of the tale of Job (likely written in Egypt sometime between 100 B.C.E. and 100 C.E.),[35] Satan attacks Job because the latter had destroyed the idol's temple in which Satan was worshipped. In the course of his assaults, the devil changes himself into other forms (μετασχηματίζεσθαι) in order to deceive Job: the devil appears as a beggar, a bread seller, and king of the Persians. Later in the narrative, Satan speaks through the person of Elious (Elihu), one of Job's so-called friends. Although persons around Job are fooled by such ruses, Job himself always discerns Satan's presence. Similarly, in Acts the devil several times works through human beings, including Ananias and Sapphira, Simon the magician, and Bar Jesus the magician.[36] But the spiritually discerning Peter and Paul are not taken in by such deception: in each case, the church leader recognizes the devil's presence and responds appropriately. The devil's deceit is no match for the spiritual perspicuity of the person of God.

In 2 Cor 11:3, Paul alludes to Satan's primal deception: the seduction of Eve. The serpent "deceived Eve by his cunning" (ἐξηπάτησεν Εὕαν ἐν τῇ πανουργίᾳ αὐτοῦ); so also the thoughts of the Corinthians may be led astray (φοβοῦμαι δὲ μή πως . . . φθαρῇ τὰ νοήματα ὑμῶν; cf. 4:4). It is true that Paul does not explicitly link the serpent with the devil, but he probably takes the association for granted.[37] Paul's subsequent reference to Satan's "disguising

---

33. In addition to the examples of deceitfulness and disguise cited in the remainder of the paragraph, see John 8:44; *T. Sim.* 2:7; *T. Judah* 19:4; *T. Dan.* 1:7; 3:6; *Mart. Isa.* 5:4–8; *Life of Adam and Eve (Vita)* 9:1–5; 11:2; *Acts of John* 70.

34. The text and translation of the *Testament of Job* being used (here and subsequently) is Robert A. Kraft et al. (ed.), *The Testament of Job According to the SV Text* (SBLTT 5; SBL Pseudepigrapha Series, 4; Missoula, MT: Scholars, 1974). According to Kraft's convention, triangular brackets enclose material that is absent from manuscript S (Messina [Sicily], San Salvatore 29), but supplied from another source. Citations follow Kraft's versification; in longer quotations his arrangement of strophes is also preserved.

35. On the provenance and date of the *Testament of Job*, see John J. Collins, "Structure and Meaning in the Testament of Job," SBLSP (2 vols.; ed. George MacRae; Cambridge, MA: Society of Biblical Literature, 1974) 1. 49–51. Collins argues for an origin in Egypt (based on the document's decription of Job as king of Egypt) and remarks that the emphasis on Job's endurance suggests a time of persecution, which points to "a date in the first century A.D. rather than earlier." In contrast, Berndt Schaller, *Das Testament Hiobs* (JSHRZ 3.3; Gütersloh: Mohn, 1979) 309–12, is skeptical about the sufficiency of the evidence for a theory of origin either in Egypt in general or, more specifically, among the Therapeutae, as proposed by M. Philonenko and others; Collins approved of this theory in the 1974 article but later modified his position in light of Schaller's work: see John J. Collins, "The Testamentary Literature in Recent Scholarship," *Early Judaism and Its Modern Interpreters* (ed. R. A. Kraft and George W. E. Nickelsburg; Atlanta: Scholars, 1986) 276. Schaller argues that the *Testament of Job* was written by a Hellenistic Jewish author from an indeterminate locale sometime between the beginning of the first century B.C.E. and mid-second century C.E. He rejects any theory of composite authorship.

36. Satan's role in these incidents is discussed in my *The Demise of the Devil: Magic and the Demonic in Luke's Writings* (Minneapolis: Fortress, 1989) chap. 3–5.

37. An association between the serpent and the devil is attested in literature from Paul's day and shortly thereafter: Wis 2:24; *Life of Adam and Eve (Apocalypse)* 16:1–5 (M. D. Johnson, "Intro-

himself [μετασχηματίζεσθαι] as an angel of light" (11:14) alludes to a related
story, according to which the devil led Eve astray a second time by disguising
himself in "the brightness of angels."[38] Paul invokes such satanic lore to imply
that his earthly opponents are in the devil's league: like the devil, they seek
to lead the Corinthians astray. Another passage insinuating that Paul's
opponents are satanic is 2 Cor 6:14–7:1. Here, as David Rensberger argues,
the term "unbelievers" (ἄπιστοι [6:14, 15]) should be interpreted in light of
Paul's usage in 4:4, where he is talking not about "unbelievers" in general but
specifically about his adversaries (see above). It is true that 2 Cor 6:14–7:1 is
often dismissed as a secondary interpolation, but Rensberger argues compel-
lingly that the passage was adapted to its present context by Paul himself, as a
negative exhortation to balance the positive one of 6:13 and 7:2. Rensberger
writes:

> No position which views 2 Cor 6:14–7:1 as an exhortation on relations with non-
> Christians or as an alien, non-Pauline piece of literature is able to explain its
> presence in its present context. For this and other reasons there seem to be
> good grounds for understanding the *apistoi* of 2 Cor 6:14 as having reference to
> Paul's opponents who have damaged his relations with the Corinthians. A
> meaning for the passage in its context is thus established. Paul is saying, "Open
> up, Corinthians! (v. 13) Not to 'unbelievers'—men of Beliar, not Christ, with
> whom you ought to have nothing to do (6:14–7:1)—but to us, who have done
> you no wrong (7:2)."[39]

The charge of alliance with Satan appears, then, to be central to Paul's
polemic against his Corinthian adversaries at the time of the composition of
2 Corinthians. Not only in 2 Cor 4:4 but also in several other passages, Paul
implies that he is able to detect the diabolical spirit behind human opponents.

   In the passages discussed above, Paul's use of satanic lore deflects accusations leveled at him back against his accusers. Peter Marshall has shown that
one of the major charges made by Paul's opponents was that the apostle was

---

duction to the *Life of Adam and Eve*," *Old Testament Pseudepigrapha* [2 vols.; ed. James H.
Charlesworth; Garden City, NY: Doubleday, 1983–85] 2. 252, dates the original composition
between 100 B.C.E. and 200 C.E., "more probably toward the end of the first Christian century").
Cf. Rev 12:9; 20:2; Rom 16:20 (possibly an allusion to Gen 3:15). These traditions are discussed in
Abraham J. Malherbe, "Through the Eye of the Needle: Simplicity or Singleness," *ResQ* 5 (1961)
125–28. Malherbe concludes (128) that "Paul's identification of the serpent with Satan is in keeping with a tradition existing at the time he wrote," but that the tradition of Eve's fall as sexual
seduction developed only after Paul. For different assessments of the latter point, see Dibelius,
Geisterwelt, 50–51 (his reference to 4 Macc 18:8 is especially suggestive); Dahl, "Der Erstgeborene Satans und der Vater des Teufels," *Apophoreta: Festschrift für Ernst Haenchen zum
sechsigsten Geburtstag* (ed. W. Eltester and F. H. Kettler; Berlin: Alfred Töpelmann, 1964) 72–74.
   38. *Life of Adam and Eve (Vita)* 9–10. In the parallel *Apoc. Mos.*, see 29:15–17 ("the form of an
angel") and 17:1–2. This second deception of Eve is said to have occurred while she was engaging
in penitence by standing in water up to her neck in the Tigris River. Cf. Barrett, *Second Epistle to
the Corinthians*, 286; Dahl, "Der Erstgeborene Satans," 72–74.
   39. Rensberger, "2 Corinthians 6:14–7:1," 40; see also Nils A. Dahl, "A Fragment and Its
Context: 2 Cor 6:14–7:1," *Studies in Paul* (Minneapolis: Augsburg, 1977) 62–69.

108 ESSAYS IN HONOR OF ABRAHAM J. MALHERBE

fickle: he changed his behavior or his mind to suit the audience or occasion.[40] This charge, associated with the stock character of the flatterer, was common in rhetorical invective and very damaging in a society that valued constancy of character. Dio Chrysostom elaborates on the nature of the flatterer (ὁ κόλαξ):

> But he who in very truth is manly and high-minded would never . . . sacrifice his own liberty and his freedom of speech for the sake of any dishonourable payment of either power or riches, nor would he envy those who change [μεταβάλλειν] their form and apparel for such rewards; on the contrary, he would think such persons to be comparable to those who change from human beings into snakes or other animals, not envying them, nor yet carping at them because of their wantonness, but rather bewailing and pitying them. . . . But as for himself, the man of whom I speak will strive to preserve his individuality in seemly fashion and with steadfastness. (*Or.* 77/78.37–38)[41]

In Marshall's estimation, charges that Paul vacillated were originally prompted by his refusal of a gift of money from the Corinthians, who likely knew that he accepted money from Macedonian Christians.[42] Alternately, Dale Martin argues that such charges can be traced to Paul's adoption of the leadership style of the "demagogue," who practices accommodation (read "vacillation") and social self-lowering in order to become like the many (οἱ πολλοί) whom he leads. The demagogue was often characterized as a flatterer by writers who disliked this model of leadership.[43] Whatever the impetus behind the original charges of inconstancy, there soon followed accusations of cunning, deceit, and more vacillation, especially with regard to Paul's travel plans (see 2 Cor 1:15–22). In 2 Corinthians, Paul turns the tables, accusing his adversaries of being allied with Satan—the acknowledged master of deceit and trickery (11:13–15). Similar rhetorical moves occur elsewhere: Paul is accused of "corrupting" (φθείρειν) or "taking advantage of" (πλεονεκτεῖν) the Corinthians (7:2; 12:17) and of being "cunning" (πανουργία [4:2]; πανοῦργος [12:16]). He insists that none of the charges is valid; moreover, he fears for the Corinthians, lest "as the serpent deceived Eve by his cunning" (ἐν τῇ πανουργίᾳ αὐτοῦ), the Corinthians' thoughts "will be corrupted [φθείρειν] from a sincere and pure devotion to Christ" (11:3; cf. 2:11). Thus, Paul deals back

---

40. Marshall, *Enmity in Corinth*, 251–57, 281–325, passim.

41. Translated by Crosby in LCL. In *Enmity in Corinth*, 70–90, Marshall delineates the ancient topos of the flatterer, quoting from numerous primary texts.

42. Marshall, *Enmity in Corinth*, 175–77, 251–57. Marshall thinks that 1 Cor 9:19–23 (Paul becomes "all things to all people") represents Paul's repetition of his critics' charge against him (308).

43. Dale B. Martin, *Slave of Christ, Slave of All: Paul's Metaphor of Slavery and 1 Corinthians 9* (diss., Yale University, 1988). According to Martin, 1 Cor 9:12–23 is Paul's own description of his leadership style. Martin argues that such a style would have been embarrassing—and unpleasantly challenging—to the elite in Corinth, who would have preferred that Paul adopt the more conventional benevolent patriarchal approach. (Martin's work will be published in revised form by Yale University Press.)

the hand and ups the ante. One sees in these instances how readily Paul could use strictly Jewish imagery (satanic lore) to interpret Hellenistic rhetoric (specifically, standard invective associated with the character of the flatterer).[44] He is able to move so easily between the two spheres of discourse because they intersect: the flatterer is known for cunning, deceitfulness, and protean changeability; so is Satan.

PAUL'S PORTRAYAL OF HIMSELF
AND HIS OPPONENTS

Paul's assertion in 2 Cor 4:4 that the god of this age has "blinded the minds" of unbelievers (ἐτύφλωσεν τὰ νοήματα) employs a motif that is common in satanic lore: Satan seeks to imprison humans in the darkness of the diabolical realm. Hence blindness and darkness are symbolic of Satan's dominion (2 Cor 6:14–15; Acts 13:4–12; 26:18; Luke 22:53; Eph 6:12; Col 1:13; T. Sim. 2:7; T. Levi 19:1; T. Judah 19:4; cf. John 12:40 [quoting Isa 6:10]). This motif of satanic darkness occurs in the Wisdom of Solomon and the Testament of Job, texts that offer parallels to aspects of 2 Cor 4:1–12. Each of these texts features an afflicted righteous figure who is opposed by persons linked with the devil. Further, the depiction of Job's confrontation with the devil in the Testament of Job exhibits considerable Stoic influence: Job, the paradigm of ὑπομονή, is "like an athlete who spars and endures hard labors and wins the crown" (4:8). A consideration of these two documents will illuminate Paul's self-portrayal vis-à-vis his opponents in 2 Cor 4:1–12.[45]

Wis 1:12–3:10 and 4:16–5:16

Borrowing a plot line found in many of the Psalms, the author of Wisdom tells the story of the testing of a righteous person by ones who "belong to the devil's party" (2:24).[46] They mock his trust in God, and—like Satan in the Job

---

44. A similar blending of traditions may be attested in Rom 16:17–20. According to Marshall, Enmity in Corinth, 311–12, Paul is here drawing on the topos of the philosopher-flatterer (see esp. v. 18b). But the term σκάνδαλα (stumbling blocks) in v. 17 and the hope expressed in v. 20 clearly associate the evil wrought by such troublemakers with the figure of Satan.

45. Kleinknecht, Der leidende Gerechtfertigte, 104–10; 133–36, briefly discusses the Testament of Job and the relevant passages of Wisdom as late examples of the tradition of "the suffering righteous one." Kleinknecht's overall thesis is that the figure of "der leidende Gerechte" has substantially influenced Paul's understanding of his apostolate. But Kleinknecht does not see the importance of Wisdom and the Testament of Job specifically. The contrast between divinely revealed knowledge and human ignorance, the association of wicked opponents with the devil, and (in the Testament of Job) the influence of Stoic traditions all make these documents especially salient for the study of 2 Corinthians.

46. In Greek, the full verse runs as follows: Φθόνῳ δὲ διαβόλου θάνατος εἰσῆλθεν εἰς τὸν κόσμον· πειράζουσι δὲ αὐτὸν οἱ τῆς ἐκείνου μερίδος ὄντες. The translators of the RSV have inferred that the antecedent of αὐτόν is θάνατος, whereas that of ἐκείνου is διαβόλου. Thus, the translators render Wis 2:24b as follows: "and those who belong to his party experience it" (italics added). But this requires a highly unusual meaning for πειράζειν. It seems more likely that the antecedent of αὐτὸν is τὸν ἄνθρωπον in 2:23a. Thus, one reads, "God created τὸν ἄνθρωπον for incorruption, and made him [αὐτόν] the image of God's own eternity; But through the devil's

account—they examine him with torture that they may "know his meekness and prove his patience" (γνῶναι τὴν ἐπιείκειαν αὐτοῦ καὶ δοκιμάσαι τὴν ἀνεξικακίαν αὐτοῦ [2:19]). They are convinced that the righteous die a miserable death. However, such wicked persons do not know the mysteries of God, "for their own wickedness blinded them" (ἀπετύφλωσε γὰρ αὐτοὺς ἡ κακία αὐτῶν [2:21–22]). The author explains this opposition between the wicked and the righteous by referring to the corresponding dualism of death versus immortality (1:13–16; 2:23–24). God did not create death and takes no pleasure in the destruction (ἀπωλεία) of the living. On the contrary: God created humans to be immortal (2:23) and to be in God's eternal image (εἰκών). But godless humans "called Death to them," "regarded it as their friend," and "made a covenant with it" (1:14–16; cf. Isa 28:15).[47] Or, as the author explains in a parallel passage (2:24), through the envy of the devil, death entered the world.

The reference to death's origin as due to the devil's "envy" (φθόνος [Wis 2:24]) cannot be explained on the basis of the OT alone, even if one assumes identification between Satan and the serpent in the garden: the Genesis account gives no hint that the serpent was "envious" of Adam. The clue to interpretation is in the preceding verse (Wis 2:23): God created humans to be in God's own "image" (εἰκών). Together the verses allude to a legend known to us from the *Life of Adam and Eve (Vita)* 11—16 (cf. 39:1–3). According to this legend, after their expulsion from the Garden (and hence from immortality), Adam and Eve ask Satan why he "enviously" pursues them "with deceit" (11:2–3). Satan tells them that when Adam was created in the image of God, Michael had commanded all the angels to worship the first man. However, Satan had replied that he would not worship one inferior and subsequent to him. Consequently, Satan and his angels were cast from their glory: "And immediately we were made to grieve, since we had been deprived of so great glory. And we were pained to see you in such bliss of delights. So with deceit I assailed your wife and made you to be expelled through her from the joys of your bliss, as I have been expelled from my glory" (*Life of Adam and Eve [Vita]* 16:2–3). The "envy of the devil" mentioned in Wis 2:24 was envy, it would seem, of Adam's likeness to immortal God (and of Adam's consequent privileges).

In 2 Cor 4:3–4, Paul claims that the god of this age has kept the perishing from seeing the light of the good news of the glory of Christ—Christ, "who is the image [εἰκών] of God" (4:4; cf. 4:6). Perhaps Paul, like the author of Wisdom, has in mind the story of Satan's jealousy over the creation of Adam/Christ in God's image. Hence Satan conceals the good news, knowing

---

envy, death entered the world, and those who belong to the party of that one [ἐκείνου = the devil] tempt/test him [τὸν ἄνθρωπον]" (italics added). This reading coheres better with 2:17, where the impious (οἱ ἀσεβεῖς [1:16]) resolve to test (πειράσαι) the righteous one.

47. The imagery used in the passage suggests that "Death" is here a personification. Cf. Dibelius, *Geisterwelt*, 116.

that those who behold the Lord's glory will themselves be changed into the Lord's image (3:18; cf. Rom 8:29; 1 Cor 15:49; Col 1:15). Paul's contrast between the "knowledge" of the saved (see esp. 2 Cor 4:6) and the "blindness" of the perishing (4:4) looks very much like the contrast in Wis 2:21–22 between those who know the "mysteries of God" and those who are "blinded" by their own wickedness. In Wisdom, the "blind" are those who oppose the righteous one; in 2 Corinthians, Paul implies that the "blind" are none other than his own adversaries, who perceive Paul as weak and dying. By casting himself into the role of the afflicted righteous one, opposed by members of the devil's party, Paul interprets his own situation vis-à-vis his opponents. Their very opposition becomes, paradoxically, Paul's vindication. They think him mad (Wis 5:4; cf. 2 Cor 5:13),[48] ridiculing his confident hope. Such ridicule points to their destruction, but to Paul's salvation—because Paul exhibits ὑπο-μονή, trusting and not "testing" God (cf. Wis 1:2; Phil 1:28).

Testament of Job

The blend of Stoicism and apocalypticism in the *Testament of Job* makes the document illuminating for the study of Paul, whose discourse was shaped by both traditions. On the one hand, the account's heavy stress on Job's patient endurance (ὑπομονή), its depiction of his unruffled calm in the face of horrendous suffering,[49] and its use of wrestling and battle metaphors to depict the struggle with hardship (4:8; 27:2, 5–8) all point to Stoic influence. On the other hand, the document's identification of Satan as the immediate cause of suffering, its portrayal of Job as recipient of knowledge from a divine messenger (3:1–4:9), and its anticipation of reward and resurrection at the consummation of the age (4:6–8) reflect the impact of Jewish-apocalyptic strains of thought.[50] The document is interesting for another reason: particularly in the latter half (the depiction of Job and his so-called friends), it bears striking resemblance to the account of the afflicted righteous one in Wisdom of Solomon.[51] The resemblance extends even to the contrast between the sufferer's knowledge of immortality and the ignorance of the wicked, who think that the sufferer is "mad" (*T. Job* 35:5–38:11; Wis 2:22; 4:4; cf. 2 Cor 5:13).

---

48. See note 54 below.

49. In the *Testament of Job*, Job is said to feel physical and emotional pain, but not with the intensity portrayed in the canonical Book of Job. Especially indicative of Stoic influence is *T. Job* 21:2–4: Job laments the humiliation experienced by his wife and then reports, "After these things I resumed my rational composure" (λογισμὸς ⟨μακρόθυμος⟩).

50. According to Collins, in the *Testament of Job*, "apocalyptic elements are placed in the service of a personal mysticism" ("Structure and Meaning," 50). In the document, the temporal dualism of the first chapters later gives way to a spatial one: the transient world below is contrasted with the eternal and unchanging heavenly realities (cf. 2 Cor 4:16–18).

51. Cf. Collins, "Structure and Meaning," 51, n. 51, citing a private communication from George Nicklesburg. Collins suggests that the specificity of some of the parallels between the two documents "strongly suggests that TJ was influenced by Wisd." On a possible relationship between canonical Job and the Psalms of lament, see Kleinknecht, *Der leidende Gerechtfertigte*, 68.

The *Testament of Job* tells the story of Job (alias Jobab), "who exhibits complete endurance" (1:3: ὁ ἐν πάσῃ ὑπομονῇ γενόμενος). The document appears to be dependent on the LXX text but expands greatly on the account, especially the material found in the prologue. The changes drastically alter the dynamics of the story. Satan is given a motive for his attack on Job: the latter had destroyed an idol's temple, "the place of Satan in which humans are deceived" (3:5: ἐν ᾧ ἀπατηθήσονται οἱ ἄνθρωποι). Job had carried out this act knowing full well that it would bring Satan's wrath upon him—but knowing also that if he endured the resulting satanic onslaught, he would be rewarded both in this life and at the consummation of the age, when he would be raised up in the resurrection (4:6–8). Hence, although the accounts of physical devastation wrought by the devil have been greatly exaggerated, the pathos of the story has diminished: Job is no longer the just one who cries out for an explanation of his undeserved suffering. Instead, he is preeminently Job *the patient one,* locked in an athletic contest with Satan the deceiver. Satan abuses Job relentlessly, seeking to make him utter blasphemy against God. The rationale seems to be that if Job blasphemes, he will relinquish authority over his soul to the devil (thus far God had given to Satan authority only over Job's body; 20:1–3). Satan even drags Job's wife, Sitis, into the fray: at the inspiration of Satan, she encourages Job to "say some word against the Lord and die" (cf. Job 2:9). Job replies to Sitis:

> Behold, I have existed for seventeen years with diseases, submitting to the worms in my body, and have not been as depressed in my soul by <the> pains as by the word you spoke: Say some word against the Lord and die. . . . Would you have it that by our speaking something against the Lord we become alienated from the great treasure? . . . But let us be patient [μακροθυμήσωμεν] in everything until the Lord in compassion shows us mercy. Do you not see the devil standing behind you and troubling your reasoning so that he might deceive [ἀπατῆσαι] even me?" (*T. Job* 26:1–7)

If Satan had succeeded in getting Job to blaspheme, then Job would be found guilty at the judgment and would forfeit his heavenly reward.[52] But Job continues to endure until Satan finally concedes defeat: "So you, Job, were underneath and diseased, but you overcame (ἐνίκησας) my wrestling holds which I applied to you" (27:8). It is then reported that Satan, ashamed, departed "for three years."

After the departure (*T. Job* 27:9), Satan makes no more bodily appearances to Job. The devil's influence has not dissipated, however; Satan continues to work through the "friends" of Job, who now enter the stage. These persons are stunned by Job's fall from prestige and power, and offended by the stench (δυσωδία) of his worm-infested body.[53] Job explains to them that he is given

---

52. See note 32 above.
53. The author is not given to understatement. Frequent reference is made to how bad Job smelled; see, for example, *T. Job* 31:2: "But since they [the kings] were about a half-stadion distant from me because of the stench of my body, they arose and approached me holding fragrant sub-

SUSAN R. GARRETT

113

strength by his confidence of heavenly reward:

My throne is eternal —
the whole world shall pass away and its splendor shall <fade> [ἡ δόξα αὐτοῦ
φθαρήσεται],
and those who cling to it shall be (caught) in its demise.
But my throne is in the holy land
and its splendor is in the unchangeable world. (33:4–5; cf. 2 Cor 4:16–18)

Such proclamations by Job cause his friends to think him mad. As Eliphas
says, "This one sits in the humiliation of worms and in a stench and at the critical moment arouses himself against us: Kingdoms are passing away, as are
their rulers, he says, but mine shall be forever!" (*T. Job* 34:4). They interro-
gate him for some time, trying to determine whether or not he is out of his
mind (35:5: μήτι ἄρα ἐξέστη αὐτοῦ ἡ καρδία; see all of 35:5–38:11). There is
irony here. Job has, in truth, experienced "ecstatic" visions of heavenly treasure (see, for example, 36:5: ἐν δὲ τοῖς ἐπουρανίοις συνέστηκεν ἡ καρδία μου),
but he is not mad.[54] The interchanges among Job and his friends display the
contrast (1) between the transience of the world and the permanence of
heavenly realities, and (2) between the ignorance and knowledge of persons
focused on each of these respective realms.[55]

The fourth friend, Elious (Elihu), is the most vehement in his attack. He
condemns Job for "boasting" (καυχᾶσθαι) that he is righteous and for speaking "grandiosely" (ὑπερβαλλόντως) about a heavenly throne (*T. Job* 41:1–6).
Later, when Job is restored, the first three friends are forgiven by God, but

---

stances in their hands, while their soldiers accompanied them and fumigated the area around me
with incense, so that they would be able to approach me. And after they spent three days supplying the incense. . . ."
54. Expressions describing Job's apparent madness are ἐξέστη αὐτοῦ ἡ καρδία and μαίνεσθαι
κατὰ ψυχήν. Expressions denoting mental health are ἐν τῷ καθεστῶτι ὑπάρχειν/εἶναι and ἔστιν
σοι φρόνησις. Apropos of 2 Cor 5:13, Marshall, *Enmity in Corinth*, 190–94, 328–33, traces the
usage in Greek literature of the opposing notions of ἐκστῆναι (or its synonym, μαίνεσθαι, "to be
irrational, frenzied, mad") and σωφρονεῖν, "to be in one's senses, practice self-control or moderation.") He points out, for example, that in Xenophon *Mem.* 1.1.16; 3.9.4–6, μανία ("madness, irrational conduct") refers to self-ignorance or self-delusion: "It is the ignorance of those who think
they are richer, possess better physical qualities, and are wiser than they are" (Marshall, *Enmity in
Corinth,* 330; Marshall points also to the discussion of self-delusion in Plato *Phlb.* 48B–49E).
Marshall then infers that in 2 Cor 5:13, Paul "appears to be responding to invective. He must
have been accused of assuming a position at Corinth for which he hadn't the appropriate qualities,
of claiming too much for himself, of not knowing his limitations" (331). Thus far Marshall's
analysis is persuasive. Less convincing is his subsequent contention (331–33) that the charges
were related specifically to Paul's uncontrolled style of speech—a style lacking in σωφροσύνη (an
all-purpose word that also served as a rhetorical technical term). It is not necessary to posit a
technical rhetorical referent for 2 Cor 5:13; the parallels from Wis 5:4 and the *Testament of Job*
suggest that the issue at stake was Paul's boasting of "knowledge" and "strength" in the midst of
apparent weakness and degradation. In 2 Cor 5:13, Paul implies that his boasts of knowledge of
"things unseen" (4:18) and his confidence despite his suffering may be taken for madness or delu-
sion. Thus, he strengthens his self-portrayal as the suffering one whom the people of this age
cannot comprehend.
55. Collins, "Structure and Meaning," 45.

Elious is declared to be "filled with Satan" (41:7).[56] The Lord reveals to Job that "the one who spoke in him [Elious] was not man but beast" (42:1). One of the first three friends laments the destruction of Elious in a hymn:

Our sin was cancelled and our lawlessness removed;
    Elious, the only wicked one, will have no memorial among the living.
And his lamp, extinguished, obliterated its light;
    and the splendor of his lantern will end in judgment against him.
For this one is <the one> of darkness and not of light,
    and the doorkeepers of darkness shall inherit his splendor and majesty.
(43:2–4; cf. Job 18:5–20 LXX)

This condemnation suggests retrospectively that Elious's "arrogant words" represented Satan's continued assault on Job.

In the *Testament of Job*, Satan's motive for attacking Job is a desire to avenge the diminution of his realm caused by Job's abolition of the idol's temple. Satan seeks to make Job blaspheme and thereby relinquish his heavenly reward. Paul's work, like Job's, serves to diminish Satan's realm: Paul "lifts the veil," so that persons may see "the light of the good news of the glory of Christ" (2 Cor 4:4). This is something that the god of this age does not want Paul to do: Satan's designs are to defraud the church of its members by keeping them in darkness. As one who, on God's behalf, proclaims that "out of darkness light shall shine" (2 Cor 4:6), *Paul puts himself in direct opposition to the god of this age.*[57]

The foregoing review of the *Testament of Job* and of relevant passages of the Wisdom of Solomon throws into sharp relief the pattern of Paul's polemic in 2 Cor 4:1–12 (and, indeed, in all of chapters 3–5). Paul contrasts his opponents' ignorance with his own divinely revealed knowledge: knowledge of Christ, the image of God, and also knowledge that his own "slight momentary affliction" is preparing for him "an eternal weight of glory beyond all comparison" (4:17). Paul's opponents ridicule his apparent weakness and smell the stench of death upon him, but their minds have been hardened, veiled, blinded. They are prisoners of the god of this age, who strives to keep them in the darkness of this perishing world by allowing them to see only that which is visible and transient. Hence they do not perceive Paul's true situation. They are not, however, merely the devil's passive victims. By their opposition to Paul, they serve Satan's aims. The Corinthians are therefore enjoined to recognize that the choice between Paul's opponents and Paul himself is nothing less than a choice between ignorance and knowledge, destruction and salvation, darkness and light, Beliar and Christ (cf. 6:14–7:1).

56. The impulse behind this singling out of Elious (Elihu) is to be found in the canonical Job account. In 42:9 it is reported that the Lord pardoned Eliphaz, Baldad, and Sophar for the sake of Job, but no mention is made of Elihu (the Elihu speeches having been interpolated into the document at a later stage of composition, according to scholarly consensus). The reference in *T Job* 41:7 to Elious's being "filled with Satan" picks up on Job 32:17–20: Elihu's report that "I am filled with words, for the spirit of my belly destroys me" (v. 18, LXX).

57. Cf. Kleinknecht, *Der leidende Gerechtfertigte,* 378–79. Cf. also *Joseph and Aseneth* 12:9–11.

The examination of the *Testament of Job* has shown the ease with which Hellenistic philosophical and Jewish apocalyptic notions of the endurance of affliction could be joined. The author uses each tradition to interpret the other, aided by their numerous points of overlap. Job the sufferer is like an athlete competing in the cosmic ἀγών; his adversary is not Fortune but Satan. Like the Stoic sage, Job exhibits perfect endurance (ὑπομονή). He is enabled to "conquer" his opponent, not only by his reasoning power (λογισμός; 21:4) but also by the divinely revealed knowledge of an eternal treasure. We should not be surprised to see Paul making analogous interpretive moves in his discussions of the endurance of affliction.

THE SOURCE OF PAUL'S AFFLICTIONS

Who or what did Paul understand to be the cause of his afflictions? Fitzgerald hypothesizes that like many Stoics, Paul regarded the hardships in which he so often found himself as a divine testing of him. Of course, the notion of divine testing is by no means limited to pagan popular philosophy. It occurs frequently in the OT and in Jewish writings roughly contemporaneous with Paul, including the Wisdom of Solomon. Among pagan and Jewish writers alike, there are varying opinions regarding the *specific* divine agent thought to be at work. Some philosophers posit Tyche or Fortuna as the cause of hardships, whereas others (such as Epictetus) refer to Zeus.[58] Jews could refer either to Satan or to God as provocation behind the afflictions that tested their fidelity. Indeed, the same writer could attribute hardships to Satan in one place and to God in virtually the next sentence.[59] Such seeming inconsistency points to writers' supposition that although Satan is the prince of this world and works to impede God's salvation of it, nonetheless, all of Satan's authority derives ultimately from God. Hence either Satan or God could be named as the source of affliction, depending on rhetorical needs or other contingencies.

Paul may have been quite willing to characterize his hardships as Satan's assaults on him. Several passages commend the hypothesis, including the statement in 1 Thess 2:18 that Satan "hindered" Paul from going to the Thessalonians at the very time when they ran the greatest danger of succumbing to Satan's tests. In other words, Paul assumes that Satan would oppose him in a

---

58. Fitzgerald, *Cracks in an Earthen Vessel*, 70–87, provides a nuanced discussion of the moralists' views of agency in hardships, distinguishing insofar as possible among the opinions of the various schools. He discusses Paul's view of agency on pp. 197–98 and 204.

59. Some Jewish writers (for example, the authors of the *Psalms of Solomon* and the author of 4 Maccabees) seldom or never mention the devil in their discussions of suffering, whereas others (for example, the author of Revelation) hold the devil responsible for virtually all affliction of the righteous. However, not all Jews regarded the options as mutually exclusive. In keeping with the book of Job (1:6–12; 2:1–6), Satan was often thought to work in cooperation with God on the matter of testing through affliction. See esp. *Jub.* 17:16–18; note also that in Wis 2:17–19, 24, wicked persons who "belong to the devil's party" assail the righteous person to "test" him, but only a few verses later (3:5–6), "testing" is attributed to God. Similarly, in *T. Job* 37:4, Job reports that it is "God" who has inflicted these maladies upon him.

direct and personal way in order to disrupt Paul's efforts to secure the salvation of believers. A second revealing passage is 2 Cor 12:7–10. Here Paul labels a "thorn in the flesh" (whatever its precise nature)[60] as an "angel of Satan" and moreover, connects his endurance of this particular affliction with his endurance of hardships more broadly construed (v. 10). A third passage suggesting that Paul held satanic forces responsible for afflictions is Rom 8:35–39, where Paul links earthly distress (v. 35) with the work of principalities and powers that would separate believers from God's love. A fourth relevant passage is 2 Cor 4:11, in which Paul writes that "we are always being given up to death" (εἰς θάνατον παραδιδόμεθα) for Jesus' sake."[61] The word παραδιδόναι designates the act of delivering someone or something over to another authority.[62] For example, in Rom 1:24–28, Paul describes God's "giving up" of wicked persons to impurity (εἰς ἀκαθαρσίαν), to dishonorable passions (εἰς πάθη ἀτιμίας), and to a base mind (εἰς ἀδόκιμον νοῦν); these forces in turn exercise control over such persons. In 1 Cor 15:24, παραδιδόναι designates Christ's final act of turning the kingdom over to God. And in 1 Cor 5:5, παραδιδόναι refers to the communal act of turning a sinner over to the authority of Satan, who is expected to bring total destruction (ὄλεθρος) upon him. In 2 Cor 4:11 also, the word designates God's act of giving Paul over to another authority: the authority of Death. Death, in turn, "does its work" (νέκρωσις; ἐνεργεῖται) on Paul (4:10, 12). Here, as in Wis 1:14–16, "Death" is personified; the one who presently holds "the power of death" is not far from view.[63]

For Paul, however—as for the afflicted righteous one in the Wisdom of Solomon, and for Job in the *Testament of Job*—it is only the unenlightened, those whose minds have been blinded, who suppose that Death will have the final say. Such godless persons see only Paul's outer, mortal self, which due to

60. "Pathological" interpretations of the passage (sometimes referring also to Gal 4:13–14 or 6:11) have, in general, been popular. For example, Dibelius, *Geisterwelt*, 45–47, argued that Paul is referring to the condition of epilepsy. Michael Barré, "Qumran and the 'Weakness' of Paul," *CBQ* 42 (1980) 216–27, strengthens the case (made by others) for interpreting Paul's "thorn in the flesh" as a human adversary (or adversaries). Jerry W. McCant, "Paul's Thorn of Rejected Apostleship," *NTS* 34 (1988) 550–72, argues that the thorn in the flesh "was the Corinthian Church's rejection of the legitimacy of Paul's apostolate" (572). McCant (550) cites Adolf Deissmann's observation that "a small library could be gathered together all dealing with Paul's illness."

61. Fitzgerald, *Cracks in an Earthen Vessel*, 180, argues that the voice of the verb is middle: Paul *gives himself up* to death, as Jesus gave himself (cf. Rom 4:25; Gal 2:20). It seems more likely, however, that it is passive, on analogy with Paul's earlier claim that "God always leads us in triumph" (2 Cor 2:14)—that is, in a triumphal procession that culminates in the prisoner's death. Paul allows God to give him over to the authority of Death.

62. In the LXX, the word occurs very frequently, most often referring to God's action of giving persons over into their enemies' hands (see, for example, Deut 7:2, 23; Josh 2:24; Judg 13:1; Pss 26[27]:12; 87[88]:8; 117[118]:18 ["The Lord has disciplined me, but has not given me up to death"]). See also note 8 above.

63. Cf. Kleinknecht, *Der leidende Gerechtfertigte*, 273. For an argument against the scholarly trend of insisting that Paul has already begun to demythologize the terminology for cosmic powers (for example, in works by Rudolf Bultmann, J. Christiaan Beker, and Walter Wink), see Clinton E. Arnold, *Ephesians: Power and Magic* (SNTSMS 63; Cambridge: Cambridge University Press, 1989) 129–32.

Death's present lordship is wasting away (2 Cor 4:16). Those who have been
blinded do not know what Christ's resurrection proved: that the one who is
given over to Satan or to Death is not defeated unless that one gives up faith.
Paul is in Death's hands, but by his endurance he exhibits Death's incapacity to
do anything more than harm his outer self.[64] Not only does the torture of Paul's
body fail to further the aims of the god of this age; more than that, Paul's ὑπομονή is helping to achieve victory in the cosmic ἀγών (cf. 1 Thess 2:2; 5:8; Rom
6:13; 8:37; 13:12; Phil 1:28–30; 2 Cor 6:7; 10:3–6; cf. Eph 6:11–12). By his
confident expectation that Death will give way before the life of Jesus (2 Cor
4:11–14; cf. 1:9–10), Paul exhibits the present impotence of the powers that
rule this age and that—like the age itself—are hastening to an end.

The influence of Hellenistic popular philosophy on Paul's portrayal of his
endurance can no longer be disputed. As Malherbe and his students have
shown, this influence extends considerably beyond a superficial borrowing of
vocabulary: Paul's literary use of the portrait of the afflicted sage shows a deep
familiarity with, and sympathy for, its functions in the works of popular philosophers. In 2 Corinthians, Paul deftly employs the motif to persuade his readers
that they ought to be proud of him, inasmuch as he—like the sages of popular
philosophy—has withstood tremendous suffering in order to advance a greater
cause.

But Paul's portrayal of his endurance also has a Jewish apocalyptic aspect.
In 2 Corinthians, Paul casts himself in the role of one opposed by the devil's
allies, who ridicule his seemingly irrational confidence in the midst of affliction.
Thus, Paul "discerns the spirit" by identifying the authority behind his human
opponents. They belong to the dominion of the god of this age, who has
blinded their minds. As prisoners of this age, they are perishing. Paul, by contrast, though he has been given over to the authority that rules this age, is
confident that on account of his endurance, God will rescue him from Death's
dominion. His confidence is a sign of his salvation, but of his opponents' destruction. Once Paul has identified his opponents with the perishing and with
the god of this age, then the ἀγών in which he is engaged begins to emerge as
more than the struggle of an individual's reason over against the passions (cf.
4 Macc 1:1). It is now seen to be the warfare of darkness against light. Paul is
not just the *sophos* whose endurance commends him, but the warrior against
the rulers of this present evil age. He battles "with the weapons of righteousness for the right hand and for the left" (2 Cor 6:7). Death tries to make Paul
stumble and fall, but in ὑπομονή he stands ever faithful.

---

64. Cf. *Mart. Isa.* 5:8–10: As Isaiah is being sawed in half, he spurns his executor's offer to cease
if he but say that he had lied: "If it is within my power to say, 'Condemned and cursed be you, and
all your hosts, and all your house!' For there is nothing further that you can take except the skin of
my body" (trans. M. A. Knibb, in Charlesworth, *Old Testament Pseudepigrapha*, 2. 164).

ACTS 17, EPICUREANS, AND THEODICY

A Study in Stereotypes

The New Testament documents were written in a milieu permeated with the ideas and slogans of Greek thinkers, whether Stoics, Cynics, or Epicureans. As the followers of Jesus moved steadily into the Greco-Roman world, they inevitably came in contact with these groups and their ideas in a variety of ways. Christians either found points of agreement with them, imitated them in terms of style and form, or engaged them in controversy. Considerable work has been done on the Stoic background of Romans 1–2 and Acts 17.[1] Furthermore, much attention has been given by Abraham J. Malherbe and several of his students to the Cynics,[2] their preaching style, and their modes of argument.[3]

Few scholars have paid much attention to the Epicureans, perhaps because their name occurs but once in the collection of NT writings, namely, Acts 17:18.[4] Malherbe himself is unusual for his interest in the Epicureans vis-à-vis the NT.[5] In spite of the single reference to them in the Areopagus speech, Malherbe has paid attention not simply to the label "Epicurean" but also to the ideas and slogans attributed to them, against which Paul, at least, seems to have reacted.

Despite lack of attention from modern scholars, the Epicureans were well

---

1. See, for example, Max Pohlenz, "Paulus und die Stoa," ZNW 42 (1949) 69–104.

2. Abraham J. Malherbe, The Cynic Epistles (SBLSBS 12; Missoula, MT: Scholars, 1977); Benjamin Fiore, The Function of Personal Example in the Socratic and Pastoral Epistles (AB 105; Rome: Biblical Institute Press, 1986).

3. For example, the Cynic diatribal style was examined by Stanley K. Stowers, The Diatribe and Paul's Letter to the Romans (SBLDS 57; Chico, CA: Scholars, 1981).

4. When the Epicureans are discussed, it is generally without any precise sense of their presence in Acts 17. See, for example, Richard B. Rackham, The Acts of the Apostles (Grand Rapids, MI: Baker Book House, 1964) 303–5; but even here, Rackham lists miscellaneous ideas attributed to the Epicureans, without indicating which Epicurean idea was operative in this particular context.

5. Abraham J. Malherbe: "The Beasts at Ephesus," JBL 87 (1968) 71–80; "Self-Definition among Epicureans and Cynics," Jewish and Christian Self-Definition (Philadelphia: Fortress, 1982) 3. 46–48; "'Not in a Corner': Early Christian Apologetic in Acts 26:26," SecCent 5 (1985–86) 196, 204–6; Paul and the Thessalonians: The Philosophic Tradition of Pastoral Care (Philadelphia: Fortress, 1987) 40–43, 101–6.

known in the Hellenistic world that cradled the NT, and known because of a variety of opinions credited to them.[6] This chapter deals with the Epicureans in the Areopagus speech in Acts 17, especially in terms of Christian preaching on theodicy as this met with Epicurean denials of the same. By theodicy I mean the argument that God's providential relationship to the world entails a just judgment of mortals, especially a judgment that takes place after death, where rewards and punishments are allotted.

Paul's speech in Athens is the clearest place in the NT where Christian theodicy is explained to Epicureans and their reaction to it recorded. Whether Acts 17 records an actual address by Paul to these very people or a creation of the author, Luke sees Christian doctrine's being compared and contrasted with an alternate doctrine, Epicureanism. It is the hypothesis of this chapter that Christian preaching about theodicy seems regularly to have come in conflict with denials of it—denials that are typically, and even specifically, characteristic of Epicureans.

LUKAN REDACTIONAL FOCUS

Before we examine Luke's narrative about the Epicureans and their reaction to Christian theodicy, we must clarify some perceptions of the Areopagus speech. The initial questions are not immediately those of cultural or intellectual background, but issues of Lukan redaction and focus. As regards the content of the Areopagus speech, Luke describes Paul's presenting in Hellenistic modes of thought "new teaching" (Acts 17:19) to Greeks at Athens, comparable to the way Paul heralded the Christian gospel in a Jewish mode of expression in the cultural contexts of synagogues. The subject matter in Acts 17, moreover, is situation specific; it is unlike that of Paul's speech to the synagogue in Antioch, which operated on a prophecy-fulfillment motif that was suited to a Jewish audience where questions of genuine leadership (Jesus) over the authentic covenant (via Abraham and David) were central, and could be argued by recourse to the Hebrew Scriptures. Acts 17 talks in a Greek mode to Greeks to make a point more relevant to the Hellenistic situation Luke perceives.

Different, too, is the modest place Jesus plays in the Areopagus speech. No mention is made of his signs and wonders, which would signal his role as a prophet attested by God (Acts 2:22). In fact, scant mention is made of Jesus' crucifixion and death, beyond the simple note about God's raising him from

---

6. Epicureans were positively known for their fellowship (Malherbe, *Paul and the Thessalonians*, 40–43; and Bernard Frischer, *The Sculpted Word* [Berkeley: University of California Press, 1982] 46–66) and for their communal meals (Dennis Smith, *Social Obligation in the Context of Communal Meals* [diss., Harvard University, 1980] 56–68). They were negatively criticized for beliefs such as "eat, drink, and be merry" (Malherbe, "Beasts at Ephesus," 75–77); and "atheism," the denial of belief in a providential god (Jerome H. Neyrey, "The Form and Background of the Polemic in 2 Peter," *JBL* 99 [1980] 409–12), about which this study is concerned.

the dead (17:31). Absent here is the pattern "you rejected/killed him, but God raised him,"[7] which functioned in other contexts to urge the hearers to "change their minds" and correct their judgments about Jesus.[8]

The God of the Scriptures, who is the Christian God, is the focus of Paul's speech,[9] in itself not an unusual focus in Paul's authentic preaching (see 1 Thess 1:9; 1 Cor 8:4–6).[10] The literary occasion of the Areopagus speech is Paul's "provocation" at seeing a city "full of idols" (Acts 17:16), which suggests that the speech will have a polemical cast to it concerning the true God. And the specific audience contains two contrasting schools of Greek thinkers about God, Stoics and Epicureans (17:18). In one sense, critical readers of Acts 17 are well aware that by and large, Paul's speech reflects Stoic ideas about God, but up to a point. What sets Paul's presentation of the Christian God apart from well-known Greek understandings of god is the very issue of Christian theodicy, the role of Jesus as Judge who will judge all peoples after death to render reward and punishment (17:30–31). However, the issue from start to finish is God and God's providential action in the world, which includes theodicy.

OLD CONCLUSIONS AND
NEW HYPOTHESES

Previous examinations of Paul's speech on the Areopagus have yielded a number of important observations and conclusions. For example, we readily recognize that the doctrine of God or natural theology in the speech is common theology,[11] common to Stoics, as well as to Jews and Christians.[12] Second, the critical remarks about the foolishness of idols (Acts 17:29) and the vanity of temples (17:24–25) reflect stock-in-trade Jewish polemic against paganism.[13] Third, some commentators, reminded of Paul's critical remarks about preaching Christ in terms of "worldly wisdom" in 1 Cor 1:17 and 2:1–5, see Paul trying just such a foolish move in Acts 17 and deservedly failing.[14]

7. See C. H. Dodd, *The Apostolic Preaching and Its Development* (London: Hodder and Stoughton, 1936); and Jacques Dupont, "Les discours missionaires des Actes des Apôtres," *RB* 69 (1962) 37–60.

8. See Jerome H. Neyrey, *The Passion According to Luke* (New York: Paulist, 1985) 89–107.

9. See Martin Dibelius, *Studies in the Acts of the Apostles* (New York: Scribner's, 1956) 26–77; Eduard Schweizer, "Concerning the Speeches in Acts," *Studies in Luke-Acts* (ed. L. E. Keck and J. L. Martyn; London: SPCK, 1966) 212–14; and L. Legrand, "The Areopagus Speech: Its theological Kerygma and Its Missionary Significance," *La notion biblique du Dieu* (ed. J. Coppens; BETL 41; Leuven, Belgium: Gembloux, 1976) 337–50.

10. See Charles H. Giblin, "Three Monotheistic Texts in Paul," *CBQ* 38 (1975) 527–47.

11. See, for example, H. P. Owen, "The Scope of Natural Revelation in Rom I and Acts XVII," *NTS* 5 (1958–59) 133–43.

12. See especially Bertil Gärtner, *The Areopagus Speech and Natural Revelation* (Uppsala: C. W. K. Gleerup, 1955) 73–143.

13. Gärtner, *Areopagus Speech,* 203–28; but it should be noted that a polemic against idols and even temples as fit places for gods is conducted also in Greek philosophy. See Hans Conzelmann, "The Address of Paul on the Areopagus," in Keck and Martin, *Studies in Luke-Acts,* 221.

14. See Legrand, "The Areopagus Speech," 338–41; and Jacques Dupont, "Le discours à

But this last remark is clearly misguided, as the following discussion will show. However one reads Paul's own apologetic remarks in 1 Cor 2:1–5,[15] Luke does not consider it wrong to speak of Christian doctrine in ways that would indicate compatibility and agreement with right-thinking people elsewhere.

As valid and valuable as these insights are, they do not adequately satisfy the Lukan logic and purpose of the Areopagus speech. I suggest the following hypotheses that refine and sharpen the above-mentioned consensus:

1. Luke's theology in Acts 17 is his clearest instance in Acts of the Apostles of his regular presentation of God in terms of providence, which was not just a Stoic idea but a general, traditional understanding of God.

2. In addition to the presentation of God's providence, Luke emphasizes a distinctively Christian view of theodicy in Acts 17:30–31. This is the forensic issue with which the hearers must grapple, the "question for judgment."[16]

3. Epicureans were popularly known in terms of stereotypes, in particular their atheism, their denial of providence, and their rejection of theodicy. Luke understands the Epicureans in Acts 17 precisely in terms of a stereotype, namely, their denial of theodicy.

4. The speech, which is a set piece of traditional theology, is delivered to contrasting groups of noted theologians, Epicureans and Stoics. Their contrasting reactions are both predictable to, and desired by, Luke.

5. Typical of Lukan narrative style, Luke portrays a divided reaction to Paul's speech: a division (schisma) takes place, and some listeners (Stoics) respond favorably to the speech, whereas others (Epicureans) reject it.

6. Because Luke does things in pairs and with parallels,[17] he intends the reader to link (a) the diverse reactions by Stoics and Epicureans to the issue of theodicy in Acts 17 with (b) the contrasting reactions by Pharisees and Sadducees to the issue of the Resurrection in 23:6–10.

7. The common point in Acts 17 and 23 is theodicy, a doctrine of three elements: (a) a divine judge, (b) survival of death/resurrection, and (c) postmortem retribution. This precise doctrine, Luke urges, is acceptable to

---

l'Aréopage (Ac 17,22–31) lieu de reoncontre entre christianisme et hellénisme," *Bib* 60 (1979) 535.

15. See Jerome H. Neyrey, *Christ Is Community* (Wilmington, DE: Michael Glazier, 1985) 204–13.

16. In terms of forensic rhetoric, speeches necessarily build toward the decision of the judged, which in classical rhetoric is called *judicatio/krinomenon* (see Cicero *Inv. Rhet.* 1.13.18 and Quintilian *Inst.* 3.11.5–6). In the speeches in Acts, this "point of judgment" is always "the resurrection"; see Jerome H. Neyrey, "The Forensic Defense Speech and Paul's Trial Speeches in Acts 22–26: Form and Function," *Luke-Acts: New Perspectives from the Society of Biblical Literature Seminar* (ed. C. H. Talbert; New York: Crossroads, 1984) 214–16.

17. See Charles H. Talbert, *Literary Patterns, Theological Themes and the Genre of Luke-Acts* (SBLMS 20; Missoula, MT: Scholars, 1974); Walter Radl, *Paulus und Jesus im lukanischen Doppelwerk: Untersuchungen zu Parallelmotiven im Lukasevangelium und in der Apostelgeschichte* (Frankfort: Peter Lang, 1975); and A. J. Mattill, "The Paul-Jesus Parallels and the Purpose of Luke-Acts: C. H. Evans Reconsidered," *NovT* 17 (1975) 15–45.

leading Jewish and Hellenistic thinkers. Conversely, those who reject this part of Christian preaching are to be labeled as eccentric, strange, and wrong—either the Epicureans or the Sadducees.

These are but hypotheses, which need to be stated more clearly and more formally argued.

ACTS 17 AND THEOLOGY

We turn first to consider the doctrine of God in Acts 17. Obviously, the speech has a polemical thrust, for the narrative describes Paul's being "provoked" at the city "full of idols." Hence part of the speech criticizes idols and their shrines and temples (17:24, 29) in service of the proclamation of the "unknown god" to be revealed (17:23). These are important aspects for Luke, who argues throughout the speech that there is a correct theology and a wrong one; the multiplicity of pagan idols is clearly wrong, whereas the remarks on the "unknown god" (17:23) point in the direction of a correct theology.[18] However, this is not the critical "question of judgment" in the speech.

ACTS 17 AND PROVIDENCE

Paul's speech is logically structured to present the Christian God under the traditional, acceptable category of providence. In Hellenistic theology, gods might be understood in a variety of ways, one of which is the complex category of god-as-provident. This synthetic idea of God would include the following elements: (1) Gods exist and are active. (2) They are wise and good, and so when they act, they act wisely and in goodness. (3) Their actions can be summarized in two ways: (a) they create, order, and maintain the world, and (b) they exercise executive and judgmental functions. (4) Hence, the gods must be both benevolent and just. (5) Providence, moreover, is shown in a variety of ways in the world: in the order and regularity of creation, in the giving of oracles and revelations to mortals, in the protective care given to good individuals, and in the just judgment of evildoers. Furthermore, a deity who is "provident" knows the future and controls the world; this deity, then, can predict the future and issue prophecies and oracles, bring things to pass, intervene in history, and so on. Such actions befit a deity who is wise, benevolent, and just.

In the Areopagus speech, Luke underscores several aspects of the popular doctrine of God's providence: (1) God is *creator* ("God, who made the world

---

18. C. K Barrett, "Paul's Speech on the Areopagus," *New Testament Christianity for Africa and the World* (ed. Mark Glasswell and Edward Fasholé-Luke; London: SPCK, 1974) 72–75. Barrett sees Paul's criticism of idols and his search for a correct doctrine of god (i.e., the "unknown god") as theological moves by the author to show some compatibility with Epicurean attacks on superstition.

and everything in it" [Acts 17:24]); (2) God is *benevolent orderer* ("God made from one every nation of men to live on all the face of the earth, having determined allotted periods and boundaries of their habitation" [17:26]); and (3) God is *just judge* ("God has fixed a day on which he will judge the world in righteousness" [17:30]). As noted above, this material draws heavily on Stoic materials and would be heard by Luke's audience as traditional, and so respectable, theology.

Luke's concern to present the Christian doctrine about God in terms of providence is not confined to the speech in Acts 17. Space does not allow for a full exposition of the Lukan portrait of God in the Acts of the Apostles in terms of providence, but the following outline suggests the fullness of fit between the abstract description of a provident deity and the Lukan God.

The Doctrine of Providence in Acts of the Apostles

A. Creation: 4:24; 14:15; 17:24.
B. Divine foreknowledge and plan.
   1. 2:23; 4:28.
   2. *Dei* (it is necessary): 14:22; 17:3.
C. Oracles of the future.
   1. Prophecy fulfillment: what God prophesied long ago has come true in Christ and his followers (2:14–21, 25–30; 3:19–22; 4:25–28).
   2. Oracles delivered during the narrative of Acts that come true (11:27–30; 21:10–14; 22:17–21; 27:23–27).
D. Benevolent control of history: the rescue of good people.
   1. Peter (4; 5; 12:1–12).
   2. Stephen (7:54–56).
   3. Paul (16:19–39; 17:1–9, 12–15; 18:5–11; 19:23–20:1; 21:27–39; 22:22–29; 23:12–31; 27:9–44; 28:1–6).
E. Just judgment of sinners.
   1. Judgment of Ananias and Sapphira (5:1–6).
   2. Judgment of Herod (12:23).
F. Theodicy: postmortem judgment.
   1. Jesus, judge of the living and dead (10:42; 17:31).
   2. Future judgment (24:25).

It would be a mistake to drive too sharp a wedge between Hellenistic god-talk and Jewish theology on the issue of providence. All of the above material would be quite intelligible to a Jewish audience in terms of its Scriptures, but equally clear to Greeks in terms of Hellenistic discussions of God. In fact, certain Jewish and Christian authors intentionally cast their traditional god-talk in terms of Hellenistic doctrine of providence.[19] Luke, I suggest, inten-

---

19. See Philo *Prov.*; Harold W. Attridge, *The Interpretation of Biblical History in the Antiquitates Judaicae of Flavius Josephus* (HDR 7; Missoula, MT: Scholars, 1976); and G. F. Moore, "Fate and Free Will in the Jewish Philosophies According to Josephus," *HTR* 22 (1929) 371–89.

tionally portrays the God of Israel in terms of providence, either because that is in fact how he, a literate person of the Hellenistic world, views the matter or because he seeks to portray Christian doctrine as traditional and acceptable to all.

ACTS 17 AND THEODICY

We are arguing two points here. First, like discussions of many topics in the ancient world, discussions of theodicy come to us in the form of a topos. Complex ideas were regularly digested and reduced to simple formulas that were easy to remember. From many discussions of theodicy, we can piece together the shape of the arguments that both defended theodicy and attacked it. Luke is quite aware of such topoi, or summaries, especially in regard to theodicy. Second, Epicureans in particular were known by their opponents in terms of stereotypes, especially the stereotype of those who deny providence and theodicy. Again, Luke is aware of this, for on these two points the Areopagus speech hinges: the topos on theodicy and the stereotype of the Epicureans.

What makes up the topos on theodicy? What regular elements were seen to make up an argument for it? A convenient discussion of this traditional doctrine can be found in Plutarch's *Delay of Divine Judgment*, which was written at the end of the first century and so is roughly contemporary with the author of Luke-Acts. In this tractate, Plutarch first voices standard anti-theodicy polemics, statements that are formally attributed to Epicureans.[20] Epicurean objections are then dealt with vigorously, although not conclusively. Finally, one of the speakers makes bold to expose the presuppositions of one of the parties to the dispute; and by doing so, he gives a précis of what makes up a belief in divine theodicy: "It is one and the same argument that establishes both the providence of God and the survival of the human soul, and it is impossible to upset the one contention and let the other stand. But if the soul survives, we must expect that its due in honour and in punishment is awarded after death rather than before."[21] From this and many other examples of the argument for theodicy, we infer that traditional belief in divine theodicy entails three elements: (1) a judge, (2) survival of death, and (3) post-mortem retribution by God.

If this is the positive presentation of belief in theodicy, the denial of it is equally informative for learning the shape of a topos on theodicy. In the ancient world, the Epicureans were accounted as the chief antagonists of belief in divine theodicy. From the writings attributed to Epicurus, we can

---

20. Although many arguments are alleged against divine providence, the Epicurean remarks in *De Sera* 548D–549D and 556E–557E urge that God is an unjust judge because punishment does not come upon the culprit himself or is visited on his children and grandchildren.

21. Plutarch *De Sera Numinis Vindicta* 560F (trans. De Lacy and Einarson in LCL) 257. See Neyrey, "The Form and Background of the Polemic in 2 Peter," 411–14.

cull the relevant elements that, when stitched together, form a coherent argument against theodicy. First, Epicurus's doctrine of God denies providence. God is neither kind nor angry, for God is not moved by passions: "A blessed and eternal being has no trouble and brings no trouble upon any other being; hence he is exempt from movements of anger and partiality, for every such movement implies weakness."[22] God, then, is not judge.

Epicurus's second Sovran Maxim affirms the finality of death: "Death is nothing to us; for the body, when it has been resolved into its elements, has no feeling; and that which has no feeling is nothing to us."[23] There is, then, no survival after death. It follows that there can be no postmortem retribution, if God does not judge and if there is no survival after death.[24] Just as traditional theodicy affirms three items (judge, survival of death, postmortem retribution), Epicurus was perceived as denying all three.

Lactantius provides a convenient and popular summary of the perception that Epicurus denies all three elements, and so denies theodicy: "If any chieftain of pirates or leader of robbers were exhorting his men to acts of violence, what other language could he employ than to say the same things which Epicurus says: that the gods take no notice; that they are not affected with anger or kind feeling; that the punishment of a future state is not to be dreaded, because the souls die after death, and that there is no future state of punishment at all."[25] Therefore, both the proponents of theodicy and its adversaries regularly cast their arguments in terms of three interrelated items that they either affirm or deny: (1) God as judge, (2) human survival of death, and (3) postmortem retribution. Such is the popular shape of the way theodicy was discussed.

Paul's presentation in the Areopagus speech of God's providential judgment fully coincides with the three expected elements of the traditional topos on theodicy. Paul declares the following:

---

22. Diogenes Laertius 10.139; see Cicero *Nat.D.* 1.85 and Lucretius *R.Nat.* 1.44–49 and 2.651. See Herman Usener, *Epicurea* (Stuttgart: Teubner, 1966) 242–44.

23. Diogenes Laertius 10.139; see Lucretius *R.Nat.* 3.830ff., Lucian *Jup. Conf.*, Cicero *Fin.* 2.31.100, and Plutarch *Non Posse* 1103D and 1104E; see also Usener, *Epicurea*, 226–28. Important studies on this topic include Traudel Stork, *Nil Igitur Mors Est ad Nos, Der Schlussteil des dritten Lukrezbuchs und sein Vermächtnes zur Konsolations Literatur* (Bonn: Rudolf Habelt, 1970), and Barbara P. Wallach, *Lucretius and the Diatribe against Fear of Death, De Rerum Natura III 830–1094* (Mnemosyne 40; Leiden: Brill, 1976).

24. We have presented the negative or reactionary side of Epicurus. In his writings he aimed at "freedom from anxiety" (ἀταραξία), a freedom that found traditional notions of a provident god and postmortem retribution all too anxiety producing. The gist of this freedom from anxiety is summarized in the famous *tetrapharmakon:* "God is not to be feared. Death is not frightful. The good is easy to obtain. Evil is easy to tolerate." See Diogenes Laertius 10.133; F. Sbordone, *Philodemi Adversus Sophistas* (Naples: Loffredo, 1947) 87; A. J. Festugière, *Epicurus and His Gods* (Oxford: Basil Blackwell, 1955) 44; and Henry Fischel, *Rabbinic Literature and Graeco-Roman Philosophy* (Leiden: Brill, 1973) 33.

25. Lactantius *Inst.* 3.17; the translation is that of William Fletcher, *The Ante-Nicene Fathers* (Grand Rapids, MI: Eerdmans, 1970) 7. 88.

1. *God as judge.* "God has fixed a day on which he will judge the world in righteousness by a man whom he has appointed" (Acts 17:31a).
2. *Human survival of death.* First, it must be noted that Paul preached "the resurrection" (17:18), which is not simply the announcement of Jesus' resurrection but the survival of death for all (see 10:42). Second, Paul specifically states that God gave assurance of the coming judgment by raising Jesus from the dead, not simply to constitute him as judge but also to give proof that there will be a resurrection unto judgment (17:31b).
3. *Postmortem retribution.* The resurrection that Paul proclaims is "resurrection unto judgment." And on that future day, God will "judge the world in righteousness" (17:31) by Jesus, whom God has appointed to "judge the living and the dead" (10:42). Those to be judged are not just Christians who are alive and Christians who have died (see 1 Thess 4:14–17), but all people, including, and especially, the dead (see Acts 24:25).

The Areopagus speech, then, is about right and wrong theology. It criticizes idols but positively affirms God's providence and, especially, theodicy.[26]

Confirmation by Comparison: Acts 24

The typical modern reader might hear Luke's doctrine in Acts 17 as vintage Christian eschatology and so pay no special attention to it as theodicy. Yet Luke is not discussing eschatology but theodicy, and so returns to just this material in two of Paul's speeches to the governor Felix.

In the first instance, Luke records Paul delivering a forensic defense of his doctrine during a solemn trial before the governor Felix (Acts 24:10–21).[27] Tertullus, the spokesman for Ananias and the priestly party, charges Paul with being a deviant ("pestilent fellow . . . agitator among all the Jews . . . ringleader of the sect of the Nazarenes" [24:5]). He implies that Paul stands totally out of the mainstream of Jewish theology and that he propounds heretical doctrines. Paul's apology defends his orthodoxy—in this case, his claim to be solidly loyal to the traditions about Israel's god. The issue is Paul's theology, his doctrine of God; more specifically, the issue is theodicy.

In the course of Paul's speech, he shapes the trial so as to make the formal "question for judgment" the general issue of "the resurrection": "With respect to the resurrection of the dead I am on trial before you this day" (Acts 24:21). Although Paul can be presumed to allude to Jesus' resurrection, his speech before Felix contains no explicit mention of Jesus at all. Rather, the reference to "the resurrection" is cast here in terms of traditional faith in the Jewish

---

26. On the very issue of right and wrong theology in Acts 17, see Barrett, "Paul's Speech on the Areopagus," 72–75.
27. For a detailed analysis of this speech, see Neyrey, *The Passion According to Luke*, 102–7; and Neyrey, "the Forensic Defense Speech and Paul's Trial Speeches," 211–16.

God; it is exclusively about the correct doctrine of God. As Paul says, "I worship the God of our fathers, believing everything laid down by the law or written in the prophets" (24:14). More specifically, Paul focuses his claim to
orthodox theology on the precise issue of theodicy: "having a hope in God
which these themselves accept, that there will be a resurrection of both the
just and the unjust" (24:15). This "resurrection," moreover, comprises both
survival of death ("resurrection") and postmortem retribution ("of both the
just and the unjust"). Paul's apologetic remarks in 24:15 can be seen to contain the three traditional aspects of theodicy: (1) a judge ("a hope in God"),
(2) survival of death ("there will be a resurrection"), and (3) postmortem retribution ("of both the just and the unjust").[28] Paul, therefore, develops his apology to Tertullus's charges with a claim to orthodox theology in general and
with belief in traditional theodicy in particular.

According to Luke's narrative, Felix does not resolve this trial. He is said to
have "rather accurate knowledge of the Way," and he later summons Paul to
"hear him speak upon faith in Christ Jesus" (Acts 24:24). But Luke's account
of Paul's further remarks to Felix has nothing whatsoever to do with "faith in
Christ Jesus"; rather they are still on the theme Paul propounded in the recent
trial: "He argues about justice, self-control, and future judgment" (24:25).
Using 17:31 and 24:15 as interpretative keys, we find in 24:25 the same three
components of traditional theodicy: a judge, survival of death, and postmortem retribution. Justice (δικαιοσύνη) is essentially forensic judgment and
implies a judge who dispenses this justice; that judge is God or God's agent,
Jesus. Survival of death is seen in "future judgment"; the future aspect of this
judgment implies that all will survive death so as to be there. Postmortem
retribution is shown in "judgment" (κρίματος τοῦ μέλλοντος). This judgment,
moreover, is a just forensic judgment rendered on the basis of the moral principle of self-control (ἐγκράτεια). If Felix was curious about Jesus in 24:24, he
is portrayed in 24:26 as "alarmed" by Paul's words because the narrative suggests that he is evil ("He hoped that money would be given him by Paul"). By
Felix's reaction, Luke indicates that he fully understood the thrust of Paul's
remarks about postmortem retribution. Whereas the Epicureans "mocked"
Paul in Acts 17, Felix is upset and dismisses him for his uncomfortable message about theodicy.

Acts 17: Division and Contrast

The whole episode in Acts 17:16–34 is so carefully crafted that notice of its
narrative logic will assist in its interpretation. As has been noted, the speech
itself is prefaced and concluded by Luke's note of contrasting reactions to
Paul.[29] Luke notes that Paul was "met by some Epicurean and Stoic philoso-

28. The reader is reminded that in the NT, when "resurrection" is mentioned, it often explicitly
means "resurrection unto judgment." See John 5:28–29; Luke 14:14; Heb 6:2; Rev 20:5–6. See
Ulrich Wilkens, "The Tradition-History of the Resurrection of Jesus," *The Significance of the Message of the Resurrection for Faith* (ed. C. F. D. Moule; SBT 2d ser. 8; London: SCM, 1968) 65–66.
29. See Robert O'Toole, "Paul at Athens and Luke's Notion of Worship," *RB* 89 (1982) 186.

phers," among whom there are initial, contrasting opinions: "Some said, 'What would this babbler say?' Others said, 'He seems to be a preacher of foreign divinities'" (17:18). The text suggests that the Epicureans call Paul a "babbler," whereas the Stoics consider him "a preacher of foreign divinities." The point lies, however, in polarized opinions from contrasting groups. At the end of the speech, moreover, Luke narrates further contrasting opinions: "Some mocked, but others said, 'We will hear you again about this'" (17:32). The rhetoric here supports this, for Luke uses the μέν-δέ (on the one hand . . . on the other hand) construction to distinguish and contrast two groups.

I suggest that Luke intends us to understand the Epicureans, who initially called Paul a "babbler," as the group who "mock him" and the Stoics, who formerly evaluated him as "a preacher of foreign divinities," as those who react more positively ("We will hear you again").[30] The text states, moreover, that from the assembled crowd of Epicureans and Stoics, "some men joined him and believed, among them Dionysius the Areopagite" (17:34). These can hardly be Epicureans, and the text might be read to infer that they were Stoics. The speech itself, then, is bracketed by contrasting opinions about Paul's doctrine.

More important, however, is the issue of whether these contrasting reactions to Paul's speech in Acts 17:32 derive from the contrasting viewpoints of Epicureans and Stoics. The answer, in large measure, rests on our observation of how Luke regularly presents characters and issues. For example, Luke frequently notes that the audience of Jesus, Peter, or Paul is "divided" over what it hears.[31] Even in Acts 17, this pattern is quite pronounced: in Thessalonica Paul first meets with success (17:2–4) but then with failure (17:5–8); likewise in Beroea, his initial success (17:10–12) is juxtaposed with failure (17:13–14). Luke has conditioned the reader to expect the same pattern of "division" among the crowds on the Areopagus during the subsequent climactic episode at Athens. Some show favor to Paul (Stoics), whereas others mock him (Epicureans).

Luke does things in twos and he favors parallels. He would seem to offer a parallel to the contrasting reactions to Paul's theodicy speech in Acts 17 in the description of the reactions to Paul's confession of "the resurrection" in Acts 23:6–10. The similarities are immediately compelling. The first similarity is contrasting audiences. Just as there are contrasting Epicureans and Stoics listening to Paul in Athens, so in Jerusalem Paul's audience consists of Sadducees and Pharisees, two groups who can be said to disagree on most things: "One part were Sadducees and the other Pharisees" (23:6a). The second similarity is the presence of allies and enemies. Just as Paul in Athens cast his

30. See Ernst Haenchen, *The Acts of the Apostles* (Philadelphia: Westminster, 1971) 526; and Barrett, "Paul's Speech on the Areopagus," 71.

31. See Jerome Kodell, "Luke's Use of LAOS, 'People,' Especially in the Jerusalem Narrative (Lk 19,28–24,53)," *CBQ* 31 (1969) 330–32; Jacob Jervell, *Luke and the People of God* (Minneapolis: Augsburg, 1972) 41–74; and Neyrey, *The Passion According to Luke*, 121–24.

doctrine in a way to elicit the favor of the Stoics as well as the mockery of the Epicureans, so in Jerusalem Paul identifies himself as a Pharisee, allying himself with them while ensuring the rejection of the Sadducees: "I am a Pharisee, the son of Pharisees" (23:6b). Third, both speeches stress resurrection. Just as the point of Paul's speech in Athens was the Resurrecton (he "preached . . . the resurrection" [17:18]), so Paul declares before the Jews "the resurrection of the dead" as the forensic point of judgment: "With respect to the . . . resurrection of the dead I am on trial" (23:6c). Finally, both speeches concern theodicy. Just as Luke could presume that his readers clearly distinguished Epicureans and Stoics on the issue of providence and theodicy, so the trial in chapter 23 works precisely because the Sadducees and Pharisees are known to hold opposite views on the central issue: "For the Sadducees say that there is no resurrection, nor angel, nor spirit; but the Pharisees acknowledge them all" (23:8). From a study of the way Luke typically presents characters and issues, then, these parallels between the contrasting reactions to Paul's speech seem persuasive enough for us to infer that Luke intends the reader to see Epicureans and Stoics holding contrasting views on theodicy in Acts 17, just as Sadducees and Pharisees differ on "the resurrection" in Acts 23.

ACTS 17 AND STEREOTYPES

It is important for a modern reader to grasp an important fact about the world of Luke. How do people in Luke's world tend to know and describe themselves and other people? Basically, they do so in terms of stereotypes.[32] For example, nations and towns were perceived in terms of stereotypes: "Cretans are always liars, evil beasts, lazy gluttons" (Titus 1:12), and "Jews have no dealings with Samaritans" (John 4:9). Towns also were stereotyped: "Can anything good come out of Nazareth?" (John 1:46).

Individual people as well are known in terms of stereotypes. For example, Jesus' new wisdom and power are incompatible with the village perception of what a carpenter's son should be like (Mark 6:2–3); Sadducees do not believe in "the resurrection," but Pharisees do. God also is known in terms of a stereotype, namely, in terms of providence and theodicy (that is, as just judge). The topos on theodicy, then, is another example of stereotypical perception.

Stereotypical perception characterizes Luke's world and is true of Luke as well. From Acts 23, we conclude that Luke obviously employs this mode of perception in regard to Sadducees and Pharisees, just as I argue that he does the same in Acts 17 in regard to the Epicureans and Stoics. More important, Luke and others in his world know both pairs, Epicureans-Stoics and

---

32. See Bruce J. Malina, *The New Testament World: Insights from Cultural Anthropology* (Atlanta: John Knox, 1981) 53–59.

Sadducees-Pharisees, stereotypically in terms of their contrasting positions on the same issue of theodicy.

Because the stereotypical perception of characters in Acts is so important to the argument of this study, let us pursue it further. Any reader of the Synoptic Gospels comes to know the Sadducees, for example, in terms of a stereotype, namely, their denial of "the resurrection":[33] "The same day Sadducees came to him, who say that there is no resurrection" (Matt 22:32); "And Sadducees came to him, who say that there is no resurrection" (Mark 12:18); and "There came to him some Sadducees, those who say that there is no resurrection" (Luke 20:27).[34] Nothing in the Synoptics suggests that this is a post-factum reaction to Jesus' own resurrection, but rather a well-known denial by Sadducees of survival after death. It is not a position attributed to them in reaction to Christian claims; rather, it is the stereotypical way in which people know them.

The stereotypical perception of Sadducees and Pharisees is not confined to the Gospels or Acts. Josephus provides a remarkable description of the Sadducees and the Pharisees that likens them to Epicureans and Stoics, respectively, and this precisely in terms of their stereotypical stand on theodicy. To explain the Pharisees to non-Jews, Josephus compares them to the Stoics,[35] relying on the stereotype of a recognized Hellenistic group (Stoics) to explain an unknown Jewish group (Pharisees).[36] In several places, Josephus describes the Pharisees (that is, the Stoics) in terms of providence and theodicy. For example, he says, "The Pharisees, who are considered the most accurate interpreters of the laws, and hold the position of the leading sect, attribute everything to Fate and to God. . . . Every soul, they maintain, is imperishable, but the soul of the good alone passes into another body, while the souls of the wicked suffer eternal punishment."[37] In this description, we find the three familiar elements of traditional theodicy: (1) God is judge ("Fate or God is all powerful"); (2) survival of death ("Every soul is imperishable"), and (3) postmortem retribution ("The soul of the good alone passes into another body, while the souls of the wicked suffer eternal punishment").[38] This text serves several purposes. First, Stoics are themselves known by their stereotypical theodicy beliefs. Second, the same stereotypical beliefs are

33. The Pharisees likewise are known by Christians in terms of certain stereotypes; they may be perceived as legalists or hypocrites for their perceived concern for keeping Torah in a strict way. In certain strands of the tradition, Jesus and his followers are perceived in comparable stereotypes, as those who do not keep Torah strictly. See Bruce J. Malina and Jerome H. Neyrey, *Calling Jesus Names* (Sonoma: Polebridge, 1988) 59–60.

34. I am presuming in this discussion that when the Sadducees are said to deny "the resurrection," this does not simply mean Jesus' resurrection but all postmortem survival. Denying "the resurrection," then, is shorthand code for rejection of afterlife and postmortem retribution. See note 28 above.

35. Josephus *Vita* 12.

36. Josephus also likens the Essenes to the Pythagoreans, *Ant.* 15.371.

37. Josephus *J.W.* 2.162–63 (trans. Thackeray in LCL) 385–87.

38. Although the primary text is Josephus *J.W.* 2.162–63, see also *Ant.* 13.172 and 18.12–15.

thought to describe the Pharisees adequately. And the topos on theodicy was well known. Stereotypes are useful all around.

Although when Josephus describes the Sadducees he never explicitly compares them to the Epicureans, this comparison is safely assumed.[39] He likewise describes them in stereotypical form as those who reject theodicy. He says, for example, "The Sadducees, the second of the orders, do away with Fate altogether, and remove God beyond, not merely the commission, but the very sight of evil. . . . As for persistence of the soul after death, penalties in the underworld, and rewards, they will have none of them."[40] Again, the three elements of the topos are evident: (1) no judge (They "remove God [even from] the very sight of evil," that is, judgment), (2) no survival of death ("As for persistence of the soul after death, . . . they will have none"), and (3) no postmortem retribution ("As for . . . penalties in the underworld, . . . they will have none").[41] Josephus's description of the position held by the Sadducees corresponds exactly with stereotypical descriptions of the Epicureans.[42]

Josephus is Luke's contemporary. He is proof positive of the stereotypical presentation of Pharisees = Stoics and Sadducees = Epicureans, and he groups both precisely in terms of the stereotype of theodicy. This is the type of understanding that Luke can assume, even if the reader did not follow the parallels between Acts 17 and 23.

Thus far we have looked at specific groups who are described in terms of stereotypes. I present one further example, this time not of specific groups but of stereotypical arguments, to help modern readers be quite clear both on the typical content of the topos on theodicy and on the widespread knowledge of the stereotype or topos. The example comes from certain targumic elaborations on Gen 4:8, the conversation between Cain and Abel about the justice of God:

> Cain answered and said to Abel:
> "I know that the world was not created by love,
> that it is not governed according to the fruit of good deeds,
> and that there is favor in Judgement.
> Therefore your offering was accepted with delight,
> but my offering was not accepted from me with delight."
> Abel answered and said to Cain:
> "I see that the world was created by love,
> and is governed according to the fruit of good deeds.
> And there is no favour in Judgement."

---

39. Josephus does, after all, call the Pharisees, Sadducees, and Essenes "three philosophies" (*J.W.* 2.119), indicating, as we noted, that Pharisees = Stoics and Essenes = Pythagoreans; it is not an unwarranted assertion that Sadducees = Epicureans.

40. Josephus *J.W.* 2.164–65.

41. See also, Josephus *Ant.* 13.173 and 18.16.

42. See Jerome H. Neyrey, *The Form and Background of the Polemic in 2 Peter* (diss., Yale University, 1978) 176–90.

Cain answered and said to Abel:
"There is no Judgement,
there is no Judge,
there is no other world,
there is no gift of good reward for the just
and no punishment for the wicked."
Abel answered and said to Cain:
"There is Judgement,
there is a Judge,
there is another world, the gift of good reward for the just
and punishment for the wicked."[43]

The conversation between Cain and Abel revolves around two issues, providence and theodicy. Cain denies that God acts providentially, that is, benignly and fairly: "The world was not created by love, . . . is not governed according to the fruit of good deeds." And like others who attacked the notion of providence, Cain cites injustice as his evidence against divine providence: "There is favor in Judgement."[44] Conversely, Abel defends providence.

From our examination of other examples of the topos on theodicy, we can readily discern the traditional three elements that make up the argument against and for theodicy:

Theodicy Denied (Cain)	Theodicy Affirmed (Abel)
1. God is not a just judge: "There is no Judge."	1. God is a just judge: "There is a Judge."
2. No survival of death: "There is no other world."	2. Survival of death: "There is another world."
3. No post mortem retribution: "There is no Judgement."	3. Postmortem retribution: "There is Judgement."

Just as Josephus described Sadducees and Pharisees in terms of their opposing points of view on theodicy, so we find Cain and Abel distinguished point for point on the same topic.

Some scholars have attempted to identify Cain and Abel with various historical groups. Sheldon Isenberg, for example, argued that the midrash on Gen 4:8 represents a Sadducee-Pharisee controversy.[45] He based his argument on the stereotype that we have already noted that Sadducees deny the Resurrection. Henry Fischel, however, argued that the midrash is Epicurean,

---

43. *Tg. Neof.* Gen 4:8; the translation is that of G. Vermes, "The Targumic Versions of Gen 4:3–16," *Post-Biblical Jewish Studies* (Leiden: Brill, 1975) 96–100. See also P. Grelot, "Les Targums du Pentateuque—Etude comparative d'après Genèse, IV, 3–16," *Sem* 9 (1959) 59–88.

44. Epicureans often cite either injustice or delay of judgment as evidence against divine providence. See Neyrey, *The Form and Background of the Polemic in 2 Peter*, 174–79.

45. Sheldon Isenberg, "An Anti-Sadducee Polemic in the Palestinian Targum Tradition," *HTR* 63 (1970) 433–41.

citing in support numerous passages from the rabbis that parallel in form and content the antitheodicy sayings attributed to Epicureans.[46]

Although the question of provenance, whether Sadducean or Epicurean, may be impossible to solve, that should not deter us from noting the persistence and pervasiveness of the topos either against or for theodicy. It matters little whether Epicureans = Sadducees = Cain or Stoics = Pharisees = Abel, for the issue is that God was perceived in terms of a stereotype, the topos about theodicy. We have ample evidence that on the topic of theodicy, there were stereotypical responses and that certain well-known parties in the Hellenistic and Jewish worlds were readily perceived in terms of their stand on theodicy. Stereotypes, then, describe both doctrine discussed and those who discussed it.

In regard to the hypotheses stated earlier in this chapter, we may now conclude the following: Among the many theological elements in the Areopagus speech, the chief issues that Luke highlights are providence and theodicy. Luke presents characters and issues in contrasting pairs and by parallel examples. The Epicureans and Stoics of Acts 17 are balanced by the Sadducees and Pharisees of Acts 23. Like other ancient writers, Luke portrays groups and parties in terms of stereotypes. Luke knows of and presents a stereotypical description of theodicy, a topos on it (Acts 17; 23; 24). Luke is not ignorant of the stereotypical perception of Epicureans and Stoics[47] and he has told the story in Acts 17:16–34 in such a way that these two parties react in contrasting fashion to Paul, both at the beginning of the speech and at its end. The stereotypical perception of Epicureans and Stoics is based on contrasting assessments of theodicy.

From this analysis, we conclude that Luke has cast the characters and the issues in such a way as to argue that Christian theology belongs to the common, acceptable doctrine of God held by good and reasonable people, whether Hellenistic Stoics or Jewish Pharisees. In regard to Paul's speech in Acts 17, we noticed that belief in providence and theodicy, while congenial to the Stoics, is not exclusive to them but is a common, orthodox doctrine. Paul's speech in Acts 24, moreover, argues that his Christian belief in God is also vintage Jewish theology, although the Sadducees, guardians of Israel's shrine, would not agree. At least Luke makes this claim to orthodoxy through Paul.

Luke, then, presents certain aspects of Christian thought (that is, theodicy) in terms acceptable to Greek and Jew alike; he would argue that this doctrine is orthodox, common, and traditional. Thus, the charge in Acts 17:6 that Paul and the Christians "turn the world upside down" must be false, for their doc-

---

46. Fischel, *Rabbinic Literature and Graeco-Roman Philosophy*, 35–50.

47. Because of the focus of this chapter, I have not attended to the stereotypical understanding of the Stoics, a task usually performed adequately in the commentaries. I remain impressed with Barrett's suggestions about the typical doctrines of the Stoics alluded to in Acts 17 ("Paul's Speech on the Areopagus," 72–74).

trine is quite in conformity with what all intelligent, good people think.[48] In fact, to be mocked by the Epicureans and then to be dismissed by the Sadducees plays into this strategy. If mockery and dismissal come from groups who can be shown to be wrong, that in itself is further confirmation of the correctness of what they mock and dismiss. Comparably, to find common ground and perhaps endorsement from groups generally considered the guardians of the basic tradition (Stoics and Pharisees) can only transfer that approbation to the new group of Christians as well. They are not mavericks.

48. See Malherbe, "'Not in a Corner,'" 195–201.

PASSION IN PAUL AND PLUTARCH
1 Corinthians 5–6 and the Polemic against Epicureans

Chapters 5 and 6 of 1 Corinthians are frequently thought to contain Paul's reply to the oral report of conditions in Corinth brought to him by "Chloe's people" (1 Cor 1:11).[1] These chapters deal with the incestuous man, lawsuits, and the frequenting of (temple)[2] prostitutes and have provided commentators with ample material from which to support theories of the socioeconomic state of the community,[3] the community's unorthodox theological tendencies,[4] Paul's similarity to his contemporary moral philosophers,[5] and Paul's views on purity.[6] This chapter will examine the writings on moral virtue and love by Paul's near contemporary Plutarch (circa A.D. 45 to 115) and Plutarch's arguments against the ideas of the Epicureans on happiness to discover some of the popular philosophical discussions of the topics to which Paul alludes, some of the philosophical-religious alternatives with which Pauline Christianity might have been in competition, and some of the argumentation used in the debates on these issues. As such, the chapter reflects the abiding interest of Abraham J. Malherbe in the Hellenistic moralists as a help to understand the content and form of expression of Paul's ideas and arguments.

Commentators have already pointed out similarities in classical writers to the arguments that Paul uses. W. Baird[7] notes that the "unheard of" situation

1. A. Robertson and A. Plummer, *First Epistle of St. Paul to the Corinthians* (ICC; New York: Scribner's, 1911) 95.
2. J. S. Glen, *Pastoral Problems in First Corinthians* (Philadelphia: Westminster, 1964) 85–86.
3. G. Theissen, *The Social Setting of Pauline Christianity: Essays on Corinth* (trans. J. H. Schuetz; Philadelphia: Fortress, 1982) 97, and W. A. Meeks, *The First Urban Christians: The Social World of the Apostle Paul* (New Haven and London: Yale University Press, 1983) 127–31, 153–54.
4. E. Fascher, *Der erste Brief des Paulus an die Korinther, Erster Teil: Einfuehrung und Auslegung der Kapitel, 1–7* (THKNT 7.1; Berlin: Evangelische Verlagsanstalt, 1984) 54–64, and D. R. MacDonald, *There Is No Male and Female* (HDR 20; Philadelphia: Fortress, 1987) 69–72.
5. H. Conzelmann, *A Commentary on the First Epistle to the Corinthians* (trans. J. W. Leitch; Philadelphia: Fortress, 1975) 94–113.
6. L. W. Countryman, *Dirt, Greed and Sex: Sexual Ethics in the New Testament and Their Implications for Today* (Philadelphia: Fortress, 1988) 196–214.
7. W. Baird, *The Corinthian Church: A Biblical Approach to Urban Culture* (New York: Abingdon, 1964) 62–63.

in 1 Cor 5:1 finds a similar "unheard of except for this case" parallel in Cicero's *Pro Cluentio*. A. Robertson and A. Plummer[8] note that the "temple of the spirit" notion in 6:19 is echoed in Epictetus's *Diss.* 2.8 ("You carry [god] within yourself and perceive not that you are polluting him by impure thoughts and dirty deeds.") H. Conzelmann[9] adds *Diss.* 1.14. They also observe that "You are not your own" in 1 Cor 6:19 is reflected in Epictetus' *Diss.* 2.8, arguing that the interlocutor is under obligation to the divine artist and creator. According to Conzelmann,[10] freedom, implied at 1 Cor 6:12, is also discussed in terms of independence from external coercion in Epictetus's *Diss.* 3.24; 4.1; 4.7 and, more to the point, is related to control over one's diet in Porphyry's *On Abstinence* 1.42. The idea of usefulness as a criterion for choice or rejection of things at 1 Cor 6:12 appears, as Conzelmann notes, in Epictetus's *Ench.* 31.4, where the philosopher relates the useful (self-interest) with piety toward the gods. The relationship of sexual purity with approach to the gods and holiness in 1 Cor 6:15–20 is noted by Conzelmann[11] in Dittenberg., *SIG* 3.117 1126–31. Material echoing Paul's on extramarital sexual indulgence in 1 Cor 6:16–20 is found in Plutarch and will be elaborated on at length below.

These are just some of the parallels found by the commentators to be suggested by 1 Corinthians 5 and 6. The material from the Cynic-Stoic Epictetus deserves a closer and more comprehensive scrutiny that goes beyond the noting of parallels to establishing a more sound determination of similarities and differences. This chapter will not pursue the material in Epictetus but will focus on the writings of Plutarch, for there, too, one finds echoes of the ideas discussed by Paul and a context of popular-philosophical debate that may have also affected the thinking in the Christian community in Corinth.

1 CORINTHIANS 5–6:
PROBLEMS AND PARENESIS

First, some attention to the features of 1 Corinthians 5–6 is in order. The entire section contains standard parenetic features:[12] prescriptions (5:7, 11, 13; 6:4, 9, 18, 20), exhortations (5:8; 6:7), disparate material in no logical order, example 5:3–5, 12; 6:12, 15), commonly known teaching (proverbs and slogans, 5:6; 6:12–13; former instruction, 5:9; Christian belief, 5:7; 6:2–3, 9, 11, 15, 16, 19; catalog of vices, 5:10, 11; 6:9), and hortatory purpose (5:5; 6:5). The rhetorical devices that render the exhortation effective also abound:

---

8. Robertson and Plummer, *First Epistle*, 128.
9. Conzelmann, *A Commentary*, 112.
10. Conzelmann, *A Commentary*, 109.
11. Conzelmann, *A Commentary*, 112.
12. See R. Bultmann, *Der Stil der paulinischen Predigt und die kynisch-stoische Diatribe* (Göttingen: Vandenhoeck & Ruprecht, 1910), and H. Thyen, *Der Stil der jüdisch-hellenistischen Homilie* (Göttingen: Vandenhoeck & Ruprecht, 1955).

hyperbole (5:1), metaphor (5:7–8; 6:19, 20), rhetorical question (5:6, 12; 6:2–7, 9, 15, 16), and exclamation (6:15). The parenetic character of the section, especially where it is expressed in prescriptions, differentiates the section from the persuasive style in the more reflective essays of Plutarch. Of course, the urgency of the community situation—both with respect to the people's unity among one another and with Paul, and also with respect to the issues of end-time salvation and the proper life of faith—gives the section, as well as the letter, a directness and finality absent from Plutarch. The moral issues are addressed in the light of final judgment (1 Cor 5:5, 12–13; 6:2–3, 9, 13–14) and the present exigencies of the Corinthians' relationship with the spirit of God and the risen Christ (5:7; 6:11, 15–17, 19–20).

The community problems dealt with in these chapters are disparate, and commentators differ on what they find to be the connecting link in Paul's treatment of the issues raised.[13] From the perspective of Jewish tradition, Paul seems to be dealing with the community faults in light of the Deuteronomic code as he refers to the problem of incest in 1 Cor 5:1–13 (see Deut 27:20), improper lawsuits in 1 Cor 6:1–8 (see Deut 16:18–20), and cult prostitutes in 1 Cor 6:12–20 (see Deut 23:17–18). Paul's comparison of the incestuous man to leaven in 1 Cor 5:6–8 (see Deut 16:4), the suggested penalty of excommunication in 1 Cor 5:19–23 (see Deut 17:7; 21:18–21), and the treatment of marriage and virginity at 1 Corinthians 7 (see Deut 22:13–30) also point to this connection.

L. W. Countryman[14] makes use of this insight into connections with biblical legislation, and his analysis of OT purity laws leads him to find in the themes of social cohesiveness and legitimate property rights a rationale that binds together Paul's otherwise disparate-seeming references. Countryman explains that sexual purity is not at issue. Paul's objection to sexual impropriety is not that it renders one unclean. Rather, Paul is concerned with an impurity of another sort. In connection with Paul's remarks at 1 Thess 4:3–8, Countryman explains that for audiences accustomed to listening to Paul, uncleanness was an equivalent of greed. Thus, πλεονεξία, or "competitive greed," contrasts with the ideal of purity of heart, the only purity that really matters. The three problems of incest, lawsuits, and frequenting prostitutes are treated by Paul as manifestations of the same greedy inclination.[15]

---

13. C. Holladay, *The First Letter of Paul to the Corinthians* (Austin: Sweet, 1979) 69–70, views Paul's criticisms as instructive reminders on how to behave in a pagan society in light of the "pathetic" immaturity of the Corinthian church. Glen, *Pastoral Problems*, 84–85, sees Paul addressing a failure to discipline with its roots in worldly wisdom and pride. Robertson and Plummer, *First Epistle*, 95, see the link in "spiritual disorder," "self-satisfied frivolity," and "self-conceit."

14. Countryman, *Dirt, Greed and Sex*, 104–9, 296–314.

15. P. Richardson, "Judgment, Immorality and Sexual Ethics in 1 Corinthians 6:1–11," *NovT* 25 (1983) 37–58, comes close to this insight in the hypothesis that the lawsuits dealt with marriage and divorce issues. However, unlike Countryman, Richardson stresses the notion of sexual morality as the uniting idea rather than ownership rights and competitive greed.

The contention of this chapter is that a look at the writings of Plutarch here further illuminates the connecting link in Paul's treatment of these three community problems. Countryman observes that Paul is concerned not with purity but with the social cohesion violated by attempts at improper possession. Although this view is consistent with the problems addressed in the letter as a whole, the letter also seems to exhibit interest in the individual's own interior movements and growth. πάθος ἐπιθυμίας, or "intemperate passion," is an explicit concern at 1 Thess 4:3–8 and might well be the underlying theme that links together the diverse topics of 1 Corinthians 5–6, with Countryman's πλεονεξία being one of its manifestations.

PLUTARCH AND PAUL ON PASSION

Plutarch's essay "On Moral Virtue"[16] suggests the possibility of such a connection, at least in the context of first-century popular philosophical discussion. He argues that the rational and irrational or passionate parts of the soul are actually two separately operating entities and states that temperance—the product of reason's curb on, or blending with, irrational passion—produces a freedom from violent changes, along with serenity and satiety (447C). He goes on to note the force of opposing, but furtive, emotions that influence the choices of some people; for example, "In the judgment of suits concerning business affairs the passions rush in unawares and cause the greatest waste of time" (447D–E). He further notes (447F–448E) these two opposing principles at work in love: of boys, of wives, of teachers. He finds that in the tempered emotion, a dutiful association that takes usefulness into consideration is later carried on to genuine affection, with reason's drawing on and persuading the passionate element. He concludes the proof that the two are separate with the observation that the passions, held in moderation, are useful when in service of reason and when they help intensify virtues (451D–452A).

In light of the relationship among the ideas argued in Plutarch's essay, the three topics of 1 Corinthians 5–6 (the immoral man, the lawsuits, and the frequenting of prostitutes), as well as the ancillary topics in the vice lists and in the slogans on eating, can all be related as expressions of irrational passion. Paul, of course, decides and urges the Corinthians to act on religious, and not on philosophical, grounds. Thus, he mentions the liturgical symbolism of Passover and leaven at 5:7–8 in connection with preserving the holiness of God's people at 6:1, the reliance on divine judgment to give or deny access to the Kingdom at 6:9, the belief in the cleansing effects of baptism at 6:11, and the spiritual reality of the body at 6:16–17, 19. Nonetheless, while he commands and provides spiritual motivation, he also tries to persuade by rational argument with language that also suggests the struggle of reason against irrational passion. Note Paul's concern with judgment at 5:3, 12, 13; 6:2, 5, 6;

16. Plutarch *Virt. Mo.* 440D–452D (trans. Helmbold in LCL).

with knowledge at 5:6; 6:2, 9, 15, 16, 19; with truth at 5:8; with wisdom at 6:5; and with deception at 6:9.

Another aspect of the unity of the section are the catalogs of vices. These are largely traditional and are suggestive of a general viciousness and irrational passion, but they often, as here, are tailored to suit the context. Thus, the greedy and robbers at 1 Cor 5:10, 11 fit the matter of unjust lawsuits at 6:1–11, whereas the additional fornicators, adulterers, boy prostitutes, and practicing homosexuals[17] at 6:9 fit the matter of sexual immorality at 5:1–13; 6:15–20; and 7. The addition at 6:10 of thieves expands the greedy; the drunkards 5:11 and 6:9 might be taken with the indiscriminate eaters, especially in light of the abuses of eating and drinking noted later at 11:21–22 at the community meals. The interrelatedness among all these in Paul's mind is noted in his easy transition from stomach and food considerations to cautions against immorality at 6:13, all of these serving as instances of the enslavement to irrational passion against which he argues.

One will have to distinguish, however, between Plutarch's philosophical idealism and Paul's pneumatic faith. Plutarch posits the goal of reason's controlling passions, turning them in service of virtue to strengthen the latter, and creating a temperate or harmonized mean that regulates their extremes ("On Moral Virtue" 443B–444E). Paul, however, recognizes the basic incapacity of human efforts to achieve virtue and thus relies on the infusion of the transforming Spirit in consequence of the death and resurrection of Christ (1 Cor 5:7; 6:11, 19–20; and see Rom 8:5–17 and Phil 3:18–21).[18] Compare, however, Paul's description of spiritual ambivalence in Rom 7:18–19 with Plutarch's description of the wise, but irresolute, person who knows what is the right choice but cannot stand by decisions made. In this respect, where Plutarch finds ultimate salvation from intemperate passion in a philosophically developed reason, Paul looks to the Spirit.

Paul's argument against the frequenting of prostitutes rests on his realistic view of the believers as members of the body of Christ[19] and also on the "two become one flesh" tradition from Genesis. Read positively, the argument presents a high ideal of the spiritual potential of licit marital sexuality to unite

17. NAB translation. See Countryman, *Dirt, Greed and Sex*, 109–23, for a discussion both of the relation of "impure" homosexual acts to the "sin" of idolatry here and at Rom 1:18–32 and of the difficulty of determining what μαλακοί and ἀρσενοκοῖται actually mean. He notes on p. 111 that the ambiguous term ἐπιθυμίαι has to be specified by its use in context. This chapter tries to establish a pejorative sense operating behind 1 Corinthians 5–6 by comparisons to 1 Thessalonians 4 and Plutarch.

18. W. Wolbert, *Ethische Argumentation und Paraenese in 1 Kor 7* (Moraltheologische Studien 8; Düsseldorf: Patmos, 1981) 60–63, establishes a parallel in argumentation between Romans 6 and 1 Corinthians 6. In describing the christological and soteriological motivation for the parenesis, Wolbert finds Paul clarifying the declaration of freedom from the law as freedom from sin, a point misunderstood by the Corinthian enthusiasts. The Christian is dead to sin, united to Christ, and living a different existence.

19. Countryman, *Dirt, Greed and Sex*, 204, and C. K. Barrett, *The First Epistle to the Corinthians* (New York and Evanston: Harper & Row, 1968) 150.

the believing couple with Christ. Paul strengthens his point by declaring the
holiness of the body, when used properly, as sanctuary of the Spirit and source
of glory for the divine presence. Plutarch speaks no less highly of the potential of the marriage relationship in his "Dialog on Love."[20] He argues that it is
not impious to claim that God has a role to play in love. On the contrary, Plutarch says that without the divine guidance of Eros, there will not develop the
lasting union of virtuous friendship, which is love's proper goal. Pleasure
(Aphrodite) can be bought but is a passing thing. Eros, in contrast (Plutarch
quotes here Melanippus), "sows secretly a delightful harvest in the desire of
man's heart," mingling what is most pleasant with what is best. In the love
relationship, sober reason and modesty temper the raging element of passion
to a radiant warmth, and then the beloved proceed through acquiescence and
affection to disregard the body and attach themselves to character, engaging in
an intercourse through reasoned discourse and moral behavior as they seek
the trace of ideal beauty in the beloved, the memory of which excited them
originally. Indeed—and now Plutarch quotes Plato—to experience the true
affection of love is to share and participate "in a power that is divine" (Plutarch "Dialog on Love" 756E–759F). In fact, when one observes that as an
effect of love, "a mean, base, ignoble soul is suddenly invaded by high
thoughts, liberality, aspiration, kindness, generosity, it would not be off the
mark to declare 'Surely some God is within!' (Homer *Od.* 19.40)" (Plutarch
"Dialog on Love" 762D–E).

Plutarch elaborates on what the union of friendship entails and notes that
from the initial physical union there grows a friendship that is "a sharing, as it
were, in great mysteries" and with it respect, kindness, mutual affection,
loyalty, and praise. This long outlasts fleeting physical pleasure. In fact, it
constitutes the greatest possible pleasure and provides unsurpassable service
to the beloved. Moreover, this friendship surpasses in beauty friendships of
all other sorts (Plutarch "Dialog on Love" 768B–769F).

Obviously, Plutarch's philosophical idealism sets him apart from Paul's
scriptural, pneumatic, and christological faith. Moreover, Plutarch's praise of
the benefits of procreation and permanence from the marital union stand in
contrast to Paul's silence on childbearing and to the impermanence of his
imminent eschatology. Nonetheless, Plutarch and Paul seem to be in battle
with similar attitudes in their societies, and their alternatives bear remarkable
resemblance to one another.

The resemblance becomes even more striking when one takes note of the
fact that throughout the "Dialog on Love," Plutarch contrasts marital love not
just with illicit heterosexual lovemaking for pleasure but also with love of boys.
The latter he argues to be ephemeral pleasure seeking and actually an assault
on the boy, not love. Paul's addition of μαλακοί and ἀρσενοκοῖται to the vice
list at 1 Cor 6:9 seems inspired by a similar association of boy-love and liaisons

---

20. Plutarch *Erotikos* 748E–771E (trans. Sandbach and Helmbold in LCL).

with prostitutes; he considers both to be pleasure-seeking vices in contrast to licit marital unions. Again, society offers both moralists the contrasting practices against which to describe their ideals. Furthermore, Plutarch describes intercourse without the inspiration of the god Eros to be like hunger and thirst, which can be sated but never achieve their noble end ("Dialog on Love" 756E). This, too, suggests the lead-in to Paul's argument against frequenting prostitutes, where at 1 Cor 6:12–13 he uses an analogy to food and the body and the calculus of usefulness. Although the notion of lawfulness suggests a freedom from kosher law as the background in his original preaching, the food-stomach-immorality association could have come from the Gentile audience's views on physical pleasure and the morality of attaining it. Both moralists studied here develop arguments against unbridled passion, but Plutarch provides an answer in terms of rational control of desires; Paul looks to the eschatological reality of the body in light of the resurrection. Once again, the answers are different, but the connection of ideas bears a striking resemblance.

ARGUMENTS AGAINST THE EPICUREANS

In the development of his ideas about the union that results from the tempering of passion by Eros, Plutarch contrasts that union with the notion in Epicurean materialism of the temporary conjunction of atoms hitting off one another ("Dialog on Love" 769F). He develops his arguments against the Epicurean position at greater length in his essay "That Epicurus Actually Makes a Pleasant Life Impossible."[21] Plutarch criticizes the Epicureans for their location of the good "in the belly and all other passages of the flesh through which pleasure and non-pain make their entrance" and for their attitude that "all the notable and brilliant inventions of civilization were devised for this belly-centered pleasure and the good expectation of this pleasure" (1087D). Plutarch, as one might expect, argues that the body also brings pain, and in greater and more lasting measure (1089F–1091B). Moreover, he says that pleasure is not just the absence of physical pain but should rather be located in the activity of the mind in the pursuit of what belongs to nature and the higher good once one is freed from pain (1091D). This higher good is found in the activity of the speculative, philosophical, honorable part—the mind—whose pleasure is knowing the truth. This pleasure surpasses the bodily gratification of eating and sex (1092E–1093B). In fact, whereas pleasures of the body demand ever fancier foods and fairer maidens, the mind seeks the good of others rather than self-gratification and actually leads one to forgo the pleasures of the body (1097D–1099D).

Plutarch also criticizes the atheism of the Epicureans as doing away not only with the harmful superstitions about divine wrath and punishment in the

21. Plutarch *Suav. Viv. Epic.* 1086C–1107C (trans. Einarson and DeLacy in LCL).

afterlife but also the confidence of divine approval in prosperity and recourse in adversity ("Dialog on Love" 1092A–C, 1101A–F). Without belief in God, in a festival the spirit is untouched by divine influence, prayers are a mummery, and the priest-sacrificer is just a butcher (1102B–C). Contrary to the Epicureans' negative opinions about the gods, the gods by nature bestow good and lend aid, and they are not angry or harmful. All things actually belong to the gods and, since humans are friends of gods, to humans also (1102E–F). Moreover, humans are not destined to be dispersed into oblivion at death but can hope for immortality and freedom of soul in a new and better life after death. The soul, destined for this high and permanent end, thus correctly concerns itself with virtue and courageous action (1103E–1106A).

Thus, Plutarch paints a grim picture of the Epicureans preoccupied with the physical pleasures of eating and sex, which lock them into an ultimately disappointing and painful pursuit of self-gratification. He finds their philosophy despicable for its self-concern, indifference, earthbound hopelessness, and misinterpretation of the gods and their relation to humans. Even their want of popular repute is a source of pain for them ("Dialog on Love" 1100C–D). These appear to be Plutarch's particular targets as he develops his positive theories about virtuous pleasure. Formidable targets they must have been, too, since, as he reports, decrees against them were passed in Rome, Messene, and Lyctos (1100C). Plutarch, writing most of his works in his hometown of Chaeronea in Boeotia, is aware of the Epicureans's pervasive influence.

Perhaps Paul, writing to the fledgling community at Corinth and finding many of the same problems of attitude and practice against which Plutarch writes, has also found it necessary to confront Epicurean influence. This influence could well have turned his teachings on freedom into the self-centered hedonism in some segments of the Corinthian community. Paul's counterarguments that rest so heavily on the disparagement of physical pleasure and enslavement to it; on the reality of the spiritual dimension of the person; on God's favor to, and actual possession of, the believers through purchase; on the confidence at being able to glorify God in the body as an optimistic counter to any presumption of divinely worked physical dissolution; on the afterlife; and on the resurrection of the body at 1 Cor 6:12–20 provide a Christian counterpart to Plutarch's idealistic treatment of the same problems raised by Epicurean atomistic materialism. At the very least, even if there were no Epicurean influences operative in the Corinthian community,[22] Paul could very well be underlining those differences between Christian and Epicurean teaching and practice that would effectively distance the community

22. M. A. Plunkett, "'All Things Are Lawful for Me': The Cynic Background of the Corinthian Theology," paper presented at the meeting of the Eastern Great Lakes Biblical Society, April 14–15, 1988, argues for a polemic with Cynic tendencies at Corinth.

from the oft-despised Epicurean movement.[23] This would forestall misinterpretations by outsiders, as well as any drift toward Epicurean thinking within.

23. Abraham J. Malherbe, *Paul and the Thessalonians* (Philadelphia: Fortress, 1987) 40–43, 84–87, 96–99, 101–6, notes Epicurean undertones in Paul's apologetic and exhortation in 1 Thessalonians and argues for Paul's deliberate effort there at distinguishing his Christian community from the Epicurean circle of friends.

BROTHERLY LOVE IN PLUTARCH
AND IN 4 MACCABEES

"The subject of brotherly love, widely discussed in popular morality, is most systematically treated by Plutarch in his tractate *On Brotherly Love*."[1] This observation by Abraham J. Malherbe serves as a beginning point for the following considerations. When Plutarch writes of brotherly love, he refers to the mutual relationships among biological brothers or sisters.[2] This is surprising when we come to Plutarch from the New Testament, where love for brothers—or, as we would better express it with inclusive language, love for brothers and sisters—is almost exclusively discussed referring to the relationships among believers within the Christian community.[3] In other words, in the Christian texts there is a thoroughgoing metaphorical use of the term *brother* and less often, of *sister*.[4] Nevertheless, 1 John 3:12 mentions one pair of biological brothers, Cain and Abel from Gen 4:1–16, as an example of brothers' hating each other.[5] And with reference to 1 John 5:1b ("Every one who loves the parent loves the child"), the commentaries, often with a reference to Plutarch, present the view that the author here employs a secular idea from contemporary experience of the family.[6] This metaphorical reference to family

---

Translation by David L. Balch.

1. A. J. Malherbe, *Moral Exhortation: A Greco-Roman Sourcebook* (Library of Early Christianity 4; Philadelphia: Westminster, 1986) 93.

2. In *Frat. Am.* 6 (480F), φιλαδελφία refers in its context to the mutual love of the Muses, clearly love between sisters. The whole tractate ends in *Frat. Am.* 21 (492D) with a practical example of love among sisters (see below).

3. For a general overview see K. H. Schelkle, "Bruder," *RAC* 2 (1954) 631–40; J. Beutler, "ἀδελφός," *EWNT* 1 (1980) 67–72. For Paul, who employs φιλαδελφία in Rom 12:10 and 1 Thess 4:9, see also A. J. Malherbe, *Paul and the Thessalonians: The Philosophical Tradition of Pastoral Care* (Philadelphia: Fortress, 1987) 96, 102, 104–5, and esp. 49: "The convert is admitted into a new family of brothers and sisters."

4. Rom 16:1; 1 Cor 7:15; 9:5; Phlm 2; Jas 2:15; 2 John 13.

5. On this text, see H. J. Klauck, "Brudermord und Bruderliebe: Ethische Paradigmen in 1 Joh 3.11–18," *Neues Testament und Ethik: Festschrift für Rudolf Schnackenburg zum 75, Geburtstag* (ed. H. Merklein; Freiburg: Herder, 1989) 151–69.

6. See as only one example N. Alexander, *The Epistles of John* (Torch Bible Commentaries; London: SCM, 1962) 115: "almost a proverb. It applies to any family"; R. Brown, *The Epistles of John* (AB 30; Garden City, NY: Doubleday, 1982) 536.

relationships occurs also in Jesus' words in the Synoptics, Mark 3:35 par. and 10:30 par., where the new congregation of believers understands itself to be constituted as the *familia Dei* (family of God) in distinction from their biological relatives (Mark 3:31 par., 10:29 par.).

Given this background, it may not appear without value to turn our attention to the theme of brotherly love, understood literally, in Plutarch.[7] The next step will be to follow the reception of these Hellenistic ideas in a short section of 4 Maccabees (13:19–14:1), a witness of that Hellenistic Judaism that in many ways served as a bridge between the Greco-Roman world and early Christianity.

BROTHERLY LOVE IN PLUTARCH

Plutarch's work *De fraterno amore* (*On Brotherly Love*; Mor. 478A–492D)[8] is number 98 in Lamprias's catalog. New editions number it 31, along with the closely related treatment of *De amore prolis* (*On Affection for Offspring*; Mor. 493A–497E), in a small collection of ethical-philosophical tractates that are connected with the Delphic dialogues but are divided from the chronologically and thematically related discussions of the ethic of friendship like *Quomodo adulator ab amico internoscatur* (*How to Tell a Flatterer from a Friend*; Mor. 48E–74E) and *De amicorum multitudine* (*On Having Many Friends*; Mor. 93A–97B).[9] It is also close in some ways to other statements of Plutarch's position about family life like *Coniugalia praecepta* (*Advice to Bride and Groom*; Mor. 138A–146A) and *Consolatio ad uxorem* (*Consolation to His Wife*; Mor. 608A–612B). In view of the length of *De fraterno amore*, in the following we cannot do much more than present the chief lines of thought[10] and point to a few matters of special interest in view of 4 Maccabees and the New Testament.

In chapter 1 (487A–D) of *De fraterno amore*, Plutarch introduces the example of the Dioscuri,[11] to whom one brings as an offering (ἀνάθημα) the

---

7. For other treatments of this theme in Greek texts, cf. Arist. *Eth. Nic.* 8.12.3–6 (1161B–1162A); Xenoph. *Cyr.* 8.7.14–16; *Mem.* 2.3.4; Hierocles in Stobaeus *Anthol.* 4.27.20 (in Malherbe's translation, *Moral Exhortation*, 93–95).

8. Trans. Hembold in LCL; the Greek text also in W. R. Paton, M. Pohlenz, and W. Sieveking, *Plutarchi Moralia* (Leipzig: Teubner, 1929) 3. 221–54. The old German translation by Kaltwasser, which Goethe already read, is found in H. Conrad, *Plutarch, Allerlei Weltweisheit: Der vermischten Schriften Dritter Band* (Klassiker des Altertums 1.13; Munich and Leipzig; Georg Müller, 1911) 65–99. The Greek text with French translation is found in J. Dumortier and J. Defradas, *Plutarque: Oeuvre morales* (Collection des Universités de France 7.1; Paris: Les Belles Lettres, 1975) 131–73.

9. On introductory questions, cf. K. Ziegler, "Plutarchos," PW 21 (1951) 636–962, here 798–800. On the whole work, H. D. Betz, "*De Fraterno amore* (*Moralia* 478A–492D)," *Plutarch's Ethical Writings and Early Christian Literature* (SCHNT 4; ed. H. D. Betz; Leiden: Brill, 1978) 231–63; E. Texeira, "A propos du *De amore prolis* et du *De fraterno amore*: La famille vue par Plutarque," *Annales de la Faculté des Lettres et Sciences Humaines de Dakar* 12 (1982) 25–41.

10. An outline from a rhetorical point of view, which does not need to be repeated here, is in Betz, *Plutarch's Ethical Writings*, 234–36.

11. Plutarch comes back to them in 483C, 484E, and 486B.

so-called beam-figures (δόκανα)—that is, two parallel wooden beams joined by two other transverse beams[12]—which Plutarch considers an entirely suitable image of the brotherly love of these gods. He understands his own work as such an offering, which he dedicates (ἀνατίθημι) to two of his Roman friends, the brothers Avidius Nigrinus and Avidius Quietus.[13] In ancient times hate of one's brother was so uncommon that the few known instances supplied material for tragedies; here a biblically informed reader thinks spontaneously of the old story of Cain and Abel in Genesis 4 and the later influence of this story, including 1 John 3:12. In the present, in contrast, brothers who love one another evoke as much astonishment as Siamese twins. After this characteristic critique of his time and culture, according to which the present is considered a period of decline, Plutarch ends the introductory paragraphs with a definition of brotherly love, which already includes essential elements from the ethic of friendship: brotherly love means "to use a father's wealth, friends and slaves in common" (478C). To illustrate, he introduces a picture that he will develop further: such a relationship is considered as incredible as for "one soul to make use of the hands and feet and eyes of two bodies" (478D).

In chapter 2 (478D–479B), nature itself (ἡ φύσις) is our best teacher (cf. 1 Cor 11:14), because the most important parts of the body, such as hands, feet, and eyes, are always created double, as brothers and even twins (ἀδελφὰ καὶ δίδυμα). Opposition among brothers then can be compared with sickness in the body (cf. 1 Cor 12:12–27). Plutarch sketches this positive counter-image with the help of a metaphor that meets us again in 4 Maccabees. According to nature, family life would be lived in agreement (συμφωνία; cf. 4 Macc 14:3) and harmony (ὁμόνοια; cf. 4 Macc 13:25). Therefore, friends and relatives will guard themselves against causing dissonance. Everything sounds like a harmonious choir (ὡς ἐμμελὴς χορός; cf. 4 Macc 13:8).

Chapter 3 (479B–D) shows that Plutarch values naturally given relationships of physical brothers over freely chosen friendships. He characterizes most friendships "as shadows, imitations and images of the first friendship which nature implanted in children towards parents and in brothers toward brothers" (479C–D). It is informative that Plutarch refers in passing to addressing a comrade in salutations and letters as "brother"—informative because in the epistolary literature of the New Testament, we often find the address "brother."[14] It would be meaningless for Plutarch to transfer this name to another as long as one avoids and hates the biological brother, just as it would be meaningless to adorn the effigy of a brother and at the same time to beat his body; in this comparison, the effigy is a friend, and the body is the brother himself (479D).

By a single example in chapter 4 (479E–480A), Plutarch shows that enmity

---

12. A picture in M. P. Nilsson, *Geschichte der griechischen Religion* (Handbuch der Altertums-wissenschaft 5.2.1; 3d ed.; Munich: C. H. Beck, 1967) 1, plate 29, no. 4 (also in no. 3, upper right).

13. On these two, see Ziegler, "Plutarchos," 691.

14. In Galatians alone, cf. 1:11; 3:15; 4:12, 28, 31; 5:11, 13; 6:1, 18.

among brothers is not compatible with the claim to be a philosopher. This concerns the universal imperative, anchored in nature and law (νόμος), to love parents. What could give parents "more pleasure than steadfast goodwill and friendship toward a brother?" (480A; cf. 1 John 5:1).

In chapter 5 (480A–D), Plutarch shows that the opposite is also true: parents are never more deeply disappointed than when they must observe their sons in an angry fight. In a clever play on words, Plutarch says that before everything else, fathers are children-loving (φιλότεκνος), not speech-, honor-, and wealth-loving (φιλόλογος, φιλότιμος, and φιλοχρήματος). The success of his sons as orators, officials, or businessmen interests the father less than whether they "love one another" (φιλοῦντας ἀλλήλους in 480C; cf. John 13:34, although the verb is ἀγαπᾶν). After two historical examples, this paragraph ends with a reversal of the main point of chapter 4: whoever hates a brother finally raises accusations against the father and mother.

The series of examples from history and literature is continued in chapter 6 (480D–481B). Two key sentences of the theme are "Excellent and just sons will not only love each other the more because of their parents, but will also love their parents the more because of each other" (480E), and "Now as regards parents, brotherly love is of such sort that to love one's brother is forthwith a proof of love for both mother and father" (480F; cf. 1 John 4:20–21 and the characteristic inversion in 1 John 5:2).

As a preliminary conclusion in chapter 7 (481B–E), Plutarch insists on avoiding every hint of hatred of brothers (μισαδελφία). For support, he points to the ruinous consequences of this hate, which appears personified as a slanderer and accuser (διάβολος[15] καὶ κατήγορος; 481B) against such alienated brothers. A broken friendship may be knit together again, but when brothers have broken their bonds, they do not readily come together again. Enmity between one person and another brings painful emotions, but when enmity is between brothers, who must share sacrifices, family rituals, and the same sepulcher and who are often neighbors, the burden is still heavier.

In diatribe style, chapter 8 (481E–482C) asks What must one who has a bad brother do? Plutarch answers: put up with him, a task that nature gives us. Plutarch reminds us that often, in chance acquaintances, we accept wrongs that are much worse than the ones of which we accuse our biological brothers.

The classic case, which other authors have handled, is a fight over the inheritance. In chapter 9 (482D–483A), where Plutarch gives us a glimpse both of his sources and of the tradition-history of his theme, he does not deal with this question but chooses to develop the concerns of chapter 8. He warns against defaming a brother to one's parents to deprive him of their goodwill. One must do just the opposite: when there is a conflict between

---

15. Cf. the "slandering slave" (οἰκέτης διάβολος) in 479A, the "slander by friends" (διαβολὰς ἑταίρων) in 483C, and the "Cynic slanderer" (ἀνθρώπους κυνικοὺς καὶ διαβόλους) in 490E.

148   ESSAYS IN HONOR OF ABRAHAM J. MALHERBE

father and son, a brother should bend every effort toward reconciliation,[16] and if necessary, appeal to a father's gullibility by substituting other terms, calling the brother's carelessness "simplicity," his stupidity "straightforwardness," and his contentiousness "inability to endure contempt."

Chapter 10 (483A–C) describes the case of a brother who has actually committed an error (ἁμάρτημα; cf. 1 John 5:16). After defending him in the manner described in chapter 9, the other should give him a brotherly rebuke, correcting the erring brother with all boldness (παρρησία). When, however, the brother was unjustly accused, one must defend him with the same boldness and, if necessary, oppose the parents, taking the risk of attracting their anger to oneself.

Chapter 11 (483C–484B) deals with the problem of the inheritance after the father's death. This is, as experience repeatedly teaches, an especially difficult situation, and Plutarch makes a special effort to address it: one brother's receiving a large share brings material gain and a momentary feeling of superiority; however, in the long run it does not pay off. Even better than a fair division, so Plutarch lets us understand, would be sharing all in common; this should at least serve as a guiding image when the property is divided. The heirs should understand that "it is the care and administration of the estate that is being distributed, but that its use and ownership is left unassigned and undistributed for them all in common" (κοινήν; 483D, citing Plato). Thereby Plutarch clearly transfers a leading ideal from the ethic of friendship to brotherly love.[17]

In chapter 12 (484B–F) Plutarch says that friendship, according to ancient conviction, assumes equality: ἰσότης φιλότης. Equality means friendship (Aristotle Eth. Nic. 1168B), which shows itself primarily, though not exclusively, in the common possession of goods: κοινὰ τὰ φίλων. Friends' possessions are common possessions (1159B). Plutarch remains within this sphere of ideas both when he quotes Plato's advice not to distinguish between "mine" and "not mine" (Plato Resp. 462C) and when he elaborates on equality (ἰσότης)[18] and its opposite in the following section. Nature and fate (φύσις and τύχη) divide gifts to brothers unequally, which makes it necessary to be concerned about equality among brothers. This addresses primarily the one who, in certain respects, has a superior position. Among the examples, especially the last one deserves attention: in his most famous dialogues, Plato intro-

16. διαλλάσσοντι (483A). Cf. in 482E the four compounds with συν- (συνεκδέχεσθαι, συν-υποδύεσθαι, συνεργεῖν, συνεισποιεῖν); similarly 483B; also 483C (συνδακρύειν, συνάχθεσθαι); 484D–E and 490F (10 examples close together); earlier already 481B–C (nine examples). To collect and analyze all the terms with συν- in this tractate would be interesting and worthwhile.

17. Cf. H. J. Klauck, "Gütergemeinschaft in der klassischen Antike, in Qumran und im Neuen Testament," in Gemeinde-Amt-Sakrament, Neutestamentliche Perspektiven (Würzburg: Echter, 1989) 69–100 (with bibliography).

18. Cf. 2 Cor 8:13–14 and, on this, H. D. Betz, 2 Corinthians 8 and 9: A Commentary on Two Administrative Letters of the Apostle Paul (Hermeneia; Philadelphia: Fortress, 1985) 67–69, with the most important sources and literature; further, Malherbe, Moral Exhortation, 154–57.

duced his brothers as his dialogue partners and so secured them immortality. One must conclude that Plutarch relates to his brothers in a similar way, at least with respect to his brother Lamprias, the leading speaker in his most important writings (for example, De defectu oraculorum and De facie in orbe lunae), as well as in relation to Timon in De fraterno amore (cf. 487E).

One of a pair of brothers is never completely perfect. In chapter 13 (484F–485C), Plutarch makes an insightful reference to the Stoic ideal of the perfectly wise person, whereas the other brother is completely wayward. Good and evil are always mixed in each person like a pair of brothers, neither of whom is completely good or evil (cf. 481F). The task of the more gifted brother is grounded on this observation.

The younger brother is thereby reminded that thousands upon thousands of other persons are more fortunate than he (chapter 14 [485C–E]). Will he constantly envy them all? If not, why make an exception of his brother? Plutarch closes these paragraphs with the observation that fundamentally, one ought to envy no one; however, when it must be, one should direct envy to outsiders, to strangers, in order to relieve the relation to brothers of such aggression. This extreme case marks the boundary of a love that no longer includes the outsider.[19]

In order to avoid competitive situations, brothers should seek out different fields of activity. This is clarified with a series of examples in chapter 15 (485E–486D). Interesting in view of 4 Maccabees is that the Syrian kings Antiochus and Seleucus and two later representatives of the dynasty (namely, Antiochus VIII Grypus and Antiochus IX Cyzicenus) are mentioned as negative examples (486A).

Chapter 16 (486D–487E) discusses how a difference in age is more important than other naturally given inequalities. It can generate a will to rule in the elder brother and unruliness in the younger. Plutarch has another recipe ready. He closes this chapter quite effectively in turning directly to his addressees, the pair of brothers Nigrinus and Quietus. They are certainly aware that for him the unbroken affection of his brother Timon transcends all the other favors of fortune.

The situation is different for brothers who are of about the same age, says chapter 17 (487E–488C). The reference to the enmity of Greek brothers who, as a consequence of their conflict, have lost their property to a tyrant (τυράν-νος in 488A) perhaps allows this work to be dated in the time after Domitian, because he is most likely the tyrant to whom Plutarch refers.[20] In 488B–C Plutarch speaks of the Pythagoreans, who are not related by birth but who share a common teaching and, therefore, "do not let the sun go down on their

19. Some exegetes see the danger that brotherly love may exclude outsiders as they interpret the command of brotherly love in the Johannine writings; cf. Klauck, "Brudermord und Bruderliebe," 151–52, 166–69.

20. Cf. Ziegler, "Plutarchos," 800. Dumortier and Defradas, Plutarque, 137, date Frat. Am. about A.D. 115.

wrath."[21] They are, so we can complete Plutarch's line of thought, despite the missing biological basis, a genuine band of brothers. Again, there is a beginning for the transfer of brotherly love to a community of another sort.

In a long series of historical examples given in chapter 18 (488C–490A), once again two Syrian kings appear who are brothers who fought a war against each other. They are Antiochus Hierax (the younger brother) and Seleucus II Callinicus (the older brother), possibly the ones referred to already in chapter 15.[22]

In chapter 19 (490A–E), Plutarch formulates the general rule that governs relationships where there are strong differences of opinion: one should cultivate the friends of one's brother and avoid his enemies. The destructive effects of enemies in friends' clothes is given further attention in chapter 19.

According to Plutarch in chapter 20 (490E–491C), Theophrastus had already formulated the fundamental maxim of the ethic of friendship: κοινὰ τὰ φίλων, "Possessions of friends are common possessions." This is interpreted to mean δεῖ κοινοὺς τῶν φίλων εἶναι τοὺς φίλους, "Friends must also have their friends in common" (490E). Plutarch extends this interpretation further to include brothers. Unity does not demand absolute agreement in their choice of friends. This shows again clearly that for Plutarch, leading ideals are taken from the ethic of friendship and transferred to the conception of brotherly love so that, therefore, a renewed interpretation of "brotherly love" referring to the mutual relationships in a Pythagorean community of friends would not be too difficult (cf. the self-designation of Johannine Christians as φίλοι, "friends," in 3 John 15, and John 15:13–15; both of the Johannine texts are to be interpreted in the context of the central position of the command of brotherly love understood metaphorically in the Johannine tradition).

The final chapter, chapter 21 (491D–492D), includes the whole family of the brother in the exhortation to brotherly love. It mentions a brother's father-in-law, brothers-in-law with their servants and households, wife, and especially children. That Plutarch reserves the final lines for the Roman festival celebrating sisters' love[23] is an indication of friendship for the pair of Roman brothers to whom the treatise is dedicated.

BROTHERLY LOVE IN 4 MACCABEES

4 Maccabees falls into two larger sections framed by an exordium (1:1–12)[24] and peroratio (17:7–18:24). The first main section (1:13–3:18) con-

21. Cf. Eph 4:26 and, on this, Betz, "De fraterno amore," 257 with n. 184.
22. On the similarity between a phrase in this chapter and the final petition in the Lord's Prayer, see Betz, "De fraterno amore," 258.
23. For further information, see G. Wissowa, Religion und Kultus der Römer (Handbuch der Altertumswissenschaft 4.5, 2d ed., 1912 reprint; Munich: C. H. Beck, 1971) 110–11.
24. Cf. H. J. Klauck, "Hellenistische Rhetorik im Diasporajudentum: Das Exordium des vierten Makkabäerbuchs (4 Makk 1.1–12)," NTS 35 (1989) 451–65; on introductory questions in general,

tains a highly theoretical treatment of the thesis that "devout reason is sovereign over the emotions" (1:1). Relevant to our theme is the thought-provoking relativizing of love for parents, spouses, children,[25] and friends: even for their sakes the law may not be broken (1:10–13). Brotherly love is missing from this series but is thematically related to love of friends. The second, much longer main section (3:19–17:6), after a transition that sketches the historical situation, narrates in order the martyrdom of Eleazar (5:1–7:23) and of the seven brothers (8:1–14:10), as well as the "martyrdom" of the mother (14:11–17:6), which consists of having to witness the death as martyrs of her sons, a narration that has one source (possibly the only source) in 2 Maccabees 6:7. Especially the first two reports of martyrdom have parallel structures, each with three parts. The beginning section has opposing speeches exchanged by the tyrant and his victims, which is followed by a central section with the last words and the death of the martyr. A final section has a philosophical reflection and an artful, rhetorically structured speech of praise with a deeply pathetic effect. In this concluding section, with its philosophical reflection and speech of praise (13:1–14:10), there are words about brotherly love. The text of 4 Macc 13:19–14:1, translated with some clarifying notes, follows:[26]

> **19** You[a] know, surely, the bewitching power of brotherly love.[b] The divine and all-wise Providence has bequeathed it through the fathers to their descendants and implants it already in the mother's womb.[c] **20** There brothers dwell the same length of time and are shaped during the same period of time; and from the same blood[d] they receive the power of their growth; the same powers of life[e] let them mature to completion. **21** They are born after an equal time of gestation; they drink milk[f] from the same fountains, through which already in babyhood[g] brother-loving [φιλάδελφοι] souls are raised.[h] **22** They grow stronger from this common nurture and daily companionship,[i] and from general education, especially through our practical discipline in the law of God. **23**

---

see idem, *4. Makkabäerbuch* (JSHRZ 3.6; Gütersloh: G. Mohn, 1989), with a complete bibliography of editions and secondary literature.

25. 4 Macc 14:11–15;12 illustrates this case by the example of the mother of the seven Maccabean martyrs, who does not allow her great love for her sons to mislead her, preventing her from suffering for the law. Here one might compare in detail Plutarch's work *De amore prolis* (Mor. 493A–497E); see Texeira, "A propos du *De amore prolis*."

26. The author's own German translation (translated into English) based on A. Rahlfs, *Septuaginta Id est Vetus Testamentum graece iuxta LXX interpretes* (Stuttgart: Württembergische Bibelanstalt, 1935) 1. 1176. Other editions and translations consulted are Brenton (1851), Bekker (1856), Fritzsche (1871), Swete (1894), Bensly (1895), Deissmann (1900), Clementz (1901), Townshend (1913), Emmet (1918), Riessler (1928), Dörrie (1938), Dupont-Sommer (1939), Hadas (1953), Schur (1956), Hartom (1967), Hyldahl (1972), López Salvá (1982), and Anderson (1985). I find it amazing that 4 Maccabees is missing in two new collections: H. F. D. Sparks (ed.), *the Apocryphal Old Testament* (Oxford: Oxford University Press, 1984), and A. Dupont-Sommer and M. Philonenko (eds.), *La Bible: Ecrits intertestamentaires* (Bibliothèque de la Pléiade 337; Paris: Editions Gallimard, 1987). For a stylistic analysis of our section, see U. Breitenstein, *Beobachtungen zu Sprache: Stil und Gedankengut des Vierten Makkabäerbuchs* (2d ed.; philological diss.; Basel: Schwabe, 1978) 114–16.

Brotherly love [φιλαδελφία] establishes a strong bond of sympathy, which is true, if in any case, for our seven brothers. 24 Educated by the same law, trained in the same virtues and intended for a life of righteousness with each other, they loved one another all the more. 25 A common zeal for ethical superiority strengthened their goodwill j and harmony[k] toward one another. 26 With the aid of their piety, they rendered[l] their brotherly love [φιλαδελφία] more fervent. 27 But although nature and companionship and virtuous habits had augmented the bewitching power of brotherly love, those who were left endured for the sake of piety, while watching their brothers being maltreated and tortured to death. 14:1 Furthermore, they encouraged them to face the torture. They not only despised their agonies, but also mastered the emotions of brotherly love [τῶν τῆς φιλαδελφίας παθῶν].[m]

a. The readers of the book are addressed.

b. A translation of τὰ τῆς ἀδελφότητος φίλτρα (the phrase occurs again in v. 27); φίλτρον (also in 15:13) means, first, a means of awakening love, a love drink or magical drink; then, the enticement by a stimulant; and finally, an inclination, goodwill.[27]

c. With the argumentation of vv. 19–21 cf. esp. Xenophon Cyr. 8.7, 14: "Those from the same seed, nurtured by the same mother, grown up in the same house, loved by the same parents . . . how should they not be close to one another?"[28]

d. Cf. Wis 7:2.

e. ψυχή in Greek; here, "the soul or the life-principle of the mother is also understood."[29]

f. γαλακτοποτοῦντες with Rahlfs and the majority of witnesses to the text; the variants are γαλακτοτροφοῦντες (S°), γαλακτοποτισθέντες (V), and γαλακτοτροφηθέντες.

g. ἐναγκάλισμα (Rahlfs) is a small child, one who is carried in arms; the improvements to ἐν ἀγκάλαις μαστῶν[30] or μητέρων[31] are unnecessary.

h. Adolf Deissmann[32] has a different translation, because he reads συν-στρέφονται instead of συντρέφονται.

27. Cf. A. Dupont-Sommer, Le Quatrième Livre des Machabées: Introduction, traduction et notes (Bibliothèque de l'Ecole des Hautes Etudes, Sciences Historiques et Philologiques 274; Paris: Librairie Ancienne Honoré Champion, 1939) 135.

28. Referred to by Dupont-Sommer; also M. Hadas, The Third and Fourth Books of Maccabees (Jewish Apocryphal Literature; 1953 repr.; New York: Ktav, 1976) 213.

29. According to C. L. W. Grimm, Kurzgefasstes exegetisches Handbuch zu den Apokryphen des Alten Testamentes, 4th fascicle: Das vierte Buch der Maccabäer (Leipzig: S. Hirzel, 1857) 348.

30. Grimm, Kurzgefasstes exegetisches Handbuch, 348, an example in minuscule 62 (according to R. Hanhart; see n. 33).

31. J. Freudenthal, Die Flavius Josephus beigelegte Schrift Ueber die Herrschaft der Vernunft (IV Makkabäerbuch), eine Predigt aus dem ersten nachchristlichen Jahrhundert (Breslau; Schetter'sche Buchhandlung [H. Skutsch], 1869) 171, simple conjecture.

32. A. Deissmann, "Das vierte Makkabäerbuch," Die Apokryphen und Pseudepigraphen des Alten Testaments (ed. E. Kautzsch; 1900 repr.; Darmstadt: Wissenschaftliche Buchgesellschaft, 1962) 2. 149–77, here 168.

i. συντροφία and συνηθεία (also in v. 27) occur together also in Plutarch (*Frat. Am.* 7.481B).
j. εὔνοια in Plutarch (*Frat. Am.* 487F, 479D, 480E, 481C, 482B–E, 483C, 487E–F, 491A, B, E). But εὔνοιαν καί is not found in A and other witnesses, which is not easy to explain but is the result of a later recension.[33]
k. ὁμόνοια in Plutarch (*Frat. Am.* 479A, 483D, 490E–F). A has not only πρὸς ἀλλήλους but τὴν πρὸς ἀλλήλους ὁμόνοιαν already at the end of v. 23, which is, however, a secondary assimilation with v. 25.
l. Deissmann[34] introduces ὁ λογισμός "reason" (a key term in the whole text), as the subject, with support only in V 577.
m. According to the text in Rahlfs, with variants discussed by André Dupont-Sommer.[35]

Immediately preceding 4 Macc 13:19–14:1 is a passage (13:6–18) that portrays well how the choir of the seven brothers (an image already in 8:4) acts on stage. First in unison, then divided into solos with individual voices, and finally again in a choral refrain, they mutually encourage one another to face certain death courageously. In this text brotherly love is mentioned, which at first gives the impression of a digression but, as becomes apparent, fits with the characteristic style of the work. The following are the numerous compounds with συν-, which linguistically express the community that the brothers have among themselves:[36] in v. 21, συν-τρέφονται; in v. 22, συν-τρο-φία and συν-ηθεία; in v. 23, συμ-παθοῦς and συμ-παθέστερον; in v. 24, συν-τραφέντες; and in v. 27, συν-ηθεία and συν-αυξόντων.

In 4 Macc 13:19–22, the author himself lets us understand that with the key phrase "brotherly love" he takes up a well-known topos—well-known both in the particular world of his readers' experience and as a common theme in moral-philosophical discussions and speeches of exhortation.[37] Correspondingly, without hesitation he works with the material and the vocabulary of the relevant Hellenistic tractates, although divine providence is the first principle, characteristically mentioned at the beginning. But then physiological data that belong in the sphere of ancient scientific knowledge follow: begetting, gestation in the mother's womb, birth, being quieted by a mother's milk. These shared experiences, which all the brothers had, even if at different times, create the best constitutional presuppositions for the ethos of brotherly love. However, social factors also contribute their part: v. 22 mentions the

33. R. Hanhart in a letter (19 July 1988); for valuable critical suggestions on the text I am thankful to R. Hanhart.
34. Deissmann, "Das vierte Makkabäerbuch," 168.
35. Dupont-Sommer, *Le Quatrième Livre*, 136.
36. For the corresponding phenomenon in Plutarch *Frat. Am.*, see n. 16 above.
37. Cf. Hadas, *The Third and Fourth Books of Maccabees*, 212: "commonplaces of the rhetorical schools, but presented by our author with uncommon virtuosity."

shared upbringing and education (παιδεία) of the brothers. So far, however, these observations remain quite general and not concerned in particular with the seven brothers, the story of whose martyrdom is being narrated. These general remarks, however, are given a specifically Jewish perspective by the closing phrase of v. 22: the discipline in the divine law, which Jews experience from childhood, makes the raising of the brothers special because the law gives an ethic concerned with daily life and social relationships a completely different foundation. Through this final phrase, the whole passage takes on an undeniably apologetic accent. It is proved not only that Judaism obviously knows the value of brotherly love, accepted by all in that cultural world, but also that brotherly love in Judaism, through its connection to the law, is qualitatively more valuable and a more powerful image than is understood and practiced elsewhere.

Introduced by οὕτως (thus), v. 23 of 4 Maccabees 13 applies the general conclusion to be deduced from the experiential values of vv. 19–22[38] to the particular case of the seven brothers. They present an unsurpassed example of realized brotherly love. In v. 24 the key terms from v. 22 are again employed—education and discipline in the law—and v. 24 concludes that this common training made the seven brothers' love more intense. Verse 26 speaks in an analogous way of a proportional growth of piety (εὐσέβεια) and brotherly love. In between, in v. 25, the leading ethical image for which the brothers strove is described with the Hellenistic term καλοκἀγαθία (nobility).[39] The result of their efforts is described in v. 25 as goodwill (εὔνοια) and harmony (ὁμόνοια), two terms that occur often in Plutarch (see notes j and k to the translation). It is noticeable that the Jewish nation before the outbreak of the Maccabean turmoil can be characterized in a similar manner: "Certain men attempted a revolution against the public harmony (ὁμόνοια) and caused many and various disasters."[40]

Until 4 Macc 13:27–14:1, one could get the impression that the author is concerned with eulogizing the seven brothers as an example of perfect brotherly love in order to demonstrate the superiority of Hellenistic, Diaspora Judaism in comparison with the ethical standards of the surrounding non-Jewish world. It seems to be more an internal apologetic to other Jews than an external one. The introduction to v. 27 emphasizes this once again: "the bewitching power of brotherly love," with whose great fame v. 19 began, was intensified in the seven brothers by nature (cf. vv. 19–21), common nurture (cf. v. 22), and virtue (cf. vv. 24–25). However, already the adversative introduction "but although" is a sign that the basic purpose of the author must be interpreted otherwise. In the following lines it becomes clear: even this exceptionally intensive brotherly love was not strong enough to overcome loyalty to the law.

38. Cf. Breitenstein, *Beobachtungen,* 115: "the content of the whole is a parable."
39. Also in 4 Macc 1:10; 3:18; 11:22; 15:9.
40. 4 Macc 3:21; εὔνοια in 4:24 is a textual variant.

For the sake of brotherly love the seven brothers would have had to save their lives for one another's sake by eating meat offered to idols. Instead, in an exemplary way, they not only endured watching the martyrdom of the others (v. 27) but even mutually encouraged one another to face death (14:1). They overcame physical tortures and the emotions (πάθη) of brotherly love.

Thereby the author has constructed a proof that "devout reason is sovereign over the emotions" (1:1) and that "it can overthrow bodily agonies . . . and all domination by the emotions" (3:18). To see brotherly love suddenly counted among the emotions or passions (πάθη) may surprise us, but it is a linguistic trick that the author uses. Πάθη is used in a very broad sense that includes the instincts, shortcomings of thought (1:6), and bodily suffering, as well as positive emotional urges. Only this equivalence of the different kinds of emotions (πάθη) enables the author to make the argument appear conclusive.

This rhetorically artistic presentation of the superiority of Jewish brotherly love to brotherly love in general serves another purpose, which is different from the one that might be presumed by looking at this section in isolation. The special purpose, which can be recognized from the conclusion, prevents brotherly love from becoming an independent theme (as in Plutarch, for example). The beginnings of a metaphorical use of the term cannot be found in this pericope but do exist in the larger text. The whole narrative has symbolic overtones that enable a typological or allegorical reading. It is no accident that the protagonist, the old priest Eleazar, has a meaningful name ("God helps"). The namelessness of the other actors heightens their representative function as characters with whom one might identify. The symbolic nature of the number seven is too well known to need elaboration. The mother who has lost her children is transparently a personification of the people Israel, who sorrows for her children (cf. Jer 15:9). As shown above, the harmony (v. 25) produced by brotherly love is simultaneously the ideal state of the whole Jewish people (3:21). At this level, brotherly love can be projected beyond the narration about the seven physical brothers. All children of Israel should practice it toward one another not as an unattached moral ideal but on the basis and within the framework of the Torah.

Plutarch's tractate *De fraterno amore* was probably written after A.D. 96 (see the comments above on chapter 17). With respect to 4 Maccabees, scholarly support for an early date in the time of Caligula (fifteen years before or after A.D. 35)[41] competes with a late date of around A.D. 100[42] or A.D.

---

41. E. J. Bickermann, "The Date of Fourth Maccabees," *Studies in Jewish and Christian History* (AGJU 9; Leiden: Brill, 1976) 1. 275–81. Freudenthal, *IV Makkabäerbuch*, 102, supports a date "in the final years before the destruction of the temple."

42. J. W. van Henten, "Datierung und Herkunft des vierten Makkabäerbuches," *Tradition and Re-interpretation in Jewish and Early Christian Literature: Essays in Honour of Jürgen C. H. Lebram* (SPB 36; ed. J. W. van Henten, H. J. de Jonge, P. T. van Rooden, and J. W. Wesselius;

117/118.[43] The question may not be answered on the basis of a single pericope. Furthermore, no one will want to suggest a direct literary dependence
of 4 Maccabees on Plutarch. Both stand in a broad history of tradition that is
older than either work. However, when one inclines to date 4 Maccabees
around A.D. 100, as I do, on the basis of various other considerations, there is a
chronological closeness to Plutarch that the similarity of content happily com-
plements. Thus some additional, mosaic-sized stones would be added to the
argument for a late date.

"Every one who loves the parent loves the child" (1 John 5:1b); "and not
like Cain who was of the evil one and murdered his brother" (1 John 3:12)—
we began with this axiom and example from 1 John. Here brotherly love is
understood literally, but at the same time, this is the basis for developing an
argument about the command of love practiced in the community among
Christian brothers and sisters. In the course of our observations, we had
several occasions to point to substantial parallels in the Johannine literature.
It might be simply accidental, but it deserves mention that 1 John belongs to
approximately the same years at the turn of the century in which, probably,
the two other works discussed were written, 4 Maccabees and Plutarch's
tractate *De fraterno amore*.

Leiden: Brill, 1986) 136–49; idem, *De joodse martelaren als grondleggers van een nieuwe orde:
Een studie uitgaande van 2 en 4 Makkabeeën* (diss. in theology, Leiden, 1986) 187–90.
43. Dupont-Sommer, *Le Quatrième Livre*, 75–85; Breitenstein, *Beobachtungen*, 13–29, 179.

WAS BARNABAS A CHILIAST?
An Example of Hellenistic
Number Symbolism in *Barnabas*
and Clement of Alexandria

Abraham J. Malherbe has demonstrated the influence of Hellenistic popular philosophy, especially in moral exhortation, on the NT writings. This
influence extends to the noncanonical writings, including those that show the
greatest concern with Jews and Judaism. A case in point is the *Epistle of Barnabas*. A feature of Hellenistic number symbolism will shed some light on a
problematic text in *Barnabas*.

THE CHILIASTIC INTERPRETATION
OF *BARNABAS*

When I was a child, I heard my paternal grandmother express her belief
that the world would come to an end in the year 2000. She explained that
God created the world in six days and rested on the seventh; a day with the
Lord is as a thousand years (2 Pet 3:8; Ps 90:4), so the world will last for six
thousand years. Accepting the chronology that placed Creation about 4000
B.C., she placed the end at about 2000. My grandmother was not an educated
person and had few intellectual contacts. As far as I know, she figured this out
for herself. If so, she has not been the only one to make such calculations.
When I grew older and began reading in patristics, I was amazed to learn what
an impressive list of thinkers could be claimed for the view that the world
would last for six thousand years. Although still not convinced, I gained new
respect for my grandmother's theological understanding.

The names of those who in some way use the equation of one day with a
thousand years for chronological speculation or who calculate the duration of
the world on the basis of the Creation week include Justin Martyr,[1] Irenaeus,[2]

---

1. Justin Martyr *Dialogue* 81 explains that Adam did not live a thousand years, because he died
in the "day" in which he sinned; chap. 80–81 refer to the millennial reign in Jerusalem followed by
the general resurrection and judgment.
2. Irenaeus *Against Heresies* 5.28.3 gives six thousand years for the world on the basis of the six
days of Creation, quoting 2 Pet 3:8; *Against Heresies* 5.33.2 identifies the subsequent millennial
kingdom as the true Sabbath; cf. 5.23.2.

Tertullian,[3] Hippolytus,[4] Lactantius,[5] Methodius,[6] Commodian,[7] Victorinus of Pettau,[8] Bardesanes,[9] and for a time Augustine.[10] With most of these, the chronology includes God's rest on the seventh day, producing a specifically premillennial framework: Jesus Christ was born during the sixth millennium and will return at its close; then will come the thousand-year Sabbath rest (the seventh millennium), followed by the eternal world. Irenaeus provides the first full exposition of this scheme.[11]

Jean Daniélou has analyzed the forms that millenarian thought took in the early church.[12] Some early Jewish Christians looked for an earthly reign of the Messiah when the saints would be at rest. The Asiatic type of millennialism (typified by Papias) added to the earthly messianic reign the expectation of material fecundity and a human life span of a thousand years. The Syriac type of millennialism, on the basis of astrological calculations of a cosmic week of seven millennia representing the seven planets, saw the seventh millennium as corresponding to the seventh day of Creation, on which God rested. Alexandrian thought, in contrast, connected the hebdomad with the world of time in contrast to the ogdoad, which is the world of eternity, a cosmological rather than a chronological perspective.

Daniélou saw *Barnabas* as an early representative of the Syrian type of millennialism whose originality lay in relating the early idea of the eschatological rest to speculations on the cosmic week. *Barnabas* brought together the Jewish idea of rest on the seventh day with the Hellenistic idea of seven millennia.[13] When one reads in *Barnabas* 15 the combination of the six days of Creation, a day with the Lord as one thousand years, and the Lord's judgment at the completion of six thousand years, it is easy to fill in, as Daniélou does,

---

3. Tertullian *On the Soul* 37 implies the millennium as 7 and Heaven as 8; *Against Marcion* 3.24 speaks of the millennial kingdom.

4. Hippolytus *Commentary on Daniel* 4.23–24 uses the six thousand years to calculate that the second coming of Christ will not be until about A.D. 500. The Sabbath is a type of the millennial kingdom of rest.

5. Lactantius *Epitome* 72 is clearest on the millennium, but *Divine Institutes* 7.22, 24, 26 contain the calculations giving a total duration of the world as seven thousand years, including the millennium.

6. Methodius *Symposium* 9.1 gives the same 6 + 1 scheme as Lactantius but bases it on the description of the tabernacle in the Law.

7. Commodian *Instructions* 43, 44 and 80—the earth will last six thousand years.

8. Victorinus of Pettau *On the Creation of the World* presents the seventh millennium as the true Sabbath, followed by the eighth age.

9. Bardesanes *On Fate* at the end says that the world will last for six thousand years.

10. Augustine *City of God* 20.7; 22.30 keeps the scheme without a literal millennium.

11. *Against Heresies* 5.23.2; 28.3; 33.2. Cf. *Didascalia* 6.18 for the Sabbath as a type of the final rest, the seventh thousand-year period; the ogdoad, or last day, is the first day.

12. Jean Daniélou, "La typologie millénariste de la semaine dans le christianisme primitif," *VC* 2 (1948) 1–16; Daniélou, *The Theology of Jewish Christianity* (Philadelphia: Westminster, 1964) 376–404, esp. 396–403.

13. Daniélou, *The Theology of Jewish Christianity*, 396–98. Daniélou is followed by G. G. Blum, "Chiliasmus II," *TRE* 7 (1981) 730.

"the archaic doctrine of the earthly reign of Christ"[14] during the seventh millennium, with the result that *Barnabas* belongs in the premillennial camp.

It is not surprising, therefore, to find *Barnabas* claimed by modern adherents of an Adventist, or premillennial, view.[15] It is more significant to find other scholars accepting this interpretation of *Barnabas*. Johannes Quasten writes, "The author is a follower of chiliasm." After the judgment "will dawn the sabbath of the millennial kingdom."[16] James A. Kleist, in *Ancient Christian Writers*, links the author of *Barnabas* with Papias as the first Christian writers to advocate chiliastic ideas, with *Barnabas*'s contribution the dividing of history into six millennia typified by the six days of Creation and followed by eschatological rest. Kleist charts the chronology as follows: days 1 through 5 were past for *Barnabas*, day 6 is the present era, day 7 will be the millennium, and "day" 8 will be eternity.[17] W. Rordorf concludes that we should regard *Barnabas* 15 as a unity with a natural progression, so that the seventh millennium in 15:8 is followed by the eighth day, a new aeon.[18]

At one time I agreed with these scholars in their reading of *Barnabas*, so it will not be understood as disrespectful if I now argue for another interpretation. Some commentators set forth the chiliastic parallels to *Barnabas* but are more cautious about saying what *Barnabas* does not say. P. Prigent warns that in spite of the one thousand years attributed to each day, *Barnabas*'s speculations must not be confounded with millennial hopes, which, he says, were not based on the cosmic week but on the expectation of a return to Paradise.[19] Prigent distinguishes 15:1–5, which draws on an earlier source, from 15:6–9, which expresses *Barnabas*'s Christianizing interpretation. In particular, 15:8 makes the eighth day, and not the seventh (as in 15:5), the type of a new world. Nevertheless, Prigent marks the parallel from Augustine *City of God* 22.30.5, according to which we are now in the sixth day; the seventh will be the great Sabbath of God, and the eighth day the eternal day of God.[20] In his later commentary for *Sources Chrétiennes*, Prigent still sees 15:1–5 as coming from another source in preference to Rordorf's view of the chapter's unity, which has received strong support from Klaus Wengst.[21] I would point out that separate sources would make unnecessary an effort to reconcile the two parts of the chapter by proposing a millennial scheme of 6 + 1 + 1. I will later attempt a nonmillennial interpretation based, however, on the unity of the chapter. Prigent notes further that as against millennialism in the technical

14. Daniélou, *The Theology of Jewish Christianity*, 398.
15. William H. Shea, "The Sabbath in the Epistle of Barnabas," *AUSS* 4 (1966) 149–75.
16. Johannes Quasten, *Patrology* (Utrecht: Spectrum, 1953) 1. 89.
17. James A. Kleist, *The Didache, the Epistle of Barnabas* . . . (ACW 6; Westminster, MD: Newman, 1948) 179.
18. W. Rordorf, *Sunday* (Philadelphia: Westminster, 1968) 93f.
19. P. Prigent, *L'Epître de Barnabé I–XVI et ses sources* (Paris: Gabalda, 1961) 67.
20. Prigent, *L'Epître de Barnabé*, 70.
21. P. Prigent and R. A. Kraft, *L'Epître de Barnabé* (Paris: Cerf, 1971) 182–88; Klaus Wengst, *Tradition und Theologie des Barnabasbriefes* (Berlin: de Gruyter, 1971) 48–51.

sense, *Barnabas* refrains even in 15:5 from explicitly interpreting the seventh day as a seventh millennium and puts at the end of the sixth or the beginning of the seventh day events that are placed in Revelation 20 after the millennium.[22] Robert Kraft does take the "rest" period as "an interim between the old and new worlds"[23] but cautions that "it might be considered strange if Pseudo-Barnabas or his tradition interpreted the 'six thousand years' *literally*."[24]

THE ARGUMENT OF *BARNABAS* 15

Chapter 15 of *Barnabas* occurs in the body of the treatise, which takes up the central practices or institutions of Judaism and gives what may be described as an allegorical, spiritual, or Christian interpretation of these: sacrifice (chapters 7–8), circumcision (chapter 9), food laws (chapter 10), washings (chapter 11), covenant (chapters 13–14), and temple (chapter 16). Chapter 15 deals with the Sabbath. It begins with three quotations, only the third of which can be definitely identified: "Now also concerning the sabbath, it has been written in the Ten Commandments, which God spoke on Mount Sinai to Moses face to face: 'Sanctify the sabbath of the Lord with pure hands and a pure heart.' And in another place he says: 'If my sons will keep my sabbaths, then I will place my mercy upon them.' The sabbath is mentioned at the beginning of creation: 'And God made the works of his hands in six days, and he completed them on the seventh day and rested on it and sanctified it'" (15:1–3).

The first quotation, although cited as coming from the Decalogue, is more like a conflation of Jer 17:22 and Ps 24:4. Several passages might suggest the thought of the second quotation, but the closest verbal parallels are provided by a combination of Exod 31:13–17 with Isa 44:3. Both the first and the second quotations are paraphrases similar to Targumim.[25] The third quotation is close to Gen 2:2–3 but follows the Hebrew massoretic text and the Aramaic *Targum Onqelos* in reading "He completed on the seventh day," rather than the Septuagint, Syriac, and Samaritan Pentateuch in reading "He completed on the sixth day." That latter reading is followed in *Barnabas*'s next verse: "Observe, children, what it says: 'He completed [his work] in six days.' This means that in six thousand years the Lord will complete all things. For a day with him signifies a thousand years. He bears me witness by saying, 'Behold the day of the Lord will be as a thousand years'" (15:4). If *Barnabas* has

22. Prigent and Kraft, *L'Epître de Barnabé*, 186.
23. Robert Kraft, *Barnabas and Didache* (vol. 3 of *the Apostolic Fathers*; ed. Robert M. Grant; New York: Nelson, 1965) 129.
24. Kraft, *Barnabas and Didache*, 128.
25. Prigent, *L'Epître de Barnabé*, 66. Prigent and Kraft, *L'Epître de Barnabé*, 183, give references for the Decalogue interpreted in a spiritual sense; this may have been the intention behind the original testimony collection, but *Barnabas*'s use is different. The fullest commentary is Hans Windisch, *Der Barnabasbrief, Die Apostolischen Väter* 3 (HNT; Tübingen: J. C. B. Mohr, 1920).

followed a testimony collection in the first three verses, the change to "sixth day" may be a correction to agree with the Greek text of Genesis or, more significantly, to avoid the idea of God's completing his work on the seventh day.[26] (If Barnabas was conscious of the variant, it might have contributed to his collapsing the numbers 6 and 7, and 7 and 8, which will be discussed below.) The scriptural support for his eschatological interpretation of the Creation account is apparently Ps 90:4, but the wording is actually closer to 2 Pet 3:8.

The purpose of this eschatological interpretation is indicated by these further comments: "'And he rested on the seventh day.' This means, when his Son comes, he will bring to an end the time of the lawless one, will judge the ungodly, and will change the sun, moon, and stars; then he will truly rest on the seventh day" (Barn. 15:5). The Second Coming of Christ will bring to an end the six thousand years of this world. The future tense rules out the possibility that the reference is to the first coming; moreover, the terminology is the usual eschatological description for the end time. Only when lawlessness is overthrown will God truly be able to rest. The true meaning of the Sabbath, in Barnabas, is the eschatological rest. The chiliastic language of 15:4 is here seen to be used not for a chronological purpose per se but to remove the Creation account as a basis for the literal observance of the seventh day.

Next, Barnabas gives another reason why the Jews are wrong in taking the Sabbath command literally, a reason designed to remove the Decalogue command as a basis for Sabbath observance. It is humanly impossible to keep the Sabbath as intended: "Moreover, he says: 'Sanctify it with pure hands and a pure heart.' If, then, anyone, by being pure in heart is able now to sanctify the day which God sanctified, we have been in every way deceived. See, therefore, that at that time when we truly rest, we will sanctify it, when we shall be able, since we will have been justified and will have received the promise, there being no more wickedness and all things being made new by the Lord. Then we will be able to sanctify it, we ourselves having first been sanctified" (Barn. 15:6–7). The repetition of the quotation in 15:1 changes the plural to the singular, bringing it closer to the form of the Decalogue and preparing for the individualized interpretation that follows. Barnabas, unlike others, concludes that no one now is able to sanctify the Sabbath, so it is not to be observed. The seventh day is eschatological. As in the Epistle to the Hebrews 4:9, "there remains a sabbath rest for the people of God"—the world to come.[27] Only when God's people have been completely sanctified and lawless-

26. Kraft, Barnabas and Didache, 127, on the reading; Prigent and Kraft, L'Epître de Barnabé, 184, for parallels in Philo; also Albert Hermans, "Le Pseudo-Barnabé est-il millénariste?" ETL 35 (1969) 863–64.
27. C. K. Barrett, "The Eschatology of the Epistle to the Hebrews," The Background of the New Testament and its Eschatology (ed. W. D. Davies and D. Daube; Cambridge: Cambridge University Press, 1956) 369–71.

ness no longer exists will it be possible genuinely to rest. *Barnabas* elsewhere affirms that complete justification before God must await the future.[28]

Having argued that the Creation Sabbath is really the eschatological Sabbath and that it is impossible for sinful human beings to sanctify the Sabbath day, the author reverts to his usual approach[29] of quoting the prophets' condemnation of Israel's ritualistic observances: "Moreover, he says to them: 'I cannot endure your new moons and sabbaths.' See, now he says, 'The present sabbaths are not acceptable to me, but that [Sabbath] which I have made, in which when I have rested in everything, I will make the beginning of the eighth day, which is the beginning of another world'" (*Barn.* 15:8). The quotation of Isa 1:13 is identical with that in 2:5, where the preceding context is included in the quotation. "Your [Jewish] sabbaths" are the Sabbaths of the present era,[30] in contrast to God's eschatological Sabbath. The author words his interpretation in the first person, as if a quotation from God, and the wording may have been influenced by some source.[31] The important point for our purposes is the shift from the seventh to the eighth day to describe this eschatological rest. Rabbinic thought interpreted the Sabbath as a figure of the world to come,[32] as the author had done in *Barn.* 15:5. *Barnabas* now, however, takes the eighth day instead of the seventh day as representative of the world to come. More attention will have to be given to the significance of this shift, but for the moment it may be noticed that it was prompted by thought of the Christian's special day, called "the eighth day" perhaps under the influence of its relation to the eschatological day: "Wherefore we keep the eighth day for rejoicing, in which also Jesus arose from the dead and when he was manifested ascended into heaven" (15:9).

Instead of using the terminology of the first day of the week, or Lord's day, *Barnabas* "trumps" the Jewish exaltation of the seventh day as the climax of Creation by connecting the day of Christian celebration with the new world of eternity. The Christian Sunday does not fit a typology of the week culminating in the seventh day, so a different eschatological symbolism is introduced, that of the ogdoad.[33] The reference to Jesus' Resurrection and Ascension emphasizes the eschatological significance of the eighth day.[34] Whether or not

28. *Barn.* 4:10; 6:19; cf. 21.
29. For example, *Barn.* 2; 3; 9; 16.
30. Kleist, *The Didache, the Epistle of Barnabas . . .*, 179.
31. Prigent, *L'Epître de Barnabé*, 69; Prigent and Kraft, *L'Epître de Barnabé*, 186f. The closest parallel is 2 *Enoch* 33:1, which may itself be a Christian interpolation—so Rordorf, *Sunday*, 235. The eighth-day symbolism occurs in *Sibylline Oracles* 7.140.
32. Tamid 7.4; *Mekhilta* on Exod 23:13.
33. H. Riesenfeld, "Sabbat et Jour du Seigneur," *New Testament Essays: Studies in Memory of T. W. Manson* (ed. A. J. B. Higgins; Manchester, England: University Press, 1959) 215–16. Daniélou affirms the Christian origin of the "eighth day"—*The Theology of Jewish Christianity*, 397–98; Daniélou, *The Bible and the Liturgy* (Notre Dame, IN: University of Notre Dame Press, 1956) 256.
34. Justin Martyr *Dialogue* 41 uses the eighth day in an anti-Jewish sense, connected with circumcision.

Barnabas means to say that the Ascension occurred on the day of the Resurrection,[35] the author does seem to put the Ascension also on an eighth day,[36] which becomes a prophecy of the new creation. As Kleist observes, *Barnabas* uses "eighth day" in two senses: for the day of eternity (the other world [15:8]) and for the first day after the lapse of the preceding week (15:9). Because Jesus arose on the eighth day in the second sense, we commemorate on it, by anticipation, the eighth day in the first sense.[37]

THE ESCHATOLOGY OF *BARNABAS*

Rordorf argues for the seventh millennium's being an interim between the six thousand years and the eighth age, since otherwise we must assume that two eschatological ideas have been forcibly yoked, with both the seventh and eighth days as the new aeon.[38] *Barnabas* may indeed have drawn on two different eschatological traditions,[39] and the whole treatise shows how little the author was interested in consistency. Whatever served to make a point could be brought in. The scheme of seven ages in the early part of the chapter relativizes the weekly Sabbath for him, and the imagery of the number 8 in the latter part of the chapter connects with the Christian's special day. The two symbolisms serve different functions in the argument, so there was no need to harmonize them. Neither serves the purpose of periodization.

To quote C. K. Barrett, "The only point that is really clear here is perhaps the only point that Barnabas really wished to make: the Jews with their Sabbaths are in the wrong, the Christians with their Sundays are in the right."[40] As the present survey of *Barnabas* 15 shows, the author was not interested in chronological calculation. He still lived in the early Christian expectation of an imminent end of all things (chapter 4). He drew on chiliastic traditions,[41] but he was not interested in them for their own sake. He subordinated chiliastic thought to another purpose—to eliminate the weekly Sabbaths, particularly the support the Creation account and its eschatological reapplication might seem to give them.

Albert Hermans has most thoroughly argued the case that *Barnabas* was not millennialist.[42] He shows that the Christian millennialists (Irenaeus, Lactantius, Victorinus, and Methodius) do not know a succession of two eschatological Sabbaths. The millennium may be called a Sabbath, but the celestial world to follow it is not so called; hence it is most unlikely that Barnabas speaks of a double final Sabbath, one during the seventh, and the other during

35. As in *Gos. Pet.* 13:56; cf. Tertullian *Against the Jews* 13.
36. Rordorf, *Sunday*, 235.
37. Kleist, *The Didache, the Epistle of Barnabas . . .* , 180.
38. Rordorf, *Sunday*, 93–94.
39. Daniélou, "La Typologie millénariste," 1–8; Windisch, *Der Barnabasbrief*, 383–84.
40. Barrett, "Eschatology," 370.
41. Rordorf, *Sunday*, 93–94.
42. Hermans, "Le Pseudo-Barnabé," 849–76.

the eighth, period.[43] Hermans advances three further arguments against the interpretation of *Barnabas* as millennialist: (1) the author's vocabulary identifies the consummation and rest at the end of the sixth period with the inauguration of the heavenly world; (2) the description of the events of the end allows only one series of future events and makes no provision for anything to bring a supposed seventh millennium to an end; and (3) the argumentation of chapter 15 sets up a correspondence between the divine rest after the first creation to the Jewish Sabbath and the divine rest of the new creation to the Christian observance of the eighth day.[44]

The second of Hermans's arguments has been strongly urged by D. H. Kromminga to establish the same point. Kromminga, as well as others, has noticed that in the usual apocalyptic scheme,[45] the judgment follows the millennial "rest." *Barnabas* 15:5 puts the judgment of the ungodly and the cosmic changes at the beginning of the seventh day, not at the end of the millennium, where they occur in the usual premillennial outline.[46]

Hermans's first and third arguments mean that for *Barnabas* the seventh and eighth ages are identical and not sequential. William H. Shea has argued against the interpretation that the seventh age is the same as the eighth, because, he says, that would mean that the Christians are keeping the Sabbath, "which is exactly what he [Barnabas] opposes."[47] Shea's reasoning should be reversed. What he says might have some force if the eighth were understood as a Sabbath, but not if the eighth superseded the seventh. Here the two forms of text at Gen 2:2–3 may have a further significance. The seventh day marks the completion of the six days of work, so the literal seventh day is joined to the sixth day as part of the created order.[48] Yet, in another sense, the seventh-day rest is really the creation of a new world and so belongs to the eighth period, the new order. *Barnabas* is so anti-Jewish that it prefers the eighth-day terminology over the seventh day for the eschatological rest. If the eighth day (*Barn.* 15:8), which is the beginning of another world, means an eighth millennium, this is inconsistent with 15:5–7, where the seventh millennium is the time when sin is overcome.[49] Moreover, *Barnabas*'s doctrine of the Sabbath really precludes the chiliastic reading of his text. Continued observance of the Sabbath amounts to a denial of our present sinfulness.[50] It is

43. Hermans, "Le Pseudo-Barnabé," 859–60.
44. Hermans, "Le Pseudo-Barnabé," 861–75. I take exception to Hermans's designation of the eighth day as the "Christian sabbath" (868).
45. Cf. *4 Ezra* 7:30.
46. D. H. Kromminga, *The Millennium in the Church* (Grand Rapids, MI: Eerdmans, 1945) 32; Prigent and Kraft, *L'Epître de Barnabé*, 186; Windisch, *Der Barnabasbrief*, 385.
47. Shea, "Sabbath," 168.
48. Cf. Kraft, *Barnabas and Didache*, 127–28.
49. Barrett, "Eschatology," 370; Windisch, *Der Barnabasbrief*, 383–84.
50. Kromminga, *The Millennium*, 34–35; Wengst, *Tradition und Theologie*, 74; Prigent and Kraft, *L'Epître de Barnabé*, 186.

hard to see how the author's negative view of the weekly Sabbath would allow for an *intermediate* seventh millennium to be a time of perfection. Another question should be raised: Is it even proper to read *Barnabas* in the light of Justin, Irenaeus, and Hippolytus and their chiliastic tradition? Is that *Barnabas*'s intellectual lineage? It is true that *Barnabas* shares with Justin similar combinations and applications of biblical texts, but this comes from a shared use of early Christian collections of testimonia.[51] On matters of fundamental doctrinal outlook, there is little in common beyond the basics of Christian faith. On such key matters as the covenant, the understanding of OT history, and the method of biblical interpretation, *Barnabas* has a completely different approach from Justin and Irenaeus.[52]

CLEMENT OF ALEXANDRIA AND *BARNABAS*

Barnabas belongs to another tradition in the early history of Christianity, an Alexandrian tradition[53] that led to Clement of Alexandria and Origen. The first attestation of *Barnabas* comes from Clement, who was clearly indebted to its author and held him in high regard. I count eight quotations in Clement's *Stromata* from *Barnabas*, the author of which is called an "apostle," companion of Paul, and one of the seventy disciples.[54] Indeed, it was reading Clement that led me to reexamine the passage in *Barnabas* and suggested another way of interpreting its author. The parallels between *Barnabas* and Clement are duly noted by the commentators but are not then pursued as to *Barnabas*'s meaning.[55] These parallels show how an early reader of the treatise reconciled the tension between 7 and 8 as types of the eschatological rest.

Before looking at the relevant section in Clement, I should explain that for Clement, 6 is the number associated with this world and the natural order, and 8 is associated with the heavenly realm. Of course, 7 is the day of rest, according to the OT.

Clement's interpretation of the Sabbath commandment in *Stromata* 6.16

51. The most recent treatment is by Oskar Skarsaune, *The Proof from Prophecy: A Study in Justin Martyr's Proof-Text Tradition* (NovTSup 56; Leiden: Brill, 1987).

52. E. Ferguson, "The Covenant Idea in the Second Century," *Texts and Testaments: Critical Essays on the Bible and Early Church Fathers* (ed. W. Eugene March; San Antonio: Trinity University Press, 1980) 135–62.

53. In support of this view, see L. W. Barnard, *Studies in the Apostolic Fathers and Their Background* (New York: Schocken, 1960) 46, and literature cited there.

54. Clement of Alexandria *Stromata* 2.6, 7, 15, 18, 20; 5.8, 10; 6.8. There may be an unreferenced allusion to *Barnabas* in *Stromata* 6.16, the chapter I see as giving a clue to *Barnabas*'s symbolic use of numbers: "By following him, therefore, through our whole life, we become impassible; and this is to rest." If *Barnabas*'s "perfected" (chap. 6) and "justified" (chap. 15) were understood by Clement as "impassible," the result would be the statement he gives.

55. Hermans, "Le Pseudo-Barnabé," 864–65, for instance, cites Clement only as an illustration of how the author's mind might have worked; Kraft, *Barnabas and Didache*, 129; Prigent and Kraft, *L'Épître de Barnabé*, 184.

will confirm Hermans's first and third arguments about the equivalence of 7 and 8 for Barnabas. Clement begins with the equivalence of the seventh day to a new beginning: "The seventh day, therefore, is proclaimed a rest—an avoidance of evils—preparing for the original day, our true rest; which, in truth, is the first beginning of light, in which all things are perceived and inherited."[56] Clement, however, is aware that Christians gave superiority to the eighth day, and he is able to accommodate that fact to the OT text: "For one may venture to say that the eighth is properly the seventh, and the seventh actually the sixth; that is the eighth is properly the sabbath, and the seventh a day of work."[57] After notices of occurrences of the number 6 in the natural order of the world, Clement observes that for the Pythagoreans, the number 7 is "motherless and childless." He connects this statement with Jesus' declaration that in the coming rest, those who are resurrected "neither marry nor are given in marriage" (Luke 20:35). The association of the number 6 with the world is illustrated by the account of the Transfiguration, where Jesus was the sixth person present (but by the Resurrection became the eighth), indicating that he was "God in a body of flesh" (Strom. 6.16).

Then comes the comment to which I would like to draw special attention: "For in the order of numbers six is included in the list, but the sequence of the letters employs the symbol digamma that is not used in writing. In this regard, each letter is kept in its position for the numbers themselves only up to seven and eight, but in the number of the letters of the alphabet zeta is six and eta seven. Yet when the symbol digamma was inserted (I know not how) into writing, if we should follow it out thus, six becomes the seven and seven the eight" (Strom. 6.16). The basis for this not-clearly-stated explanation is that the numeral 6 in Greek was the letter digamma, which had dropped out of the alphabet and was used only for the numeral or as a contraction. If one did not count the digamma, then the letter that stood for 7 (zeta) was actually the sixth letter in the alphabet, and the letter that stood for 8 (eta) was the seventh. With this explanation made, Clement can proceed to an extended praise of the number 7 in the nature of things, as supported by many pagan writers. His premise seems to be that the seventh day of the Law was to be identified with the Christian's first (eighth) day. Not that Clement advocated keeping the first day in the way Jews kept the seventh day, as later Christian Sabbatarians would: he has in mind "abstinence from evil"[58] and especially the eschatological rest. That puts him in the tradition of the Epistle to the Hebrews (4:1–11) and, I would add, the tradition of Barnabas.

56. Clement is borrowing from Aristobulus, a passage preserved in Eusebius Preparation for the Gospel 13.12.9–11. Aristobulus identified the first day and the seventh day. Prigent and Kraft, L'Epître de Barnabé, 185.
57. Cf. a similar play in Stromata 4.25.
58. The spiritual interpretation of the prohibition of work on the Sabbath as meaning an abstinence from evil was common in the early church—see R. J. Bauckham, "Sabbath and Sunday in the Post-Apostolic Church," From Sabbath to Lord's Day (ed. D. A. Carson; Grand Rapids, MI: Zondervan, 1982) 265–69, for metaphorical interpretations of the Sabbath command.

Clement's identification of 8 with 7, by way of the peculiar relation that obtained between the Greek alphabet and Greek numerals, may give an explanation for *Barnabas*'s apparent inconsistency in combining two different eschatological schemes as if they were one. What appears to us as, at worst, a chronological contradiction or as, at best, a sample of muddleheadedness was of no concern to the author. And that fact itself separates him from a chiliastic mentality. There is no intermediate millennial kingdom in *Barnabas*. The seventh age of heavenly rest, according to one set of terms, was also the eighth period according to another terminology. And the difference is one of terminology, not of eschatological schemes.

Having delivered *Barnabas* from the chiliasts, have we delivered him to the Gnostics?[59] After all, many of them were connected with Alexandria. Clement was likely acquainted with the numerical speculations of the Valentinian Gnostic Marcus.[60] The latter refers to the intervention of Jesus (whose name in Greek has six letters) in transforming the hebdomad (represented by *Anthropos* and *Ekklesia*) into the ogdoad (represented by *Logos* and *Zoe*).[61] But there is nothing to connect *Barnabas*, who was earlier, with these speculations. *Barnabas*'s gnosis has little, if anything, in common with the Gnosticism of a Basilides or a Valentinus. Moreover, the number symbolism in *Barnabas* has a quite different significance. For the Gnostics, the number 7 (the hebdomad) stood for the seven planetary spheres, in contrast to the fixed stars of Heaven above (the ogdoad).[62] The number 7 represented the world of time, and the ogdoad was the world of eternity. Gnostics gave the numbers a cosmological significance; *Barnabas* gave them an eschatological significance (but not in the same way as chiliasts). Although chronology as such was not his main concern, the six thousand years remained a chronological concept.

No, Barnabas was not a chiliast, nor was he a Gnostic. There were other options possible in the mixture of Jewish and Hellenistic traditions available to early Christians.

---

59. As Robert Grant perceptively asked on hearing a first reading of this paper.
60. Clement *Strom.* 6.16 (cited above) makes the same reference as Marcus (Irenaeus *Adv. haer.* 1.14.6) does to Jesus as one of six persons on the mount of Transfiguration.
61. Irenaeus *Adv. haer.* 1.14.5. Cf. Daniélou, *The Theology of Jewish Christianity*, 399.
62. Daniélou, *The Bible and the Liturgy*, 259; cf. Daniélou, *The Theology of Jewish Christianity*, 403.

PART TWO

HELLENISTIC LITERATURE
AND RHETORIC

NARRATIVE MODELS
FOR IMITATION IN LUKE-ACTS

Hellenistic rhetorical and literary conventions of moral exhortation used personal examples as a common device, as Abraham J. Malherbe notes.[1] Most scholars agree that Greco-Roman education and rhetoric, as well as works (including narratives) that were written under their influence, emphasize models, paradigms, or exempla for imitation by pupils or readers.[2] In this vein, Benjamin Fiore cites Pliny's letter to Titius Aristo (8.14) as claiming an

---

1. Abraham J. Malherbe, *Moral Exhortation: A Greco-Roman Sourcebook* (Library of Early Christianity 4; Philadelphia: Westminster, 1986) 135–38, esp. 135. Cf. Karlheinz Stierle, "L'Histoire comme exemple, l'exemple come histoire: Contribution à la pragmatique et à la poétique des textes narratifs," *Poétique* no. 10 (1972) 176–98. Stierle indicates that ancient rhetoric on exemplum and its theory of history as teacher of life (Cicero's *Historia magistra vitae*) found a close link between history and moral philosophy. Thus, ancient history could be called paradigmatic (p. 184). On p. 185, he cites R. Koselleck, "Historia magistra vitae: Über die Auflösung des Topos im Horizont neuzeitlich bewegter Geschichte," *Natur und Geschichte, Karl Löwith zum 70. Geburtstag* (Stuttgart: Kohlhammer, 1967) 196–218, who traces the loss of the ancient philosophical-moral link with history and the loss of the exemplum from the end of the eighteenth century.

2. See Benjamin Fiore, *The Function of Personal Example in the Socratic and Pastoral Epistles* (AnBib 105; Rome: Biblical Institute Press, 1986), esp. chap. 3, "Example in Rhetorical Theory, Education, and Literature," 26–44, and his bibliography. Cf. Pedro Gutierrez, *La Paternité spirituelle selon S. Paul* (Paris: Gabalda, 1968); Willis P. de Boer, *The Imitation of Paul: An Exegetical Study* (Kampen, Netherlands: J. H. Kok, 1962); Henri Crouzel, "L'imitation et la 'suite' de Dieu et du Christ dans les premiers siècles chrétiens, ansi que leurs sources gréco-romaines et hébraiques," JAC 21 (1978) 7–41, esp. 7–30; and Eduard Cothenet et al., "Imitation du Christ," *Dictionnaire de Spiritualité* 7 (1971) 1536–1601. G. W. Trompf, *The Idea of Historical Recurrence in Western Thought: From Antiquity to the Reformation* (Berkeley: University of California Press, 1979) 106, asserts that "Polybius was probably trained as a rhetorician, and though placing truth before rhetorical embellishment . . . he had a feeling for incidents possessing universal and paradigmatic qualities (and thus having affinities with the rhetorician's stock of pertinent examples)." For Jewish use of literary models of heroes and anti-heroes and for teachers and fathers as models in Jewish education, see P. Höffken, *Elemente kommunikativer Didaktik in frühjüdischer und rabbinischer Literatur* (Religionspädogogik in der Blauen Eule 1; Essen: Die Blaue Eule, 1986). But note Meeks's caution against mere imitation of behavior described in Matthew: "It is not only a model for the present but also a basis which is different from the present and which therefore requires different responses" (Wayne A. Meeks, *The Moral World of the First Christians* [Library of Early Christianity; Philadelphia: Westminster, 1986] 142; see also p. 141). Likewise, Trompf insists on Polybius's desire not only to write history paradigmatically but also to do justice to the data (*The Idea of Historical Recurrence*, 105–6).

ancient custom of instruction by the example of one's father or equivalent figure: "But in the olden time it was an established rule that Romans should learn from their elders, not only by precept, but by example, the principles on which they themselves should one day act, and which they should in turn transmit to the younger generation. . . . The father of each youth served as his instructor, or, if he had none, some person of years and dignity supplied the place of the father. . . . Thus they were taught by that surest method of instruction, example, the whole conduct of a senator."[3] Charles H. Talbert quotes a similar emphasis by Seneca on the effect of the teacher's life upon disciples: "Cleanthes could not have been the express image of Zeno, if he had merely heard his lectures; he also shared his life, saw into his hidden purposes, and watched him to see whether he lived according to his own rules. Plato, Aristotle, and the whole throng of sages who were destined to go each his different way, derived more benefit from the character than from the words of Socrates. It was not the classroom of Epicurus, but living together under the same roof, that made great men of Metrodorus, Hermarchus, and Polyaenus."[4]

Beverly Roberts Gaventa calls attention to how narratives impose "order" on narrated events, shaping events according to the writer's view, in "what Hayden White calls the intrinsic 'moralism' of narrative."[5] One aspect of such moralism is the paradigmatic uses of narrative. Wesley A. Kort argues that even contemporary fictional characters, who differ so starkly from religious heroes in ancient literature, "provide us with paradigms that illuminate the human potential for good and evil."[6] David Aune maintains that such paradigmatic purposes were quite explicit in ancient biographies: "The subjects of most ancient biographies are depicted as static personalities presented as paradigms of either traditional virtues or vices, rarely as a mixture of both."[7]

3. Trans. Radice in LCL; cited in Fiore, *The Function of Personal Example*, 35, n. 28. Cf. 34–37; Malherbe's citation of Pliny *Letter* 8.13, on imitating one's father (*Moral Exhortation*, no. 55, p. 137); Gutierrez, *Paternité spirituelle*, esp. 172–97; and Rainer Riesner, *Jesus als Lehrer: Eine Untersuchung zum Ursprung der Evangelien-Überlieferung* (Tübingen: J. C. B. Mohr [Paul Siebeck], 1981), esp. 70–79, on previous work on Jesus as teacher; chap. 2, 97–245, on Jewish popular education; chap. 3, on Jesus' authority, esp. 277–98, on prophet-disciple relations; chap. 5, on teaching of disciples, esp. 408–34, on their life together; 503–68, bibliography.

4. Charles H. Talbert, "Biographies of Philosophers and Rulers as Instruments of Religious Propaganda in Mediterranean Antiquity," *ANRW* 2.16.2, 1643, quotation of Seneca *Epistle* 6.5–7, trans. Gummere in LCL.

5. Beverly Roberts Gaventa, "Toward a Theology of Acts: Reading and Rereading," *Interpretation* 42 (April 1988) 152. Cf. Stanley Hauerwas, "Story and Theology," *Religion in Life* 45 (1976) 341: "Stories . . . are not told to explain as a theory explains, but to involve the agent in a way of life."

6. Wesley A. Kort, *Narrative Elements and Religious Meanings* (Philadelphia: Fortress, 1975) 41. See his whole chapter, "Character and Paradigm," 40–58.

7. David E. Aune, "Greco-Roman Biography," *Greco-Roman Literature and the New Testament: Selected Forms and Genres* (ed. David E. Aune; SBLSBS 21; Atlanta: Scholars, 1988) 110. Aune also compares the function of the Gospels as legitimizing Christian practices "by appealing to the paradigmatic role of the founder," as subjects of Greco-Roman biographies exemplified Hellenistic cultural values (p. 122). Trompf, *The Idea of Historical Recurrence*, 4–178, compares to Polybius such (often moralistic) examples of historical recurrence in Luke-Acts as reenactment

This chapter will demonstrate that that consensus about ancient paradigmatic uses of narratives holds also for the narrative of Luke-Acts,[8] by pointing out similar concerns to provide models for imitation in other narratives from the Lukan Greco-Roman and Hellenistic-Jewish milieu. It thus illustrates for narrative forms Malherbe's observations about the explicit and more subtle implicit uses of examples in many literary forms.[9] The chapter further aims to relate what we know of Hellenistic rhetorical emphasis on narrative models for imitation as evidenced in Luke-Acts to contemporary concern for implicit moral exhortation to implied readers of narratives. It thus attempts to relate a historical-critical study of rhetorical models for imitation to recent narrative-critical concerns. Because the primary focus of the chapters in this book is historical, some preliminary definition of the key contemporary literary term *implied readers* is in order.

NARRATIVE CRITICAL CONCEPTS

A significant contribution of literary narrative criticism is the notion of the readers who are implied by the narrative.[10] Although no text can be used to identify fully its real readers, who are outside the text (as are twentieth-century readers), the text itself produces and gives evidence for its implied readers, which are the kinds of readers demanded by the text, or the readers as the writer imagines them.[11] A writer's audience is *always* a fiction, as Walter J. Ong has demonstrated.[12] Because writers compose in the absence of their readers, they must imagine readers' concerns and how they would react to what is being written, unlike oral storytellers, who can adjust to listeners' actual reactions. Implied readers are the kinds of readers who are imagined

---

of OT events and retributive principles, citing the paradigmatic qualities of the sins and appropriate penalties of Ananias, Sapphira, and Elymas (p. 173).

8. See Robert W. Wall, "The Acts of the Apostles in Canonical Context," *BTB* 18 (1988) 16–24, who claims that in a canonical setting, Acts provides the epistles' principle of "imitate the apostles" with a narrative framework. "The moral situation of the apostolic community is always understood as analogous to those situations addressed by the apostolate: to see the world and react to its contingencies as they did, to imitate their character, is to follow God's Christ into God's kingdom" (p. 23). Cf. Richard D. Nelson, "David: A Model for Mary in Luke?" *BTB* 18 (1988) 138–42, who cites the parallel roles of David and Mary in Luke-Acts as exemplary believers in God's promises (140).

9. Malherbe, *Moral Exhortation,* 136.

10. Cf. Seymour Chatman, *Story and Discourse: Narrative Structure in Fiction and Film* (Ithaca: Cornell University Press, 1978) 147–51.

11. For a discussion of readers demanded by the text, see Terence J. Keegan, *Interpreting the Bible: A Popular Introduction to Biblical Hermeneutics* (New York: Paulist, 1985) 96–98. For a discussion of readers as imagined, see William S. Kurz, "Narrative Approaches to Luke-Acts," *Bib* 68 (1987) 195–220, esp. 201. Cf. William S. Kurz, "The Beloved Disciple and Implied Readers," *BTB* 19 (1989) 100–107.

12. Walter J. Ong, "The Writer's Audience Is Always a Fiction," *Interfaces of the Word: Studies in the Evolution of Consciousness and Culture* (Ithaca: Cornell University Press, 1977) 53–81. Cf. Susan Sniader Lanser, *The Narrative Act: Point of View in Prose Fiction* (Princeton: Princeton University Press, 1981) 114–20.

or expected by the writers, and they therefore influence the way the text is expressed and can be reconstructed from the text itself.

Narratives differ from direct persuasion in that narrators normally do not address their readers directly but rather simply "show" the action taking place for the readers to observe, as it were. When narrators do directly address their audience, it is normally through prefaces, asides, and similar devices that precede or intrude upon the actual narration of the events. Thus, the narrator in Acts 20 does not directly exhort implied readers to imitate Paul but simply shows them Paul enjoining the Ephesian elders, who carried on his authority after his departure, to do so. However, it is not much of a further logical step for the implied readers to interpret Paul's actions as paradigmatic for later Christian leaders in general. This is particularly true in view of the ordinary first-century practice for teachers to urge their disciples to learn by their example, and the widespread Christian awareness that Paul himself had done so, as the narrative claims.

EXPLICIT EXEMPLA IN THE LUKAN CORPUS

The presence in Luke-Acts of at least two explicit exempla warrants our search for implicit uses of narrative models elsewhere in the Lukan corpus and in related literature contemporary to it.[13] The farewell addresses in Acts

13. For an overview of research on the exemplum stressing the exemplarity of the past for discourse, see Jacques Berlioz and Jean-Michel David, "Introduction bibliographique," *Rhétorique et histoire: L'exemplum et le modèle de comportement dans le discours antique et médiéval* (Mélanges L'Ecole Française de Rome 92.1; Rome: Ecole Française de Rome, 1980) 15–23. Cf. Jean-Michel David, "*Maiorum exempla sequi*: L'*exemplum* historique dans les discours judiciares de Cicéron" (*Rhétorique et histoire* 67–86, esp. 81–82, 84–86). He concludes, "Les chaines d'*exempla* qui réduisent les individus à des comportements répétitifs, sont autant de précédents qui fixent le *mos maiorum* et l'organisent en un système conceptuel et mnémonique. . . . L'*exemplum* lui-même développe en revanche une image exemplaire qui se vivifie de ce qui reste de la mémoire collective de son héros. Il autorise alors des phénomènes d'identification et de répulsion paradigmatique" (p. 86). Hans Robert Jauss, "Levels of Identification of Hero and Audience," *New Literary History* 5 (1974) 293, illustrates how the exemplary facilitates transition from aesthetic to moral identification with a quotation from Ambrose on the exemplum: "quia cui verba satis non faciunt, solent exempla suadere" (PL, 17, 236). Admiring identification with personal models "can consolidate experience of history and pass it on from generation to generation" (p. 304). Cf. M. Gaillard, "'Auctoritas exempli': pratique rhétorique et idéologie au Ier siècle avant J.-C.," *Revue des études latines* 56 (1979) 34: "Comment impose-t-on son *auctoritas*? En acquiesçant à la *consuetudo*, en suscitant l'imitation—c'est-à-dire en devenant un *exemplum historicum.*" A helpful treatment with bibliography is Arthur Wirt Robinson, *Cicero's Use of People as Exempla in His Speeches* (diss., Indiana University, 1986). See Klaus Döring, *Exemplum Socratis: Studien zur Sokratesnachwirkung in der kynisch-stoischen Popularphilosophie und im frühen Christentum* (Hermes Einzelschrift 42; Wiesbaden: Steiner, 1979); A. Lumpe, "Exemplum," *RAC* 6 (ed. Theodor Klausner; Stuttgart: Anton Hiersemann, 1966) cols. 1229–57; Thomas R. Lee, *Studies in the Form of Sirach 44–50* (SBLDS 75; Atlanta: Scholars, 1986) 99–103; and Moses Gaster, *The Exempla of the Rabbis: Being a Collection of Exempla, Apologues and Tales Culled from Hebrew Manuscripts and Rare Hebrew Books* (prolegomenon by William G. Braude; New York: Ktav, 1968).

20:17–38 and Luke 22:14–38 draw explicit attention to Paul and Jesus as models to be imitated. As Malherbe observes, Paul's farewell to the Christian elders of Ephesus in Acts 20 uses the standard procedures of moral philosophers of juxtaposing rival teachers (stereotypically portrayed as "wolves," Acts 20:29–30) to his own example to be imitated (20:31–35), described in normal parenetic style.[14] The farewell provides an occasion to make explicit the paradigmatic character of Paul's life and mission for later Christian leaders and perhaps, by further implication, for other Christians as well. Thus, Paul is shown reminding the Ephesian elders of their knowledge of how he went among them teaching (Acts 20:18). He calls them to be on guard, remembering how he had admonished them for three years. Memory of how Paul admonished them is to guide how they are to admonish communities that they in turn oversee. Paul also points to his example of providing for his own needs and not seeking the Ephesians' money: "All these things I showed you [πάντα ὑπέδειξα ὑμῖν] that thus [οὕτως] working you should provide for the weak and remember the words of the Lord Jesus" (20:35). The narrative thus appeals to two authoritative guides for how Christian leaders are to act: to the example of Paul and to the words of Jesus (independently of whether this saying happens to be authentic). The accounts in Acts of Paul's activities provide sources for learning Paul's apostolic example, and the Lukan Gospel supplies collections of the sayings of Jesus.

Similarly, in Jesus' farewell address in Luke, Jesus twice asks the apostles to imitate an action of his.[15] The traditional and textually problematic Eucharistic statement "Do this in memory of me" (Luke 22:20a) is a call for imitation, but not a formal exemplum. It is rather the imitation of a stylized liturgical action in a set ritual. The apostles are directed to do exactly the same set of actions that Jesus does—taking, blessing, breaking, and giving the bread to others to eat as his body. Such ritualized imitation does not tend to generalizations that interpret other actions of Jesus as analogously paradigmatic.

However, later in the farewell address (in Luke 22:24–27), where Jesus is teaching his apostles an explicit lesson about authority as service, he illustrates his point by using his own behavior as an exemplum: "For which is greater, the

14. Abraham J. Malherbe, "'Not in a Corner': Early Christian Apologetic in Acts 26:26," *SecCent* 5 (1985–86) 200. For imitation of Jesus and Paul in Pauline writings, see L. W. Hurtado, "Jesus as Lordly Example in Philippians 2:5–11," 113–26, and David Stanley, "Imitation in Paul's Letters: Its Significance for His Relationship to Jesus and to His Own Christian Foundations," 127–41, both in *From Jesus to Paul: Studies in Honour of Francis Wright Beare* (ed. Peter Richards and John C. Hurd; Waterloo, Ontario: Wilfrid Laurier University Press, 1984); William S. Kurz, "Kenotic Imitation of Paul and of Christ in Philippians 2 and 3," *Discipleship in the New Testament* (ed. Fernando F. Segovia; Philadelphia: Fortress, 1985); and David Stanley, "'Become Imitators of Me': Apostolic Tradition in Paul," *The Apostolic Church in the New Testament* (Westminster, MD: Newman, 1965) 371–89, besides the works cited in note 2 above.

15. On Luke 22 as farewell address, see William S. Kurz, "Luke 22:14–38 and Greco-Roman and Biblical Farewell Addresses," *JBL* 104 (1985) 251–68; and Jerome Neyrey, *The Passion According to Luke: A Redaction Study of Luke's Soteriology* (Theological Inquiries; New York: Paulist, 1985) 5–48.

one lying at table or the one serving? But I am in your midst as one who serves [ὁ διακονῶν]" (22:27). Jesus' own example illustrates how Christian authority differs from secular authority. Although secular authorities lord their authority over their subjects and insist on honors for themselves, this reversal of expectations likens Jesus' authority to that of a table waiter.

This exemplum within Jesus' farewell address invites the implied readers to reflect on other narratives of how Jesus conducted himself in authority over his followers, to illustrate in Jesus' actions how authority is in fact a form of service. Inviting implied readers to see Jesus' actions as models for their own alerts them to notice the paradigmatic features for Christian imitation in other Lukan narratives about Jesus.

This chapter will advance two hypotheses: (1) From exempla and explicit statements about narratives as behavior models in prefaces and intrusive narrators' asides, it seems reasonable to expect that in other narratives in the same works where the narrator is unobtrusive, a similar *implicit* paradigmatic intention may be present, especially in biblical writings that use narrative asides far more sparingly than do secular Hellenistic works.[16] (2) Even though the normally unobtrusive narrator in Luke-Acts seldom expressly mentions models for imitation, the author of Luke-Acts would most likely be quite familiar with such paradigmatic functions and use them more often than in only the overt exempla. The chapter will gather representative explicit references to paradigmatic functions of narratives from a wide spectrum of narratives within the Lukan milieu to illustrate how widespread was the rhetorical motif of imitation of models in narrative literature. With this background, it will then illustrate how both explicit exempla and more implicitly paradigmatic narratives within Luke-Acts exhibit a similar pattern and concern.

HELLENISTIC CONCERN ABOUT NARRATIVE MODELS FOR IMITATION

So far this chapter has discussed Hellenistic use of narrative models within the broader context of imitation and exempla in education and rhetoric. Pedagogical emphases colored the writing of narratives of many sorts— biographical, historical, even novelistic. Biographies presented lessons for living. Histories provided lessons for the future from the past. Novels tended to be moralistic.[17] Paradigmatic concerns are common to most of the major

16. By *intrusive narrator,* I mean a narrator who makes his or her presence known to readers or audiences by directly addressing them or providing information that is not directly part of the plot narrated, such as translations of foreign terms. Such narrators are normally said to be using a "telling point of view." Unobtrusive narrators simply "show" the plot unfolding, so audiences do not normally avert to the fact that someone is narrating the story. This is called the "showing point of view." Cf. Francis Martin, *Narrative Parallels to the New Testament* (SBLRBS 22; Atlanta: Scholars, 1988) 10–11. Focus on implicit paradigmatic intentions applies to narrative remarks about subtle uses of examples in autobiography and pseudonymous letters in Malherbe, *Moral Exhortation,* 136.

17. On models in biographies, see Malherbe, *Moral Exhortation,* 137; on the past as lessons for

genres of narratives in the Lukan milieu. Therefore, the thesis about the use of narratives as models for imitation can be argued without entering the debate over the genre or genres of Luke and Acts. Focus on paradigmatic elements common to several genres of narratives is applicable to Luke-Acts as a narrative, however its genre or genres may be classified.

Historiographical Imitation of Models

Historiographical concerns that the past should provide lessons of profit for the future provide one of the rationales for Hellenistic paradigmatic use of narratives.[18] These concerns influenced later biblical historiography such as 1 and 2 Maccabees, as well as writers like Polybius, Dionysius of Halicarnassus, and Josephus. Thus, Polybius, in his preface (1.1), claims there is no more ready corrective of conduct than knowledge of the past (ἑτοιμοτέραν . . . διόρθωσιν τῆς τῶν προγεγενημένων πράξεων ἐπιστήμης). His claim that the best education and training for political life is study of history (παιδείαν καὶ γυμνασίαν . . . ἱστορίας μάθησιν) implies a protreptic approach that uses historical examples as paradigms of behavior (1.2). Thus, he claims that a method for learning to bear bravely the vicissitudes of fortune (διδάσκαλον τοῦ δύνασθαι τὰς τῆς τύχης μεταβολὰς γενναίως ὑποφέρειν) is to recall the calamities of others (ἀλλοτρίων περιπετειῶν ὑπόμνησιν [1.2]). Despite the stereotyped nature of such prefaces, they provide evidence for actual expectations of Hellenistic readers—expectations grounded in their familiarity with rhetoric.

Statements toward the beginning of the life of Apollonius of Tyana (Philostr. VA 1.3) that the author hopes this biography may have some use (ὠφέλειαν), along with the tongue-in-cheek comments in Lucian's How to Write History, 9, that history has one task and end—the useful (τὸ χρήσιμον) that comes from truth and not primarily the pleasurable (τὸ τερπνόν), such as that which comes from eulogies—provide evidence that this rhetorical tradition continued into the second century. Lucian later uses Thucydides as his authority that usefulness (τὸ χρήσιμον) is the purpose of sound history: "That if ever again men find themselves in a like situation [τὰ ὅμοια] they may be able, he says, from a consideration of the records of the past to handle rightly

---

the future in histories, see Trompf, The Idea of Historical Recurrence, 74–79, 83, 97–101, and passim. On novels, cf. Ronald F. Hock, "The Greek Novel," in Aune, Greco-Roman Literature and the New Testament, 127–46, esp. 134, on the overall plot structure of Greek novels as humiliation and trials of hero and heroine because of fidelity to their mutual love until they are restored to live happily ever after. In Jewish novels, Aseneth is a paradigm of a convert and Tobit, of hospitality to fellow Jews (Tob 1:16–20).

18. Trompf, The Idea of Historical Recurrence, 97–101. Charles William Fornara, The Nature of History in Ancient Greece and Rome (Eidos Studies in Classical Kinds; Berkeley: University of California Press, 1983) 104–20, traces the rise of paradigmatic history from rhetorical influence, beginning especially with Polybius (113), so that Diodorus Siculus could treat history as philosophy by example (116–17).

what now confronts them [πρὸς τὰ προγεγραμμένα ἀποβλέποντες εὖ χρῆσθαι τοῖς ἐν ποσί]" (Lucian *Hist. conscr.* 42; trans. Kilburn in LCL).

In his preface to *Roman Antiquities,* Dionysius of Halicarnassus mentions historical truth as the source of both prudence and wisdom (τὴν ἀλήθειαν . . . ἀρχὴν φρονήσεώς τε καὶ σοφίας οὖσαν [*Ant. Rom.* 1.1.2; trans. Cary in LCL]), thus emphasizing its practical value for action. Historians ought "to make choice of noble and lofty subjects and such as will be of great utility to their readers [πολλὴν ὠφέλειαν τοῖς ἀναγνωσομένοις φερούσας]" (1.1.2). Dionysius refers to the rhetorical expectation by readers that writers admired lives like those about which they wrote (ὅτι τοιούτους ζήλωσαν αὐτοὶ βίους, οἵας ἐξέδωκαν τὰς γραφάς [1.1.3]). Dionysius will present lives of illustrious ancestors as an incentive to their descendants: "And again, both the present and future descendants of those godlike men will choose, not the pleasantest and easiest of lives, but rather the noblest and most ambitious, when they consider that all who are sprung from an illustrious origin ought to set a high value on themselves and indulge in no pursuit unworthy of their ancestors [μέγα ἐφ᾽ ἑαυτοῖς προσήκει φρονεῖν καὶ μηδὲν ἀνάξιον ἐπιτηδεύειν τῶν προγόνων]" (1.6.4).

The narrator's asides during Dionysius's narrative reinforce these statements in his proem by explicit references to his history's paradigmatic dimension. For example, before summarizing how Larcius handled matters as Rome's first dictator, the narrator interjects the following: "For I look upon these matters as being most useful to my readers [ταῦτα ἡγούμενος εἶναι χρησιμώτατα τοῖς ἀναγνωσομένοις], since they will afford a great abundance of noble and profitable examples [καλῶν καὶ συμφερόντων παραδειγμάτων], not only to lawgivers and leaders of the people, but also to all others who aspire to take part in public life and to govern the state" (Dionysius *Ant. Rom.* 5.75.1).

It is therefore not surprising to see Rome's founder Romulus treated as an exemplar of Roman values, which the intrusive narrator contrasts with contemporary shortcomings in asides to the implied readers. Thus, the narrator describes Romulus's simple victory triumph and remarks: "Such was the victorious procession . . . which the Romans call a triumph, as it was first instituted by Romulus. But in our day [ἐν δὲ τῷ καθ᾽ ἡμᾶς βίῳ] the triumph has become a very costly and ostentatious pageant, . . . and it has departed in every respect from its ancient simplicity [καὶ καθ᾽ ἅπασαν ἰδέαν ἐκβέβηκε τὴν ἀρχαίαν εὐτέλειαν]" (Dionysius *Ant. Rom.* 2.34.3). This moralistic narrator's aside contrasts the ancient simplicity of the triumphs as instituted by Romulus and the ostentation of contemporary triumphs, holding it up as an example for imitation in the present day. The narrators' other asides point to Romulus as a model promoter of civic virtues and of simple religion that rejects blasphemous myths about the gods (2.18; 2.23.4–6).

In a later moralistic aside, the narrator turns to the implied readers after describing the austere virtue of Lucius Quintius: "I am led to relate these particulars for no other reason than to let all the world see what kind of men the

WILLIAM S. KURZ 179

leaders of Rome were at that time, that they worked with their own hands, led frugal lives, did not chafe under honourable poverty, and, far from aiming at positions of royal power, actually refused them when offered. For it will be seen that the Romans of today do not bear the least resemblance to them, but follow the very opposite practices in everything—with the exception of a very few by whom the dignity of the commonwealth is still maintained and a resemblance to those men preserved" (Dionysius *Ant. Rom.* 10.17.6). Thus, Dionysius intersperses notices of his paradigmatic intentions throughout his multivolumed narrative.[19]

Luke's contemporary Josephus modeled his *Antiquities of the Jews* on Dionysius's *Antiquities of the Romans*, so it is not surprising to find similar paradigmatic concerns in his work. Josephus's preface makes a comparable statement about publishing for the public benefit (εἰς κοινὴν ὠφέλειαν [*Ant.* 1 proem 1 § 3]), just as Dionysius desires to write about noble subjects that will be of great utility to his readers (πολλὴν ὠφέλειαν τοῖς ἀναγνωσομένοις φερούσας [*Ant. Rom.* 1.1.2]). Josephus makes explicit a moral lesson for his complete work: "But, speaking generally, the main lesson to be learnt from this history by any who care to peruse it is that men who conform to the will of God, and do not venture to transgress laws that have been excellently laid down, prosper in all things beyond belief, and for their reward are offered by God felicity; whereas, in proportion as they depart from the strict observance of these laws, things (else) [*sic*] practicable become impracticable, and whatever imaginary good thing they strive to do ends in irretrievable disasters" (Josephus *Ant.* 1 proem 3 § 14; trans. Thackeray in LCL). Not only does Josephus have this stated moralistic purpose, but he also calls attention to the worthy conception of God as he describes him in his work (in contrast to unseemly myths [1 proem 3 § 15]). He presents this purified portrayal of God as a model to be imitated: "Be it known then, that that sage [Moses] deemed it above all necessary, for one who would order his own life aright and also legislate for others, first to study the nature of God, and then, having contemplated his works with the eye of reason, to imitate as far as possible that best of all models and endeavor to follow it [οὕτως παράδειγμα τὸ πάντων ἄριστον μιμεῖσθαι, καθ' ὅσον οἷόν τε, καὶ πειρᾶσθαι κατακολουθεῖν]" (1 proem 4 § 19).

Josephus goes on to argue that without such a model and vision of God, Moses would be unable to find truth, "nor would anything that he should write in regard to virtue avail with his readers [οὔτε τῶν γραφησομένων εἰς ἀρετῆς λόγον οὐδὲν ἀποβήσεσθαι τοῖς λαβοῦσιν]" (1 proem 4 § 20). God must be seen, as Moses portrayed him, as bestowing retribution on both good and evil

19. John Lilley gathered these references in his April 1, 1989, paper, "Hellenistic Historiography and Ethico-Religious Paradigm in Luke's Gospel," for my graduate course. Other paradigms of behavior in Dionysius's history that Lilley refers to include "Numa Pompilius (2.76), Gaius Marcius (6.92–94; 8.60–62), and Tarquinius, a tyrant whose treachery, theft and murder mark him as an extraordinarily *negative* example (4.68; cf. 4.78)" (p. 12).

conduct: "God, as the universal Father and Lord who beholds all things [πάντα ἐπιβλέπων], grants to such as follow Him a life of bliss, but involves in dire calamities those who step outside the path of virtue [τοῖς μὲν ἑπομένοις αὐτῷ δίδωσιν εὐδαίμονα βίον, τοὺς ἔξω δὲ βαίνοντας ἀρετῆς μεγάλαις περιβάλλει συμφοραῖς]. Such, then, being the lesson which Moses desired to instill [τοῦτο δὴ παιδεῦσαι βουληθεὶς Μωυσῆς τὸ παίδευμα] into his fellow citizens . . ." (1 proem 4 § 20). Josephus's paradigmatic purpose could hardly be clearer.

Narrators' asides continue to call attention to both positive and negative examples throughout Josephus's Antiquities. Thus, Josephus uses Ahab as an explicit negative exemplum: "And further, with the king's history before our eyes, it behooves us to reflect [λογίζισθαί τε πάλιν ἐκ τῶν περὶ τὸν βασιλέα γεγενημένων] on the power of Fate" (Ant. 8.15.6 § 418–20). Also regarding Antipater, the narrator says, "I shall relate the whole story of this in order that it may be an example and warning to mankind to practise virtue in all circumstances [παράδειγμα τῷ ἀνθρωπείῳ γενησόμενον τοῦ ἀρετῇ πολιτεύσοντος ἐπὶ πᾶσιν]" (17.3.3 § 60).

As a positive model for imitation, the narrator proposes the witch of Endor for her generosity toward someone (Saul) who could not repay her: "It is well, then, to take this woman for an example [καλὸν οὖν ἐστι μιμεῖσθαι τὴν γυναῖκα] and show kindness to all who are in need, and to regard nothing as nobler than this or more befitting the human race or more likely to make God gracious and ready to bestow on us His blessings" (Josephus Ant. 6.14.4 § 342).[20]

Synoptic comparison between the treatments of Mattathias's farewell in Josephus and his source, 1 Maccabees, illustrates Josephus's stronger Hellenistic emphasis on presenting oneself as a model. In 1 Macc 2:49–70, the Maccabean patriarch Mattathias presents only biblical models for his sons to emulate; in Josephus's? Antiquities, Mattathias uses his own spirit (φρόνημα) as an example for his sons' imitation: "I myself, my sons, am about to go the destined way, but my spirit I leave in your keeping, and I beg you not to be unworthy guardians of it, but to be mindful of the purpose of him who begot you and brought you up, and to preserve our country's customs [παρατίθεμαι δὲ ὑμῖν τοὐμὸν φρόνημα καὶ παρακαλῶ μὴ γενέσθαι κακοὺς αὐτοῦ φύλακας, ἀλλὰ μεμνημένους τῆς τοῦ φύσαντος ὑμᾶς καὶ θρεψαμένου προαιρέσεως ἔθη τε σώζειν τὰ πάτρια]" (12.6.3 § 279–84).

2 Maccabees gives an explicit exemplum in the farewell address of the aged martyr Eleazar: "Wherefore now, manfully changing this life, I will show myself such a one as my age requires, and leave a notable example to the young [τοῖς δὲ νέοις ὑπόδειγμα γενναῖον καταλελοιπώς] to die willingly and

20. Jack Lilley's "Paradigm" gathered most of these citations, as well as the following further ethico-religious paradigms in Josephus's Antiquities (p. 16, n. 10). Positive models include Abraham (1.7.1; 1.13.2; 1.17), Joseph (2.4.1–2), and David (7.15.1–2); negative exempla include Joab (7.1.5), Rehoboam (8.10.2, 4), Asa (8.12.6), Ahab (8.15.6), and Caius (19.1.2).

courageously for the honorable and holy laws" (2 Macc 6:27–28). The narrator immediately reemphasizes the exemplary nature of Eleazar's death in the eulogy of him: "And thus this man died, leaving his death for an example of a noble courage, and a memorial of virtue, not only unto young men but unto all his nation [οὐ μόνον τοῖς νέοις, ἀλλὰ καὶ τοῖς πλείστοις τοῦ ἔθνους τὸν ἑαυτοῦ θάνατον ὑπόδειγμα γενναιότητος καὶ μνημόσυνον ἀρετῆς καταλιπών]" (6:31). By pointing out how Eleazar's death is a model not only within the narrative for the young men to whom Eleazar hoped to give a good example but for "all his nation," the narrator includes among those who should imitate Eleazar the implied readers of the narrative, who were being implicitly addressed (6:31).

The preface to 2 Maccabees confirms the presence of such a concern by the implied author to provide models for the implied readers. The three stated goals in epitomizing Jason's account are "that those who want to read may have delight, that those who want to memorize might have easy work, and that all into whose hands it falls may have profit [ὠφέλειαν]" (2 Macc 2:25). The Greek word for "profit" here is the same expression as that found in the prefaces of *Apollonius of Tyana*, Dionysius, and Josephus and is a synonym of the word χρήσιμον used by Lucian. That the expected profit included lessons from history appears in such narrator's asides as that in 2 Macc 4:17: "For it is no light thing to show irreverence to the divine laws—a fact which later events will make clear" (RSV).

On the spectrum of biblical and Hellenistic historiography, Luke-Acts lies between 1 and 2 Maccabees. 1 Maccabees more closely resembles biblical historiography than does 2 Maccabees, with no preface and a much less obtrusive narrator. Still, the narrator in 1 Macc 2:26 compares the action of Mattathias in killing the apostate Jew to that of Phinehas, a biblical paradigm of zeal for God's law (cf. Numbers 25): "Thus he burned with zeal for the law, as Phinehas did against Zimri the son of Salu" (RSV). By implication, Mattathias also becomes a paradigm of zeal for God's law for the implied readers.

Mattathias's farewell address (1 Macc 2:49–70) repeats in 2:54 the narrator's reference in 2:26 to Phinehas as paradigm of zeal for God's law. The context of his exhorting his sons to "be zealous for the law" in remembrance of the deeds of their fathers (2:50–51) clearly shows the same concern for imitation of narrative models as the narrator had in 2:26.[21] One of the common literary functions of farewell addresses is to address the time and concerns of the implied readers after the time of the story.[22] Mattathias's exhortation to zeal for the law according to the example of Abraham, Joseph,

21. By calling Phinehas "our father" and stating that his zeal obtained the covenant of an everlasting priesthood, Mattathias's speech also makes the narrative claims that the Hasmonean priesthood is grounded in that of Phinehas, both by blood descent and by imitation of his zeal.
22. Cf. William S. Kurz, S.J., *Farewell Addresses in the New Testament* (Michael Glazier Books; Collegeville, MN: Liturgical, 1990).

Phinehas, . . . Hananiah, Azariah, Mishael, and Daniel presents their paradigm for imitation not only by his sons within the story but by the implied readers.

Biographical Imitation of Models

Similar references to imitation of models appear in biographies. Thus, Plutarch defends his use of negative as well as positive examples among the lives he chose to describe:

> The most consummate arts of all, namely, temperance, justice, and wisdom, since their function is to distinguish, not only what is good and just and expedient, but also what is bad and unjust and disgraceful, have no praises for a guilelessness which plumes itself on its inexperience of evil, nay, they consider it to be foolishness, and ignorance of what ought especially to be known by men who would live aright [ἄγνοιαν ὧν μάλιστα γινώσκειν προσήκει τοὺς ὀρθῶς βιωσομένους]. Accordingly, the ancient Spartans would put compulsion upon their helots at the festivals to drink much unmixed wine, and would then bring them into the public messes, in order to show their young men what it was to be drunk. And though I do not think that the perverting of some to secure the setting right of others is very humane, . . . still, when men have led reckless lives, and have become conspicuous, in the exercise of power or in great undertakings, for badness, perhaps it will not be much amiss for me to introduce a pair or two of them into my biographies, though not that I may merely divert and amuse my readers by giving variety to my writing. . . . So, I think, we also shall be more eager to observe and imitate the better lives [καὶ ἡμεῖς προθυμότεροι τῶν βελτιόνων ἔσεσθαι καὶ θεαταὶ καὶ μιμηταὶ βίων] if we are not left without narratives of the blameworthy and the bad. (*Demetr.* 1.3–6; trans. Perrin in LCL)[23]

Philo also emphasizes the theme of the importance of lives of virtuous people as models for readers' imitation. In the introduction to his life of Abraham, he announces he will preface discussion of specific laws by looking at the lives on which they are based:

> Let us postpone consideration of particular laws, which are, so to speak, copies [εἰκόνων] and examine first those which are more general and may be called originals of those copies [καθολικωτέρους καὶ ὡς ἂν ἀρχετύπους]. These are such men as lived good and blameless lives, whose virtues stand permanently recorded in the most holy scriptures, not merely to sound their praises but for the instruction of the reader and an inducement to him to aspire to the same [καὶ ὑπὲρ τοῦ τοὺς ἐντυγχάνοντας προτρέψασθαι καὶ ἐπὶ τὸν ὅμοιον ζῆλον ἀγαγεῖν]; for in these men we have laws endowed with life and reason [οἱ γὰρ ἔμψυχοι καὶ λογικοὶ νόμοι ἄνδρες ἐκεῖνοι γεγόνασιν]. (*Abr.* 1.3–5; trans. Colson in LCL)

Philo goes on to say that Moses extolled these people for two reasons: to show that enacted ordinances do not contradict nature, and to show that those wish-

23. Much of this is quoted in Malherbe, *Moral Exhortation*, no. 56, pp. 137–38.

ing to follow the laws could see that others before them have followed them in
their unwritten state with ease, so that one could call the enacted laws
"memorials of the life of the ancients [ὑπομνήματα εἶναι βίου τῶν παλαιῶν]"
(1.5). Even if one grants rhetorical conceits in such statements, they provide
evidence of, and function within, cultural conventions that expect narratives of
lives to be paradigmatic.

Charles H. Talbert refers to Philo's similar treatment of Moses himself as
prototype: "Philo, in his 'Life of Moses', depicted Moses as a perfect example
of Hellenism's ideal king. Having perceived the invisible good, Moses so
modelled his own life after it that he became a paradigm for his subjects.
Moses is νόμος ἔμψυχος, the incarnate representation of supreme and universal virtue."[24]

Lucian's humorous biography of the philosopher Demonax also uses the
rhetoric of presenting a model for aspiring young philosophers to follow: "It is
now fitting to tell of Demonax for two reasons—that he may be retained in
memory [διὰ μνήμης] . . . and that young men of good instincts who aspire to
philosophy may not have to shape themselves by ancient precedents alone
[ἔχοιεν μὴ πρὸς τὰ ἀρχαῖα μόνα τῶν παραδειγμάτων σφᾶς αὐτοὺς ῥυθμί-
ζειν], but may be able to set themselves a pattern from our modern world and
to copy that man, the best of all the philosophers whom I know about [ἀλλὰ
κἀκ τοῦ ἡμετέρου βίου κανόνα προτίθεσαι καὶ ζηλοῦν ἐκεῖνον ἄριστον ὧν
οἶδα ἐγὼ φιλοσόφων γενόμενον]" (Demon. 2; trans. Harmon in LCL).[25]

Imitation of Models in Other
Narrative Genres

Not only history and biography, but other narrative genres as well, use
narratives as exempla for imitation. The biblical romance Tobit presents
Tobit moralistically as a model of obedience to the law (Tob 1:10–12) and of
self-sacrificing care of fellow Jews (1:16–20); it also treats Tobias and Sarah's
behavior on their wedding night in a moralistic fashion (8:7). Luke's familiarity with Tobit and its moralism is supported by Richard I. Pervo's claim that
"Daniel 1–6, with its Greek additions, Tobit, Judith, and Esther, were almost
certainly known to the author of Acts."[26]

Likewise, Sirach's praise of the fathers (Sir 44:1–50:24) presents poetic
narratives of ancestors as inspiring models and both positive and negative
types of virtue or sin. Thus, the first ancestor mentioned, Enoch, was taken
up as an example of repentance to the generations (μετετέθη ὑπόδειγμα μετα-
νοίας ταῖς γενεαῖς [44:16]). Although the narrator uses the term ὑπόδειγμα
expressly only for Enoch, it is also implied in the ways the other figures are
well-known biblical types of virtues or vices. For example, the perfect and

24. Talbert, "Biographies of Philosophers and Rulers," 1644.
25. Malherbe, Moral Exhortation, no. 54, pp. 136–37, quotes all of Demonax 1–2.
26. Richard I. Pervo, Profit with Delight: The Literary Genre of the Acts of the Apostles
(Philadelphia: Fortress, 1987) 119.

righteous Noah was taken in exchange so that a remnant was left to the earth (44:17). Abraham kept the law and covenant and, when tested, was found faithful (καὶ ἐν πειρασμῷ εὑρέθη πιστός [44:20]), so God swore to him that in his seed the nations would be blessed and they would inherit the land (44:21). The general pattern in these capsuled accounts of ancestors is that good deeds find rewards from God, whereas sinners like Rehoboam and Jeroboam receive God's wrath (cf. 47:23–25). This, of course, is closely related to the Deuteronomic theology and is deeply ingrained in much of Luke's OT.[27] Luke's implied readers expected to find in OT narratives both lessons and examples for living as God's people and could be assumed to be alert to such a use of narrative in Luke-Acts.

One particular retributive pattern in Sirach 48 seems to have become a plot outline for Luke-Acts. Just as the wonder-working prophet Elijah was followed by his disciple Elisha, who worked similar miracles, so Jesus the wonder-working prophet like Moses is followed by his wonder-working apostles in Acts: "For all this the people did not repent ['Εν πᾶσιν τούτοις οὐ μετενόησεν ὁ λαός], and they did not forsake their sins, till they were carried away captive from their land and were scattered all over the earth [καὶ διεσκορπίσθησαν ἐν πάσῃ τῇ γῇ]; . . . Some of them did what is pleasing to God, but others multiplied sins" (Sir 48:15–16 RSV). The mixed reception of some believing and some rejecting the Twelve and Paul is a pattern running throughout Acts to its very end, so Jesus' prophecies of the destruction of Jerusalem and captivity among the nations in Luke 21:20–24 were to come true, as had happened after Elijah and Elisha.[28] Thus, a pattern in Sirach becomes a typology in Luke-Acts, indicating probable use by Luke of Sirach's hymn to the ancestors. If this is so, then the use of the ancestors as prototypes in Sirach provided yet another model for Luke's own paradigmatic treatment of people in Luke-Acts.

Implicit Paradigmatic Intentions Elsewhere

The many explicit references to paradigmatic functions of narratives across a wide spectrum of narratives from the Lukan milieu thus provide support for two contentions of this chapter. First, the fact that a preface or intrusive narrator's aside draws attention to several narratives as examples to be imitated by implied readers warrants the hypothesis that an unobtrusive narrator may also have such an *implicit* paradigmatic intention in many other narratives in the same works. This seems especially true in the biblical traditions, which use narrative asides far more rarely than do pagan and secular Hellenistic sources. The second contention is that the author of Luke-Acts would be quite familiar with such paradigmatic functions and likely to be using them

27. Cf. Trompf, *The Idea of Historical Recurrence*, on retributive logic in the OT and Hellenistic Jewish writings (156–70) and in Luke-Acts (170–74).
28. Cf. William S. Kurz, "Acts 3:19–26 as a Test of the Role of Eschatology in Lukan Christology," SBLSP 11 (1977) 314–16.

even when the normally unobtrusive narrator does not draw explicit attention to that fact. With this in mind, we can look at some examples of possibly paradigmatic uses of narratives in Luke and Acts beyond the explicit exempla in the farewell addresses in Luke 22 and Acts 20.

PARADIGMATIC PORTRAYALS IN LUKE-ACTS

An obvious place to begin looking for implicit paradigmatic narratives is in the Passion of Jesus in Luke, which commentators have long agreed has taken a more martyrological and less soteriological approach than that of Mark. Brian E. Beck has recently summarized the issues of martyrological interpretations of the Lukan Passion in view of the imitation-of-Christ motif.[29] Although acknowledging Luke's probable knowledge and use of Daniel and 2 Maccabees, as well as the many martyrological motifs undoubtedly present in Luke's Passion, Beck argues strongly that many important martyrological motifs are missing and that something more is at stake than Jesus' dying a martyr's death. It is a consensus that Luke's Passion has no emphasis on death as expiation, which is common in martyrologies, despite the Eucharistic language of Luke 22:19–20 and the comment in Paul's farewell in Acts 20:28, which more likely indicate partially assimilated tradition than a leading motif in Luke's own narrative.[30] Luke also lacks other martyrdom features like condemnation of persecutors, stress on physical pain, educative value of suffering for Jesus or Stephen, and a clear cause or issue and an easy way to defect (as by eating pork in 2 Macc 6:18–20).[31]

Beck points to the garden scene in Luke 22:39–46 as particularly decisive for interpreting the Lukan Passion account. When his explanation is supplemented by that of Jerome Neyrey and other observations, a strong case emerges for seeing the Lukan redaction as portraying Jesus as a model for imitation.[32] Both Beck and Neyrey argue that the disputed verses of the angel and the blood (22:43–44) are genuine, on internal criteria especially. In any case, the scene focuses on Jesus' struggle against temptation (πειρασμός) as an example to his disciples and as a contrasting exemplum to their failure to pray lest they succumb to temptation.

The redactional differences from Mark highlight especially Jesus' lesson in

29. Brian E. Beck, "'Imitatio Christi' and the Lucan Passion Narrative," *Suffering and Martyrdom in the New Testament: Studies Presented to G. M. Styler by the Cambridge New Testament Seminar* (ed. William Horbury and Brian McNeil; Cambridge: Cambridge University Press, 1981) 28–47.
30. Beck, "'Imitatio Christi,'" 34, 37; cf. Kurz, "Luke 22:14–38," 258–59, n. 21.
31. Beck, "'Imitatio Christi,'" 35.
32. Beck, "'Imitatio Christi,'" 37–40: "The idea of Jesus as an example is strongly emphasized" (40); Neyrey, *Passion According to Luke*, chap. 2, "Jesus in the Garden (Lk 22:39–46)," 49–68, which appeared in an earlier form as "The Absence of Jesus' Emotions—the Lukan Redaction of Lk. 22,39–46," *Bib* 61 (1980) 153–71.

prayer to his disciples. The Lukan introduction emphasizes the customary nature of Jesus' going to the Mount of Olives and the fact that "the disciples followed him," setting the stage for a lesson by the master (Luke 22:39; contrast Mark 14:32). Only Luke has Jesus begin by the command "Pray lest you succumb to temptation" (Luke 22:40), which Jesus repeats at the end just before his arrest (22:46), thus providing a frame for his own example to them of praying (22:41–45). In Luke, Jesus keeps all the disciples with him—not just Peter, James, and John, as he does in Mark. Unlike Mark's portrayal of Jesus' grief, where he falls on his face and fruitlessly looks three times for support from his closest followers, Luke shifts to the disciples the reference to debilitating grief (22:45) and shows Jesus manfully praying on his knees (22:41). His prayer has echoes of the Pater: πάτερ . . . μὴ εἰσενέγκῃς ἡμᾶς εἰς πειρασμόν (11:1–4). There is a typical Lukan emphasis on the Father's will (εἰ βούλει . . . πλὴν μὴ τὸ θέλημά μου ἀλλὰ τὸ σὸν γινέσθω [22:42]). If 22:43–44 is not genuine, this simple acceptance by Jesus of the Father's will provides a model of prayer for the disciples, whom he now finds sleeping (therefore missing his example), whom he awakens, and to whom he repeats his instruction to "pray lest you enter into temptation" (22:45–46). If the verses are genuine, Jesus' example includes evidence of God's help through an angel and the model of more insistent prayer in the face of intense struggle leading to sweat as drops of blood. In either case, Jesus instructs his disciples on the need to pray lest they enter temptation, then provides his own example of doing just that and rejecting temptation by accepting the Father's difficult will for him, and finally repeats his instruction to pray not to enter temptation. Because the disciples in the story missed much of Jesus' example by sleeping, the paradigm is clearly addressed to the implied readers, who are the only witnesses of the entire scene that the narrator depicts.

The death of Jesus in Luke 23 and the death of Stephen modeled on it in Acts 7 also readily come to mind as clearly paradigmatic portrayals in Luke and Acts. The Lukan tendency to downplay negative emotions of Jesus, such as those found in the Markan Passion traditions, is well known. The loud cry of apparent dereliction in Mark and Matthew based on Ps 22:2 is missing in Luke. Instead, Jesus calmly hands over his spirit into his Father's hands (citing Ps 31:6) as he dies. If Luke 23:34 is genuine, Jesus exemplifies the forgiveness of enemies that he preached, as in Luke 17:3–4 (frequent forgiveness of someone who sins against you), and that he gave as an example of how to pray: "Father . . . forgive us our sins, for we ourselves forgive everyone who is indebted to us" (11:4 RSV). After enduring in silence the mockery of his enemies (23:35–39), Jesus peacefully assures the repentant crucified evildoer who defended him that "today" they would be together in Paradise (23:43). All of this is in sharp contrast to Mark's picture of Jesus in torment. In Mark, Jesus asks loudly why his Father has abandoned him and dies after a loud cry. The Lukan redactional themes all go in the direction of portraying Jesus as a model of how to die, as Plato had presented Socrates.

The frequently noted similarities between Stephen's death in Acts 7 and Jesus' death on the cross confirm one's initial sense that Lukan redaction has highlighted the paradigmatic aspects of Jesus' death. Luke accentuates the exemplary aspects of Jesus' death and passes over emphases on Jesus' distress that were probably in his sources. By narrating the death of a disciple, Stephen, which echoes the exemplary aspects of Jesus' death, Luke signals clearly his intention to use Jesus' death as a model for that of Christians. Thus, like Jesus, Stephen is taken outside the city to be killed (Acts 7:58). Like Jesus, he gives his spirit over as he is about to die, but to the Lord Jesus rather than to the Father (7:59). And Stephen forgives his enemies, which parallels the disputed verse in Luke 23:34. His dying forgiveness of those who killed him, among whom Saul is intrusively mentioned (Acts 7:58; 8:1–3), prepares for Saul's later conversion in Acts 9, just as Jesus' forgiveness of those "who know not what they do" at his crucifixion opened the way for their conversion in Acts 2–3 after their sinning in ignorance (Acts 3:17; cf. 13:27; 17:30) by rejecting him.[33]

Acts provides balancing positive and negative exempla: the good example of Barnabas' and the negative example of Ananias's and Sapphira's giving proceeds to the apostles from their selling of fields (Acts 4:34–5:11). Barnabas obviously embodies the narrator's generalization that there was no needy person among the believers, but those who had fields sold them and laid the proceeds at the feet of the apostles (4:34–35). In the very next sentence after this general statement, the narrator introduces Barnabas and tells of his sale of a field and how he lay the proceeds at the apostles' feet (4:36–37). Through the disjunctive particle δέ in the next sentence, the narrator immediately contrasts to Barnabas's example Ananias's and Saphhira's false imitation of that act and of the community principle of laying proceeds from unneeded possessions at the feet (and disposal) of the apostles.[34]

Neither incident has an obtrusive narrator who applies it to the audience, as so many Hellenistic works do. But the narrator implicitly draws attention to the paradigmatic nature of both good and bad acts. First, the narrator states the general lesson of community sharing and generosity, which in the light of the Jesus tradition can be understood as an inspiration for Christian readers, whether or not strict imitation was envisaged. Next the narrator shows first a positive, then a negative, instance of the principle. After giving the negative case of Ananias and Sapphira, the narrator stresses how fear fell upon all who heard of it (Acts 5:11).[35] In light of the frequent drawing of les-

---

33. All these thematic links between parallel forgiveness and ignorance motifs provide strong internal evidence of the genuineness of Luke 23:34, despite the serious external textual counterevidence. See Josef Ernst, *Das Evangelium nach Lukas* (RNT; Regensburg: Friedrich Pustet, 1977) 634–35.

34. Cf. Malherbe, *Moral Exhortation,* 136, on antithetical examples.

35. John Andrew Darr, *"Glorified in the Presence of Kings": A Literary-Critical Study of Herod the Tetrarch in Luke-Acts* (diss., Vanderbilt University, 1987) 319 and passim, understands Herod as a similar negative paradigm of response to Jesus.

sons from narratives in the Lukan milieu, this bears the mark of a Christian educator using both Barnabas and Ananias and Sapphira as examples for positive and negative imitation in analogous ways in the implied readers' circumstances. But unlike many Hellenistic intrusive narrators who call attention to such paradigmatic usages, biblical narrators rarely draw explicit morals from their stories, and Luke-Acts imitates the biblical narratives in this respect.[36]

IMPLICIT MORAL EXHORTATION TO
IMPLIED READERS OF NARRATIVES

This sampling illustrates the Lukan use of the ancient practice of narrative models for imitation. This section sketches briefly how this archaic Hellenistic practice relates to contemporary literary critical insights into communication with implied readers through narratives. This, in turn, provides a link facilitating ethical use of Lukan (and other biblical) narratives today.

The notion of implied reader implies a communication model for writing and reading: the writer communicates to potential readers concerning some referent.[37] In communicating narratives, writers relate to their potential readers real or imaginary events. But since writers are not writing merely for their own amusement but for intended readers, it is legitimate to ask what goals they have in thus narrating events to them. This question plainly overlaps with the ancient rhetorical concerns that influence most writing from the Lukan milieu. Narratives that Hellenistic rhetoric would treat as models for behavior would, in this contemporary approach, be aimed at influencing the implied readers. Ancient rhetoric can thus provide clues for contemporary literary readings of a text. Hellenistic rhetoric indicates the likelihood that the author of Luke-Acts intended some of his narratives about Jesus and the disciples to be models for behavior. This provides in the text itself a justification for contemporary uses of such stories as models, that such uses are in continuity with the original intentions of the text and not mere eisegesis or pious accommodation.

Thus, the Hellenistic rhetorical paradigmatic use of narratives provides a

---

36. These are some among many possible samples of narrative paradigms in Luke-Acts. Other presentations of Jesus as model include the following instances: victory over temptation (Luke 4:1–13), persistent prayer (6:12; 9:18, 28; 11:1–13; 18:1), positive and negative examples of resolute obedience to God (9:51–53 vs. 9:57–62), friendship with sinners (15:1–2), ministry to sinners (19:1–10), and confronting unjust accusation (22:66–23:12). This list is adapted from Lilley, "Paradigm."

37. These personal reflections have more in common with the approach of thinkers like Paul Ricoeur and Susan Lanser than with most forms of deconstruction. See Wallace Martin, *Recent Theories of Narrative* (Ithaca: Cornell University Press, 1986) 155: "Susan Lanser, in *The Narrative Act,* integrates speech-act theory with point-of-view criticism to produce a comprehensive account of the communication between writers and readers." Cf. Lanser, *The Narrative Act,* and her appendix on speech-act theory and the status of fictional discourse (283–94) and bibliography (295–300).

grounding in the text for typical ethical, homiletic, and other church uses of
Lukan stories as models for contemporary Christian behavior. Such paradigmatic uses of Luke-Acts today are in continuity with the paradigmatic uses
originally envisaged for such texts. Although hermeneutical considerations are
evidently required when spanning centuries and cultures, Lukan narrative
does provide models for imitation, not only for Luke's original implied readers
but also for Christians today.

The Luke-Acts narratives have never legitimately been interpreted as
primarily moralistic, but the use of some of them as models for imitation is
one of their functions. This is indicated not only by the rhetorical expectations
concerning many kinds of narratives from the biblical and Hellenistic milieus,
including Luke-Acts, but by the fact that Luke and Acts themselves have also
been used for moral examples throughout Christian history. Here there is
space to mention only some obvious instances. Early Christian martyr literature, such as the *Martyrdom of Polycarp,* seems to have been influenced by
Stephen's death in imitation of his Lord's in Acts.[38] The Western monastic
tradition provides a second conspicuous example of imitation of Acts narratives. In its origins, monasticism interpreted the Acts summaries about sharing of goods as ethico-religious models for imitation and considered itself as
literally imitating their ideals and practices.[39] Luke T. Johnson has proposed
the "Council of Jerusalem" in Acts 15 as a model for community decision making.[40] The Lukan Gospel has provided Christians of many generations and cultures even more models for Christian reflection and imitation than has Acts.
Thus, Mary's Magnificat canticle has frequently been interpreted, especially in
liberation exegesis, as encouraging and exemplifying a preferential option for
the poor by Christians. The story of Martha and Mary has for centuries been
interpreted as a model for the contemplative calling. Jesus' word of forgiveness on the cross has from earliest times to the present been held up in homi-
lies as a model of forgiveness of one's enemies.

This survey of Hellenistic rhetorical ideals and examples from Luke-Acts
and its milieu indicates that many such common paradigmatic uses of Luke-
Acts are not far from the original intention of the text. A significant number of
the narratives in Luke and Acts are specially shaped and redacted to provide
clear models for imitation by implied readers.

---

38. See *Mart. Pol.* 17.3: "but the martyrs we love as disciples and imitators of the Lord [ὡς
μαθητὰς καὶ μιμητὰς τοῦ κυρίου]." Cf. 19.1. See also Eusebius *Hist. Eccl.* 23.16–17, citing
Hegesippus on the martyrdom of James portrayed with echoes of Stephen's and Jesus' deaths in
Luke-Acts.
39. Cf. Luke T. Johnson, *The Literary Function of Possessions in Luke-Acts* (SBLDS 39;
Missoula, MT: Scholars, 1977) 1–2, n. 3, and the primary texts he cites.
40. Luke T. Johnson, *Decision Making in the Church: A Biblical Model* (Philadelphia: Fortress,
1983).

PAUL, THE ANCIENT
EPISTOLARY THEORISTS, AND
2 CORINTHIANS 10 – 13
The Purpose and Literary Genre
of a Pauline Letter

Ancient epistolography has been an interest of NT scholars since the time of Adolf Deissmann, who sought to relate the letters of primitive Christianity to the private letters found among the papyri.[1]

PAUL AND ANCIENT EPISTOLARY THEORY

As is well known, Deissmann distinguished the nonliterary papyrus "letters" *(Briefe)* from the literary "epistles" *(Episteln)* of writers such as Cicero and Seneca, and he claimed that Paul's letters were "real letters, not epistles."[2] This understanding of Paul's writings coincided with Deissmann's assessment of the low social level of Pauline Christianity. Because of his conviction that primitive Christianity "was a movement of the lower classes,"[3] he neglected the literary epistles and made only occasional use of the works of ancient epistolary theorists.[4]

Subsequent scholarship, in general, has followed Deissmann's lead and concentrated on actual papyrus letters. The results of this concentration have often been useful in establishing the form and function of the various parts of

I wish to express my gratitude to Daniel L. Pals, J. Stephen Sapp, and Katherine G. Evans for their comments on a previous draft of this article.

1. See esp. Adolf Deissmann, *Bible Studies* (Edinburgh: Clark, 1901) 1–59; Deissmann, *Light from the Ancient East* (rev. ed.; New York: Harper & Bros., 1927) 146–251; and Deissmann, *Paul: A Study in Social and Religious History* (2d ed.; London: Hodder and Stoughton, 1926) 8–11. On Deissmann and his influence, see J. C. Hurd, *The Origin of I Corinthians* (New York: Seabury, 1965) 3–4; and A. J. Malherbe, *Social Aspects of Early Christianity* (2d ed.; Philadelphia: Fortress, 1983) 31–59 passim.

2. Deissmann, *Light from the Ancient East*, 234.

3. Deissmann, *Light from the Ancient East*, 9.

4. For Deissmann's occasional use of the ancient epistolary theorists, see *Bible Studies*, 4, nn. 1, 3; 6, n. 1; 31, n. 6; 35, n. 2; and *Light from the Ancient East*, 167, n. 7; 177, n. 4; 178, nn. 3, 7; 191, n. 2; 228, n. 1; 296, n. 2.

early Christian letters.[5] As the study of ancient letter writing and the NT has progressed, however, some of Deissmann's errors have been exposed. For instance, his distinction between letters and epistles has been shown to be conceptually flawed and of limited validity.[6] Again, recent sociological analyses of early Christianity have demonstrated that Deissmann woefully under-estimated the number, and especially the importance, of people in the Pauline congregations who came from the upper classes.[7] This growing appreciation of mixed social levels in Pauline Christianity has coincided with the skillful use of some of the more "literary" letters to help understand Paul's correspondence. Not only Seneca's *epistulae*[8] but also the Cynic epistles,[9] for example, have been effectively used to explicate writings in the Pauline corpus.

In addition, there is currently an increasing awareness by NT scholars that

5. The bibliography on ancient epistolography is immense. Important general studies include F. X. J. Exler, *The Form of the Ancient Greek Letter of the Epistolary Papyri* (Washington, DC: Catholic University of America, 1923; repr. Chicago: Ayer, 1976); H. Koskenniemi, *Studien zur Idee und Phraseologie des griechischen Briefes bis 400 n. Chr.* (Annales Academiae scientiarum fennicae, ser. B, 102.2; Helsinki: Suomalainen Tiedeakatemian, 1956); J. Sykutris, "Epistolographie," PWSup 5 (1931) 185–220; and K. Thraede, *Grundzüge griechisch-römischer Brieftopik* (Monographien zur griechischen und lateinischen Altertumswissenschaft 48; Munich: Beck, 1970), who concentrates on the "literary" letters. Among the many studies of the letters of the NT, see esp. K. Berger, "Hellenistische Gattungen im Neuen Testament," ANRW 2.25.2 (1984) 1031–1432, 1831–85, esp. 1326–63; M. Bünker, *Briefformular und rhetorische Disposition im 1. Korintherbrief* (GTA 28; Göttingen: Vandenhoeck & Ruprecht, 1984); N. A. Dahl, "Letter," IDBSup (1976) 538–41; W. G. Doty, *Letters in Primitive Christianity* (Guides to Biblical Scholarship, NT ser.; Philadelphia: Fortress, 1973); R. W. Funk, "The Letter: Form and Style," in his *Language, Hermeneutic, and Word of God* (New York: Harper & Row, 1966) 250–74, and Funk, "The Apostolic *Parousia*: Form and Significance," *Christian History and Interpretation: Studies Presented to John Knox* (ed. W. R. Farmer, C. F. D. Moule, and R. R. Niebuhr; Cambridge: Cambridge University Press, 1967) 249–68; B. Rigaux, *The Letters of St. Paul: Modern Studies* (Chicago: Franciscan Herald, 1968) 115–46; O. Roller, *Das Formular der paulinischen Briefe: Ein Beitrag zur Lehre vom antiken Briefe* (BWANT 58; Stuttgart: Kohlhammer, 1933); J. Schneider, "Brief," RAC 2 (1954) 563–85; P. Schubert, *The Form and Function of the Pauline Thanksgivings* (BZNW 20; Berlin: Töpelmann, 1939); S. K. Stowers, *Letter Writing in Greco-Roman Antiquity* (Library of Early Christianity 5; Philadelphia: Westminster, 1986); J. L. White, *The Form and Function of the Body of the Greek Letter* (SBLDS 2; 2d ed.; Missoula, MT: Scholars, 1972); White, "New Testament Epistolary Literature in the Framework of Ancient Epistolography," ANRW 2.25.2 (1984) 1730–56; White, *Light from Ancient Letters* (FFNT; Philadelphia: Fortress, 1986); and White, "Ancient Greek Letters," *Greco-Roman Literature and the New Testament: Selected Forms and Genres* (ed. D. E. Aune; SBLSBS 21; Atlanta: Scholars, 1988) 85–105.

6. See, for example, the comments by Paul Wendland, *Die urchristlichen Literaturformen* (HNT 1:3; 2d, 3d eds.; Tübingen: Mohr, 1912) 344; Doty, *Letters in Primitive Christianity*, 24–27; and Dahl, "Letter," 540.

7. See esp. W. A. Meeks, *The First Urban Christians: The Social World of the Apostle Paul* (New Haven: Yale University Press, 1983) 51–73.

8. On Seneca's epistles, see esp. H. Cancik, *Untersuchungen zu Senecas epistulae morales* (Spudasmata 18; Hildesheim: Olms, 1976). For the use of Seneca to elucidate Romans, see S. K. Stowers, *The Diatribe and Paul's Letter to the Romans* (SBLDS 57; Chico, CA: Scholars, 1981), esp. 69–75.

9. The text and translation of the Cynic epistles is now conveniently available in the edition of A. J. Malherbe (ed.), *The Cynic Epistles: A Study Edition* (SBLSBS 12; Missoula, MT: Scholars, 1977). Among the letters included in this edition are the Socratic epistles, which have been used by B. Fiore to illuminate the Pastoral Epistles. See Fiore, *The Function of Personal Example in the Socratic and Pastoral Epistles* (AnBib 105; Rome: Biblical Institute, 1986).

ancient epistolary theory is highly relevant to the investigation of Pauline literature. For instance, parts of Paul's writings clearly conform to recognized epistolary types in the ancient theory of letter writing.[10] As Abraham J. Malherbe has observed, "Sensitivity to the classifications of letters provided by ancient handbooks on letter writing" has already "contributed to a different perspective on Paul's letters."[11] However, "what is needed is not simply further investigation into Paul's style in light of the rhetorical theory and practice of his time, but an examination of his letters in light of the epistolary theory and practice of his time. Ancient writers had an interest in what constituted the proper subject matter and style of a letter, and Paul's letters will be illuminated by their prescriptions for letter writing as well as by the letters of the men who were familiar with the theory."[12]

It is in keeping with this desideratum that the investigation in this chapter is undertaken. The scope of this study is limited to 2 Corinthians 10–13, which forms a literary unit that is often the subject of separate examination. It is offered in tribute to Professor Malherbe, who has greatly enhanced our understanding of early Christianity and the Greco-Roman world in which it arose. Among his many contributions,[13] Malherbe has sharpened our appreciation of the role of rhetoric in the NT world,[14] demonstrated the relevance of ancient epistolary theory for the interpretation of Paul's letters,[15] and clarified some of the philosophical traditions employed in 2 Corinthians 10–13.[16] The present chapter builds upon Malherbe's contributions in these three areas, using ancient epistolary theory and rhetoric to illuminate aspects of 2 Corinthians 10–13.

As will be demonstrated, 2 Corinthians 10–13 has affinities with several different epistolary types discussed in the handbooks of Ps.-Demetrius (second century B.C.E. to third century C.E. and Ps.-Libanius (fourth to sixth centuries C.E.).[17] The manual of Ps.-Demetrius (*Epistolary Types*) contains descriptions

10. See esp. Dahl, "Letter," 539–40. Cf. also Stowers, *Letter Writing*, esp. 51–57; and White, *Light from Ancient Letters*, 189–91, 202–3.
11. Malherbe, *Social Aspects*, 58. Among the contributions Malherbe mentions, emphasis should be given to the unpublished paper of N. A. Dahl, "Paul's Letter to the Galatians: Epistolary Genre, Content, and Structure," SBL Seminar "Form and Function of the Pauline Letters," 1973.
12. Malherbe, *Social Aspects*, 58.
13. See the bibliography in this book.
14. See, for example, Malherbe, *Social Aspects*, 54–59.
15. See, for instance, A. J. Malherbe, *Ancient Epistolary Theorists* (SBLSBS 19; Atlanta: Scholars, 1988). For Malherbe's application of epistolary theory to Paul's letters, see his "Exhortation in First Thessalonians," *NovT* 25 (1983) 238–56, esp. 241–42; 246, n. 38; and 255.
16. A. J. Malherbe, "Antisthenes and Odysseus, and Paul at War," *HTR* 76 (1983) 143–73, now in his *Paul and the Popular Philosophers* (Minneapolis: Fortress, 1989) 91–120.
17. The first commentator to use the epistolary handbooks of Ps.-Demetrius and Ps.-Libanius in an interpretation of 2 Corinthians was apparently Hans Windisch, who did so in his magisterial *Der zweite Korintherbrief* (MeyerK; Göttingen: Vandenhoeck & Ruprecht, 1924) 8–9, 75, 82, 84, 211, 221, and 414. Subsequent commentators usually have either ignored these handbooks or have been content to make passing allusions to them. In this chapter, references to Ps.-Demetrius and Ps.-Libanius are to the page and line of Malherbe's edition (see note 15 above). The translations of these authors are those provided by Malherbe.

and examples of twenty-one kinds of letters.[18] That of Ps.-Libanius (*Epistolary Styles*) is more extensive, providing definitions and examples for forty-one letter types.[19] Both handbooks presuppose an audience of advanced students who already have been instructed in both epistolary form and rhetorical technique. Consequently, the manuals probably "were used in the training of professional letter writers,"[20] for "letters were written as an exercise in style early in the tertiary stage of the educational system."[21] Inasmuch as this instruction in epistolary style was provided by teachers of rhetoric, the correspondence of Paul's letters to the styles and letter types given by Ps.-Demetrius and Ps.-Libanius is highly significant. It provides another piece of evidence that Paul's educational level was high and that he had received training in rhetoric.[22]

In what follows, the focus of attention is on the text of 2 Corinthians 10–13. The affinities of material there with the epistolary styles and types of Ps.-Demetrius and Ps.-Libanius are indicated primarily in the notes to this chapter. The points of correspondence can be best indicated by means of an analysis of the purpose and literary genre of 2 Corinthians 10–13, and it is to this analysis that we now turn.

THE PURPOSE AND LITERARY GENRE
OF 2 CORINTHIANS 10–13

First, like 1 Cor 1:10–4:21, the final four chapters of 2 Corinthians constitute an appeal made by the apostle.[23] Recent interpretation has focused on other dimensions of these chapters and has devoted insufficient attention to the fact that Paul begins this section with the verbs παρακαλῶ (I entreat

18. For a bibliography and a discussion of Ps.-Demetrius, see esp. Malherbe, *Ancient Epistolary Theorists*, 4–7; 9, nn. 29–35.

19. There are two manuscript traditions of the *Epistolary Styles;* one attributes the work to the rhetorician Libanius and the other to the neo-Platonist philosopher Proclus. For a bibliography and discussion, see Malherbe, *Ancient Epistolary Theorists*, 5–7; 10, nn. 42–45.

20. Malherbe, *Ancient Epistolary Theorists*, 7. Cf. also the comments of R. Schubert, "Form and Function of the Pauline Letters," *JR* 19 (1939) 365–77, esp. 367.

21. Malherbe, *Social Aspects*, 59.

22. See esp. the important work by H. D. Betz, "The Problem of Rhetoric and Theology According to the Apostle Paul," *L'Apôtre Paul: Personnalité, style et conception du ministère* (ed. A. Vanhoye; BETL 73; Leuven, Belgium: Leuven University Press, 1986) 16–48. To the list of those arguing that Paul had been trained in rhetoric, add now P. Marshall, *Enmity in Corinth: Social Conventions in Paul's Relations with the Corinthians* (WUNT 2:23; Tübingen: Mohr, 1987) esp. 400. Cf. also Malherbe, *Social Aspects*, 59, for the implications of Paul's epistolary style for his educational level.

23. Ps.-Demetrius assigns appeals, petitions, and requests (δεήσεις) to the "supplicatory" (ἀξιω-ματικός) type of letter; see *Epistolary Types* 12 (36,27 Malherbe). The "requesting" (παρακλη-τική) type of epistolary style is discussed by Ps.-Libanius *Epistolary Styles* 7 and 54 (68,14 and 74,16–19 Malherbe). Cf. also Philostratus *On Letters* (42,20 Malherbe). The elements and the form of petitions are discussed by T. Y. Mullins, "Petition as a Literary Form," *NovT* 5 (1962) 46–54. Cf. also J. L. White, *The Form and Structure of the Official Petition* (SBLDS 5; Missoula, MT: Scholars, 1972). For the hortatory character of 1 Cor 1:10–4:21, see J. T. Fitzgerald, *Cracks in an Earthen Vessel: An Examination of the Catalogues of Hardships in the Corinthian Correspondence* (SBLDS 99; Atlanta: Scholars, 1988) 117–28.

[2 Cor 10:1]) and δέομαι (I beg [10:2]). As a consequence, the ultimately hortatory character of 2 Corinthians 10–13 has not received due emphasis.[24] Yet all that Paul says in these chapters is ultimately in service to his appeal as he makes a final,[25] passionate effort to persuade the Corinthians by verbal petition. He appeals "by the meekness [πραΰτητος] and gentleness [ἐπιεικείας] of Christ" (10:1), for he wishes, now as before, to avoid a display of his apostolic power and to come to them in a spirit of meekness (1 Cor 4:21).[26]

If, however, his pleas should prove unpersuasive or fall on deaf ears, Paul is prepared to resort to power and force. The strategy is much the same as in 1 Cor 4:16–21. Paul is coming to the Corinthians in any case (1 Cor 4:19; 2 Cor 12:14; 13:1). *How* he comes depends on them (1 Cor 4:21; 2 Cor 12:20). He can come in the power of the rod or with meekness (1 Cor 4:20–21). He can come as a storm trooper (2 Cor 10:3–6) or in the weakness that he displayed when he was first among them (1 Cor 2:3). The decision is theirs, and they will come to the right decision only if they realize that Paul is God's approved apostle (10:18)—that Christ does indeed speak in him (13:3).

Paul's express purpose in writing is to persuade the Corinthians of this very fact. In 2 Cor 13:6 he says, ἐλπίζω δὲ ὅτι γνώσεσθε ὅτι ἡμεῖς οὐκ ἐσμὲν ἀδό-

---

24. An important exception to this general tendency is V. P. Furnish, *II Corinthians* (AB 32A; Garden City, NY: Doubleday, 1984) 48, who correctly calls attention to "the overall hortatory character" of these chapters. See also C. H. Talbert, *Reading Corinthians: A Literary and Theological Commentary on 1 and 2 Corinthians* (New York: Crossroad, 1987) 129, who refers to "the hortatory purpose of the whole of 2 Cor 10–13."

25. 2 Corinthians 10–13 constitutes Paul's final appeal not merely in the sense that it chronologically *may* be part of his last letter to the Corinthians. It is final in the more important sense that it represents his last-ditch verbal effort to persuade the Corinthians and to avoid the use of discipline. For Paul's other appeals in the Corinthian correspondence, see 1 Cor 1:10; 4:16; 16:15; 2 Cor 2:8; 5:20; 6:1. For recent advocates of the view that 2 Corinthians 10–13 reflects a situation later than 2 Corinthians 1–9, see esp. F. F. Bruce, *1 and 2 Corinthians* (NCB; London: Marshall, Morgan & Scott, 1971) 166–70; C. K. Barrett, *A Commentary on the Second Epistle to the Corinthians* (HNTC; New York: Harper & Row, 1973) 11–25, 243–45; Furnish, *II Corinthians*, 35–48; and R. P. Martin, *2 Corinthians* (Word Biblical Commentary; Waco: Word, 1986) xxxviii–xlvi. For recent advocates of the view that 2 Corinthians 10–13 is chronologically prior to at least part of 2 Corinthians 1–9 (esp. 2 Cor 1:1–2:13; 7:5–16), see esp. R. Bultmann, *The Second Letter to the Corinthians* (Minneapolis: Augsburg, 1985) 18; H. D. Betz, *2 Corinthians 8 and 9* (Hermeneia; Philadelphia: Fortress, 1985); F. Lang, *Die Briefe an die Korinther* (NTD 7; Göttingen: Vandenhoeck & Ruprecht, 1986) 12–14; M. Carrez, *La deuxième épître de Saint Paul aux Corinthiens* (CNT, 2d ser., 8; Geneva: Labor et Fides, 1986) 14–18; and Talbert, *Reading Corinthians*, xviii–xxi.

26. Πραότης (meekness) and ἐπιείκεια (gentleness) are the virtues that create goodwill and make the use of force unnecessary. As early as Thucydides, these terms appear in contexts dealing with foreign policy and the use of military might. Ἐπιείκεια is the virtue of those who voluntarily do not make full use of the power that their superior position justly allows. See esp. J. de Romilly, "Fairness and Kindness in Thucydides," *Phoenix* 28 (1974) 95–100, and, for the ancient controversy concerning the place of power and goodwill in politics, de Romilly, "Eunoia in Isocrates or the Political Importance of Creating Good Will," *JHS* 78 (1958) 92–101. Paul's discussion of his ἐξουσία (authority) shows that he not only appeals by the ἐπιείκεια of Christ but also that he himself is ἐπιεικής in his use of authority. For a discussion of ἐπιείκεια (modesty) as a rhetorical style, see esp. Hermogenes *De ideis* 2.6. A useful translation of this work from the second century C.E. has recently been provided by C. W. Wooten, *Hermogenes' On Types of Style* (Chapel Hill: University of North Carolina Press, 1987).

κιμοι, "And I hope that you will understand that we are not counterfeit."[27] The goal is less modest than that of 1:12–14,[28] but the situation that prompts it is more pressing. The one who is not ἀδόκιμος (counterfeit) is obviously δόκιμος (genuine), and as such has *God's* commendation (10:18; cf. 1 Thess 2:4).[29] This is the decisive factor, and Paul is convinced that once his genuineness as an apostle is recognized, the Corinthians' esteem for him and his ministry will increase (2 Cor 10:15)[30] and they will begin to take all the actions appropriate to that recognition.

If this happens, Paul will be able to avoid the use of force. In 2 Cor 13:10 he brings his appeal to an end and gives the ultimate purpose for which he has aired his hopes and fears, issued his pleas and threats, and used all his literary devices: "I write this while I am away from you, in order that when I come I may not have to be severe in my use of the authority which the Lord has given me for building up and not for tearing down" (RSV). The Lord has given him authority for constructive rather than destructive purposes (cf. also 10:8). All that Paul has said has been aimed at οἰκοδομή (edification [12:19]).[31] He has no desire to use his authority (ἐξουσία) in a severe and abrupt manner (ἀπο-τόμως), for such a use would be destructive. At both the beginning and the end of his appeal, he airs his reluctance to act in this fashion (10:2; 13:10), because it can only result in casualties and sorrow (12:21; cf. also 2:3–4). But he will not refrain from doing so at all costs, for he is not willing to forfeit the Corinthian church completely. He wants the God of peace to be with the church and for the church to be at peace (13:11). However, he will go to war, if necessary, and demolish the fortifications of his opponents in order to secure the Corinthians' obedience (10:3–6).

Paul's appeal is thus, in the second place, also an ultimatum that carries a threat (2 Cor 10:6; 13:2), a *Drohrede* that carries with it a call for repentance (cf. 12:21).[32] The ἀποτομία (severity) that he mentions (13:10) is diametrically

27. As is widely recognized, the δόκιμος word group plays a crucial role in Paul's Corinthian correspondence. See 1 Cor 3:13; 9:27; 11:19, 28; 16:3; 2 Cor 2:9; 8:2, 8, 22; 9:13; 10:18; 13:3, 5–7. On this word group and the concepts of testing and attestation, see the discussions by W. Grundmann, "δόκιμος, κτλ.," *TDNT* 2 (1964) 255–60; and H. Haarbeck, "δόκιμος," *The New International Dictionary of New Testament Theology* (ed. C. Brown; 3 vols.; Grand Rapids, MI: Zondervan, 1975–78) 3. 808–11.
28. On 2 Cor 1:12–14, see Fitzgerald, *Cracks in an Earthen Vessel*, 148–51, 157–58.
29. Important observations on the idea of the divine commission in Paul and the philosophers are made by Abraham J. Malherbe in his highly influential article "'Gentle as a Nurse': The Cynic Background to 1 Thess ii," *NovT* 12 (1970) 203–17, esp. 214–16.
30. On 2 Cor 10:15, see J. E. Belser, *Der zweite Brief des Apostels Paulus an die Korinther* (Freiburg: Herder, 1910) 307–8; Windisch, *Der zweite Korintherbrief,* 312–13; W. G. Kümmel in the appendix to H. Lietzmann, *An die Korinther* (HNT 9; 5th ed.; Tübingen: Mohr, 1969) 209; Barrett, *Second Corinthians,* 267; and esp. Furnish, *II Corinthians,* 473.
31. On οἰκοδομή in early Christian literature, see esp. P. Vielhauer, *Oikodome* (TBü 65; Munich: Kaiser, 1979) 1–168.
32. For "threatening" (ἀπειλητικός) letters, see Ps.-Demetrius *Epistolary Types* 8 (36,1–6 Malherbe; cf. also 38,15 Malherbe) and Ps.-Libanius *Epistolary Styles* 13 and 60 (68,23 and 74,37–39 Malherbe). Windisch, *Der zweite Korintherbrief,* 8, refers to this letter type in connection with the threat in 2 Cor 13:2. The function of such letters is to instill fear (φόβος) through the threat of punishment for wrong conduct. The threatened punishment is connected with a con-

opposed to the πραΰτης (meekness) and ἐπιείκεια (gentleness [10:1]) by
which he appeals (Ps.-Plut. Mor. 13D; Dion. Hal. Ant. Rom. 8.61.1–2; cf. Rom
11:22). Although Paul clearly wishes to avoid ἀποτομία by threatening its use,
he provides the Corinthians with a sample of such severity in his letter. That
2 Corinthians 10–13 has at points a sharp and biting tone is undeniable.
Letters written ἀποτόμως are not unknown in antiquity (cf. Cic. Att. 10.11.5).
But Paul's use of severity in chapters 10 through 13 is restricted, a stern tone
warning of sterner actions. He prepares for discipline, but he also prays
(εὐχόμεθα)[33] for the rectification of the Corinthians that will make the need
for severe action superfluous (13:7, 9).

In this regard, Paul shows himself to be a good father, a role that he as the
founder of the congregation (2 Cor 10:13–16) has not forgotten in this section
(11:2; 12:14). Ps.-Plutarch not only advises fathers who are concerned for the
good upbringing of their children to drive away flatterers who might corrupt
them (Mor. 12F–13C); he also exhorts them not to be too harsh and severe
themselves: "As physicians, by mixing bitter drugs with sweet syrups, have
found that the agreeable taste gains access for what is beneficial, so fathers
should combine the abruptness [ἀποτομίαν] of their rebukes with mildness
[πραότητι]" (13D; trans. F. C. Babbitt in LCL). This is precisely what Paul
does as he combines a gentle appeal with the threat of severe action if the
entreaty goes unheeded.

Third, 2 Corinthians 10–13 is an apology (12:19).[34] This fact is widely
recognized, rendering the need for detailed discussion of the point unnecessary. It may be helpful, however, to call attention to 13:1. One finds here a
quotation of Deut 19:15 with its regulation concerning the number of

---

templated visit of the person writing the letter: "Pray with all your soul and strength that I not
come. For if I did come, you would experience many evils you had hoped never to experience"
(Ps.-Libanius Epistolary Styles 60 [74,37–39 Malherbe]). Compare Ps.-Libanius's "letter of
declaration," in which a harsh judgment (ἀπότομον κρίσιν) is rendered and carried out (Epistolary Styles 38 and 85 [70,31–32 and 80,17–20 Malherbe]); for the expression harsh judgment, cf.
also Wis 6:5. The idea of frightening readers by means of letters appears in 2 Cor 10:9 (ἐκφοβεῖν
ὑμᾶς διὰ τῶν ἐπιστολῶν) in connection with the idea that Paul's letters are βαρεῖαι and ἰσχυραί
(10:10). Inasmuch as βαρύς is the opposite of ἐπιεικής (Hermogenes On Types of Style 2.6
[348,8–9 Rabe = 2.371,30–31 Spengel]), there is an effective contrast between Paul's gentle
appeal (2 Cor 10:1) and the opponents' assessment that his letters are harsh (10:10). For the idea
that a "blaming" letter should not be harsh, see Ps.-Demetrius Epistolary Types 3 (32,27
Malherbe).
    33. Ps.-Libanius Epistolary Styles 12 and 59 (68,22 and 74,34–36) identifies the "praying"
(εὐκτική) style as one in which "we pray" (εὐχόμεθα) and express our hopes (ἐλπίζω) for certain
things.
    34. The "apologetic" (ἀπολογητικός) letter type is defined by Ps.-Demetrius Epistolary Types
18 (40,1–2 Malherbe) as follows: "The apologetic type is that which adduces, with proof, arguments which contradict charges that are being made." See notes 35 and 36 below and also Philostratus On Letters (42,21 Malherbe). Windisch, Der zweite Korintherbrief, 8, had already pointed
to Ps.-Demetrius Epistolary Types 18 in connection with 2 Corinthians 1–7, 10–13. F. Young and
D. Ford also cite Ps.-Demetrius in support of their argument that 2 Corinthians as a whole is an
apologetic letter. See their Meaning and Truth in 2 Corinthians (Grand Rapids, MI: Eerdmans,
1988) 39–40. For the use of apology to refer to a letter written in "conciliatory" style, see the
comment by Ps.-Libanius Epistolary Styles 19 (68,33–34 Malherbe).

witnesses needed at a trial. The quotation is important, coming as it does after the mention of an "apology" in 12:19. The two belong together and serve to provide a quasi-legal setting for Paul's literary apology.

The situation presupposed in 2 Corinthians 10–13 also conforms to the typical apologetic *Sitz im Leben*. The case involves three parties: Paul, the Corinthians, and the opponents. The accusations against Paul have been raised by the opponents (the third party), but Paul (the first party) does not respond directly to them. The apology is instead directed to the Corinthians (the second party). Ps.-Demetrius presupposes precisely this situation in an example of an apologetic letter, with the first party's response to the third party's charges being directed to the second party.[35]

Hans Dieter Betz has attempted to locate 2 Corinthians 10–13 more precisely in the apologetic traditions of antiquity. According to Betz's provocative thesis, Paul's apology belongs to the Socratic tradition.[36] It is a philosophical apology rather than a rhetorical one. That is, Paul defends himself in the manner appropriate to a philosopher, not with the rhetorical devices of the Sophist. In so doing, he presents himself as the true, but ταπεινός, philosopher and his opponents as pretentious Sophists.

Betz's work has the great merit of bringing into scholarly discussion a number of key texts that shed light on Paul's apologetic method in 2 Corinthians 10–13, and his insights are often brilliant. But his attempt to restrict 2 Corinthians 10–13 to the narrow tradition of Socratic apology is not fully persuasive. Paul's apology not only fails at key points to conform to the Socratic apologetic tradition[37] but also has definite points of contact with the

35. Ps.-Demetrius *Epistolary Types* 18 (40,3–16 Malherbe) gives the following example of an apologetic letter:

> Fortune has served me well by preserving for me important facts to be used in the demonstration of my case. For at the time they say I did this, I had already sailed for Alexandria, so that I happened neither to see nor meet the person about whom I am accused. Since there has been no disagreement between you and me, it is absurd for you to accuse someone who has wronged you in no way. But those who brought the accusation appear themselves to have perpetrated some foul deed, and, suspecting that I might write you something about them, they (took care) to slander me in anticipation. If you have believed their empty accusations, tell me. On the other hand, if you persevere with me as you should, you will learn everything when I arrive. In fact, one could be confident that, if I had at any time spoken against other people to you, I would also have spoken against you to others. So, wait for my arrival, and everything will be put to the proof, so that you may know how rightly you have judged me to be your friend, and I may prove you by your actions. I dare say that those who accused us will rather attack each other and choke themselves.

36. Hans Dieter Betz, *Der Apostel Paulus und die sokratische Tradition* (BHT 45; Tübingen: Mohr, 1972). See p. 40 for Betz's reference to Ps.-Demetrius *Epistolary Types* 18.

37. See, for instance, the discussion of Betz's thesis by E. A. Judge in his "St. Paul and Classical Society," *JAC* 15 (1972) 19–36, esp. 35, and, in more detail, in his "St. Paul and Socrates," *Interchange: Papers on Biblical and Current Questions* 14 (1973) 106–16. See also the objections raised by J. M. Dillon, "Critique of H. D. Betz's Paper," in H. D. Betz, *Paul's Apology, II Corinthians 10–13, and the Socratic Tradition* (Protocol Series of the Colloquies of the Center for Hermeneutical Studies in Hellenistic and Modern Culture 2 = Protocol of the Second Colloquy: 5 December 1970; Berkeley: Center for Hermeneutical Studies, 1975) 17–20, esp. 19. Cf. A. T.

broader rhetorical tradition of self-defense.[38] In short, 2 Corinthians 10–13 is more broadly apologetic than Betz's thesis suggests.

At the same time, however, 2 Corinthians 10–13 is not simply an apology made to the Corinthians. It contains, in the fourth place, a counteraccusation against Paul's opponents. Paul accuses them of illegitimacy and ignorant pretentiousness, the very charges they have brought against him (10:2, 7, 12, 15; 11:5, 13–15; 12:11).[39] The presence of such a counteraccusation in a letter is not surprising, for this is one of the letter types recognized by Ps.-Libanius (*Epistolary Styles* 22 [70,1–2 Malherbe]): "The counter-accusing style [ἀν-τεγκληματική] is that in which we bring a countercharge against someone by accusing him of what is brought against us, thus turning the charge around upon the accuser."[40]

Implicit in this counteraccusation there is, in the fifth place, a sharp accusation and reproach directed to the Corinthians for allowing themselves to fall prey to Paul's opponents (2 Cor 11:3–4) and for being ungrateful for the benefits he has conveyed to them (11:7–11; 12:13–15).[41] This ingratitude is made all the more contemptible and culpable by the emphasis that their unrequited benefactor is none other than their own parent (12:14). Such behavior is unjust and worthy of condemnation (cf. esp. Xen. *Mem.* 2.2.1–14). Letters of accusation and reproach that deal with unacceptable conduct are found in the epistolary handbooks. In light of the situation in Corinth, the examples of the accusing letter provided by Ps.-Demetrius and the letter of reproach given by Ps.-Libanius are especially pertinent. Just as Paul accuses the Corinthians of receiving those who malign him, so also Ps.-Demetrius's letter writer complains that the recipient has caused him grief by befriending someone who has unjustly accused him of improper conduct.[42] Again, just as Paul reproaches

---

Lincoln, *Paradise Now and Not Yet: Studies in the Role of the Heavenly Dimension in Paul's Thought with Special Reference to His Eschatology* (SNTSMS 43; Cambridge: Cambridge University Press, 1981) 73.

38. I hope to demonstrate some of these points of contact in a paper, still in preparation, on Paul and Isocrates.

39. The standard treatment of Paul's opponents in 2 Corinthians remains that of Dieter Georgi, *Die Gegner des Paulus im 2 Korintherbrief* (WMANT 11; Neukirchen-Vluyn: Neukirchener, 1964), now available in a slightly revised English version: *The Opponents of Paul in Second Corinthians* (Philadelphia: Fortress, 1986). For a minimalist reconstruction of the opponents' criticisms of Paul, see S. N. Olson, *Confidence Expressions in Paul: Epistolary Conventions and the Purpose of 2 Corinthians* (diss., Yale University, 1976) 21–27. Cf. also Betz, *Der Apostel Paulus*, 43–137; G. Theissen, *The Social Setting of Pauline Christianity: Essays on Corinth* (Philadelphia: Fortress, 1982) 44–46; Furnish, *II Corinthians*, 48–54; Marshall, *Enmity in Corinth*, 325–40; and Talbert, *Reading Corinthians*, 111–13.

40. For Ps.-Libanius's example of a letter of counteraccusation, see *Epistolary Styles* 69 (76,34–37 Malherbe).

41. Valuable observations on 2 Cor 11:3 are provided by Abraham J. Malherbe in his "Through the Eye of the Needle: Simplicity or Singleness?" *Restoration Quarterly* 5 (1961) 119–29.

42. Ps.-Demetrius *Epistolary Types* 17 (38,28–36):

The accusing type is that which consists of an accusation of things that have been done beyond the bounds of propriety. For example: It was not pleasant for me to hear what was being said against me, for it was at variance with my upright conduct. On the other hand,

the Corinthians for failing to be properly appreciative of his sacrifices for them, Ps.-Libanius's letter of reproach castigates the recipient for lack of gratitude toward his benefactor.[43]

Therefore, 2 Cor 12:19–13:9 contains a strong strain of both accusation and reproach, but especially of accusation. If Paul is reluctant to admit that he is defending himself to the Corinthians, this is not simply because he may be drawing upon a philosophical tradition.[44] It is also because he is preparing to take the witness stand to *accuse* the Corinthians. When he says that he speaks "before God" (12:19), he is indicating that his testimony is being given before the Lord, as in Deut 19:17.[45] The catalogs of vices (12:20–21) function as the indictment he is preparing against them, with at least two of the items (καταλαλιαί [slanders] and ψιθυρισμοί [gossiping]) having special reference to himself.[46] In short, the Corinthians, too, are on trial and in danger of being found ἀδόκιμοι (counterfeit [13:5]). In order to avoid punishment, the Corinthians must test themselves, set their own affairs in order, and take appropriate action (13:5–7). That will include repentance of their sins (12:21), as well

---

you, too, conducted yourself badly when you placed yourself in the hands of the man who was speaking against me, even though you knew him to be a slanderer and liar. Speaking in general, you continue to cause (me) grief, for you have as friend someone whom you know to be an enemy of all men. Nor have you weighed this one fact, that the man who brings accusations against (absent) people while he is with you and others, is likely to do the same thing against you. Him, therefore, I blame because he does this, but you (I blame) because, although you seem to be intelligent, you nevertheless have no discrimination with regard to the friends you keep. For Windisch's reference to this text, see *Der zweite Korintherbrief*, 8.

43. Ps.-Libanius *Epistolary Styles* 64 (76,12–16 Malherbe): "You have received many favors from us, and I am exceedingly amazed that you remember none of them but speak badly of us. That is characteristic of a person with an ungrateful disposition. For the ungrateful forget noble men, and in addition ill-treat their benefactors as though they were enemies." Cf. also Ps.-Libanius *Epistolary Styles* 17 (68,29–30 Malherbe), Ps.-Demetrius *Epistolary Types* 4 (34,1–7 Malherbe), and Windisch, *Der zweite Korintherbrief*, 8. For the concept and practice of benefaction that lies back of Paul's argument, see now F. W. Danker, *II Corinthians* (Augsburg Commentary on the New Testament; Minneapolis: Augsburg, 1989) 201, and the more extensive treatment of the subject in Danker, *Benefactor: Epigraphic Study of a Graeco-Roman and New Testament Semantic Field* (St. Louis: Clayton, 1982). According to Hermogenes *De ideis* 2.8 (364 Rabe), "Indignation is found in all reproachful thoughts whenever the speaker who is discussing his own benefactions says by way of criticism that he has received little or no gratitude for them" (trans. Wooten, *Hermogenes*, 97). Indignation (βαρύτης) involves the use of irony, of which Paul makes heavy use in 2 Corinthians; cf. note 48 below.

44. So Betz, *Der Apostel Paulus*, 13–42, esp. 15.

45. It should be recalled that Deut 19:15 is quoted in 2 Cor 13:1 and that Paul sees himself as accused by unjust witnesses (cf. Deut 19:16).

46. On lists of vices, see Abraham J. Malherbe, *Moral Exhortation: A Greco-Roman Sourcebook* (Library of Early Christianity 4; Philadelphia: Westminster, 1986) 138–41; and J. T. Fitzgerald, "Virtue/Vice Lists," forthcoming in the *Anchor Bible Dictionary*. For an ancient popular philosophical work that makes an extensive allegorical use of virtues and vices, see J. T. Fitzgerald and L. M. White (trans.), *The Tabula of Cebes* (SBLTT 24; Chico, CA: Scholars, 1983). For the "censorious" (ἐπιτιμητικός) letter type used to rebuke people for sins already committed and to summon them to stop sinning, see Ps.-Demetrius *Epistolary Types* 6 (34,20–30 Malherbe) and Ps.-Libanius *Epistolary Styles* 34 and 81 (70,24 and 80,1–3 Malherbe). Cf. Windisch, *Der zweite Korintherbrief*, 8.

as recognition of Paul's legitimacy. "The Corinthians' δοκιμή must show itself precisely in their acknowledgment of Paul's δοκιμή."[47]

Finally, in addition to those letter types already identified, parts of 2 Corinthians 10–13 correspond to other epistolary types, such as the "ironic" letter[48] and the "provoking" letter.[49] These other types are not singled out here for comment, since the preceding discussion has already made it abundantly clear that 2 Corinthians 10–13 is an excellent example of a mixed letter type.[50] The outward structure is that of an appeal, but a strong use is made of elements from a legal setting. It is within this quasi-legal setting that Paul boasts and defends himself; threatens, accuses, and reproaches the Corinthians; and launches a counterattack on the superapostles. But the self-laudatory, apologetic, admonitory, and polemical elements are in service to the appeal, and not vice versa. Paul is, of course, vitally concerned with his apostolic legitimacy,[51] but he is more concerned that the Corinthians do right. Their salvation is more important than his giving them the decisive, but destructive, δοκιμή (proof) of his apostleship (13:3). Their restoration to wholeness (13:9) is more crucial than his self-vindication, and for that reason he is even willing to keep his authority in abeyance and appear ὡς ἀδόκιμοι (as though we were counterfeit [13:7]). That might seem more foolish than noble, but it is appropriate to one who gives a "foolish discourse"[52] and boasts of his weaknesses.

47. Bultmann, *Corinthians*, 246.
48. For irony as an epistolary style and type, see Ps.-Demetrius *Epistolary Types* 20 (40,24–30 Malherbe) and Ps.-Libanius *Epistolary Styles* 9 and 56 (68,17–19 and 74,23–27 Malherbe). Betz, *Der Apostel Paulus*, 52, n. 57, refers to Ps.-Demetrius's definition of an ironic letter in his discussion of 2 Cor 10:1. For 2 Cor 11:19 as an example of Pauline irony, see Fitzgerald, *Cracks in an Earthen Vessel*, 206–7. For other letter types in 2 Corinthians, see Windisch, *Der zweite Korintherbrief*, 8–9.
49. See Ps.-Libanius *Epistolary Styles* 24 and 71 (70,4–5 and 78,4–8 Malherbe). Cf. Windisch, *Der zweite Korintherbrief*, 9.
50. This observation in regard to 2 Corinthians as a whole was already made by Windisch, *Der zweite Korintherbrief*, 9. He is followed in this judgment by Betz, *Der Apostel Paulus*, 41, who, however, contends that 2 Corinthians 10–13 stands closest to the "apologetic" letter. For the mixed letter type, see Ps.-Libanius *Epistolary Styles* 45 and 92 (73,6 and 80,37–41 Malherbe).
51. See esp. E. Käsemann, *Die Legitimität des Apostels: Eine Untersuchung zu II Korinther 10–13* (Darmstadt: Wissenschaftliche Buchhandlung, 1956). This essay by Käsemann appeared earlier in ZNW 41 (1942) 33–71. For some important modifications and corrections of Käsemann's argument, see J. H. Schütz, *Paul and the Anatomy of Apostolic Authority* (SNTSMS 26; Cambridge: Cambridge University Press, 1975), esp. 1–21, 165–86.
52. Among recent treatments of 2 Cor 11:1–12:10, see esp. J. Zmijewski, *Der Stil der paulinischen "Narrenrede"* (BBT 52; Cologne and Bonn: Hanstein, 1978).

L. MICHAEL WHITE

13

MORALITY BETWEEN
TWO WORLDS
A Paradigm of Friendship in Philippians

BETWEEN TWO WORLDS

"There will be tribulation and anguish for every living person who practices vice [τὸ κακόν], for the Jew first and for the Greek; but there will be glory, honor, and peace for all who do the good [τὸ ἀγαθόν], for the Jew first and for the Greek" (Rom 2:9–11). A world of dualisms—Jew and Greek, good and evil, virtue and vice—these are polarities within Paul's thought, a glimpse at the way he saw the moral structure of the world. Paul, like many other Jews of the Diaspora, stood between two worlds and felt the tensions this position produced. Typically, we have characterized this dilemma in Paul in terms of the dialectic between law and grace (for example, in Romans and Galatians). Paul, then, becomes the "apostle of freedom and liberty" from the constraints of Jewish legalism.[1] However, the very theology of freedom produced for Paul a moral dilemma as to the constraints and responsibilities of personal freedom. I wonder, though, if we have not overly individualized the notions of freedom and grace,[2] and if what is at stake for Paul is rather a corporate moral ideal. There is in Philippians a communal ideal of virtue in Christ Jesus, a Pauline adaptation of the Hellenistic moral paradigm of φιλία (friendship).

We have tended to portray the Pauline dialectic as an abrogation of the ethics of Torah legalism in favor of a new ethic based solely on the gospel of love. However, two cautionary comments need to be made here in passing. First,

---

Τῷ Ἄβε : "ὁ παιδευτὴς ὁ κοινός,
  ὁ παιδαγωγός,"
  καὶ ὁ φίλος μου ὁ πιστός.

1. So one notes the classic formulations of Richard Longnecker, *Paul, Apostle of Liberty* (New York: Harper & Row, 1964), and F. F. Bruce, *Paul, Apostle of the Heart Set Free* (Grand Rapids, MI: Eerdmans, 1977).

2. Here I follow the caution on Paul suggested by Krister Stendahl, "The Apostle Paul and the Introspective Conscience of the West," *HTR* 56 (1963) 199–215. My own further suggestions of how this perspective might be used to reevaluate the development of the Christian cultural tradition may be found in L. Michael White, "Shifting Sectarian Boundaries in Early Christianity," *BJRL* 70 (1988) 7–24.

recent scholarship has amply demonstrated that this is an oversimplification of Jewish views on Torah and ethics.[3] Instead, there was considerable diversity of applications of law and purity.[4] We should be cautious, then, of any overtly monolithic portrayal of Judaism in the period. After all, the Wisdom tradition, Qumran, and even Jesus himself represent a rather broad spectrum of moral ideology within first-century Palestine, not to mention others like Philo and Paul in the Diaspora. There is now ample evidence of Jewish communities in the Diaspora, such as at Delos, Sardis, or Aphrodisias, that were highly acculturated to their environments.[5] The result is that the Pauline language of "freedom" and "the end of the Law" must be seen in this same context.[6]

Second, we should not assume that the claim of "freedom" as a moral ideal was uniquely Pauline or necessarily antinomian. The Cynic, too, boasted of freedom, meaning not just the lack of social constraint, as in the infamies perpetrated by Diogenes the Dog. Rather, such exemplary tales were meant to embody the Cynic paradigm of moral purpose (προαίρεσις) unfettered by vice, desire, or compulsion.[7] One sees the paradox of inner freedom as a moral paradigm in Epictetus's description of the ideal Cynic:

> What sort of things do you imagine the good to be? Serenity, happiness, freedom from restraint. . . . Here then you see that there is something within you which is naturally free. But to desire, or to avoid, or to choose, or to refuse, or to prepare, or to set something before yourself—what man among you can do these things without first conceiving an impression of what is profitable, or what is not fitting? No one. You have, therefore, here, too, something unhindered and free. Poor wretches, develop this, pay attention to this, seek here your good. (*Diss.* 3.22.38–44; trans. Oldfather in LCL)[8]

The Stoics spoke of self-sufficiency (αὐτάρκεια) and indifference (ἀδιά-

3. Cf. E. P. Sanders, *Paul and Palestinian Judaism* (Philadelphia: Fortress, 1977) 9–27; Sanders, *Paul, the Law, and the Jewish People* (Philadelphia: Fortress, 1983) 143–69; and Shaye J. D. Cohen, *From the Maccabees to the Mishnah* (Philadelphia: Westminster, 1987) 215–25.

4. See the suggestive overview of Wayne Meeks, *The Moral World of the First Christians* (Philadelphia: Westminster, 1986) 68–96.

5. L. Michael White, "The Delos Synagogue Revisited: Recent Fieldwork in the Graeco-Roman Diaspora," *HTR* 80 (1987) 133–60; White, *Building God's House in the Roman World: Architectural Adaptation among Pagans, Jews, and Christians* (Baltimore: Johns Hopkins University Press, 1990) chap. 4; A. T. Kraabel, "The Social Systems of Six Diaspora Synagogues," *Ancient Synagogues: The State of Research* (ed. J. Gutmann; BJS 8; Chico, CA: Scholars, 1981) 79–91; Kraabel, "The Roman Diaspora: Six Questionable Assumptions," *Essays in Honor of Yigael Yadin* (ed. G. Vermes and J. Neusner) *JSS* 33 (1982) 445–64; Kraabel, "The Impact of the Discovery of the Sardis Synagogue," *Sardis from Prehistoric to Modern Times* (ed. G. M. A. Hanfmann; Cambridge: Harvard University Press, 1983) 178–90.

6. Cf. Lloyd Gaston, *Paul and the Torah* (Vancouver: University of British Columbia Press, 1988).

7. Abraham J. Malherbe, "Hellenistic Moralists and the New Testament," *ANRW* 2.27.1 (forthcoming).

8. Cf. Epictetus *Diss.* 3.22.38–44 and 4.1.1 (trans. Oldfather in LCL). Both are quoted and discussed in Abraham J. Malherbe, *Moral Exhortation: A Greco-Roman Sourcebook* (Philadelphia: Westminster, 1986) 36, 158.

φορα), by which they meant the freedom that comes from following the natural will, or what some Stoics would even call God.[9] Thus, a philosopher such as Seneca or Musonius Rufus would say that one is truly free who cares nothing for pain, exile, death, or wealth and status, and that one is free when training in want and self-discipline, after the example of Diogenes, enables one to live in virtue. Such a person is living in the "image of God."[10] Epictetus can say, "There is no bad man who lives as he wills, and accordingly no bad man is free. And who wishes to live in grief, fear, envy, pity . . . ? No one at all. Thus, we find that no bad man is free" (*Diss.* 4.1.1–5). Here, *freedom* is still the watchword of virtue, despite a high degree of Stoic determinism. For the Stoics, like many of the Platonists,[11] human reason in accord with the precepts of divine nature stands at the pinnacle of a moral world view. From Plato's day there was posited a set of four cardinal virtues—usually prudence (φρόνησις), justice (δικαιοσύνη), courage (ἀνδρεῖα), and temperance (σωφροσύνη)—which served as the starting point for Hellenistic ethical instruction.[12] They stand above matters of practical ethical interpretation, yet they also serve as the core of a semantic complex that is loaded with the symbolic valuation of a moral world view. Hence, for a Plutarch, Epictetus, or Musonius, only to mention a loaded term such as *freedom* is to call to mind a whole complex of associated ideas as part of the moral paradigm.

HELLENISTIC VIRTUES AND MORAL PARADIGMS

A good example comes from the Roman Stoic Musonius, who was noted for his thoroughly practical ethical concerns and for denigrating abstract metaphysics despite his apparent willingness to offer theological justification for his

9. Meeks, *Moral World,* 47; cf. Cleanthes *Hymn to Zeus* with Epictetus *Diss.* 1.16 (on providence); cf. H. W. Attridge, "The Philosophical Critique of Religion under the Early Empire," *ANRW* (1979) 2.16.1, 45ff.

10. See Musonius Rufus frag. 17 (Lutz, 109):

> In general, of all creatures on earth man alone *resembles* [μίμημα] God and has the same virtues that He has, since we can imagine nothing even in the gods better than *prudence, justice, courage, and temperance.* Therefore, as God, through the possession of these virtues, is unconquered by pleasure or greed; is superior to desire, envy, and jealousy; is *high-minded, beneficent, and kindly* [μεγαλόφρων δὲ καὶ εὐεργετικὸς καὶ φιλάνθρωπος] (for such is our conception of God), so also man in the *image* [μίμημα] of Him, when living in accord with nature, should be thought of as *being like* [ὁμοίως ἔχειν] Him. [My emphasis.]

Cf. Epictetus *Diss.* 2.14.12, Cicero *Leg.* 1.8.25, Seneca *Ep.* 75, and Ps.-Diogenes *Ep.* 6 or Ps.-Crates *Ep.* 7 (which emphasizes the example of Diogenes). For the last two especially, see the collection of Abraham J. Malherbe, *The Cynic Epistles: A Study Edition* (Missoula, MT: Scholars, 1977) 59, also discussed in his *Moral Exhortation,* 159.

11. Cf. Plutarch *Mor.* 439B or 441D.

12. Thus, note the inclusion of these virtues in Musonius frag. 17 L. (quoted in note 10 above), where they are both attributes of God and virtues to be inculcated by humans in imitation of the divine.

moral philosophy.[13] For Musonius, all aspects of day-to-day living derive from personal inculcation of one or another of the cardinal virtues. Typically, when Musonius lists commonplace attributes of the "good woman" (frag. 3 Lutz), such as being a good overseer of the household, chaste, not a slave to desire, or not lavish in expense or dress, these all come under the heading of the virtue of self-control (σωφροσύνη). By the same token, the "good woman's" service to husband and children, working with her hands, and being a good example to others are listed under the virtue of courage (ἀνδρεῖα). Thus, Musonius can sum up: "These are the things that the teachings of philosophy transmit, and the person who has learned [μαθών] them and practices [ἀσκήσας] them would seem to me to have become a well-ordered and fitting character, whether man or woman" (frag. 3.22–25 L. 41). Such "essentialism" assumes that the virtues stem from a paradigm of natural order to which all humans should conform. Likewise, Musonius can apply the same pattern of argument from the cardinal virtues to practical ethics and behavior in claiming that both women and kings should study philosophy, just like the sage.[14] What we begin to see is that the call to virtue as the basis for ethics and freedom is really more a Greek than a Jewish way of shaping moral identity. To place the emphasis instead on virtues, even among observant Jews of the Diaspora, is to move into a different world view and a different arena of moral self-definition.

An example of such a synthesis of moral world view can be seen in the work of Philo, the Jewish philosopher from Alexandria. Philo was an astute interpreter of scripture and a devout proponent of keeping the Decalogue as the defining mark of Jewish identity. Yet these traditionally Jewish values come wrapped in a new cloth. The story of Abraham is, for Philo, the model of "a virtue-loving soul" (*Abr.* 68); the wanderings of Abraham, who is called the "friend of God," represents the migration of the soul through virtue to happiness and freedom (*Migr. Abr.*).[15] The Law given by Moses was the source for Plato's philosophy, so that truth, even from a Gentile philosopher, still comes from God. After all, Philo can appeal to "nature's right *reason*, the sole source and fountain of virtues" (*Vit. Mos.* 1.48; trans. Colson in LCL).

Of course, we recognize the typically Hellenistic structure of Philo's Middle Platonism, yet one further element should be noted. The term *reason* is the Greek λόγος, which holds a position similar to that of σοφία (wisdom) in Sirach. For Philo, the Logos was that man created "in the Image of God" (Gen 1:26) who existed in the world of Forms as the beginning of the created

13. See Cora E. Lutz, *Musonius Rufus: The Roman Socrates* (Yale Classical Studies 10; New Haven: Yale University Press, 1947), for an introduction to the life and works of Musonius, as well as the standard English translation of his surviving works.

14. Musonius frag. 3, 4, 8, 14 L.

15. For more on Philo's background and philosophic roots, see E. R. Goodenough, *An Introduction to Philo Judaeus* (2d ed.; Oxford: Blackwell, 1962), esp. 112–18; cf. Meeks, *Moral World*, 81–85. Meeks's assertion (based on *Migr. Abr.* 89–93) that one is ill advised simply to read Philo as an acculturated Greek apologist, and not also as an observant Jew, is well taken as a point of intersection between the two moral worlds.

order (*Op. Mund.* 19–26; *Leg. All.* 1.31). This divine Logos, then, is the form or source for the moral structure of the cosmos, since the physical creation was necessarily inferior due to its corruptible nature. The physical world was "without order or soul . . .; it was full of inconsistency, ill-adjustment, and disharmony," yet God gave it the possibility of undergoing a "change to the best, the very contrary of these [its innate state] to order, quality, life, correspondence, identity, likeness, perfect adjustment, and harmony, to all that is characteristic of the more excellent model [that is, the Logos]" (*Op. Mund.* 22). In Philo, then, Hellenistic virtue and vice lists define a world order modeled on that of Plato, yet projected through Creation in Genesis. Philo was at home in two worlds, yet the paradigm by which he came to define his moral world was finally a Hellenistic synthesis. This is part of the dilemma of transition between moral worlds, where cardinal virtues, laden with symbolic cultural value as well as ethical imperatives, become the signposts for synthesis.[16]

PHILIPPIANS: A TEST CASE FOR
PAULINE MORAL PARADIGMS

As we turn our attention to Paul, we may begin to see that he would have been very much at home in Philo's world—much more so than, say, in the highly stigmatized worldview of apocalyptic dualism at Qumran.[17] We have come to recognize the importance of Paul's social environment in his dependence upon Hellenistic moral conventions, especially through Abraham J. Malherbe's work on the moralist literature and the Cynic tradition, and most recently his work in applying these perspectives to understanding 1 Thessalonians.[18] Such studies continue to show how Paul adapted his Jewish heritage to Hellenistic culture, especially in his use of commonplaces and conventions of theology and rhetoric. Although most of the Pauline corpus has been examined from this perspective, less has been done on the Philippian letter. It is to it that I wish to turn as a test case of Paul's moral world view.

I choose Philippians in part because it seems to have so little that is Jewish in its content, its tone, or its ethical exhortation. There is no midrashic play on

16. Chasing this elusive rabbit through the biblical briar patch reflects what is called a "cultural linguistic approach" to religion and socialization. Cf. Meeks, *Moral World*, 12–17.
17. It is precisely because such overtly Jewish sectarian language, such as that found in 2 Cor 6:14–7:1, sounds so un-Pauline that its authenticity is subject to debate. Whether or not such a preformed apocalyptic unit may have been used by Paul as an integral part of the letter, one must conclude that Paul's own move (as in 1 Cor 5:9–11) was to shift away from the sectarian boundary definition that such language had originally represented. So see my suggestions in White, "Shifting Sectarian Boundaries," 20.
18. Thus, see the bibliography of Malherbe's works listed separately in this volume. Especially on 1 Thessalonians, see his *Paul and the Thessalonians: The Philosophic Tradition of Pastoral Care* (Philadelphia: Fortress, 1987), which was first presented as the Haskell Lectures at Oberlin College for 1985. This chapter is offered as a small return in kind for laborers in the same vineyard.

the OT, as there is in Romans 4, Galatians 3 and 4, or even 1 Corinthians 10, nor is there an overtly Jewish social idiom presupposed, as in the claim to apocalyptic "visions" of 2 Corinthians or the eschatological section of 1 Thessalonians. Even the section in Phil 3:2–11 (where Paul rattles off his Jewish pedigree) gives the impression of being decidedly negative toward the tradition. It may be significant, then, that Philippi, like nearby Thessalonica, represents Paul's first work on the Greek mainland (in Macedonia) and was likely made up predominantly of Gentile converts.[19]

Philippians, like 1 Thessalonians, is primarily a friendly hortatory letter and holds to conventions seen in the epistolary theorists.[20] The Eucharisto (thanksgiving) section (Phil 1:6–11) incorporates a similar sense of compassion and expectation as the philosophic missionary of 1 Thess 2:3–8. Parenetic forms of appeal intrude even on the body of the letter (in Phil 2:1, 12) before being resumed formally in the Parakalo (exhortation) section (in 4:2).[21] As we shall come to see, much of the language of the letter comes from several interrelated semantic complexes commonly found in the moralist tradition. Most notably we shall observe an emphasis on terms associated with the virtue of friendship (φιλία).[22] If we look carefully at the ethics endorsed in this

19. As Malherbe has aptly demonstrated for Thessalonica; cf. *Paul and the Thessalonians*, 46ff. This view of Paul's missionary strategy is shared by Sanders, *Paul, the Law, and the Jewish People*, 179–89.

20. Malherbe, *Paul and the Thessalonians*, 68–72. See also Malherbe, "'Gentle as a Nurse': The Cynic Background to 1 Thess. ii," *NT* 12 (1970) 203–17; Malherbe, *Ancient Epistolary Theorists* (Atlanta: Scholars, 1988) 21, 31–41; and S. K. Stowers, *Letter Writing in Greco-Roman Antiquity* (Philadelphia: Westminster, 1986) 58ff., 94–105.

21. We shall not take space here to discuss matters relating to the date and composition of the letter, both of which are complex and much-debated issues in Philippian studies. It is hoped, rather, that these observations on the tone and world view of the letter may shed light on its historical setting. It is worth noting here, however, that I am generally assuming for the sake of discussion that the Philippian correspondence comes from the so-called Ephesian imprisonment. In terms of both date and tone, Philippians seems closest to the social setting and language of the Philemon letter. Through what follows I will also be suggesting that the letter seems to be a single, integral composition, at least for the sections contained in 1:1–2:30 and 4:2–23. It seems to me that the section from 3:1–4:1 is more problematic and may have the best claim for derivation from a separate letter. Nonetheless, I do not find the threefold partitioning of the letter assumed by many scholars (going back to B. D. Rahtjen) to be persuasive. Cf. H. Koester, "The Purpose of the Polemic of a Pauline Fragment (Phil. iii)," *NTS* 8 (1961–62) 317–32; Koester, "Philippians," *IDBSup*, 665ff.; B. D. Rahtjen, "The Three Letters of Paul to the Philippians," *NTS* 6 (1959–60) 167ff.; and G. Bornkamm, "Der Philipperbrief als paulinische Briefsammlung," *Neotestamentica et Patristica, Freundesgabe O. Cullmann* (NovTSup 6; Leiden: Brill, 1962) 192ff. In favor of literary integrity see Victor Paul Furnish, "The Place and Purpose of Philippians iii," *NTS* 10 (1964) 88; Robert Jewett, "The Epistolary Thanksgiving and the Integrity of Philippians," *NT* 12 (1970) 53; and Duane F. Watson, "A Rhetorical Analysis of Philippians and Its Implications for the Unity Question," *NT* 30 (1988) 57–88. A good summary of the questions relating to Paul's opponents is given by Joseph Tyson, "Paul's Opponents at Philippi," *Perspectives in Religious Studies* 3 (1976) 82–95.

22. The use of topoi associated with "friendship" will be discussed in greater detail in "The Christ-Hymn and Its Moral Context." Here I would note that the consistency with which the semantic complex of "friendship" (and its related fields) appears through the various sections of the letter is one of the chief arguments in favor of its literary integrity. Cf. D. Garland, "The Composition and Unity of Philippians: Some Neglected Literary Factors," *NT* 27 (1985) 141–73;

parenetic exhortation, we find them to follow the pattern of Hellenistic virtue
and vice lists: "Finally, brethren, whatever is honorable, whatever is just,
whatever is pure, whatever is lovely [προσφιλῆ], whatever is gracious
[εὔφημα], if there is any virtue [ἀρετή], and if there is anything worthy of
praise [ἔπαινος], think on these things" (Phil 4:8–9). There is nothing
uniquely Christian or Jewish in this list; it espouses the highest ideals of Hellenistic virtue.[23] Thus, what makes it applicable in Paul's thoroughly Christian
ethic? The answer lies in the way that commonplaces from the Hellenistic
moralist tradition are infused with a grounding in Christ Jesus.[24] The passage
in Phil 2:1–4 makes the linkage clearer: "If there is any *exhortation* [παράκλη-
σις] {in Christ}, any *consolation* [παραμύθιον] {of love}, any *partnership*
[κοινωνία], *compassion* [σπλάγχνα], and *sympathy* [οἰκτιρμοί] {of spirit},
complete my joy by *having the same mind* [τὸ αὐτὸ φρονῆτε]."[25] Thus, as the
passage continues, the common vices and virtues that follow this exhortation
("Do nothing from selfishness or conceit, but in humility count others better
than yourself"; Phil 2:3) are also derived from Hellenistic terms of moral
exhortation, yet rooted in Christ and Spirit. A clue to the implicit structure of
Paul's synthesis to form this moral world can be seen in the linkage between
this extended ethical exhortation (2:1–4) and the Christ-hymn that follows in
2:6–11.

THE CHRIST-HYMN AND
ITS MORAL CONTEXT

The hymn of Phil 2:6–11 is generally accepted (since Ernst Lohmeyer) to
be a pre-Pauline liturgical unit.[26] Thus, it forms a confessional foundation that

---

and P. T. O'Brien, "The Fellowship Themes in Philippians," *Reformed Theological Review* 37
(1978) 9–18.
    23. Notice also the hortatory tone of the imperative to "think on these things" (ταῦτα λογίζεσθε)
in comparison with that of Epictetus *Diss.* 3.22.44 (quoted above). The thoroughly Hellenistic
character of this list, evidenced by the use of two hapax legomena (προσφιλής and εὔφημος) and
by the absence of the latter from the Septuagint, was first observed by Martin Dibelius, *An Die
Thessalonicher I, II, An Die Philipper* (HNT 11; 3d ed.; Tübingen: J. C. B. Mohr [Paul Siebeck],
1937) 95, and followed by S. Wibbing, *Die Tugend- und Lasterkataloge im Neuen Testament*
(BZNW 25; Berlin: Töpelmann, 1959) 101ff.; cf. Victor Paul Furnish, *Theology and Ethics in Paul*
(Nashville: Abingdon, 1968) 46, 88. Also on the catalogs of virtues and vices as a topos or commonplace of the moralist tradition, see Malherbe, *Moral Exhortation,* 138–40. The full incorpora-
tion of the topos of lists of virtues and vices into the moral template can be seen in the
personification of vices and virtues, usually as women, following the Prodicus myth (cf. Xenophon
Mem. 2.1.21–34). It is seen in Dio Chrys. *Or.* 4.83–96 and 113–14, which may depend upon the
more elaborately drawn allegory of *The Tabula of Cebes* (see J. T. Fitzgerald and L. M. White, *The
Tabula of Cebes: Text and Translation with Introduction and Notes* (Chico, CA: Scholars, 1983)
14–16.
    24. Furnish, *Theology and Ethics,* 89–91.
    25. The rendering is my own in order to emphasize the structure of the passage. It relies on
parallel clauses made up of commonplace terms from the parenetic tradition (italicized) set off by
prepositional phrases (set in braces) to add the Christian flavor.
    26. Lohmeyer's observation, first presented in *Kyrios Jesus* (Heidelberg: C. Winter, 1928), is

is assumed to go back to the roots of the Jewish-Christian movement. The nature and the wording of the Jewish *Vorlage* (source) have been the subject of considerable conjecture.[27] In its present form, however, the unit has been redacted by Paul into the parenetic function of the larger section 2:1–18, and this adaptation bears directly on the form and content of the hymn.[28] Ernst Käsemann (and others) are correct in suggesting that there remains little that is exclusively Jewish in the hymn, at least in its present form.[29] Even if one were to posit analogues from the acculturated Jewish Diaspora, as has been suggested,[30] one would tend to expect different terminology. Most notably, in v. 6 one would have expected εἰκὼν τοῦ θεοῦ (image of God) instead of μορφή (form), on the analogy of usage both in Philo and in the supposed hymnic fragment in Col 1:15.[31] Ralph Martin is surely correct when he concludes that in the hymn, Paul "stands at the juncture of two cultures."[32] We may begin with this observation, then, to look to the paradigms of synthesis as a way of interpreting the hymn's present moralizing context.

The crux that links the hymn to the parenesis (of Phil 2:1–4) is v. 5: Τοῦτο φρονεῖτε ἐν ὑμῖν ὃ καὶ ἐν Χριστῷ Ἰησοῦ (RSV: "Have this mind among your-selves, which is yours in Christ Jesus"). Although it is somewhat awkward, we see that the phrase must end with a reference to Jesus in order to set up the transitional relative construction, which regularly introduces such preformed hymnic materials. The pivot, then, is the first phrase, Τοῦτο φρονεῖτε (have this mind), which points back directly to the seemingly redundant exhortations in v. 2: τὸ αὐτὸ φρονῆτε (have the same mind) and τὸ ἓν φρονοῦντες (have one mind). One longstanding difficulty in interpreting the content of the

---

reprinted in *Kyrios Jesus, Eine Untersuchungen zu Phil 2, 5–11* (2d ed.; Heidelberg: C. Winter, 1961) 7. See also Dieter Georgi, "Der vorpaulinische Hymnus Phil 2.6–11," *Zeit und Geschichte, Dankesgabe an Rudolf Bultmann*, ed. J. M. Robinson (Tübingen: J. C. B. Mohr [Paul Siebeck], 1964) 263–66; Günther Bornkamm, "On Understanding the Christ-Hymn: Philippians 2.6–11," *Early Christian Experience*, trans. by P. L. Hammer (New York: Harper & Row, 1969) 112–22; and Ralph P. Martin, *Carmen Christi: Philippians ii.5–11 in Recent Interpretation and in the Setting of Early Christian Worship* (Cambridge: Cambridge University Press, 1967) 36–39.

27. Cf. Martin, *Carmen Christi*, 184ff. Most recently, see J. Fitzmyer, "The Aramaic Background of Philippians 2.6–11," *CBQ* 50 (1988) 470–83.

28. So Ralph P. Martin, *Philippians* (NCB Commentary; rev. ed.; Grand Rapids, MI: Eerdmans, 1985) 109, following Georg Strecker, "Redaktion und Tradition im Christus-Hymnus," *ZNW* 55 (1964) 63–78 (and contra M. D. Hooker, *Jesus and the Servant: The Influence of the Servant Concept of Deutero-Isaiah in the New Testament* [London: SPCK, 1959], 121). For the lines of the redaction, see esp. F. W. Beare, *Epistle to the Philippians* (HNTC; New York: Harper & Row, 1959) 77; and Martin, *Carmen Christi*, 36ff., 198.

29. Ernst Käsemann, "Kritische Analyse von Phil 2.5–11," *ZTK* 47 (1950) 313–60; cf. Beare, *Epistle to the Philippians*, 77; and Martin, *Philippians*, 113.

30. Cf. J. T. Sanders, *The New Testament Christological Hymns* (Cambridge: Cambridge University Press, 1971) 66–69; and Georgi, "Vorpaulinische Hymnus," 292–93. The strongest arguments seem to be in favor of an original Jewish core built around the "suffering servant" imagery of Isaiah 53, but which Martin (*Carmen Christi*, 304, 318–19) thinks had already been adapted to a Jewish-Christian mission in the Diaspora before this Pauline redaction.

31. Modifying the argument of J. Jervell, *Imago Dei* (Göttingen: Vandenhoeck & Ruprecht, 1960) 206–9; cf. Martin, *Carmen Christi*, 81.

32. Martin, *Carmen Christi*, 297.

hymn comes in the middle of v. 5, the eliptical connecting phrase ἐν ὑμῖν ὃ καὶ ἐν. Older interpretations of the hymn tended to see its function primarily as a moral example, an *imitatio Christi*, pointing to self-humiliation and asceticism as the ideal moral life for the Christian.[33] Following this view, it has been typical to supply the missing verb in the ellipsis of v. 5 with some form of *to be*: "Have this mind in yourself which *was* also in Christ Jesus."[34] A difficulty with this reading is that Paul, after the fashion of Hellenistic moral philosophers, typically calls on the Philippians to "imitate" himself, not Christ (3:17).[35]

Following Käsemann,[36] this interpretation has generally been replaced in more recent scholarship by what is called a soteriological interpretation. Thus, the hymn is seen as a statement of the mechanism of salvation, not an exemplar to be followed. In this view, the emphasis has tended to shift toward the content of the hymn, focusing on the notion of the μορφὴ θεοῦ (form of God) and ἐκένωσεν (emptied [Phil 2:7]) as core features of the earliest kenotic incarnational Christology.[37] In this vein, Phil 2:5 is read as an ecclesiological or soteriological disposition: "Let this disposition be in you as is proper for those who are in Christ Jesus."[38] The soteriological drama described in the hymn is seen to effect a transformation in the disposition, the moral outlook, of the Christian. In support of this reading is the technical sense given to the phrase ἐν Χριστῷ (in Christ) consistently in Paul and seen in the parallel structure of 2:1 and 2:5.[39]

Interpretations following the kenotic theory (like older incarnational interpretations) have often gone too far, by trying to read into the Philippian hymn a fully developed Christian doctrine of the incarnation. That may not be Paul's intent at all.[40] Instead, I would agree to some extent with Georg Strecker that the either/or debate between the *imitatio Christi* versus the

33. Martin, *Carmen Christi*, 84.
34. As found in the traditional rendering of the KJV and NIV; cf. W. P. de Boer, *The Imitation of Paul: An Exegetical Study* (Kampen: Kok, 1962) 60.
35. As Malherbe has shown on the basis of the moralist tradition; cf. his *Paul and the Thessalonians*, 52–54. Cf. also Benjamin Fiore, *The Function of Personal Example in the Socratic and Pastoral Epistles* (AnBib 105; Rome: Pontifical Biblical Institute, 1986).
36. Käsemann, "Kritische Analyse," 313–35.
37. The soteriological interpretations improved on the older incarnational theologies read into the hymn, as in J. B. Lightfoot, *St. Paul's Epistle to the Philippians* (12th ed.; London, 1888; repr. Grand Rapids, MI: Zondervan, 1953) 110–11, 127–28. Cf. Beare, *Philippians*, 76, 159–74 (an appendix "Kenotic Christology" by E. R. Fairweather); Martin, *Philippians*, 96–97; Martin, *Carmen Christi*, 84–95.
38. So the rendering of the RSV; cf. Martin, *Philippians*, 91f.
39. Käsemann, "Kritische Analyse," 335; Martin, *Carmen Christi*, 85–86.
40. From the perspective of an assumed Jewish *Vorlage* based on the "suffering servant," it would not be necessary to assume an incarnational theology as the theological ground. Although few have been willing to relinquish the notion of preexistence as an element of the hymn, I am no longer so sure. Cf. C. H. Talbert, "Pre-existence in Philippians 2.6–11," *JBL* 86 (1967) 141–53; and Georgi, "Vorpaulinische Hymnus," 278. We may take special note of Strecker's reservations (in "Redaktion und Tradition," 68–69), since the notion of preexistence (and hence incarnation) seemed not to fit any of the parenetic functions of the passage.

soteriological readings is unnecessary; both elements may be represented in the hymn, but neither is primary to the parenetic function.[41] The main problem lies still in the opening parenetic phrase of Phil 2:5: τοῦτο φρονεῖτε (have this mind). In both of the traditional interpretations, φρονεῖν is taken literally as a disposition of mind. Instead, the phrase τὸ αὐτὸ φρονεῖν (and its several variations in Philippians) should be read as referring to social relations and, hence, to ethical behavior in Christ, as suggested in the variation of C. F. D. Moule: "Adopt toward one another in your mutual relations, the same attitude which was found in Christ Jesus."[42]

It is just here, then, that we must turn our attention to the paradigms of social ethics that are reflected both in the content of the hymn and in the moral appeal of the letter. Paul Sampley, following this line in Moule, has shown the technical use and social dimensions of several characteristic Pauline terms and phrases.[43] They include especially κοινωνία (and its cognates) and the phrase τὸ αὐτὸ φρονεῖν. Both give the sense of "partnership" in a social sense and are regularly found in the legal-contractual vocabulary of consensual agreements (which Sampley calls by the Latin societas). Good examples of this social sense are to be found in Paul in Philemon 17 (in the framework of hospitality conventions) and in Phil 4:15 (which further uses commercial/monetary language of the relationship).[44] Sampley argues, therefore, that Paul saw his relationship with the Philippian congregation as one of contractual reciprocity grounded in their common goal of spreading the gospel and in their common experience of salvation in Christ.[45]

Sampley's view of the social context of such language is basically correct. Its significance is to be seen in the way conventionalized terms reflect patterns of communal expectations and obligations. It carries inherently ethical implications; however, I think more nuance is called for in two regards, by broadening the semantic field and by showing its various applications throughout the Philippian letter. First, Sampley has drawn his semantic field too narrowly by limiting it to the quasi-legal setting of contractual societas. The technical vocabulary (including κοινωνία, τὸ αὐτὸ φρονεῖν, and others, such as ἀγάπη) actually reflects a broader semantic field. In fact, these same terms can be used in slightly different combinations in several semantic complexes, each of which has a distinct set of social relations and conventions. They include the important social function of hospitality (φιλοξενία) and the

41. Strecker, "Redaktion und Tradition," 63–78.
42. C. F. D. Moule, "Further Reflections on Phil. 2.5–11," Apostolic History and the Gospel: Biblical and Historical Essays Presented to F. F. Bruce (ed. W. W. Gasque and R. P. Martin; Grand Rapids, MI: Eerdmans, 1970) 265. In this sense it seems that the NEB rendering is on the right track: "Let your bearing toward one another arise out of your life in Christ Jesus."
43. Paul Sampley, Pauline Partnership in Christ: Christian Community and Commitment in the Light of Roman Law (Philadelphia: Fortress, 1980) 51–72.
44. These similarities in language further suggest a proximity in setting for the composition of Philippians and Philemon. See note 59 below.
45. Sampley, Pauline Partnership, 67–68.

closely related conventions of recommendation letter writing (συστατικὴ ἐπιστολή) and patronage/benefaction (εὐεργεσία). These areas are widely represented in the social organization of Paul's communities.[46] But as Malherbe has recently reminded us, in the exhortation in 1 Thessalonians, we should recognize that the legal/contractual complex, the hospitality/recommendation complex, and even the patronage/benefaction complex have a common social grounding in the technical language of friendship (φιλία).[47] It is this underlying social convention that serves as the key moral paradigm for understanding both the hymn and its context in the Philippian letter.

From the classical Greek period, friendship had become an ideal of social relationships that could be applied in a number of different arenas of social action. Whereas it had originally defined a relation between equals, it could also be applied (since Aristotle's time) to relations between unequals, such as in benefactions. By the Roman period, the notion was taken over into the Latin *amicitia*. However, the conceptual field was broadened substantially, so Roman social forms of political and economic patronage (*patrocinium*) could be expressed in terms of the technical language of friendship.[48] Thus, the semantic fields for the social conventions of patronage, hospitality, and letters of recommendation, as well as consensual contracts and commercial exchange, had begun to intersect and converge in practical application. One often finds, then, that the code word for the moral paradigm is the overarching category of friendship.[49]

From the Hellenistic moralist tradition, the ideal of friendship included "having all things in common" (κοινωνία) and "having one mind" (ἐπὶ τὸν αὐτὸν ὄντες, μία ψυχή).[50] This ideal is most directly expressed ethically by Aristotle, Plutarch, and others in terms of the "mutual love" (using both φίλος and ἀγάπη) and "kindly affection" (φιλοφρόνησις) that friends hold for one another.[51] In common usage, letters (which represented the absent "friend"),

46. Cf. Abraham J. Malherbe, *Social Aspects of Early Christianity* (2d ed.; Philadelphia: Fortress, 1983) 61ff.; and F. W. Danker, *Benefactor: Epigraphic Study of a New Testament and Greco-Roman Semantic Field* (St. Louis: Clarion, 1982).

47. Malherbe, *Paul and the Thessalonians*, 69–72.

48. Cf. Erich Gruen, *The Hellenistic World and the Coming of Rome* (2 vols.; Berkeley: University of California Press, 1985) 1. 9, 58–59; R. P. Saller, *Personal Patronage under the Early Empire* (Cambridge: Cambridge University Press, 1982) 1–40; M. Gelzer, *The Roman Nobility* (Oxford: Blackwell, 1975) 62–122; and G. Herman, *Ritualized Friendship and the Greek City* (Cambridge: Cambridge University Press, 1987) 1–35.

49. For an excellent analysis of the Corinthian correspondence from this perspective, see Peter Marshall, *Enmity at Corinth: Social Conventions in Paul's Relations with the Corinthians* (WUNT; Tübingen: J. C. B. Mohr [Paul Siebeck], 1987) 91–164. Marshall also provides a useful comparative analysis of the friendship language as applied to the financial relations of Paul with the Philippians from Phil 4:8–10 (cf. 157–64). Cf. L. L. Welborn, "On the Discord in Corinth: 1 Corinthians 1–4 and Ancient Politics," *JBL* 106 (1987) 85–111, who also recognizes the implications of the patronage/benefaction language in issues of social and economic inequality.

50. Aristotle *Eth. Nic.* 8.1167b; Plutarch, "How to Tell a Flatterer from a Friend" (*Mor.* 65A,B). Cf. Phil 1:27.

51. Aristotle *Eth. Nic.* 8.1155; Plutarch, "Flatterer" (*Mor.* 51B); Lucian *Toxaris* 62.

"joy," and "mutual exhortation" were by-products of such friendly relations.[52] Also, Plutarch says παρρησία ("frankness, boldness" of speech) is "the voice of φιλία."[53] Finally, Aristotle (*Eth. Nic.* 8.1156) makes friendship a virtue or, to be precise, the most essential social reflection of the cardinal virtue of justice, and he derives beneficence from it as friendship between unequals (*Eth. Eud.* 7.1238b). Friendship, then, in the Hellenistic conceptual world, was far more than a simple relationship and had profound social and ethical implications. Thus, the ethical implications for Paul's extensive appropriation of this language throughout Philippians points to the framework of a paradigm of virtue.

Second, having thus broadened the social purview of this technical vocabulary, one may gain more insight into its application as a theological paradigm throughout the argument of Philippians. Sampley's legal and contractual interpretation of τὸ αὐτὸ φρονεῖν is most appropriate to the commercial language found in Phil 4:10–20 (cf. 1:5–6), but this contractual sense (especially in Phil 2:5) has little to connect the social implications of the partnership language directly to the moral structure of the soteriological drama in the hymn. Here is where I think the larger category of friendship both as a social convention and as an ideal of virtue may help, remembering that the contractual vocabulary derives from these social conventions as well. We must return to the hymn for a moment and notice that Eduard Schweizer has suggested that μορφή should be understood as a condition or "status," as opposed to either "existence" (οὐσία) or "outward appearance" (σχῆμα).[54] The essential play of the hymn's soteriological drama entails Christ's eschewing his "status" of equality with God in order to lower himself to the status of "slave." The result of his "humiliation" and "subjection" (v. 8), then, is God's "exaltation" and "elevation" (v. 9).

Whatever might have been the original Jewish moorings of the Christ-hymn or its original christological affirmations, in its present form in Philippians it has been adapted to a new moral paradigm. The model of selflessness, the willingness to give up one's own status and share another's troubles, is the ultimate sign of true friendship. As Aristotle says, "To a noble man there applies the true saying that he does all for the sake of his friends . . . if need

52. Aristotle *Eth. Nic.* 8.1156. Compare Phil 1:9, 2:1–2, 4:1–4, 10.
53. Plutarch, "How to Tell a Flatterer from a Friend" (*Mor.* 51B). Compare Phil 1:20; Philemon 8; 2 Cor 3:12, 7:4. On παρρησία as an attribute of philosophic moral instruction and parenesis, cf. Malherbe, *Moral Exhortation*, 48–53; Malherbe, *Paul and the Thessalonians*, 23.
54. Eduard Schweizer, *Erniedrigung und Erhoehung bei Jesus und seinen Nachfolgern* (Zurich: Zwingli, 1956), ET: *Lordship and Discipleship* (London: SCM, 1960) 61–64; cf. "Μορφή," *TDNT* 6. 394–449. Schweizer further asserts that it is not necessary to read "Jesus *became* a 'man'" (p. 63, emphasis mine). His assertion comes close to the understanding of human nature among the Stoics, in which one is already an imperfect likeness of God seeking moral perfection. Cf. Musonius Rufus Frag. 17 (quoted above in note 10). See also the discussion of Epictetus's notion of human nature as "sons of God" in E. Hatch, *The Influence of Greek Ideas on Christianity* (New York: Harper & Row, 1957) 155–58.

be, even to the point of death" (*Eth. Nic.* 9.1169a; trans. Rackham in LCL; cf. *Eth. Eud.* 7.1245b).

Something of the moral paradigm behind this notion of friendship may be seen in Lucian's *Toxaris*, just one example from among the many Hellenistic treatises on the topic. The treatise purports to be a contest between two men over who can tell the best stories to epitomize the Greek ideal of friendship. One of the anecdotes (chap. 29–34) recounts the relationship between a certain young noble, named Demetrius, and his slave Antiphilus.[55] In the course of events, Antiphilus was wrongfully accused of a crime and imprisoned. The loyal Demetrius constantly comforted his slave in the horrible jail. But when the guards would no longer allow Demetrius to visit freely, he got himself arrested on a trumped-up charge. To be with Antiphilus, he would even throw away his wealth, status, and freedom for imprisonment, disgrace, and want. In prison, Demetrius served Antiphilus and ministered to his needs through illness and distress until such time as the wrong was righted. In other words, Demetrius demonstrated his friendship by exchanging roles with his slave, and the treatise is full of standard friendship topoi and language.[56] We may suggest, then, that in the present form of the Philippian hymn, Christ's "emptying" and "humbling" himself to take the "form of a slave" is being portrayed, at least in part, as an all-surpassing act of selfless love—that is, the supreme virtue of friendship.[57]

If this is a correct reading of the moral paradigm at work in the Philippian hymn, notice how it links the parenesis of Phil 2:1–4. It picks up on cognates of ταπεινοῦν (to humble [vv. 3, 8]) and three variations on φρόνησις (vv. 2, 5). The sense of "reckoning" status similarly is repeated in vv. 3, 6. I would render the ellipsis of v. 5 by repeating the phrase τουτὸ φρονεῖτε as follows: "*Have this mind* with one another as you also *have this mind* with Christ Jesus." Thus, Paul has grounded the fundamental ethical imperative of the Christian's social relationships within the community in the Greek ideal of virtue (friendship) exemplified in Christ's own actions. Christ, then, becomes the cosmic repository of virtue (much like Philo's Logos) and, thus, a divine source for Paul's exhortations to live in accord with the highest ideals of Greek culture.

---

55. The slave's name is, of course, a word play on the φιλία topos. It means "in the place of a friend" and proves ironic in the twist of the tale.

56. The story also includes a potentially disastrous prison escape (much like the case of the Philippian jailer in Acts 17) wherein Demetrius and Antiphilus, out of loyalty, refuse to flee. Their high morals, then, are a key to their eventual release and the ultimate restoration of their status. Thereafter Antiphilus was manumitted by Demetrius and lived comfortably as a freedman.

57. Compare also 2 Cor 8:9, which in rich/poor language follows the same status-loss and elevation pattern to describe the soteriological drama of Christ and its bearing on the Christian. This may also be closely related to the common motif (found both in inscriptions and in literature) of the endangered benefactor—that is, one whose gift is reckoned as more spectacular and worthy of praise because it placed the benefactor at risk. Cf. Danker, *Benefactor*, 413–14.

This helps us to put the hortatory and ethical tone of the Philippian letter into perspective. The virtue of selfless, loving friendship is recognizable in the technical language of the semantic complex, especially in the terms κοινωνία, χαίρειν, and τὸ αὐτὸ φρονεῖν. The virtue is also seen in the specific ethical behaviors enjoined through parenesis, such as humility (ταπεινοφροσύνη [Phil 2:3; cf. 3:21]). We should notice the structure of this cardinal virtue. The same humility that is exemplified in Christ's "emptying" himself to take "the form of a slave" (2:8) is also the proper disposition to be maintained in all Christian relationships (2:3; cf. 3:10, 21) and especially in the situation of Euodia and Syntyche (4:2). Paul also claims to have exemplified this virtue to the Philippians, as he calls himself δοῦλος Χριστοῦ (a slave of Christ [1:1]), and he cites his own experience of "humiliation and want" (4:12) in his service to them. From this distress he says that he "learned self-sufficiency" (ἔμαθον αὐτάρκης [4:11]), and in turn, the Philippians should imitate him. The characteristic terms and affections of friendship appear throughout the Philippian letter, despite the fact that φιλία (friendship) itself is absent.[58]

Paul takes the ideal of a Greek virtue and applies it directly to the social life of the Philippian community and to his dealings with them. We notice the appeal to reciprocal affections (Phil 1:7; 4:10) between Paul and the community. Also, his financial dealings with them (reflected in the extensive use of commercial language in 1:6 and 4:10–20) further show contacts to the letter of recommendation for the returning Epaphroditus (2:25–30). Given the tone of 4:10–12, where Paul "disdains" his financial distress, we may begin to suspect that the bonds of their friendship had become strained either by Paul's or Epaphroditus's situation.[59] Reading the whole as a letter of reconcili-

---

58. Malherbe (*Paul and the Thessalonians*, 101–2) has suggested that Paul might have intentionally avoided using the key term φιλία precisely because it had become associated with Epicurean communities. Thus, the extensive use of the rest of the semantic complex becomes a circumlocution to avoid confusion. Κοινωνία and φρόνησις (with their cognates) occur a total of seventeen times in the letter. Concentrations of compounds using συν- (with; a total of twelve times) further convey the tone of social actualization of the moral paradigm within the framework of the community. Nor is it insignificant that the technical terms related to friendship (and its associated semantic conventions) tend to cluster at the critical points of the letter. Note especially (a) the thanksgiving (Phil 1:4–10), (b) the letter of receipt and thanks for their gift (4:10–20), and (c) the parenetic appeal of 2:1–5 (anchored by the hymn).

59. Here I would largely agree with Peter Marshall's suggestions regarding the use of money, the "partnership [ἐκοινώνησεν] of giving and receiving" in Phil 4:15, as a sign of friendship offered or withheld; cf. Marshall, *Enmity at Corinth*, 157–58. My own suspicion is that one or another of Paul's house church patrons (perhaps either Euodia or Syntyche) had decided no longer to support Paul, thus creating the sense of crisis and distress. In this way, Sampley's suggestions regarding the situation behind the stress on partnership language is also helpful. Yet it seems to me that Paul is calling on the Philippians to fulfill their obligations to him as "friends," which may mean a play on patron-client relations as well. In this sense, Paul may be suggesting the same kind of relationship to the Philippians as he does with Philemon. There, he claims an obligation (the requested hospitable reception for the runaway Onesimus) from Philemon as his spiritual client. But it is precisely the irony of the letter that Paul must resort to such social claims because he was indebted to Philemon as his missionary patron. It is noteworthy, then, that we find some of the same interrelated topoi of friendship, hospitality, and patronage as in Philemon 17: "if you hold me as a *partner* [κοινωνόν], receive him as you receive me." Cf. L. Michael White, "Social Authority in the House Church Setting and Eph. 4.1–16," *ResQ* 29 (1987) 214–21.

ation, then, the appeal to reestablish those bonds of friendship, through partnership in Christ, was a central concern. Thus, Paul adopted the style, as well as the ideal, of φιλία through friendly parenesis to the Philippians to live the virtuous life in Christ. By grounding the Greek virtue in the divine will, through the soteriological drama of Christ's humility and exaltation, Paul created a moral paradigm for understanding the world of the Philippians.

In the case of Philippians, Paul's presentation of his "distress" (Phil 1:12–26; 2:25–30; 4:10–20) serves to liken his sufferings on their behalf to those of Christ, as a kind of endangered benefactor. Thus, he is their spiritual patron, just as they are his economic patron. The reciprocal obligations of this relationship are the basis for their bond of friendship with one another, just as with Christ.

THOMAS H. OLBRICHT   14

AN ARISTOTELIAN RHETORICAL
ANALYSIS OF 1 THESSALONIANS

In the 1980s, scholars published numerous rhetorical analyses of biblical documents, especially the Pauline epistles. Early in the decade, the studies focused on Galatians, perhaps as the result of Hans Dieter Betz's landmark, rhetorically informed commentary.[1] More recently, 1 Thessalonians has received special attention through the work of Bruce C. Johanson and Robert Jewett.[2] The emphasis has been on arrangement or structure. Scholars have begun, however, to give more attention to proofs, for example, Yehoshua Gitay in his study of Second Isaiah and Johanson on 1 Thessalonians.[3] Wilhelm Wuellner has proposed, "Better than any other modern critical approach it [rhetorical criticism] brings to comprehension . . . what all exegetical methods want 'to explain'—the text's power."[4] One may not agree with Wuellner, but

---

1. Hans Dieter Betz, *Galatians: A Commentary on Paul's Letter to the Churches in Galatia* (Philadelphia: Fortress, 1979). Other materials include James D. Hester, "The Rhetorical Structure of Galatians 1:11–2:14," *JBL* 103 (1984) 223–33. See also Wilhelm Wuellner, "Where Is Rhetorical Criticism Taking Us?" *CBQ* 49 (1987) 448–63; J. Muilenburg, "Form Criticism and Beyond," *JBL* 88 (1969) 1–18; Bernard Hungerford Brinsmead, *Galatians—Dialogical Response to Opponents* (Chico, CA: Scholars, 1982); Steven J. Kraftchick, *Ethos and Pathos Appeals in Galatians Five and Six* (diss., Emory University, 1985); James D. Hester, "The Use and Influence of Rhetoric in Galatians 2:1–14," *TZ* 42 (1986) 386–408; H. Hübner, "Der Galaterbrief und das Verhältnis von Antiker Rhetorik und Epistolographie," *TLZ* 109 (1984) 241–50; and Robert M. Berchman, "Galatians (1:1–5): Paul and Greco-Roman Rhetoric," *New Perspectives on Ancient Judaism* (ed. Jacob Neusner and Ernest S. Frerichs; New York: University Press of America, 1987) 1–15.

2. Bruce C. Johanson, *To All the Brethren: A Text-Linguistic and Rhetorical Approach to 1 Thessalonians* (Stockholm: Almqvist & Wiksell, 1987); Robert Jewett, *The Thessalonian Correspondence: Pauline Rhetoric and Millenarian Piety* (Philadelphia: Fortress, 1986). Other studies not discussed below include Frank W. Hughes, *The Literary Rhetoric of II Thessalonians* (diss., Northwestern University, 1983); R. Lee and C. Lee, "An Analysis of the Larger Semantic Units of I Thessalonians," *Notes on Translations* 56 (1975) 28–42; Karl Thieme, "Die Struktur des ersten Thessalonischer-Briefes," *Abraham unser Vater* (ed. O. Betz, M. Hengel, and P. Schmidt; Leiden: Brill, 1963) 450–58; and Glenn S. Holland, *The Tradition That You Received from Us: 2 Thessalonians in the Pauline Tradition* (Tübingen: J. C. B. Mohr [Paul Siebeck], 1988).

3. Yehoshua Gitay, *Prophecy and Persuasion: A Study of Isaiah 40–48* (Bonn: Linguistica Biblica, 1981). Bruce Johanson, *To All the Brethren: A Text-Linguistic and Rhetorical Approach to 1 Thessalonians*.

4. Wilhelm Wuellner, "The Rhetorical Structure of I Thessalonians," 17, paper presented at the 1988 Colloquium Biblicum Lovaniense, which focused on 1 Thessalonians.

his declaration is an appropriate point of departure, since whether rhetorical criticism does in fact make a contribution depends upon how it helps us comprehend something about the text that we did not understand before.

RHETORICAL STUDIES ON 1 THESSALONIANS

Abraham J. Malherbe, admired former colleague as a Harvard student and Abilene Christian professor, mentor, and friend, has published at least four works that directly or indirectly have influenced the growing bibliography on rhetorical analyses of 1 Thessalonians.[5] Because of Malherbe's in-depth studies on the Thessalonian correspondence, his work will influence rhetorical criticism of these epistles for decades to come. We turn now to placing his research in the context of the rhetorical criticism of 1 Thessalonians.

Hendrikus Boers's 1976 article adumbrated the growing interest in rhetorical studies on 1 Thessalonians.[6] Under the rubric of "form criticism," Boers was interested in the structure according to consensus epistolary theory. He concluded that the letter followed the normal form: prescript, 1:1; thanksgiving, 1:2–10; apostolic apology, 2:1–12; apostolic parousia, 2:17–3:13; exhortation, 4:1–5:22; and conclusion, 5:23–28. Boers did not employ the term *rhetorical,* but ten years later Jewett labeled the same concerns *rhetoric analysis.*[7] Helmut Koester, in 1979, utilized Boers's work as a foil and argued, very significantly, that 1 Thessalonians is more than old forms under new auspices; "rather it is a composition using inherited themes in the context of a new counterpoint."[8]

In 1983 *Semeia* articles, Elizabeth Struthers Malbon and Daniel Patte approached 1 Thessalonians from the standpoint of structural exegesis.[9] Malbon first posited a traditional structure not too different from that proposed by Boers, but she turned quickly to syntagmatic and paradigmatic dimensions.[10] Patte focused upon dialogic and warranting levels.[11] In both cases, the authors probed depths beyond the traditional epistolary structure, noting repeated phraseology, narrative, and dialogic maneuvers. Although the analysis of Mal-

5. Abraham J. Malherbe, "Exhortation in First Thessalonians," *NovT* 25 (1983) 238–56; Malherbe, *Paul and the Thessalonians* (Philadelphia: Fortress, 1987); Malherbe, "Ancient Epistolary Theorists," *Ohio Journal of Religious Studies* 5 (1977) 3–77; and Malherbe, *Moral Exhortation: A Greco-Roman Sourcebook* (Philadelphia: Westminster, 1986).

6. Hendrikus Boers, "The Form-Critical Study of Paul's Letters: I Thessalonians as a Case Study," *NTS* 22 (1975–76) 140–58.

7. Jewett, *Thessalonian Correspondence.*

8. Helmut Koester, "I Thessalonians: Experiment in Christian Writing," *Continuity and Discontinuity in Church History* (ed. F. F. Church and T. George; Leiden: Brill, 1979) 44.

9. Elizabeth Struthers Malbon, "'No Need to Have Any One Write'? A Structural Exegesis of I Thessalonians," *Semeia* 26 (1983) 56–83; Daniel Patte, "Method for a Structural Exegesis of Didactic Discourses: Analysis of I Thessalonians," *Semeia* 26 (1983) 85–129.

10. Malbon, "'No Need,'" 66, 80.

11. Patte, "Method for a Structural Exegesis," 89.

bon and Patte obviously does not fall under the rubric of classical rhetoric, certain modern rhetorical analyses influenced by structuralism are similar.[12]

In his chapter on rhetoric in *The Thessalonian Correspondence: Pauline Rhetoric and Millenarian Piety*, Jewett professed to make use of classical rhetoric but continued, "I believe that the New Rhetoric and closely associated linguistic theories offer a more comprehensive grasp of epistolary communication."[13] In particular, he had in mind the focus of the rhetorics upon the audience, as well as the expectation that such inferences drawn from structure and genre will provide the identity and social roles of both audience and speaker.[14] Jewett therefore proceeded to discuss genre and structure, with a few citations of classical rhetoric but none, in fact, of the new rhetoric. Based upon analysis of genre and structure, he sought to posit in the succeeding chapter the situation of the Thessalonian congregation. Jewett gave no attention to invention and proofs.

Johanson's *To All the Brethren: A Text-Linguistic and Rhetorical Approach to 1 Thessalonians* is one of the most balanced of all the attempts at rhetorical analysis of biblical materials of the 1980s. Johanson proposed to use "both modern and ancient rhetorical theory. . . . A justification of this approach lies not only in the consideration that there appears to be a basic or 'deep' human rhetoric universal to mankind, but also the fact that Paul lived in a culture where rhetoric was very much alive and highly conceptualized."[15] In his monograph, Johanson proceeded to analyze "textual structures and persuasive strategies."[16] He, too, employed extensively the vocabulary and insights of structuralism.[17]

Much is commendable about Johanson's analysis. The problem, as I see it, is that he attempted, using the building block method, to locate the structure and purpose inductively. Although such an approach is admirable and, as Johanson observed, keeps one immersed in the text, writers typically have some vision of the whole before they set out to write, so it is not clear that this "scientific approach" is preferable to ascertaining first the basic arrangement and fitting the parts in later. Furthermore, although Johanson made several astute observations on the classical proofs, they are in the confines of the unit structures, and unfortunately, he did not draw conclusions on the overall

12. See Michael McGuire, "The Structure of Rhetoric," *Philosophy and Rhetoric* 15 (1982) 149–69; R. Scholes, *Structuralism in Literature: An Introduction* (New Haven: Yale University Press, 1971).
13. Jewett, *Thessalonian Correspondence*, 64.
14. Jewett, *Thessalonian Correspondence*, 65. Jewett quotes Bernard L. Brock and Robert L. Scott, *Methods of Rhetorical Criticism* (Detroit: Wayne State University Press, 1980) 267, to the effect that the traditional perspective is speaker oriented. This is much more the case with the Scottish rhetoricians George Campbell, Richard Whately, and Hugh Blair, however, than with Aristotle, whose three genres were different audiences, not different speaker intentions.
15. Johanson, *To All the Brethren*, 34.
16. Johanson, *To All the Brethren*, 49.
17. See esp. Johanson, *To All the Brethren*, 33. He draws heavily on E. Gülich and W. Raible, *Linguistische Textmodelle* (Munich: Uni-Taschenbücher, 1977) 130.

nature of proofs in 1 Thessalonians. More important, the reasons for Paul's rhetorical strategies tend to get lost in the maze of details.

The most recent studies were presented at the 1988 Colloquium Biblicum Lovaniense by Wuellner, A. Vanhoye, J. Chapa, J. Menken, R. Kieffer, and J. Lambrecht.[18] These likewise focused on structure. I will single out the paper by Wuellner, who argues that the interpretation of 1 Thessalonians is best served "by prioritizing our concern for rhetorical rather than the epistolary genre."[19] He focuses, by his own admission, on rhetorical structure but offers occasional observations on ethos and pathos. I find myself applauding much of what Wuellner has written. I think that more than any other scholar undertaking rhetorical analysis of biblical materials, Wuellner has pursued arguments with purpose and theology as determinative, rather than frozen in rhetorical forms. He sees the goal of 1 Thessalonians as pastoral and revolving about the oxymoron "tribulations with joy."[20] He thereby sidesteps such conundrums as the so-called long thanksgiving section interjected by Paul Schubert.[21]

The last decade, therefore, has seen the emergence of rhetorical criticism of 1 Thessalonians that in some measure has superseded epistolary analysis. The focus has been on structure, but recently scholars have made limited comments on the rhetorical proofs. Each of these studies has contributed to an understanding of the structure and, in some cases, other strategies of Paul, but the studies have not been strong on relating rhetorical observations to Paul's theology so as to ascertain why he proceeded as he did. Only to a modest extent have these studies helped us to comprehend better the text's power. Rhetoric, after all, was not in the forefront of Paul's mind as he penned 1 Thessalonians. Theology and purpose led, not rhetoric. Scholars for centuries have identified theology, purpose, and argument with considerable success without labeling their investigations "rhetorical criticism."

Malherbe's contribution to the rhetorical discussion, at least as yet, lies not so much in comments on structure or proofs as in observations on the characteristics and categories of the letters and their component parts. He has especially explored similarities to, and differences with, Hellenistic discourse and letters. Limiting the investigations to Hellenistic backgrounds and foregrounds is one-sided, as Malherbe recognizes, but his prodigious efforts highlight similarities and differences and often explain how the Greco-Roman

---

18. All these papers are as yet unpublished: W. Wuellner, "The Rhetorical Structure of I Thessalonians"; Albert Vanhoye, "La composition de 1 Thessaloniciens"; J. Chapa, "Consolatory Patterns (I Thess 4, 18; 5, 11)"; M. J. Menken, "The Structure of 2 Thessalonians"; R. Kieffer, "L'eschatologie en 1 Thessaloniciens dans une perspective rhetorique"; and J. Lambrecht, "Thanksgiving in 1 Thess 1–3."

19. Wuellner, "The Rhetorical Structure," 1.

20. Wuellner, "The Rhetorical Structure," 4. He does, however, labor more over the triadic rhetorical genre formula than I think is warranted, as I will argue later.

21. Paul Schubert, *Form and Function of the Pauline Thanksgivings* (BZNW 20; Berlin: Verlag von Alfred Töpelmann, 1939).

cultural milieu influenced the "package" in which Paul's theology is contained, as well as his personal missionary approaches.[22]

ARISTOTELIAN RHETORICAL ANALYSIS

This examination limits rhetorical analysis to the perspective developed by Aristotle in *The Rhetoric*.[23] I will refrain from reference to later versions of Aristotelian rhetoric, whether those of Chaim Perelman and L. Olbrechts-Tyteca,[24] I. A. Richards,[25] Lester Thonssen and A. Craig Baird,[26] or P. J. Corbett.[27] Aristotelian rhetoric has had its advocates and detractors through the centuries, but it is now, in an era of postdeconstruction criticism, once again enjoying a resurgence, both literary and oral.[28]

An Aristotelian rhetorical analysis of 1 Thessalonians involves proofs (πίστις), style (λέξις), and arrangement (τάξις). The five classical divisions of rhetoric were (1) invention, (2) style, (3) arrangement, (4) delivery, and (5) memory.[29] In Aristotle's rhetoric, most of the space was assigned to what others called *invention,* a term that Aristotle did not use; he rather used *proofs,* with lesser attention to style and arrangement.[30] He made clear this threefold explication in *The Rhetoric:* "There are three things which require special attention in regard to speech: first, the sources of proofs; secondly, style; and thirdly, the arrangement of the parts of the speech" (3.1.1). Delivery and memory are applicable to oral presentations, but not to NT letters. Recently, as pointed out, arrangement has been the driving force of

---

22. Chapa faults Malherbe for neglecting Jewish influences in regard to consolatory patterns. For a recent reflection on the history of emphasis on Hellenistic versus Jewish influences, see W. D. Davies, "My Odyssey in New Testament Interpretation," *Bible Review* 5 (1989) 10–18.

23. The translation quoted throughout is Aristotle *The Art of Rhetoric* (trans. Freese in LCL).

24. Chaim Perelman and L. Olbrechts-Tyteca, *The New Rhetoric: A Treatise on Argumentation* (trans. John Wilkinson and Purcell Weaver; Notre Dame, IN: University of Notre Dame Press, 1969).

25. I. A. Richards, *The Philosophy of Rhetoric* (New York: Oxford University Press, 1936).

26. Lester Thonssen and A. Craig Baird, *Speech Criticism* (New York: Ronald, 1948).

27. P. J. Corbett, *Classical Rhetoric for the Modern Student* (New York: Oxford University Press, 1971).

28. Olivier Reboul, *La Rhétorique* (Paris: Presses Universitaires de France, 1985); Reboul, "Can There be Non-Rhetorical Argumentation?" trans. Henry W. Johnstone, Jr., *Philosophy and Rhetoric* 21 (1988) 220–33; Robert J. Connors, Lisa S. Ede, and Andrea A. Lunsford (eds.), *Essays on Classical Rhetoric and Modern Discourse* (Carbondale: Southern Illinois University Press, 1984); James W. Hikins and Kenneth S. Zagacki, "Rhetoric, Philosophy, and Objectivism: An Attenuation of the Claims of the Rhetoric of Inquiry," *Quarterly Journal of Speech* 74 (1988) 201–28; Richard J. Berstein, *Beyond Objectivism and Relativism: Science, Hermeneutics, and Praxis* (Philadelphia: University of Pennsylvania Press, 1983); Eugene Garver, "Aristotle's Rhetoric as a Work of Philosophy," *Philosophy and Rhetoric* 19 (1986) 1–22; Paul G. Bator, "The 'Good Reasons Movement': A 'Confounding' of Dialectic and Rhetoric?" *Philosophy and Rhetoric* 21 (1988) 38–47.

29. Quintilian *Inst.* Aristotle did not list these together. He discussed the first four but said nothing about memory as a division.

30. In most of the first two books of *The Rhetoric*, 343 pages are on proofs (Freese in LCL, both Greek and English), as compared with 80 pages on style with a few comments on voice, and 45 pages on arrangement.

biblical critics, whereas in a prior age of traditional Protestant hermeneutics, beginning with J. C. G. Ernesti, style was the dominant focus of rhetorical analysis.[31]

It is obviously possible to analyze 1 Thessalonians from the standpoint of any rhetoric, as the studies on 1 Thessalonians mentioned above indicate, but one that may have influenced Paul should also receive its day in court.[32] If Paul was affected by rhetoric, it was Greek rather than Roman. It is interesting that Betz, in his Galatians commentary,[33] cites largely the *Rhetorica ad Herenium*,[34] Cicero,[35] and Quintilian.[36] It seems highly unlikely that Paul was influenced by any of the three. *The Rhetoric* of Aristotle, written about 330 B.C., made a far deeper impression on Hellenistic culture.[37] Whatever rhetorical instruction Paul may have received, if any, or whichever literary documents he read and imitated would have been influenced by Aristotle through contemporary Hellenistic handbooks.[38]

The claim here is not that Paul knew *The Rhetoric* but that some indirect influence may have filtered into his letters. One may dispute whether Paul, in fact, knew rhetoric at all.[39] Rhetoric, however, so permeated Hellenistic culture that it seems inconceivable for Paul to have escaped altogether rhetorical insight or, at minimum, a familiarity with Greek literature so affected.[40]

31. J. C. G. Ernesti published several works on rhetoric, including *Initia rhetorica* (Lipsiae: C. Fritsch, 1784); *Lexicon technologiae Graecorum rhetoricae* (Lipsiae: C. Fritsch, 1795); and *Lexicon technologiae Latinorum rhetoricae* (Lipsiae: C. Fritsch, 1797). These works in turn influenced his approach to hermeneutics, *Institutio interpretis Novi Testamenti* (Lipsiae: Weidmanni et Reichium, 1775). So also Wuellner's assessment, "Where Is Rhetorical Criticism Taking Us?" 450–55.

32. In the middle 1960s I was part of a study group of philosophers, rhetoricians, and linguists at The Pennsylvania State University who looked at documents of various sorts—including orations, plays, and poetry—from the standpoint of several different rhetorics. We discovered that any rhetoric can be superimposed on any piece, but that certain rhetorics are more helpful in regard to specific documents. What surprised us the most was that the orations of Demosthenes did not readily conform to the recommendations set forth in Aristotle's *Rhetoric*.

33. Betz, *Galatians*, 114, nn. 128–30. Betz drew heavily upon Heinrich Lausberg, *Handbuch der literarischen Rhetorik* (2 vols.; Munich: Hueber, 1960).

34. Published about 86 B.C.

35. Cicero's *De oratore*, *Brutus*, and *The Orator*, written between 55 and 46 B.C.

36. Quintilian's *Institutio oratoria*, written about A.D. 95, that is, after Paul's death.

37. John Henry Freese, "Introduction" to Aristotle, *The Rhetoric*, xxii.

38. George Kennedy, *The Art of Persuasion in Greece* (Princeton: Princeton University Press, 1964) 264–66.

39. The most recent effort to build a case for the influence of Hellenistic rhetoric on Judaism, not only outside Palestine but even in Jerusalem, is James L. Kinneavy, *Greek Rhetorical Origins of Christian Faith: An Inquiry* (New York: Oxford University Press, 1987) 80–91. Paul, according to Kinneavy, was clearly influenced by rhetoric and its vocabulary. Although Kinneavy establishes an interesting case, it is more dependent on scholarly conclusions than on primary data. See also Bernard Hungerford Brinsmead, *Galatians—Dialogical Response to Opponents* (Chico, CA: Scholars, 1982) 37–46, who drew heavily upon Martin Hengel, *Judaism and Hellenism* (2 vols.; London: SCM, 1974).

40. Abraham J. Malherbe, *Social Aspects of Early Christianity* (rev. ed.; Philadelphia: Fortress, 1983) 54–59, is open to the possibility that Paul's training included Hellenistic rhetoric, whether in Tarsus or Jerusalem. Gerald M. Phillips, in a study of the talmudic academies, argued that not only are there no signs of Hellenistic rhetoric, but that the rabbis were unaware of it. "Thus, it is apparent, that even though there is no specific mention of rhetoric in the Talmud, and though it is

A PERSPECTIVE ON
ARISTOTLE'S RHETORIC

Before commenting on 1 Thessalonians, it is appropriate to set forth the manner in which *The Rhetoric* may serve as a manual for rhetorical criticism.[41] Many studies have undertaken mechanical superimpositions of categories from *The Rhetoric* without investigating Aristotle's basic assumptions.[42] In Aristotle's own words, rhetoric is the "faculty of discovering the possible means of persuasion in reference to any subject whatever" (*Rhet.* 1.2).[43] This definition aptly depicts *The Rhetoric*, for in it Aristotle reflects on the major genres coming under his purview, in respect to both common and distinctive rhetorical features. For this reason it is a formidable task to employ *The Rhetoric* as a handbook for rhetorical or literary criticism. The work is not a precise compendium of rules tailor-made for effortless adjudica-

---

likely that the rabbis were not even aware of the existence of an art of rhetoric in any other culture, the whole Jewish culture of the Talmudic period rested upon the art of rhetoric in use." What he meant by the latter is that one can obviously talk about a rhetoric of the rabbis even though they knew nothing of Greco-Roman rhetoric. "An implicit theory of rhetoric can be drawn from the Talmud. The discovery of God's law applied to specific situations would correspond to invention. Communication of God's law through lecture and disputation would involve arrangement, style, and delivery, and the existence of an art of memory." (Gerald M. Phillips, "The Place of Rhetoric in the Babylonian Talmud," *Quarterly Journal of Speech* 43 [1957] 303. Also Gerald M. Phillips, "The Practice of Rhetoric at the Talmudic Academies," *Speech Monographs* 26 [1959] 37–46.) I think we should pay attention to Phillips, but I think he has overstated the case. It is hard to conceive that the rabbis were unaware of rhetoric. However, they were a closed society and followed their own approach to discourse. A helpful study would ascertain the similarity and differences between the discourse of the rabbis and Hellenistic practitioners. A recent work by Richard E. Cohen, "The Relationship between Topic, Rhetoric and Logic: Analysis of a Syllogistic Passage in the Yerushalmi," in Neusner and Frerichs, *New Perspectives on Ancient Judaism*, 87–125, is a step in the right direction but does not compare the conclusions with Hellenistic rhetoric.

41. The more recent commentaries on *The Rhetoric* are William Grimaldi, *Aristotle, Rhetoric I: A Commentary* (Bronx, NY: Fordham University Press, 1980); and less technical, but a helpful introduction, Larry Arnhart, *Aristotle on Political Reasoning: A Commentary on The "Rhetoric"* (DeKalb: Northern Illinois University Press, 1981). Also, Lawrence D. Green (ed. and trans.), *John Rainolds's Oxford Lectures on Aristotle's Rhetoric* (Newark: University of Delaware Press, 1986).

42. Some, but very limited, information is obtained from such applications. A recent instance is the work of Kinneavy, *Greek Rhetorical Origins*. Because of the thesis he is pursuing, that the NT concept of faith (πίστις) is derived from Hellenistic rhetoric, Kinneavy is especially constrained to show that Christian discourse conforms admirably to the procrustean bed of Aristotelian rhetoric (pp. 106–20). But what Kinneavy fails to take into account is that Aristotle invites us not only to see what he has seen but also to ascertain whether the discourse we examine differs. Kinneavy does not seriously entertain the possibility that Christian discourse is significantly different in certain fundamental ways.

43. Rhetoric, therefore, focuses upon what happens within a discourse. Aristotle clearly did not mean that in a discourse one could or should use all the available means, nor that a speaker need locate all the possible means of persuasion. Rather, the rhetorical theorist needs a systematic treatise on rhetoric needs to set out the ground rules for all the possible means of persuasion. I therefore conclude that George A. Kennedy did not think through his comment that "classical rhetoricians generally think that an effort should be made to assemble and evaluate all possible arguments. Paul clearly does not do this." (Kennedy, *New Testament Interpretation through Rhetorical Criticism* [Chapel Hill: University of North Carolina Press, 1984] 151.)

tion but rather observations and recommendations that are operable only if granted specified variables.[44] Identifying the right variable for a specific situation, whether proof or style, either in presenting or criticizing, is no simple matter.[45]

Aristotle argued that rhetoric is an art rather than an exact science and forewarned anyone presuming otherwise: "But in proportion as anyone endeavours to make of Dialectic or Rhetoric, not what they are, faculties [δύναμις],[46] but sciences, to that extent he will, without knowing it, destroy their real nature, in thus altering their character, by crossing over into the domain of sciences, whose subjects are certain definite things, not merely words" (*Rhet.* 1.4.6). In my view, the same is true of all modern rhetorics as well as ancient, and whatever the value of rhetorical criticism, we can never expect assured or consensus results regarding the rhetorical features of any biblical materials. Such would be the case even if biblical scholars settled on a common rhetorical method, which is far from the situation at present.

How did Aristotle arrive at his principles of rhetoric? It is obvious, first of all, that he collected whatever rhetorical works were then available, just as he collected the constitutions of the city-states so as to amass a body of data from which to generalize about political systems.[47] From the extant rhetorics, he incorporated appropriate insights but weighed and sifted the conclusions, often creating new categories or adding examples from speeches, literature, and observations. He did not claim to have exhausted the discipline. He made no effort to dissuade others from building on his foundations and methodologies.[48] We therefore are the most faithful to Aristotle when we add to his categories and observations, both in respect to commonalities and diversities. Any use of *The Rhetoric* that treats it as a frozen corpus is not faithful to the presuppositions of its author. We are indebted to Aristotle more for his methodology than for the completeness of his categories or conclusions.

---

44. It can further be observed that the work is not organized as rigorously as one might hope; for example, 2.18–26 seems better located before 2.1–17. Arnhart, *Aristotle on Political Reasoning,* however, argues that this location makes sense if ethos is viewed as an enthymeme (111, 112). He has persuaded me on the latter point, but I'm not convinced that the arrangement of this section is the most helpful.

45. "Examples are most suitable for deliberative speakers, for it is by examination of the past that we divine and judge the future. Enthymemes are most suitable for forensic speakers, because the past, by reason of its obscurity, above all lends itself to the investigation of causes and to demonstrative proof." (*Rhet.* 1.9.40.) "But we must not lose sight of the fact that a different style is suitable to each kind of Rhetoric. That of written compositions is not the same as that of debate; nor, in the latter, is that of public speaking the same as that of the law courts." (3.12.1.)

46. Perhaps best translated as "capabilities," "gifts," or a "knack," that is, skills in the same category as those of the artist.

47. See Freese, "Introduction" to Aristotle, *The Rhetoric,* vii–xxi, for Aristotle's predecessors.

48. George A. Kennedy, *Classical Rhetoric and Its Christian and Secular Tradition from Ancient to Modern Times* (Chapel Hill: University of North Carolina Press, 1987) 61, makes the same point. Kennedy's section on Aristotle, pp. 60–85, is perhaps the best short introduction to the background and basic features of *The Rhetoric.* But see the discussion in note 49 below in regard to the three genres.

Aristotle was well aware of imprecision in categories and strategies. His famous situation genres—deliberative, forensic, and epideictic (*Rhet.* 1.2.3)[49]—have been applied far more perfunctorily by biblical critics than Aristotle contemplated. Are the genres precisely delineated categories in respect to persuasion strategies? For example, if the predominant concern of a discourse is praise and blame, do we automatically categorize it as epideictic, since praise and blame are endemic to that genre? Aristotle warned that the categories overlap and that praise and blame may be indispensable, as well, to both deliberative and forensic discourse (1.9).

Finally, for Aristotle, rhetorical strategies are inextricably immersed in the matter at hand. For that reason, it is questionable whether experts in rhetoric can make perceptive observations about a discourse, the content and context of which they know little or nothing: "First of all, then, it must be understood that, in regard to the subject of our speech or reasoning, whether it be political or any other kind, it is necessary to be also acquainted with the elements of the question, either entirely or in part; for if you know none of these things, you will have nothing from which to draw a conclusion" (*Rhet.* 2.22.4). In *The Rhetoric*, the presumption is that the communicator knows the subject matter at hand; therefore, Aristotle's observations have to do with the manner by which the discourse can be marshaled so as to bring about the optimal persuasiveness. From the standpoint of rhetorical criticism, however, we are left with a major hiatus, since one cannot appropriately depict rhetorical technique without attending to content. Aristotle supplies no instructions for assessing the subject matter.

RHETORICAL CRITICISM OF
1 THESSALONIANS

To uphold the spirit as well as the letter of *The Rhetoric* in our examination of 1 Thessalonians demands guidelines, based on Aristotle's presuppositions, that recognize the unique features of 1 Thessalonians. Such an approach fully fleshed out would generate the optimal analysis, especially if pertinent insights from later rhetorical studies were incorporated, but would extend this effort to monographic proportions.[50] I shall therefore foray beyond *The Rhetoric* only in those aspects essential to the task at hand. Likewise, it is not possible to scrutinize every pericope in 1 Thessalonians, but I have attempted to address all the major rhetorical matters.

A useful point at which to commence Aristotelian criticism is identification of the genre. Aristotle astutely observed three major contexts for public

---

49. There are not three different rhetorics, as the Greek text makes clear, but three rhetorical genres: καὶ ἰδία περὶ ἕκαστον γένος (Aristotle *Rhet.* 3.12.6).

50. For a helpful insight into the history of rhetorical studies, see Winifred Horner (ed.), *The Present State of Scholarship in Historical and Contemporary Rhetoric* (Columbia: University of Missouri Press, 1983).

address in his world: the political assembly; the law court; and locations for encomium, such as the marketplace. Where is 1 Thessalonians to be located, since as to setting, it is none of the above? Must we force 1 Thessalonians into one of the categories, regardless? In the spirit of Aristotle, I think not; rather, we should add a genre.[51] Aristotle did not include the Christian assembly, since it did not as yet exist.[52] Had Aristotle lived in the fourth century A.D., his modus operandi would have driven him to this fourth genre.[53] But does this mean that we now are without assistance from *The Rhetoric*? The answer is no, since according to Aristotle, certain rhetorical features are common to all genres.[54] Various attempts have been made to locate 1 Thessalonians among the three genres. I conclude, however, that to do so is precarious.[55]

In certain features, 1 Thessalonians is deliberative, and yet the concern of Paul with praise and blame makes Aristotle's observations on the latter insightful.[56] In my view, however, we benefit the most by starting from Aristo-

51. In this regard Kennedy and I apparently understand Aristotle differently. Kennedy may be right that to some extent (in some cases very limited), the three genres are "in fact applicable to all discourse" (*New Testament Interpretation,* 19). But Aristotle clearly identified types of discourse where even rhetoric itself is not applicable, much less the three genres (*Rhet.* 1.2.20–22). Examples are discourses on philosophy, physics, and medicine. Aristotle makes it clear that the province of rhetoric is ethics, hence politics (1.2.7). I regard rhetoric as far more inclusive than Aristotle did, affirming that all forms of discourse have rhetorical dimensions (see Thomas H. Olbricht, *Informative Speaking* [Chicago: Scott, Foresman, 1968]; and Olbricht, "The Self as a Philosophical Ground of Rhetoric," *Pennsylvania Speech Annual* 21 [1964] 28–36). But further, I argue throughout this chapter that it is not helpful to promote a hardening of Aristotle's categories, especially in view of his own warnings against such a stance.

52. The synagogue is another similar context, but if there were synagogues in Aristotle's time, they were essentially unknown in his orbit. Of course, Aristotle accounted for other forms of public orality that are apart from rhetoric and its three genres—for example, philosophical argumentation (dialectic), poetry, and theatre (*The Poetics*)—as well as written forms, including contracts, constitutions, and letters. It is interesting how like a freeze-frame Aristotle's three genres have become. Stanley K. Stowers, in his inventive book on ancient letters, sets forth in an Aristotelian mode to break out of insular typology and descriptively delineate new features and boundaries of ancient epistolary genre, but he does not propose additional rhetorical genres. Certain of his observations are in keeping with Aristotle's perspectives—for example, that letters differ from public speaking and that their contents overflow the three categories—but he does not observe that Aristotle himself made the same observations (Stanley K. Stowers, *Letter Writing in Greco-Roman Antiquity* [Philadelphia: Westminster, 1986] 51–57.)

53. Hugh Blair, who was familiar with *The Rhetoric,* also set forth three genres, but epideictic is replaced with pulpit speaking: "I have already treated the Eloquence of Popular Assemblies, and of the Eloquence of the Bar. The subject which remains for this Lecture is, the strain and spirit of that Eloquence which is suited to the Pulpit" (Hugh Blair, *Lectures on Rhetoric and Belles Lettres* [London: W. Strahan, T. Cadell, 1783; repr. and ed. Harold F. Harding; Carbondale: Southern Illinois University Press, 1965]) 2. 101.

54. For example, "It remains to speak of the proofs common to all branches of Rhetoric, since the particular proofs have been discussed" (Aristotle *Rhet.* 2.20.1).

55. Kennedy makes a persuasive case for 1 Thessalonians's being deliberative (*New Testament Interpretation through Rhetorical Criticism,* 142–44). Johanson declares it closer to the deliberative than any other (*To All the Brethren,* 166). Jewett, however, identifies it as demonstrative/epideictic (*Thessalonian Correspondence,* 71), whereas Wuellner ("The Rhetorical Structure," 5–7) focuses on epideictic, more specifically paradoxical encomium, as also does Frank Witt Hughes ("New Testament Rhetorical Criticism and Its Methodology," SBL paper, Atlanta, 1986).

56. For example, Aristotle's comments on the epideictic exordium seem more helpful in respect to 1 Thessalonians than those on either the forensic or deliberative genres (*Rhet.* 3.14.15).

tle but delineating a new genre. Biblical scholars newly interested in rhetorical criticism should pay attention to Amos N. Wilder, who wrote in 1964, "The
whole compendium of Israel's literature is built upon peculiar rhetorics that
find no place in the textbooks of Aristotle or Quintilian."[57] Johanson con-
curred: "It is questioned here whether the rhetorical genres as defined by
Aristotle are of a sufficiently general and inclusive character to be so univer-
sally applicable as Kennedy and many others appear to allow."[58] Johanson also
pointed out that Aristotle did not know about sermons, but he did not go on to
suggest a new genre.[59]

We shall designate this new genre "church rhetoric." What, then, are the
distinctive features of church rhetoric?[60] I have developed these characteristics at some length in an article, "An Aristotelian Rhetorical Analysis of Galatians." Here I can state that certain aspects of the Christian vision differ from
Aristotle's. In the Christian view, the world is the arena in which God
(through God's Son and the Spirit) carries out divine purposes among
humans. In popular Greek thinking, the gods also acted, but since there were
many gods, there were many goals, often at cross-purposes. In Aristotle's
view, God had no involvement in human life, and therefore "humanity is the
measure of all things" (*Nic. Eth.* 10.8). All truths, proofs, and positions are in
the final analysis human. In the Christian rhetoric, in contrast, a recitation of
the acts of God in the community of believers plays a major role, affecting
proofs, arrangement, and style. That which is eternal is not so much immut-
able laws but the one-for-all actions of God.[61]

57. Amos N. Wilder, *The Language of the Gospel: Early Christian Rhetoric* (New York: Harper
& Row, 1964) 15. Helmut Koester likewise argued for a distinctive theological dimension of
1 Thessalonians and criticized Boers for ignoring the differences ("I Thessalonians Experiment,"
34–36).

58. Johanson, *To All the Brethren*, 39.

59. Johanson, *To All the Brethren*, 40. See also D. A. G. Hinks, "Tria Genera Causarum," *Classical Quarterly* 30 (1936) 170–76. I think that rhetorical criticism of biblical materials has suffered at the hands of those who inflexibly apply ancient and modern categories without perceiving
differences incurred by the "different" Christian vision. Throughout this study I have highlighted
those scholars who have recognized this difference. I applaud those in epistolary analysis, and that
is most of the scholars, who have not been infected with the same malaise, as, for example, has not
John L. White, *Light from Ancient Letters* (Philadelphia: Fortress, 1986).

60. The use of *church* is consistent with Aristotle's designating genre according to location. I
have refrained from labeling it "religious rhetoric," because I am limiting observations to Christian
discourse. Although I think many of the same features pertain to the synagogue, there are also
differences. *Church* is a larger category, with various subsets, as Wilder points out (*The Language
of the Gospel*, 26–47) including poetry, gospel, apocalyptic, narrative, epistles, and so on. These
various subsets, however, are related in the Christian topoi, to use Aristotle's terminology. On this
as a genre, I cite Albert Vanhoye, even though he was not specifically discussing genre: "Toute la
lettre est *ecclésiale* (on cherchera en vain cette catégorie dans les traites de rhétorique classique!)"
("La composition de 1 Thessaloniciens," 19; and Karl Thieme, "ekklesialparänetische" in "Die
Struktur," 458).

61. "An Aristotelian Rhetorical Analysis of Galatians" is as yet unpublished. Aristotle quotes
Sophocles concerning universal law in regard to burying the dead: "For neither today nor yester-
day, but from all eternity" (*Rhet.* 1.13.2). He also quotes Empedocles in regard to the sanctity of
life: "And a universal precept, which extends without a break throughout the wide-ruling sky and
the boundless earth" (*Rhet.* 1.13.2).

It is helpful, in addition, to delineate a subset for 1 Thessalonians. In the analysis of Galatians, I designated the subset "confrontational." The appropriate designation for 1 Thessalonians is "reconfirmational," or we may follow Malherbe in employing the more classical "exhortation" or "paraenesis."[62] It might be said that Paul's purpose in the letter was to do precisely what he said he did when he was there "encouraging [παρακαλέω], comforting [παραμυθέομαι] and urging [παρτύρομαι] you to lead lives worthy of God" (1 Thess 2:12), which was likewise the reason he sent Timothy "to strengthen [στηρίζω] and encourage [παρακαλέω] you" (3:2), and the reason behind the charge to the Thessalonians: "Therefore encourage [παρακαλέω] one another and build each other up [οἰκοδομέω], just as in fact you are doing" (5:11).[63] This is to say that the power of God, Christ, and the Spirit, and of the discourse that announces their power, through reconfirmation brings the community to deeper commitment. Ascertaining the text's power is therefore to delineate the contours of that reconfirmation.

Proofs

Before examining specific proofs, it is important to identify the larger purpose of 1 Thessalonians. I agree with those who think that in 1 Thessalonians, Paul chiefly sought to reconfirm the young congregation in the matters on which it had been taught, and secondarily to clear up eschatological misconceptions.[64] The congregation had been forewarned in regard to persecution, but Paul was fearful that while they had been prepared mentally, they were ill equipped for the actuality. The letter is essentially praise, with almost no blame. We will return to the arrangement later, but at this point it may be helpful to offer an outline on 1 Thessalonians that reflects the purpose: indicators of past and present confirmation (1:1–10), Paul's ministry confirmed in the believers (2:1–16), the effort at reconfirmation

---

62. Malherbe, "Exhortation in First Thessalonians," 238. Others who use the same description but different terminology are Daniel Patte, *Paul's Faith and the Power of the Gospel* (Philadelphia: Fortress, 1983) 126 ("strengthening further in their faith"); Boers, "Form Critical Study," 158 ("to spur them on to a way of life pleasing to God"); and Johanson, *To All the Brethren*, 189 ("a delicate combination of consolation and correction without reproof"). Johanson's observation is essentially recommended by Wuellner, "Form Critical Study," 7.

63. We have no doubt much to learn in regard to this genre by examining "the Greco-Roman tradition of moral exhortation" (Malherbe, "Exhortation in First Thessalonians," 239), but here we are specifically interested in spelling out the ramifications of Aristotle's rhetoric. Juan Chapa, "Consolatory Patterns," 5–7, argues that the consolatory patterns are more Jewish, citing 2 Macc 7:5, 14, 20, as well as additional extensive bibliography. He also points to the differences in content in regard to the resurrection and return, as compared with a word from a friend that has no higher origin. Johanson likewise emphasized Jewish backgrounds (*To All the Brethren*, 173–87).

64. I am therefore taking the position of Malherbe, *Paul and the Thessalonians*, 68–78, and Wuellner, "The Rhetorical Structure," 4, against Johanson, *To All the Brethren*, 58, who argued, "It was the deaths of fellow Christians before the parousia that constitutes the primary exigence to which the various persuasive strategies of the letter as a whole are directed," and Helmut Koester, "I Thessalonians," 33–44.

through Timothy (2:17– 3:13), and reconfirmation of the believing community by letter (4:1–5:28).[65]

Ethos. Paul implements ethos in 1 Thessalonians in a classic Aristotelian manner. In fact, I am prepared to argue that the major form of proof from an Aristotelian standpoint in 1 Thessalonians is ethos, as contrasted with Galatians, where it is logos. This marks a difference between reconfirmational and confrontational rhetoric. Basically, Paul shows goodwill toward the "brothers" and avows his own virtue. Aristotle was well aware that a speaker brings an image or reputation with him to the dais. But the rhetorician is concerned with the manner in which the speaker may enhance his image once the speech commences: "The orator persuades by moral character when his speech is delivered in such a manner as to render him worthy of confidence. . . . But this confidence must be due to the speech itself, not to any preconceived idea of the speaker's character" (Aristotle *Rhet.* 1.2.4).[66] What are the ways within speeches that speakers can show that they have good sense, virtue, and goodwill and that those they oppose have the opposite traits, regardless of the audience's preconceived notion about them? (2.1.6). Aristotle set out the components of virtue as "justice, courage, self-control, magnificence, magnanimity, liberality, gentleness, practical and speculative wisdom." He held that justice and courage are the most esteemed (1.9.3–6).

Because *The Rhetoric* is not a manual for rhetorical criticism, we are given few procedural guidelines for scrutinizing ethos.[67] I shall therefore call attention to the statements in 1 Thessalonians in which Paul seeks to establish his goodwill toward the readers and affirm his own virtue.

It is interesting that after establishing his goodwill by speaking of his constant prayers for, and memory of, the Thessalonians, in the rest of chapter 1, Paul praises the believers for their Christian virtues: "faith, love and hope" (1:2, 3), "He has chosen you" (1:4), "You became imitators of us and of the Lord" (1:6), "You welcomed the message with joy" (1:6), "You became a model" (1:7), "Your faith in God has become known everywhere" (1:8), "They report what kind of reception you gave us" (1:9),[68] and "They tell us how you

65. It is clear from this outline that I understand *reconfirmational* in a continuing, not a one-time, sense.

66. It is of interest to note that Aristotle wrote: "In deliberative oratory, it is more useful that the orator should appear to be of a certain character, in forensic, that the hearer should be disposed in a certain way" (*Rhet.* 2.1.4). Paul, in 1 Thessalonians, used much more ethos than pathos. On this ground, 1 Thessalonians should be classified as deliberative, therefore supporting Kennedy against Jewett. But to complicate the matter, when Aristotle took up ethos, he referred the reader back to epideictic wherein he discussed virtue (2.1.7). The failure of church rhetoric to conform to any of the three genres lends additional support to the contention that we should demarcate a new genre.

67. If Arnhart (*Aristotle on Political Reasoning*, 51–53) is correct, we should treat ethical proofs from the perspective of enthymemes. I think his point is appropriate, but because of space limitations, I will set out the enthymemes without showing their full syllogistic forms.

68. Johanson, *To All the Brethren*, 85, notes that Aristotle identifies the witness or opinion of others as ethos (*Rhet.* 3.17.16).

turned to God from idols" (1:10). In addition, he addressed them as "brothers," as he did seventeen more times in the letter.[69]

In the next longer section, 1 Thess 2:1–3:6, in contrast, Paul focused almost
exclusively on his own virtue as it related to his relationship with the believers.
Jewett called this section the "apostolic example" and "the desire for apostolic
visit."[70] These affirmations of virtuous action are too numerous to set forth
here, so I will cite only some of the most obvious: "We had previously suffered
and been insulted in Philippi, as you know" (2:2); "We are not trying to trick
you" (2:3); "We speak as men approved by God" (2:4); "You know we never
used flattery, nor did we put on a mask to cover up greed" (2:5); "We worked
night and day in order not to be a burden to anyone" (2:9); and "We kept telling you that we would be persecuted. And it turned out that way" (3:4).
Although Aristotle did not discuss these sorts of particulars, they are Hellenistic topoi for the moralists, as Malherbe has shown.[71]

From 1 Thess 3:6 on, most of the ethos in the letter is Paul's praise or show
of goodwill to the believers; for example, "We are encouraged about you
because of your faith" (3:7); "You do love all the brothers throughout
Macedonia" (4:10); "You are the sons of light and the sons of day" (5:5); and
"Therefore encourage one another and build each other up, just as in fact you
are doing" (5:11). Ethos, therefore, basically follows the outline above and
reflects the differing purposes of the main points.

Although Paul placards his virtues in good Aristotelian manner, the character of those virtues grow out of Christian values rather than Hellenistic
morals.[72] This is shown in their Holy Spirit empowerment (1 Thess 1:5, 6),
their imitation of the Lord (1:6), Paul's dependence on God for speech (2:4),
the motivations for ethics because of the Lord (4:1, 2), and the relationships
being God based (3:12; 4:9). Malherbe expressed it well: "His use of the traditional hortatory material is marked by profound change as he reshapes it to
express his experience of God working in him, or stresses the theological and
religious dimensions of ethics, or uses traditional Christian material to address
issues also of concern to pagan consolers."[73]

Aristotle's observations on ethos may be of particular help as we read
1 Thessalonians. In these reconfirmational remarks, Paul drew heavily upon
ethos, and did so because of his effort to bring together a new community of
persons responsive to God and one another. Confidence in, and the credibil-
ity of, God, God's messengers, and the members of the community are
imperative if Paul's program is to succeed. Paul summed it up in his hopes for

---

69. On the significance of this, see Malherbe, *Paul and the Thessalonians*, 48. Johanson, *To All
the Brethren*, 83–86, also identifies the main proof in this section as ethos.

70. Jewett, *Thessalonian Correspondence*, 73–74.

71. Malherbe, "Exhortation in First Thessalonians."

72. On Aristotle's delineation of ethical characteristics, see *Rhet.* 2.1.6.

73. Malherbe, "Exhortation in First Thessalonians," 256. Cf. his remarks in *Moral Exhortation*,
15.

the community: "May the Lord make your love increase and overflow for each other and for everyone else, just as ours does for you. May he strengthen your hearts so that you will be blameless and holy in the presence of our God and Father when our Lord Jesus comes with all his holy ones" (1 Thess 3:12, 13).

Pathos. Paul utilizes very little pathos in 1 Thessalonians in the Aristotelian sense of proof. Many of his statements, no doubt, have affective overtones, but he does not draw often on the wellsprings of emotion explicitly as a strategy. According to Aristotle, "The orator persuades by means of his hearers, when they are roused to emotion by his speech; for the judgements we deliver are not the same when we are influenced by joy or sorrow, love or hate" (*Rhet.* 1.2.5).[74]

The cases in which Paul does seek to arouse the emotions draw on his relationships with God and the believers. This means that the emotion is more dependent on close family and community metaphors than Aristotle anticipated.[75] For example, "We were gentle among you, like a mother caring for her little children. We loved you so much that we were delighted to share with you not only the gospel of God but our lives as well, because you had become so dear to us" (1 Thess 2:7);[76] "We dealt with each of you as a father deals with his own children" (2:11); "We were torn away from you for a short time (in person, not in thought), out of our intense longing we made every effort to see you" (2:17); and "For this reason, when I could stand it no longer, I sent to find out about your faith" (3:5). All these instances had to do with Paul himself and the reason he sent Timothy. The only exception is the statement about the Jews "who killed the Lord Jesus and the prophets and also drove us out" (2:15).[77] Paul characteristically did not utilize the mawkish pathos resorted to in the Hellenistic law courts. He depended rather on understanding and ethos.

Logos. Logical proof[78] is derived from enthymemes, or rhetorical syllo-

---

74. The main discussion of pathos is in a section on the emotions (Aristotle *Rhet.* 2.1.8–17.6). There Aristotle discussed the different emotions and their outcomes in regard to age and status. He criticized those rhetoricians who "chiefly devote their attention to matters outside the subject; for the arousing of prejudice, compassion, anger, and similar emotions has no connexion with the matter in hand, but is directed only to the dicast" (1.1.3–4). He favored pathos that is more closely related to the subject matter. See Arnhart, *Aristotle on Political Reasoning*, 115–21.

75. Johanson, *To All the Brethren*, 85, identified 1 Thess 1:6 as pathos because of the imitation, so *Rhet.* 2.11.1–7; but I think as employed here, ethos is more obviously Paul's intention. Also in contrast with Johanson, p. 86, I think that 1 Thess 2:1–12 contains more pathos than 1:2–10. Johanson argued that reference to God is pathos (p. 113), and cited Kennedy in support (*Classical Rhetoric*, 121).

76. Also identified as pathos by Johanson (*To All the Brethren*, 93), as well as 1 Thess 2:17–20 (p. 101), 3:5 (p. 104), and 3:9–13 (p. 108).

77. I agree with Johanson, *To All the Brethren*, 96–99, that this is Pauline, as against Boers, "Form Critical Study," 151, 152, and many others, who take it to be an anti-Jewish interpolation. Johanson (p. 98) also designated 1 Thess 2:15, 16 as pathos, and a special form, "vituperatio."

78. In the quotation above "upon the speech itself."

gisms, and examples, or rhetorical induction (Aristotle *Rhet.* 1.2.8). Examples are especially useful in deliberative speaking, and enthymemes in forensic (1.9.40–41).[79] The enthymeme, Aristotle contended, "generally speaking, is the strongest of rhetorical proofs" (1.1.11), and the example is the lesser (1.2.11).

Enthymemes are consensus propositions, sometimes stated, sometimes assumed.[80] When employed, enthymemes are found in regular sentences and not formalized after the manner of the logician's syllogism.[81] Rhetorical enthymemes are normally probable, not certain.[82] Paul is a master at advancing and weaving enthymemes.[83] But enthymemes are much more in evidence in discourse in which Paul has specific opponents to refute, as in Galatians, than in praise and encouragement.

It is not simple to describe Paul's logical proofs in 1 Thessalonians on Aristotelian grounds. With the exception of the argument on eschatology (4:13–5:11), in which enthymemes are obviously operative, the rest of the letter seems best depicted as rhetorical induction couched in the framework of an "umbrella" enthymeme. Aristotle described such use: "Examples must be used as evidence and as a kind of epilogue to the enthymemes" (*Rhet.* 2.20.9).

Let us take up the argument of the first major point. In 1 Thess 1:2–10, Paul commended the believers for the manner in which they exhibited evidences of election. The fully fleshed out syllogism follows:

Believers exhibit concrete marks of election by God.
The believers in Thessalonica exhibit such concrete marks.
Therefore, the believers in Thessalonica have been elected by God.

As to the marks exhibited by the believers in Thessalonica, the specifics or examples follow:

1. They did works of faith.
2. They performed labors of love.

79. It is interesting that those who assure us that specific epistles belong to one of the three genres pick and choose among the characteristics of that genre. Kennedy, for example, designates Galatians "deliberative" contra Betz, but he finds neither the deliberative topics nor the example as proof useful in his rhetorical criticism of the letter (*New Testament Criticism*, 144–52).
80. In this regard, Aristotle should be suggestive for reader response criticism: "That which is persuasive is persuasive in reference to someone" (*Rhet.* 1.2.11).
81. The literature on enthymemes is vast. For a judicious statement that recognizes the history of different perspectives, see James C. Raymond, "Enthymemes, Examples, and Rhetorical Method," *Essays on Classical Rhetoric and Modern Discourse* (Carbondale: Southern Illinois University Press, 1984) 140–51, and his bibliography, 280–81. For Johanson's comments on Paul's use of enthymemes, see *To All the Brethren*, 89.
82. Convenient access to these matters may be found in Keith Erickson (ed.), *Aristotle: The Classical Heritage of Rhetoric* (Metuchen, NJ: Scarecrow, 1974); and Erickson (ed.), *Aristotle's Rhetoric: Five Centuries of Philological Research* (Metuchen, NJ: Scarecrow, 1975).
83. Paul did not often generalize from examples (inductive), as did the writer of Hebrews who drew conclusions based on the faith of several heroes of old (Hebrews 11).

3. They exhibited steadfastness of hope.
4. Their acceptance of the Gospel had power with the Holy Spirit.
5. Their acceptance of the Gospel had deep conviction.
6. They imitated Paul.
7. They imitated the Lord.
8. They welcomed the message with the joy given by the Holy Spirit, despite suffering.
9. They became a model for all believers in Macedonia and Achaia.
10. Their faith was known everywhere.
11. It has been reported by others that they accepted Paul with open arms.
12. They turned from idols to serve the living God.
13. They wait for God's Son from Heaven.

In like manner in the next section, Paul cites numerous examples of the manner in which his ministry reflected a genuine commitment to a holy, loving God.

In the section on the Parousia, Paul's arguments depended on enthymemes. One manner by which to pinpoint these enthymemes is to lay out the underlying syllogisms so as to reveal the hidden assumptions.[84] There are three basic arguments. In each case, it is only the conclusion or perhaps the minor premise of the syllogism that is explicit. The rest of the syllogism, as Aristotle noted, is unstated:

> All believers share the hope of the Parousia through Christ's care.
> The believers who have died continue in Christ's care.
> Therefore, the believers who have died share in the Parousia.

> All believers will be caught up by Christ to be with God.
> The believers who have died will be raised.
> Therefore, they will be caught up with Christ to be with God.

> No one knows the time when Christ will return, so everyone must be ready.
> The Thessalonians do not know when Christ will come.
> Therefore, the Thessalonians must be ready for the return of Christ.

Clearly, 1 Thessalonians contained proofs of the sort noticed by Aristotle, with emphasis on ethos. Whether Paul knew of the three forms of proof is not certain. However, Aristotle did not claim that only those aware of the three proofs utilized them. Rather, he believed they were employed by all communicators, whether consciously or unconsciously. Better means of ascertaining Paul's persuasive strategies may exist, but these help pinpoint

---

84. For Johanson's analysis of the proofs in 1 Thess 4:13–18, see *To All the Brethren*, 121–26. Johanson criticizes Malherbe for rejecting instruction or logos in this section (p. 126). But he fails to ascertain Malherbe's intent, which is not to deny a cognitive dimension but to highlight consolation and maintain against Koester that parallels in the moral philosophers may be discovered in respect to consolation.

Paul's conviction that confirmation grows from that active love of God that supplies humankind a place in reality and community, now and in the end time.

Style

Aristotle declared that good style is characterized by perspicuity, purity, loftiness, and propriety (*Rhet.* 3.3.1–12.6). He argued that style should be suited to each genre and form, whether written or spoken. He believed that the written style is more precise than the spoken and lends itself less to the repetition of words and asyndetons. Deliberative style is like a rough sketch, whereas forensic is more polished but contains fewer rhetorical devices. The epideictic style is especially suited for written composition. In all cases, the mean is the most desirable (3.12.1–6).

Aristotle helps us locate certain stylistic features of 1 Thessalonians, but not others. Taking up his characteristics of good style in reverse order, even though 1 Thessalonians is uplifting, endearing, or affective,[85] and also powerful and direct, a stylistic balance pervades the letter. Paul employed several rhetorical devices,[86] but these are unobtrusive and do not detract from the task at hand.[87] Most characteristic are parallelisms, especially those having to do with faith, love, and hope (1 Thess 1:3; 3:6–8; 5:8), as well as the building up of instances as we have noted in the "Logos" section.

A precision of language and a tone of encouragement is obvious. The style, therefore, is appropriate to the genre and form, and it shows propriety in vocabulary and stylistic devices. "Loftiness" seems not a befitting appellation, but the letter is suitably elevated for the context. Paul's Greek, although not sophisticated Classical Attic, is adequately pure for his readers.[88]

We must now comment in more detail on the perspicuity of 1 Thessalonians with Aristotle as our guide. The discourse that exhibits perspicuity uses appropriate nouns and verbs—fresh, creative words, but natural.[89] It is the metaphor (including epithets and similes) above all that gives the discourse this quality (Aristotle *Rhet.* 3.2.1–4).[90] Paul's nouns and verbs

---

85. See Malherbe, *Paul and the Thessalonians,* 73–76.

86. George Milligan, *St. Paul's Epistles to the Thessalonians* (repr.; Grand Rapids, MI: Eerdmans, 1908) lvii, wrote of Paul's "almost complete absence of the rhetorical figures, so largely practiced in his own day," but went on to identify meiosis (1 Thess 2:15) and chiasmus (5:6).

87. G. G. Findlay, *The Epistles of Paul the Apostle to the Thessalonians* (Cambridge: Cambridge University Press, 1925) lviii, wrote, "The Apostle's style is the most natural and unstudied in the world. It is, as Renan said, 'conversation stenographed.'"

88. Milligan, *St. Paul's Epistles,* lv, wrote, "St Paul, when not directly indebted to the Greek O. T., was mainly dependent upon the living, spoken tongue of his own day, borrowing from time to time more or less consciously from ethical writers, but otherwise showing little or no dependence upon the literature of classical or later times."

89. Findlay, *Epistles of Paul,* lv–lvii, spoke of Paul's use of new words (fifty-four hapax legomena in 1 and 2 Thessalonians), but the majority were compounds of types prevailing in later Greek. Findlay concluded, "There is nothing in the Greek of these Epistles that would present any difficulty to a contemporary reader moderately acquainted with the Hellenistic phraseology of the Jewish synagogues and schools of the Diaspora."

90. For Johanson's comments on tropes and figures, see *To All the Brethren,* 94–96.

appear accurate and suited to his purposes. We have many difficulties with nuances and implications, but we have to assume that Paul's readers had somewhat less, since they had heard him many times and were familiar with his thought patterns and vocabulary, as well as the situation.[91] We can further observe, with some degree of confidence, that Paul used vocabulary in a fresh, commanding way. Although he exhibits recurring patterns, we discover, as we look through his letters, no overworked formulas, clichés, or platitudes.[92]

Paul employed a number of metaphors in 1 Thessalonians, but they are perhaps not as fresh as those in Galatians, since all of them were also used by the Hellenistic moralists, as Malherbe has conclusively shown. Perhaps, however, those who heard Paul had not frequented the lectures of the moralists and therefore heard them as fresh analogies. At minimum, we find the following: "gentle as a nurse" (2:7), "father with his children" (2:11), "torn away" (2:17), "the crown in which we glory" (2:19), "like a thief in the night" (5:2, 4), "sons of light" (5:8), "love as a breastplate" (5:8), "the hope of salvation as a helmet" (5:8), and "the Spirit's fire" (5:19). These metaphors indeed gave 1 Thessalonians a clarity and liveliness, as Aristotle affirmed.

A few additional observations, first in regard to Paul's direct style, are appropriate; they are compatible with the spirit of Aristotle, but not that in *The Rhetoric*. Paul's manner of discourse is not unique, since it is found in Cynic letters, but few Greek orations were so forthright.[93] Paul employed first and second person pronouns (mostly plural) almost exclusively throughout 1 Thessalonians.[94] In the sections and places at which he praised the Christian attributes of the believers, he addressed them in second person plural. In sections in which he spoke of his own ministry, he employed first person plural consistently except in two places, in which he refers to the challenge of Satan (2:18, 3:5). In this regard, 1 Thessalonians and even 2 Thessalonians tend to be unique among Paul's letters. In polemics, for example, in Galatians, Paul almost always employs the first person singular. It could be that the plural is more the language of exhortation and praise, though I have not found it in the Hellenistic moralists.[95] It is significant, however, that Paul was interested in divine community building, and these first person plurals highlight the need for the involvement of all in mutually growing conviction and excitement.

91. Malherbe, "Exhortation in First Thessalonians," established the common devices and vocabulary among the moral teachers, which Paul in turn utilized.

92. For Johanson's description of Paul's language, *To All the Brethren*, 117, 140–41, 190. Cf. Martin Dibelius, *From Tradition to Gospel* (trans. B. F. Woolf; New York: Scribner's, 1933) 238–44.

93. The most obvious example is the twenty-eighth letter of Diogenes (Abraham J. Malherbe, *The Cynic Epistles* [Missoula, MT: Scholars, 1977] 121–25). Examples of Greek orations are Isocrates, "Panegyricus," and Demosthenes, "The Philippics," though "On the Crown" is more direct.

94. I have labeled this style reconfirmational rather than exhortation, advice, praise and blame, parenesis, admonition, rebuke, or reproach, for although it is all of these, none singularly captures the flavor of 1 Thessalonians. These are categories employed by Stowers, *Letter Writing in Greco-Roman Antiquity*.

95. Neither have I located a scholar who addressed this difference.

Furthermore, 1 Thessalonians is sprinkled with references to God, Christ, the Holy Spirit, prayer, holiness, and persecution, thereby producing a repetitiveness that Aristotle eschewed but that provides divine reinforcement for Paul's argument.

Arrangement

Aristotle was explicit about the arrangement of a speech. He contended that delineated parts should characterize all speeches. He therefore criticized those who multiplied the divisions: "So then the necessary parts of a speech are the statement of the case and proof. These divisions are appropriate to every speech, and at the most the parts are four in number—exordium, statement, proof, epilogue" (*Rhet.* 3.13).

What happens if we follow Aristotle's lead, both in the four parts as well as in his observations on the parts? Because 1 Thessalonians is a letter, I think it well that we emulate other scholars in identifying a prescript and postscript, then reflect on the four divisions.[96] I offer the following outline:

Prescript, 1:1.
I. Exordium, 1:2, 3.
II. Statement, 1:4–10.[97]
III. Proof, 2:1–5:11.[98]
IV. Epilogue, 5:12–24.
Postscript, 5:25–28.[99]

The truth of the matter is that Aristotle's divisions of arrangement are not nearly as helpful in understanding 1 Thessalonians as they are in understanding Galatians. We can pinpoint these parts in 1 Thessalonians, though the statement is difficult to identify. But the section in which Aristotle's observations are the least helpful is the proof, since the differences in the materials of this section are not at all nuanced by his comments. In the case of 1 Thessalonians, attention to epistolographic features is instructive, as Malherbe argues: matters of thanksgiving, friendship, presence and absence, and

---

96. Boers, "Form Critical Study," 140, and Malbon, "'No Need,'" 66, who use *greeting* in both cases. See also Stowers, *Letter Writing in Greco-Roman Antiquity.* For a helpful chart, see Jewett, *Thessalonian Correspondence,* 216–21, who sets out patterns of arrangement from sixteen scholars who follow thematic analysis, six who employ epistolary analysis, and four who use the classical rhetorical divisions. R. Lee and C. Lee, "An Analysis," 39, employing modern divisions, propose the following: introduction, 1 Thess 1:1–10; body, 2:1–5:24; conclusion, 5:25–28.

97. With Wuellner, "Rhetorical Structure," 11, and Johanson, *To All the Brethren,* 157–60, 172; and against Jewett, *Thessalonian Correspondence,* 121, and the Funk school, who argue for a long thanksgiving section—Robert Funk, *Language, Hermeneutic, and the Word of God* (New York: Harper & Row, 1966). Wuellner, p. 1, designates 1 Thess 1:1–10 "insinuatio." This is not Aristotelian and, although insightful, is perhaps not completely convincing.

98. Wuellner, "Rhetorical Structure," 12, designates 1 Thess 2:1–5:22 the "Main Argument."

99. Wuellner, "Rhetorical Structure," 16, designates 1 Thess 5:23–28 the "peroration." Johanson, *To All the Brethren,* 142, declares 5:12–24 the conclusion of the whole, and not so much a peroration.

parenesis.[100] But even more helpful, as Wuellner contends, is to assess the argument apart from both ancient epistolary and rhetorical structures.[101] That, I believe, is done by ascertaining the flow of purpose through the argument's divisions, as I did at the beginning of "Proofs." Paul's progression moves from the love and power of God in the Thessalonians, to Paul himself, and on to the believing community by his presence and later Timothy's presence, to their love for one another, and ultimately beyond the end time in which God, Christ, the Spirit, the believers, and the missionaries will all be one.

If help in understanding a document is the end of rhetorical criticism, then Aristotle's rhetoric assists us in certain specifics to gain access to the meaning of 1 Thessalonians.[102] I conclude that church rhetoric is a distinctive genre with various subgenres, including reconfirmational, the genre of 1 Thessalonians. This genre has parallels in Greco-Roman exhortation and parenesis but also has its own distinctive thrusts. The text's power lies in declaring the action of God, Christ, and the Holy Spirit—past, present, and future—rather than in exhibiting the universal principles and friendship factors of Aristotle's civilization. The result is a powerful community of faith, sustained by recurring exhortatory communication, which in turn creates faith and brotherly love despite affliction, or paradoxically, joy through tribulation. Because of Paul's world view, his rhetorical strategy exuded personal dimensions reflecting distinctive Christian perspectives on ethos, the premises of enthymemes, language, metaphor, and arrangement.

Aristotle himself maintained that rhetoric is an art and must follow the conventions of the time, the nature of audiences, the purposes of the speaker, and perhaps chiefly the contours of the subject matter. To address all these facets, we must employ *The Rhetoric* as a fountainhead of insight rather than as a leveed, controlled stream. We need to draw upon whatever conventions and later rhetorical insights may be of help. In my judgment, however, we must steer clear of esoteric modern criticisms that obfuscate rather than clarify.

---

100. See Malherbe, *Paul and the Thessalonians,* 68–78, and his extensive bibliographical citations. I think Malherbe is correct not to invest so much effort in discussing the matter of thanksgiving as the key to understanding the structure, as does Paul Schubert, *Form and Function of Pauline Thanksgivings* (BZNW 20; Berlin, 1939). Cf. Lambrecht, "Thanskgiving in 1 Thess 1–3."
101. Wuellner, "Rhetorical Structure," 1. He uses *rhetoric,* but not here limited to classical divisions of arrangement. Johanson, too, in *To All the Brethren,* 188–90, eschews the epistolary but finds it more suggestive than does Wuellner.
102. Wuellner, "Rhetorical Structure," 17, argues that rhetorical analysis is the most valuable of all modern critical approaches, but he has in mind a mixture of modern German, French, and American rhetoric, not Aristotelian rhetoric. From one perspective I can agree, in that I think that what Wuellner really has in mind is an analysis of the argument in biblical documents. My misgiving is that scholars have long analyzed arguments under a different appellation than *rhetoric* and therefore as a component of other forms of modern criticism.

15

THE BEGINNINGS OF THE
CHURCH AT THESSALONICA

In Acts, Luke tells the story of how Paul first came to Thessalonica accompanied by Silas (17:4, 10) and Timothy. Timothy was last mentioned in 16:1–3 but reappears again in 17:14. Paul, according to Luke's story, went into the synagogue. He had some success there, even among the devout Greeks (especially among their women), but was rejected by the "jealous" Jews. When they could not lay their hands on him, they dragged Jason and some of the "brethren" before the city authorities and denounced them and the Christians in general, accusing them of actions against the decrees of Caesar. After having received assurances, Jason and the others were set free, and nothing further is said about them. By night Paul and Silas (and Timothy) left Thessalonica for Beroea, where they again went to the synagogue of the Jews, who, according to Luke, were "more noble than those in Thessalonica" (17:11). But the Jews of Thessalonica followed them there, and so Paul had to leave Beroea for Athens. Silas and Timothy stayed in Beroea and did not meet with Paul again before he had arrived in Corinth (18:5). In Acts 19:21, Luke tells us that some years later Paul planned a journey from Ephesus to Macedonia and Achaia, a plan that he subsequently carried out (20:1–2), staying in Greece for three months. After that he came back to Macedonia, accompanied by some brothers, among them Sopater of Beroea and Aristarchus and Secundus of Thessalonica. From there they left for Troas (20:6) and Miletus (20:15), with the final objective of going to Jerusalem.

THE EVIDENCE FROM ACTS COMPARED
WITH PAUL'S LETTERS

The story as Luke tells it raises some questions when we compare it with the evidence we have from Paul's own letters. That Paul came to Thessalonica from Philippi and left Thessalonica for Athens agrees with 1 Thess 2:2 and 3:1. The latter verse, however, shows that at least Timothy was with him in Athens

I am grateful to Hendrikus Boers for his revision of my English text.

and did not stay in Beroea, as Luke has it. Both Silvanus (the Silas of Acts) and Timothy were with Paul when he wrote his letter to the Thessalonians (1 Thess 1:1), but before that Paul had sent Timothy back to Thessalonica from Athens (3:2). Timothy brought him good news of the Thessalonians' faith and of their love and ongoing remembrance of him. Therefore, when he wrote his letter to the Thessalonians, Paul must have been either in Athens or in Corinth. Those are the alternatives exegetes have discussed since the early colophons of the manuscripts.[1] The entire picture fits in a "traditional" chronology of Paul based on the sequence of events from his conversion to his arrival in Galatia (Gal 1:15–3:1; Acts 9:1–16:6). In this picture there is no place for a mission to Thessalonica in the early forties.[2] Thus, we can date this letter in the year A.D. 50 or 51, that is, in the begining of Paul's missionary activities around the Aegean Sea, after he had broken his connections with the church of Antioch and had gone west.

Up to this point, the information Luke gives us agrees in general with Paul's own letters. The exception is the report that Silas and Timothy remained in Beroea, since in fact Timothy must have gone with Paul to Athens and was then sent back to Thessalonica. Luke's story as a whole, however, follows a certain pattern, which Luke himself indicates by saying that Paul entered the synagogue in Thessalonica "as he usually did" (Acts 17:2). According to Luke, he did so in Philippi as well (16:13), in Beroea (17:10), in Corinth (18:4), and in Ephesus (18:19; 19:9). In all these places Paul achieved some success but was always rejected by the Jewish leaders, after which he turned to the Greeks. He was then denounced by the Jews before the local or the Roman authorities but was never sentenced, and he finally left the city in question. What Luke tells about Thessalonica is the story of how it always went in this area. To what degree can this be corroborated by Paul's own letters?

According to Luke, Paul's stay in Thessalonica lasted for three "sabbaths" only. The Greeks of those times did not yet have the week as a unit of seven days, and therefore also had no word for it. Luke, as well as other early Christian writers, uses the Hebrew term "sabbath" in the sense of either every seventh day or of a week. Although Luke speaks only of three "sabbaths" on which Paul argued in the synagogue, no reader would think of a period much longer than three weeks. In Phil 4:16, however, Paul thanks the Philippians for having sent him aid *twice* while he had been in Thessalonica. Therefore, he must have been there for a longer time, in any case for more than three weeks. Here again we have to question a detail in Luke's story.

1. Cf. the note under "subscriptio" in Nestle-Aland, 26th ed., 538.
2. Contra esp. G. Lüdemann's chronology in *Paul: Apostle to the Gentiles* (Philadelphia: Fortress, 1984). The questions below have been treated by many exegetes in different contexts. I shall give the reasons for my own view without always indicating to whom I am indebted. For a survey of recent scholarship, see R. F. Collins, *Studies on the First Letter to the Thessalonians* (BETL 66; Leuven: University Press–Uitgeverij Peeters, 1984) 3–75.

That a story follows a certain pattern is not in itself an argument that what it tells did not actually happen. Even life follows certain patterns. But an author may take some features from a pattern where there is no information by assuming that things always went the way they usually did. That may be the case when Luke says that Paul, "as he usually did," also in Thessalonica went to the synagogue. Acts 17:1, in fact, is the only mention we have of a synagogue in Thessalonica at that time. Archaeology has until now provided only *six* pieces of Jewish origin, among them a remarkable inscription of a Samaritan synagogue of the fourth century A.D.[3] In general, archaeological evidence for Jews in Macedonia in those days is quite rare compared with other regions.[4] That may depend more on archaeological conditions in the area than on the historical situation of the time. But even the famous passage from Philo's *Embassy to Gaius* (281), where he tries to show how widespread Judaism was at the time, counts Macedonia only in general among other provinces, not Thessalonica specifically, as he does Corinth. So neither archaeology nor ancient authors give support to Luke's mention of a synagogue or a Jewish community in Thessalonica in Paul's time. However, neither do they contradict it.

Paul, however, addresses his readers as people who "turned to God from idols" (1 Thess 1:9) and who have suffered the same things from their countrymen as the churches in Judea did from the Jews (2:14). Thus, no reader of this letter would think of former Jews among the Thessalonians if they had not been so informed by Luke. Paul sees them as former pagans who converted to his proclamation of Jesus, the Son of God, whom God had raised from the dead (1:10). If there had been Jews among them, he could never have said that only recently they had begun "to serve the living and true God" (1:9). That Paul nowhere in this letter quotes the OT is of minor importance: we do find allusions to it, and Paul's language here, as elsewhere in his letters, is the language of the Jewish Greek tradition.[5]

If we take 1 Thess 1:9–10 as a summary of Paul's initial preaching in Thessalonica, he proclaimed the living and true God, who raised Jesus, his

3. Even in recent publications, only one gravestone is mentioned: *CII* 1.693, that of "Abrameos and his wife Theodote." In the "Prolegomenon" to the reprint of *CII* 1 (New York: KTAV, 1975) 75–76, B. Lifshitz added "two sarcophagi with the symbols of the menorah" (693b); a tomb with an inscription at its marble door, "Beniames also called Dometios" (693c); and an inscription with the dedication "To God the Most High according to the command," followed by the letters ΙΟΥΕΣ (693d), which have "been interpreted by the first editors as an attempt to transliterate the name of Yahve." In no case is a date given. *CII* 1.693a (pp. 70–75) is a bilingual (Greek and Samaritan) inscription that has parallels in Samaritan inscriptions in Israel, especially that of ᾿Imwās; see F. Hüttenmeister and G. Reeg, *Die antiken Synagogen in Israel, Teil 2: Die samaritanischen Synagogen* (Wiesbaden: Dr. Ludwig Reichert Verlag, 1977) 603–9.

4. But see the inscription of the synagogue at Stobi *CII* 1.694 of the third century and the two inscriptions from Beroea *CII* 1.694a–b.

5. For example, in 1 Thess 4:9 Paul takes up the Greek concept of φιλαδελφία but interprets it with ἀγαπᾶν ἀλλήλους, which is close to the Old Testament command to love one's neighbor. Cf. also Abraham J. Malherbe, "Exhortation in First Thessalonians," *NovT* 25 (1983) 239–56, esp. 252.

son, from the dead, "who will deliver us from the wrath to come." In Acts 17:3, however, we read that Paul argued from the Scriptures "that it was necessary for the Christ [the Messiah] to suffer and to rise from the dead" and that he said, "This Jesus, whom I proclaim, is the Christ." So, according to Luke, Paul first gave a definition based on the Scriptures of what the Messiah had to be and then made it reasonable that Jesus would meet just that definition. For Paul, indeed, Jesus *is* the Christ as the one who died and was raised according to the Scriptures (cf. 1 Cor 15:3–4). Thus, Luke may summarize what he knew from Mark (8:31) and what he took over in his Gospel (Luke 9:22), "that the *Son of man* must suffer many things, and be rejected by the elders and the chief priests and the scribes, and be killed and after three days rise again." He may also have referred to Paul's summary of the gospel that the Messiah had to suffer and rise from the dead.

In Acts 17:7, however, the "jealous Jews" accused the Christians of saying "that there is another king, Jesus." What Luke wants to show is that the Jews twisted what Paul had "actually" said. According to Luke, Paul only spoke about Jesus. The Jews made it into a challenge for the Roman Empire. Thus, according to Luke, there was no reason for the authorities of the empire to suspect the Christians. The content of Paul's preaching, seen together with the Jewish accusations, belongs to the apologetic flow of Luke's story, in which he denounced the Jews to the Roman authorities as troublemakers in contrast to the Christians, who were loyal to the Roman Empire. The Romans of Luke's time knew of the trouble caused by the Jews, the arch of Titus being a reminder of it.

It is interesting, however, that Paul, after his departure from Antioch, not only tried to get to Rome (cf. Rom 1:13; 15:22) but also on his way to Rome, entered the main Roman centers around the Aegean Sea: Philippi, Thessalonica, Corinth, and Ephesus. In every place, he got into trouble with the Romans—even in Ephesus, where he was imprisoned according to a well-established consensus of many exegetes, Acts 19 notwithstanding. 1 Cor 15:32 and 2 Cor 1:8 (cf. 11:23) are the proof texts, and so Phil 1:3–3:1 (if not the whole of Paul's letter to the Philippians) and his letter to Philemon may have been written from the praetorium at Ephesus (Phil 1:3). According to Acts, however, Paul nowhere had serious trouble, so Luke's picture appears very optimistic. The reason again is the apologetic flow in the presentation of Acts: Christianity does not contradict the Roman Empire.

The only name Luke mentions in Acts 17:1–9 is Jason. There is a Jason among those who send their greetings in the last chapter of Romans, which was probably written from Corinth (Rom 16:21), along with Sosipater, whose name comes close to that of Sopater, the delegate from Beroea, according to Acts 20:4.[6] Paul calls both of them his kinsmen, Jewish Christians therefore as

6. For the names of persons, see W. H. Ollrog, *Paulus und seine Mitarbeiter* (WMANT 50; Neukirchen: Neukirchener Verlag, 1979).

he himself was. Of the names that Luke connects with Thessalonica in Acts 20:4, an Aristarchus is also mentioned in Acts 19:29 and 27:2; a person with the same name is among Paul's co-workers in Philemon 24 (cf. Col 4:10). A Secondus, however, can nowhere be found among the persons Paul mentions in his letters.

In his letter to the Thessalonians, Paul does not address any person by name. Perhaps he was not sure who of those he knew still remained in the congregation. He always calls his readers his "brothers and sisters"[7] or, simply, "you." Thus, we cannot be sure that the Jason of Acts 17:5, 9 is the Jewish Christian Jason of Rom 16:21, nor can we say that he and the So(si)pater of Acts 20:4 and Rom 16:21 prove that among the Thessalonian Christians there had been former Jews, which would be a contrast with the picture we get from Paul's letter that the Christians in Thessalonica were of Greek extraction, and not former Jews.

To sum up, all Luke tells us about the beginnings of the church in Thessalonica is that these beginnings had been as always—that, to repeat the story, Paul preached at the synagogue, had some success, was rejected by the Jews, and eventually left the city. The details of this story are confirmed in general by Paul's letters, but at some points his letters contradict the story. Obviously, Luke did have some information, but he modeled the story after what he thought Paul usually did. More important is what we get to know from Paul's own letter to the Thessalonians about these beginnings. Up to now we have only started to look at the evidence we have from this letter.[8]

THE BEGINNINGS AS THEY ARE
REFLECTED IN 1 THESSALONIANS

In none of his other letters does Paul remind his readers of their beginnings as frequently as in 1 Thessalonians. He refers to what they can "remember" (2:9), what they "know" (1:5; 2:1, 2, 5, 11; 3:3, 4; 4:2, 4, 5), what he had "told them beforehand" (3:4; 4:6), what they had "received" (2:13; 4:1), and what his "instructions" had been (4:2, 11). He reminds them of "the afflictions" they had to endure (1:6; 2:14; 3:3–4), and above all, again and again he refers to his initial preaching and to their response to it (1:5, 9; 2:1, 9–12;

7. It is worth mentioning that already in 1976 or earlier the late Gerhard Friedrich, in his commentary on 1 Thessalonians (NTD 8), changed his former translation of ἀδελφοί as "Brüder" to the German inclusive term "Geschwister."
8. As many others do, I take 2 Thessalonians to be deutero-Pauline, imitating 1 Thessalonians in its structure and wording but at a crucial point contradicting it in the statement that Paul never proclaimed, not even in a letter, the imminence of the *parousia* (2 Thess 2:2). I do not make use of 2 Thessalonians for my reconstruction of the beginnings of the church at Thessalonica; the author of a deutero-Pauline letter may have reacted to a situation elsewhere that looked similar to that of the Thessalonians.

3:3–4; 4:1–6, 10–12).[9] The letter indeed provides more and better information about the beginings than does Luke's account.

What does Paul want the Thessalonians to remember of his initial preaching? Among the other points, it is noticeable that Paul reminds them that he had worked as a "laborer" (1 Thess 2:9) so as not to burden them, as he says, when he preached the gospel in their city. Luke, too, knows about that, and it is from Acts 18:3 that we are informed about his profession as a "tent maker" or "saddler," or someone working with leather. Nowhere, however, does Luke show that Paul's laboring caused conflicts with his congregations. But in 1 Corinthians 9, Paul had to defend this as his and Barnabas's special way compared with the other apostles, who made use of their rights to be subsidized by the congregations (1 Cor 9:6; cf. 4:12). Obviously, Paul did not convince the Corinthians, for in 2 Cor 11:9 he had to raise the question of his financial independence again.

There are indeed early Christian traditions that explicitly understand proclaiming the gospel as "labor" that has to be paid for. So, in the mission discourse in the Synoptic Sayings Source Q, the missionaries are called "laborers" who deserve their wages or their food (Luke 10:2, 7 par.; Matt 9:37; 10:10).[10] Paul himself knows about such claims when he quotes a commandment of the Lord "that those who proclaim the gospel should get their living by the gospel" (1 Cor 9:14). In a different context, however, he denounces as "peddlers of the word of God" (2 Cor 2:17) those who make use of this privilege, which is not only an allowance but a commandment of the Lord; and in Phil 3:2, he calls his opponents "false laborers" (cf. 2 Cor 11:13).

In early Christianity, therefore, it was already a matter of dispute whether missionaries should get a salary or not, whether their work was to be esteemed as labor or not. Paul's claim was favored by his profession. Fishers like Peter (cf. 1 Cor 9:5) were not able to earn their living in Jerusalem, Corinth, or elsewhere, but Paul could take his bag, buy materials, and open a shop wherever he came, and then earn money and discuss the Christian faith with his customers.[11] That he received aid from the Philippians while he was in Thessalonica (Phil 4:16) and when in Corinth from Macedonia (2 Cor 11:9; does this aid include gifts from the Thessalonians?) does not contradict his general attempt not to burden his congregations and not to make the proclamation of the gospel an occasion for profit. He takes the Philippians' gift as a proof of their kindness "to share in his troubles" (Phil 4:14) at Thessalonica, at Corinth, and at Ephesus, from where he writes his letter to the Philippians.

His "troubles" lead us to another point that Paul wants the Thessalonians to remember, their own "troubles" or "afflictions." He says that he had foretold to them that "afflictions" would be necessary (1 Thess 3:4),[12] and indeed, they

---

9. I think indeed all the passages listed above refer to what Paul remembers about the beginnings of, and therefore suggests his readers can know about, his initial preaching.
10. Cf. 1 Tim 5:18; *Did.* 13:2.
11. Cf. R. Hock, *The Social Context of Paul's Ministry* (Philadelphia: Fortress, 1980).
12. A topic well known from apocalypticism since at least Dan 12:1.

had to suffer such afflictions and still do when Paul writes his letter (3:7). The matter of afflictions also goes back to the very beginning (1:6), and this may be the basis for Luke's story that the afflictions started with Paul's initial preaching of the gospel, when he had to hide and leave the city by night while Jason and the others were arrested (Acts 17:5–10). According to Luke, those afflictions were caused by the Jews. According to Paul, however, it was the readers' own kinsmen, in contrast with the Jews of Judea, who persecuted the Thessalonians (2:14). Luke's picture corresponds to the general apologetic flow in Acts that in every city, the Romans or their representatives declared Paul innocent and that everywhere the Jews were the troublemakers. But even from Luke's story we can learn that Paul had trouble in cities dominated by the Romans. Obviously, Luke, writing at the end of the first or at the beginning of the second century, wanted to show that in former times the Roman authorities had always welcomed Christianity and only recently, maybe under Domitian or Trajan, had changed their policies and persecuted the Christians.

Thus, when Paul wrote his letter, he knew that the persecution of the church at Thessalonica still continued. He was informed by Timothy, but he also received the good news that the Thessalonians held to their faith and love, and that they still remembered Paul and his preaching of the gospel (1 Thess 3:5–8). The faith that, to Paul's own surprise, they still had was "believing in the living and true God" (1:9); their love was the "brotherly love" that they "have been taught by God" (4:9).

Coming to the reconstruction of Paul's initial proclamation of the gospel at Thessalonica, we have already referred to 1 Thess 1:9–10—that the Thessalonians have "turned to God from the idols, to serve the living and true God, and to wait for his Son from heaven, whom he raised from the dead, Jesus who delivers us from the wrath to come." According to this summary, Paul's proclamation consisted in the first place of preaching the one living and true God in contrast with the idols of the pagan world, who therefore are dead and false idols. This topic went back to the Jewish heritage, where the one God, creator of heaven and earth, was opposed to the idols. Thus, it was not a newly revealed god whom Paul proclaimed, nor had he introduced a "young" god in contrast with the old one or old ones, but the same God of old of the Jewish religion. That God, however, was identified in a new way as the one who had raised his son Jesus from the dead. So Jesus, according to Paul, was neither a new god nor the young god, but the son of the living God, himself living as the one raised from the dead. For the Thessalonians, former pagans, however, the god whom Paul proclaimed must have appeared as a new god who had raised his son Jesus from the dead.

Throughout Paul's letters it remains unclear how exactly one should see the relation between God and the Son, and during the following centuries the early church had to solve the question how one could proclaim one God *and* Jesus, but not proclaim Jesus as a secondary or second god and still hold on to the heritage of Jewish as well as Hellenistic monotheism. This question led to the distinctions of the early councils, that were challenged by Gnosticism with its claim that Jesus had revealed a new god, hitherto unknown—a god who was no longer seen as the creator of the heaven as well as of this world. Orthodoxy, or what came to be acknowledged as orthodoxy, tried to define itself in terms of Greek philosophy as a monotheism, declaring Father, Son, and Holy Spirit as one and the same God. The orthodox may have mixed up church politics with theology, but their fundamental question remained the relation between the one God and the Son[13] (and the Holy Spirit).

The Son is the one awaited "from heaven . . . who delivers us from the wrath to come" (1 Thess 1:10). Part of Paul's proclamation, therefore, had been "the wrath to come," God's final judgment, the annihilation of sin and death. God *is* an "avenger" (4:6). This eschatological perspective of Paul's theology may not be neglected.[14] As God had vindicated his son Jesus, so Jesus will deliver the believers from the coming wrath. Therefore, the eschatological "coming" of Jesus before the wrath of God, his παρουσία, had been part of Paul's initial preaching in Thessalonica. He refers to it throughout the letter (1 Thess 2:19; 3:13; 4:15; 5:23).

In the meantime, however, some of the members of the congregation had died, perhaps due to the "afflictions" they had to suffer. Thus, Paul had to answer questions about what happens to those who had died before Christ's παρουσία (1 Thess 4:13–18). According to Paul, there was to be no difference between those who were still alive and those who had died: all believers would always be with the Lord Jesus, whom God had raised from the dead (4:18). The "times and seasons" (5:1) of Jesus' coming need no further instructions, Paul says, but he nevertheless reminds his readers of what they must know, "that the day of the Lord will be like a thief in the night" (5:2). This is a widespread motif in early Christian eschatology, used for different purposes.[15]

Readers who have access to Paul's later letters may be surprised that in 1 Thessalonians Paul mentions the expiatory effect of Jesus' death only once, toward the end of the letter (5:10), revealing that Paul presupposed that this was something his readers knew. Thus, Jesus' expiatory death must also have belonged to his initial preaching, as it did in Corinth, according to what Paul repeats as the gospel he preached there from the beginning (1 Cor 15:1–8). It is not part of his summary in 1 Thess 1:9–10, but that can be explained as being due to the position of this passage in the letter. These verses belong to the *prooemium;* at the same place in his first letter to the Corinthians, Paul also refers to the final revelation of Jesus, not to his death and resurrection (1:7–8). In another summary of the faith where the concept of expiation is missing, 1 Thess 4:14, Paul's point is "life and death." More important is that

13. Cf. the formula of 1 Cor 8:6, with its parallel sentences on the one God and the one Lord.
14. Cf. E. Brandenburger, "Gericht Gottes III: Neues Testament," *TRE* 12. 469–83, esp. 475–78.
15. See W. Harnisch, *Eschatologische Existenz* (FRLANT 110; Göttingen: Vandenhoeck & Ruprecht, 1983) 84–116.

in the repetition of this section, Paul mentions Jesus' death "for us" (5:10). That Jesus died "for us," "instead of us," or "for our sins" is the condition of our deliverance (1:10) from the coming judgment. So, what Paul in 1 Cor 15:1–8 summarizes as the essential and initial gospel can also be found in his letter to the Thessalonians.

Paul's initial preaching had also included ethics.[16] In 1 Thess 4:1 he reminds his readers of what they have received from him regarding "how you ought to live and please God" (cf. 4:6). The Greek text, with the definite article and the infinitive, sounds like the headline of a topos that Paul wants them to remember as part of his preaching—comparable to the headlines in ancient ethical teaching. In what follows, Paul summarizes as "sanctification" what had been the essence of his instructions (4:2–12). His concept of sanctification, however, is not that the readers have to aim for it; it is their stance already, and he simply wants them "to do so more and more" (4:1, 10). Thus, it is a progress as well as their stance.

As elsewhere, especially in catalogs of vices,[17] Paul starts with the topic "fornication" (1 Thess 4:3). The opposed moral value is given in the next sentence (4:4), which is rendered, not only in the RSV but also in many translations, including German, as "that each one of you know *how to take a wife for himself* in holiness and honor" (my emphasis). A footnote gives this as an alternative for the italics: "how to control his own body." This alternative is not based on a variant in the transmission of the text; there is no doubt about the crucial word in this case, σκεῦος in all the manuscripts. The dictionaries show that this word has to be translated "vessel."[18]

The question of how Paul wanted his readers to *understand* this metaphor has been discussed since his earliest interpreters; some say "wife" and others, "body."[19] Those who choose "wife" take Paul as addressing the male members of the congregation only. This seems unlikely, as 1 Corinthians 7 shows, where he also deals with "fornication" (cf. 1 Cor 6:18; 7:2). Paul had to answer a question of the Corinthians concerning sexual relations between men and women. They obviously had wanted him to agree that "it is well for a man not to touch a woman" (7:1). Thus, it had been a question about men's relations to women only. The Greek words in this case are ἄνθρωπος and γυνή. Paul, however, gives strictly parallel sentences for man (ἀνήρ) and woman (γυνή), respectively (7:2–5; cf. 7:10–16), and makes the plural ἄνθρωποι an inclusive term for both genders: "I wish that all men [men and women] were

16. On the following, see especially F. Laub, *Eschatologische Verkündigung und Lebensgestaltung nach Paulus* (BU 10; Regensburg: Verlag Friedrich Pustet, 1973); Malherbe, "Exhortation."
17. Cf. 1 Cor 6:9; Gal 5:19, etc.
18. In a similar case, 1 Cor 11:10, the RSV has "veil," but a footnote informs the reader: "Greek *authority* (the veil being a symbol of this)." That is more information than what the RSV provides in the case of 1 Thess 4:4.
19. For the older literature, see E. von Dobschütz, *Die Thessalonicher-Briefe* (KEK 10; 7th ed.; Göttingen: Vandenhoeck & Ruprecht, 1909) 163–67.

as I myself am" (7:7)—that is, he wants all to live as ascetics, as he did. For
Paul, then, in questions of sexual ethics, as well as ethics in general, it is not
only the man who is addressed, but the woman as well. 1 Corinthians 7 is one
example of how he understood that there is "neither male nor female" in the
congregation (cf. Gal 3:28); both genders, not only the men, are equally subjects of ethical admonitions.[20]

Whence, then, the old tradition of interpreting σκεῦος in 1 Thess 4:4 as
"wife"? In the early church it goes back to traditions in which the *you* of the
ethical admonitions was taken as only the free male person who had to be restricted in his possibilities of behavior outside the "house," whereas, as the
Pastoral Epistles show, women had their duties and responsibilities inside the
"house" only and were subordinate to their husbands. This social structure of
the house, the household, the family was the basic condition of ethics in the
OT as well as in Greek tradition, where books "on economy" or on "how to run
the household" have been part of practical philosophy.[21] And the household
has been the basic social structure of all preindustrial societies; it still survives
in rudimentary forms in our day wherever the household is still the place of
economics (for example, at farms and shops of craftspeople). Surprisingly,
Paul in 1 Corinthians 7 saw women as having the same rights as their husbands at the very basic level of matrimony, which is the elementary presuppo-
sition of a "house" that includes parents, children, and servants. Thus, in view
of 1 Corinthians 7, nothing demands an understanding of "vessel" in 1 Thess
4:4 as the "wife" of the male member of the congregation, because it is not
only the male who is addressed in the admonition.

The modern variant of the earlier interpretation is based on two arguments.
The first is 1 Pet 3:7, where the husbands in such a "household code" are
admonished to get together with their wives, honoring them, because the
wives are heirs of the grace of life even though they are the "weaker vessels."
This phrase, however, presupposes the opposition of "stronger vessels,"
namely, the males. Therefore, the use of the word *vessel* in 1 Pet 3:7 can by
no means prove that *vessel* in general, and therefore also in 1 Thess 4:4, has to
be a term for "wife," since even in 1 Pet 3:7, it is an inclusive term for men
and women.

More influential has been an argument from the history of religion, namely,
that Paul's usage of the term *vessel* is said to follow a common Hebrew phrase

20. Cf. M. McGehee, "A Rejoinder to Two Recent Studies Dealing with 1 Thess 4:4," *CBQ* 51
(1989) 82–89. He argues against Collins, *Studies on the First Letter*, 299–325, and O. L.
Yarbrough, *Not Like the Gentiles: Marriage Rules in the Letters of Paul* (SBLDS 80; Atlanta:
Scholars, 1985). Abraham J. Malherbe, however, though referring to Yarbrough (*Paul and the
Thessalonians* [Philadelphia: Fortress, 1987] 51), has *not* accepted this view (against McGehee,
p. 82, n. 3).

21. See the most recent study by D. L. Balch, "Household Codes," *Greco-Roman Literature and
the New Testament: Selected Forms and Genres* (ed. D. E. Aune; SBLSBS 21; Atlanta: Scholars,
1988) 25–50.

in which "women" in general, and not only "wives" are seen as "vessels."[22] Following a recent interpreter, who, though reluctantly, prefers "wife" to "body," I think the rare Rabbinic texts quoted in favor of this view need not be repeated here.[23] They obviously tend to pornography, taking the vagina as the vessel for the man, and thereby take women in general, not only wives, as only vessels.

Again, it seems unlikely that Paul, who favors sexual asceticism (1 Cor 7:7), should follow male presuppositions of this kind, making the women in his congregations and his female co-workers subject to male discrimination. Thus, with his warning against fornication, as well as with his other admonitions, Paul does not address only the male members of the Thessalonian congregation.

Neither 1 Thessalonians nor the parallel account in Acts gives us as much information about the Thessalonians as we have especially for the Corinthians. But if Gal 3:28 can be taken as a basic formula for the communities founded by Paul, any understanding of 1 Thess 4:4 in the sense of "to take a wife for himself" is excluded. In Gal 3:28, it is not only the differences between Jews and Greeks and between slaves and free people that are denied in the congregations but also the differences between males and females; all of these distinctions, according to the ancient understanding, are "by nature."[24] The alternative in the RSV, "to control his [or her] own body," must be considered correct, which is supported by 2 Cor 4:7, where "vessel" is the body in general, neither male nor female.

The warnings against "fornication" in the Pauline texts are often connected with warnings against "idolatry."[25] This is not explicitly the case here in 1 Thess 4:1–8. 1 Thess 4:5, however, refers to the gentiles "who do not know God"; they serve the idols. The summary in 1:9–10 shows that the Thessalonians had moved away from idolatry, and their afflictions had been caused by their conversion from the idols to the living God. But different from the situation in Corinth (cf. 1 Corinthians 8–10), idolatry is no longer a problem for the Thessalonians.

The instruction that follows in 1 Thess 4:6 is concerned with "greediness," a topic well known from comparable passages in other Pauline letters.[26] As Paul had introduced the whole as part of what his readers knew from his initial preaching, he now, at the end, repeats that this is what he said and witnessed in the beginning (4:6). That God is an "avenger" calls to mind the "wrath to come" of the summary in 1:9–10. "Sanctification" had been the main issue of his proclaiming the gospel (4:7), corresponding to the Holy Spirit given to all

22. See C. Maurer, "σκεῦος," TDNT 7. 361–62, 365–67.
23. T. Holtz, Der erste Brief an die Thessalonicher (EKK 13; Zürich: Benzinger; Neukirchen: Neukirchener Verlag, 1986) 157.
24. Cf. Dieter Lührmann, "Wo man nicht mehr Sklave oder Freier ist," WD 13 (1975) 53–83.
25. Cf., for example, 1 Cor 6:9.
26. Cf., for example, 1 Cor 5:10.

of them (4:8). So again, sanctification is not what they have to aim for, but what they already have.

The passage 1 Thess 4:3–8 has its closest parallels in the catalogs of vices that we find throughout Paul's letters, describing behavior inappropriate to faith. Thus, 4:9–10a in turn has its parallels in the catalogs of virtues, where "love" is not only mentioned first, but is the origin and the principle of all other kinds of behavior in accordance with faith. Elsewhere Paul quotes this concept as the command of the Hebrew Bible to love one's neighbor as oneself from Lev 19:18 (cf. Gal 5:14; Rom 13:9). Here, however, he uses the Greek term φιλαδελφία (cf. Rom 12:10), meaning "to love (ἀγαπᾶν) one another."[27] The Greek term ἀγαπᾶν instead of φιλεῖν shows that Paul has in mind Lev 19:18, the "neighbors" being the "brothers and sisters," their fellow Christians in Macedonia, those who are of the "household of faith" according to Gal 5:10. Such an interpretation of Lev 19:18, however, different from the meaning of the original, does not recognize a restriction on whom to love; 3:12 shows that the consequence would not be to hate those outside the "household of faith," but love should be "love to one another *and to all people*" (my emphasis).

All these instructions are not seen as additions to Paul's initial preaching; they had been part of it. They are only to remind the readers of the beginnings, and as 1 Thess 4:1–2 makes clear, in 4:10b–12 Paul only repeats that he wants his readers "to abound more and more" in what they are already doing. The word of God that he had brought to them proved itself not to be empty (cf. 2:1) but enabled them to live in times of affliction.

CONCLUSIONS

Luke's account shows how, according to his view, the beginnings in Thessalonica were the same as beginnings in every other city. An analysis of Paul's own letter to the Thessalonians, written immediately after these beginnings and itself still part of those beginnings, allows for a more vivid picture of what happened. In Luke's time there had been a Christian congregation in Thessalonica, as there had been elsewhere around the Aegean Sea. Paul, however, could not have been sure in his time about the future of the congregations he had founded. What happened subsequently, however, shows that indeed the word of God proclaimed by Paul in Thessalonica and elsewhere had not been "empty." Since A.D. 49 there has been a continuous history of the congregation in Thessalonica.

The analysis of 1 Thessalonians leads to some remarkable, if not surprising, results, at least for someone who has been trained in form criticism. The two summaries of the initial preaching of the gospel to which Paul draws his readers' attention (1:9–10 and 4:1–12) do not fit clearly into the picture that

27. See note 5 above.

form criticism postulated about the essentials of the kerygma. Although we can recognize the motif of expiation through Christ's death in 1 Thessalonians (5:10), the emphasis in 1:9–10 is on the proclamation of the "coming wrath" from which Jesus, the Son of God, will deliver the believers. Therefore, the imminent judgment and the παρουσία of the Son of God were at least within the horizon of Paul's preaching, if not a major feature of it.

The second surprise—and this is the more important result of the analysis—is that ethics had not been a second, and by no means a secondary, aspect of Paul's initial proclamation of the gospel. Form criticism has taught us that ethics became a topic in early Christian theology only after the delay of the παρουσία, when the believers had to accept the conditions of the existing world and no longer waited for its consummation. 1 Thess 4:1–12, however, shows that "how you ought to live and please God" had been part of Paul's initial preaching in Thessalonica. The imperatives of which he reminds his readers are not derived from an indicative, as it is in the somehow classical sentences in Gal 5:1 and 13. Paul does not admonish his Thessalonian readers on how they may live and please God; he only wants them to proceed in what they were already doing. So ethics is not the question of being delivered from the "wrath to come" but a question of pastoral care for a newly founded congregation that exists even into the present.

I need not repeat what one can read better in Abraham J. Malherbe's various essays and in his *Paul and the Thessalonians*, to which I merely wanted to add a short appendix on how it all began. His recent volume of collected essays,[28] as well as his expected commentary on this letter of Paul, will challenge some presuppositions of Paul's interpreters. My intention here is to give support to his views.

---

28. *Paul and the Popular Philosophers* (Minneapolis: Fortress, 1989).

PART THREE
_____

HELLENISTIC ANTHROPOLOGY

PAUL ON THE USE AND
ABUSE OF REASON

What do Paul's letters have to say about reason? On the one hand, this question might seem misguided. After all, the apostle was not a philosopher, and he nowhere explicitly discusses reason. Even incidental uses of terms for reason and reasoning are infrequent.[1] On the other hand, in spite of these facts, certain texts from Paul's letters have had as much impact on Western views about the functions and limits of reason as the writings of Plato and Aristotle.

The oppositions that the thinkers of the Enlightenment used against traditional Christianity—reason versus faith, revelation, grace, authority, and tradition—had already been defined by the intellectual tradition of the medieval West following Augustine. The tradition agreed that faith preceded reason, but that reasoning had a significant role to play, both apart from faith and in the maturation of faith. Texts from Romans 1 and 2, which supposedly taught natural revelation or natural theology, were used to support the limited value of "natural reason" in the religious sphere.[2] Texts from 1 Corinthians 1–4 were used to legitimate the subordination of reason to faith, revelation, authority, and tradition. Augustine had appealed to Romans 1 in claiming that

I would like to thank Katherine Eldred and my colleagues Wendell Dietrich, Susan Harvey, and John G. Milhaven for reading this chapter and making valuable suggestions. I am also indebted to Anne Hart and the members of my seminar on "Early Christian Psychagogy" for being lively partners in discussion.

1. Terms for reasoning are, however, more frequent than the literature on Paul would suggest. *Reason*, for example, is missing from most Bible dictionaries and reference works. Paul does not use λόγος as "reason," but this is understandable, since there is hardly a context in his letters for such an abstract and quasi-metaphysical concept. Interpreters also fail to realize that its use is even infrequent in some philosophers and moralists, for whom the more concrete λογισμός and λογίζεσθαι are more apt. The following are some texts where the meanings "reason," "reasoning," or "faculty or ability to deliberate" are appropriate: λογισμός (2 Cor 10:4; Rom 2:15), διαλογισμός (Rom 1:21; 14:1), λογίζεσθαι (1 Cor 13:11; 2 Cor 3:5; 10:2, 7; Phil 4:8), λογικός (Rom 12:1), νοῦς (Rom 1:28; 7:23, 25; 12:2; 14:5; 1 Cor 14:4, 15, 19; Phil 4:7; 2 Thess 2:2), φρήν (1 Cor 14:20), φρόνιμος (Rom 11:25; 12:16; 1 Cor 4:10; 10:15; 2 Cor 11:19), and φρονεῖν (Rom 12:3, 16; 14:6; 15:15; 1 Cor 13:11; 2 Cor 13:11; Phil 2:2, 5; 3:15, 19; 4:2, 10).

2. I will not treat the texts from Romans due to limitations of space and because I believe that they concern not human nature but the state of the Gentile peoples.

the faculty of reason had been distorted, although by no means destroyed, in the Fall. I want to suggest that these formulations are anachronistic as readings for these texts. They do not fit Paul in his Hellenistic context.

There are several compelling reasons for attempting to reassess the traditional understandings of what Paul says about intellect and rationality. One is the new standpoint toward reason apparent in recent philosophy. As one after another of the twentieth-century attempts to "naturalize" reason have failed, it has become clear that the Enlightenment oppositions between reason and faith, tradition, and authority are either misleading or simply wrong.[3] Philosophy itself, to a large extent, has repudiated the view of reason as a fortress (like God) in which one could be secure from the vulnerability of human finitude.[4] Reason is not a faculty or capacity that can make itself free from cultural and historical context. Talk of the true and false, the right and wrong, make sense only within the context of particular human traditions, even if those traditions can also be criticized.[5] Thus, the tendency is to talk about reason and characterize rationality in much more modest ways than has been traditional. In the past, conceptions of faith and reason that carried highly anachronistic metaphysical programs with them have often been read into the Pauline texts. My subject, then, concerns Paul's view of the value and proper functions of valid arguments, providing reasons, and justifications of belief. Admittedly, our sources make this task difficult, since they are occasional pieces (letters) and preclude comprehensive and systematic discussion of topics.[6]

Another stimulus toward reassessing Paul on reason is provided by a remarkable shift in the understanding of some central aspects of his thought in recent scholarship. Until recently, there has been a broad consensus that Paul's central message was about the saving effects of faith. A person is justified or made righteous before God by an act of believing. This "central message" is sometimes treated as a quasi-epistemological doctrine: Paul was advocating the religious centrality and value of belief where there is no good evidence to justify the belief. Pauline texts were used to support various degrees and kinds of fideism. Now, however, there is a growing consensus, supported by extremely weighty arguments, against this reading of Paul. It has been shown that the expression πίστις χριστοῦ does not mean "faith in

---

3. Hilary Putnam, "Why Reason Cannot Be Naturalized," *Synthese* 52 (1982) 305–27; Putnam, *Reason, Truth and History* (New York: Cambridge University Press, 1982).
4. This repudiation has not gone far enough for some. For example: Richard Rorty, *Philosophy and the Mirror of Nature* (Princeton: Princeton University Press, 1979).
5. In addition to Putnam, Rorty, and others, another to argue strongly is Alasdair MacIntyre: *After Virtue* (2d ed. with postscript; Notre Dame, IN: Notre Dame University Press, 1984); and *Whose Justice? Which Rationality?* (Notre Dame, IN: Notre Dame University Press, 1988).
6. Stanley K. Stowers, *Letter Writing in Greco-Roman Antiquity* (Library of Early Christianity 5; Philadelphia: Westminster, 1986); Abraham J. Malherbe, *Ancient Epistolary Theorists* (SBS 19; Atlanta: Scholars, 1988). On the inappropriateness of systematic discussions and technical matters, see Ps.-Demetrius *On Style* 230–31.

Christ" but rather the "faith of Christ" or the "faithfulness of Christ."[7] This latter understanding robs the older position of virtually all of its textual evidence. Paul certainly assumed that the followers of Christ ought to believe in Christ and in God, but he made no epistemological point that legitimated irrational belief in regard to religious matters.

Yet another stimulus comes from advances in placing Paul within his proper Greco-Roman social and cultural context. More than anyone else, Abraham J. Malherbe, whom we justly honor in this volume, has demonstrated that Paul moved and thought in the world of Hellenistic philosophers and moralists. Paul certainly belongs to other cultural environments as well, but the central significance of the popular philosophical context can no longer be doubted. This means that the interpreter can sidestep the anachronistic faith/reason formulations of later Christianity and compare Paul to contemporary figures for whom reason was of central importance.

A CRITIQUE OF EPISTEMIC VICES
IN 1 CORINTHIANS 1–4

The classic texts where Paul supposedly subordinates reason to faith and the authority of revelation are in 1 Corinthians 1–4. The discussion in 1:18–2:5 revolves around the antithesis between the wisdom of God and the wisdom of the world. It is easy to understand how a superficial reading could lead one to conclude that Paul was subordinating reason to revelation and, in general, denigrating the value of human reasoning and rationality. The most important text for this view is 1:18–25:

> For the word of the cross is folly to those who are perishing, but to us who are being saved it is the power of God. For it is written,
>
> "I will destroy the wisdom of the wise,
> and the cleverness of the clever I will thwart."
>
> Where is the wise man? Where is the scribe? Where is the debater of this age? Has not God made foolish the wisdom of the world? For since, in the wisdom of God, the world did not know God through wisdom, it pleased God through the folly of what we preach to save those who believe. For Jews demand signs and Greeks seek wisdom, but we preach Christ crucified, a stumbling block to Jews and folly to Gentiles, but to those who are called, both Jews and Greeks, Christ the power of God and the wisdom of God. For the foolishness of God is wiser than men, and the weakness of God is stronger than men. (RSV)

Richard Popkin's comment from "Fideism" in *The Encyclopedia of Philosophy*

---

7. For arguments and bibliography, see Richard Hays, *The Faith of Jesus Christ* (SBLDS 56; Chico, CA: Scholars, 1983) 157–92. Also, recently, Sam K. Williams, "Again *Pistis Christou*," *CBQ* 49 (1987) 431–47; Morna D. Hooker, "*Pistis Christou*," *NTS* 35 (1989) 321–42.

is a rather tyical understanding of Paul's thought in 1 Corinthians: "Starting with St. Paul's contention that the central doctrine of Christianity was non-sensical by Greek philosophical standards and with Tertullian's announcement *credo quia absurdum* (I believe that which is absurd), there have been theologians who have insisted that religious truths are contrary to those which might be supported or justified by reasonable evidence and that rational activities are not proper means to arrive at such truths."[8] Calvin, just to mention one influential commentator, building on Augustine, used 1 Corinthians 1–2 to depict humans as beings with severe damage to their capacities for knowledge due to the Fall.[9]

There is no clear consensus among the modern commentators about exactly what Paul is doing in 1 Corinthians 1–4.[10] This lack of consensus, I believe, is largely due to the common approach whereby interpreters begin asking the highly speculative question of who the opponents were or what the theologies were of the parties Paul was supposedly arguing against, and then proceed to construct a reading over against this image. Such mirror reading not only begs all kinds of questions but also is completely unnecessary. Paul explains exactly what he is doing in terminology from Hellenistic rhetoric and moral instruction in 4:6, 14.

In 1 Cor 4:14, Paul says, "I am not writing these things to shame you but to admonish you as my beloved children." As Paul indicates, 1:10–4:16 is packed with typical features of admonition through which he tries to criticize effectively the Corinthians and yet avoid the harsher forms of blame that might produce negative results.[11] The specific criticism has two main aspects: First, the Corinthians have broken into factions (or perhaps only strife) over their favorite teachers (1:10–13) and the wisdom of their teachings (implied in 1:17). Second, Paul relates this factionalism to false attitudes and beliefs about wisdom and knowledge (1:17–3:4). The latter seem to be the cause of the former, although Paul does not fully clarify the relationship between the two.[12]

In 1 Cor 4:6, Paul reveals one of the techniques of admonition that he has been using and gives his reasons for using it: "With regard to these things, brethren, I have used veiled allusion pertaining to myself and Apollos for your sake, so that you might learn, 'not to go beyond what is written,' so that you might not be puffed up with arrogance favoring one person and opposing

---

8. Paul Edwards (ed.), *The Encyclopedia of Philosophy* (New York: Macmillan and the Free Press, 1967) 3. 201.

9. *Commentary on First Corinthians*, on chap. 1 and 2; see esp. on 1:21.

10. The exegetical literature is vast. Useful guides are John C. Hurd, *The Origin of 1 Corinthians* (2d ed.; Macon, GA: Mercer University Press, 1983); and Hans Conzelmann, *1 Corinthians* (Hermeneia; Philadelphia: Fortress, 1975). See also John Fitzgerald, *Cracks in an Earthen Vessel* (SBLDS 99; Atlanta: Scholars, 1988) 117–48.

11. On admonition in letters, see Stowers, *Letter Writing*, 125–32.

12. For an excellent discussion of the argument and rhetoric in 1 Corinthians 1–4 see Fitzgerald, *Cracks in an Earthen Vessel*, 117–48.

STANLEY K. STOWERS

257

another."[13] Veiled or covert allusion (λόγος ἐσχηματισμένος; cf. μετασχη-
ματίζειν in 4:6) was a well-known and widely discussed technique among
rhetoricians, Sophists, and philosophers.[14] As an example of its proper use,
Ps.-Demetrius (Eloc. 288) gives the example of Plato's (Phaedo 59c) criticizing
Aristippus and Cleombrotus by indirectly comparing their actions to the
actions of others and thus avoiding λοιδορία (abuse), which would have been
unproductively harsh. Such allusion proves particularly effective against the
haughty pride of kings and tyrants (Eloc. 289). It is perhaps not a coincidence
that Paul follows with these ironic exclamations: "Already you are filled!
Already you have become rich! Without us you have become kings! And
would that you did reign, so that we might share the rule with you!" Rhetoricians noted that veiled allusion was closely associated with irony.[15] The technique was also associated with admonition (νουθεσία) and the use of positive
contrastive models.[16] That admonition was gentle criticism that used indirection to soften the censure was almost a cliché in antiquity.[17]

Benjamin Fiore has persuasively argued that the ταῦτα in 1 Cor 4:6 refers
back to all of 1:10–4:5.[18] In three sections, Paul contrasts his own behavior
while working with the Corinthians with their current behavior and attitudes
(1:18–2:5; 2:6–3:4; 3:5–4:5).[19] Not only were the Corinthians not chosen
because of their worldly stature (1:26–31), but also Paul did not use "worldly
wisdom" (2:1–5). He had spiritual wisdom and teachings when he was with
the Corinthians, but they were too fleshly and immature for it (3:1–4). In contrast to the conceit and strife of the Corinthians, Paul and Apollos had
cooperated in their work, considering themselves servants of God and attributing the growth of the community to him rather than to themselves (3:5–9).
Paul's admonition becomes less and less allusive until he becomes completely
explicit in 4:6. "Not to go beyond what is written" is an adage that plays upon
the practice of students learning to write letters of the alphabet by tracing
models provided by the teacher.[20] Paul thus recommends Apollos and himself
as models of constructive cooperation in the community. In 4:16 he explicitly
calls for imitation. The ultimate purpose of all this exhortation and admonition is to counter the conceit that has caused the Corinthians to split into warring factions (4:6c).

But what is this false wisdom that is the root of the problem? Whereas
traditional interpreters tended to understand wisdom in a general way as
human reason, recent critical scholars have looked for some particular histori-

---

13. My translation.
14. Benjamin Fiore, "Covert Allusion in I Cor 1–4," CBQ 47 (1985) 85–98.
15. Quintilian Inst. 9.2.65; Dion. Hal. Rhet. 9.323.1; Fiore, "Covert Allusion," 90–91; Fitzgerald,
Cracks in an Earthen Vessel, 121.
16. Fitzgerald, Cracks in an Earthen Vessel, 120–22.
17. Stowers, Letter Writing, 126–27.
18. Fiore, "Covert Allusion," 93–94, 98.
19. Fiore, "Covert Allusion," 87–89, 94–96.
20. Persuasively argued by Fitzgerald, Cracks in an Earthen Vessel, 123–26.

cal problem such as Gnostic speculation, Jewish wisdom teachings, or even sophistic rhetoric. It seems clear that Paul is not referring to reasoning as such or to the faculty of reason, even in 1 Cor 1:18–25. At most, as the reference to Greeks and Jews might suggest (1:24), the opposition might be to certain traditions of rationality. Nevertheless, it is extremely difficult to detect any criticism of a particular kind of wisdom, and scholars have produced nearly endless speculations on the subject.[21] In fact, Paul seems to have no concern about countering the content of any particular teachings. Rather, his focus is entirely on wrong attitudes and behavior in relation to the pursuit of wisdom. This is perhaps why he uses such a vague and general term as *wisdom*. Wisdom as such, or its pursuit, is not condemned. In fact, there is a genuine wisdom from God (1:30; 2:6–3:4; 3:18). Paul attacks "worldly" and "fleshly" wisdom. This he defines by referring to aspects of the Corinthians' behavior in each of the three sections where he uses allusion.

The first section, 1 Cor 1:27–29, speaks of God's using what is weak in the world to shame the worldly-wise so that no human might boast before God. Opposed to this worldly-wise boasting is a wisdom and a boasting that is legitimate because the basis for both is acknowledged to be God himself (1:30–31). The conclusion of the second section reveals what Paul means by calling the Corinthians worldly and fleshly: "For while there is jealousy and strife among you, are you not of the flesh—for one says, 'I belong to Paul,' and another, 'I belong to Apollos'" (3:3–4). In the third section, the themes of boasting and division are related directly to the Corinthians' situation. There are those who think themselves wise according to this age (3:18) and who boast of men (3:21), but this belief is a kind of self-deception (3:18) that God has chosen to deflate (3:19–20). The Corinthians do not need to boast of humans, because Paul, Apollos, and Cephas are already present for them as gifts (3:22). Mention of these three is an unambiguous counter to the Corinthian division into factions over these teachers mentioned in 1:11–13.

Worldly and fleshly wisdom is certainly not reason and not a particular set of beliefs such as those one might find in a Hellenistic philosophy.[22] Rather, this false wisdom is any wisdom characterized by certain moral and epistemic vices. It is when the pursuit and use of knowledge is characterized by conceit, arrogance, and bragging.[23] In Paul's view, this conceit has led to another condition that is epistemologically, morally, and "religiously" unproductive: the breakdown of the community into opposing factions. The Corinthians have treated their teachers as if each represented yet another philosophical school competing to outdo all others. Paul will suggest throughout 1 Corinthians that

21. For the major issues and some bibliography, see Gordon D. Fee, *The First Epistle to the Corinthians* (NTCNT; Grand Rapids, MI: Eerdmans, 1987) 64–65, esp. n. 79.
22. In the following section, I am in debt on several points to Paul W. Gooch, *Partial Knowledge: Philosophical Studies in Paul* (Notre Dame, IN: University of Notre Dame Press, 1987) 16–51.
23. Gooch, *Partial Knowledge*, 40–42.

certain cooperative virtues and a mutually enhancing life together are conditions for the attainment of knowledge and wisdom. In 5:1–13 and 6:1–11, he
mentions two cases that illustrate that the Corinthians lack practical wisdom as
a community; they have failed in crucial tests of community judgment.

Some aspects of Paul's critique are familiar. Both Paul and certain traditions in Greek philosophy treat these vices of conceit, arrogance, and contentiousness as patterns of deception and self-deception. The braggart (ὁ ἀλα-
ζών), the conceited person, and the arrogant person claim to know, or think
they know, what they really do not know. The classic example of treating such
self-deceit is, of course, Socrates: "the soul can receive no benefit from teachings offered to it until someone by refutation (ἐλέγχειν) brings the one who is
being refuted to shame, by removing the opinions that hinder the teachings
and thus purifying him and leading him to think that he knows only what he
really knows, and no more" (Plato Sophist 230c–d).[24] The goal is to rid students of the conceit of wisdom (δοξοσοφία [231b]) and "high and stubborn
opinions about themselves" (230b). Plato's Socrates also corrects that false
wisdom that is characterized by contentiousness. The students of Phaedrus
are difficult to get along with, since they are "wise in their own conceit instead
of truly wise" (Plato Phaedrus 275B).

Moralists from Paul's own era not only frequently refer to the example of
Socrates' admonition of conceit but also claim it for themselves as the starting
point for the guidance of souls. They connect conceit with unprofitable contentiousness. Plutarch says that Socrates reproved Sophists who were "full of
self-conceit, and loved unprofitable and contentious debates." By divine and
spiritual guidance, Socrates used reproof and freed them from conceit,
pretentiousness, and error (Plutarch Plat. Quaest. 999E). The chief obstacles
of training in a philosophical school are envy, malice, and hostility (Plutarch
Aud. 39D). Students tend to be reckless and contentious lovers of disputation
rather than lovers of the truth. Therefore, it is "even more necessary to take
the wind of self-opinion and conceit out of the young, than to deflate wine-
skins, if you wish to fill them with something useful; otherwise, being full of
bombast and inflation, they have no room to receive it" (Aud. 39D; trans. Babbitt in LCL).

In the following passage, Plutarch warns against typical problems that block
the progress of the one who aspires to love wisdom:

> Most of all must we consider whether the spirit of contention and quarrelling
> over debatable questions has been put down, and whether we have ceased to
> equip ourselves with arguments, as with boxing-gloves or brass knuckles, with
> which to contend against one another, and to take more delight in scoring a hit
> or a knockout than in learning and imparting something. For reasonableness
> and mildness in such matters, and the ability to join in discussions without wran-
> gling, and to close them without anger, and to avoid a sort of arrogance over

24. The translations of Plato are my own.

success in argument and exasperation over defeat, are the marks of a man who is making adequate progress. (*Prof. Virt.* 80B–C; trans. Babbitt in LCL)

Not only do Paul and Plutarch share a similar association of conceit, false wisdom, and contentiousness but they also associate these with a lack of progress, however different their respective goals might be. The Corinthians are babies who have to be fed with milk rather than solid food (1 Cor 3:1–2). This immaturity is manifested in their jealousy and strife (3:3–4). For this reason, Paul could only give them basic instruction and nothing more advanced (2:14–3:3).

Although the parallels between 1 Corinthians 1–4 and the Hellenistic moralists are extensive, there are obviously important aspects of the discourse peculiar to Paul. He, like the Hellenistic moralists, employs techniques such as veiled allusion, irony, a hardship list, and general admonition to deflate the conceit of the Corinthians. Unlike the moralists, however, he stresses that God has acted in history through Jesus Christ as a kind of divine psychagogue to challenge conceit and pretension to wisdom. Like an ancient moralist admonishing others truly to open their minds, God shames the wise (1:27) and aims to eliminate arrogant boasting (1:29). "He catches the wise in their craftiness" (3:19). All of this is so that those who think they are wise may truly become wise (3:18). The problem with Jews and Greeks is that they have closed minds blinded by their own traditions of rationality. They dismiss the Cross as foolishness, because they already know what truth and wisdom are about (1:22–25).

John T. Fitzgerald has shown that the theme of foolishness in 1 Corinthians 1–4 reflects the influence of Hellenistic philosophy at various points. Here the motif of the righteous sufferer as the "foolish" wise one is particularly important.[25] Paul develops this motif 4:8–13 with the ironic list of hardships, but he already prepares for it in chapter 1 by stressing that his teachings are considered foolish by worldly standards. Hardship lists, which demonstrated the virtue and endurance of the philosopher in adversity, are important in the philosophical-ethical literature of the early empire. Because philosophy was a way of life in opposition to common conceptions of what is true and good, the wise might be considered fools and even abused for their virtue. Seneca writes, "Let some men think you even a fool. Allow any man who so desires to insult you and work you wrong; for if virtue dwells in you, you will suffer nothing" (*Ep.* 71.7). Paul depicts the Corinthians as if they described themselves by the Stoic paradoxes: "Only the wise man is rich" and "Only the wise man is king" (1 Cor 4:8).[26] In contrast, the apostles hunger and thirst; are ill-clad, buffeted, and homeless; work with their hands; and are reviled, slandered, and

---

25. Fitzgerald, *Cracks in an Earthen Vessel,* chap. 3, 4, esp. 100–103 on the "foolish wiseman."
26. On the Stoic paradoxes and their use by the Corinthians, see Stanley K. Stowers, "A 'Debate' over Freedom: I Corinthians 6:12–20," *Christian Teaching: Studies in Honor of LeMoine G. Lewis* (ed. Everett Ferguson; Abilene, TX: Abilene Christian University, 1981) 59–71, esp. 62–67; Fitzgerald, *Cracks in an Earthen Vessel,* 135–43.

persecuted (4:11–13). The Corinthians are honored, strong, and wise (φρόνιμοι), but the apostles are dishonored, weak, and fools for Christ's sake (4:10).
Although Paul is using the same rhetorical device and the same motifs as the
philosophers, there is a different attitude toward reason implied. The philosophers employed hardship lists to illustrate the invincibility of their reason.[27]
Nothing could affect their inner tranquility and virtue. Paul, in contrast, uses
hardship lists to show that he and other Christians are truly fragile and vulnerable. Any power that they do have to succeed and endure such hardships
comes from God and not an inner bulwark. They succeed in spite of human
vulnerability rather than by overcoming it. In fact, it is the Corinthians who
Paul suggests are like the philosophers.

Far from opposing faith and tradition to reason, 1 Cor 1:18–4:21 criticizes a
lack of openness to that which is new and different, as well as epistemic vices
such as conceit and bragging. The latter are not only matters of self-deception
but also create conditions in the community that make difficult the pursuit of
knowledge and the exercise of practical reason.

Before treating other texts that bear upon Paul's understanding of reason, I
will deal with a possible objection to my reading of 1 Corinthians 1–4. In
2:6–3:4, Paul has been widely understood to say that all knowledge of God and
"the things of God" can only come by revelation in which human reason or
wisdom plays no part. Thus, religious propositions and beliefs can only appear
as foolishness to human reason. What Paul actually says is quite different.
For the mature, Paul and his fellow workers do have a secret and hidden wisdom "which God decreed before the ages for our glorification" (2:7). The
authorities responsible for crucifying Jesus did not understand this wisdom
(2:6, 8). This plan of God for the world's future was revealed to Paul by the
Spirit. Only those who possess the Spirit can receive such revelations from it
(2:10–16). Paul implies that such mysteries are revealed to some and not to
others. Because of the Corinthians' immaturity, now epitomized by their conceit and contentiousness, Paul could not teach them these mysteries when he
was with them (3:1–4).

It is particularly important to notice that this revelation is something
entirely different from the basic teachings that Paul brought to the Corinthians and is apparently unessential to their Christian life.[28] The apostle never
questions their basic security "in Christ." The Corinthians are among those
being saved; they have received the Spirit and gifts of the Spirit, and Paul has
full confidence in their ability to make progress (1 Cor 1:4–7; 12:1–11). Paul
seems to view their present immaturity as a temporary problem that will be
overcome in time. The teachings and beliefs by which the Corinthians were
constituted are completely separate from the mysteries for the mature. Thus,

27. An important point developed in Fitzgerald, *Cracks in an Earthen Vessel*, chap. 3–4.
28. A point that I have taken from Gooch, *Partial Knowledge*, 44–45. Gooch, I believe, is
unwarranted in his tentativeness about this conclusion.

basic beliefs about God and the narrative of Jesus' life, death, and resurrection are not placed on the side of some kind of special knowledge through revelation in 1 Corinthians. Whatever conception of revelation might be deduced from Paul's letters, one cannot extract a basic opposition between reason and faith or revelation.[29]

MODELS OF RESPONSIBLE DELIBERATION

Thus far, my results have been primarily negative: 1 Corinthians 1–4 does not subordinate reason to faith, revelation, or authority. There are, however, some positive results that I wish to develop. Paul's admonition of the Corinthians has certain epistemic implications. These primarily concern social conditions for the productive exercise of rationality. First, I will argue that after concluding his admonition, Paul, in 6:12 through chapter 14, not only advocates certain qualities of community as an antidote but also tries to illustrate the proper sort of openness and humility in his own reasoning and discussion of particular issues in the letter. Second, I will argue that Paul does criticize a specific misuse of reason, and I will attempt to set this critique within its historical and cultural context. I have already suggested the direction of this critique in pointing out that Paul describes the attitudes of the Corinthians in terms of the Stoic wise man in contrast to his own vulnerability.

I will illustrate my first point by briefly discussing 1 Cor 6:12–20 and 7:1–40. The former text is a transition from Paul's admonition that ends in 6:11 and an introduction to his discussion of specific questions that he had received in a letter from the Corinthians.[30] He seems to treat these questions under the general rubric of "rights and freedom." Paul certainly had very strong negative reactions to the attitudes and actions of the Corinthians. His admonition of them becomes more and more intense through chapters 1 through 4 and reaches its height in his condemnation of specific actions in 5:1–13 and 6:1–11. One might expect Paul, as an apostle and a religious leader, to go from criticism to a set of authoritative and even authoritarian directives. This Paul does not do. In fact, chapters 7 through 14 are remarkable for their exemplification of the style and rhetoric of the letter of advice.[31] These chapters largely treat what moderns would describe as ethical issues. Paul's arguments concern ethical justification, but he does not settle matters with any simple appeal to authority.

Many scholars believe that the Corinthian questions and Paul's answers to them reflect libertine and ascetic factions or tendencies within the Corinthian community.[32] It is at least plausible to say that Paul's rhetorical audience is

---

29. This applies also to Romans 1–2, which has been grossly misused on this subject. I will address these texts in forthcoming publications on Romans.
30. On 1 Cor 6:12–20, see Stowers, "'Debate' over Freedom."
31. Stowers, *Letter Writing*, 91–112.
32. Hurd, *Origin of 1 Corinthians*.

sometimes well described as libertine and at other times as ascetic. In 1 Cor
6:12–20, he takes up slogans concerning moral freedom. I have shown elsewhere that Paul employs the dialogic style of the diatribe and that the text is
best understood as a dialogue between Paul and an imaginary interlocutor
who represents the "libertine position":[33]

Interlocutor:	All things are permitted for me.
Paul:	But not all things are profitable.
Interlocutor:	All things are permitted for me.
Paul:	But I will not be enslaved to anything.
Interlocutor:	Food is meant for the stomach and the stomach for food and God will destroy both one and the other.
Paul:	But the body is not for immorality but for the Lord, and the Lord for the body. God raised the Lord, and he will raise us through his power. Do you not know that your bodies are members of Christ? Then shall I make the members of Christ members of a prostitute? God forbid! Do you not know that he who joins himself to a prostitute becomes one body with her? For "the two shall become one flesh" [Gen 2:24].... Flee immorality!
Interlocutor:	Every sin which a man commits is apart from the body.
Paul:	But the immoral man sins against his own body. Or do you not know that your body is a temple of the Holy Spirit within you? ... Glorify God in your body.[34]

In this little exchange, the interlocutor first repeats the slogan "All things
are permitted," which seems to be a well-attested version of the Stoic paradox
"Only the wise man is truly free."[35] In the second two responses, the interlocutor reveals the reasons for the "libertine" position: Material things, including
the body, are irrelevant to questions of right and wrong. The body is morally
irrelevant. In light of the strong negative reactions, sometimes turning into
excoriation, that Paul himself (1 Cor 5:1–13) and moralists like Musonius
Rufus, Dio Chrysostom, and Plutarch exhibit against what counts for them as
sexual immorality, Paul's response in 6:12–20 is mild and reasonable. His
responses to the interlocutor's slogans and "theology" are a series of reasons
for qualifying the interlocutor's concept of freedom. Paul does not dismiss the
slogan but first appeals to two nonreligious reasons for modifying this conception of liberty: freedom of action should be guided by what is beneficial to the

33. Stowers, "'Debate' over Freedom," 68–69; Stowers, *The Diatribe and Paul's Letter to the Romans* (SBLDS 57; Chico, CA: Scholars, 1981).
34. The translation follows the RSV where possible.
35. Stowers, "'Debate' over Freedom," 63–67; Robert M. Grant, "Hellenistic Elements in I Corinthians," *Early Christian Origins: Studies in Honor of Harold R. Willoughby* (Chicago: Quadrangle, 1961) 60–66.

actor, and behavior that leads to loss of freedom should be avoided. To the interlocutor's "spiritualizing" theological reasons for his ethic, Paul provides counter theological arguments: the resurrection of Jesus is a divine affirmation of bodily life; membership in Christ's community makes union with a prostitute a serious matter; the presence of the Holy Spirit is an affirmation of the value of bodily life.

We can see the significance of this exchange as a model for the Corinthians if we imagine that they had broken into libertine and ascetic factions, each responding to the claims of the other with conceit and boasts about their own wisdom and that of their teachers. The authority of moral traditions in larger Greco-Roman and Jewish culture would put the libertines at a disadvantage in justifying their position and make it difficult for them to even get a hearing. And yet, before going on to a question from the ascetic faction in 1 Corinthians 7, Paul provides a model for a calm and friendly exchange of "reasons" with the libertine group. The dialogue makes even more sense as a model when we notice that Paul explicitly urges the Corinthians to imitate him in 4:16 and 11:1. The latter appeal forms the closing exhortation of a section (10:23–11:1) that sums up and concludes his discussion of the Corinthians' questions under the rubric of freedom and rights. In 10:23 he again quotes the libertine slogan, thus referring back to 6:12–20. He concludes, "Be imitators of me as I am of Christ," and he seems here, as elsewhere, to view Jesus primarily as a model of forbearance and concern for the needs and interests of others.[36] The call to imitation extends to Paul's manner of discussing the Corinthians' issues.

In 1 Cor 7:1, Paul quotes from the Corinthian letter: "It is good for a man not to touch a woman."[37] Again, one might expect a dogmatic reply and a call for obedience. But on the contrary, Paul's ethical justifications rarely appeal to commands of God and never require an abdication of moral autonomy.[38] Again, as with the libertine slogan, Paul does not simply dismiss the ascetic position but raises a series of considerations that would radically qualify it. Moreover, he commends these considerations in such a way that the Corinthians are encouraged to think through the issues themselves and to arrive at their own conclusions in light of Paul's advice.[39]

These points can be illustrated by examining the way Paul appeals to ethical authorities in giving his advice.[40] Paul considers his own advice to carry

36. On Jesus as a model, see Richard B. Hays, "Christology and Ethics in Galatians," *CBQ* 49 (1987) 276–83. In what is otherwise a very fine article, Hays descends into apologetic (283–88) and tries to argue that the paradigm of Christ is unique. Not only does he do an injustice to the Greco-Roman traditions about self-sacrifice but he also thereby misses what really is distinctive for the lack of a nuanced and systematic comparison.

37. On what I take to be decisive arguments for reading 1 Cor 7:1b as a quotation from the Corinthians, see Hurd, *Origin of 1 Corinthians*, 154–69; and O. Larry Yarbrough, *Not Like the Gentiles: Marriage Rules in the Letters of Paul* (SBLDS 80; Atlanta: Scholars, 1985) 93–96.

38. This has been demonstrated for 1 Corinthians 7 by Gooch, *Partial Knowledge*, 85–101.

39. A point emphasized by Gooch, *Partial Knowledge*.

40. Here I, in part, follow Gooch, *Partial Knowledge*, 92–96.

authority, but he never appeals to his apostleship to support the authority of that advice. Instead, his moral authority comes from being more experienced and mature in the life and practices of the Christian community. Moreover, he carefully qualifies, and provides nuance to, the weight that he expects particular pieces of advice to carry. In 1 Cor 7:2–4, he puts forth a reason why the ascetics should prefer marriage to celibacy. Verse 5 is a concession to the spirituality of the ascetics and makes explicit that it is advice to be considered: "I say this by way of concession [κατὰ συγγνώμην] rather than command [κατ᾽ ἐπιταγήν]." In v. 7, Paul adds, "I wish [θέλω] that all were as I myself am." He goes on to say, however, that each has his or her own special conditions and thus reasons upon which to base a decision. To a particular subgroup in the community, he says that it is "well" (καλός) for them to adopt a certain policy. But as an exception, under certain conditions, "they *should* marry."

In 1 Cor 7:10, he has an "instruction not from himself but from the Lord." Paul clearly considers Jesus' teaching on a subject to be more authoritative than his own, although not a fundamental source of rules and teachings for the community, since he only cites teachings of Jesus twice in his letters (1 Cor 7:10; 9:14). In 7:12, he is careful to distinguish his own authority from that of Jesus: "To the rest I say, not the Lord." After a series of arguments and exhortations on various matters (vv. 12–24), he passes to the subject of the unmarried: "I have no command of the Lord, but I give my opinion as one who by the Lord's mercy is trustworthy" (v. 25). Then he introduces a section that brings to light the underlying reason for his whole line of advice in the chapter with "I think [νομίζω] that it is well" (v. 26).

These examples make it clear that Paul did not expect blind, unreasoning obedience to his authority. Even more interesting, he is very free about modifying, extending, and reinterpreting divine authorities for new and different circumstances. Paul as a Jew certainly knew that the command to marry and reproduce is one of the central teachings of the Scriptures. However, he feels free to qualify "God's command" in light of his own speculations (his "opinion" [1 Cor 7:25]) about the approaching end of the age and the tribulations of the final period (7:25–35). He also knows that Jesus forbade divorce, yet he feels free to make an exception to Jesus' teaching and allow it if the circumstances seem to warrant divorce (7:10–11, 12–16). Similar observations could be made about Paul's treatment of circumcision and "God's gifts and calling."[41]

All of this points to the fact that Paul expected the Corinthians to be responsible moral agents and to choose the right course of action for themselves. This expectation is not only implicit throughout the discussion but also mentioned explicitly. In 1 Cor 7:37, a certain decision is deemed correct as long as the person made it not under constraint (ἀνάγκη) but out of his or her own free will and with due deliberation. Paul's stance is well summarized in

41. Gooch, *Partial Knowledge*, 97.

7:35: "I say this for your own benefit [τὸ σύμφορος], not to place any constraint upon you but for your decorum [εὐσχήμων] and undistracted attention to the Lord."⁴² The term συμφέρειν is important both in Hellenistic philosophical ethics and in rhetoric, where it is the kind of argument that characterizes the symbouleutic rhetoric of advice.⁴³ "Your own benefit" points to the fact that Paul's arguments are often nontheological and consequentialist (for example, 7:9, 14–16, 35, 36). To justify his advice, Paul often uses not divine authority but the desirability of the consequences. By τὸ σύμφορος, Paul means that the Corinthians as individuals and as a community ought to make decisions with a view to their own advantage. It is also worth pointing out that τὸ σύμφορος is the first qualification Paul makes of the libertine position: freedom should be exercised in a way that is to one's advantage (6:12). Another purpose for Paul's advice is to facilitate the Corinthians' decorum (or "good order" or "nobility" [εὐσχήμων]). This is a Greek moral ideal that includes aesthetic elements.⁴⁴ The last justification of Paul's advice giving contains a theological reference but is not itself theological in any direct sense—for example, obedience to a divine command.⁴⁵ Rather, Paul understands the development of the community itself to be the goal of Christ's and his own work. The "undistracted attention" points the Corinthians to the leading agent of that goal. Both 6:12–20 and chapter 7 suppose and even stress the moral autonomy of the audience.

Now we can see why Paul is so concerned about the conceit of wisdom and factious strife of the Corinthians. Such "immaturity" prevents them from engaging in the kind of free, cooperative, and open moral deliberation that Paul models for them in 1 Cor 6:12–20 and chapter 7. As he sees it, their moral and epistemic vices have prevented them from carrying on reasonable discussion and from making responsible choices (for example, 5:1–13; 6:1–6). Far from advocating that rational deliberation be subordinated to blind faith, authoritative revelation, or Paul's authoritative leadership, 1 Corinthians 1–7 stresses the legitimacy of reason and moral autonomy in the context of a particular community with its particular goals.

AN ASSAULT ON THE
FORTRESS OF REASON

If Paul's complaint about reason is not that it is inferior to faith and religious authority, then what is his complaint? One clue comes from his likening of the "wise" Corinthians to the invincible Stoic sage. With impressive skill and erudition, Malherbe has shown that 2 Cor 10:3–6 employs military imagery that ultimately goes back to Antisthenes but became popular with

42. Gooch, *Partial Knowledge*, 98–100.
43. Stowers, "'Debate' over Freedom," 64–67.
44. Gooch, *Partial Knowledge*, 98.
45. Gooch, *Partial Knowledge*, 99.

later Stoics and Cynics for the purposes of self-description.[46] Malherbe's reading of 2 Corinthians 10, I believe, has implications for our question. In summary, Malherbe writes:

> Two military images which were popular in the first century were derived from Antisthenes. He applied the image of a city fortified against a siege to the wise man's rational faculties with which he fortifies himself, and he applied the image of a soldier's personal armor to the garb of Odysseus the proto-Cynic, who through his versatility and self-humiliation adapted himself to circumstances in order to gain the good of his associates and save them. The imagery of the fortified city was adopted by Stoics and developed in their description of the sage who is secure in the citadel of his reason. The imagery of the philosopher's garb as his armor became popular among Cynics, who do not appear to have used the imagery of the fortified city to any great extent to describe the philosopher's personal security.[47]

In 2 Cor 10:3–6, Paul uses both images, in conjunction with one another, to introduce this polemical section of the letter. He describes his own weapons in terms approximating the self-description of the rigoristic Cynics and describes his opponents' fortifications in terms strongly reminiscent of the Stoic sage.

2 Corinthians is a very different kind of letter from 1 Corinthians.[48] Relations between Paul and the Corinthians had deteriorated, and teachers had entered the community who apparently attacked Paul and his way of working with the congregation. In chapter 10 he responds to charges that he is humble (ταπεινός), fleshly, and weak (ἀσθενής) in person, and that his manner of speech amounted to nothing (10:1–2, 10). All of this seems to be related to the charge that Paul was inconsistent. The adaptability of approach in working with the community, which Paul viewed positively (for example, 1 Cor 9:19–23), the Corinthians and the new teachers viewed as a weakness.[49] In response, Paul writes: "I do live in the flesh, but I do not make war as the flesh does; the weapons of my warfare are not weapons of the flesh, but divinely strong to demolish fortresses—I demolish reasonings [λογισμοί] and any rampart thrown up to resist the knowledge of God, I take captive every mind [or thought (νόημα)] to make it obey Christ, I am prepared to court-martial anyone who remains insubordinate, once your submission is complete."[50] In response to those who have challenged him, Paul boasts that he will demolish their fortress of reason. But what exactly does it mean to understand reason as a fortress, and why does Paul oppose this understanding?

46. Abraham J. Malherbe, "Antisthenes and Odysseus, and Paul at War," *HTR* 76 (1983) 143–73.
47. Malherbe, "Antisthenes and Odysseus," 165.
48. Victor Paul Furnish, *2 Corinthians* (AB 32A; Garden City, NY: Doubleday, 1984).
49. Clarence Glad is currently writing a dissertation at Brown University on the subject of "Adaptability in Epicurean and Early Christian Psychagogy: Paul and Philodemus."
50. Malherbe, "Antisthenes and Odysseus," 166. I have slightly modified the translation of Moffatt that Malherbe uses.

The Stoics wanted to make the "good" in life invulnerable to life's vicissitudes. The best-planned human pursuits and goals are often brought to nothing by sickness, death, and conflict with other humans.[51] Values and pursuits, each good in themselves, often come into conflict. Appetites and emotions make humans vulnerable by drawing them toward actions and involvements that may be in conflict with values and long-term commitments. The person who is on her way to an important business meeting and sees an old lady being mugged, for example, may respond suddenly with anger and indignation at the injustice. Her involvement may not only ruin the most important business opportunity of her life but could cost her her life or her health. Or an "emotional response" might draw a person to do things that are illegal or that he considers immoral. Aristotle argues against Plato's ascetic solution to these problems: human fragility and vulnerability are a part of what makes human life good and beautiful and cannot be overcome without grave cost.

The Stoics in several respects adapted a strategy closer to Plato's. The only good in life is to be virtuous, which for the Stoics means to live in harmony with reason or nature. Everything else is a matter of indifference, although some things, such as life and health, might be preferred even if having no ultimate value. Because the wise act only according to reason, they know that death, illness, pain, and such are not real evils and that pleasure, wealth, health, and such are not real goods. The wise cannot be harmed or have their happiness diminished. In Paul's time, Stoics tended to treat emotions as diseases that could be eliminated. Stoics found reason as a fortress to be a particularly apt metaphor in their exhortations and descriptions of the wise man. Thus, for example, Seneca can give the following exhortation because of "reason which distinguishes between the desirable and the undesirable" (*Ep.* 82.6; trans. Gummere in LCL). "Therefore, gird yourself about with philosophy, an impregnable wall. Though it be assaulted by many engines, Fortune can find no passage into it. The soul stands on unassailable ground, if it has abandoned external things; it is independent in its own fortress; and every weapon that is hurled falls short of the mark" (82.5–6). Furthermore, the wise man, "full of virtues human and divine, can lose nothing. His goods are girt about by strong and insurmountable defences. Not Babylon's walls, which an Alexander entered, are to be compared with these, not the ramparts of Carthage or Numantia, both captured by one man's hand, not the Capitol or citadel of Rome,—upon them the enemy has left his marks. The walls which guard the wise man are safe from both flame and assault, they provide no means of entrance,—are lofty, impregnable, god-like" (Seneca *De Const.* 6.8; trans. Basore in LCL). For Marcus Aurelius, the mind "is a very citadel, for a

---

51. In my discussion of the ascetic strategy, I have drawn upon Martha C. Nussbaum, *The Fragility of Goodness: Luck and Ethics in Greek Tragedy and Philosophy* (Cambridge: Cambridge University Press, 1986), esp. pt. 1 and 2.

man has no fortress more impregnable wherein to find refuge and be untaken forever" (*Med.* 8.48; trans. Haines in LCL).

The view of reason as a fortress could be integrated into forms of Judaism. This adaptation by Jews is of interest because the "superapostles" who appear in 2 Corinthians and whom Paul has in view in 2 Cor 10:3–6 were Jewish. Philo uses fortress-of-reason language, but it is 4 Maccabees that is most relevant.[52] The oldest title of 4 Maccabees is "On the Sovereignty of Reason" (λογισμός).[53] According to this work, people who are dominated by their emotions have "weak [ἀσθενής] reason" (4 Macc 7:20). The story tells of how Jewish martyrs fanatically and uncompromisingly endure gruesome torture because of their reason rather than disobey the law. The mother does not even shed a tear as she watches her seven sons burned, dismembered, and flayed (14:11–16:12). The work is informed by Stoicism and the ideal of the Stoic martyr for philosophy.[54] In describing the martyr's reason and the tyrant's attack on it, the work uses the same military imagery as the Stoics and Paul in 2 Cor 10:3–6.[55] Speaking of Eleazar's endurance, the narrator says: "No city besieged with numerous and ingenious works has offered such resistance as did that perfect saint. When his holy soul was set aflame with rack and torture, he overcame his besiegers through the bulwark of his religion-reason [λογισμός]. Making his mind taut like a jutting crag, our father Eleazar shattered the frenzied surge of the emotions" (4 Macc 7:4–5).[56]

Like 2 Cor 10:3–6, 4 Maccabees uses the imagery of a siege against a fortified city to describe the invincibility of reason (λογισμός). For this writer, reason and the law are means that God gives to the faithful. Through these they can transcend the normal weaknesses of humans.

Although Paul employs the same imagery, he is the one besieging the fortress of reason. Those who would become superhuman are in rebellion against God. They do not understand the gospel of Jesus' weakness and God's power, of which Paul believes his ministry is a model.[57] Even in his weakness, through the power of God, Paul will take the rebellious Corinthians captive

52. André Pelletier, "Les passions à l'assault de l'âme d'après Philon," *Revue des études grecques* 78 (1965) 52–60.

53. Stanley K. Stowers, "4 Maccabees," *Harper's Bible Commentary* (ed. James L. Mays; San Francisco: Harper & Row, 1988) 922–34.

54. Stowers, "4 Maccabees," 924; R. Renehan, "The Greek Philosophic Background of Fourth Maccabees," *Rheinisches Museum* 115 (1972) 221–38.

55. In addition to 4 Macc 7:4–5 cited below, see 9:18–23; 11:21–22; 13:3–8, which Moses Hadas, *The Third and Fourth Books of Maccabees* (New York: Harper & Bros., 1953), translates as follows: "by the reason which is commended by God they got the better of emotions, over which the superiority of reason is thus made evident; for they overcame both emotion and suffering. How is it then possible not to admit, considering these men, right reason's sovereignty over emotion, when they did not shrink from the agonies of fire? Even as towers constructed at the mouths of harbors break the threatening waves, and render the anchorage calm for those that sail into it, so the seven-turreted right reason of these young men fortified the harbor of religion, and overcame the unruliness of the emotions."

56. Translated by Hadas, *The Third and Fourth Books.*

57. See especially 2 Cor 12:9–10; cf. 4:7–11.

and make them obedient to God (2 Cor 10:5–6). Elsewhere, Paul speaks of the gospel, the story of Jesus' self-giving life and death, as God's power (Rom 1:16; 1 Cor 1:18). The means of God's power through which Paul will conquer the super-Christians at Corinth is nothing other than the persuasiveness of the gospel that Paul attempts to model for them in his own weakness. He will persistently speak with them employing irony, indirection, metaphors, and examples, just as he does in 2 Corinthians 10–13. His manner of teaching and speech are themselves signs of realism in the face of the limitations of human knowing.

Paul's response to his opponents in 2 Corinthians 10–13 is charcterized by self-deprecating irony that has a strongly Cynic flavor.[58] Like rigoristic Cynics, he describes his teaching task with the imagery of the armament of the gods, which distinguishes him from other sorts of missionaries.[59] He will wage war against those who view their reason as a fortress in three stages: he will destroy their fortifications, take captives, and punish the resistance. Paul's armament by which he will defeat those with the fortress of reason is his own humble life, through which the power of God is manifested. 2 Cor 10:2 displays some sarcasm in describing those who have criticized Paul: "certain people who *reason* that we are behaving according to the flesh" (emph. mine). To these "reason people" he affirms that he lives in the flesh (10:3). He has not become invulnerable to human vicissitudes. Nevertheless, his behavior as a teacher, community founder, and builder—his warfare—is not weak and powerless.

When the "reason people" charged Paul with conducting his work as a teacher-missionary in a fleshly manner, they seem to have focused on what they understood as Paul's duplicity and inconsistency.[60] In 2 Cor 1:17, Paul protests that his failure to carry through with stated plans was not a matter of unreliability or duplicity. In 1:12–14 he seems to be defending himself against accusations that he was insincere, inconsistent, and unclear. These things seem also related to the charge that his speech was weak and ineffective (10:10; 11:6). To complete the pattern of weakness, Paul also refused to be supported by patrons and instead worked with his hands at a socially despised craft so that he could preach the gospel free of charge and preserve his own freedom of speech.[61]

Between Paul and his opponents in Corinth there are conflicting sets of values and different understandings of what the teaching-missionary task is about. The significance of these oppositions is not obvious to the modern reader. Fortunately, very similar issues were debated among Hellenistic philosophers and moralists, and their debates can help us to place the issues

58. Malherbe, "Antisthenes and Odysseus," 167; Johannes Geffcken, *Kynika und Verwandtes* (Heidelberg: Winter, 1909) 55–56.
59. Malherbe, "Antisthenes and Odysseus," 169–72.
60. Malherbe, "Antisthenes and Odysseus," 167–69.
61. Ronald F. Hock, *The Social Context of Paul's Ministry* (Philadelphia: Fortress, 1980) 50–68.

between Paul and his antagonists within a cultural context. Ronald F. Hock
has shown that the issue of whether to accept financial support or to be free
but socially humbled was an issue among philosophical teachers, especially
Cynics.[62] Malherbe has demonstrated that Paul sides with philosophers who
believed that their exhortations and teachings should be adapted to the needs
of each individual rather than be indiscriminate "preaching to the masses."[63]
In each case, the other apostles who had come into the Corinthian community
may have taken the opposite side on these well-established debates. These are
certainly aspects of the syndrome in 2 Corinthians, but there are features of
the discussion that the debates about the philosopher's support and the
teacher's adaptability do not illuminate.

In 2 Cor 1:12–14, Paul solemnly testifies to the Corinthians that he has
acted toward them with clarity and sincerity, although not with worldly wisdom.[64] "Worldly wisdom" echoes 1 Corinthians 1–4. As we have seen, worldly
wisdom is wisdom characterized by conceit and other epistemic and moral
vices. Indeed, Paul alludes to his characterization of this false wisdom in 1:12
by ironically calling his godly sincerity his "boast." He then goes on to support
(1:13) his claim to clarity and sincerity. He does not write things in his letters
that the Corinthians cannot read and understand. They have indeed only
understood him in part, but he hopes that they will come to understand him
fully. The implication is unambiguous. The Corinthians had complained that
Paul's letters were unclear, difficult to read, and insincere. They also charged
that Paul's duplicity extended to other aspects of his behavior (1:15–20).

The charge about Paul's letters would include 1 Corinthians. What in
1 Corinthians would have been unclear and have given the Corinthians occasion to view Paul as insincere? The use of veiled allusion, irony, and metaphor
might have been cause for the charges of difficulty in understanding. Furthermore, all of these techniques were sometimes understood as forms of insincer-
ity. To speak with irony is purposely to say the opposite of what you mean.
The Corinthians themselves, then, attributed epistemic vices to Paul. Each
side seems to have thought that the other was characterized by habits that
made knowledge, deliberation, and communication difficult. The Corinthians
may also have thought that Paul's dialogic style in 1 Cor 6:12–20 and his carefully qualified, undogmatic, and varied arguments in 6:12–20 and chapter 7
(also chapters 8 through 14) manifested a lack of consistency, confident
knowledge, and conviction. The very approach that Paul considered a model
of epistemic responsibility was considered irresponsible by the Corinthians.

The protestations in 2 Cor 4:2–3 make the Corinthian view of Paul's

62. Hock, *The Social Context*, 37–49.
63. Abraham J. Malherbe, "Gentle as a Nurse: The Cynic Background of I Thess. 2," *NovT* 12
(1970) 203–17.
64. I am assuming either that 2 Corinthians is a unity or that it is composed of two letters (chap.
1–9 and 10–13), and that chap. 10–13 was sent subsequent to 1–9. See Furnish, *2 Corinthians*, on
these questions.

272   ESSAYS IN HONOR OF ABRAHAM J. MALHERBE

methods quite clear: "We have renounced shameful hidden ways; we do not behave with trickery or disguise the word of God, but by the open truth we commend ourselves to everyone's conscience ... and even if our gospel is veiled, it is veiled only to those who are perishing."[65] Paul's indirect methods and lack of dogmatism on points important to the Corinthians were taken as signs of duplicity, hypocrisy, and deceit.

In 2 Corinthians 10 and 11 (whether part of the same letter or one subsequent to chapters 1 through 9), Paul reaffirms his approach against those people who view reason as a fortress. He reaffirms his humble approach—his weakness—and revels in his use of irony. He responds to charges that his way of speaking is ineffective and asserts the value of his self-humiliation. For the Corinthians, Paul's humility, vulnerability, and self-deprecating irony show his ineffectiveness as compared with the superapostles. For Paul, this fragility is a way of manifesting God's message and God's power. Again, there are two opposing views of responsible behavior, with both moral and epistemic implications.

For those who know Hellenistic philosophy, this debate will have a familiar ring. It is in just such terms that Epicureans and those in the Socratic tradition debated about the proper methods of the moral guide.[66] Epicurus knew everything that was essential for wisdom and the good life. His followers faithfully transmitted and inculcated his teachings for centuries. For converts, it was a matter of learning and habituating Epicurus's doctrines with the help of more advanced members of the community.[67] People outside the community suffered from diseases of the soul. The task was to apply the medicine and save lives.

For Epicureans, Socrates represented exactly the wrong way to go about philosophy. He and those who followed his approach were extensively criticized throughout the history of Epicureanism.[68] In *On Vices,* Philodemus cari-

---

65. My translation.
66. Mark T. Riley, "The Epicurean Criticism of Socrates," *Phoenix* 34 (1980) 55–68; Knut Kleve, "*Scurra Atticus:* The Epicurean View of Socrates," *SYZETESIS: Studi sull'epicureismo greco e romano offerti a Marcello Gigante* (Biblioteca della Parola del Passato 16; Naples: Gaetano Macchiaroli, 1983) 227–53; "The Philosophical Polemics in Lucretius: A Study in the History of Epicurean Criticism," *Entretiens sur l'antiquité classique* 24 (1978) 39–75.
67. For conversion in Epicureanism, see Bernard Frischer, *The Sculpted Word: Epicureanism and Philosophical Recruitment in Ancient Greece* (Berkeley: University of California Press, 1982). Frischer's study is important, but too narrow concerning methods of missionary work. On Epicurean nurturing in the community, see Norman De Witt, "Organization and Procedure in Epicurean Groups," *CP* 31 (1936) 205–11; Marcello Gigante, "Philodème: Sur la liberté de parole," *Actes du VIIIe Congrès, Assoc. Guillaume Budé* (Paris: Sociéte D'édition "Les Belles Lettres," 1969) 196–217; Gigante, "Per l'interpretazione dell' opera Filodemea <Sulla liberta di parola>," *Cronache Ercolanesi* 2 (1972) 59–65; Gigante, "Motive paideutici nell' opera Filodemea sulla liberta de parola," *Cronache Ercolanesi* 4 (1974) 37–42; Ilsetraut Hadot, *Seneca und die griechisch-römische Tradition der Seelenleitung.* (Berlin: Walter de Gruyter, 1969) 47–71; Hadot, "Epicure et l'enseignement philosophique hellenistique et romain," *Actes du VIIIe Congres, Assoc. Guillaume Budé* (Paris, 1969) 347–54; Paul Rabbow, *Seelenführung: Methodik der Exerzitien in der Antike* (Munich: Kosel, 1954); and Abraham J. Malherbe, *Paul and the Thessalonians: The Philosophic Tradition of Pastoral Care* (Philadelphia: Fortress, 1987) 85–88.
68. See note 66 above.

catures Socrates as a typical ironic person, the εἴρων being one who displayed the traditional Greek vice of dissimulation (εἰρωνεία):[69]

> Usually he praises the man he will censure, but always minimizes and blames himself and those like himself, thereby perverting what he wants to say. He is, however, well aware of his own cleverness to deceive and give a trustworthy impression. . . . If somebody praises him or asks him to say something, or they say that he will be remembered, he exclaims: "Oh, what do I know, except that I know nothing?" And: "Why speak about me?" And: "If anybody will remember me!" Often he says: "Happy those, if there really are any, for their character or power or good luck!" . . . Sometimes he makes a display of wisdom, but ascribes it to others, as Socrates to Aspasia and Isomachus. . . . When he arrives at a party he gives the impression of being panic-stricken both with regard to appearance, self-estimation and speech, and full of admiration for those present. If somebody asks him to take part in the discussion, he becomes afraid and asserts that he does not think himself able to contribute even with the slightest argument. If laughed down, he remarks: "It is quite right of you, who are such an important person, to despise me. I even despise myself." And: "I wish I were young and not old, so I could have been your pupil." If somebody in the party has spoken about a thing quite clearly, and the important person asks, for instance: "But why do you say so," our man will exclaim with his hands outstretched: "How quickly you have caught it! I am disabled, of wits slow and dull." He listens with open mouth to a man who will prove something, then mocks him covertly by nodding to others, and sometimes he bursts out laughing. To people in whose company he happens to be, he may say: "Dear friends, please arrest my ignorance and my other shortcomings, and do not let it pass unnoticed if I behave unseemly!" And: "Please tell me about the success of Mr. So-and-so, that I may rejoice and imitate him, if I can." But why say more? Get hold of the Socratic Memorabilia, everything (can be read there).[70]

The εἴρων both praises and admonishes the same people. He has a self-deprecating modesty, especially about his wisdom. Epicurus had said, "The wise man will dogmatize and not suspend judgment" (Diogenes Laertius 10.121; frag. 562 Usener). The εἴρων is a hypocrite and is inconsistent because he claims to be less than what he really is. He is thus a deceiver, and his modesty is a kind of boasting. According to Philodemus, Socrates and philosophers like him are not only εἴρωνες but also boasters (ἀλαζόνες).[71] Epicureans thought that Socrates' openness and quest for truth was the worst attitude one could take toward the sick of soul in desperate need of a cure. Socrates used not only irony but also hyperbole, dialogue, and metaphor instead of precise scientific language. Furthermore, he tried to lead people to find the truth for themselves rather than plainly speaking the truth to the lost.

---

69. Otto Ribbeck, "Über der Begriff des EIPΩN," *Rheinisches Museum* 31 (1876) 381–400; Riley, "Epicurean Criticism," 60–68; Kleve, "*Scurra Atticus,*" 246–49.
70. Translated by Kleve, "*Scurra Atticus,*" 246–47.
71. Riley, "Epicurean Criticism"; Kleve, "*Scurra Atticus.*"

274   ESSAYS IN HONOR OF ABRAHAM J. MALHERBE

In contrast to Paul's and Socrates' self-proclaimed foolishness, Epicurus said, "He who has become wise never again assumes the opposite habit and does not even seem to be unwise" (10.117). The εἴρων attributes any wisdom he might have to others. Socrates even attributed his wisdom to a god.[72]

The conflict between Paul and the people at Corinth who championed reason as a fortress and who considered themselves wise is in many ways analogous to the conflict between the Socratics and the Epicureans. The opponents at Corinth must have thought that Paul never attained the right level of seriousness and honesty. Paul clearly thought that their pretensions to knowledge and wisdom and their self-comparing superiority over others, including Paul himself, reflected a most basic misunderstanding of the good news.

In 2 Corinthians 11, we find the sharpest irony in Paul's letters. The Jesus that the superapostles preach is a different one from Paul's (11:4). The model of their Jesus leads one into the invulnerable fortress of reason, and the model of Paul's Jesus, to a recognition that God supports his people in the midst of their human frailty. The superapostles' gospel results in feelings of superiority over the less rational, and Paul's gospel, in humility and self-giving mutual enhancement. These, I believe, are the basic oppositions that Paul sets up with his irony in chapters 10–13. He claims that he has knowledge (11:6) but is a fool compared with the wise Corinthians (11:19–21), and he boasts of his weakness as manifested by his hardships (11:23–32). For him, the medium of his behavior as a missionary is part of the message. This prominently included his self-support, at which the Corinthians took offense (11:7, 27).

It is less easy to understand the Corinthian side. Paul's sarcastic irony naturally does not provide a sympathetic perspective. Moreover, it is far from clear just how the patterns we have seen fit together. Paul uses language popular among Stoics to describe his opponents, but the Corinthian criticisms of Paul resemble criticisms made by Epicureans. I want to argue that we can make sense of this puzzling evidence and understand both sides of the debate better if we recognize that some Corinthians had adopted a therapeutic model of Christianity. In Paul's day, both Epicureans and Stoics understood philosophical activity in terms of an analogy with medical practice. According to Epicurus, "Empty is that philosopher's argument, by which no passion of a human being is therapeutically treated. For just as there is no use in a medical art that does not cast out the sicknesses of bodies, so there is no use in philosophy, if it does not throw out passion from the soul" (Usener 221 = Porph. Ad Marc. 31 p. 209, 23N).[73] I will use Epicureanism in order to illustrate the therapeutic model of philosophy, although very similar things could be said of Stoics from the early empire.[74] It is also important to realize that the

72. Kleve, "Scurra Atticus," 247–50.
73. Translation cited from Martha Nussbaum, "Therapeutic Arguments: Epicurus and Aristotle," The Norms of Nature (ed. M. Schofield and Gisela Striker; Cambridge: Cambridge University Press, 1986) 31.
74. In addition to Nussbaum, "Therapeutic Arguments," see Marcello Gigante, "'Philosophia

therapeutic model had become a part of the philosophical koine known to cultured and educated people in the empire.

As Epicureans saw it, human misery was largely the result of anxiety and disturbance in the soul, which was caused by false beliefs about the nature of the world. False beliefs about the world and about value generated empty desires and passions. Because people thought that the gods could harm them, they were filled with fear and anxiety. In desiring wealth, prestige, and power, they filled their lives and souls with trouble and care. Epicureans and Stoics agreed: If one could get rid of false beliefs, then the passions and anxieties of the soul would be eliminated. The object is to have a healthy soul. False beliefs produce diseases of the soul, unnatural passions, and empty desires. The therapy may require dissolving, purging, or amputating the diseased portions of the soul. The means for these medical procedures is the employment of reasoning (λογισμός) and wisdom (φρόνησις).[75] This is the same language that Paul uses to describe his opponents in 2 Corinthians 10 and 11. They feel secure in the fortress of their reasonings (λογισμοί [10:5, cf. Paul's ironic use of λογίζεσθαι, 10:2, 7, 11]).[76] Paul boasts of his foolishness (ἄφρων), whereas they are wise (φρόνιμοι [11:19, cf. 1 Cor 4:10; 10:15]).

Reasonings (λογισμοί) often took the form of brief nuggets of thought that those seeking to become wise employed as spiritual exercises.[77] Thus, the Stoic Musonius Rufus says, "The reasonings (λογισμοί) which I use for my own benefit so that I will not be troubled by exile, I would like to say to you— these things I used to repeat to myself" (frag. 9, 50.15.5 Hense). The λογισμοί are things such as "Exile does not prevent you from possessing virtue." The so-called slogans introduced by "we know" in 1 Cor 8:1, 4 and the so-called confession in 8:5–6 sound very much like λογισμοί.

Epicurus said that the flesh (σάρξ) acts as if there were no limits to the enjoyment of pleasure, but "the mind, having attained a reasoned understanding of the ultimate good of the flesh and its limits and having dissipated fears of the time to come, supplies us with the complete life" (*Key Doctrines* 20).[78] Furthermore, "it is sober reasoning (λογισμός) that searches out the causes of all pursuit and avoidance and drives out the beliefs from which a very great disturbance seizes the soul" (Epicurus *Ep. Men.* 132).[79] Epicureans and other kinds of philosophers, then, would apply arguments and reasonings based on

---

Medicans' in Filodemo," *Cronache Ercolanesi* 5 (1975) 53–61. For an early Christian example, see Abraham J. Malherbe, "Medical Imagery in the Pastoral Epistles," *Texts and Testaments* (ed. W. A. March; San Antonio: Trinity University Press, 1980) 19–35.

75. Nussbaum, "Therapeutic Arguments," 36–53.

76. For λογίζεσθαι as a slogan of the Corinthians, see Dieter Georgi, *The Opponents of Paul in Second Corinthians* (Philadelphia: Fortress, 1986) 230, 232, 235.

77. Epicurus often employed διαλογισμός in reference to basic nuggets of reasoning (Rabbow, *Seelenführung*, 338). Cf. Rom 14:1.

78. Translated by Cyril Bailey, *Epicurus: The Extant Remains* (Oxford: Oxford University Press, 1926) 99.

79. Translated by Nussbaum, "Therapeutic Arguments," 36.

the doctrines of their schools to sick members, in order to drive out false beliefs and heal the diseases of their souls.

THE PROBLEM OF THE WEAK

Is there evidence, however, that anyone at Corinth had actually adopted such a procedure? A positive answer, I believe, lies in 1 Corinthians 8. The pattern of discourse is already familiar from the discussion of 6:12–20 and especially chapter 7. Paul again cites views of the Corinthians (cf. 6:12; 7:1) that he partly accepts but then rather drastically qualifies. Again, he gives advice by arguing in a dialectical fashion, first raising considerations on one side and then on the other.[80] Without attempting to discuss all of the extremely complex exegetical problems of the chapter, I will draw attention to a few features that suggest that some Corinthians had adopted the therapeutic model and its assumptions about the role of reason.

The great majority of commentators agree that either "All of us possess knowledge" or "We know that all of us possess knowledge" (1 Cor 8:1) is a kind of slogan that Paul quotes from the letter sent by certain Corinthians.[81] Likewise, "An idol has no real existence" (8:4) is from the same people. Some scholars also believe that all or at least part of the statement about monotheism in 8:5–6 comes from the Corinthians.[82] From our perspective, it is interesting to note along with numerous commentators that the formulation in 8:6 finds its closest parallels in philosophical texts about divinity.[83] Finally, it is also widely agreed that "the weak" is a designation that the "wise" Corinthians used. At any rate, Paul also employed the concept independently of the Corinthians (for example, 1 Thess 5:14). It seems clear that the Corinthian letter presented Paul with an ideology that is reflected in the quotations and in practices to which Paul responds in talking about the problem of the weak.

One of the challenges for Pauline scholarship has been to identify the historical context for the Corinthian ideology and practice. Unfortunately, more obvious and commonplace Greco-Roman scenarios frequently have been overlooked for wildly unlikely ones—for example, a Gnostic party at Corinth. The Corinthians whom Paul quotes were making much of their freedom from belief in the gods and the power of the gods. Such "rationalizing" of popular religion could be found in different forms among Stoics and especially Cynics, but even among Platonists.[84] It was such a central tenet in Epicureanism,

---

80. On the manner of argument, see Wayne A. Meeks, *The Moral World of the First Christians* (LEC 6; Philadelphia: Westminster, 1986) 133–36.
81. Wendell Lee Willis, *Idol Meat in Corinth: The Pauline Argument in 1 Corinthians 8 and 10* (SBLDS 68; Chico, CA: Scholars, 1985) 67–70.
82. Willis, *Idol Meat*, 83–97.
83. Conzelmann, *1 Corinthians*, 144–45.
84. M. Dragon-Monachou, *The Stoic Arguments for the Existence and the Providence of the Gods* (Athens, 1976); D. E. Hahn, *The Origins of Stoic Cosmology* (Columbus: Ohio State University Press, 1977); Helmut Rahn, "Die Frömmigkeit der Kyniker," *Paideuma* 7 (1960) 280–92; Theodore Gomperz, *Greek Thinkers* 2 (New York, 1908) 164–66; Abraham J. Malherbe, "Self-

however, that Epicureans and early Christians were sometimes lumped together as "the atheists" by detractors (Lucian *Alex*. 25.38).[85] The first four of Epicurus's *Principle Doctrines* were known as the *tetrapharmakos*, the four-fold drug. The first remedy for the cure of humanity concerned the gods: "The blessed and immortal nature is not itself troubled, nor does it trouble another, so that it is not affected by anger or favor. For all such things are only in the weak [ἐν ἀσθενεῖ]."[86]

Epicurus taught that people could be as blessed and untroubled as the gods if they could give up certain false beliefs. The principal concern that troubled humanity was its fear of the gods and belief in divine influence in the affairs of life. The cure was to drill into the patient "true beliefs" summed up in the first remedy of the *tetrapharmakos*. This knowledge could best be instilled in the weak and troubled soul by reasonings (λογισμοί [cf. 2 Cor 10:4]) based on Epicurus's teachings.[87] Epicureans viewed the cure as an extended process in which those who had already become wise (οἱ σοφοί) helped the less mature to learn and become habituated to the master's teachings. The new convert had to reflect upon the rational teachings and practice acting correctly upon these teachings until deep habits of character were formed. When new converts entered the Epicurean community, they were first instructed to give up the traditional false beliefs and superstitions about the gods and then taught true knowledge based upon reason. Epicureans were allowed, and indeed even encouraged, to worship the traditional Greek gods as long as they did so with the proper rational understanding that the gods did not involve themselves in this world and that rituals had no effect.[88]

Some of the Corinthians were very proud of their true beliefs about the divine and the power of those beliefs to desacralize the world.[89] Because they knew that an idol had no real existence and that there was only one transcendent God, they could enjoy festivities in pagan temples and eat meat dedicated to the gods. The gods and the lords existed only as false beliefs in peoples' minds (1 Cor 8:5–6). Their new-found beliefs meant an end to

---

Definition among Epicureans and Cynics," *Self-Definition in the Greco-Roman World* (vol. 3 of *Jewish and Christian Self-Definition*; ed. B. E. Meyer and E. P. Sanders; Philadelphia: Fortress, 1982) 57–59; Harold W. Attridge, "The Philosophical Critique of Religion under the Early Empire," *ANRW* 2.16.1, 45–78. On Platonism, see Ramsey MacMullen, *Paganism in the Roman Empire* (New Haven: Yale University Press, 1981) 73–79.

85. A. D. Simpson, "Epicureans, Christians, Atheists in the Second Century," *TAPA* 72 (1941) 372–81.

86. My translation. On Epicurean criticism of traditional religion, see D. Lemke, *Die Theologie Epikurs* (Zetemata 5.7; Munich, 1973); A. J. Festigière, *Epicurus and His Gods* (Oxford: Oxford University Press, 1955) 51–65; Knut Kleve, *Gnosis Theon* (Symbolae Osloenses supp. 19; Oslo, 1963).

87. See note 67 above.

88. W. Schmid, "Epikur," *RAC* 5, cols. 732–35; Knut Kleve, "Lukrez und Venus (*De rerum natura* 1.1–49)," *SO* 41 (1966) 91; Norman De Witt, *Epicurus and His Philosophy* (Minneapolis: University of Minnesota Press, 1954) 280–81; J. M. Rist, *Epicurus* (Cambridge: Cambridge University Press, 1972) 156, n. 5.

89. Meeks, *Moral World*, 136.

superstitions about foods: that which one ate could neither win divine favor
nor provoke divine wrath (8:8). Paul has no quarrel with their basic beliefs.
Indeed, he provided the very arguments that persuaded the Corinthians that
the gods and lords did not exist and that there was only one transcendent God.
In commenting on the reception of his initial missionary teaching, he speaks of
"turning from idols to serve a living and true God" (1 Thess 1:9) and of being
in "bondage to beings that by nature [φύσις] are not gods" before coming to
know the true God (Gal 4:8–10). The latter text reflects the family of rationalizing explanations and arguments known as Euhemerism, which had been
adopted by Jews long before Paul's time in their critiques of polytheism.[90]

Paul's criticism does not concern the true beliefs or the reasonings of the
Corinthians as such, but the way that these have been used in arrogant disregard (1 Cor 8:4) of those who had not yet achieved such wisdom. Thus,
chapter 8 seems to provide a concrete illustration of the epistemic irresponsi-
bility that Paul attacks in chapters 1–4. His criticism of these "wise" Corinthians focuses on their attitude toward the "weak." Again, a context for understanding the "weak" is to be found in the therapeutic models of the Hellenistic
philosophies.

To illustrate the widespread use of this concept, I will provide examples
from various authors and schools. The word ἀσθενής means not only "weak"
but also "sick"; in fact, it and its noun form are the most common NT words
for illness.[91] The term, then, is natural to the medical metaphor. For Stoics,
one of the most important characteristics of weak or sick people is their inability to make consistent judgments. Epictetus writes, "Precisely as in a diseased
body, suffering from a flux, the flux inclines now in this direction and now in
that. Such is also the sick mind [ἀσθενὴς ψυχή]; it is uncertain which way it is
inclined, but when vehemence also is added to this inclination and drift, then
the evil gets past help and past cure" (Diss. 2.15.20; trans. Oldfather in
LCL).[92] As Anthony A. Long explains, "Rather, if he is not a sage whose life is
on a consistently even keel, he is liable to sudden changes and fluctuations of
his governing-principle. At one moment he may assent to the true Stoic pro-
position that pain is not a bad thing; but if this judgment is insecurely based it
will not be strong enough to reject a contrary judgment, that pain is something
very bad, which comes to mind and is accompanied by a bodily reaction as the
dentist starts drilling his tooth. The Stoics distinguished good men from
others by reference to the consistency of their logos."[93]

---

90. Hans Dieter Betz, *Galatians* (Hermeneia; Philadelphia: Fortress, 1979) 214; Klaus Thraede,
"Euhemerismus," *RAC* 6, 877–90.

91. David Black, *Paul, Apostle of Weakness: Astheneia and Its Cognates in the Pauline Literature* (New York: Peter Lang, 1984) 15–17; Gustav Stählin, "ἀσθενής," *TDNT* 1. 490–93. Neither
Black nor Stählin has anything to say about the use of these terms within this therapeutic model or
in Greco-Roman practices connected with the guidance of souls.

92. For other Stoic texts about the "weak," see *Stoicorum Veterum Fragmenta* ed. H. von Arnim
(Leipzig: Teubner, 1903–5) (hereafter *SVF*) 3.121.1; 123.1; 124.5.

93. Anthony A. Long, *Hellenistic Philosophy: Stoics, Epicureans, and Skeptics* (2d ed.; Berkeley:
University of California Press, 1986) 177.

The weak, in 1 Corinthians 8, are described in similar terms. They know the same propositions about the true God and the nonexistence of idols as the other Corinthians. They would even imitate their healthier, more rational brethren in eating meat dedicated to an idol (8:7, 10). But because they have not broken the habituation (συνήθεια [8:7]) of their false beliefs and emotions and habituated the true beliefs and emotions, their wavering minds will be filled with bad feelings (ἡ συνείδησις μολύνεται). Their consciences—that is, their awareness of the rights and wrongs they have done—are weak, because they are not guided by a firm and unwavering conviction of the new beliefs.[94]

The last part of Epictetus *Diss.* 2.15.20 mentions that the weak soul may become so sick that it is beyond cure. Elsewhere, Epictetus speaks of the struggle of divine reason ("Great the struggle, divine the task; the prize is a kingdom, freedom, serenity, peace. Remember God; call upon him to help you and stand by your side" [2.18.28–29] to judge consistently and rightly the circumstances of life. For example, one should refuse to fear death: "But if you be once defeated and say that by and by you will overcome and then a second time do the same thing, know that at last you will be in so wretched a state and so weak [ἀσθενῶς] that by and by you will not so much as notice that you are doing wrong, but you will even begin to offer arguments in justification of your conduct" (2.18.31–32). Weakness is a state of illness in which the patient may be past the point of return to health. In such cases, a drug or treatment might only kill the patient. To give an Epicurean example, fear of the gods and holy places might be so deeply habituated that the disciple is too weak for help. Such a person has become calloused by constantly reverting to old feelings and beliefs (cf. 1 Tim 4:2; Titus 1:15). "The weak" was a category adopted by those in Corinth who considered themselves wise. For these wise people, the weak were too sick for concern. They and their "sick" consciences were simply ignored as the wise went about acting on their knowledge.

Weakness also held a place in more theoretical Stoic explanations of the medical model. Stoics discussed degrees of illness and states of disease (Cicero *Tusc.* 4.10; *SVF* 3.421–30).[95] First came the predisposition to illness (εὐεμπτωσία, *proclivitas* [*SVF* 3.421; *Tusc.* 4.27]). Some people are prone to anger and others, to fear or lust. Second is illness or passion (πάθος, *affectus* [*SVF* 3.391, 447; cf. Seneca *Ep.* 75.12]). The third stage is disease (νόσημα, *morbus* [*SVF* 3.421; *Tusc.* 4.23]). Here the false beliefs and passions have

---

94. On "conscience," the literature is considerable but often informed by anachronistic theological considerations. Especially helpful are C. A. Pierce, *Conscience in the New Testament* (SBT 1.5; London: SCM, 1955); Gooch, *Partial Knowledge*, 117–20; and Gooch, "'Conscience' in the New Testament," *NTS* 33 (1987) 244–54. Gooch's discussion is particularly lucid and helpful. The comment in *A Greek-English Lexicon of the New Testament* (s.v. συνείδησις) is perceptive: "*a weak conscience*, one that cannot come to a decision."

95. Hadot, *Seneca*, 144–46; Michel Foucault, *The Care of the Self* (vol. 3 of *History of Sexuality*; New York: Random House, Vintage, 1986) 54–55.

established themselves in the soul as habits. A fourth stage is sickness (ἀρρώστημα, aegrotatio), defined as "disease [νόσημα] accompanied by weakness
[ἀσθένεια] (SVF 3.421; Tusc. 4.23–24). "Weakness" occurs as the distinguishing mark of sickness, the stage before inveterate, incurable disease (ἁμάρτημα
ἀπὸ σκληρᾶς διαθέσεως [SVF 3.529]).

The theory of "sickness" (ἀρρώστημα) coincides remarkably well with the
descriptions of the weak in Paul's letters.[96] Stoics defined a passion-disease
(πάθος) as an impulse (ὁρμή) carried to excess. This condition results when
people value something as highly desirable when it should not be so valued.
Examples the Stoics gave of such diseases are love of women, love of wine,
love of money, and gluttony (SVF 3.421, 427). But at least some Stoics held
there to be a second class of παθή.[97] This is the ἀρρώστημα, defined as
"disease accompanied by weakness."[98] In this kind of "sickness," the impulse
(ὁρμή) is deficient rather than excessive. This comes about because people
are subject to many impulses that can result in the collision (προσκοπή, offen-
sio) of opposing impulses.[99] Cicero, who has little patience with the subtleties
of Stoic theory and wants to get to the heart of the matter, describes this
conflict as follows: "So the disturbing effect of wrong beliefs warring against
one another robs the soul of health and introduces the disorder of disease"
(Tusc. 4.23).[100] For example, an excessive fear of eating meat or of the gods
may conflict with an excessive fondness for eating meat or for worship of the
gods. If the two impulses collide, both will be weakened, but one will prevail.
If fear prevails, then the person will, in the one case, loathe meat and become
a vegetarian or, in the other case, develop a superstitious fear of things associated with religion.

Cicero describes this state of deficient or weak impulses as "an unwhole-
some aversion and loathing for certain things" (Tusc. 4.23). As examples of
this kind of sickness with weakness he gives misogyny, misanthropy, and fear
of strangers (4.25). Stobaeus adds hatred of wine (2.7.10e, p. 93, 6–9 = SVF
3.421). Cicero also gives the following information: "The product of aversion
moreover is defined as an intense belief, persistent and deeply rooted, which
regards a thing that need not be shunned as though it ought to be shunned;

---

96. For the following account of ἀρρώστημα, I am indebted to George B. Kerford, "Two Prob-
lems Concerning Impulses," On Stoic and Peripatetic Ethics: The Work of Arius Didymus (ed.
W. W. Fortenbaugh; Rutgers University Studies in Classical Humanities 1; New Brunswick, NJ:
Transaction Books, 1983) 87–93; cf. 99–106.

97. SVF 3.421 may consist of distinctively middle Stoic formulations, perhaps of Posidonius. See
Ian G. Kidd, "Euemptosia-Proneness to Disease," in Fortenbaugh, Stoic and Peripatetic Ethics,
107–17; and Anthony Preus, "Comments on Professor Kerferd's Paper," in Fortenbaugh, Stoic
and Periaptetic Ethics, 99, 102.

98. For a different kind of weakness in the soul caused by weak τόνος, see Adolf Bonhöffer,
Epiktet und die Stoa (Stuttgart, 1890). Bonhöffer was mistaken to equate this weakness with
ἀρρώστημα.

99. Kerferd, "Two Problems Concerning Impulses," 93.

100. Translated by J. E. King, Cicero: Tusculan Disputations (Cambridge: Harvard University
Press, 1945). I have also used King for the other texts of Cicero cited below.

further this sort of belief is an act of judging that one has knowledge where one has none" (*Tusc.* 4.26).

The importance of this material lies not so much in the technical Stoic theory as in what that theory suggests about more popular conceptions of the weak. The category of "the weak" and the types of aversions existed independently of Stoic theory. The Stoics tried to give scientific explanations to commonly recognized phenomena. Cicero and the Stoic discussions show that "weakness" was associated with mental and emotional conflict over differing beliefs. They also connect weakness with unreasonable avoidance of, and repulsion for, certain things. The "healthy" attributed this to false beliefs. Finally, Cicero shows us that the wise characterized people in a condition of weakness as thinking that they know what they really do not know. At root, the problem of the weak is their lack of genuine knowledge and their self-deception about knowledge.

In Romans 14, the weak are people who shun meat and eat only vegetables, as well as people who have scruples about certain days. Like the Stoic sources, Rom 14:21 provides the example of abstinence from wine. In 1 Corinthians 8, the weak are those who have conflict and aversion concerning things associated with pagan cults. The weak and weak in conscience are not a specific group but, as even Paul's hypothetical language shows, people who have a certain disposition. As Cicero says, these are people who "regard a thing that need not be shunned as though it ought to be shunned" (*Tusc.* 4.26). Paul's discussion suggests that the weak in conscience are subject to something like "opposing impulses" and "aversions." In his example, they are former pagans who have rejected their past and developed a deep aversion to that which they formerly valued. The example may suggest "God-fearing" Gentiles who had been taught by Jewish teachers that idol meat was polluting. Now that these Gentiles were followers of Christ, more rational fellow members were telling, or perhaps only showing them by example, that idol meat posed no threat of religious pollution, since the gods and idols did not really exist. According to Paul, the problem arises when these people follow the example of the more rational and eat idol meat. Because their consciences are weak, their consciences will be "polluted" and "wounded" if they eat that to which they have an aversion. Cicero, the Stoics, and Paul agree that the problem of weakness results from false beliefs and inadequate knowledge. Paul has to remind the wise Corinthians that some people lack knowledge, are weak, and are therefore subject to damaging conflicts and aversions (1 Cor 8:7).

The Hellenistic philosophies assumed that people entered their schools and communities in various states of illness. The main activity of the school, community, or individual spiritual guide was to provide a therapy and, if possible, a cure for vice and false belief. The "wise" Corinthians, who called some of their brethren "weak," most likely believed that they were following Paul in holding similar assumptions. In the context of Hellenistic spiritual therapy, the questions about the weak are whether they can be cured and whether an attempt to cure their condition is worth the effort. The weak person's belief in the power of the gods and the reality of idols might be so deeply habituated that a change of belief and feeling is impossible. An attempted cure might even drive away the spiritually sick altogether.

Philodemus of Gadara put together a handbook, On Frank Criticism, as a guide for mutual admonition in Epicurean communities.[101] Philodemus describes some members of the community as weak. The weak are people who are unable to be healed (ἀναλθής) by constructive criticism of their false beliefs and bad habits (59.1–11). The weak are prone to renounce the love of wisdom altogether (59.1–2). Some think that one should admonish the weak with frank criticism (παρρησία); others resort to bitter criticism (λοιδορία [60.1–6]). Plutarch says that the incurable are characterized by an inability to receive criticism and an unwillingness to confess their faults to others (Profect. in Virt. 92; cf. Seneca Ep. 94.24). Plutarch also speaks of those who have made "an admirable beginning for their salvation" but who lose it because of their weakness when they are unable to endure reproof (Aud. 46E–F).

"The weak" and "weakness," then, were established concepts in Greco-Roman society. The weak were people inconsistent and insecure in what they professed. From the perspective of the therapeutic metaphor, they were people who brought very deeply entrenched false beliefs and emotions from their former lives and were in danger of succumbing to these diseases. Paul does not dispute that there are weak people in the community any more than he denies that the knowledge of the wise about God and the gods is true. Rather, he objects to the conceit that belongs to the Corinthian view of wisdom, reason, and knowledge. Conceited wisdom is a kind of knowing that is without love and that therefore puffs up the knowers (1 Cor 8:1). The wise seem to have written off the weak. Paul must remind the wise that the weak are people who have not assimilated the true beliefs about God and the gods (8:7). The old beliefs are still so deep that their consciences are divided.

According to a popular misreading of the text that projects back an anachronistic understanding of conscience, Paul asks the wise to allow their behavior to be determined by the false beliefs of the weak.[102] But Paul says no such thing. Rather, he tells the wise to take seriously the severely ill state of the weak, to be sensitive to the acuteness of the pain that strikes the divided mind of the weak when they are "wounded" (τύπτειν) by the insensitive behavior of the wise (1 Cor 8:12). Paul's concern has parallels among the Greek and Roman moralists who wrote about the weak. Paul, like Philodemus and Plutarch, fears that insensitivity toward the weak might destroy them altogether, driving them away from their new commitments (8:10–11).

---

101. A. Olivieri (ed.), Philodemi ΠΕΡΙ ΠΑΡΡΗΣΙΑΣ (Leipzig: Teubner, 1914). For critical appraisal and modification of Olivieri's text, see the articles by Gigante in note 67 above.

102. Gooch, Partial Knowledge, 102–23; Gooch, "'Conscience' in the New Testament," 244–54.

The apostle seems to have learned something from his experience with those at Corinth who viewed Christianity as a kind of Hellenistic philosophy where, through knowledge and reason, they could become wise. In Rom 14:1–15:6, Paul guards against this understanding and its attendant problems. His advice in Gal 6:1–5 already anticipates the problem. There is to be mutual edification, where those who are more advanced work gently with the less advanced (Gal 6:1–2). He warns sternly, however, that conceit about one's spiritual status is a form of self-deception (6:3). Both this text and Romans 14 and 15 deserve careful study in light of Greco-Roman psychagogic practices in philosophical communities and among friends.[103] Similarly, even in the earliest letter he exhorts the Thessalonians to "tenaciously persevere with the weak" (1 Thess 5:14).[104]

For my purposes, Rom 14:1 is significant: "Take the weak under your wings in trust, not for judgments about reasonings" (μὴ εἰς διακρίσεις διαλο-γισμῶν). The other alternative to ignoring the weak, either because they are too far gone or because their illness is not taken seriously, is actively to attempt a cure. This would be primarily a matter of trying to dispel the false beliefs and false reasonings of the weak by means of more rational arguments. "Judgments about reasonings" is Paul's way of referring to this kind of activity.[105]

Epicurus said that "philosophy is an activity which brings about the happy life by means of arguments and reasonings" (λόγοις καὶ διαλογισμοῖς [Usener 219]).[106] Did Paul and Epicurus take completely opposite stands on the role of reason? Did Paul rule out rational discussion in the community? The answer to the second question is clearly no, as I have emphasized in my discussion of 1 Corinthians 1–4. In general, Paul believed that important issues should be rationally and constructively discussed in the community. The key to Rom 14:1–15:13, like that to 1 Corinthians 8, is to understand that the text describes reason's functioning in a therapeutic situation of the more rational and the weak. Paul's examples of issues reasoned about—meat eating versus vegetarianism, and holding some days holy or not—provide an important clue for understanding Romans 14. Wayne A. Meeks has perceptively noted that these issues are typical of works against superstition, such as those by Theophrastus and Plutarch.[107] Those who have a more rational view of religion are

103. Glad, "Adaptability," treats a number of these issues.
104. I owe the translation and exegesis of 1 Thess 5:14 to Themistocles Adamopoulo, who is currently writing a dissertation at Brown University on "The Concept of Endurance in Paul's Letters."
105. Συζητητής in 1 Cor 1:20 should be understood along the same lines. The word συζήτησις, meaning "joint inquiry," perhaps more than any other term characterizes the philosophical ideal of mutual psychagogy. The word is particularly important for Epicureans.
106. My translation. On διαλογισμοί as being just the sort of basic argument for more "rational" beliefs and practices as is found in Romans 14, see Rabbow, Seelenführung, 338.
107. Wayne A. Meeks, "Judgment and the Brother: Romans 14:1–15:13," Tradition and Interpretation in the New Testament: Essays in Honor of E. Earle Ellis (ed. G. F. Hawthorne with Otto Betz; Grand Rapids, MI: Eerdmans, 1987) 292–93.

not to act as if the goal of life in Christ is to relieve the weak of every irrational belief by means of arguments over arguments. Paul again identifies himself with the more rational. They are right, but he wants to make it clear that the goal of the kind of community that he advocates is not minds purged of all irrational belief. In fact, the point of the section as a whole is that such a narrow view is counterproductive in achieving an inclusive and mutually enhancing community.

I have tried to show that Paul opposes a view of reason's function in 2 Corinthians 10, 1 Corinthians 8, and Rom 14:1 that is best understood along the lines of the therapeutic metaphor in Hellenistic philosophy, especially Stoicism and Epicureanism. The question of why Paul opposed this view of reason is extremely difficult to answer with precision because of the irony and indirection that he uses in criticizing the champions of wisdom. It lies far beyond the scope of this chapter to provide a full discussion of why Paul criticized the view of reason I have outlined. I will, however, advance some theses and observations that I hope will lead to further discussion.

First, Paul believed that this view of reason was epistemically irresponsible. It entailed an overblown view of one's wisdom that amounted to a kind of self-deception. It also produced a kind of contentiousness, elitism, and dogmatism that destroyed conditions for rational individual and communal deliberation. Paul stressed the limitations of human knowing over against the "wise." It seems safe to say that for him, reason is not a faculty that can somehow guarantee certainty in religious or other matters. The exact position of the "wise" is unclear, but it is reflected in their claims to the status of wise; their dogmatic use of propositions about God and the gods; and their negative reaction to Paul's irony, indirection, and lack of dogmatism on certain matters. His model of pursuing ethical knowledge is dialogical and polyphonic.[108] Over against the "wise," Paul stresses how imperfect and incomplete human knowledge is, especially religious knowledge ("If anyone thinks he knows something, he does not yet know as he ought to know" [1 Cor 8:2]; our knowledge is imperfect, our reasoning is childish, we know God indirectly [1 Cor 13:9, 11–12]), and he contrasts knowledge to love, which includes the more important knowledge of persons.

The second thesis is that the "Christianity" that Paul envisaged did not conform to the therapeutic model. This thesis is made difficult to see and is arguable because later schemes of sin and salvation that do owe much to the therapeutic model have been read into Paul. He was an apostle to the Gentile peoples, and the goal of his work was communal. His concern was not the human condition and human nature but the state of the non-Jewish cultures who had, in his view, rejected the one true God. He does not begin by making human nature problematic and then proceed to offer a therapy. Thus, he

---

108. Wayne A. Meeks, "The Polyphonic Ethics of the Apostle Paul," *Annual of the Society of Christian Ethics* (1988) 17–29.

opposes the ascetic strategy of certain Corinthians. In Romans, he does speak of enslavement to passions and desires, but not as the human dilemma. Rather, God has handed the Gentile peoples over to their passions and desires as a punishment for rejecting him (Rom 1:18–32). The solution to this problem is not a therapy of the passions through reason but allegiance to the one God and his agent, Jesus Christ, for the creation of renewed communities of Gentiles.

The third thesis is that Paul opposed the understanding of reason as a fortress because he held that "human nature" could be transformed but not transcended, at least in this life. At the return of Christ, Paul believed, a new age would begin in which the "sons of God" would have their bodies changed so that they would be no longer normally subject to death and fragility. In his discussions of this age to come, Paul seems to attempt something that may be impossible. He wants to envisage this future life as truly human life but to eliminate or drastically reduce normal human fragility. People can imagine themselves continuing to live indefinitely without aging, but a human culture without aging or death would be so radically different from what we know that the question arises as to whether it would make sense to call it human.

About this life, however, Paul is unambiguous: one is not to attempt to transcend human fragility. Much of his language of weakness aims to persuade his readers that they cannot and should not seek escape from human finitude.[109] Whereas the fortress-reason people and the ascetics believed that they could and should transcend this condition of weakness, Paul believed that human limitedness and vulnerability should be accepted as opportunities for service to others and for the display of God's mercy and power. Indeed, to aid the weaknesses of another is what it meant to imitate Christ. Paul's answer to the problem of weakness was a community based on this principle: the strength of one will supplement the weakness of another. This is why there was no question for Paul of ignoring or abandoning the weak as terminally ill, beyond hope. At the end of the section that begins at Rom 14:1, Paul writes, "We who are strong ought to bear the frailties (infirmities [KJV]) of the weak and not to please ourselves. Let each of us please his neighbor for his good, with his development in view. For Christ did not please himself" (15:1–3a).[110]

Some Corinthians believed that they could, like Stoic and Epicurean saints, become wise people through right reasonings and rise above human weakness. Sometime before Paul wrote 2 Corinthians, those whom he sarcastically calls superapostles entered the community and became champions of these "wise" Corinthians. As part of his rhetorical strategy in both Corinthian letters, Paul develops the theme of weakness over against these people. God chose the weak to shame the strong and wise (1 Cor 1:27). Paul and his fellow workers are weak; the Corinthians are strong (4:10). After chapter 8 and before

109. Black, *Paul, Apostle of Weakness*, esp. 228–34.
110. My translation.

resuming his discussion of idol meat in chapter 10, Paul presents himself as an example of one who voluntarily gives up his own rights and freedom for others. Paul based his strategy of adaptability to the needs and conditions of others on this principle of forgoing rights. He does not demand that others rise to his level before he will deal with them, but rather he begins where they are. Here he says, "To the weak I became weak that I might benefit the weak" (9:22). In the community, likened to a body with its parts, the weaker members are absolutely indispensable (12:22). Human weakness, as it turns out, provides the conditions for human generosity, love, and community.

The fourth thesis is that Paul held that the view of reason as a fortress of the wise was elitist and individualistic, whereas the goal of his work was communal. The person who lives in a fortress looks down on other people from behind thick walls. Here Paul is closer to Epicureans, with their emphasis on community and love, than to Stoics. But he is fundamentally different from both in the nature of his goal. For Stoics and even Epicureans, the basic goal is the inner health of individuals. Community often seems to serve only an instrumental function toward that telos. For Paul, the goal is the community itself, a community of a certain quality to which the mutual enhancement of individuals is intrinsic.

Finally, this is the place to remember that constructions of psychology and anthropology are always related to issues of power. The inner mythologies of various psychologies always belong to particular social arrangements. The distinctions between reason, passions, feelings, and appetites have functioned in the West to produce an order of higher and lower activities. The descending scale of men, women, children, barbarians, and slaves was a movement from the more rational to the less in Paul's world. The more rational were born to rule and the more emotional, to serve. In making distinctions between the healthy and the weak, the "wise" Corinthians were creating a hierarchy in the new community. It is very highly probable that the "wise" were also those who "humiliate the have-nots" (1 Cor 11:22). Those who were richer and of a higher social stratum differentiated themselves from those who were poor and of a lower stratum during community meals so that some went hungry while others feasted. Gerd Theissen has argued that there is a correlation between the more "rational" attitudes about idol meat and a higher social stratum.[111] Paul replies to this situation by saying that such distinctions are a complete reversal of what the Lord's Supper ought to mean. Whatever else one might say about Pauline social ideas, Paul does not use reason as a principle of social hierarchy. What he commends is identification with the plight of the weak: "Who is weak, and I am not weak? Who is made to fall, and I am not indignant?" (2 Cor 11:29).

111. Gerd Theissen, *The Social Setting of Pauline Christianity* (Philadelphia: Fortress, 1982) 69–102.

SARAH'S SEMINAL EMISSION
Hebrews 11:11 in the Light of Ancient Embryology

Many translators and commentators have racked their brains over Heb 11:11:

Πίστει καὶ αὐτὴ Σάρρα στεῖρα δύναμιν εἰς καταβολὴν σπέρματος ἔλαβεν καὶ παρὰ καιρὸν ἡλικίας. (Nestle-Aland²⁶)

The problem is obvious: καταβολὴ σπέρματος is the *terminus technicus* for a seminal emission by a male person or animal,[1] so it would seem impossible to say that Sarah received power to emit semen. Hence there are many evasive translations: "Through faith also Sarah herself received strength to conceive seed" (KJV); "By faith even Sarah herself received strength to conceive" (NEB); "It was by faith that even Sarah got strength to conceive" (Moffatt); "It was equally by faith that even Sarah was made able to conceive" (JB); "Also by faith Sarah personally received potency for conception" (Berkeley Version); "By faith Sarah herself received power to conceive" (RSV); "It was faith that made Abraham able to become a father, even though . . . Sarah herself could not have children" (GNB). This last translation reflects a cutting of the Gordian knot based upon the way Heb 11:11 is printed in the UBS *Greek New Testament* (third edition): πίστει—καὶ αὐτὴ Σάρρα στεῖρα—δύναμιν εἰς καταβολὴν σπέρματος ἔλαβεν. As Bruce Metzger explains in the *Textual Commentary to the Greek New Testament* (672–73), this way of printing the text is based upon the assumption that Abraham, who is the grammatical subject in vv. 8–10 and in v. 12, most probably is also the subject in v. 11, and the words καὶ αὐτὴ Σάρρα στεῖρα are a parenthetical and semiticizing circumstantial clause ("even although Sarah was barren"), as Matthew Black has already proposed.[2] The

---

I am grateful to Prof. J. Mansfeld and Dr. J. N. Pankhurst for their valuable suggestions on both the form and the content of this chapter. I take full responsibility for errors in grammar and substance.

1. See the instances collected in BAGD *s.v.* καταβολή 2, especially the many passages collected by J. J. Wettstein in his *Novum Testamentum Graecum* (Amsterdam: Dommerian, 1752) 2. 425–26.

2. M. Black, *An Aramaic Approach to the Gospels and Acts* (3d ed.; Oxford: Oxford University Press, 1967) 87–88. Black here refers to K. Beyer's discussion of the "Zustandssätze" in his *Semitische Syntax im Neuen Testament* (Göttingen: Vandenhoeck & Ruprecht, 1961), esp. 117ff.

authors of the *Translator's Handbook on the Letter to the Hebrews*[3] also opt for this solution, albeit not without hesitation.[4]

In commentaries on the Epistle to the Hebrews, one finds a variety of other solutions to this problem. H. Windisch assumes that the text is corrupt; if it were about Sarah, one would expect εἰς ὑποδοχὴν σπέρματος; since the author uses καταβολὴ σπέρματος, which can only be said of Abraham, there must be a textual corruption.[5] Both O. Michel and H. Braun assume that an original dative αὐτῇ Σάρρᾳ has been misread as a nominative αὐτὴ Σάρρα; thus, one should translate, "By faith he (namely, Abraham) received power, together with Sarah, to deposit seed." They find less likely the solutions to regard the words καὶ αὐτὴ Σάρρα στεῖρα as a later gloss or to take them as a circumstantial clause.[6] A. F. J. Klijn assumes that the author has mixed two different thoughts, one about the faith of Abraham and one about Sarah's becoming pregnant.[7] H. W. Montefiore says that one should not press the expression δύναμιν εἰς καταβολὴν σπέρματος to have a literal meaning; the translation "power to conceive" can stand.[8] H. A. Kent proposes as the least forced solution a translation as follows: "Sarah received power with regard to [Abraham's] depositing of the seed."[9] Of the commentators, as far as I have consulted them, it is only C. Spicq who assumes that the author may have literally meant what he seems to write. In his earlier commentary, Spicq only remarks that the ancients believed that a woman, as well as a man, could emit semen; for evidence he refers to an article by H. J. Cadbury.[10] In his later commentary Spicq says that some pre-Socratics (Empedocles, Parmenides, and Democritus) believed that women emit their own semen and that the physician Galen had the same opinion, and he quotes Lactantius as stating that Varro and Aristotle shared this view.[11] Cadbury and Spicq seem to me to be on the right track. This chapter will demonstrate that the view that women had their own seminal emissions was not an eccentric, but a quite current, opinion in antiquity and that this idea did not remain limited to Greek scholarly circles but penetrated into other strata of society as well. It will also demonstrate that this theory was well known in early Judaism.[12]

---

3. P. Ellingworth and E. A. Nida, *Translator's Handbook on the Letter to the Hebrews* (London, New York, and Stuttgart: United Bible Societies, 1983) 261.

4. Cf. also the remark in the *Translator's New Testament* (London: British and Foreign Bible Society, 1973) 528: "The verse could also be translated with reference to Abraham: 'By faith— though Sarah herself was barren—he received power to deposit seed.'"

5. H. Windisch, *Der Hebräerbrief* (Tübingen: Mohr, 1913) 92–93.

6. O. Michel, *Der Brief an die Hebräer* (6. Aufl.; Göttingen: Vandenhoeck & Ruprecht, 1966) 395–96; H. Braun, *An die Hebräer* (Tübingen: Mohr, 1984) 358–59.

7. A. F. J. Klijn, *De Brief aan de Hebreeën* (Nijkerk: Callenbach, 1975) 123.

8. H. W. Montefiore, *The Epistle to the Hebrews* (London: Black, 1964) 194.

9. H. A. Kent, *The Epistle to the Hebrews* (Grand Rapids: Baker Book House, 1972) 226.

10. C. Spicq, *L'épitre aux Hébreux* (Paris: Gabalda, 1953) 2. 348f. He refers to H. J. Cadbury, "The Ancient Physiological Notions Underlying John I 13 and Hebrews XI 11," *The Expositor*, ser. 9, vol. 2 (1924) 430–39.

11. C. Spicq, *L'épitre aux Hébreux* (Paris: Gabalda, 1977) 188.

12. Cadbury was the first to study Heb 11:11 in the light of "ancient physiological notions" (see

PRELIMINARY REMARKS

Three preliminary remarks are in order here. First, it should be borne in mind that although it was known since Herophilus[13] that women had ovaries, the ovum itself was unknown throughout antiquity (and remained so until it was discovered by C. A. von Baer in 1827).[14] Second, when the ancients discussed female ejaculation, this probably had little or nothing to do with observation of the so-called G-spot (discovered by W. Grafenberg in 1950),[15] but it did have to do with a theoretical problem in their doctrines of heredity. Third, this theoretical problem was created by the fact that the widespread and traditional notion that the father alone makes the child and provides the substance for its coming into being and development could not explain why children often resemble their mothers. This traditional theory already occurs in "a context innocent of pretensions to biological investigation,"[16]—namely, in Aeschylus's *Eumenides* (657ff.), where the god Apollo says: "This too I will tell you and mark the truth of what I say. She who is called the child's mother is not its begetter, but only the nurse of the newly sown embryo. The begetter is the male, and she as a stranger preserves for a stranger the offspring, if no god blights its birth."[17] Aeschylus here clearly reflects the common assumption of the superiority of the male role, a theory that had obvious implications for the evaluation of the position of women. As G. E. R. Lloyd has stated, "The question must still be pressed, on what grounds alternative views— dissenting from the assumption of the determining role of the male and allotting equal importance to the female—were put forward."[18]

Alternative views were developed by some of the pre-Socratic philosophers.[19] The doxographical excerpt in Censorinus, *De die natali* 5:4, clearly

---

note 10 above), but his evidence is extremely limited, and he does not discuss at all the relevant rabbinic material.

13. On Herophilus, the famous third century B.C.E. Alexandrian anatomist, and his role in ancient medical science, see L. Edelstein, "The History of Anatomy in Antiquity" (1932), reprinted in his *Ancient Medicine* (ed. O. Temkin and C. L. Temkin; Baltimore and London: Johns Hopkins University Press, 1967; repr. 1987) 247–301; but now esp. H. von Staden, *Herophilus: The Art of Medicine in Early Alexandria* (Cambridge: Cambridge University Press, 1988).

14. See for the details J. Needham and A. Hughes, *A History of Embryology* (2d ed.; Cambridge: Cambridge University Press, 1959). When ovaries were discovered in the Hellenistic period, they were regarded as the depositories of female sperm and called testes!

15. On which see A. K. Ladas, B. Whipple, and J. D. Perry, *The G-Spot and Other Recent Discoveries about Human Sexuality* (London: Corgi Books, 1983).

16. Thus G. E. R. Lloyd, *Science, Folklore and Ideology: Studies in the Life Sciences in Ancient Greece* (Cambridge: Cambridge University Press, 1983) 86.

17. Translation (slightly adapted) by H. Lloyd-Jones, *The Eumenides by Aeschylus: A Translation and Commentary* (Englewood Cliffs: Prentice-Hall, 1970) 51–52. Cf. also Euripides *Orestes* 552–53.

18. Lloyd, *Science, Folklore and Ideology*, 87.

19. What follows is based largely upon E. Lesky, *Die Zeugungs- und Vererbungslehren der Antike und ihr Nachwirken* (Mainz: Akademie der Wissenschaften und der Literatur, 1951). Other and shorter presentations can be found in W. Gerlach, "Das Problem des 'weiblichen Samens' in der antiken und mittelalterlichen Medizin" (Sudhoff's) *Archiv für Geschichte der Medizin* 30 (1937–38) 177–93; T. Hopfner, *Das Sexualleben der Griechen und Römer von den An-*

states: "Illud quoque ambiguam facit inter auctores opinionem, utrumne ex patris tantummodo semine partus nascatur, ut Diogenes et Hippon Stoicique scripserunt, an etiam ex matris, quod Anaxagorae et Alcmaeoni nec non Parmenidi Empedoclique et Epicuro visum est" ("On another point as well these authors [namely, the philosophers] have divergent opinions, namely whether an embryo originates solely from the seed of the father, as Diogenes and Hippo and the Stoics have written, or also from the seed of the mother, which is the view of Anaxagoras, Alcmaeon, Parmenides, Empedocles, and Epicurus").[20] The five authors mentioned as defenders of the view that female semen is also needed to form an embryo were not the only ones—we will meet others later—nor were their theories uniform. There existed at least three different theories on the coming-into-being of human sperm: (1) the encephalo-myelogenic doctrine, (2) the pangenesis doctrine, and (3) the hematogenic doctrine.

THREE GREEK THEORIES

The encephalo-myelogenic doctrine[21] holds that there is a continuum of "brains—spinal marrow—sperm"; hence "sperm is a drop of brain," as Diogenes Laertius (8.28) presents Pythagoras's view. And the Pythagorean(?) Alcmaeon of Croton is reported to have said that sperm is ἐγκεφάλου μέρος (Aetius 5.3.3). Although this theory was rather quickly superseded by the pangenesis doctrine, its influence is still noticeable in Plato's *Timaeus*. In *Tim.* 77D Plato speaks of the "generative marrow," and in 91A he says that "marrow runs from the head down the neck and along the spine and has, indeed, in our earlier discourse been called seed" (referring back to 73C, 74B, 86C).[22] And

---

fängen bis ins 6. Jahrhundert nach Christus 1/1 (Prag: Calve, 1938) 132–36; P. M. M. Geurts, *De erfelijkheid in de oudere Griekse wetenschap* (Nijmegen and Utrecht: Dekker & van de Vecht, 1941); E. Lesky and J. H. Waszink, "Embryologie," *RAC* 4 (1959) 1228–42; H.-J. von Schumann, *Sexualkunde und Sexualmedizin in der klassischen Antike* (Munich: UNI-Druck, 1975) 102–4; Lloyd, *Science, Folklore and Ideology*, 86–94. A. Rousselle, *Porneia: On Desire and the Body in Antiquity* (Oxford: Blackwell, 1988) 27–32, is idiosyncratic. A short survey of other (more primitive, often magical) theories of conception in antiquity is F. Kudlien, "Zur Erforschung archaisch-griechischer 'Zeugungslehren,'" *Medizinhistorisches Journal* 16 (1981) 323–39. A survey of the study of ancient gynecology in general in the last decade can be found in D. Gourevitch, "Les études de gynécologie antique de 1975 à aujourd'hui," *Centre Jean Palerne, Université de Saint-Etienne, Informations* 12 (March 1988) 2–12 (I owe this reference to the kindness of Dr. M. Stol).

20. N. Sallmann, *Censorini de die natali liber* (Leipzig: Teubner, 1983) 8 *ad loc.*, gives the pertinent references to the fragments of the authors mentioned, as does R. Rocca-Serra, *Censorinus: Le jour natal* (Paris: Vrin, 1980) 45 (his French translation is on p. 8). In 6. 5 and 6. 8 Censorinus discusses Parmenides' and Anaxagoras's ideas on the role of female semen.

21. Discussed by Lesky, *Zeugungs- und Vererbungslehren*, 9–30; but see esp. the extensive discussion in R. B. Onians's classic *The Origins of European Thought about the Body, the Mind, the Soul, World, Time, and Fate* (Cambridge: Cambridge University Press, 1951; repr. 1988) passim. A concise doxographical survey of several theories on this matter is to be found in Aetius *Placita* 5.3–11 (in H. Diels, *Doxographi Graeci* [4th ed.; Berlin: W. de Gruyter, 1965] 417–22).

22. Translation by F. M. Cornford, *Plato's Cosmology* (London: Routledge and Kegan Paul, 1937) 356.

although Aristotle speaks out strongly against this theory, which gave an extra impetus to its decline, even in the imperial period it still had some adherents, albeit by then in various amalgamated forms.[23]

It is clear that this doctrine in principle leaves room for a female contribution in the process of conception, the brains–spinal marrow–semen continuum not being restricted to males. And, indeed, we find that several of its adherents adopt the *epikrateia* principle as far as heredity is concerned. The principle of ἐπικράτεια (predominance) is best illustrated by the short statement in Censorinus *De die natali* 6.4, "Ex quo parente seminis amplius fuit, eius sexum repraesentari dixit Alcmaeon" ("Alcmaeon said that the sex of that parent would be realized [namely, in the embryo] whose semen was most abundant [namely, in coition]"; frag. 24A14, Diels-Kranz). That is to say, if the woman's sperm prevails in quantity, a girl will be born, and if the man's, a boy. This principle, that the seed of either parent can be "overpowered" by the other's seed, is not limited to Pythagorean circles but occurs with various modifications in several ancient theories of sex differentiation (again, in spite of Aristotle's opposition to every double-seed theory; see especially *De generatione animalium* 1.20).[24] The existence of female semen and the occurrence of female ejaculation is the necessary basis of the *epikrateia* principle and is affirmed by authors like Parmenides (frag. 28B18 Diels-Kranz),[25] Empedocles (frag. 31B63 D.-K.), Democritus (frag. 68A142 D.-K.), and several Hippocratic writers (see below). Let us look briefly at two theories concerning sex differentiation that imply a double-seed doctrine.

Empedocles thought that some parts of the embryo had their origin in the man's seed and others, in the woman's seed. However, he seems to have combined this with a theory about the determining influence of the temperature of either the uterus or the seed.[26] A late tradition (in Censorinus *De die natali* 6.6–7) schematizes this theory as follows:

Mw + Fw > Mm   Mc + Fc > Ff   Mw + Fc > Mf   Mc + Fw > Fm

M = male; m = resembling the male parent; F = female; f = resembling the female parent; w = warm seed; and c = cold seed.

Although this tradition may not fully go back to Empedocles himself, it gives a good idea of one of the ancient theories of sex differentiation and heredity.

23. On which see Lesky, *Zeugungslehren*, 20–22.
24. For example, *Gen. anim.* 1.20.727b33ff.: "Some think that the female contributes semen in coition because the pleasure she experiences is sometimes similar to that of the male, and also is attended by a liquid discharge; but this discharge is not seminal."
25. On this difficult fragment, preserved only in a late and free Latin rendering (and beginning with "femina virque simul Veneris cum germina miscent," ["When a woman and a man together mix the germs of love"], see the discussion by J. Mansfeld, *Parmenides en Zeno: Het leerdicht en de paradoxen* (Kampen: Kok-Agora, 1988) 76–77.
26. On the problems caused by the lack of clarity in the doxographical tradition on this point, see Lesky, *Zeugungslehren*, 31–38. The relevant fragments are 31A81, 31B63, 31B65 D.-K.

Parmenides' view on this matter is different, because he has a combination of a double-seed doctrine with a left-right theory.[27] This is the theory that the sex of the child is determined by its position in the right or left part of the uterus (right for males and left for females). A later modification of this theory by Anaxagoras (frag. 59A107 D.-K.) seems to have introduced the idea that the sex of the embryo was determined by the part (left or right) of the body from which the seed had been formed.[28] This results in the following schema:

Mr + Fr > Mm   Ml + Fl > Ff   Mr + Fl > Mf   Ml + Fr > Fm

M = male; m = resembling the male parent; F = female; f = resembling the female parent; r = seed formed in the right part of the body; and l = seed formed in the left part of the body.

Later, other amalgamated forms of the left-right theory and of other pieces of embryological speculation developed, and it is probable that these theories had become widely accepted even outside scientific circles.[29]

Anaxagoras brings us to the second theory concerning the origin of semen, the so-called pangenesis doctrine of which he is the *auctor intellectualis* (see frag. 59B10 D.-K.).[30] This theory was refined in the school of the atomistic philosophers. According to Aetius (*Plac.* 5.3, 6), Democritus said that sperm is formed from all parts of the body, like bones and flesh and sinews (frag. 68A141 D.-K.). Democritus is also quoted as saying: "Coition is a slight attack of epilepsy, for man gushes forth from man and is separated by being torn apart with a kind of shock" (frag. 68B32 D.-K.). Democritus believed that in women, too, sperm was formed from all the parts of the body. Aristotle tells us that the *epikrateia* principle was an important factor in Democritus's embryological system: "Democritus of Abdera also says that the differentiation of sex takes place within the mother; however, he says, it is not because of heat and cold that one embryo becomes female and another male, but that it depends on the question which parent it is whose semen prevails—not the whole of the semen, but that which has come from the part by which male and female differ from one another" (*De generatione animalium* 4.1.764a6–11 = frag. 68A143 D.-K.).

The pangenesis doctrine was the dominant theory in several Hippocratic writings, especially in *On Airs, Waters, Places; The Sacred Disease; On Gen-*

27. See esp. Lesky, *Zeugungslehren,* 39–69; O. Kember, "Right and Left in the Sexual Theories of Parmenides," *JHS* 91 (1971) 70–79; G. E. R. Lloyd, "Parmenides' Sexual Theories," *JHS* 92 (1972) 178–79.

28. On the ambiguities in the doxographical tradition about Anaxagoras's embryology, see Lesky, *Zeugungslehren,* 51–61.

29. Lesky, *Zeugungslehren,* 62, points to passages in Varro, Pliny, and Horapollo that indicate that these theories had become popular lore.

30. On the question of whom is to be credited with the invention of this theory, Lesky, *Zeugungslehren,* 70ff., should be corrected; see A. Preus, "Galen's Criticism of Aristotle's Conception Theory," *Journal of the History of Biology* 10 (1977) 65–85, esp. 72.

eration; On the Nature of the Child; and *On Diseases* (4).[31] A few quotations
will suffice. *On Generation* 8.1–2 says, "Sperm is a product which comes from
the whole body of each parent. . . . [The child] must inevitably resemble each
parent in some respect, since it is from both parents that the sperm comes to
form the child." *On Generation* 4.1 says, "A woman also emits something
from her body, sometimes into the womb, which then becomes moist, sometimes externally as well, if the womb is open wider than normal. . . . If her
desire for intercourse is excited, she emits before the man."[32] *On Diseases*
4.32.1 says, "The sperm, coming from all parts of the body both of the man
and the woman to produce a human being and falling into the uterus of the
woman, coagulates."[33] An interesting new feature is that the author of *On
Generation* stresses that "both male and female sperm exists in both partners"
(7.1). This thesis, in fact a principle of complete parity, results in the following schema:[34]

$$M + / F + > M \quad M - / F - > F \quad M - + / F + - > M \text{ or } F \quad M + / F - > M \text{ or } F$$
$$M - / F + > F \text{ or } M.$$

M = male; + = male determining seed; F = female; − = female determining
seed; M or F −F or M = depending upon the *epikrateia*.

We see here a far-reaching theory with immensely important implications for
an anthropology in which equality of the sexes is sought.

   The hematogenic doctrine holds that semen originates from the blood—in
fact, is nothing but blood in a certain state of coagulation. It is not certain
who the author of this theory is,[35] but it was already held by Diogenes of Apol-
lonia (frag. 64B6 D.-K.), as is clearly stated in a long quotation from his work
by Aristotle (*Historia animalium* 3.2.511b31ff.). Aristotle himself is the one
who promoted this theory to its influential position,[36] which it held until far
into the Middle Ages. Aristotle's *De generatione animalium,* book 1, is our
main source for his ideas on spermatogenesis. Of course, the basic principle is

---

31. See the references in Lesky, *Zeugungslehren,* 77, and in I. M. Loney, *The Hippocratic
Treatises "On Generation," "On the Nature of the Child," "Diseases IV"* (Berlin and New York:
W. de Gruyter, 1981) esp. 19ff.

32. Translation by Loney. Loney, *The Hippocratic Treatises,* 119, makes the pertinent comment: "The question of what the mother contributes to the formation of her child has an obvious
importance socially, legally, and economically, as well as on a more personal level. The kind of
relevance this question had is illustrated by the passage in the *Eumenides* of Aeschylus (657–666)
in which Apollo supports the case of Orestes by the argument that it is the father who forms the
embryo, while the mother nourishes it and preserves it."

33. The three Hippocratic treatises *De Gen., De nat. pueri,* and *Morb.* 4 originally formed one
whole; see, besides Loney, *Hippocratic Treatises,* also R. Joly, *Le niveau de la science hippocra-
tique* (Paris: Les Belles Lettres, 1966) 70–119, esp. 111–16, "L'infériorité de la femme").

34. Lesky, *Zeugungslehren,* 84.

35. See Lesky, *Zeugungslehren,* 120–25.

36. On Aristotle, see Lesky, *Zeugungslehren,* 125–59, and V. Happ, *Hyle: Studien zum aristotelischen Materie-Begriff* (Berlin and New York: W. de Gruyter, 1971) 746–50.

teleology. Aristotle holds that the woman contributes to the embryo nothing but ὕλη (material)—that is, she is the *causa materialis* (material cause)—whereas the man contributes τέλος (end), εἶδος (form), and ἀρχὴ τῆς κινή-σεως (source of movement)—that is, he is the *causa finalis* (final cause), the *causa formalis* (formal cause), and the *causa efficiens* (efficient cause). This male contribution is semen, but the female contribution is not semen but menstrual blood (τὰ καταμήνια). Semen is a residue of food. The body converts food into blood by means of a process of "concoction" (πέψις). Blood is the substance from which flesh, bones, and so on come into being. Because in childhood all (food >) blood is needed for the growth of the body and its parts, no semen or menstrual blood is produced. Once the body has become full-grown, it produces a residue (περίττωμα) of blood (< food), and in a process of further concoction, this residue is transformed into semen or menstrual blood. The essential element in this concoction process (food > blood > semen) is bodily heat. Because males have greater bodily heat than females, their blood can be "cooked" enough to reach the stage of semen; a female can never reach this stage and hence can produce no semen, only (menstrual) blood.[37] In the process of fertilization the semen brings form and movement into the matter (ὕλη) of the menstrual blood. The state of aggregation of this blood changes only by the impact of the greater heat of the semen, "for the menstrual blood is semen not in a pure state but in need of working up" (*Gen. anim.* 1.20.728a26). Only semen in a pure state can "inform" the powerless female matter so as to make it develop into an embryo. It is clear that in Aristotle's version of the hematogenic doctrine, the female contribution to embryogenesis is very much reduced as compared with the pangenesis and the encephalo-myelogenic doctrines.[38]

Aristotle heavily influenced not only Stoic doctrines of spermatogenesis[39] but also the doctrines of the medical school of the so-called pneumatics, founded in the first century C.E. by Athenaeus of Attaleia.[40] More important in this respect, however, is the influential Galen, since this great physician tried to combine Aristotelian elements with insights of pre-Socratic and Hippocratic writers as regards embryology.[41] Galen did assume on the one hand that

37. Happ, *Hyle*, 747, puts it concisely: "Die Katamenien sind also sozusagen 'halbgares' Sperma, das Sperma ist 'gares' Menstruationsblut."
38. See J. Morsink, "Was Aristotle's Biology Sexist?" *Journal of the History of Biology* 12 (1979) 83–112.
39. It should be noted, however, that whereas Aetius in *Plac.* 5.5.2 states that Zeno, like Aristotle, did not believe that women produce sperm, the same doxographer says about the Stoics in *Plac.* 5.11.4 that they believe προΐεσθαι δὲ καὶ τὴν γυναῖκα (the woman also produces [sperm]). On the Stoics, see also Censorinus, *De die natali* 5:4, quoted above.
40. Lesky, *Zeugungslehren*, 163–77. F. Kudlien demonstrates also the Stoic influence on the pneumatics in his article "Pneumatische Ärzte," PWSup 11 (1968) 1097–1108.
41. See R. E. Siegel, *Galen's System of Physiology and Medicine* (Basel and New York: Karger, 1968) 1. 224ff.; Preus, "Galen's Criticism of Aristotle's Conception Theory"; M. Boylan, "Galen's Conception Theory," *Journal of the History of Biology* 19 (1986) 47–77; J. Kollesch, "Galens Auseinandersetzung mit der aristotelischen Samenlehre," *Aristoteles, Werk und Wirkung* (FS P. Moraux; ed. J. Wiesner; Berlin: W. de Gruyter, 1987) 17–26.

women contributed their own sperm, but on the other hand he followed Aristotle in attributing a much lower value to this contribution: female sperm is by far less perfect, thinner, and colder than male sperm. During coition, female seed is expelled from the "ovaries" in such a way that both seeds meet in the womb, mix, and form a membrane; thereafter, the female sperm serves only as food for the male semen in its development into an embryo (see for all this especially Galen's extensive treatise *De semine*).[42] As a real eclectic, Galen tries to run with the hare and hunt with the hounds. Nonetheless, despite Aristotle's influence, Galen maintains the concept of female sperm: ψευδῶς λέγεται τὸ μόνου τοῦ πατρὸς εἶναι τὸ σπέρμα (It is falsely said that sperm is only from the father) (*Sem.* 2.1; 608 [ed. Kühn]) and transmits this theory to many a writer in the Middle Ages.[43]

We could go on discussing ancient Greek testimonies concerning female seed,[44] but I will turn now to a few references to Latin authors. In Lucretius *De rerum natura* 4.1208–87, we find a long and interesting passage on matters of procreation. I quote lines 1208–17 (in the prose translation of R. E. Latham):[45]

In the intermingling of seed it may happen that the woman by a sudden effort overmasters the power of the man and takes control of it. Then children are conceived of the maternal seed and take after their mother. Correspondingly children may be conceived of the paternal seed and take after their father. The children in whom you see a two-sided likeness, combining features of both parents, are products alike of their father's body and their mother's blood. At their making the seeds that course through the limbs under the impulse of Venus were dashed together by the collusion of mutual passion in which neither party was master or mastered.[46]

This is a very clear instance of a double-seed theory based upon the pangenesis doctrine combined with the *epikrateia* principle. The influence of earlier philosophers is obvious. Less influenced by philosophy is Ovid, who warns women in his *Ars amatoria* 3.767–68: "It is not safe to fall asleep during

---

42. See also the notice on Galen by Nemesius, *De natura hominis* 247 (ed. M. Morani; Leipzig: Teubner, 1987) 86–87: Γαληνός δὲ καταγινώσκων Ἀριστοτέλους λέγει σπερμαίνειν μὲν τὰς γυναῖκας καὶ τὴν μῖξιν ἀμφοτέρων τῶν σπερμάτων ποιεῖν τὸ κύημα. Galen's reproductive system as presented in his *De usu partium* books 14 and 15 is excellently summarized in M. Tallmadge May, *Galen on the Usefulness of the Parts of the Body* (Ithaca: Cornell University Press, 1968) 1. 56–58; see also 2. 631–32 n. 24.

43. Gerlach, "Das Problem," 190ff. Soranus, too, takes an eclectic position: females as well as males emit sperm (*Gyn.* 1. 30–31), but female sperm does not contribute to the formation of the embryo (*Gyn.* 1. 12). See O. Temkin, *Soranus' Gynecology* (Baltimore: Johns Hopkins University Press, 1956).

44. Short but interesting doxographical accounts on this matter can be found in Aetius, *Placita* 5. 3–9, esp. 5. 5 (on the question εἰ καὶ θήλεα προΐενται σπέρμα); cf. H. Daiber, *Aetius Arabus: Die Vorsokratiker in arabischer Überlieferung* (Wiesbaden: Harassowitz, 1980) 487 (on *Plac.* 5. 3).

45. *Lucretius: The Nature of the Universe* (trans. R. E. Latham; Harmondsworth: Penguin, 1951) 168.

46. Cf. also Lucretius *De rerum natura* 4.1227–32.

a meal, for much can happen during sleep that one may feel ashamed of." It is very probable that the poet is making an allusion here to the phenomenon of female wet dreams. The pseudo-Aristotelian author of the tenth book of *De generatione animalium* states that when women have erotic dreams, they too emit semen into the region in front of the womb (10.2.634b30–31).[47] And other authors discuss the same phenomenon.[48]

The material surveyed so far covers the period of roughly 500 B.C.E. to 200 C.E. It has shown us that throughout this period, a theory about female sperm had its place side by side with a theory that denied females a contribution to embryogenesis. Widely differing ideas circulated concerning the origin of human semen. I have briefly discussed three of them, and we have seen that all three left room for one or other form of a double-seed theory. Even Aristotle, the most staunch opponent of the idea of female semen, did not deny that a woman contributed her *katamenia* to the embryogenesis and that this menstrual blood was in fact from the same origin as male semen, albeit that it had stopped halfway in its development into semen "pur sang." We have seen that many philosophers, physicians, poets, and others held that the contributions of men and women to the formation of a fetus were strictly equal.

JEWISH THEORIES

If, however, we want to make it a probable thesis that the author of the Epistle to the Hebrews could have known this theory, it does not suffice to point out its existence in the Greco-Roman world. We will have to demonstrate that a Jewish author—and this the author of Hebrews certainly was— could have known such a theory, either because it had penetrated into early Jewish circles or because similar ideas were already current in Jewish tradition itself.

Let us first go back in history and look at whether ancient Israel could possibly have met such a theory in one of its surrounding cultures. When we turn to Egypt, we do not find any evidence. This matter has been studied extensively by the Dutch Egyptologist B. H. Stricker in his impressive multivolume enterprise *De geboorte van Horus*, but in this elaborate commentary on an ancient Egyptian embryological treatise he has not been able to point to any unambiguous passage from Egyptian literature that supports a double-seed theory.[49] If we continue our search in Mesopotamia, the harvest is far from

47. Aristotle himself denies that the occurrence of wet dreams in women has anything to do with emission of sperm (*Gen. anim.* 2.4.739a20–26), but it is apparent from this passage that the occurrence of nocturnal emissions in women had been used as one of the arguments that females, as well as males, emit sperm. Cf. also *Hist. anim.* 10.6.637b28.

48. See Hopfner, *Sexualleben*, 134, and esp. A. Rousselle, "Observation féminine et idéologie masculine: Le corps de la femme d'après les médecins grecs," *Annales (économies, sociétés, civilisations)* 35 (1980) 1100–1101.

49. B. H. Stricker, *De geboorte van Horus* (5 vols.; Leiden: Ex Oriente Lux, 1963–89; see esp. 1968, 2. 131.

rich, but perhaps there is something to be found. There is an ancient Mesopotamian potency incantation in which the following line occurs: "If either a man or a woman is [. . . ?] and their semen flows copiously, . . ."[50] The most recent editor of this text remarks that the Babylonian word *rihutu* (sperm) is "here used exceptionally of a woman's secretions."[51] However, it should be conceded that this cuneiform tablet is partly restored here, and that even if the restoration would seem acceptable, this single instance would stand too isolated to enable us to speak of a double-seed theory in Mesopotamia.[52]

When we turn to the OT, again we find only one single text that could possibly be interpreted as implying a theory of female seed. The text is Lev 12:2: "Say to the people of Israel: If a woman *tazri'a* and bears a male child, then she shall be unclean seven days; at the time of her menstruation she shall be unclean." The word *tazri'a* is the hiphil (causative form) of *zr'* (to sow), which is used in the OT only here and in Gen 1:11–12, where it is said of plants in the sense of "produce seed, yield seed, form seed." When a form of *zr'* means "to become pregnant, to be impregnated," the niphal form is always used (see, for example, Num 5:28; Nah 1:14). Because the hiphil form cannot mean anything else than "make seed," commentators have got into trouble over this verse and proposed emendations of the text, because they found the thought expressed impossible.[53] But one should beware of overhasty conclusions and leave open the possibility that the author of Leviticus 12 meant what he seems to write, that is, that a woman can produce semen. We shall see later that this is exactly what the rabbis understood this biblical verse to mean. However, before looking at the rabbinic evidence, let us cast a quick glance at earlier postbiblical Jewish material.[54]

The earliest postbiblical passage to be quoted is *1 Enoch* 15:4, where the Ethiopic text runs as follows: "Surely, you [namely, the Watchers], you (used to be) holy, spiritual, the living ones, (possessing) eternal life; but (now) you have defiled yourselves with women and with the blood of flesh you have begotten children; you have lusted with the blood of the people [or: after the daughters of men],[55] like them producing blood and flesh, (which) die and

50. See R. D. Biggs, *SA.ZI.GA: Ancient Mesopotamian Potency Incantations* (Locust Valley, NY: Augustin, 1967) 66. The text is usually referred to as BAM 205:40.
51. Biggs, *SA.ZI.GA*, 68. See also the comments in the review by R. Labat in *Bibliotheca Orientalis* 25 (1968) 357a, and M. Stol, *Zwangerschap en geboorte bij de Babyloniërs en in de Bijbel* (Leiden: Ex Oriente Lux, 1983) 5.
52. My colleague Karel van der Toorn drew my attention to the fact that in the *Chicago Assyrian Dictionary* (1984) 5. 349b, our passage (BAM 205:40) is quoted but not translated, being too uncertain.
53. See, for example, A. B. Ehrlich, *Randglossen zur hebräischen Bibel* 2 (Hildesheim: Olms, 1968, repr. of the 1909 ed.) 40: "Bei der durch *zr'* ausgedrückten Handlung kann das Weib nur als der passive Teil gedacht werden; vgl. Num. 5, 28. Aus diesem Grunde ist für das hier unmögliche [!] *tazri'a* entschieden *tivra'* zu lesen."
54. A very short survey of this material can be found in Cadbury, "Ancient Physiological Notions," 433–34, and in Lesky and Waszink, "Embryologie," 1241.
55. On the text-critical problem here, see M. Black, *The Book of Enoch or 1 Enoch* (Leiden: Brill, 1985) 152.

perish."[56] The expression "with the blood of flesh you have begotten children" seems to be a reference to the Aristotelian theory of the καταμήνια (menstrual blood) as one of the two components in the generative process. That this theory was known in Jewish circles seems certain in view of Wis 7:1–2: "In my mother's womb I was sculpted into flesh during a ten months' space, curdled in blood by virile seed and the pleasure that is joined with sleep" (καὶ ἐν κοιλίᾳ μητρὸς ἐγλύφην σὰρξ δεκαμηνιαίῳ χρόνῳ, παγεὶς ἐν αἵματι ἐκ σπέρματος ἀνδρὸς καὶ ἡδονῆς ὕπνῳ συνελθούσης).[57] D. Winston rightly points out in his commentary that the author here reflects passages like Aristotle's *De generatione animalium* 1.19–20. The same probably holds true for 4 Macc 13:20: "There do brothers abide for a similar period and are molded through the same span and nurtured by the same blood and brought to maturity through the same vitality"[58] ([τῆς μητρῴας γαστρὸς] ἐν ᾗ τὸν ἴσον ἀδελφοὶ κατοικήσαντες χρόνον καὶ ἐν τῷ αὐτῷ χρόνῳ πλασθέντες καὶ ἀπὸ τοῦ αὐτοῦ αἵματος αὐξηθέντες καὶ διὰ τῆς αὐτῆς ψυχῆς τελεσφορηθέντες). And we can add Philo *Quaestiones ad Genesim* 3.47: "The matter of the female in the remains of the menstrual fluids produces the fetus. But the male (provides) the skill and the cause. And so, since the male provides the greater and the more necessary (part) in the process of generation, it was proper that his pride should be checked by the sign of circumcision."[59] And compare his *De opificio mundi* 132: "(The menstrual blood) too is said by physical scientists to be the bodily substance of embryos"[60] ([τὰ καταμήνια] λέγεται γὰρ οὖν καὶ ταῦτα πρὸς ἀνδρῶν φυσικῶν οὐσία σωματικὴ βρεφῶν εἶναι).

These five passages all clearly use Aristotelian terminology or show reminiscences of it, so one cannot but conclude that at least this form of the hematogenic doctrine of seed was known in educated Jewish circles. And it has been suggested that it is against this background that one should consider a passage in the NT, John 1:13: οἳ οὐκ ἐξ αἱμάτων οὐδὲ ἐκ θελήματος σαρκὸς οὐδὲ ἐκ θελήματος ἀνδρὸς ἀλλ᾽ ἐκ θεοῦ ἐγεννήθησαν. The expression ἐξ αἱμάτων ἐγεννήθησαν (born of blood)[61] is best explained as a reference to the Aristotelian *katamenia* theory. Be that as it may, the evidence for knowledge of (originally) Aristotelian theories in Judaism does not prove the existence of a theory of female semen. As far as I know, there is no direct evidence for that outside rabbinic literature. However, it should be borne in mind that

56. Translation (slightly adapted) by E. Isaac in *The Old Testament Pseudepigrapha* (ed. J. H. Charlesworth; Garden City: Doubleday, 1983) 1. 21. The square brackets are mine; the round brackets are Isaac's. The passage refers, of course, to Gen 6:1–4.

57. The translation is by D. Winston, *The Wisdom of Solomon* (Garden City: Doubleday, 1979) 162. See his commentary on 163–64.

58. The translation is by M. Hadas, *The Third and Fourth Books of the Maccabees* (New York: Ktav, 1953) 213.

59. The translation of the ancient Armenian version is by R. Marcus in LCL.

60. The translation is by F. H. Colson and G. H. Whitaker in LCL.

61. For the plural αἵματα (bloods) cf. Euripides *Ion* 693 ἄλλων τραφεὶς ἐξ αἱμάτων, and see, besides the commentaries *ad loc.*, especially Cadbury's article mentioned in n. 10.

knowledge of Aristotle's ideas very probably implied knowledge of the ideas he combatted so firmly, that is, knowledge of double-seed theories. It may be pure coincidence that these theories are nowhere mentioned (besides being a testimony to Aristotle's influence and prestige), for we meet them often in early rabbinic literature.

In the Talmud and the Midrashim, we meet the same variety of opinions as in Greek (or Latin) literature. Of course, there is the traditional theory that the woman does not contribute anything to the formation of the embryo, for example, in *Lev. Rab.* 14.6.[62] This need not detain us here, although it is interesting to see that in one of the passages that reflect this view, we find a marked concurrence with, if not influence of, Greek terminology: In *Gen. Rab.* 17.8 we read: "Why does a man deposit sperm within a woman while a woman does not deposit sperm within a man? It is like a man who has an article in his hand and seeks a trustworthy person with whom he may deposit it." The word for "deposit" used here is a hiphil form of *pqd*, which, according to the dictionaries, means "to give in charge, to deposit." When one looks up καταβάλλω and καταβολή in Liddell-Scott-Jones, one finds there exactly the same meaning, "(to) deposit." This can hardly be coincidence, and I am inclined to detect here the influence of Greek terminology for seminal emission.

That there was indeed Greek influence on rabbinic embryology[63] is proved beyond any doubt by several passages, of which I will quote only the most illuminating.[64] The Aristotelian position seems to be reflected in the short remark in *b. Ketub.* 10b: "It has been taught in the name of Rabbi Meir: Every woman who has abundant (menstrual) blood has many children."[65] A combination of an Aristotelian and a double-seed theory is found several times—for example, in a baraita in *b. Nid.* 31a:

> Our rabbis taught: There are three partners in (the conception of) man, the Holy One—blessed be He—, his father, and his mother. His father supplies the semen of the white substance out of which are formed the child's bones, sinews, nails, the brains in his head and the white in his eye. His mother sup-

62. See, for example, J. Feliks, "Biology," *EJ* 4 (1972) 1019ff.; I. Simon, "La gynécologie, l'obstétrique, l'embryologie et la puériculture dans la Bible et le Talmud," *Revue d'histoire de la médecine hébraïque* 4 (1949) 35–64; J. Preuss, *Biblical and Talmudic Medicine* (trans. F. Rosner in 1911 ed.; New York: Sanhedrin, 1978) 375–431 (Gynecology and Obstetrics). Unfortunately, I have not been able to obtain a copy of the dissertation by E. Szarvas, *Les connaissances embryologiques et obstétricales des Hébreux jusqu'à l'époque de clôture du Talmud* (Paris, 1936).
63. That there was Greek influence on rabbinic anthropology in general was proved more than fifty years ago by R. Meyer, *Hellenistisches in der rabbinischen Anthropologie* (Stuttgart: Kohlhammer, 1937).
64. Some passages are discussed by F. Rosner, *Medicine in the Bible and the Talmud* (New York: Ktav, 1977) 173–78. Cf. also D. M. Feldman, *Birth Control in Jewish Law: Marital Relations, Contraception and Abortion as Set Forth in the Classic Texts of Jewish Law* (Westport: Greenwood Press, 1980) 132–40. Several passages are also mentioned by Stricker, *De geboorte van Horus*, passim, esp. 2. 121ff. with notes.
65. I use throughout the Soncino translation of the Talmud and the Midrash Rabba.

plies the semen of the red substance out of which is formed his skin, flesh, hair, blood and the black of his eye. The Holy One—blessed be He—gives him the spirit and the breath, beauty of features, eyesight, the power of hearing, the ability to speak and to walk, understanding and discernment.

Almost identical passages can be found in *b. Qidd.* 30b, *Qohelet Rabba* 5.10.2, *Midrash Yetsirat ha-Walad* vol. 1, p. 156, 18ff. Jellinek,[66] et al. The Aristotelian element is, of course, that the menstrual blood is regarded as the female contribution to the embryogenesis (although, in a sense, quite different from that of the Stagirite), whereas the fact that the *katamenia* are explicitly called semen classes this statement with the double-seed theory.

The double-seed theory is also explicitly referred to in *b. B. Qam.* 92a, where the rabbis discuss the fact that in Gen 20:18 ("For the Lord had closed up all the wombs of the house of Abimelech"), the Hebrew text has two forms of the verb *close*, the infinitive and the finite verb (MT has ʿatsor ʿatsar):

> Rabbi Eleazar said: Why is "closing up" mentioned twice? There was one closing up in the case of males, semen, and two in the case of females, semen and the giving of birth. In a baraitha it was taught that there were two in the case of males, semen and urinating, and three in the case of females, semen, urinating and the giving of birth. Rabina said: Three in the case of males, semen, urinating and anus, and four in the case of females, semen and the giving of birth, urinating and anus.

Interestingly enough, within the framework of a double-seed theory, the rabbis developed their own version of the *epikrateia* principle. This version simply held that if a man emits his semen first, the child will be a girl, but if the woman emits her semen first, the child will be a boy (see, for example, *b. Ber.* 54a and *Nid.* 70b–71a).[67] This theory—strange at first sight—of crosswise sex determination was supported by an exegesis of Lev 12:2 and Gen 46:15 (Lev 12:2 being the only OT text mentioned above). In *b. Nid.* 31a we read the following discussion:

> "Rabbi Isaac citing Rabbi Ammi [or: Assi] stated: If the woman emits her semen [hiphil of *zrʿ*, like Lev 12:2!] first, she bears a male child; if the man emits his semen first, she bears a female child; for it is said: 'If a woman emits semen and bears a male child' (Lev 12:2). Our Rabbis taught: At first it used to be said that 'if the woman emits her semen first, she will bear a male child, and if the man emits his semen first, she will bear a female,' but the Sages did not explain the reason, until Rabbi Zadok came and explained it: 'These are the sons of Leah whom she bore unto Jacob in Paddan-Aram, with his daughter Dinah' (Gen 46:15). Scripture thus ascribes the males to the females and the females to the males."

66. German translation of this midrash in A. Wünsche, *Aus Israels Lehrhallen* (Hildesheim: Olms, 1967; repr. of 1909 ed.) 3. 221.

67. These and other passages are discussed by Rosner, *Medicine in the Bible and the Talmud*, 173ff.

This last sentence makes clear how Gen 46:15 was understood: because this biblical text speaks of "sons of Leah" and of "his daughter Dinah," Scripture evidently implies that the fact that sons were born was due to Leah and that a daughter was born was due to Jacob. This fact, combined with the datum that the unique hiphil form of zrʿ in Lev 12:2 implies female seminal emission, seems to lead inevitably to this specifically rabbinic doctrine of *epikrateia* and sex differentiation.[68] The obvious problem of a double pregnancy with both a male and a female embryo is solved as follows: "It may equally be assumed that both [man and woman] emitted their semen simultaneously, the one resulting in a male and the other in a female" (*b. Nid.* 25b and 28b).

In this context, it should be added that although the Targumim on Leviticus all have a verb meaning "to become pregnant" for the hiphil of zrʿ in Lev 12:2, and the halakic midrash *Sifra* has no remarks *ad locum*, the haggadic midrash *Lev. Rab.* 14.9 remarks on our verse: "It [namely, the determination of the embryo's sex] may be likened to two artists, each of whom executes the likeness of the other; thus it is always that the female is formed from [the seed of the] man and the male from [the seed of the] woman. This is indicated by what is written . . . (Lev. 12:2 and Gen. 46:15). The process may be likened to two entering a bath house: whichever perspires first is the first to come out."

Several other aspects of rabbinic embryology clearly betray the influence of Greek medical ideas, but I have limited myself to the concept of female seed. It may be clear that this concept was not the fruit of an indigenous development of Jewish ideas about semen, nor was it the result of exegesis of Lev 12:2 and Gen 46:15. The fact that these biblical texts are only adduced in a context of discussion of *epikrateia* as the dominant principle of sex determination makes it highly probable that these biblical passages were only taken into service a posteriori as a scriptural prop to this theory. The Greek theory had probably already been adopted by the rabbis before the exegetical justification was there. It seems to me that in this respect, too, the rabbis were in the debt of Hellenistic culture.[69]

CONCLUSION

I have surveyed evidence for a theory of female semen from approximately 500 B.C.E. to approximately 500 C.E. I have demonstrated that there was continuous support for the theory during this millennium (and the demonstration could have covered the next millennium as well).[70] What has become over-

---

68. The sequel of this passage in *b. Nid.* 31a goes on to discuss this theme but need not be reproduced here. All embryological, sexological, and gynecological lore in the tractate *Nidda* betrays a great deal of knowledge of Greek medical theories.

69. For another example in the field of embryology, see Pieter Willem van der Horst, "Seven Months' Children in Jewish and Christian Literature from Antiquity," *ETL* 54 (1978) 346–60.

70. For the persistence of this doctrine in the Middle Ages in Greek, Latin, and Hebrew literature, see the studies by Needham, Gerlach, Lesky, and Rosner referred to in notes 14, 19, and 64.

whelmingly evident is that nothing prevents us from assuming that the author of Hebrews could easily have had knowledge of this widely current idea (much more current than Cadbury and Spicq had surmised). The fact that this author uses the term καταβολὴ σπέρματος, whereas in almost all other texts about female ejaculations this term is not used—the most current terms are προΐεσθαι, ἀποκρίνειν, ἐκκρίνειν σπέρμα, and σπερμαίνειν—is not a valid objection, since these other terms were used indiscriminately for male and female emissions as well. Hence we cannot but concur with Cadbury, who said sixty-five years ago: "The author of Hebrews meant what he seems to say."[71]

It should be added in fairness, however, that nine centuries before Cadbury, an early commentator on our Epistle, the Byzantine exegete Theophylactus, wrote in his *Expositio in Epistulam ad Hebraeos* 11:11: "δύναμιν εἰς καταβολὴν σπέρματος ἔλαβε"· τουτέστι, ἐνεδυναμώθη εἰς τὸ ὑποδέξασθαι καὶ κρατῆσαι τὸ καταβληθὲν εἰς αὐτὴν σπέρμα τοῦ Ἀβραάμ. Ἢ ἐπειδή φασιν οἱ ταῦτα ἀκριβωσάμενοι, καὶ τὴν γυναῖκα οἷόν τι σπέρμα ἀφ᾽ ἑαυτης συνεισάγειν, μήποτε οὕτως ἐκληπτέον τὸ "εἰς καταβολὴν σπέρματος" ἀντὶ τοῦ εἰς τὸ καταβαλεῖν καὶ αὐτὴν σπέρμα ("She received strength for a seminal emission": That is, she obtained strength to receive and retain Abraham's seed that was emitted into her. Or, because those who have studied these matters in detail say that a woman too, in a sense, produces seed of her own, perhaps the words "for a seminal emission" should be taken to mean this: "so that she herself too could emit semen").[72]

71. Cadbury, "Ancient Physiological Notions," 439. On p. 430 Cadbury rightly remarks on sexological notions of the ancients: "Such notions as they had, they were wont to express with directness without euphemism and false delicacy even in untechnical writing, as in poetry and religious literature."

72. *PG* 125, 348. On the knowledge of double-seed theories among patristic authors of the earlier period (second to fourth centuries), see esp. Waszink in *RAC* 4 (1959) 1242–44, and also his monumental *Tertulliani De Anima* (Amsterdam: Meulenhoff, 1947) 342–48. One can only speculate about the possibility that the author of the *Odes of Solomon* had a theory on female seed in mind when he wrote: "(Mary) brought forth, like a man, by will" (*Odes* 19.10a). See, however, J. Legrand, "How Was the Virgin Mary 'Like a Man'?" *NovT* 22 (1980) 97–107.

PART FOUR

HELLENISTIC SOCIAL BEHAVIOR

THE CIRCLE OF REFERENCE
IN PAULINE MORALITY

For Aristotle, the context in which character is formed and the arena in which virtue is exercised is the polis.[1] For the sect or cult of early Christianity, obviously the polis does not have the same force, but what precisely took its place? The first groups that emerge clearly into what little light is cast by our surviving sources are the communities to which Paul wrote his letters. Because those letters are primarily instruments intended for moral instruction and formation, they are particularly precious sources for questions about the scope of moral perceptions and obligations in the Christian movement, at least as Paul understood them. Moreover, the research by Abraham J. Malherbe and his students over the past two decades has put into a quite new context the question, How large was the moral world of Paul, his fellow workers, and their communities?

THE SOCIOLOGY OF MORAL REFERENCE

Before turning to the sources and to the insights Malherbe has won for us, let me try to make the object of our inquiry clearer by introducing one notion from sociological theory: reference groups. This term was coined in 1942 by the social psychologist Herbert H. Hyman,[2] who used it to point out that the

1. On the social context of Aristotle's ethical thought, see Jonathan Lear, *Aristotle: the Desire to Understand* (Cambridge: Cambridge University Press, 1988), chap. 5. Werner Jaeger's exposition remains the definitive treatment of the polis as the context of all Greek ethical thought and of the public character of virtue and conscience, not only in Aristotle but also in the whole classic tradition (*Paideia: The Ideals of Greek Culture* [Oxford; Oxford University Press, 1948]). For example, "The polis is the social framework of the whole history of Greek culture" (1. 78). For a superficial survey of some of the problems imposed on this polis-ideal in the empires of the Diadochoi and Rome, see Wayne A. Meeks, *The Moral World of the First Christians* (Philadelphia: Westminster, 1986) 19–39. Eckhard Plümacher, *Identitätsverlust und Identitätsgewinn: Studien zum Verhältnis von kaiserzeitlicher Stadt und frühem Christentum* (*BTS* 11; Neukirchen-Vluyn: Neukirchener Verlag, 1987), has sketched a picture of anomie caused by the political changes among the sub-decurional classes and, later, even the urban elites. Some of these people, he argues, found in Christianity an alternative "city" either practically or symbolically.

2. Herbert H. Hyman, "The Psychology of Status," *Archives of Psychology* 269 (1942) 5–38, 80–86; abridged in Herbert H. Hyman and Eleanor Singer (eds.), *Readings in Reference Group*

groups with reference to which people shape their attitudes may or may not be the same as the groups to which these people belong—the latter's being labeled usually membership groups or in-groups. Harold H. Kelley observed that reference groups may act on people normatively, by affecting their motivations, or comparatively, by affecting their perceptions and giving them a standard for self-evaluation. He also pointed out that the relationship may be negative as well as positive.[3] Tamotsu Shibutani emphasized the perceptual side of reference group function and connected it both with G. H. Mead's "taking the role of the generalized other" and with the concept of *culture* as used by anthropologists. Shibutani's definition will serve our purposes well: "any collectivity, real or imagined, envied or despised, whose perspective is assumed by the actor," where *perspective* means "an ordered view of one's world—what is taken for granted about the attributes of various objects, events, and human nature."[4] It will also be important to keep in mind Hyman's observation, in his original article, that there may be reference individuals who affect us in much the same way as reference groups—and these, too, may be "real or imagined, envied or despised."

The notion of reference groups and reference individuals will help us understand how broad were the moral horizons of Pauline Christianity. It will, of course, help us with only one dimension of Paul's moral world. In particular, it will not directly enable us to talk about the circle of moral responsibility that Paul tried to draw for his audiences. The composite of a person's reference groups does not necessarily comprise all those for whom the person may feel responsible.[5]

We can put our question in this way: In his admonitions, what reference groups and individuals did Paul assume would be effective, or did he want to make effective, for the people to whom he was writing? A related question is this: What are Paul's own overt or implied reference groups and individuals? Who were those whom Paul might imagine looking over his shoulder, or the shoulders of his audience? Who were those before whom they would like to feel proud or fear being shamed, by whom they would be praised or blamed? Who were those whose values Paul's audience had internalized? Whose picture of the way things are do they take for granted? We are limited, of course, to what Paul takes to be the case and wishes to make the case; unfortunately,

---

Theory and Research (New York: Free Press; London: Collier-Macmillan, 1968) 147–65. The latter is a collection of the articles that figured most importantly in the development of reference group theory.

3. Harold H. Kelley, "Two Functions of Reference Groups," in Hyman and Singer, *Readings*, 77–83.

4. Tamotsu Shibutani, "Reference Groups as Perspectives," in Hyman and Singer, *Readings*, 103–13; quotations from 105. Further on, Shibutani restates his definition more concisely: "A reference group, then, is that group whose outlook is used by the actor as the frame of reference of his perceptual field" (107).

5. Prof. Susan Garrett helped me to understand this point; I am grateful for her careful reading of this chapter and her helpful suggestions at several points.

we cannot interview his addressees to see whether the reference groups and individuals Paul assumes or proposes were in fact effectual among the people who heard his letters read out in church. Pauline Christianity is thus inevitably an idealized construct. It is nevertheless neither uninteresting nor irrelevant to the interpretive concerns mentioned above.

MORALS FOR CONVERTS
1 THESSALONIANS

A good place to begin is with 1 Thessalonians, especially in view of the extraordinary new insights that Malherbe has introduced into our understanding of this earliest extant Christian letter.

The Movement as Reference Group

In 1 Thess 1:7–10, Paul says that the Thessalonian Christians have become a τύπος for converts in other Macedonian cities, as well as in Achaia. We could almost translate τύπος as "reference group." Paul puts this notion of the Salonicans' "modeling" for other converts into the context of his notion of μίμησις, "imitation," which would become a standard part of his parenetic repertory (v. 6: "You have become imitators of us and of the Lord"). The chain of imitation is thus extendable: Christ/Paul, Silvanus, and Timothy/Thessalonian Christians/other converts. In 2:14, Paul inserts another link: the Thessalonian Christians, by suffering at the hands of their peers and relations, have become imitators of the Judean churches. Paul's praise, in this philophronetic portion of the letter, serves as a reminder to the addressees of the attitudes and behavior that they exhibited in their initial response to Paul's missionary preaching and that they are expected to continue, and at the same time as a reminder of the other groups that are, as it were, witnesses to their good behavior. The apostles, the other churches that Paul has founded near and far from them, and the earlier Christian groups in Judea, as well as the idealized picture of themselves at the beginning, thus constitute the reference circle with which the Thessalonian Christians ought to compare themselves and within which the norms that Paul will state and imply in the admonitions of the letter are validated.

Reference Individuals

Paul has also introduced reference individuals—not only himself, his fellow workers, and (in 1 Thess 5:12–13) local leaders and patrons who are explicitly identified as moral guides (καὶ νουθετοῦντες ὑμᾶς [5:12]), but also Christ. For these Gentile converts in Macedonia, Christ is, of course, an *imagined* individual. That is, the converts are dependent, for their picture of the features of Christ by which they are to guide their lives, upon the things that the apostles have told about him and that are reiterated in the group's ritual and song.[6] Some elements of that narration are recalled in the letter: suffering, being raised from the dead, expected return from Heaven, action "saving us from the coming wrath," and companionship with the living and dead believers in the future.

Not only Christ but also God become here, though the phrase sounds crude, reference individuals. The comprehensiveness of the relationship is implied by the words that recall the addressees' conversion: "how you turned to God from the idols to serve a God living and real" (1 Thess 1:9). Paul makes the reference function explicit in 2:12, "to the end that you behave in a way worthy of the God who calls you into his kingdom and glory," and in 4:1, "how you must behave and (so) please God" (to the last, compare Paul's declaration of his own integrity in 2:4, οὐχ ὡς ἀνθρώποις ἀρέσκοντες ἀλλὰ θεῷ [not as pleasing humans but God]). As in the case of Christ, the way in which God serves as model is explicitly tied to the Christian narrative and to the addressees' experience of conversion: "worthy of the God *who calls you*" (italics added). The underlying conception of God, nevertheless, is not exclusively Christian but broadly Jewish and includes many elements familiar in the larger culture (for example, "the God who tests our hearts" [2:4]).

It is obvious that Paul quite deliberately presents himself as a model to be imitated, in a way typical of philosophical parenesis,[7] and thus, in our sociological jargon, as a reference individual. Throughout the first three chapters of 1 Thessalonians, Paul's reminders and self-references serve to reinforce his own position (along with Silvanus and Timothy) in that role. His allusions to his own feelings may serve the same function. For example, in 3:5 he recalls the anxiety that made him send Timothy to find out about the recent converts: μή πως ἐπείρασεν ὑμᾶς ὁ πειράζων καὶ εἰς κενὸν γένηται ὁ κόπος ἡμῶν (lest the Tester had tested you and *our labor had come to naught* [emphasis added]). An ancient audience would doubtless hear an allusion to Paul's concern about his honor; failure of the Thessalonian Christians to endure would bring shame on Paul. Paul makes no explicit mention of honor, but he does speak of the addressees as his ἐλπὶς ἢ χαρὰ ἢ στέφανος καυχήσεως (hope and joy and proud diadem [2:19]) and as ἡ δόξα ἡμῶν καὶ ἡ χαρά (our glory and joy [2:20])—though in the specifically Jewish and Christian context of final judgment and Jesus' Parousia (2:19; cf. 3:13). The "public" before which the apostle's shame or honor will be manifest is not a crowd of citizens in the agora of the polis but a transcendent community: God and Christ and their

6. Norman R. Petersen, *Rediscovering Paul: Philemon and the Sociology of Paul's Narrative World* (Philadelphia: Fortress, 1985) 200–286; Martin Hengel, "Hymns and Christology," *Between Jesus and Paul* (Philadelphia: Fortress, 1983) 78–96.
7. Abraham J. Malherbe, "1 Thessalonians as a Paraenetic Letter," paper presented at the SBL Seminar on Paul in Los Angeles in 1972; Malherbe, "Exhortation in First Thessalonians," *NovT* 25 (1983) 238–56; Malherbe, *Paul and the Thessalonians: The Philosophic Tradition of Pastoral Care* (Philadelphia: Fortress, 1987). For a detailed treatment of the use of personal examples, see the work by Malherbe's student Benjamin Fiore, S.J., *The Function of Personal Example in the Socratic and Pastoral Epistles* (AnBib 105; Rome: Pontifical Biblical Institute, 1986).

"holy ones." The motif of being blameless at the Parousia reappears at the end of the letter (5:23) in the form of a wish or prayer that at the same time serves as a reminder of the ultimate sanction of the admonitions.

The Thessalonians are not so dependent upon report and imagination for their conception of Paul as for their images of God and Christ, for they have seen and talked with the apostle. Nevertheless, Paul takes some pains in 1 Thess 2:1–12 to be sure that the image they have of him is appropriate—appropriate precisely for one who sets himself as a reference individual for them. The interesting thing is that the language he uses, as Malherbe has shown, is drawn from typical self-descriptions of moralizing philosophers, as found especially in the debate between rigoristic Cynics and milder curers of souls.[8] Thus, as Paul supports his position as a reference individual for his audience, by reminding them of his credentials to give them moral advice, he does so in terms that are familiar and approved in the larger society. Those philosophers and orators—an intellectual elite—are in some important sense a reference group for Paul and, at some remove, also for the audience, or so Paul must assume. Still, he does not mention Cynics or even philosophy by name; the audience of the letter need not recognize the implied reference in order to understand Paul's point. Further, Paul has interwoven the Cynic themes with specifically Christian phrases: ἐπαρρησιασάμεθα (we exercised bold speech [good Cynic language]) but "in our God" (2:2); οὐδὲ ἐν δόλῳ (not by guile [a familiar philosopher's self-defense]), but καθὼς δεδοκιμάσμμεθα ὑπὸ του θεοῦ πιστευθῆναι τὸ εὐαγγέλιον (as we stood God's test to be entrusted with the gospel [2:4]); "as Christ's apostles" (2:7); "the gospel of God" (2:8, 9); and "worthy of the God who calls you into his own kingdom and glory" (2:12). Paul's reference to moralists of the dominant culture is thus tacit, whereas specific Christian references are explicit.

Outsiders as Reference Group

We may doubt that Paul wants prestigious circles of pagan society to provide positive moral reference points for his converts, because at several places in 1 Thessalonians, "Gentile" society as a whole is explicitly a *negative* reference group. Thus, the marriage precept, handed on by Paul as (Jewish-Christian) tradition and recalled by way of example in 4:4–7, is accentuated by contrast with alleged behavior of "the gentiles who do not know God" (4:5). Similarly, the consolation passage 4:13–5:11 uses apocalyptic commonplaces to distinguish the Christians from "the rest who do not have hope" (4:13b; cf. 4:6, μὴ ... ὡς οἱ λοιποί), the "sons of light" and "sons of the day" from the children of darkness and night (5:8), and so on. Such negative stigmatization of the social world from which the converts have "turned" is, of course, an essential feature of the language of conversion.[9] Malherbe has shown how

8. Abraham J. Malherbe, "'Gentle as a Nurse': The Cynic Background to I Thess ii," *NovT* 12 (1970) 203–17.

9. Compare the classic discussion of "nihilation" by Peter Berger and Thomas Luckmann,

much of Paul's pastoral appeal to the Thessalonian Christians interprets and builds upon the real pain of separation that every convert experiences.[10] However, Malherbe has also pointed out, building on earlier work by A. D. Nock, that in antiquity, apart from Judaism, it was preeminently in the philosophical schools, not least in the Cynic letters and in friendly accounts of Cynic philosophers, that conversion stories were told.[11] Thus, we find Paul urging the Christians to distinguish themselves from the world around them, but doing so in terms that were at home in the "philosophical koine" of that world. Even the content of Paul's admonitions reveals the same ambivalence. The sex life of the "Gentiles who do not know God" is characterized by πάθος ἐπιθυμίας, "passion to possess" (1 Thess 4:5)—just the language a Stoic or Cynic (and many Middle Platonists, including the Jew Philo) would use to characterize the chief obstacle to a rational moral life. And the monogamy here set forth as required of Christians and avenged by God was, in fact, the ideal of most pagan moralists as well.[12] Further, Malherbe has shown that beginning with περὶ δὲ τῆς φιλαδελφίας, "concerning affection for brothers," in 4:9, Paul is employing "well-known topoi": minding one's own business, decorum, self-sufficiency, quietism, and love.[13] Malherbe thinks that Paul may be urging the Christians not to behave like Epicureans, and that Paul's neologism in 4:9, θεοδίδακτοι (God-taught), may be a deliberate rejection of Epicurus's claim to be αὐτοδίδακτος (self-taught).[14] Be that as it may, it is clear that here, as in Stoic and Academic criticism of the Epicureans, the implied reference group is a generalized public, the polis. The ἡσυχία (quiet life) of the Christians is not, as opponents complained of the Epicurean withdrawal, opposed to the good order of the city. Paul makes this explicit in 4:12: ἵνα περιπατῆτε εὐσχημόνως πρὸς τοὺς ἔξω ("that you behave decently vis-à-vis the outsiders").[15]

The Social Construction of Reality: A Treatise in the Sociology of Knowledge (Garden City, NY: Doubleday, Anchor, 1967) 156–62; and, for a survey of recent studies of conversion and application to conversion in Paul, Beverly Gaventa, From Darkness to Light: Aspects of Conversion in the New Testament (Philadelphia: Fortress, 1986), and Alan Segal, Paul the Convert (New Haven and London: Yale University Press, 1990).

10. See esp. Malherbe, "Exhortation in First Thessalonians" and Paul and the Thessalonians.

11. Abraham J. Malherbe, "'Not in a Corner': Early Christian Apologetic in Acts 26:26," SecCent 5 (1985–86) 193–209; A. D. Nock, Conversion: The Old and the New in Religion from Alexander the Great to Augustine of Hippo (Oxford: Clarendon, 1952).

12. See O. Larry Yarbrough, "Not Like the Gentiles": Marriage Rules in the Letters of Paul (SBLDS 80; Atlanta: Scholars, 1985).

13. See Malherbe, "Exhortation in First Thessalonians," 252, and the references given there.

14. Malherbe, "Exhortation in First Thessalonians," 253.

15. See W. C. van Unnik, "Die Rücksicht auf die Reaktion der Nicht-Christen als Motiv in der altchristlichen Paränese," in his Sparsa Collecta (NovTSup 30; Leiden: Brill, 1980) 2. 307–22.

THE OTHER LETTERS

The reference individuals and groups that we have identified in Paul's parenesis in 1 Thessalonians appear throughout the later letters that are generally recognized to be undoubtedly by Paul, though the emphasis and tone vary considerably according to the issue and the situation. What turns out to be most characteristic of Paul's moral universe is precisely the multiplicity of reference. The categories we found in 1 Thessalonians provide a rough map.

The Movement as Reference Group

When Paul invokes specifically Christian teachings or practices as warrants for admonitions about behavior, the implicit reference group is the Christian movement itself—for example, 1 Cor 6:12–20. The common theme of 1 Corinthians 5–6 is the internal purity of the groups. Specific Christian traditions (παραδόσεις) can be the basis for praise or blame (1 Cor 11:2, 17, 23). Over against common "status-specific expectations" in the larger society for standards at meals provided by patrons of extended household gatherings,[16] Paul sets the concern for the ἐκκλησία τοῦ θεοῦ (God's meeting) and, on the part of those who are better provided, the concern for "those who haven't [namely, houses? anything?]" (τοὺς μὴ ἔχοντες [11:22]). Citation of the tradition about the Last Supper provides the warrant for behavior that will be "worthy" when one "discerns the body" (11:29). Paul's preference for prophecy over tongue speaking in the meetings at Corinth is explicitly for the sake of the community itself as the object of moral concern: "but one who prophesies speaks to human persons words of construction [οἰκοδομή] and exhortation and consolation" (14:3); "that the Meeting may be built up [οἰκοδομὴν λάβῃ]" (14:4, cf. 14:12). Yet in this same context, Paul also expresses concern for outsiders' opinions (14:23–25).

Next to 1 Corinthians, 2 Corinthians is perhaps the most interesting of Paul's letters for the historian of morality, because it gives an extended picture, however clouded at places, of conflict and attempts to deal with it within one of the Pauline congregations and between it and Paul.[17] In a hermeneutical tour de force, Paul wants to persuade the Corinthians to see the grief (λύπη) he has caused them by his previous visit and letter (2 Cor 2:1–4; 7:8–12) and the grief they, especially one of them, have caused him (2:5–11) within the category of "the sufferings of Christ" (1:5), the θλίψεις in which God provides comfort. The conflict between them can thus be managed and, he hopes, reconciliation made possible. The circle of responsibility thus seems at the outset strictly "sectarian": the conflict is internal to the Christian

16. The phrase and, in part, the interpretation are from Gerd Theissen, "Die Starken und Schwachen in Korinth: Soziologische Analyse eines theologischen Streites," EvT 35 (1975) 155–72.

17. I take the first eight chapters (at least) of 2 Corinthians to be, in spite of all the oft-noted aporias, one letter, the theme of which is enunciated in the opening blessing: παράκλησις ἐν θλίψει (comfort in affliction).

movement, and the interpretive framework is distinctively Christian, even distinctively Pauline. At one point, Paul, to be sure, extends this interpretive framework to "cosmic" dimensions: the reconciliation of their quarrel belongs to the process of God's "reconciling the world to himself" (5:18–21). But that image of cosmic reconciliation is itself peculiar to the Christians and to some other varieties of Judaism. The circle of action and the circle of reference are still limited to the Christian groups, even though the terms imply an ultimate responsibility for the world.

As in 1 Thessalonians, Paul in the other letters sometimes calls attention to churches in other places as models or witnesses. There are three places in 1 Corinthians where Paul refers to "all the churches" or the equivalent, twice in explicit warrants for recommended behavior (1:2; 11:16; 14:33b—though the first and last of these are often regarded as later interpolations). Shame and honor figure largely in Paul's exhortation about the collection in 2 Corinthians 8–9, explicitly at 9:2–4 but implicitly from the beginning of the comparison of the addressees with the Macedonian Christians (8:1–7: the Macedonians, despite their "abysmal poverty," have given abundantly; how much more the Corinthians, who "abound" in all kinds of gifts, should give). The public before whom this shame, both of the Corinthians and of the apostles, might be displayed (9:4) is the representatives of the Macedonian churches. Paul introduces instructions for the collection in 1 Cor 16:1–4 by referring to the directive he gave to the Galatian Christians.

The principle of equity (ἰσότης) that Paul enunciates (2 Cor 8:13) is, of course, a commonplace in Greco-Roman moralizing; Aristotle had already expatiated on equity in the transactions that make the κοινωνία of friendship or of civic life possible (for example, his discussion of friendship in *Eth. Nic.* 7.7.1–3, or of "corrective justice" in 5.4). For Paul, however, it is not the city or ordinary friendship that forms the circle of reference but the various Christian communities. The ἄλλοι ("others") in 2 Cor 8:13 is perhaps deliberately vague, encompassing both the proportional obligation between the Gentile communities and the Jerusalem center, which Paul will later enunciate in Rom 15:27, and the friendly competition between the Macedonians and the Corinthians, which Paul introduces at the beginning of this chapter and again in 9:2–4.

The Aristotelian (or common Greco-Roman) sense of proportion is altered here in one fundamental respect. For Aristotle (and evidently in common custom, even in law), ἰσότης entails that the socially superior party always receive more—honor, affection, goods, whatever—than the inferior. Here, however, a different model is introduced: the "grace [χάρις, the same word Paul uses for the gift (2 Cor 8:4, 6, 7, 19; 1 Cor 16:3)] of our Lord Jesus Christ, that for your sakes he being rich impoverished himself, that by his poverty you should be enriched" (2 Cor 8:9). Note that this description of Christ's action parallels the earlier description of the Macedonians' gift: "their abysmal poverty abounded to the wealth of their integrity" (8:2b). Paul is thus making the pattern of Christ's self-giving a model by which to revise the notion of equity within the Christian movement. At the same time, his citation of Exod 16:18 (2 Cor 8:15) undoubtedly indicates that, at least in his own mind, the movement is continuous with Israel and that therefore the same pattern of equity is to be seen in God's dealings with (biblical) Israel.

In the Letter to Philemon, Paul forcefully and adroitly invokes the reference circle of the Christian community, both local and extended, to put Philemon into a situation of obligation.[18] By addressing the letter not to Philemon privately but to the whole κατ᾽ οἶκον ἐκκλησία (the household meeting), by naming Apphia and Archippus, by including greetings from five "fellow workers" (23–24), and by announcing that he will visit Philemon soon, Paul emphatically portrays the normative group in sight of which Philemon must make his decision. And, of course, Paul at the same time underscores his own role as a reference individual.

Despite the years that have intervened, Philippians reminds us in several ways of the first of Paul's extant letters, addressed to nearby Thessalonica. Even more than in the earlier letter, elements of the friendship topos of Greco-Roman rhetoric pervade Philippians—without a single use of φίλος or φιλία.[19] As usual, friendship is understood as a relationship of exchange, so language that sounds to our ears "commercial" provides many of the metaphors—contracts, giving and receiving, payments and receipts, making up the balance, profit and loss, and bankruptcy.[20] Although the aim of the parenetic portion of the letter is like that of much of 1 Corinthians, the promotion of unity and concord within the community—the "political" commonplaces of parts of that letter[21]—is here replaced almost entirely by the more intimate language of friendship. Moral commonplaces from the language of philosophy appear again: the list of urbane values in Phil 4:8 (the true, the grand, the pure, the amiable, the reputable, and any virtue and anything praiseworthy) as well as the virtue of αὐτάρκεια, "self-sufficiency," so cherished by the Cynics (4:11–13). The correspondence thus again takes place within the reference circle implied by sophisticated public and private talk, a circle within which the importance of "those of Caesar's household" (4:21) is self-evident. Yet again, as in the Thessalonian letters, this educated circle of reference is taken for granted. In the foreground is the specific set of relationships that constitute the Christian community itself.

We noticed above that when the Christian movement as a whole serves as the reference group for Paul's admonitions, he often represents it as continu-

---

18. See, besides the commentaries, Petersen, *Rediscovering Paul.*

19. Ken Berry is currently completing a dissertation on this topic at Yale University, under Professor Malherbe's direction. See also the essay in this volume by L. Michael White.

20. See Peter Marshall, *Enmity in Corinth: Social Conventions in Paul's Relations with the Corinthians* (WUNT 23, 2d ser.; Tübingen: J. C. B. Mohr [Paul Siebeck], 1987) 160–62.

21. Robert M. Grant, "Political Ideas in Paul," paper delivered at Haverford College, 4 March 1983; L. L. Welborn, "On the Discord in Corinth: 1 Corinthians 1–4 and Ancient Politics," *JBL* 106 (1987) 85–111.

ous with biblical Israel.[22] Implicitly, that is the case whenever Paul appeals to Scripture or to traditional interpretations, as in 1 Cor 10:1–22 or 5:6–8, or when he contrasts his audience with "the Gentiles," as in 1 Thess 4:5; 1 Cor 5:1; 12:2; cf. Gal 4:8–9. In Galatians, when the terms of entry for Gentiles into the community are the center of controversy, Paul sketches a narrative of God's dealings with Israel and the world (chapters 3 through 4), so one might say that the eschatological people of God—an idealized construct from the biblical account of Israel's history, transformed by eschatological hopes and by peculiarly Christian exegesis based on the kerygma of Christ's death and resurrection—is the central reference group to which all others are subordinated. In Romans, which evidently contains fruit of Paul's reflections on the Galatian controversy, Paul declares the history, scriptures, and destiny of Israel to be of utmost relevance to the mostly Gentile congregations of Rome, and the complex dialectic governing Paul's understanding of that relevance becomes the central theme of the letter. The letter itself, to be read in all the housechurches that make up the "fractionated" Roman church,[23] is designed to be a practical instantiation of the interconnectedness of all such Christian groups—hence Paul's account of his expanded mission area, of the planned journey to Jerusalem, and the greetings from Corinth and to the many separate groups in Rome. As in Galatians, but in much more carefully nuanced and elaborated terms, the ultimate reference group is an ideal entity, the eschatological people of God, comprising the Israel of God's choosing and promises and the Gentile Christians who have been "grafted into" it; and, potentially, πᾶς ἄνθρωπος—"every human person."

Reference Individuals

It hardly requires documentation that Christ and God are the primary imagined reference individuals, either explicitly or implicitly, in all Paul's letters. As in 1 Thessalonians, we see in the other letters a fairly narrowly drawn narrative of Christ as not only reference individual but also model. Also, as in the early letter, we find a much broader conception of God that is, however, often focused by relating specific actions: raising Christ from the dead, making and keeping promises, calling his people, and acting as judge. Consider only the way in which Paul's quotation of the liturgical poem in Phil 2:6–11 presents the mythic picture of Christ's ταπείνωσις (humility) as model for the φρόνησις (way of thinking) appropriate to the Christian community.[24] The narrative structure of Galatians 3–4 and Romans 1–11 not only portrays the idealized community's history, as noted above, but also offers a picture of

---

22. Compare the comment above on 2 Cor 8:15.

23. Peter Lampe, *Die stadtrömischen Christen in den ersten beiden Jahrhunderten: Untersuchungen zur Sozialgeschichte* (WUNT 18, 2d ser.; Tübingen: J. C. B. Mohr [Paul Siebeck], 1987) pt. 5.

24. The extended debate over whether Christ appears here as *Vorbild* or *Urbild* need not concern us; I have tried to address one aspect of that question in a chapter of a forthcoming book.

God as active agent by which, in varied and subtle ways, the behavior and attitudes of the Christian groups ought to be measured.

Paul's self-portrayal as reference individual is as pervasive as the christological and theological references. For example, in his rebuking letter to the Galatians, his account of his own prophetic call, his interaction with the Jerusalem apostles, and his previous relationship with the converts are an integral basis for his appeal for them to alter their behavior. Examples abound in the Corinthian letters. In 1 Corinthians 1–4, Paul, of course, presents himself as a reference individual, as he sums up in 4:6–21; note especially v. 6: "I have used these figures of myself and Apollo for your sakes, so that you could learn by us." Again, in 1 Corinthians 9, he makes himself the imitator of Christ and the model to be emulated, as he reiterates in 10:32–11:1.

As was the case in 1 Thess 5:12–13, patrons and leaders of local congregations can be singled out as reference individuals—for example, "such people" as Stephanas and his household and Fortunatus and Achaicus (1 Cor 16:15–18; comparing the language in Phil 2:30 and Philemon 7, 20). The same is probably implied of Phoebe in Rom 16:1–2 and the people greeted explicitly as heads of households where meetings are held, like Prisca and Aquila in Rom 16:3–5a and 1 Cor 16:19, and probably others among the named individuals who would be known by the recipients to have such roles.

Outsiders as Reference Group

The places where Paul explicitly refers to outsiders to back up his admonitions are few. One instance of a positive reference is 1 Cor 14:23–25, where Paul warns that ἰδιῶται ἢ ἄπιστοι, if they "enter" a meeting dominated by undisciplined tongue speakers, would think them possessed of a (Dionysian?) frenzy. In 1 Corinthians 5–6, the common theme of which is the internal purity of the Christian groups, the "outsiders" (κόσμος οὗτος [5:10], οἱ ἔξω [5:13]) are excluded from the circle of reference, though eventually the ἅγιοι (saints) will judge them (6:2). Certainly the institutions of judgment of the "unbelievers" are not to be resorted to in disputes among the Christians. Gentiles are a negative reference group in 1 Cor 12:2–3 ("when you were Gentiles") and, though with double-edged irony, in 5:1 ("not even among the Gentiles").

In contrast, if we consider also the standards of value that are implicit in Paul's style and argumentative strategies, the map of his effective reference groups becomes more complex. Malherbe and his students have taught us that Paul often depends tacitly upon the reference circle of the rhetorically or philosophically educated elites of Greco-Roman society. To be sure, he appeals to their values often with ambivalence, and sometimes he expressly contradicts or modifies them. 1 Corinthians 1–4 is a telling example. The dissension that Chloe's people have reported to Paul is rooted in the pride of partisans for different apostles, primarily—perhaps solely—Paul and Apollos (N.B. 4:6–7). The "boasting" involved in this partisanship is like that indigenous to the sophistic tradition, so Paul distances himself throughout from the pride of rhetoric, as well as from the boasts of the σοφός in the philosophical schools. As two of Malherbe's students have pointed out,[25] Paul's irony in 4:8 uses language familiar from the early Stoics, who coined the watchword μόνος ὁ σοφὸς βασιλεῦς (only the wise person is a king).[26] The philosophical parallels do not explain Paul's emphasis on baptism as the focal point of the divisions (1:14–17) nor all of Paul's references to πνεῦμα in chapters 2 and 3, but they are sufficient to show that we do not need to posit a proto-Gnostic movement to explain what Paul is opposing. However rational or irrational was the wisdom the Corinthians thought they received in baptism, Paul identifies their divisive boasting with the "wisdom of the world" set opposite to the "wisdom of God" (1:18–2:5). Thus, he treats the intellectual world of Sophists and philosophers as a negative reference group—even as, in typical fashion, he demonstrates his ability to use the rhetorical devices of that world against it.

The ambivalence is even more vivid in Paul's ironic polemic of 2 Corinthians 10–13, where again he mixes his implied reference groups in a most complex way. He both tacitly appeals to, and sarcastically undermines, the values of the educated elite that apparently underlie the attack on him by the opposing apostles. As Malherbe has shown,[27] Paul employs a familiar tradition to defend the propriety of a philosopher's being ταπεινός, "humble," and to deride the hubris of his opponents. He uses, and at the same time parodies and mocks, the rhetorical strategies of boasting and invective.[28] He equally employs citations of Scripture and allusions to Jewish haggadic traditions (10:17; 11:3, 14; 13:1) and, like his opponents, appeals to indicators of status within Israel (11:22). And, of course, he appeals to peculiarly Christian beliefs and traditions, as well as to his own apostolic autobiography, which itself conforms both to the philosophical use of catalogs of circumstances to prove virtue and, ironically, to the inversion of values in the cross-and-resurrection kerygma (especially 11:23–33 and the whole passage on "visions and revelations" [12:1–10]).[29]

Not only are multiple reference groups and individuals implicit in the exhortations of Paul's letters, but in any given instance, several different bases

25. See Stanley K. Stowers, "A 'Debate' over Freedom: 1 Corinthians 6:12–20," *Christian Teaching: Studies in Honor of Lemoine C. Lewis*, ed. Everett Ferguson (Abilene, TX: Abilene Christian University, 1981) 59–71; and John T. Fitzgerald, *"Cracks in an Earthen Vessel": An Examination of the Catalogues of Hardships in the Corinthian Correspondence* (SBLDS 99; Atlanta: Scholars, 1988)—another dissertation directed by Professor Malherbe—135–44.

26. Attributed to Chrysippus in *Stoicorum Veterum Fragmenta* 3. 81,31 (frag. 332); 158,35 (frag. 617).

27. Abraham J. Malherbe, "Antisthenes and Odysseus, and Paul at War," *HTR* 76 (1983) 143–73.

28. Marshall, *Enmity in Corinth*, chap. 9; and E. A. Judge, "Paul's Boasting in Relation to Contemporary Professional Practice," *AusBR* 16 (1968) 37–50.

29. For the way Paul transforms the philosophical use of catalogs of circumstances within this self-reference, see Fitzgerald, *"Cracks in an Earthen Vessel."*

of reference may be operative, sometimes in tension with one another. One of the more complex examples is the discussion of εἰδωλόθυτα (idol-sacrifices) in 1 Corinthians 8–10. Paul requires the audience of his admonitions to keep in mind a remarkable number of implicit reference groups: the "knowing" Christians and their social peers among the pagans of Corinth (whose invitations to dinner presumably have precipitated the controversy [10:27]); "the weak," whose consciences these more sophisticated Christians ought to respect; the Israel of Scripture and tradition (especially 10:1–22, but also v. 26); Paul himself as personal example (chapter 9); but above all, the whole Christian community, with its special traditions (for example, 8:6), made up of "brothers for whom Christ died" (8:11). If we had to rank the reference groups to which Paul implicitly appeals, this last would be at the top, yet he does not himself simplify the process of moral formation by stating a hierarchy. It is in the give and take of dialogue that the community itself must work out what is σύμ-φερον (advantageous) what οἰκοδομεῖ (builds up [10:23]).[30] Most expansive of all are the circles of reference depicted or implied in the Letter to the Romans. All humankind (1:18–3:20; 5:12–21), even all the creation (8:19–22), are brought within the scope of Paul's "gospel." The political order is affirmed in quite traditional terms (13:1–7). The history, scripture, and destiny of Israel are of fundamental importance. All the Christian groups founded by Paul among the Gentiles, the multiple household groups to which the letter is to be read, the church at Jerusalem to which Paul is taking the collection—all are included in the context within which Paul's protreptic discourse is to be heard.[31]

The dominant reference groups and individuals in Paul's admonitions are peculiar to the movement, and outsiders are often a negative reference group, yet the Pauline stance is not simply countercultural. The Torah of God, which once worked to keep God's people "locked in" (Gal 3:23) and firmly maintain the "separation" (διαστολή) between Jew and Gentile, has now become in the Pauline groups a witness to the liberation that faith brings and to the unity of Jew and Greek, slave and free, male and female in the New Human, Christ. Although God has chosen things foolish and weak in the world to put to shame the σοφοί (wise) and the δυνατοί (powerful), that does not keep Paul from making use of the traditions and strategies of the σοφοί in his moral arguments, nor from depending upon the (relatively) δυνατοί as patrons of his household meetings. However dualistically Paul can sometimes portray "this world," it remains the creation of God that "groans in travail" for its liberation, for its reconciliation, in which the apostle's efforts and the inner life of the Christian groups are implicated.

30. See Wayne A. Meeks, "The Polyphonic Ethics of the Apostle Paul," *Annual of the Society of Christian Ethics (1988)*, 17–29.
31. See above, pp. 313–14.

IS PAUL DEVELOPING
A SPECIFICALLY CHRISTIAN
ETHICS IN GALATIANS?

Abraham J. Malherbe's career-long fascination with the historical and cultural setting of the NT, and more specifically, with the indebtedness of these writings to Greek culture, lends a distinctive character to his scholarly work. This interest is not surprising. Few contemporary scholars are better equipped to deal with this vast area of research. Over the years, Malherbe has explored many of its facets and has guided a generation of scholars to appreciate the importance of this material for the understanding of the NT.

It is also not surprising that Paul has occupied a special place in Malherbe's own research. This "enigmatic figure," as Malherbe calls Paul,[1] epitomizes in his personal history and in his theological reflection so much of the interaction and cross-pollination between early Christianity and Hellenistic culture that Malherbe constantly returns to the apostle's writings. Without denying the importance of Jewish influences on Paul, it is his Greco-Roman side that commands Malherbe's attention. The title of one of his recent essays expresses this interest well: "Paul: Hellenistic Philosopher or Christian Pastor?"

It is in the context of this dialectical relationship that I would like to explore a related, but secondary, question: Is Paul developing specifically Christian ethics in Galatians? To do full justice to this question, it should be considered against the background of Paul's other writings and in the context of his theology as a whole. The aim of this chapter, restricted to one letter and to one aspect of Paul's thought, is much more modest. I would like to concentrate only on two theological motifs that seem to play an important role in shaping Paul's ethical thinking in this letter. The one affects the *nature* of Paul's ethics (*ethics* understood as a system of rules or as the responsibility for independent and founded decision making); the other has to do with its *style* (the ideal of a participating and creative ethics).

In the first section, the wider background of the question is briefly outlined. In the second, the nature and function of Paul's ethical instructions in Gala-

---

1. A. J. Malherbe, "Paul: Hellenistic Philosopher or Christian Pastor?" *ATR* 68 (1986) 3.

tians are examined, in order to look at two specific, theological motifs in the third section. Finally, a provisional conclusion is formulated.

THE WIDER CONTEXT OF PAUL'S ETHIC

An examination of the ethics of a single Pauline letter forms part of at least two wider issues: the development of Paul's theology as a whole and the relationship between his theology and his ethics.

The development of Paul's theology has been the focus of extensive research and intense debate in recent years. At stake is a whole complex of historical, sociological, and theological issues. It has become customary in some circles to distinguish between an "early" and a "late" Paul, coupled with attempts to reconstruct the different stages in Paul's theological evolution.[2] How these attempts influence specific theological issues can be seen in the recent discussion on the function of the law in the Pauline letters.[3] Whatever the relative values of these different hypotheses may be, there can be little doubt that the changing circumstances of Paul's ministry and the new challenges he had to meet forced him to rethink and revise key concepts of his theology.[4] Any consideration of ethical questions peculiar to Galatians must be seen against this wider backdrop, and conclusions are not necessarily representative of the full Pauline position.

Furthermore, Paul's ethics forms an integral part of his theology. Whereas in Hellenistic thought there is no necessary connection between religion and ethics, Paul's ethics is a consequence of his theology. As W. Schrage has shown,[5] Paul uses a variety of theological motifs—soteriological, christological, sacramental, pneumatological, and eschatological—as basis for his ethics. It is therefore not surprising that the different models proposed by interpreters—for example, R. Hasenstab's distinction between parenetic, Paracletic, reception-historical, and autonomous models[6]—to serve as the framework for Paul's ethical statements are all theological in nature. Any statement on the ethics of Galatians will have to take this relationship into

2. See, for example, S. Schulz, *Neutestamentliche Ethik* (Zürich: Theologischer Verlag, 1987) 290–93.

3. See, for example, H. Hübner, *Das Gesetz bei Paulus* (3. Aufl.; Göttingen: Vandenhoeck & Ruprecht, 1982); E. P. Sanders, *Paul, the Law and the Jewish People* (Philadelphia: Fortress, 1983); J. D. G. Dunn, "Works of the Law and the Curse of the Law (Galatians 3.10–14)," *NTS* 31 (1985) 523–42; H. Räisänen, "Galatians 2.16 and Paul's Break with Judaism," *NTS* 31 (1985) 543–53; D. Moo, "Paul and the Law in the Last Ten Years," *SJT* 40 (1987) 287–307; H. Räisänen, *Paul and the Law* (WUNT 29, 2d ed.; Tübingen: Mohr, 1987); J. C. Beker, "Paul's Theology: Consistent or Inconsistent?" *NTS* 34 (1988) 364–77.

4. H. D. Betz, "Das Problem der Grundlagen der paulinischen Ethik (Röm 12,1–2)," *ZTK* 85 (1988) 199.

5. W. Schrage, *Ethik des Neuen Testaments* (4. Aufl.; Göttingen: Vandenhoeck & Ruprecht, 1982) 155–76.

6. R. Hasenstab, *Modelle paulinischer Ethik* (TTS 11; Mainz: Matthias Grünewald, 1977).

account. As we shall see, the peculiar role of ethics in this letter is directly related to changes in Paul's theological orientation.

The relationship between Pauline and extrabiblical material involves a wide range of issues.[7] It could relate to matters of style, to the actual content of ethical instructions or statements, or to the (theological) origins and function of these statements. What follows will deal mostly with aspects that belong to the last category.

AN ETHICAL DEFICIT IN GALATIANS?

A remarkable feature of Galatians is the apparently underdeveloped nature of Paul's ethical statements. Although opinions differ on how the epistolary structure should be understood,[8] there is general agreement that only chapters 5 through 6 could be classified as parenesis. But even a superficial look at these chapters reveals the relative scarcity of explicit ethical commands or directions. The first definite parenetic statements appear only in 5:13ff. Even then, however, specific instructions are given only in 5:13 and 16—the rest is either theological motivation for the instructions or illustrations of what is meant.

The lack of a comprehensive set of rules for ethical conduct is all the more surprising if one considers the rhetorical situation in which the letter is written. However difficult it may be to come to a full understanding of the anti-Pauline opposition in Galatia,[9] it is clear that this group was very successful on at least one point. They were able to convince the Galatians that they should—in addition to having faith in Christ—obey the Torah and adopt a Jewish way of life. Considering the background of most of the Galatians, it is not difficult to understand why the argument was so persuasive. Their conversion to the Christian faith implied a complete reorientation of both their value system and their life-style. For Jews, this transition was difficult enough but did not entail the abandonment of their own tradition—it was rather understood as its continuation and completion. For Gentiles, however, the break was much more incisive. They found themselves at a double disadvantage—they were new to the Christian faith, but also unfamiliar with its Jewish roots. As Johnny-come-latelies they were in desperate need of practical advice to guide their day-to-day life in an environment not very sympathetic or suppor-

---

7. For an indication of the issues involved, see Betz, "Das Problem der Grundlagen," 200–204; Malherbe, "Paul," 4–11; W. A. Meeks, "Understanding Early Christian Ethics," *JBL* 105 (1986) 3–11; G. Strecker, "Autonome Sittlichkeit und das Proprium der christlichen Ethik bei Paulus," *TLZ* 104 (1979) 865–72; Schrage, *Ethik*, 189–92; Schulz, *Neutestamentliche Ethik*, 386–95.

8. See H. D. Betz, *Galatians: A Commentary on Paul's Letter to the Churches in Galatia* (Hermeneia; Philadelphia: Fortress, 1979) 14–25; H. Hübner, "Der Galaterbrief und das Verhältnis von antiker Rhetorik und Epistolographie," *TLZ* 109 (1984) 241–50; J. D. Hester, "The Use and Influence of Rhetoric in Galatians," *TZ* 42 (1986) 386–408; H. D. Betz, *Der Galaterbrief: Ein Kommentar zum Brief des Apostels Paulus an die Galater* (Munich: Kaiser, 1987) 1–4.

9. See Betz, *Galatians*, 5–9.

tive of their new convictions. Thus, they became easy targets for the proponents of "another gospel" (Gal 1:6).

For whatever reason, Paul has—at least in their own understanding of the matter—not given them enough practical guidelines to survive as believers under these circumstances.[10] That is why they are so susceptible to the argument of the opponents. Faith in Christ is—also in the opponents' view—essential, but to translate that into action and to make it workable in everyday life, one needs a set of time-tested rules for the practice of this faith. That is exactly what the Jewish way of life can offer—it has stood the test of time; it has guided the Jewish people through the most testing and adverse times of their long history. Not only does it offer a practical guide to the Galatians, but it also provides the means to become part of an age-old tradition, to become fully initiated and accepted by the central leadership in Jerusalem. In view of the psychologial needs of new converts—their acceptance into the group and their self-identity and sense of security after being cut off from their natural environment—this is a very attractive and persuasive argument.

It is therefore all the more surprising that Paul does not use the opportunity to present a more coherent and directive set of instructions in his letter. He studiously avoids spelling out in more detail how the congregation should behave in different situations (unlike the practical advice he gives, for example, in 1 Corinthians). Instead, he contents himself with a few general and rather vague remarks: "You are set free. Do not abuse this freedom" (Gal 5:13). When he does make use of a virtue list, this is not in the form of direct instructions but rather an indirect summary of what the fruits of the Spirit and of the flesh, respectively, are—as if this were common knowledge and as if the readers should be able to work out the consequences for themselves. What is argued extensively throughout the letter, and in particular in chapters 3 and 4, is the theological basis of the new life. On the one hand, there seems to be an "ethical deficit" in Galatians; on the other hand, when ethical matters are discussed, Paul apparently adopts the common values of the Hellenistic environment in which the Galatians found themselves.

It is this phenomenon I would like to consider in a little more detail. My hypothesis is that apart from historical and cultural factors, there are fundamental theologial considerations that shape Paul's ethical thinking in this letter.

A structural analysis of the so-called parenetic section of the letter (Gal 5:1–6:10) reveals that two pivotal commands provide the framework for the series of loose ethical injunctions in the rest of the section. The first is the command to stand in the freedom that Christ has made possible (5:1); the second is the command to walk in the Spirit (5:25). The two are structured in a parallel way. Both appear twice in this section: the call to freedom in 5:1 and 13, and the walk in the Spirit in 5:16 and 25. In both, the indica-

10. Betz, "Das Problem der Grundlagen," 206.

tive/imperative sequence is clear: "Christ has set us free for freedom. Stand therefore firm [in this freedom]" and "If we live through the Spirit, let us walk in the Spirit." This parallelism extends to other elements in the parenetic section, resulting in a series of binary oppositions in which *freedom, Spirit,* and *fruit of the Spirit* are set off against *the yoke of slavery, flesh,* and *works of the flesh.*

The freedom/Spirit motif therefore forms the backbone of the ethical injunctions of the last two chapters and provides an insight into the way Paul's ethics function. Three observations are of importance.

First, the strong and almost overwhelming theological basis of Paul's ethics is clear. Everything that is said in chapters 5 and 6 is closely connected and flows from the preceding theological argument. This argument is even extended into the parenetic section. After the freedom statement in Gal 5:1, the apostle interrupts himself to recap the theological rationale for this call in 5:1–12. In a similar way, the ethical injunctions are interspersed with theological dictums (for example, 5:14, 18, 24; 6:3, 5, 7–8).

Second, the style of Paul is very subdued, almost conciliatory. There is no attempt to lay down the law, and there is no reference to his authority as apostle in this section. An appeal is made to what his readers already know or should know, and the consequences of the two life-styles (in the Spirit and in the flesh) are set out as something self-evident. In contrast to earlier parts of the letter, where the distance and tension between Paul and his audience are underlined, inter alia, by the use of second person pronouns, the inclusive first person sets the tone for the parenetic section ("Christ has set *us* free . . ." [Gal 5:1], "if *we* live by the Spirit, let *us* . . ." [5:25], "let *us* not become boastful . . ." [5:26], and "let *us* not grow weary of doing good . . ." [6:10]). Although the loose collection of sententiae is not without some kind of structure,[11] there is no attempt to develop a rigid system of conduct or a complete set of rules that is then prescribed in an authoritarian style to the readers as a new or alternative code of law.

The way in which Paul refers to the law in these chapters is very instructive. In 5:14 it is deliberately used in the form of its classic summary and not in the sense of a casuistic system. At the end of the list of virtues in 5:22–23, the cryptic comment is added: "No law is against these things." The fruits of the Spirit do not constitute a new law. They are not cast in the form of commands or instructions, but represent a summary of the self-evident results flowing from a life controlled by the Spirit. At the same time, they do not contradict any kind of law—to the contrary. Paul is describing the characteristics of the new existence in faith, which is attained without mediation of, or recourse to, the law. Responsible ethical conduct is possible without enablement by the law. For a proper understanding of what constitutes ethical behavior for Paul, this is an important clue, to which we shall return later.

11. Betz, *Galatians,* 292.

Finally, the enigmatic reference to the "law of Christ" in 6:2 is probably an ironic play on the opponents' defense of the Mosaic Torah[12] and certainly not an endorsement of the law.

Third, when the content of the ethical instructions is considered, there is very little (if anything at all) that could be described as distinctly "Christian." In particular, the list of virtues and vices in Gal 5:19–23 is a typical Hellenistic phenomenon. Such lists express those values and ideals that reflect the moral conventions of the time, and one gets the impression that Paul, rather than developing a Christian ethic that is distinctive in content, is demonstrating that the fruit of the Spirit is neither in conflict with Jewish custom nor with current Hellenistic morality.

When taking all these factors into consideration, one might be justified to talk of an "ethical deficit" in Galatians. In the light of the Galatians' need for practical guidelines and more concrete help in forging a new life-style as believers, this deficit is all the more puzzling. Why did Paul have this apparent reluctance to develop a fuller and more distinctive ethics? I would like to suggest that the key to this question lies in two important theological concerns that shaped Paul's thinking in these matters. The first relates to a shift in the theological basis for Christian action, and the second has to do with a new understanding of what it means to be ethically responsible.

THE NATURE AND FUNCTION OF
PAUL'S ETHICAL GUIDES

In his interaction with the Galatian churches, Paul has, in the first place, gained a clearer understanding of the relationship between faith and action. The heart of the theological argument in his letter is that salvation does not come from the "works of the law" (that is, being rewarded by God for doing the law) but from "faith" (that is, trusting God's promise of justification, made possible by the event of the cross [Gal 3:1–14]). This basic shift was motivated, inter alia, by the surprisingly positive reaction to his preaching by non-Jews (including the Galatians). Because these converts initially accepted the gospel without the law—that is, without a Jewish background and without prior knowledge of the Torah—Paul was forced to rethink his understanding of the function of the law. Could it be—contrary to all that he as a Jew unquestionably accepted thus far—that the law was *not* essential for salvation? Could it be that the law even could prevent believers from understanding the true nature of salvation? The fundamental shift from the dominance of the law was, for Paul, an experience of liberation. And this liberation, at the same time, became the hallmark of a new existence in faith—an existence in which also the ethical conduct of the believer could only be understood in terms of freedom (5:1, 13).

12. See Betz, *Galatians*, 300–301.

ESSAYS IN HONOR OF ABRAHAM J. MALHERBE

The implication of this freedom from the law for the ethical conduct of believers is twofold. First, such conduct can no longer be conceived of as motivated either by fear (punishment) or by gain (reward). It is now understood as the exercise of responsibility—a responsibility that flows from the theological self-understanding of the believer, which implies discretion and which must be executed in freedom. The change from *works* to *faith*[13] therefore alters the essential nature of ethical conduct. It is this change that is threatened by the message of Paul's opponents—purportedly offering practical guidelines for the everyday life of the believer, but in actual fact relieving him or her of the responsibility of independent ethical decisions. This would mean a return to the flesh after the Galatians have started with the Spirit (Gal 3:2).

It is for this reason that Paul avoids any misunderstanding that he is replacing the Torah with a new law or that the believers now only have to follow a new set of rules. There is no new system to be learned or to be played.[14] Despite the attractiveness of his opponents' message, Paul resists the temptation to offer a similar solution, for fear that it will merely confirm the misunderstanding he is trying to rectify. That is why he provides his readers with the barest essentials to illustrate what the nature of the new life should be. What appears to be an "ethical deficit" is, in fact, an "ethical minimum," which is the consequence of the theological nature of the new existence in faith.

The second implication of cutting the umbilical cord of the law is that the believer is no longer restricted to one ethical tradition. But it also implies that the theological basis of Christian ethics up to that point has fallen away and will have to be redefined.[15] This redefinition has already been given in the concentrated christological formulation of Gal 2:19–20. Paul uses the metaphor of death in a double sense: to explain, on the one hand, the finality with which the law is left behind and, on the other hand, why the cross is the start of a new existence. In this way, the cross mediates between two modes of existence. This mediation concerns not only the theological basis of the transformation but also the ethical content of the new life.[16] It is a life in faith and a life for God, of which the ethical "style" is at the same time exemplified by the event of the cross. The mode is one of love and of service (2:20: ἀγαπήσαντος and παραδόντος). Theology and ethics remain inseparable in Paul's thinking.

On the one hand, then, the severance from the law makes it possible in principle for Paul to consider all kinds of ethical traditions, including espe-

13. See Betz, "Das Problem der Grundlagen," 202; he sees the *proprium Christianum* expressed by *faith* in contrast to *doing*, which would decribe the essence of Jewish ethics.
14. See Strecker, "Autonome Sittlichkeit," 871: "Das christliche Ethos ist nicht wirklich normschöpferisch, weil es im Gegebenen die aktuelle Forderung Gottes entdeckt."
15. Betz, "Das Problem der Grundlagen," 200.
16. See B. C. Lategan, "Is Paul Defending his Apostleship in Galatians?" *NTS* 34 (1988) 429–30.

cially Hellenistic codes.[17] On the other hand, the theological redefinition provides the criterion for how these traditions are to be used.

According to H. D. Betz, the rejection of the law as basis for Christian ethics also makes it impossible for Paul merely to take up the ethical teaching of the historical Jesus. It is the kerygma of the risen Christ that provides this foundation for Paul's ethics.[18] It may be asked whether such a contrast between the historical Jesus and the kerygmatic Christ is really functional in this case. Paul makes extensive, but not exclusive, use of Hellenistic concepts. In Gal 5:14, he explicitly refers to the essence of the law as expressed in Lev 19:18—exactly the formulation that, according to the synoptic tradition (Matt 19:19; Luke 10:27; Mark 12:31), is accorded primary status by Jesus, together with Deut 5:6. Jesus' criticism of a legalistic interpretation of the law (cf., for example, the antitheses of the Sermon on the Mount, the handling of Sabbath laws in Matt 12:1–14) is already indicative of the nonlegalistic ethic that comes to fruition in Paul.

The Hellenistic context of the Galatian churches makes it only natural that Paul will concentrate on traditions and concepts with which his audience will be most familiar. But this does not mean that he takes over Hellenistic material at random and uncritically. Exactly because of his new theological *Selbstverständnis*, ethical injunctions cannot be added arbitrarily or exist as a separate body of instructions, unrelated to his theology. At the same time, the generalized dictums, metaphors, precepts, and codes of his Hellenistic environment were not without their religious undertones. As Betz says, "Religiös betrachtet war daher die antike Moral keineswegs neutral, sondern sie war 'heidnisch'"[19] (Examined theologically, classical Greek ethics are in no sense neutral, but "pagan"). The development of a responsible and functional ethical approach therefore required from Paul not only a careful sifting of available material but also a consideration of its compatibility with his theological principles. One of these principles, as we have seen, is that of the freedom to make responsible choices and the freedom to consider all traditions. There is a certain universality that characterizes the new Christian existence and that makes Hellenistic moral concepts a natural area for consideration— an opportunity that Paul exploited to the fullest.[20] But it was also crucial to place that which was compatible within a theological framework. Galatians gives clear evidence of how Paul goes about achieving this. The list of (common Hellenistic) vices is characterized as "works of the flesh" (5:19), whereas the list of virtues comes under the caption "fruit of the Spirit" (5:22). In this way the link with the theological framework is made; as we have seen, *flesh* and *Spirit* function as code words for the two modes of existence (5:16–18).

17. See Strecker, "Autonome Sittlichkeit," 871; V. P. Furnish, *Theology and Ethics in Paul* (Nashville: Abingdon, 1968) 72.
18. Betz, "Das Problem der Grundlagen," 202.
19. Betz, "Das Problem der Grundlagen," 200–201.
20. See Malherbe, "Paul," 13.

In a similar way, the theological thread runs all through the sententiae that follow in 6:1–10: "those who are spiritual" (6:1), "the law of Christ" (6:2), "God"
(6:7), "flesh" and "Spirit" (6:8), and "faith" (6:10). In this way, substance is
given to the freedom and universality of the new existence in faith, but understood in the context of its theological framework.[21]

The second theological concern that guides the development of Paul's ethical thinking in Galatians is the ideal of a creative and participating ethics. On
the one hand, Paul is seeking to enable and empower his readers, and on the
other hand, he is enticing them to participate in and to follow a hands-on
approach. It is because of the former—the issue of empowerment—that the
indicative/imperative sequence is such a fundamental feature of Paul's ethical
teaching.[22] Because one is free, one must exercise freedom (Gal 5:1); if one is
spiritual, one must act in a spiritual way (5:25). It is part of the apostle's pastoral concern for his readers that he does not tire of reminding them who they
are. They are liberated, and therefore they must think and act in a liberated
way. He expects them to be responsible and independent. Then they will
need neither him nor the crutches of a casuistic system.

Together with empowerment, Paul is aiming at participation. In the context of reception theory, much attention has been given to the production of
meaning and the role that the indeterminacy of the text plays in this process.
An important concept developed by Wolfgang Iser is that of intentional "gaps"
in the text.[23] These gaps usually refer to breaks in the narrative sequence
when the story is approached from a different perspective or suddenly
developed in another direction. The imagination and participation of the
reader is required in order to fill these gaps. Although Galatians is not a narrative text, the concept of indeterminacy is useful to explain the peculiar
strategy Paul is following in his parenetic instructions. He restricts himself to
the bare minimum and describes the duties of believers in very general terms,
forcing them to fill in the details and use their imaginations in doing so. Typical is his concluding exhortation: "Let us work for the common good of all, but
in particular for the good of fellow-believers!" (5:10).

Complementing the general and open-ended nature of his ethical injunctions is another typical feature of Paul's literary style, namely, his tendency to
use concentrated and abbreviated language.[24] Although this feature is to be
found throughout the letter, it is especially noticeable in the parenetic section.[25] Cryptic references to "the law of Christ" (Gal 6:2) and the "carrying of
one's own burden" (6:5) require of Paul's readers not only some previous

21. For an indication of how Paul achieves a theological setting in 1 Thessalonians in the same
way, see Malherbe, "Paul," 12.
22. See Schrage, *Ethik*, 156–61.
23. For a discussion of this concept, see R. C. Holub, *Reception Theory: A Critical Introduction*
(New York: Methuen, 1984) 92–95.
24. See Lategan, "Is Paul Defending His Apostleship?" 420, n. 2.
25. Betz, *Galatians*, 292, refers to the "very general sense" of the values mentioned in 5:25–6:10,
which are only "exemplaric."

knowledge of what is implied but also their active participation in order for them to understand. The same can be said of the sententiae that appear in 5:25–6:10. These unconventional and often paradoxical sayings are designed to stimulate the imagination and critical reflection of the reader. "His goal [with the parenesis] is to induce self-examination and self-criticism, in order to keep the level of ethical awareness high."[26]

Instead of giving his readers detailed instructions that would relieve them of making independent decisions and that would encourage the drift back into the old mind-set of earning their salvation and gaining points for good ethical behavior, Paul deliberately leaves them with gaps and cryptic remarks that require their cooperation, imagination, and creativity. Gaps in the text of Galatians are therefore more than a literary device to ensure participation. Gaps and cryptic remarks form an essential element of what Paul considers to be the proper mental attitude and ethical orientation of converts to the gospel. By encouraging independent decisions and responsible ethical behavior, he is preparing his readers for both his absence and for the future. Not only will the Galatians have to cope on their own, but also future generations will have to discern what the gospel requires from them in a particular situation and find the courage to act accordingly.

A PROVISIONAL CONCLUSION

Is Paul developing a specifically Christian ethics in Galatians? The answer is both no and yes. It is no in the sense that in terms of content, he is neither introducing new concepts nor proposing a line of conduct that is in conflict with the conventional morality of the time. He builds on what was familiar to his audience and accepted in their social context. It would even seem that he is bent on demonstrating the compatibility and universality of his moral precepts. The answer is yes in the sense that Paul develops a new understanding of what ethical responsibility entails—an understanding that flows directly from his theological assessment of the new existence in faith. There can be no relying on rules or on the gaining of awards, and no relinquishing of responsibility. Paul presents an ethical minimum to his readers to stimulate a creative and responsible application of basic theological principles in new situations. What started off as a crisis of misunderstanding and absence became (inadvertently and perhaps unintentionally) an opportunity to gain a clearer understanding of the universal and durable nature of the gospel. Paul reaches beyond the constraints of place and time, and in doing so, he demonstrates that it is a message that functions not only in a Palestinian environment but also in a Hellenistic context, giving hope for generations to come. For many who also find themselves in the throes of cultural and political transition— who still have to experience what liberation means—this perspective provides

26. Betz, *Galatians*, 292.

a strong motivation to reach beyond themselves, to give new substance to freedom, to use freedom imaginatively and creatively, and in doing so, to guarantee its survival for future generations.

20

TACITURNITY AND
TRUE RELIGION
James 1:26–27

The careful attention to speech in the Letter of James reveals its roots in the wisdom traditions of the ancient world. Like other Hellenistic moralists, James insists that speech find consistent expression in deeds (1:22–25; 2:14–26).[1] Of equal importance, however, are speech-acts themselves. The way James shares, yet also differs from, the perceptions of his world concerning proper speech is the focus of this chapter offered in fond tribute to a teacher who exemplifies, ὡς ἐν ἐσόπτρῳ (as in a mirror), the virtues here discussed.[2]

The ancient world agreed that the wise person was also taciturn. Silence was generally better, and always safer, than speech. Brevity in speech was preferred to loquacity. The evidence is everywhere: in the Wisdom literature of the OT (LXX),[3] Hellenistic Jewish[4] and other Jewish writings,[5] and early

1. "In the first place I require that the consistency of men's doctrines be observed in their way of living," Plutarch *Stoic. Rep.* 1 (Mor. 1033B). In addition to the passages in Stobaeus's *Anthologium* II, 15 (Hense 185–96), see also Seneca *Ep.* 20.1; Diog. Laert. 1.53; and 9.37; Plut. *De Prof. Virt.* 14 (Mor. 84B); Philo *Vit. Mos.* 1.6.29; 2.8.48; *Spec. Leg.* 2.14.53; *Congr.* 13.67; *The Sentences of Sextus* 177; *Did.* 2.5, as well as the references in L. T. Johnson, "Friendship with the World/Friendship with God: A Study of Discipleship in James," *Discipleship in the New Testament* (ed. F. Segovia; Philadelphia: Fortress, 1985) 183, n. 66.

2. Like the other students of Abraham J. Malherbe, I have enjoyed and benefited from the Malherbian apothegms, delivered in his inimitable style. In this essay, I emulate Professor Malherbe's scholarly example of making appropriate distinctions in order to clarify specific traditions.

3. The biblical passages (LXX) include Prov 10:8, 14, 19, 31; 11:12–13; 12:13, 18; 13:3; 14:3; 15:2; 17:27–28; 18:4, 6–7; 21:23; 29:20; Eccl 5:1–2, 6; 10:14; Wis 1:11; 8:12; Sir 1:22–24; 4:23, 29; 6:33; 7:14; 8:3; 9:18; 11:8; 13:12–13; 19:5–12, 16; 20:1, 5–8, 18, 27; 21:26; 22:27; 23:8; 32:4, 8. The widespread use of the theme in the ancient Near East is shown by *The Instructions of Shuruppak* 21 and 130 (*ANET* 595); *Instructions of Ptah-Hotep* 535 and 575 (*ANET* 414); *Instructions for King Mei-ka-re* 30 (*ANET* 415); *The Instruction of Ani* 4.1 (*ANET* 420); *The Instruction of Amen-Em-Opet* 3.15; 11.15; 22.15 (*ANET* 422–24); *The Words of Ahiqar* 7.95–110 (*ANET* 428–29).

4. Cf., e.g., *The Sentences of Pseudo-Phocylides* 20; 57; 69; 123–24. Among many places in Philo are *Fug.* 16.136; *Som.* 2.40.262–70; 2.42.276; *Det. Pot. Ins.* 13.42; 27.102; *Spec. Leg.* 2.14.50; *Abr.* 3.20; *Mut. Nom.* 41–42.240–43; *Leg. All.* 3.53.155; *Plant.* 42.176.

5. See 'Abot 1:5, 9, 11, 15, 17; 3:14; 5:7, 12; and 'Abot R. Nat. 13, 22, 26, 37; also *The Sentences of the Syriac Menander* 311, 312, 313.

Christian literature.[6] The topic was so widely discussed by Greek writers that it was anthologized under several different rubrics.[7]

In the NT, James gives most direct expression to this ideal: "Let every one be quick to hear, slow to speak, slow to anger" (Jas 1:19). He devotes considerable (if complex) attention to the power and peril of speech in 3:1–12.[8] The person who can control the tongue, he says, is "perfect" (τέλειος [3:2]).[9] His statements seem at home within the standard distinction between the laconic and loquacious, in which short is always better than long.[10]

Another of James's statements, however, is more puzzling: "If anyone thinks that he is religious [θρησκός], not curbing his tongue [χαλιναγωγῶν γλῶσσαν] but deceiving his heart, this person's religion [θρησκεία] is vain [μάταιος]" (Jas 1:26).[11] Why and how should speech be connected to authentic religion?

Jas 1:26 raises the question of why silence was preferred to speech, the pithy to the prolix. This chapter surveys the rationalizations given in Hellenistic moral literature[12] and examines James against that background. The rela-

6. *1 Clem.* 21.7; 30.4; Ign. *Phld.* 1.1; *Eph.* 15.1–2; *Barn.* 19.7–8; Herm. *Vis.* 2.3; *Mand.* 11.12. Striking similarities to James can be found in *The Sentences of Sextus* 155–57; 162a; 163b; 171; 185; 253a; 350–51; 361; 366; 426–27; 430–32.

7. Stobaeus's *Anthologium* contains pertinent entries in these chapters: Περὶ σιγῆς (["concerning silence"] 3.33; Hense, 678–82); Περὶ τοῦ εὐκαίρως λέγειν (["concerning speaking at the appropriate time"] 3.34; Hense, 682–87); Περὶ βραχυλογίας (["concerning taciturnity"] 3.35; Hense, 687–90); and Περὶ ἀδολεσχίας (["concerning garrulity"] 3.36; Hense, 690–98). Many passages particularly from historians and rhetoricians are considered by G. Schnayder, *De Antiquorum Hominum Taciturnitate et Tacendo* (Traveaux de la Société des Sciences de Wrocław 56; Wrocław, 1956). Among the noteworthy passages not contained in the above sources are Diog. Laert. 1.35, 69, 70, 88, 92, 104; 9.2; Lucian *Demon.* 64; Plut. *Lib. Educ.* 14 (Mor. 10F); and those discussed below. For the continuation of the ideal in Western monasticism, cf. A. G. Wathen, O.S.B., *Silence: The Meaning of Silence in the Rule of St. Benedict* (Cistercian Studies Series 22; Washington, D.C.: Cistercian Publications, 1973), esp. 109–76.

8. The NT has much to say about appropriate and inappropriate modes of speech as in Matt 6:7; Col 3:8; Eph 5:4; 1 Tim 1:6; Titus 1:10) but little about speech as such. The term ἡσυχία in 1 Thess 4:11 and 2 Thess 3:12 refers to the quiet life. Paul's use of σιγάω (to be silent) in 1 Cor 14:28–30 is purely functional. The notable exception is the silence imposed on women in the assembly (1 Cor 14:34; 1 Tim 2:11–12).

9. For a careful discussion of the exegetical problems in Jas 3:1–12, with a rich selection of material illustrating the metaphor of "reining the tongue," see M. Dibelius, *A Commentary on the Epistle of James* (rev. H. Greeven; trans. M. Williams; Hermeneia; Philadelphia: Fortress, 1976) 181–206; and J. B. Mayor, *The Epistle of St. James* (3d ed.; London: Macmillan, 1910) 107–25. Neither supplies the best parallel to James's assertion concerning the "perfection" of someone who controls speech; it is in Philo *Poster. C.* 24.88 (cf. also *Migr. Abr.* 13.73).

10. A variety of terms are used for both "laconic" and "loquacious," the most common being βραχυλογία (*brevitas*) and ἀδολεσχία (*garrulitas*). For the rough equivalent of σιγᾶν and σιωπᾶν (to be silent), cf. Schnayder, *Taciturnitate*, 51, n. 41; for that between *silere* and *tacere*, cf. Wathen, *Silence*, 13–19.

11. Θρησκός is a hapax legomenon, but θρησκεία is common, having perhaps a slight emphasis on cultic observance (cf. BAGD 363). Thus, Philo opposes εὐσεβεία and ὁσιότης to θρησκεία in *Det. Pot. Ins.* 7.21. The "vain" character of religion (μάταιος) can also be read as "foolish," suggesting a wisdom/folly contrast in the statement, which reinforces the connection of taciturnity to wisdom (cf. Liddell-Scott, s.v.).

12. The largest number of exhortations to silence or brevity lack explanation. The fullest discussions are found in the Greek materials. I concentrate on them, noting passim points of agreement or disagreement in Jewish literature.

tive rarity of explicit rationalization should not be surprising. Perceptions that are pervasive often appear to those holding them to be so obvious and experientially confirmed as to require no theoretical support. Enough evidence remains available to suggest a fairly intricate web of perceptions governing the preference for concision in speech. A line of at least implicit logic can be traced through the three realms of the rhetorical, the ethical, and the religious.

SILENCE AND SPEECH IN THE HELLENISTIC WORLD

Brevity Is Best

In rhetorical discussions, the quality of speech known as βραχυλογία (*brevitas* [conciseness]) holds an honored, but for the most part minor, place. Aristotle does not use the term. In several places, he does assert that in style, "the mean" (τὸ μέσον) between the overly concise and overly diffuse (ἀδολέσκη) is to be observed (*Rh.* 3.2.3; 3.12.6; 3.16.4). He recognizes that brevity communicates knowledge quickly (3.11.9) and that "laconic apothegms and riddles" have their uses.[13] Cicero scarcely adverts to *brevitas* when discussing figures of thought and speech (*De Or.* 3.53.202). Only slightly more attention is given by the author of *Rhetorica ad Herennium*, who links *brevitas* to the figure aposiopesis.[14] Quintilian declares that the "praise awarded to perfect brevity is well deserved" because it expresses a great deal in a few words, but he warns that failure to achieve such perfection results in obscurity (*Inst.* 8.3.82). In his extensive treatise on rhetoric, he gives meager attention to βραχυλογία (expressions not linked by conjunctions or other grammatical connectors) as a form of asyndeton (9.3.50; cf. 9.3.99). Brevity is considered only in passing as well by "Longinus," who characterizes garrulousness as a sign of old age and who, like Aristotle, recommends a middle ground between excessive brevity and prolixity in speech (*Subl.* 9.14; 42.1–2; cf. also Philostr. *Vit. Ap.* 8.2).

In contrast, the treatise "On Style" attributed to Demetrius pays considerably more attention to brevity. Demetrius thinks lengthy sentences appropriate to an elevated style, but when they grow too long, garrulousness results (*Eloc.* 4.204, 212–14). In the same way, sentences that are too short fail to make an impression on hearers (1.4). Demetrius nevertheless shows unusual fondness for βραχυλογία. He attaches three qualities to brevity.

---

13. His phrasing is: τὰ Λακωνικὰ ἀποφθέγματα καὶ τὰ αἰνιγματώδη, Arist. *Rh.* 2.21.8.

14. *Rhet. Her.* 4.54.67–68. *Brevitas* has this admiring definition: "Brevitas est res ipsis tantummodo verbis necessariis expedita" ("Conciseness is the expressing of an idea by the very minimum of essential words" [trans. Caplan in LCL]). Plutarch's characterization comes very close. He states that the orator Phocis had βραχυλογία and was considered the most clever in speaking because "his speech contained the most meaning in the fewest words" (*Praec. Ger. Reip.* 7 [Mor. 803E]).

First, short sentences are forceful (δεινός). Excessive length paralyzes intensity, but βραχυλογία, because it packs "much meaning in a brief form[,] is more forcible" (Demetr. *Eloc.* 5.241; trans. Roberts in LCL; cf. also 5.274).[15] Like Longinus, Demetrius considers garrulousness a sign of old age, occurring then "because of their weakness." In contrast, the people he associates with βραχυλογία are the vigorous Lacedaemonians (1.7).

Second, because of its force, brevity is appropriate to apothegms and maxims. It thereby reveals great skill in speakers or writers by "putting much thought in little space." Demetrius cites two sorts of examples. From the Spartans, he quotes the response to the tyrant Philip, "Dionysius at Corinth." From the pre-Socratic sages, he cites the apothegms "Know thyself" and "Follow God" (*Eloc.* 1.9; cf. also 5.241).

Third, Demetrius says that brevity leads to a certain inevitable ambiguity. This makes it useful for symbolism. The hearer is forced to supply interpretation (*Eloc.* 5.242). In this respect, βραχυλογία resembles aposiopesis (5.253, 264). Demetrius can thus call the statement "Dionysius at Corinth" an "allegory" (2.102).

As the art of rhetoric developed, it left behind βραχυλογία except as one figure of speech or thought among others.[16] But the rhetorical sources still contain intriguing traces of another way of viewing brevity. Garrulousness is a sign of age and weakness. Brevity represents youth and power. Is there, in these associations, a nostalgia for perhaps an earlier time, when speech was the sign of a certain kind of character rather than a matter of making proofs? (Philo *Plant.* 38.157–58). The examples of the sages and Spartans would make us suspect that it was not the professional speakers, but rather the professedly virtuous, who would treasure βραχυλογία as the ideal mode of speech.

Speech as Self-control

The moralist was concerned with βραχυλογία as a sign of character. The connection between style and character is suggested by Demetrius in his discussion of epistolary style, because letters are an "image of one's soul" and enable the reader to "see the character of the writer." One epistolary virtue is brevity, but its exaggeration is sententiousness (Demetr. *Eloc.* 4.227–32).[17]

Seneca makes the most explicit connection between virtue and style. In

15. The same connection between βραχυλογία and δύναμις is made by Philo *Rer. Div. Her.* 21.102.

16. Dio Chrysostom, for example, acknowledges the reputation of Lysias for brevity and simplicity but does not recommend him for imitation (*Or.* 18.11). Dio was confident that speech could express everything (12.64–65). His philosopher need "never keep silence" or be at a loss for words (71.1). With the exceptions noted below, Philo often expressed the same sentiments concerning the power of speech. Cf. *Jos.* 44.269; Philo *Migr. Abr.* 14–15.78–81; *Det. Pot. Ins.* 35.129–31.

17. Advice and proverbs are appropriate to letters, but maxims and exhortations are not (Demetr. *Eloc.* 4.232).

one place he argues that the style not only of individuals but also of peoples at a particular time reveals private and public character (*Ep.* 114.2). A luxurious life-style is reflected in overly ornate (or even preciously clipped) speech (114.9–14, 17). Not surprisingly, Seneca recommends care for the soul as a prerequisite for appropriate speech. When the soul is sound and strong, "the style too is vigorous, energetic, manly; but if the soul loses its balance, down comes all the rest in ruins" [illo sane ac valente oratio quoque robusta, fortis, virilis est; si ille procubuit, et cetera ruinam sequuntur] (114.22; trans. Gummere in LCL).

Elsewhere, Seneca argues that speech should be unadorned and plain. Above all, it should be controlled: "Quomodo autem regere potest quae regi non potest? [But how can that speech govern others which cannot itself be governed?]" (*Ep.* 40.4). Speech that runs too fast or too elaborately reveals a loss of self-control and with it, the loss of modesty (*pudor* [40.13]). Seneca concludes with the clearest possible connection between speech and the sage: "Just as a less ostentatious gait becomes a philosopher, so does a restrained style of speech, far removed from boldness. Therefore the ultimate kernel of my remarks is this: I bid you be slow of speech [tardilocum esse te iubeo]" (40.14).[18]

Taciturnity, then, is associated with the philosophical life. The pre-Socratic sages,[19] and in particular the Pythagoreans, are consistently characterized by silence and βραχυλογία.[20] The necessity of silence for becoming wise is obvious: one must hear in order to learn. Silence is the precondition for the learning of wisdom.[21] Garrulous people can become neither wise nor virtuous simply because they never stop talking (Sir 8:3; Plut. *De Garr.* 1 [Mor. 502C]).

Silence is also safer. If one does not speak, then one cannot misspeak. Silence is therefore a protection against error. It is the mute symbol of per-

18. The connection between style and character is made with equal force by Plut. *De Prof. Virt.* 7. (Mor. 79B); *Lib. Educ.* 9 (Mor. 6B–7B); *Quomodo Adul.* 12 (Mor. 33F).

19. See the sayings in Diogenes Laertius attributed to Thales (1.35); Chilon (1.69–70); Bias (1.88); Cleobolus (1.92); Anacharsis (1.104), and Heracleitus (9.12). Note as well Diogenes Laertius's own characterizations of Chilon, βραχυλόγος τε ἦν (1.72); Zeno, βραχυλόγος ὤν (8.8), and Heracleitus (9.7). Similar characterizations are found in Plut. *Pyth. Or.* 29–30 (Mor. 408E–409D) and *De Garr.* 17 (Mor. 511B). Zeno's heroic refusal to divulge names to the tyrant made a great impression; cf. Plut. *De Garr.* 8 (Mor. 505D); Philo *Omn. Prob. Lib.* 16.108; *Det. Pot. Ins.* 48.176.

20. The Pythagoreans demanded a five-year period of silence as part of initiation (Diog. Laert. 8.10), and silence was a well-known aspect of the Pythagorean regimen (Lucian *Demon.* 64). The maxims of Pythagoras are fine examples of βραχυλογία (cf. Diog. Laert. 8.17). Apollonius of Tyana was a spectacular representative of this tradition (Philostr. *Vit. Ap.* 1.1; 1.14; 6.11). Philostratus repeatedly refers to the βραχυλογία of the sage (*Vit. Ap.* 1.17; 4.33; 5.32; 7.35), and the letters attributed to Apollonius both discuss and manifest that style (cf., e.g., *Ep.* 8). Cf. also B. E. Perry, *Secundus the Silent Philosopher* (Philological Monographs 22; Ithaca: Cornell University Press, 1964), esp. 69.

21. Zeno says, "The reason why we have two ears and only one mouth is that we may listen the more and talk the less," Diog. Laert. 7.23; cf. also 1.92; Luc. *Demon.* 51; Philostr. *Vit. Ap.* 6.11; Plut. *De Garr.* 2 (Mor. 502E); Prov 17:27–28; Sir 6:33; 11:8; Philo *Rer. Div. Her.* 3.10–13; *'Abot* 5.12; *Sentences of Sextus* 171, a–b.

fection.[22] Once something is spoken, furthermore, it enters the public realm. Its consequences cannot be controlled (see Plut. *Lib. Ed.* 14 [Mor. 10F]; Wis 1:11). The results of loose speech can be disastrous both for speaker and hearers. The speaker is discredited[23] and the listeners put in peril.[24]

In the Hellenistic world, self-control (ἐγκράτεια) was an inarguable virtue. Emotions and their expression in speech ought to be directed by reason.[25] Lack of self-control (ἀκρασία) is a vice. It is revealed above all in drunken speech[26] and in speech driven by anger.[27] People who speak when angry not only show lack of self-control and thereby shame themselves;[28] they also can do real injustice to others.[29]

Rhetoricians define βραχυλογία in terms of compression, and the moralists define it in terms of self-control. Together, these definitions point to power and authority in speech. It is therefore not surprising to find alongside the sages the Lacedaemonians of old as the exemplars of taciturnity.[30] Their "laconic" speech was literally proverbial.[31] By extension, it seems natural as well that brevity should be a quality of lawgivers.[32]

22. Cf. Diog. Laert. 7.26; Epict. *Ench.* (in Stobaeus 3.35, 10); Apollonius of Tyana *Epp.* 81–82; Plut. *Lib. Educ.* 14 (Mor. 10F); *Rect. Aud.* 4 (Mor. 39C); *De Garr.* 23 (Mor. 515A); Prov 12:13; 13:3; 21:23; Sir 20:18; 22:27; Philo *Fug.* 14.136; *Som.* 2.40.262–70; *Det. Pot. Ins.* 13.42.

23. Prov 10:18; 12:13; 13:3; 18:6–7; Sir 9:18; 20:5, 8; 23:8; Epict. *Diss.* 4.13.11, 17; Plut. *Cap. Util.* 8 (Mor. 90C); *De Garr.* 4–7 (Mor. 504C–F); 16 (Mor. 510D); Philo *Spec. Leg.* 1.9.53; *Fug.* 34.191; *Mut. Nom.* 43.247; *Det. Pot. Ins.* 47.174.

24. See Prov 18:6; Plut. *Lib. Educ.* 14 (Mor. 10F); *Cohib. Ira* 4 (Mor. 455B); *De Garr.* 3 (Mor. 503C); 7 (Mor. 504F–505A).

25. Cf. Diog. Laert. 1.70; 1.104; 7.24; Philostr. *Vit. Ap.* 6.11; Epict. *Ench.* 33.1–2; Plut. *Lib. Educ.* 14 (Mor. 10B); *Cap. Util.* 7–8 (Mor. 90B–C); *De Garr.* 3 (Mor. 503C); 9–11 (Mor. 506D–507F); 14 (Mor. 510A); 17 (Mor. 510E); Philo *Spec. Leg.* 2.14.50; *Conf. Ling.* 13.53–55; *Cong.* 14.80; *Det. Pot. Ins.* 19.68; *The Sentences of Sextus* 253b; 294; 429–30.

26. Cf. Diog. Laert. 1.69; Plut. *De Garr.* 4 (Mor. 503E–540C); Philo *Leg. All.* 3.53, 155; *Plant.* 42.176.

27. Cf. Prov 29:11; Eccl 7:9; Sir 1:22–24; Diog. Laert. 1.70; 8.23; Luc. *Demon.* 51; Plut. *Cap. Util.* 8 (Mor. 90C); *Cohib. Ira* 3 (Mor. 454F); 7 (Mor. 461C); 16 (Mor. 464B–C); *Lib. Educ.* 14 (Mor. 10B); Philo *Leg. All.* 3.42–44, 123–28.

28. In contrast, the person who controls speech maintains dignity and modesty; cf. Plut. *De Garr.* 4 (Mor. 504b); *Cap. Util.* 8 (Mor. 90D); *De Prof. Virt.* 10 (Mor. 80E–81B); Philo *Conf. Ling.* 10.37; Sen. *Ep.* 40.13. Those, in turn, who can make their meaning clear even without words are even more to be admired (Plut. *De Garr.* 17 [Mor. 511C]).

29. Plut. *Cohib. Ira* 9 (Mor. 457D); 14 (Mor. 462C); *Sera* 5 (Mor. 551A).

30. Cf. Thuc. 4.12.16; Hdt. 4.77; 7.135; 7.226; Arist. *Rh.* 3.21.8; Demetr. *Eloc.* 1.7; 2.102; Dio Chrys. *Or.* 12.55; Plut. *De Garr.* 17 (Mor. 510F); *Lyc.* 19.1–4; *Apophth. Epameinodes* 16 (Mor. 193D); *Charillus* 1 (Mor. 189F): When Charillus the king was asked why Lycurgus enacted so few laws, he replied that "people who used few words had no need for many laws." Cf. also *Apophth. Lac. Charillus* 1 (Mor. 232C). In Plutarch, the view is nostalgic; cf. *Inst. Lac.* 42 (Mor. 239F). Clement of Alexandria also attaches brevity to the Lacedaemonians in particular, *Stromateis* 1.14.42–43.

31. Cf. the examples in Plut. *Apophth. Lac.* Agis 7 and 9 (Mor. 215E–F), and Diaphon 2 (Mor. 232E), as well as *Inst. Lac.* 39 (Mor. 239C); *Lyc.* 20.1–6.

32. Cf. Philostr. *Vit. Ap.* 1.17; Luc. *Demon.* 51; Plut. *Praec. Ger. Reip.* 14 (Mor. 810D). Plutarch says that those who receive a royal and noble education "learn first to be silent, and then to speak," *De Garr.* 9 (Mor. 506C).

Religious Silence and Speech

Two religious rationalizations appear in the Hellenistic literature. Silence is legitimated by the Mysteries, and brevity by the Delphic Oracle. Because the Mysteries demanded silence of their initiates,[33] silence itself could, by extension, take on a sacred quality.[34] In the Pythagorean tradition, this is clearly the case.[35] And following from the religious value of silence, the reception of teachings could also have a religious connotation. The sayings of a sage or legislator were like oracles.[36] Finally, the Mysteries can be understood as providing a religious legitimation for the keeping of human secrets.[37]

The practice of taciturnity—and its legitimation—centers on the shrine of Pythian Apollo at Delphi. The connections are complex and interwoven. In the first place, the oracles delivered by the prophetess at the shrine were themselves marked by βραχυλογία. As a result, they were also obscure (sometimes notoriously so).[38] Around the shrine at Delphi, furthermore, were inscribed the gnomic sayings of the Seven Sages. Visitors, when confronted with them on the way to consult the god, found themselves forced to reflect and interpret these sayings:[39] "Know thyself" (Diog. Laert. 1.40), "Nothing too much" (1.4), and most intriguingly, "Follow God."[40]

In the most obvious way, therefore, a person who used brevity in speech imitated the sages and, more impressively, "imitated the god" as well, in this case the Pythian Apollo.[41] Plutarch explicitly aligns the apothegms of the sages

---

33. Hdt. 2.171; Plut. De Def. Or. 14 (Mor. 417C); Philo Cher. 14.48.

34. τὸ σέμνον καὶ τὸ ἅγιον καὶ τὸ μυστηριῶδες τῆς σιωπῆς ("the solemn, holy, and mysterious character of silence"), Plut. De Garr. 17 (Mor. 510E) trans. Helmbold in LCL; also Philostr. Vit. Ap. 3.26; Plut. De Prof. Virt. 10 (Mor. 81E).

35. Cf. Philostr. Vit. Ap. 1.1; 6.11. Philo is fond of defining Judaism in terms of its "lesser and greater mysteries" (Vit. Mos. 1.11.62). Consistent with the symbolism attached to the Mysteries in the Greek world, he repeatedly invokes silence as one of their chief components, as in Op. mund. 1.14; Fug. 16.85–86; Sac. A. C. 15.60; Cher. 12.42; Vit. Cont. 10.75. In particular, read Sac. A. C. 16.62.

36. Philostr. Vit. Ap. 6.11; Plut. Is. et Os. 10 (Mor. 354F). For Philo, Moses spoke like a prophet in oracles (Vit. Mos. 1.10.57). He learned the secrets of the holy mysteries and revealed them to those with purified ears (Gig. 12.54). Even the translators of the LXX were like prophets and priests of the Mysteries (Vit. Mos. 2.7.40).

37. "Men of olden times established the rites of initiation into the mysteries, that we, by being accustomed to keeping silence there, may transfer that fear which we learned from the divine secrets to the safekeeping of the secrets of men," Plut. Lib. Educ. 14 (Mor. 10F); also De Garr. 8 (Mor. 505F). Schnayder, Taciturnitate, 51, n. 42, touches on this in passing.

38. Plut. Pyth. Or. 29–30 (Mor. 408E–409D). Among the many examples of obscure oracles, the most notorious may be the one that told Croesus he would destroy a mighty empire (Hdt. 1.53) and the one assuring the Athenians that they would be saved from the Persians by a "wooden wall" (Hdt. 7.139–43; 8.51).

39. Plut. Ei ap. Delph. 2–3 (Mor. 385D–E). For the legend of the sages meeting at Delphi, cf. Diog. Laert. 1.41.

40. For the attribution of ἕπου θεῷ to Pythagoras, cf. Stobaeus Anth. 2.7.16 (Hense, 49), as well as Iamb. Vit. Pyth. 28.137. Diverse traditions make Pythagoras himself the Apollo of Delos (Diog. Laert. 8.10), or worshiping exclusively at Apollo's altar (8.13), or receiving his doctrines from the Delphic priestess Themistocles (8.21).

41. For "following God" as the "imitation of God," cf. Plato Tht. 176B–D; Phdr. 248A; Epict. Diss. 1.12.8; Plut. Sera 5 (Mor. 550D).

and the oracles of the god, even noting that both were formerly delivered in verse but, in his day, only in prose (*Pyth. Or.* 18, 24 [Mor. 402F, 406E]). The tripod that was used when delivering prophecies at Delphi also excited comment and speculation among visitors (Plut. *Eiap. Delph.* 2 [Mor. 385D]). The symbol of the tripod was portable. The Seven Sages, according to one tradition, were supposed to have passed the tripod to one another in succession, according to the command of the Delphic Oracle that the one who was most wise should have the tripod (Diog. Laert. 1.28, 82). Because the tripod ended up at Delphi, we are to assume that Apollo is always most wise. The association of tripod, prophecy, wisdom, and βραχυλογία occurs frequently in the literature.[42]

Finally, the Greeks most renowned for their βραχυλογία were also most widely known for their devotion to the Delphic Oracle.[43] There is even a tradition that has Lycurgus's Spartan Constitution revealed by the oracle itself.[44] Seers, sages, and Spartans come together at Delphi. For such as these, "following God" in speech means the practice of taciturnity, for "the god himself [is] fond of conciseness and brevity in his oracles [φιλοσύντομός ἐστι καὶ βραχυλόγος ἐν τοῖς χρησμοῖς]" (Plut. *De Garr.* 17 [Mor. 511B]; trans. Helmbold in LCL).

SPEECH AND RELIGION IN JAMES

The Shared Tradition

Much of what James says about speech fits comfortably within the conventions of Hellenistic wisdom. At the rhetorical level, James deserves high marks for his own βραχυλογία. Although Jas 3:1–12 is one of James's longer "essays," it is a marvel of brevity, compressing a variety of conventional motifs with unconventional conciseness.[45]

Many of the Hellenistic ethical concerns are also found in James. He links speech and character. He emphasizes the importance of hearing. Speech should be slow. Incontinent speech he connects to anger, and anger to the doing of injustice (Jas 1:19–20). He thinks control of speech particularly important for the sage (διδάσκαλος [3:1]). He uses the stereotypical meta-

42. As priest of Apollo at Delphi, Plutarch might be expected to have more than ordinary interest in this symbolism, and such is the case: cf. *Sera* 17 (Mor. 560D); 29 Mor. 566D); *Conv. Sept. Sap.* 10 (Mor. 154A); *Ei ap. Delph.* 6 (Mor. 387C–D); *Pyth. Or.* 24 (Mor. 406D); *De Def. Or.* 7 (Mor. 413B). But traces can be found also in Hdt. 1.144; 4.179. Philostratus likens one who prophesies (as did Apollonius) to the Delphic Oracle, clasping the tripod to the breast and uttering oracles (*Vit. Ap.* 3.42). His taciturn sage is himself said to speak ὥσπερ ἐκ τρίποδος (as from a tripod [*Vit. Ap.* 1.17]).

43. Cf., e.g., Hdt. 1.51; 1.66; 1.67; 5.42–43; 5.62–63; 5.91; 6.52; 6.57; 6.66; 6.76; 6.86; 7.220; 7.239; 8.114; 8.141; Thuc. 2.7.55; 3.11.92; 4.13.118; 5.15.17.

44. Hdt. 1.65; Plato *Leg.* 1.624A; 632D; Plut. *Lyc.* 5.3; 6.5. To complicate matters still further, Plutarch in one place suggests that Lycurgus was also influenced by Thales (4.2)!

45. Compare Jas 3:1–12 with Plutarch's *De Garrulitate*, a compendium of the themes here under review, marred only by its own garrulousness (cf. esp. Mor. 511F–515A)!

phors: the rudder of a ship, the bit for a horse, the taming of wild animals.[46] Equally commonplace are statements on the tongue's disproportionate power to do both good and evil (3:5, 9–12).[47]

In several decisive ways, however, James differs from the standard treatment of speech. He is, for one thing, far more pessimistic. Hellenistic moralists recognize the difficulty in controlling speech but do not really doubt its possibility.[48] In contrast, James denies that anyone can truly control speech (Jas 3:8).[49] He also heightens the tongue's potential for evil. He personifies the tongue as though it were indeed completely independent: "It boasts of great things" (3:5). He also makes the tongue a cosmic force. It is a "world of wickedness," a fire that is "lit from Gehenna" (3:6). This mention of Gehenna introduces the most important difference between James's treatment of speech and that of Hellenistic wisdom: in James, the religious valuation of speech is distinctive, more fundamental to his exhortations, and more pervasive.

James's Distinctive Approach

The first and most startling thing one notices in turning to James from the Hellenistic materials is that he entirely lacks the religious motivations found in those writings. He makes no mention of the Mysteries or of the Delphic Oracle. James's monotheism is not sufficient reason for his abstinence, for Philo appropriated both themes into his system. James's entire outlook is distinctive. He has a relational or, perhaps better, a covenantal perspective, in which the speech and actions of humans are fundamentally qualified by the speech and action of the God who chooses to be involved with humans.

Three elements in the essay of Jas 3:1–12 provide important clues to James's perspective. First, the "double-mindedness" (cf. 1:8; 4:8) of human speech is manifested by the same tongue, both blessing God and cursing humans (3:9). The cursing of people is wrong, because they are "created in the image of God." This is an assertion that is derived from something other than the observance of behavior. Second, when James mentions Gehenna, he not only invokes the symbolic world of Torah but also points to the conviction that the rule of God in the world is opposed by the devil. This theme is developed in the call to conversion that immediately follows the essay on the tongue (3:13–4:10).[50] Third, teachers who fail in speech are not simply "foolish," failed sages. They are instead liable to a "greater judgment," obviously from God (3:1).

---

46. Cf. the fine collection of passages in Dibelius, *James*, 185–90.

47. In most dramatic fashion, Prov 18:21 says, "Life and death are in the power of the tongue." Cf. also Anacharsis in Diog. Laert. 1.105 and Bias in Plut. *Rect. Aud.* 2 (Mor. 38B); also *Lib. Educ.* 14 (Mor. 10B); *De Garr.* 8 (Mor. 506C).

48. Cf. Diog. Laert. 1.69; Plut. *De Garr.* 1 and 19 (Mor. 502E and 511F).

49. Cf. Dibelius, *James,* 191. The sentiment closest to James is found in Sir 19:16: "Who has not sinned with his tongue?"

50. Cf. L. T. Johnson, "James 3:13–4:10 and the *Topos* περὶ φθόνου," *NovT* 25 (1983) 327–47.

These small touches alter the reader's view of James's traditional material. They direct us to the central religious polarity in James between the "wisdom from above," which leads to "friendship with God," and the "wisdom from below," which manifests itself in a "friendship with the world" (Jas 3:13–16; 4:4).[51] All human activity, certainly including speech, is lived within these competing norms and allegiances.

The theological weighting is present as well in Jas 1:19–20, the passage with which this essay began. James's command to be "quick to hear, slow to speak, slow to anger," is classically Hellenistic. So also, as we have determined, is the connection between rash speech, anger, and the doing of injustice. Notice, however, that for James, it is *human* anger that does not work *God's* justice. The two levels of activity are intertwined with an intensity that would be unsettling to a Plutarch.[52]

James's commandment, furthermore, is framed by two statements that show that taciturnity is more than a matter of self-control. In Jas 1:18, readers are told that they have been given birth by a "word of truth" (λόγῳ ἀληθείας) that has made them "first-fruits of creation." In 1:21, they are ordered to "receive with meekness the implanted word [τὸν ἔμφυτον λόγον] that is able to save your souls." Human speech is qualified by reference to the creating and saving word of God. God's word determines a form of identity and behavior not measured by the world or its wisdom.

James's transcendental reference point is stated succinctly in Jas 2:22: "So speak and act as those who will be judged by the law of freedom." By the law of freedom, James means the law of love (2:8), derived from Lev 19:18 and explicated by the Decalogue, the scriptural context of Lev 19:12–18, and the words of Jesus.[53] Thus, James categorically condemns slander (4:11), mutual grumbling (5:9), and the taking of oaths (5:12). As in 3:1, these sins of speech bring a person under God's judgment (see the warrants in 4:12; 5:9; 5:12).

Less directly, but no less emphatically, James condemns speech that distorts the proper relationship between humans and God:[54] arrogantly boasting about human projects without reference to God's will (Jas 4:15); claiming that temptation has its source in God (1:13); and praying with a double mind, either with doubt (1:5) or "wickedly" as a means of self-gratification (4:3). James likewise condemns religious language that does not manifest itself in moral action. It is useless to pronounce a benediction ("Go in peace") while denying to the needy the food or clothing that they require (2:14–16). This is precisely to bless God and curse humans made in God's image (3:9). In James's covenantal perspective, religion and ethics are inseparable. The line

---

51. Johnson, "Friendship with the World," 169–77.
52. But cf. Plut. *Cohib. Ira* 16 (Mor. 464B–D).
53. Cf. L. T. Johnson, "The Use of Lev. 19 in the Letter of James," *JBL* 101 (1982) 391–401.
54. Two passages that touch on the same concern, though in very different fashion, are Eccl 5:1–2 and Philo *Spec. Leg.* 2.2.7.

from claiming to be religious to "visiting orphans and widows" is a direct one (1:26–27).

James has few positive instructions on speech. He prefers listening and acting. But he does add a few characteristic commands: say "if God wills" and mean it (Jas 4:16), and let your "yes be yes and your no be no" (5:12). Most of all, he stresses the speech that builds the community. In every circumstance, members of the community are to pray and sing (5:13). When a brother or sister is ill, the elders are to be called for the prayer and anointing of the sick person (5:14). They are to confess their sins to one another and pray for one another (5:16). They are to turn a brother or sister from the path of error back to the truth (5:20). These are the uses of speech that match the measure of friendship with God and express the wisdom from above. Without them, even the claim to be "religious" is a dangerous failure to "control the tongue" (1:26).[55]

55. Johnson, "Friendship with the World," 172–73; B. C. Johanson, "The Definition of 'Pure Religion' in James 1:27 Reconsidered," *ExpTim* 84 (1973) 118–19.

RACHEL'S VIRTUOUS BEHAVIOR
IN THE *TESTAMENT*
OF ISSACHAR

The *Testament of Issachar* in the *Testaments of the Twelve Patriarchs* begins with the story of Reuben's finding the mandrakes in the field in the days of the wheat harvest. *T. Iss.* 1:3–15 retells Gen 30:14–18 (LXX) with significant dramatizing changes and additions. It is followed by a number of additional remarks in 2:1–5 emphasizing Rachel's virtuous behavior in the matter.[1] They reflect what is told in Gen 30:19–24 about Leah's giving birth to a sixth son, Zebulun, and God's remembering Rachel and opening her womb. According to the biblical story, she called her son Joseph, hoping to receive another son.

In the *Testament of Issachar* 2, these themes are treated in a remarkable way. Leah is portrayed as wanting to give up anything for intercourse with Jacob; Rachel is a paradigm of continency: "She despised intercourse with a man and chose continency" (2:1); the Lord saw "that for the sake of children she wished to have intercourse with Jacob and not for lust of pleasure" (2:3). She gave up Jacob yet another night, for there were two mandrakes (called *apples,* as in Gen 30:14 LXX). On this account the Lord listened to Rachel (*T. Iss.* 2:4; cf. v. 2). An angel of the Lord announces to Jacob that Rachel will bear two children because of this virtuous behavior (2:1). Leah, by way of contrast, is punished: instead of eight sons, she will bear six, the other two now being allotted to Rachel. And in case anyone would think that Rachel, after all, was keen on the sweet-smelling apples (see 1:3), we are told that "though she desired them she did not eat them but dedicated them in the house of the Lord, offering them to the priest of the Most High who was there at the time."

This very special interpretation of Gen 30:14–24 propagates a distinct view of sex and marriage. Sexual intercourse between spouses should be for the sake of children and not for lust of pleasure (φιληδονία), and continency

---

1. On the *Testament of Issachar* see also M. de Jonge, *The Testaments of the Twelve Patriarchs: A Study of their Text, Composition and Origin* (Assen: Van Gorcum, 1953) 77–81; "Testament Issachar als 'typisches' Testament" (*Studies on the Testaments of the Twelve Patriarchs: Text and Interpretation* (ed. M. de Jonge; SVTP 3; Leiden: Brill, 1975) 291–316; and H. W. Hollander and M. de Jonge, *The Testaments of the Twelve Patriarchs: A Commentary* (SVTP 8; Leiden: Brill, 1985) 233–52.

(ἐγκράτεια) should be preferred to intercourse (συνουσία). This idea is not unknown. In the section on "Conventional Subjects" of his *Moral Exhortation: A Greco-Roman Sourcebook*,[2] Abraham J. Malherbe prints fragment 12, "On Sexual Indulgence," from Musonius Rufus, in which we read:

> Men who are not wantons or immoral are bound to consider sexual intercourse justified only when it occurs in marriage and is indulged in for the purpose of begetting children [ἐπὶ γενέσει παίδων], since that is lawful, but unjust and unlawful when it is mere pleasure-seeking [τὰ δέ γε ἡδονὴν θηρώμενα], even in marriage.... But furthermore, leaving out of consideration adultery, all intercourse with women which is without lawful character is shameful and is practiced from lack of self-restraint [δι' ἀκολασίαν]. So no one with any self-control [μετά γε σωφροσύνης] would think of having relations with a courtesan or a free woman apart from a marriage, no, nor even with his own maidservant.[3]

Musonius's attitude toward sex and marriage as expressed in this fragment (as well as in the fragments 13A and 13B on "What Is the Chief End of Marriage?") is representative of the teaching of Greek philosophers of various schools. That people have to marry for the procreation of children, so that the human race may continue and a new generation will be able to serve society in general and the state in particular, is a commonplace.[4] The opposition between the pursuit of pleasure and one's responsibility for the perpetuation of the human race is also emphasized by Ocellus Lucanus in his *De Universi Natura* 44–45.[5] Musonius is stricter than others in forbidding pleasure seeking even in marriage. Seneca agrees when he advocates temperance in marital intercourse and puts intemperance in sexual matters on a par with adultery.[6]

2. This book appeared as vol. 4 in the Library of Early Christianity (ed. W. A. Meeks; Philadelphia: Westminster, 1986).

3. See pp. 152–54. Malherbe gives the translation of Cora E. Lutz, *Musonius Rufus: "The Roman Socrates"* (Yale Classical Studies 10; New Haven: Yale University Press, 1947) 84–89. I have added some Greek words from this edition.

4. On p. 152 of his sourcebook, A. J. Malherbe refers to extracts given earlier, one from Maximus of Tyre *Discourse* 36, 6b: "Ask a married man, 'What is your reason for marrying?' He will answer, 'To have children'" (p. 78); and one from the section "On Marriage" in Hierocles, *On Duties* (see pp. 100–104). For other examples see, for instance, H. Preisker, "Die Umwelt des Christentums in ihrer Stellung zur Ehe. 1: Das hellenistisch-römische Heidentum," *Christentum und Ehe in den ersten drei Jahrhunderten* (Berlin: Travitzsch und Sohn, 1927) 13–65; A. Oepke, "Ehe I (Institution)" *RAC* 4 (1959) 650–66; G. Delling, "Geschlechtsverkehr" *RAC* 10 (1978) 812–29; and N. Geurts, *Het Huwelijk bij de Griekse en Romeinse Moralisten* (diss., University of Utrecht, 1928). See also O. Larry Yarbrough, *Not Like the Gentiles: Marriage Rules in the Letters of Paul* (SBLDS 80; Atlanta: Scholars, 1985) 31–63 ("Marriage Precepts in the Greco-Roman Tradition").

5. In *Neue Philologische Untersuchungen* (vol. 1; ed. R. Harder; Berlin: Weidmann, 1926). Cf. Iamblichus *De Vita Pythagorica* 210 (ed. L. Deubner; Lipsiae: Teubner, 1937).

6. "Nihil est foedius quam uxorem amare quasi adulteram," in a fragment from Seneca's *De Matrimonio* preserved by Hieronymus in his first book against Iovinianus (no. 85 on p. 434 in F. Haase, *L. Annaei Senecae, Opera quae supersunt* (vol. 3; Lipsiae: Teubner, 1878). On pp. 373–94 of his *Diatribe in Senecae Philosophi Fragmenta* (vol. 1 of *Fragmenta de Matrimonio;* Leipzig: Teubner, 1915), L. Bickel has given a critical text of Hieronymus *Adversus Iovinianum* 1. 41–49, indicating what may be considered to go back to Seneca's work. Bickel regards the sentence at the beginning of this note as coming from Seneca.

How are we to explain this parallel between the *Testament of Issachar* and a well-known representative Stoic philosopher of the first century A.D.? In order to answer this question, we shall first have to examine the position of these statements in *T. Iss.* 2:1, 3 in the *Testaments of the Twelve Patriarchs*. Next, we shall have to look at early Jewish and early Christian writings in which the views expressed by Musonius return. Finally, we shall ask whether our investigation sheds light on the hotly debated question of the origin of the *Testaments of the Twelve Patriarchs*.

CHASTITY AND SIMPLICITY
IN THE *TESTAMENT OF ISSACHAR*

After the fashion of Gen 49:14–15 (LXX), the *Testament of Issachar* depicts Issachar as a farmer living a simple and good life. The central virtue in this testament is ἁπλότης, a word that may be translated as "simplicity," "single-mindedness," or "integrity."[7] "Singleness of heart" occurs parallel to "uprightness" (εὐθύτης; see *T. Iss.* 3:1, 2; 4:6). It leads to complete obedience to the essentials of the Law, love for the Lord and for one's neighbor:

> Keep, therefore, the law of God, my children,
> and acquire simplicity
> and walk in guilelessness,
>   not meddling with the commandments of the Lord
>   and the affairs of your neighbor.
> But love the Lord and your neighbor,
> show mercy to the poor and the weak. (5:1–2; cf. 7:6)

The hardworking farmer shows his gratitude to God by bringing offerings from the fruits of labor (*T. Iss.* 3:6; 5:3; cf. Rachel in 2:5). The farmer cares for all who are in need (3:8; 5:2; 7:5) and is therefore blessed by God (3:7; 4:1; 5:4–6). Toiling away and living a simple life, Issachar is able to avoid a number of bad habits and vices (3:2–3; 4:2–6; 7:2–4). In short, desire and love of pleasure do not get a hold on him. We may note here that Musonius advocates the life of a farmer or shepherd as the ideal occupation of a philosopher: "What is there to prevent a student while he is working from listening to a preacher speaking about self-control or justice or endurance [περὶ σωφρο-σύνης ἢ δικαιοσύνης ἢ καρτερίας]?"[8]

Self-control is also characteristic of the attitude of a simple man toward

---

7. See J. Amstutz, ΑΠΛΟΤΗΣ: *Eine begriffsgeschichtliche Studie zum jüdisch-christlichen Griechisch* (Theophaneia 19; Bonn: P. Hanstein, 1968). On *T. 12 Patr.* see pp. 64–85.

8. Edited by Lutz, *Musonius Rufus*, 82–83. The quotation is from Frag. 11: "What Means of Livelihood Is Appropriate for a Philosopher." For other parallels to Musonius see Hollander and de Jonge, *Commentary*, esp. on 4:2, referring to R. Vischer, *Das einfache Leben: Wort- und motivgeschichtliche Untersuchungen zu einem Wertbegriff der antiken Literatur* (Göttingen: Vandenhoeck & Ruprecht, 1965). Vischer shows that the ideal of simplicity was an important topic in the work of Hellenistic moralists.

women. Issachar took a wife when he was thirty years old. Labor wore away his strength, and because of his toil, sleep overcame him; he simply did not think of pleasure (ἡδονή) with a woman (*T. Iss.* 3:5). He assures his sons: "Except my wife I have not known any woman. I did not act impurely by the uplifting of the eyes" (7:2; cf. *T. Benj.* 6:2–3). There and elsewhere in the *Testaments* there is a direct connection between seeing and sexual impurity (πορνεία). The statement about Issachar's marriage in 3:5 immediately follows the clause "walking in singleness of eyes." The single-minded man who is free from all sorts of desires (4:2) will not be overpowered by the spirits of evil. He is able to avoid various temptations. The first thing mentioned is that "he does not look to welcome the beauty of a woman lest he would pollute his mind with perversion" (4:4). In short, "he walks in uprightness of life and looks at all things in simplicity" (4:6).

SELF-CONTROL, CHASTITY, AND SEXUAL IMPURITY IN THE OTHER TESTAMENTS

In the *Testaments* Joseph is the paradigm of virtue.[9] The *Testament of Benjamin* hails him as a good and holy man (chap. 3–8), and the first part of Joseph's own testament describes at some length the ten temptations to which he did not succumb in his struggle against the wiles of Potiphar's wicked wife (*T. Jos.* 2:7–10:4; cf. Gen 39:6–18). Joseph's self-control (σωφροσύνη) and purity (ἁγνεία), together with his patience and humility of heart, are praised and held out to his sons and brothers as an example to be imitated (*T. Jos.* 10:2). Also in the second section of the *Testament of Joseph,* which concentrates on Joseph's attitude toward his brothers (10:5–18:4), the Memphian woman figures prominently. All along, Joseph's humility (ταπείνωσις [10:2]) and patience (ὑπομονή [2:7; 10:1, 2; 17:1] or μακροθυμία [2:7; 17:2]) are praised. It was because of his patience that Joseph took as his wife the daughter of his masters (18:3).

Joseph is the counterpart of his brother Reuben. According to *T. Reub.* 4:8–10, the magicians and love potions of the Egyptian woman had no effect on Joseph because "the disposition of his soul did not admit an evil desire" (v. 9). Indeed, "he purged his thoughts from all impurity [πορνεία]" (v. 8). Therefore, God delivered him "from all visible and invisible death" (v. 10). Reuben's sons are told: "If impurity does not overcome the mind, also Beliar will not overcome you" (v. 11).

Reuben, on the contrary, did fall "into the great iniquity [ἀνομία]." After he had twice seen Bilhah naked (*T. Reub.* 3:11–14), he could not restrain himself from doing "the abominable thing" (v. 12) that can only be classified as

9. See H. W. Hollander, *Josephus as an Ethical Model in the Testaments of the Twelve Patriarchs* (SVTP 6; Leiden: Brill, 1981).

"impiety" (ἀσέβεια [vv. 14–15]). The patriarch repeatedly warns his sons against sexual impurity, which is especially dangerous in the case of young people (1:6–10; 3:9–6:4). Preparing the way for the admonitions of his brother Issachar, Reuben exhorts his sons:

Pay no heed, therefore, to the beauty of women,
and do not set your mind on their affairs.
But walk in singleness of heart,
    in the fear of the Lord
    and laboring in works
    as well as wandering about in literature and with your flocks
until the Lord will give you a wife, whom he wants. (4:1)

Reuben warns strongly against women; they are all potentially dangerous. Joseph, he says, "guarded himself from every woman" (*T. Reub.* 4:8a). Men will do wise to keep at a distance (3:10; 4:1; 6:1–4). "Beware, therefore, of impurity, and if you wish to be pure in mind, guard your senses from every woman" (6:1). The *Testament of Reuben* 5 is downright misogynistic. Women, having no strength or power over men, use their wiles to take them in. Their makeup, their adornments, their beguiling glances bewitch people. In a very radical variant of the story of the union between women and the angelic "Watchers" before the Flood, the women are the ones who take all initiative (5:6–7; cf. *T. Napht.* 3:5, which holds the Watchers responsible).[10]

In between the two references to the Bilhah story in *T. Reub.* 1:6–10 and 3:9–15, we find a remarkable double excursus. In 2:1–2 we hear about Reuben's insight into the machinations of the seven spirits of deceit (πλανή) commanded by Beliar—an insight received by him in the seven years during which he repented (1:9–10; 4:2–4). The first of those spirits, "that of impurity [πορνεία] is seated in the nature and the senses"; it is linked with "the spirit of insatiate desire [ἀπληστία],"[11] "located in the belly" (3:3). Before the patriarch, however, comes to speak about the seven spirits of deceit, he describes "seven spirits given to man at creation" (2:3–9).[12] For the purpose of our present investigation, two verses are of importance.

The second spirit in this category is "the spirit of sight, with which desire comes" (*T. Reub.* 2:4b)—also sexual desire, as illustrated in *T. Reub.* 3:10–14; 4:1; and 6:1; and, in a different way, in 5:3 and 6:7 (cf. *T. Iss.* 4:4; 7:2; and *T. Benj.* 6:3; 8:2).[13] The seventh spirit is listed as "the spirit of procreation

---

10. See M. Küchler, *Schweigen, Schmuck und Schleier: Drei neutestamentlichen Vorschriften zur Verdrängung der Frauen auf dem Hintergrund einer frauenfeindlichen Exegese des Alten Testaments im antiken Judentum* (NTOA 1; Freiburg: Universitätsverlag; Göttingen: Vandenhoeck & Ruprecht, 1986) 439–60.

11. The opposite of ἁπλότης in *T. Iss.* 4:5; 6:1.

12. For Stoic parallels, see Hollander and de Jonge, *Commentary*, 93–94.

13. On Judah being deceived by his eyes, see note 16 below. Joseph remained steadfast while Potiphar's wife "used to bare her arms and breasts and legs," when she "very beautiful and splendidly adorned, tried to beguile him" (*T. Jos.* 9:5).

[σπορά] and intercourse [συνουσία] with which through love of pleasure [φιληδονία] sin comes in" (*T. Reub.* 2:8). It is "the last (in the order) of creation, but the first (in the order) of youth"; this constitutive aspect of human life brings with it very great dangers for young people (2:9).

These two verses bring us back to *T. Iss.* 2:1, 3. There is a natural link between intercourse and procreation. "For there is a season (for a man) to have intercourse with his wife, and a season to abstain therefrom for his prayer," Naphtali says in *T. Napht.* 8:8 (echoing Eccl 3:5; 1 Cor 7:5), and he adds, "So there are two commandments, and if they are not done in their order, they bring sin." The trouble is, however, that abstention (ἐγκράτεια) is often not practiced because φιληδονία (love of pleasure) prevails.

Another slave of (the spirit of) πορνεία (impurity) in the *Testaments* is Judah. His unfortunate marriage with Bath-shua, the daughter of Barsan, the king of Adullam, and his misery about his children receive much attention (*Testament of Judah* 8; 10–11; 13–14; 16–17; 19). The fact that Bath-shua was a Canaanite is duly emphasized (10:2, 6; 11:1, 3; 13:3; 14:6; 16:4; 17:1). Judah knew "that the race of Canaan is wicked" (11:1) and that he transgressed God's commandments by marrying Bath-shua (13:7; 14:6). Yet in the admonitions to his sons, Judah does not explicitly warn against marrying non-Israelite women,[14] and the descriptions of his meeting with Bath-shua highlight the dangers connected with an encounter with any woman. This time it is not only Bath-shua's beauty and her adorning that lead Judah astray (13:5; 17:1),[15] but also the fact that she poured large quantities of wine (11:2; 13:5) and that her father showed a boundless store of gold on his daughter's behalf (13:4). Consequently, Judah warns his sons at great length concerning the evil effects of drinking too much wine (especially in chap. 5, 14, and 16)[16] and of love of money (φιλαργυρία [17:1; 18:2; 19:1–2]).

Also in the story of the meeting of Judah and his daughter-in-law Thamar (*Testament of Judah* 12; cf. 13:4; 14:5; chap. 15), not only Thamar's beauty, her dress, and her adorning receive attention (12:1, 3), but especially the fact that Judah did not recognize her because of his drunkenness (12:3, 6; 14:4–5). Strangely enough, Thamar's legitimate wish to have children, denied to her by her husband and his family (Genesis 38), does not receive attention. Judah, of

---

14. The same applies to Levi and his sons, as I have argued in my contribution "Die Paränese in den Schriften des Neuen Testaments und in den Testamenten der Zwölf Patriarchen: Einige Überlegungen," *Neues Testament und Ethik: Für Rudolf Schnackenburg* (ed. H. Merklein; Freiburg, Basel, and Wien: Herder, 1989) 538–50. *T. Levi* 9:9–14 (including the warning against the spirit of πορνεία and the command to marry an Israelite wife without blemish or defilement) goes back to similar instructions in the Aramaic fragments of Levi. For the author or authors of the *Testaments* these instructions apply only to Levi and his offspring during the period of the priesthood that has come to an end with the appearance of Jesus Christ.

15. Because Judah boasted of the fact that in his many wars (cf. *Testament of Judah* 3–7, 9) no comely woman's face had ever deceived him, and reproved his brother Reuben, "the spirit of jealousy and impurity" engineered his downfall (13:3).

16. Note, again, the influence on the eyes: "Wine turned away the eyes" (*T. Jud.* 13:6); "wine . . . leads the eyes into error" (14:1).

course, is the one to be blamed for all that happened. Yet in *T. Jud.* 15:5–6 women are portrayed as beings to beware of (in the manner of the *Testament of Reuben* 5):

> And the angel of God showed me
> that women have dominion over king and beggar alike, for ever;
> and from the king they take away the glory
> and from the valiant man the power
> and from the beggar even that little which is the stay of his poverty.

Summing up, we may say that warnings against πορνεία, a broad term denoting a variety of undesirable sexual relations, are very prominent in the *Testaments*. Self-restraint and caution should prevail in the relationships between men and women, who should behave modestly. In some instances, women are described in negative terms (*Testament of Reuben* 5, cf. *T. Jud.* 15:5–6), but meeting with women is almost always dangerous for men who do not observe God's commandments—which are, in fact, the common laws of decency as taught by Hellenistic philosophers. Desire, love of pleasure, and lust (ἡδονή, φιληδονία, ἐπιθυμία) are always there and are to be held in check. The only legitimate union between man and woman is marriage. The purpose of marriage is procreation. Therefore, also within marriage, continency has a place. It is interesting that in the *Testaments,* which address men (because in all testaments the sons—and sometimes the brothers—of the patriarch are pictured as standing around his deathbed), there is at least one example of a virtuous woman whose self-restraint is praised: Rachel.[17]

FLAVIUS JOSEPHUS ON THE ESSENES

In *J.W.* 2.8.2–14 §§119–66, Josephus describes the tenets and practices of the Essenes, Pharisees, and Sadducees. As in *Ant.* 18.1.2–6 §§11–25, he treats these religious groups as philosophical schools. In his *Jewish War,* the Essenes receive a great deal of attention (only §§162–66 are devoted to the Pharisees and the Sadducees), for, as Josephus tells us, they "have a reputation for cultivating peculiar sanctity" (§119).[18] In *Ant.* 15.10.4 §371, he describes the Essenes as "a group which follows a way of life taught to the Greeks by Pythagoras."

At the beginning of *J.W.,* Josephus speaks about the Essenes' attitude toward marriage: "They shun pleasures [ἡδοναί] as a vice and regard temperance [ἐγκράτεια] and the control of the passions as a special virtue. Marriage they disdain, but they adopt other men's children. . . . They do not, indeed, on

---

17. Küchler, *Schweigen, Schmuck und Schleier,* concentrates on the stories about Potiphar's wife and about Bilhah, Bath-shua, and Thamar and so gives a one-sided picture of the attitude toward women in the *Testaments.*

18. The translations from Josephus's works in this section are those by Thackeray, Marcus, Wikgren, and Feldman in LCL.

principle, condemn wedlock and the propagation thereby of the race, but they wish to protect themselves against women's wantonness [ἀσελγείαι] being persuaded that none of the sex keeps her plighted troth to one man" (§§120–21).

At the end of his description of the Essenes (§§160–61), Josephus introduces another order of Essenes that differs in its attitude to marriage: "They think that those who decline to marry cut off the chief function of life, the propagation of the race [διαδοχή—a word also used in §121]. . . . They have no intercourse with them [namely, their wives] during pregnancy, thus showing that their motive in marrying is not self-indulgence but the procreation of children [τὸ μὴ δι' ἡδονὴν ἀλλὰ τέκνων χρείαν γαμεῖν]." This special group of Essenes is mentioned only here by Josephus. In Ant. 18.1.5 §21 he states that the Essenes do not bring wives into the community.[19] For our purpose, we need not determine the actual situation, nor is it necessary to compare the description in these passages of Josephus with what the documents and archaeological remains tell us about the community at Qumran.[20] In the context of this present contribution, it is interesting to note a few clearly Hellenistic notions.

According to Josephus, both groups of Essenes regard the propagation of the human race as the purpose of marriage. Both shun passion and pleasure (ἡδονή), the first group opting for complete ἐγκράτεια (abstention) and the second abstaining from sexual intercourse during pregnancy.[21] Josephus returns to this issue when, in an apologetic treatment of various essential commandments of the Law in Ag. Ap. 2.22–30 §§190–219, he speaks about marriage laws. His first statement follows: "The Law recognizes no sexual connections, except the natural union of man and wife, and that only for the procreation of children [τέκνων ἕνεκα]" (§199). A little further, H. St. J. Thackeray translates a difficult passage as "none who has intercourse with a woman who is with child can be considered pure" (§202).[22] If this translation is correct, we have another parallel with Josephus's description of the second Essene group.

The final clause in J.W. 2 §121 shows an extremely low opinion of women in general. It is only surpassed by Philo (as quoted by Eusebius Prep. Ev. 8.11.1–18), who explains that the Essenes prefer continency (ἐγκράτεια) to marriage because "a wife [or woman] is a selfish creature, excessively jealous

19. Compare Philo in Eusebius Prep. Ev. 8.11–18 (to be discussed below in the section on Josephus), and Pliny HN 5.17: "sine ulla femina, omni venere abdicata."
20. On this, see Todd S. Beall, Josephus' Description of the Essenes Illustrated by the Dead Sea Scrolls (SNTSMS 58; Cambridge and New York: Cambridge University Press, 1988).
21. In the fragment mentioned in note 6, Seneca also regards intercourse during pregnancy as undesirable: "Certe qui dicunt se causa reipublicae et generis humani uxoribus iungi et liberos tollere, imitentur saltem pecudes et postquam uxorem venter intumuerit, non perdant filios, nec amatores uxoribus se exhibeant sed maritos." Bickel, Diatribe, ascribes this statement to Jerome.
22. The crucial expression is εἴ τις ἐπὶ λεχοῦς φθορὰν παρέλθοι. The clause follows on the prohibition of abortion and destruction of a fetus. See also Ps. Phoc. 186, "Lay not your hand upon your wife when she is pregnant," and P. W. van der Horst's comment in his The Sentences of Pseudo-Phocylides (SVTP 4; Leiden: Brill, 1978) 234–35.

and an adept at beguiling the morals of her husband [or a man] and seducing him by her continued impostures [γοητείαι]. For by the fawning talk which she practises and the other ways in which she plays her part like an actress on the stage she first ensnares the sight and hearing, and when these subjects as it were have been duped she cajoles the sovereign mind."[23]

Here we are very near to the assessment of women found in the *Testament of Reuben* 5 (and the emphasis in the *Testaments* that desire comes with sight—see *T. Reub.* 2:4). Yet the two passages concerned are not typical of Philo (as we shall see presently) or of Josephus, according to whom even the more radical Essenes were not against marriage on principle. Of course, the Law tells people to marry for the sake of children, not for pleasure's sake. As a final example, in *Ant.* 4.8.24 §261, parents have to tell their rebellious children (Deut 21:18) "that they came together in matrimony not for pleasure's sake [οὐχ ἡδονῆς ἕνεκα], nor to increase their fortunes by uniting their several properties to one, but that they might have children who should tend their old age and who should receive from them everything that they needed."[24]

In all instances concerned, Josephus writes with outsiders in mind, and this accounts for the manner in which he expresses the essentials of the Jewish law and the Essene way of life.[25] Of course, G. Vermes is right when, in his comments on the summary of the Law in *Ag. Ap.*, he remarks: "Apropos of marriage laws, which are listed in conjunction with sexual impurity, Josephus maintains firmly that the purpose of marital union is procreation (199), thereby echoing the common teaching based on the divine commandment, 'Be fruitful and multiply' (Gen 1:28)."[26] The opposition—sexual union for pleasure or for the sake of children—however, is certainly Hellenistic.[27]

---

23. Translated by Colson in LCL. Cf. *Quaest. in Gn.* 1.43 (on Gen 3:8). "It was the more imperfect and ignoble element, the female, that made a beginning of transgression and lawlessness, while the male made the beginning of reverence and modesty and all good, since he was better and more perfect" (trans. Marcus in LCL).

24. Cf. *Ant.* 3.12.1 §273: "Adultery he absolutely prohibited, deeming it blessed that men should be sane-minded concerning wedlock and that it was to the interest alike of the state and the family that children should be legitimate."

25. This general statement holds true whether Josephus and others portraying the essentials of the Jewish law wrote with a missionary or an apologetic purpose, or in order to remind Jews in the Diaspora of the central tenets of their religion and way of life. On these questions, see, for example, J. E. Crouch, *The Origin and Intention of the Colossian Haustafel* (FRLANT 109; Göttingen: Vandenhoeck & Ruprecht, 1972) 99, who speaks of missionary activity of Jewish propagandists receptive to Hellenistic influences; John J. Collins, *Between Athens and Jerusalem: Jewish Identity in the Hellenistic Diaspora* (New York: Crossroad, 1983) 167–68, who links Jewish identity and the appeal to Gentiles; and K. W. Niebuhr, *Gesetz und Paränese* (WUNT 2. 28; Tübingen: J. C. B. Mohr, 1987) 69, who uses the term "Apologetik nach innen."

26. See G. Vermes, "A Summary of the Law by Flavius Josephus," *NovT* 24 (1982) 289–303; quotation from p. 296.

27. See the introductory section on Musonius and the section on Philo directly below.

PHILO'S IDEAS ON MARRIAGE
AND PROCREATION

The two quotations from Philo given in the preceding section underscore Wayne A. Meeks's negative assessment of this philosopher's attitude toward women.[28] Meeks calls Philo the most blatant example of misogyny, reminding us that Philo "commonly uses the female figures as symbols of *aisthēsis* [sense-perception] or *pathos* [emotion], but the male for *nous* [mind] and *logos* [reason]" and that he "associates with woman an extraordinary number of pejorative expressions." Yet, as Meeks remarks, "Philo is both Jewish and Greek enough to regard marriage as natural and necessary—but the husband's relationship to his wife is like that of father to children and owner to slaves."

In fact, in many places in his voluminous oeuvre, Philo links marriage and procreation, very often adding a negative remark about pleasure (*Op. Mund.* 161; *Det. Pot. Ins.* 102; *Cher.* 43, 50; *Congr.* 12; *Abr.* 137, 248–49; *Jos.* 43; *Vit. Mos.* 1.28; *Decal.* 119; *Spec. Leg.* 3.9, 32, 34–46, 112–13; *Virt.* 207; *Praem. Poen.* 108–9; *Quaest. in Gn.* 3.21; 4.86). There is no need to discuss all examples here, for Philo is clearly dealing with an issue familiar to him and his readers. We should note that in *Op. Mund.* 161, in an invective against φιλη-δονία (love of pleasure) in which the serpent of Genesis 3 is said to symbolize ἡδονή (pleasure), Philo concedes: "And certainly the first approaches of the male to the female have pleasure to guide and conduct them, and it is through pleasure that begetting and the coming of life is brought about."[29] In *Spec. Leg.* 3.112, however, he follows the usual pattern: "For they are pleasure-lovers [φιλήδονοι] when they mate with their wives, not to procreate children and to perpetuate the race, but like pigs and goats in quest of the enjoyment which such intercourse gives"[30] (cf. *T. Iss.* 2:3).

In *Spec. Leg.* 3.32, Philo comments on the prohibition found in Lev 18:19 of intercourse with a menstruating woman. His argumentation is in line with that probably used by members of the second group of Essenes, those refusing to have sexual union with their pregnant wives. Philo says that one must respect the law of nature and also "remember the lesson that the generative seeds should not be wasted fruitlessly for the sake of a gross and untimely pleasure." In *Spec. Leg.* 3.34–36, this rule leads to the interdiction of intercourse with a barren woman. Those who knowingly want to marry such a woman are clearly moved by "an inordinate frenzy and incontinence

28. In Wayne A. Meeks, "The Image of the Androgyne: Some Uses of a Symbol in Earliest Christianity," *HR* 13 (1974) 165–208. Quotations from pp. 176–77.
29. Translated by Colson in LCL. Cf. Musonius in frag. 14, "Is Marriage a Handicap for the Pursuit of Philosophy?": "For, to what other purpose did the creator of mankind first divide our human race into two sexes, male and female, then implant in each a strong desire for association and union with the other [ἐπιθυμία ἰσχυρὰ τῆς θ' ὁμιλίας καὶ τῆς κοινωνίας], instilling . . . a powerful longing [πόθος] each for the other. . . ." The purpose is a life together, producing and rearing children together [γένεσις παίδων καὶ τροφή] (text and trans. Lutz, *Musonius Rufus*, 92–93).
30. Translated by Colson in LCL.

[ἀκρασία] past all cure." Only those who married maidens not knowing whether or not they would be able to bear children are to be pardoned when they refuse to dismiss their wives after prolonged childlessness. Otherwise, Philo remains adamant: "Those persons who make an art of quenching the life of the seed as it drops, stand confessed as the enemies of nature."

Particularly in his treatment of relations with a barren woman, it becomes clear that Philo is more radical than rabbinic tradition, as I. Heinemann[31] and S. Belkin[32] have pointed out. Marital relations were considered a biblical command, even if they were not necessarily for the sake of begetting children.[33] Marriage of a priest with a sterile woman was allowed if he already had a wife or children (m. Yebam. 6:5).[34] The problem arises when a man has not fulfilled the command of Gen 1:28, that is, does not have at least two children. After he has been married to a woman who does not bear children for ten years, he has to marry another by either taking a second wife (not a common practice) or by divorcing the first one. The duty to be fruitful and multiply falls on the man, not on the woman (m. Yebam. 6:6). It is this duty that is under discussion, not the relation between sexual intercourse and pleasure. With regard to that matter, Philo introduced Hellenistic categories.

EARLY CHRISTIAN AUTHORS ON MARRIAGE AND PROCREATION

Hellenistic ideas about procreation as the purpose of marriage have been taken over by Christian authors from the second century onward. Relevant texts have been assembled by J. Stelzenberger,[35] whose crown witness among Greek theologians is Clement of Alexandria. The first authors to be mentioned in this context are, not surprisingly, a number of apologists. Justin, in Apol. 1.29.1, and Minucius Felix, in Oct. 31.5, emphasize that Christians either do not marry at all or marry only one woman in order to procreate.

31. I. Heinemann, Philons griechische und jüdische Bildung: Kulturvergleichende Untersuchungen zu Philons Darstellung der jüdischen Gesetze (Breslau: H. und H. Marcus, 1929–32; repr. Darmstadt: Wiss. Buchgesellschaft, 1962) 261–73.
32. S. Belkin, Philo and the Oral Law: The Philonic Interpretation of Biblical Law in Relation to Palestinian Halakah (HSS 11; Cambridge: Harvard University Press, 1940) 219–22.
33. Belkin, Philo and the Oral Law, 219, points out that Philo is (of course) aware of this, when in Quaest. in Gn. 3.21 he writes about Abraham and Hagar: "For with the concubine the embrace was a bodily one for the sake of begetting children. But with the wife the union was one of the soul harmonized to heavenly love."
34. The Sages disagree with R. Judah, who equates a sterile woman with the harlot spoken of in Lev 21:7.
35. In J. Stelzenberger, Die Beziehungen der frühchristlichen Sittenlehre zur Ethik der Stoa: Eine moralgeschichtliche Studie (Munich: M. Hueber, 1933) 403–38 (on marriage and procreation, in Clement and other Greek theologians, see pp. 416–23). See also Preisker, Christentum und Ehe; Oepke, "Ehe I"; and Delling, "Geschlechtsverkehr." Peter Brown, The Body and Society: Men, Women and Sexual Renunciation in Early Christianity (New York: Columbia University Press; London and Boston: Faber and Faber, 1988–89), appeared too late to be used in this chapter.

Athenagoras, in *Suppl.* 33.1–2, introduces again the topic of pleasure and lust: "Since we hope for eternal life, we despise things of this life, including even the pleasures of the soul. Thus each of us thinks of his wife, whom he married according to the laws we have laid down, with a view to nothing more than procreation. For as the farmer casts seed into the ground and awaits the harvest without further planting, so also procreation is the limit that we set for the indulgence of our lust [καὶ ἡμῖν μέτρον ἐπιθυμίας ἡ παιδοποιία]."[36]

An illustrative example of the Christian attitude toward ἐγκράτεια (continence) and criticism of φιληδονία (love of pleasure) is found in the *Sentences* of Sextus, a document characteristic of nonsectarian Encratism also favored by Clement.[37] This collection of maxims no doubt had a very complicated history. H. Chadwick has argued[38] convincingly that it was composed by a Christian author about A.D. 180 to 210. Subtly christianizing pagan maxims (many of them characteristic of neo-Pythagorean ethics and religious piety) and at the same time "paganizing" Christian maxims, this author created a collection that could attract pagans to the Christian church, keeper of all that is true. But this collection, composed for an apologetic purpose, exercised a great influence in Christian circles, as Origen tells us.

An interesting group of sentences on marriage is formed by Sextus's *Sentences* 230a–240.[39] Married people may renounce marriage in order to live as "companion to God" (230a), yet marriage is not at all forbidden: "Marry and beget children knowing that both are difficult; if you know this, as you know that a battle would be hard and that you would be brave, then marry and have children" (230b). However, restraint is called for: "Every unrestrained husband [ἀκόλαστος] commits adultery with his wife" (231) and "Do nothing for the sake of mere sensual pleasure [ψιλὴ ἡδονή]" (232). Wives should be modest in dress: "Let moderation [σωφροσύνη] be the normal attire of a believing wife" (234). Indeed, "A modest [σώφρων] wife is her husband's glory" (237). Husband and wife should respect one another (238). The marriage of believers should be "a struggle for self-control [ἐγκράτεια]" (239). "As you control your stomach, so you will control your sexual desires" (240, cf. 428).

A few further sentences on ἐγκράτεια (continence) and φιληδονία (love of pleasure) complement this picture. "Self-control is the foundation of piety.

---

36. *Athenagoras, Legatio and De resurrectione* (ed. and trans. W. R. Schoedel; Oxford: Clarendon, 1972).

37. See H. Chadwick, *The Sentences of Sextus: A Contribution to the History of Early Christian Ethics* (TextsS N.S. 5; Cambridge: Cambridge University Press, 1959); and R. A. Edwards and R. A. Wild, S.J., *The Sentences of Sextus* (SBLTT 22; Chico, CA: Scholars, 1981). Cf. also H. Chadwick, "Enkrateia," *RAC* 5 (1962) 343–65.

38. See Chadwick, *The Sentences of Sextus*, 159–62, esp. 160: "His purpose is evident; it is to bring the moral wisdom of the Greek sages under the wing of the church, to whom all truth belongs. With adjustments here and there the language of Stoic or Pythagorean wisdom could pass in Christian circles. *Pythagoras saepe noster* might be his motto. His kindred spirit is Clement of Alexandria."

39. See Chadwick, *The Sentences of Sextus*, 99–100, 172–73 (notes). The translations are from Edwards and Wild, *The Sentences of Sextus*.

The goal of piety is friendship with God" (Sextus *Sentences* 86ab); "For the sage even sleep is a matter for self-control" (253b); "Self-control is the wealth of a philosopher," and "A faithful man is nurtured in self-control" (438). Self-control and temperance are eminent virtues:

> The temperate [σώφρων] man is pure in God's sight.
> Flee licentiousness [ἀκολασία].
> Exercise prudence.
> Master pleasures.
> Conquer the body in every way.
> If you love pleasure [φιληδονία], you will not escape licentiousness.
> God does not listen to one who loves pleasure.
> Luxurious living results in ruin. (67–72)[40]

RACHEL'S CONTINENCY: A JEWISH OR A CHRISTIAN IDEAL?

Early Christian authors, including the person responsible for the *Sentences of Sextus* in their present form, would no doubt concur with the praise bestowed upon Rachel, Issachar, and Joseph in the *Testaments*, as well as with the criticism leveled at Reuben, Judah, and other people led away by their desires. Josephus and Philo, in their efforts to present an acceptable picture of Jewish piety and ethics to a Hellenistic audience, also would concur, as would leading Hellenistic moralists like Musonius. They, after all, exercised great influence on Hellenistic-Jewish and early Christian thinking about sexual morality. With regard to the point under discussion in this chapter, there is also a remarkable continuity in ideas between Jews and Christians living in the same Hellenistic environment.

Consequently, our investigation does not allow any conclusion with regard to the question of the origin of the *Testaments of the Twelve Patriarchs*. The ideas about marriage expressed in the *Testament of Issachar* 2 may stem from a Jewish author and may have been taken over unaltered when the *Testaments* were adapted for use in Christian circles. They may also have been introduced into the Issachar story by Christians, either when they composed it or when they redacted an earlier Jewish testament. The *Testaments* themselves testify to the continuity in ethical thought in Hellenistic-Jewish and early Christian circles.[41]

---

40. Cf. Sextus *Sentences*, 139–40:

> The body by nature causes little disturbance for the soul.
> Love of pleasure makes the body unbearable.
> Every excess is an enemy of man.

and 172: "A man full of pleasure is useless in every respect."

41. On this question, see Hollander and de Jonge, *Commentary*, 82–85; de Jonge, "Die Paränese" (n. 14); and "The Testaments of the Twelve Patriarchs, Christian and Jewish: A Hundred Years after Friedrich Schnapp," *NedTTs* 39 (1985) 265–75.

PART FIVE

ARCHAEOLOGY

MELIKERTES AT ISTHMIA
A Roman Mystery Cult

Solutions of problems in the interpretation of ancient materials are not always readily available. Abraham Malherbe, the scholar and friend whom we honor in this volume, has demonstrated that the careful presentation and evaluation of materials from the world of the NT always have their merits. Thus, I am offering here a discussion of an Isthmian cult without any claim to a final solution, but in the hope that the discussion of this important Corinthian sanctuary will interest those who want to learn about the world of the apostle Paul. After all, a reference to the Isthmian Games seems to appear in 1 Cor 9:24–25: "Do you not know that in a race all runners compete, but only one receives the prize? . . . They do it to receive a perishable wreath."

ISTHMIA AND POSEIDON

The ancient sanctuary of Isthmia is situated near the Saronic Gulf in the eastern part of the Isthmus of Corinth, the narrow strip of land that connects the Peloponnesus with the Greek mainland. This sanctuary was the site of the Isthmian Games which were conducted there every two years in honor of the god Poseidon. The center of the sanctuary was the Temple of Poseidon. The Classical Temple of Poseidon that replaced an archaic structure was a Doric peripteros with 6 columns on the eastern and western sides and 13 columns on the north and south on a stylobate that measured 23 by 53 m. In dimensions and plan, it was very similar to the Temple of Zeus in Olympia and was probably built at the same time (468–460 B.C.E.).[1] Partially destroyed during the sack of Corinth by Mummius in 146 B.C., it was restored in its original

---

1. On the Temple of Poseidon in Isthmia, see Oscar Broneer, *Isthmia: Excavations by the University of Chicago under the Auspices of the American School of Classical Studies at Athens* (3 vols.; Princeton, N.J.: American School of Classical Studies, 1971–1977), 1:3–55; idem, "Isthmia Excavations, 1952," *Hesperia* 22 (1953) 111–17. For Broneer's first detailed presentation of the similarities of the Classical Temple at Isthmia with the Temple of Olympia, see his "The Temple of Poseidon at Isthmia," in Χαριστήριον εἰς Ἀναστάσιον Κ. Ὀρλάνδον III (Athens: Βιβλιοθήκη τῆς ἐν Ἀθήναις Ἀρχαιολογικῆς Ἑταιρείας 54, 1966).

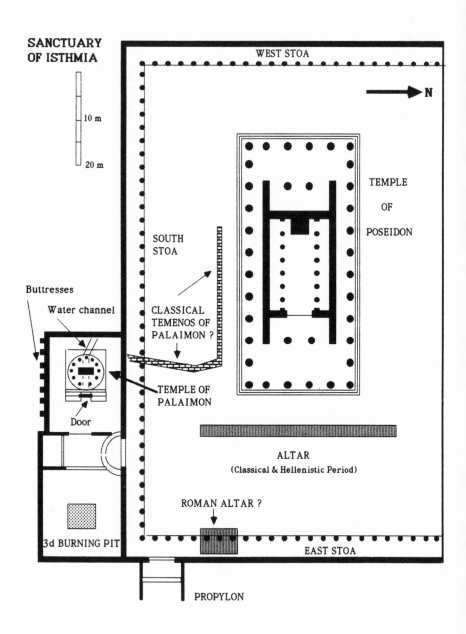

SANCTUARY OF ISTHMIA

10 m

20 m

WEST STOA

N

TEMPLE OF POSEIDON

SOUTH STOA

Buttresses

Water channel

CLASSICAL TEMENOS OF PALAIMON ?

TEMPLE OF PALAIMON

Door

3d BURNING PIT

ALTAR
(Classical & Hellenistic Period)

ROMAN ALTAR ?

EAST STOA

PROPYLON

form after the refounding of Corinth as a Roman colony a hundred years later.

The Altar of Poseidon, situated 9 m east of the temple and centered on its eastern entrance, measured 40 m from north to south. One of the largest altars of the Greek world, it was destroyed during the sack of Corinth by Mummius in 146 B.C.E. and never rebuilt.[2]

Building activities surrounding the Temple of Poseidon in the Roman period include a structure measuring ca. 8 by 10 m of which the foundations and the two lower steps are preserved.[3] This may have been the later altar of Poseidon, built in the Julio-Claudian period, although it lies ca. 20 m to the southeast of the Temple of Poseidon and is not centered on its east entrance. In the Antonine period stoas were built on the eastern, southern, and western side of the Temple of Poseidon; the steep slope to the north prevented the construction of the stoa on that side. The Roman altar southeast of the temple was dismantled at that time: the Antonine east stoa runs across the altar foundations.[4] Nothing is known about an altar of Poseidon after that period.

Poseidon, to be sure, together with his traditional consort Amphitrite, continued to be the primary deity of Isthmia. It was these two deities to whom Herodes Atticus gave a new gold and ivory statue group in the middle of the second century C.E. that Pausanias saw in the temple.

MELIKERTES PALAIMON IN THE
CLASSICAL PERIOD

Other archaeological finds from the Roman period seem to suggest that the worship in liturgy, ritual, and sacrifice emphasized the presence of another deity: Melikertes-Palaimon. He may already have been associated with Isthmia in the Classical period.[5] In a fragment from an Isthmian Ode of Pindar, the Nereïds request of Sisyphus to establish games in honor of Melikertes: "They commanded Sisyphus, the Aeolid, to determine a widely visible honor for the dead child Melikertes" (Pindar, frag. 5 Snell; frag. 4 Tusculum). Another Pindar fragment recalls the myth of Ino who, fleeing the madness of her husband, threw herself and her son into the sea: "Ino snatched the child out of the fire and threw him into the waves where she joined the fifty daughters of full-bosomed Doris" (Pindar, frag. 128d Snell; frag. 104 Tusculum).[6]

2. Broneer, *Isthmia* 1: 98–101.
3. On this Roman altar foundation see Broneer, *Isthmia* 2: 73–75. The exact measurements are 10 m north to south, 8.2 m east to west at the foundation level, 9 m by 7.61 m at the first course.
4. The Antonine stoas are described in Broneer, *Isthmia* 2: 75–85.
5. All ancient materials related to Melikertes are listed in J. G. Frazer, *Pausanias's Description of Greece* (New York: Biblo and Tannen, 1965) 2: 549.
6. Frag. 128e Snell (= frag. 105 Tusculum) speaks of Leukothea (Ino) and requests that the dirge be sounded aloud.

But the information remains very scanty. Unfortunately that is also true with respect to the archaeological record. Professor Elizabeth R. Gebhard has suggested that an enclosure just south of the Classical Temple of Poseidon may mark the place where Melikertes-Palaimon was worshiped in the Classical period.[7] But she also points out that, without further excavation, "the best support at present for the identification of this enclosure as the Classical temenos of Melikertes-Palaimon is its resemblance to the shrine of Opheltes-Archemoros at Nemea," another cult for a dead child that was associated with the Nemean Games. The use of wild celery in the victory crown of both Nemea and Isthmia[8] may also be evidence for the worship of Melikertes in the Classical period: wild celery is worn as a sign of mourning for a dead person.[9]

Otherwise, there is very meager literary information from the Classical period about Melikertes-Palaimon. We know the story of Ino's jump into the sea with her son, as she was fleeing from her husband Athamas, who had been stricken with madness by Hera.[10] The identification of Ino with the sea goddess Leukothea occurs as early as Homer's *Odyssey* (5.333–34).[11] Euripides speaks of the "Lord Palaimon, son of the goddess Leukothea" (both sea divinities); but he does not connect Leukothea with Ino.[12] Nowhere in Classical literature is Palaimon connected or identified with "Melikertes"—a name that appears only once, that is, in the Pindar fragment quoted above. On the other hand, Palaimon is related to Herakles in several passages. Lycophron (third century B.C.E.), *Alexandra* 229, says of the "hero" Palaimon of Tenedos: "And now Palaimon to whom babes are slain beholds [the Greek ships sailing in from Troy]." In another passage (*Alexandra* 663) he identifies Palaimon with Herakles: "And he shall see the remnant that was spared by the arrows of Keramynthes (= Herakles Alexikakos) Paukeus Palaimon." An association of

---

7. Orally and in a paper presented at the Corinth Symposium, January 22, 1987: "The Early Sanctuary of Poseidon at Isthmia." In this paper, Professor Gebhard says: "The temenos is located immediately south of the Classical Temple of Poseidon and west of the early Stadium. The use of blocks from the Archaic Temple securely places the construction after the temple fire and the temenos wall is so close to the south pteron of the temple as to suggest that the two are contemporary. The size and the finish of the blocks also point to a 5th c. date."

8. The victory crown is discussed by Oscar Broneer, "The Isthmian Victory Crown," *American Journal of Archaeology* 66 (1962): 259–63. For a marble head of an orator crowned with pine, ca. second century C.E. (Isthmia Museum inv. number 15 351), see Mary C. Sturgeon, *Isthmia IV: Sculpture I: 1952–1967* (Princeton, N.J.: American School of Classical Studies, 1987), 131–32, number 56, plate 61A; and *Mind and Body: Athletic Contests in Ancient Greece* (Athens: Ministry of Culture, 1989), 236, number 127. Broneer also remarks that the use of wild celery, which withers quickly, may have prompted Paul to speak of "a perishable wreath" in 1 Cor 9:25. Apparently, at the end of the first century C.E. a change took place: victory crowns were henceforth made of pine branches, but celery crowns were still also used.

9. Suggested by Professor Gebhard, "The Early Sanctuary."

10. See the Pindar fragment quoted above.

11. Homer says that the sea goddess Leukothea, "Ino, Kadmos' daughter," was once a human woman but was now receiving divine honors in the sea.

12. Euripides *Iph. Taur.* 270–71: "Son of Leukothea, guardian of ships, lord of the sea Palaimon, be merciful to us."

these two divinities appears in Plautus (*Rudens* 160): "[At the sight of two girls drifting in the sea:] O Palaemon, sancte Neptuni comes, qui Herculis socius esse diceris [O Palaemon, holy friend of Neptune, you who are said to be a companion of Hercules]."

Although there can be little doubt that Melikertes-Palaimon was somehow connected to the Isthmian Games and its rituals, at least as early as the fifth century B.C.E., the figure remains elusive, and even the attestation of his story is so fragmentary that it would be impossible to reconstruct it solely on the basis of the surviving Classical evidence. In stark contrast, the evidence for Melikertes-Palaimon and for his cult is overwhelming as soon as one enters the Roman period. This is true of the literary, as well as of the archaeological, materials.

ARCHAEOLOGICAL EVIDENCE FOR
MELIKERTES - PALAIMON FROM
THE ROMAN PERIOD

During the excavations of Isthmia by Oscar Broneer, three pits for the burning of sacrificial animals were discovered.[13] All three are situated 20 to 40 m to the southeast of the Temple of Poseidon. The oldest of these pits is roughly rectangular and measures 3.70 by 2.00 m and 1.30 m deep. The north side was lined with rough stones which were cracked from intense heat. The pit was surrounded by an enclosure wall, measuring ca. 9 m square. When the pit was found, it was filled with ashes, animal bones, pottery and lamps. According to the date of the pottery, the pit must have been in use during the first half of the first century C.E.; the pit was closed half a century later. The animal bones from this pit, as well as in the other two pits, have been identified as those of bulls. A second burning pit, slightly larger than the first, was built 3 m to the southeast. A new enclosure wall with sides measuring between 16 and 19 m surrounded both the first and second burning pit.

A third burning pit was built 15 m to the southeast of the second pit. It is the largest of the three, measuring 4.05 m from east to west and 3.57 m from north to south. Its preserved height is 1.10 m. All stones lining its walls were blackened and had partially disintegrated from intense heat. This points to a long period of use. Also this pit was filled with ashes, animal bones, and a very large quantity of lamps to a depth of 0.75 m. It was probably built at the beginning of the second century C.E. and may have been in use for as long as a hundred years.

Together with many lamps of various ordinary shapes, a large quantity of lamps of an unusual form have been found in and near the three burning pits. They are round bowls with a high funnel in the center that served to hold the

---

13. Oscar Broneer, "Excavations at Isthmia, Fourth Campaign 1957–1958," *Hesperia* 28 (1959): 312–17; idem, *Isthmia*, 2:100–106.

wick and they vary in size from 10 to 25 cm in diameter. The excavator Oscar Broneer dated these lamps into the early first to the late second century C.E. Lamps of this type have not been found anywhere else in Greece.

To the west of this third burning pit, but like it just outside of the southeastern corner of the stoas surrounding the Temple of Poseidon in the Antonine period, the concrete core of the foundations of a structure from the early second century C.E. was discovered.[14] It is 2 m high and almost square, measuring 8.00 m from north to south and 8.80 m from east to west. There is a passage in the center of the foundations which is the end of a water channel which brought water from a reservoir lying to the west. The passage is now 1.70 m wide; but it was originally lined with poros blocks on both sides of which the lowest course is preserved, leaving a passage that was only 0.73 m wide. At the eastern end was a door with a threshold 1 m above the floor of the channel. There are no traces of any steps leading down into the channel from the threshold. The walls and the bottom of the channel were lined with thick waterproof stucco to the northwestern end where it is joined to the older Greek stucco of a channel that was originally built for the supply of water for the basins of the archaic stadium. The new function of this water channel is difficult to explain.

Two bronze coins minted in Corinth in the second century C.E. show a monopteros standing on a podium with several steps leading up to the floor level of the temple. There is a door in the center of the steps to the podium. One coin shows a bull standing to the left of the temple: a pine tree is visible behind the animal.[15] The other coin shows, between the columns of the temple, the sculpture of a dolphin with a figure lying prostrate on its back, and a pine tree on either side of the temple.[16] A variant of this coin shows Melikertes on the dolphin in a monopteros with the pine tree behind.[17]

The preserved foundations and the evidence provided by the coins make it possible to reconstruct the temple that stood on these foundations. It was a monopteros without walls and with 11 Corinthian columns and a domed roof, standing on a square foundation that is typical for Roman podium temples with stairs leading up to the stylobate from the east. Pausanias (2.2.1), describing his visit to Isthmia, speaks of this structure as "a temple of Palaimon with images in it of Poseidon, Leukothea, and Palaimon himself." The latter is most likely the figure lying on the back of the dolphin as depicted by the coin. When the Temple of Palaimon was built, the western rectangle of

14. Oscar Broneer, "Excavations at Isthmia, Third Campaign, 1955–1956," *Hesperia* 26 (1957): 15–17; idem, "Excavations at Isthmia, Fourth Campaign 1957–1958," *Hesperia* 28 (1959): 317–19; idem, *Isthmia* 2:106–12.

15. Coin of Corinth, Marcus Aurelius; B. V. Head, *Catalogue of Greek Coins: Corinth, Corinthian Colonies, etc.* (London: Trustees of the British Museum, 1889) 78, number 613, plate 20 number 14; *Sylloge Nummerum Graecorum Copenhagen: Corinth* (Copenhagen: Einar Munksgaard, 1944) number 360, plate 8.

16. Coin of Corinth, Lucius Verus; Head, *Catalogue*, 80, number 623, plate XX, number 22.

17. *Sylloge Nummerum Graecorum Copenhagen: Corinth*, number 342, plate 7.

the earlier enclosure for the third burning pit, lying to the east of the temple, was enlarged, and the enclosure walls were raised to the height of several meters and reinforced by strong buttresses. On the northern side, the back wall of the new Southern Stoa of the Temple of Poseidon now served as the enclosure wall for this district. Thus, the entire area—the Temple of Meli-kertes-Palaimon, as well as the third, large burning pit—was surrounded by high walls that would have made it impossible for anyone outside to witness the rituals performed inside.

There is also epigraphic evidence for the building activities at the Palaimon Temple in the Roman period. An inscribed statue base, found in Isthmia during the excavation of the site (now in the Corinth Museum), carried a statue of "Iuventianus, the Priest."[18] The date of the inscription is the early second century C.E. This Iuventianus is known from another inscription (now in the Museo Lapidario in Verona; *IG* IV, 203). This latter inscription gives the full title of Iuventianus and lists his benefactions as follows:

> To the ancestral gods and to the fatherland. Poplius Licinius, son of Poplius, Aemiklia Priscus Iuventianus, high-priest for life, has constructed the guest-lodgings for the athletes who come from all over the world to the Isthmian games. The same also made out of his own funds the Palaimonion with its decorations and the place for the offerings for the dead [ἐναγιστήριον] and the sacred entry-way and the altars for the ancestral gods with their enclosing walls and the pronaos and the houses for the examination of the athletes and the temple of Helios and the statue in it and the enclosing wall and the enclosing walls of the sacred grove and the temples of Demeter and Kore and Dionysos and Artemis in it with their statues and decorations and pronaoi; and he reconstructed the temples of [Demeter] Eueteria and Kore and the Ploutoneion and the passage-ways and their substructures which had been weakened by earthquakes and age. When he held the office of Agoranomos he also erected the stoa at the stadium with the vaulted chambers and decorations.

Another priest from Isthmia is mentioned in a third inscription which has since disappeared. It was reported by Johann Joachim Winckelmann over two hundred years ago, in the year 1764, in his famous *Geschichte der Kunst des Altertums* (2: 383):[19] "A large and beautiful statue of Neptune which together with a Juno, so-called, was excavated about twelve years ago at Corinth, was probably executed either in the time of Julius Caesar or not long afterwards. The style of the workmanship also points to about this time, and from it, though more from the shape of the letters in a Greek inscription on the head of a dolphin at the feet of the statue, it can be proved that it was not made before the destruction of the city. The inscription tells that the statue was

---

18. Oscar Broneer, "Excavations at Isthmia, Third Campaign, 1955–1956," *Hesperia* 26 (1957): 15–17; idem, "Excavations at Isthmia, Fourth Campaign 1957–1958," *Hesperia* 28 (1959): 317–19; idem, *Isthmia* 2:106–12.

19. English translation: Johann Joachim Winckelmann, *History of Ancient Art* (2 vols.; New York: Unger, 1968) 2: 280–81.

erected by Publius Licinius Priscus, a priest of Neptune. It is as follows: 'P. LIKINIOS PRISKOS IEREUS.'" Winckelmann is describing an entire statue group from Isthmia. It is unlikely that this group, although apparently monumental, came from the temple of Poseidon, because a part of the statues from the Temple of Poseidon appears to have been found in the recent Isthmian excavations. The torso of a monumental female statue, found in a trench at the west end of the Temple of Poseidon,[20] is most likely a part of the statue of Amphitrite that Pausanias (2.1.7) saw in the pronaos of the Temple of Poseidon, where it was standing next to a statue of Poseidon. These statues must have been the original temple statues of the naos of the Temple of Poseidon which were moved into the pronaos, when Herodes Atticus dedicated new gold and ivory statues of Poseidon and Amphitrite. Pausanias (2.1.7–8) describes this later group as a four-horse chariot (the bodies of the horses gilded except for the hooves which were made of ivory), with two tritons beside the horses and Poseidon and Amphitrite standing in the chariot. Pausanias also says that the boy Melikertes, standing upright, was part of the group depicted in this new temple statuary that Herodes Atticus dedicated. Thus the statues that Winckelmann saw in Rome must be the group mentioned by Pausanias: Poseidon, Leukothea, and Palaimon on the dolphin from the Temple of Palaimon.

LITERARY EVIDENCE FOR
MELIKERTES - PALAIMON FROM
THE ROMAN PERIOD

Roman writers of the Augustan time were quite familiar with the story of Ino and Melikertes. Vergil, in the *Georgica* (436–37) mentions both deities: "And the sailors, safe in port, shall pay their vows on the shore to Glaucus and to Panopea and to Melicerta, Ino's son." Horace refers to the "tearful Ino" (*Ino flebilis; Ep.* 2.3 = *Ars poetica* 123).

The myth about Ino and Melikertes is recorded in full for the first time by Ovid in his *Metamorphoses* (416–542): He tells of Juno's wrath against Ino, because she had nursed her sister Semele's infant Bacchus, and of Ino's flight and mad jump into the sea from a high rock together with her son Melicerta. But Venus requests Neptune to change the two into sea-gods. Neptune complies, stripping away their mortality and renewing them, changing both form and name: "And he called the new god Palaemon, and his goddess mother Leucothoe."

In his *Fasti* (6.485–550)—written in 8 C.E., just before the exile and about a year after the completion of *Metamorphoses*—Ovid adds that Ino and her son

---

20. Oscar Broneer, "Isthmia Excavations, 1952," 189–91. Definitive publication by Mary C. Sturgeon, *Isthmia IV*, cat. number 17A: pp. 83–99 (discussion), 99–100 (catalogue entry), plates 34–40.

Melicerta whom she had snatched from the cradle are brought to Italy to the mouth of the Tiber, where Hercules rescues them from the Maenads: on their flight, they encounter a Tegean priestess, who prophesies to them their future divine status: "Thou shalt be a divinity of the sea, thy son, too, shall have his home in ocean. Take ye both different names in your own waters. Thou shalt be called Leucothoe by the Greeks and Matuta by our people; thy son will have all authority over harbors; he whom we name Portunus will be named Palaemon in his own tongue . . . Their troubles ceased, they changed their names: he is a god and she is a goddess." In the *Fasti* (6.495–96) it is also clear that the sanctuary in which the two are worshiped is situated on the narrows of the Isthmus: "A land there is, shrunk with narrow limits, which repels twin seas and, single in itself, is lashed by twofold waters."

The relationship of Melikertes and Isthmia is explicit also in Ps.-Apollodoros *Bibliotheca* 3.4.3, a mythography probably written in the first century C.E.; however, here it is presumed that Melikertes was already dead when Ino jumped into the sea: "Ino threw Melikertes into a boiling cauldron, then carrying it with the dead child she sprang into the deep. She is called Leukothea, and the boy is called Palaimon—this is what they are called by the sailors, because they help those who are tossed by a storm. The Isthmian Games were instituted in honor of Melikertes by Sisyphus."

In the second century C.E., the mythographer Hyginus (*Fabulae* 2) gives a full account of the story. He tells how Ino had parched the grain in order to make it infertile; how Athamas, stricken with madness, sacrificed Ino's older son Phrixus; how Ino, saved by Liber, threw herself into the sea together with her younger son. Hyginus concludes the story with a reference to the Roman identification of Leukothea as Mater Matuta and of Melicerta-Palaemon as Portunus.

The fuller accounts of the myth by Roman writers may be related to the renewal of the Isthmian cult when Caesar had refounded Corinth and returned the control of the Isthmian Games to the new colony—the games had been held at Sikyon during the hundred years in which Corinth lay in ashes. These accounts also seem to confirm the archaeological record, that is, that the cult of Melikertes-Palaimon had moved to center stage in Isthmia. Very little can be learned from these accounts about the cult itself. But it seems clear that the Isthmian Games were understood as games in honor of Melikertes-Palaimon. That is also evident in Pausanias's report about his travel from Megara along the coast of the Saronic Gulf from Athens: "Further on the pine still grew by the shore at the time of my visit, and there was an altar of Melikertes. At this place, they say the boy was brought ashore by a dolphin; Sisyphus found him lying and gave him burial in the Isthmus, establishing the Isthmian Games in his honor" (2.1.3).

This dating of the founding of the games to the legendary Corinthian king Sisyphus is confirmed by an archaeological find. A statue base, found at the site and dated to the second century C.E., bears the inscription "Sisyphus" both in front and in the back of the base.[21] Thus, the statue that stood on this base must have been displayed prominently somewhere within the precinct of the Temple of Palaimon.

THE MYSTERY CULT OF
MELIKERTES - PALAIMON

Pausanias, however, also gives some indication of the character of the cult of this deity. After having described the Temple of Palaimon and its statues, he goes on to say this: "There is also another what is called secret holy place (ἄδυτον) and an underground descent leading into it, where they say that Palaimon is concealed. Whoever, whether Corinthian or stranger, swears falsely here, can by no means escape from the oath" (2.2.1). The excavations, however, have not brought to light anything that could be identified with this "adyton." It is possible that Pausanias associated it with the door in the middle of the staircase leading up to the temple. But the water channel that ended behind this door is very narrow and not easily accessible from the threshold lying about 1 m above the floor of the channel (see above). Pausanias says nothing about the rituals in honor of Palaimon; he only mentions the swearing of oaths—hardly the oaths that the athletes had to swear before the games.

That the rituals were secret is clearly stated by Plutarch (*Theseus* 25). He reports Theseus' arrival on the Isthmus, after killing the giant Skeiron, and says that Theseus founded the Isthmian Games in honor of Poseidon, emulating Herakles who had founded the Olympian Games for Zeus. Then Plutarch continues: "But what is dedicated to Melikertes in that place is performed at night, and its order involves a mystical rite [τελετή] rather than a public festival and celebration." Although the character of the ritual is clearly designated as a secret rite, no other details are given.[22]

More detailed information comes from Philostratus in his description of a picture entitled "Palaimon," whom he also calls Melikertes (*Imagines* 2.16). He describes the people of Corinth sacrificing on the Isthmus, the king—"we will think that it is Sisyphus"—and the sacred grove of Poseidon in which the pine needles whisper the story of Ino and Palaimon. Whereas Ino-Leukothea is not pictured, though her story is told briefly, the painting apparently includes the scene of Palaimon arriving asleep (not dead) on the back of a dolphin who is obedient to his will; Poseidon announces the child's coming. Then Philostratus continues his description of the painting: "For him who arrives, a sanctuary [ἄδυτον] breaks forth on the Isthmus as the earth splits open on Poseidon's command; it seems to me that Poseidon has also foretold

---

21. Oscar Broneer, "Excavations at Isthmia, Third Campaign, 1955–1956," 22–23.
22. The terms τελετή and ὀργιασμός are also used by Aelius Arist., p. 375 (Keil), for the cult of Palaimon.

to Sisyphus here the arrival of the boy and that it would be necessary to sacrifice to him. He [Sisyphus] sacrifices a black bull—I think that he took it from the herd of Poseidon. The meaning of the sacrifice, the garb worn by those who conducted it, the offerings [ἐναγίσματα], my child, and the method of slaughtering [τὸ σφάττειν] must remain hidden for the rites [ὄργια] of Palaimon, for the doctrine is holy and altogether secret, as the wise Sisyphus has clothed them in mystical language [ἀποθειώσαντος]." In agreement with Pausanias, Philostratus calls the sanctuary an "adyton" and, like Plutarch, he points to the secrecy of the rites. The unusually high temenos walls of the Palaimonion testify to the exclusion of the public. The sacrificing of a bull is confirmed by the excavation of the burning pits. Ἐναγίσματα and/or σφάγια are sacrifices to the dead, to heroes, and to chthonic deities; in a σφάγιον, the blood is poured into a bothros, and nothing of the sacrificed animal is eaten.[23] But there is no indication in Philostratus's description that the bull was meant to become a whole-burnt offering.

There can be no doubt about the mystery character of the cult of Melikertes-Palaimon in the Roman period. The secret rites of offerings to a hero are affirmed in several sources and borne out by the archaeological finds. Closely related is the renewed propagation of the story—the cult myth— among writers of the Roman period. About the third element constituting a mystery cult, the community that celebrated this cult, nothing is known. Possibly, this community was related to the celebration of the Isthmian Games, but that must remain speculation.

It is difficult to determine whether, and in which way, this Roman mystery cult of Melikertes-Palaimon was related to any Classical cult for this hero. Neither the full cult myth nor the ritual are attested in the Classical period, although tantalizing fragments of this myth appear in several writers. The burning of whole large animals in pits was apparently not practiced in Classical times; rather, the animals were cut up and burned piece by piece in small pits. It is possible that there was no direct connection to whatever Palaimon cult existed in the Classical period and also that the cult rituals for Melikertes-Palaimon, as they are evidenced by writers and archaeological finds, were created in the Roman period, when Corinth was reestablished by Caesar.

It is not possible, however, to explain this Roman cult or the name Melikertes as a completely novel creation of that time. To be sure, the name Melikertes (which possibly means "honeycutter") is a strange Greek name and not otherwise attested. It is also not possible to find an explanation for the identification of Palaimon with Melikertes.[24] The attempt has been made to explain Melikertes as Greek transcription of the Syrian god Melqart[25] who was

---

23. See Martin P. Nilsson, *Geschichte der griechischen Religion* (2 vols.; Handbuch der Altertumswissenschaft 5.2; 2nd ed.; Munich: Beck, 1955) 1: 186–87; Paul Stengel, *Opferbräuche der Griechen* (Darmstadt: Wissenschaftliche Buchgesellschaft, 1972), 92–104.

24. Cf. Albin Lesky in Pauly-Wissowa, *RE* 29 (1931): 514–21.

25. A full statement of this hypothesis and a listing of older literature can be found in John G. Hawthorne, "The Myth of Palaemon," *TAPA* 89 (1958): 92–98.

associated very early with Herakles.[26] Since Herakles is Παλαιμώνιος as well as Μέλκαθρος,[27] the identification of Palaimon with Melikertes would find a natural explanation.[28] However, all this must remain idle speculation because of the attestation of the name Melikertes in the Pindar fragment quoted above. This name, its association with Palaimon, and an older cult for this hero in Isthmia clearly predates the reorganization of the cult in the Roman period.

However, the Roman mystery cult of Melikertes-Palaimon deserves attention. The Classical period knew of the child who was tragically killed by his mother's mad jump into the sea. In the later versions, the child is once dead and buried in his adyton (Pausanias), once sleeping on the dolphin (Philostratus), once standing upright with Poseidon and Amphitrite as they ride the sea (the statue group in the Temple of Poseidon as described by Pausanias)— a hero who was once dead and rose to new life. What was the significance of the nocturnal rites, illuminated by strange lamps, in which bulls were sacrificed in a secret ritual and burned in a pit? What did the worshiper experience, and what was the meaning of this ritual? We may never know the answers, but we should continue to discuss the hero Melikertes-Palaimon and his cult in the context of the mystery religions of the Roman period and—last but not least—in the context of Paul's stay in Corinth.

26. See Karl Preisendanz, Pauly-Wissowa, *RE* suppl. 6. 293–97.
27. Μέλκαθρος is the usual Greek transcription of Melqart. That the Thassian Herakles came from Tyre in Syria is already stated by Herodotus 2.44.
28. I have discussed this thesis in more detail in my essay, "The History-of-Religions School, Gnosis, and the Gospel of John," *ST* 40 (1986): 123–26. I acknowledge gratefully the helpful criticisms of Professor Elizabeth R. Gebhard, and I have revised my presentation accordingly.

BIBLIOGRAPHY
Works by
Abraham J. Malherbe

A bibliography is never complete. The following record, while including some unpublished papers, wants several more. Surely many book reviews also remain fugitive. Gratefully, Abraham's steadfastly fertile mind and active pen are the chief reasons this list remains unfinished.

Stephen L. Peterson, *Librarian*
Yale Divinity School

BOOKS

Paul and the Popular Philosophers. Minneapolis: Fortress, 1989.
Ancient Epistolary Theorists. Atlanta: Scholars, 1988. Based on the earlier article "Ancient Epistolary Theorists," 1977.
Paul and the Thessalonians: The Philosophic Tradition of Pastoral Care. Philadelphia: Fortress, 1987.
Moral Exhortation: A Greco-Roman Sourcebook. Philadelphia: Westminster, 1986.
Gregory of Nyssa: The Life of Moses. New York: Paulist, 1978.
Social Aspects of Early Christianity. 2d ed. enl. Philadelphia: Fortress, 1983. First edition: Baton Rouge, LA: Louisiana State University Press, 1977.
The Cynic Epistles: A Study Edition. Missoula, MT: Scholars, 1977.
The World of the New Testament. The Living Word Commentary, vol. 1. Austin, TX: Sweet, 1967.

Special thanks are due Don L. Meredith, Librarian of Harding University Graduate School of Theology, for supplying citations from Church of Christ indexes maintained in the Harding Library.

ARTICLES

"Hellenistic Moralists and the New Testament." In *Aufstieg und Niebergang der Rom-ischen Welt*, vol. 26, edited by Wolfgang Haase and H. Temporini. Berlin and New York: Walter de Gruyter, in press.
"Epicureans."
"Hospitality."
"Stoics."
In *The Oxford Companion to the Bible*, edited by Bruce M. Metzger. Oxford: Oxford University Press, in press.
"Traditions and Theology of Care: The New Testament." In *Dictionary of Pastoral Care and Counseling*, edited by Rodney J. Hunter. Nashville: Abingdon, 1990.

1989

"Graeco-Roman Religion and Philosophy and the New Testament." In *The New Testament and Its Modern Interpreters*, edited by Eldon Jay Epp and George MacRae, 1–26. Atlanta: Scholars, 1989.

1988

"Herakles." *RAC* 14 (1988) 559–83.

1987

"New Testament Ethics and the Church Today." Christian Scholars Conference, Pepperdine University, July 1987. Unpublished. Copy located at Harding University Graduate School of Theology.

1986

"'Not in a Corner': Early Christian Apologetic in Acts 26:26." *SecCent* 5 (1985–86) 193–210.
"A Physical Description of Paul." In *Christians among Jews and Gentiles: Essays in Honor of Krister Stendahl on His Sixty-Fifth Birthday*, edited by George W. E. Nickelsburg with George W. MacRae, 170–75. Philadelphia: Fortress, 1986. Also published in *HTR* 79 (1986) 170–75.

1985

"Paul: Hellenistic Philosopher or Christian Pastor?" *American Theological Library Association Proceedings* 39 (1985) 86–98. Also published in *ATR* 68 (1986) 3–13.

1984

"'In Season and Out of Season': 2 Timothy 4:2." *JBL* 103 (1984) 235–43.

1983

"Antisthenes and Odysseus, and Paul at War." *HTR* 76 (1983) 143–73.
"Exhortation in First Thessalonians." *Novum Testamentum* 25 (1983) 238–56.

1982

"Early Christianity and Society: A Contemporary Academic Interest." In *Freedom, Order and the University*, edited by James R. Wilburn, 69–82. Malibu, CA: Pepperdine University Press, 1982.

"Self-Definition among Cynics and Epicureans." In *Jewish and Christian Self-Definition*, edited by Ben F. Meyer and E. P. Sanders, 3. 46–59, 192–97. Philadelphia: Fortress, 1982.

1981

"Crescens and Justin." In *Christian Teaching: Studies in Honor of LeMoine G. Lewis*, edited by Everett Ferguson, 312–27. Abilene, TX: Abilene Christian University Bookstore, 1981.

1980

"Continuities in Scholarship: The Work of Nils Dahl." *Reflection* 78 (1980) 8–12.

"*Mē genoito* in the Diatribe and Paul." *HTR* 73 (1980) 231–40.

"Medical Imagery in the Pastoral Epistles." In *Texts and Testaments: Critical Essays on the Bible and Early Church Fathers: A Volume in Honor of Stuart D. Currie*, edited by W. Eugene March, 19–35. San Antonio, TX: Trinity University Press, 1980.

1979

"Soziale Ebene und Literarische Bildung." In *Zur Soziologie des Urchristentums*, edited by Wayne A. Meeks, 194–221. Munich: Kaiser, 1979.

1978

"Pseudo Heraclitus, Epistle 4: The Divinization of the Wise Man." *JAC* 21 (1978) 42–64.

1977

"Ancient Epistolary Theorists." *Ohio Journal of Religious Studies* 5 (1977) 3–77.

"The Inhospitality of Diotrephes." In *God's Christ and His People: Studies in Honour of Nils Alstrup Dahl*, edited by Jacob Jervell and Wayne A. Meeks, 222–32. Oslo: Universitetsforlaget, 1977. Also published as chap. 4 in *Social Aspects of Early Christianity*. 2d ed. enl. Philadelphia: Fortress, 1983.

1976

"Cynics," 201–3.

"Epictetus," 271.

In *Interpreter's Dictionary of the Bible*, Supplementary vol. Nashville: Abingdon, 1976.

1972

"Inception of Christian Apologetics," 707–11.

"Publication of Celsus' True Word," 731–36.

"Emergence of Theology as a Concept," 757–61.

"Crystallization of the New Testament," 779–83.

In *Great Events from History: Ancient and Medieval Series*, edited by Frank N. Magill. Englewood Cliffs, NJ: Salem, 1972.

1971

"The Household of God." *RelSoc* 4 (1971) 17–24.

1970

"Athenagoras on the Location of God." *TZ* 26 (1970) 46–52.

"The Apologetic Theology of the *Preaching of Peter.*" *ResQ* 13 (1970) 205–23.

"Athenagoras on the Poets and Philosophers." In *Kyriakon: Festschrift Johannes Quasten,* edited by P. Granfield and J. Jungmann, 214–25. Munster Westfalen: Aschendorff, 1970.

"'Gentle as a Nurse': The Cynic Background to I Thess ii." *NovT* 12 (1970) 203–17.

1969

"Athenagoras on Christian Ethics." *JEH* 20 (1969) 1–5.

"The Holy Spirit in Athenagoras." *JTS* N.S. 20 (1969) 538–42.

"A People under the Word: Theological Interpretation." In *The Concept of the Believers' Church: Addresses from the 1967 Louisville Conference,* edited by James L. Garrett, Jr., 207–23. Scottdale, PA: Herald, 1969. Abridged version: "A People under the Word." *Mission* 1 (September 1967) 16–20.

"The Structure of Athenagoras, 'Supplicatio pro Christianis.'" *VC* 23 (1969) 1–20.

1968

"The Beasts at Ephesus." *JBL* 87 (1968) 71–80.

"Towards Understanding the Apologists: A Review Article." *ResQ* 11 (1968) 215–24.

1967

"Life in the Graeco-Roman World." In *The World of the New Testament,* edited by Abraham J. Malherbe, 4–36. Austin, TX: Sweet, 1967.

"The Mission of the Church." *Mission* 1 (July 1967) 7–8.

1965

"Peter: The Serving Leader." *20th Century Christian* 27 (May 1965) 5–6.

"Recent New Testament Introductions." *ResQ* 8 (1965) 143–53.

"Surveying New Testament Research." *ResQ* 8 (1965) 82–87.

"To Today's Intellectual Challenges." In *Lift up Your Eyes,* 177–200. Abilene Christian College Annual Bible Lectures, 1965. Abilene, TX: Abilene Christian College, 1965.

1964

"The Singing of the Early Church." *20th Century Christian* 27 (November 1964) 7–10.

"The Student and Church Life." *20th Century Christian* 26 (September 1964) 10–11.

1963

"Apologetic and Philosophy in the Second Century." *ResQ* 7 (1963) 19–32.

1962

"Through the Eye of the Needle: The Doctrine of Christ." *ResQ* 6 (1962) 12–18.

1961

"An Introduction: The Task and Method of New Testament Exegesis." *ResQ* 5 (1961) 169–78.

"Through the Eye of the Needle: Simplicity or Singleness?" *ResQ* 5 (1961) 119–29.

1960

"Impetus to Activity." *20th Century Christian* 22 (July 1960) 5–6.

1959

"The Corinthian Contribution." *ResQ* 3 (1959) 221–33.

"Gnosis and Primitive Christianity: A Survey." *ResQ* 3 (1959) 99–107; 4 (1960) 16–29.

1958

"Christology in Luke-Acts." *ResQ* 2 (1958) 62–66, 115–27.

"The Unity of the Church in Paul." *ResQ* 2 (1958) 187–96.

1957

"Notes on Religious Washings in the Graeco-Roman World." *ResQ* 1 (1957) 152–58.

REVIEWS

Banks, Robert. *Paul's Idea of Community.* Exeter: Paternoster, 1979; Grand Rapids, MI: Eerdmans, 1980. Reviewed in *ResQ* 24 (1981) 242–43.

Betz, Hans Dieter, ed. *Plutarch's Ethical Writings and Early Christian Literature.* Leiden: Brill, 1978. Reviewed in *JBL* 100 (March 1981) 140–42.

Kemmler, Dieter W. *Faith and Human Reason.* Leiden: Brill, 1975. Reviewed in *JBL* 96 (March 1977) 149–50.

Koester, Helmut. *Introduction to the New Testament.* Philadelphia: Fortress, 1982; Berlin and New York: Walter de Gruyter, 1982. Reviewed in *RelSRev* 10 (1984) 112–16.

Lohse, Eduard. *The New Testament Environment,* translated by J. E. Steely. Nashville: Abingdon, 1976; London: S.C.M., 1976. Reviewed in *Interpretation* 31 (April 1977) 211–12.

O'Neil, Edward N., ed. *Teles, the Cynic.* Missoula, MT: Scholars, 1977. Reviewed in *JBL* 97 (December 1978) 599–600.

Penella, Robert J. *The Letters of Apollonius of Tyana: A Critical Text with Prolegomena, Translation, and Commentary.* Leiden: Brill, 1979. Reviewed in *SecCent* 3 (Summer 1983) 100–102.

INDEX OF
CLASSICAL AND EARLY LITERATURE

[All page references are in **bold** type.]

INDEX OF
JUDEO-CHRISTIAN SCRIPTURES

[All page references are in **bold** type.]

HEBREW BIBLE

APOCRYPHA

APOCRYPHAL LITERATURE

12, **345**
13-14, **345**
13:3, 4, **345**
13:5, **345**
13:6, **345 n.16**
13:7, **345**
14:1, **345 n.16**
14:4-5, **345**
14:6, **345**
15, **345**
15:5-6, **346**
16-17, **345**
16:4, **345**
17:1, **345**
18:2, **345**
19, **345**
19:1-2, **345**
19:4, **106 n.33, 109**

T. Levi
9:9-14, **345 n.14**
19:1, **109**
T. Moses 3:11, **15 n.66**
T. Napht.
3:5, **344**
8:8, **345**
T. Reuben
1:6-10, **344**
1:9-10, **344**
2:1-2, **344**
2:3-9, **344**
2:4, **344, 348**
2:8, **345**
2:9, **345**
3:3, **344**
3:9-6:4, **344**
3:9-15, **344**

3:10-14, **344**
3:10, **344**
3:11-14, **343**
4:1, **344**
4:2-4, **344**
4:8-10, **343**
4:8, **344**
4:11, **343**
4:14-15, **344**
5, **344, 346, 348**
5:3, **344**
6:1, **344**
5:6-7, **344**
6:1-10, **344**
6:1-4, **344**
6:7, **344**
6:11, **344**
T. Sim. 2:7, **106 n.33, 109**

NEW TESTAMENT

Matthew
1:24-25, **11 n.43**
4:1-11, **105 n.28**
4:8, **87 n.35**
5, **46, 47, 48**
5:2, **48**
5:3-12, **45**
5:3, **47, 50**
5:10, **47**
5:11, **45**
5:48, **47**
6:7, **330 n.8**
8:4, **87 n.35**
8:11-12, **44**
9:37, **242**
10:10, **242**
10:22, **105 n.30**
11:5, **44**
11:6, **47**
12:1-14, **325**
13:16, **48**
16:21, **87**
17:19-20, **90**
19:19, **325**
21:21, **90**
22:32, **130**
23:39, **48**
24:13, **105 n.30**

Mark
1:13, **105 n.28**
1:44, **87 n.35**
2:18, **44**
3:28-29, **105 n.29**
3:31 *par*, **145**

3:35 *par*, **145**
6:2-3, **129**
6:48 *par*, **4 n.2**
8:31, **240**
10:29 *par*, **145**
10:30 *par*, **145**
12:18, **130**
12:31, **325**
14:15, **87 n.35**
14:25, **44**
14:32, **186**
14:58, **76**

Luke
1:1, **58**
1:14, **44**
1:26, **11 n.43**
1:41, 44, 46-55, **44**
1:68-79, **44**
2:10, **45**
3:23, **11 n.43**
4:1-13, **105 n.28, 188
 n.36**
4:5, **87 n.35**
4:6, **104 n.23**
4:18-19, 21, **45**
4:22, **11 n.43**
5:14, **87 n.35**
6, **46, 47**
6:12, **188 n.36**
6:20-25, **45**
6:20-22, **39**
6:20, **47, 50**
6:22, **45**
7:23, **47**

9:18, **188 n.36**
9:22, **240**
9:28, **188 n.36**
9:51-53, **188 n.36**
9:57-62, **188 n.36**
10:2, **7 *par*, 242**
10:23, **48**
10:27, **325**
11:1-13, **188 n.36**
11:1-4, **186**
11:4, **186**
11:28, **48**
12:22-31, **49**
12:37, **48**
12:43, **48**
13:35, **48**
14:14, **127 n.28**
15:1-2, **188 n.36**
17:34, **186**
18:1, **188 n.36**
20:24, **87 n.35**
20:27, **130**
20:35, **166**
21:20-24, **184**
21:24, **54**
21:25-26, **55**
22, **175 n.15, 185-86**
22:12, **87 n.35**
22:14-38, **175, 185 n.30**
22:24-27, **175**
22:27, **176**
22:31-32, **100 n.8, 105
 n.28**
22:39-46, **185 n.32**
22:53, **109**

INDEX OF
MODERN AUTHORS

22; 85 nn.25-31; 88 n.38,
89 n.39, 93 n.47, 118 n.2,
171, 172 n.3, 192 n.9, 209
n.35, 257, 308 n.7
Fischel, Henry, 125 n.24,
132, 133 n.46
Fitzgerald, John T. (Jr.), xiv,
99, 100 n.5, 101 n.10, 103
nn.18-21; 115 n.58, 116
n.61, 193 n.23, 195 n.28,
199 n.46, 200 n.48, 207
n.23, 256 nn.10, 12; 257
nn.15, 16, 20; 260, 261
n.27, 316 nn.25, 29
Fitzmyer, J., 208 n.27
Fletcher, William, 125 n.25
Ford, D., 196 n.34
Fornara, Charles William,
177 n.18
Fortenbaugh, W. W., 280
n.96
Fortunatus, 315
Foucault, Michel, 279 n.95
Frazer, J. G., 357 n.5
Freese, John Henry, 221
n.37, 223 n.47
Frerichs, Ernest S., 216 n.1,
222 n.40
Freudenthal, J., 152 n.31,
155 n.41
Fridrichsen, A., 80 n.4, 81
nn.6, 7, 8; 81- 82 n.12, 82
n.15, 89 n.40, 92 n.46, 96
n.48
Friedrich, Gerhard, 241 n.7
Frischer, Bernard, 119 n.6,
272 n.67
Fritsche, 151 n.26
Fritz, K. von, 40 n.6, 60
n.34, 62 n.42, 66 n.53, 70
n.73
Fuchs, Harold, 56
Funk, Robert W., 192 n.5,
235 n.97
Furnish, Victor Paul, 101
nn.11, 12; 102 n.16, 104
n.24, 194 n.24, 194 n.25,
195 n.30, 198 n.39, 206
n.21, 207 nn.23, 24; 267
n.48, 325 n.17

Gager, John G., 69 n.73, 70
Gaillard, M., 174 n.13
Gaius Marcius, 179 n.19
Galinsky, G. Karl, 4 n.4, 6
n.19, 10 n.36
Garland, D., 206 n.22

Garrett, Susan R., xiii, 306
n.5
Gärtner, Bertil, 73 n.89, 75-
78, 120 nn.12, 13
Garver, Eugene, 220 n.28
Gasque, W. W., 210 n.42
Gaster, Moses, 174 n.13
Gaston, Lloyd, 202 n.6
Gaventa, Beverly Roberts,
172, 310 n.9
Gebhard, Elizabeth R., 358,
366 n.28
Geffcken, Johannes, 68
nn.67, 68; 60 nn.70, 71; 71
n.77, 72 n.82, 270 n.58
Gelzer, M., 211 n.48
George, T., 217 n.8
Georgi, Dieter, 102 nn.15,
16; 198 n.39, 208 n.26,
208 n.30, 275 n.76
Gerlach, W., 289 n.19, 295
n.43, 301 n.70
Geurts, N., 341 n.4
Geurts, P. M. M., 290 n.19,
Giblin, Charles H., 120 n.10
Gigante, Marcello, 272 n.67,
274 n.74, 282 n.101
Gigon, Olof, 53 n.7, 60 n.34,
62 n.43, 66 n.56, 70 n.73
Gilbert, C. D., 61 n.39
Gitay, Yehoshua, 216
Glad, Clarence, 267 nn.49,
50; 283 n.103
Glasswell, Mark, 122 n.18
Glen, J. S., 135 n.2, 137 n.13
Gompers, Theodore, 276
n.84
Gooch, Paul W., 258 nn.22,
23; 261 n.28, 264 nn.39,
40; 265 n.41, 266 nn.42,
44-45; 279 n.94, 282 n.102
Goodenough, E. R., 204
n.15
Gourrevitch, D., 290 n.19
Grafenberg, W., 289
Grant, Robert M., 82 n.12,
160 n.23, 167 n.59, 263
n.35, 313 n.21
Grässer, Erich, 13-14 n.57,
14 n.58, 15 n.65, 67 n.63
Green, Lawrence D., 222
n.41
Greeven, H., 330 n.9
Grelot, P., 132 n.43
Grimaldi, William, 222 n.41
Grimm, C. L. W., 152 nn.29,
30
Gruen, Erich, 211 n.48

Grundmann, W., 195 n.27
Guelich, R. A., 46
Gülich, E., 218 n.17
Gummere, 268
Gunkel, Hermann, 55
Guthrie, W. K. C., 5 n.13, 7
Gutierrez, Pedro, 171 n.2,
172 n.3
Gutmann, J., 202 n.5

Haarbeck, H., 195 n.27
Haase, F., 341 n.6
Haase, W., 82 n.13,
Hadas, Moses, 84 n.23, 151
n.26, 152 n.28, 153 n.37,
269 nn.55, 56; 298 n.58
Hadot, Ilsetraut, 272 n.67,
279 n.95
Haenchen, Ernst, 128 n.30
Hafemann, Scott, 103 n.18
Hahn, David E., 58 n.24, 59,
61-62, 66, 276 n.84
Hammer, P. L., 208 n.26
Hanfmann, G. M. A., 202
n.5
Hanhart, R., 152 n.30, 153
n.33
Hanson, M. B., 13 n.57
Happ, V., 293 n.36, 294 n.37
Harder, R., 341 n.4
Harding, Harold S., 225 n.53
Harnack, Adolf von, 69 n.73,
80 n.3, 81 n.12
Harnish, W., 244 n.15
Harrisville, R. A., 16 n.71
Hart, Anne, 253
Hartom, 151 n.26
Harvey, Susan, 253
Hasenstab, R., 319
Hatch, E., 212 n.54
Hauck, F., 40 n.5
Hauerwas, Stanley, 172 n.5
Hawthorne, G. F., 283 n.107
Hawthorne, John G., 365
n.25
Hays, Richard B., 102 n.17,
255 n.7, 264 n.36
Heinemann, I., 350
Hembold, 145 n.8, 335 n.33
Hengel, Martin, 14 n.60, 216
n.2, 221 n.39, 308 n.6
Henle, Jane, 4n.5
Héring, J., 80 n.6, 82 n.15,
83 n.17
Herman, G., 211 n.48
Hermans, Albert, 161 n.26,
163, 164, 165 n.55